Beholding Beauty

Beholding Beauty

Saʿdi of Shiraz and the Aesthetics of Desire in Medieval Persian Poetry

By

Domenico Ingenito

BRILL

LEIDEN | BOSTON

Originally published in hardback in 2020 as Volume 41 in the series Brill Studies in Middle Eastern Literatures.

Cover illustration: Folio with heading, Sa'di's *Kulliyāt*, 725/1325, King Muhammad Zahir Shah's Personal Library Collection © National Archives of Afghanistan.

The Library of Congress has cataloged the hardcover edition as follows:

Names: Ingenito, Domenico, author.
Title: Beholding beauty : Sa'di of Shiraz and the aesthetics of desire in medieval Persian poetry / by Domenico Ingenito.
Description: Leiden ; Boston : Brill, 2021. | Series: Brill studies in Middle Eastern literatures, 15715183 ; volume 41 | Includes bibliographical references and index.
Identifiers: LCCN 2020037597 (print) | LCCN 2020037598 (ebook) | ISBN 9789004435896 (hardback) | ISBN 9789004435902 (ebook)
Subjects: LCSH: Sa'di—Criticism and interpretation. | Aesthetics in literature.
Classification: LCC PK6546 .I46 200 (print) | LCC PK6546 (ebook) | DDC 891/.511009—dc23
LC record available at https://lccn.loc.gov/2020037597
LC ebook record available at https://lccn.loc.gov/2020037598

Typeface for the Latin, Greek, and Cyrillic scripts: "Brill". See and download: brill.com/brill-typeface.

ISBN 978-90-04-73344-2 (paperback, 2025)
ISBN 978-90-04-43589-6 (hardback)
ISBN 978-90-04-43590-2 (e-book)

This book is printed on acid-free paper and produced in a sustainable manner.

گفتم یکی به گوشه چشمت نظر کنم
چشمم در او بماند و زیادت مقام شد

I thought I'd gaze upon you only once, with the corner of my eye
My eyes lingered, and I kept beholding him
Over and over

SAʿDI SHIRĀZI

Contents

Acknowledgments XIII
Abbreviations XV
Note on Dates, Names, and Transliteration XVI
Plates XVII

Introduction: The Mufti of the Masters of Gazes 1
1 New Directions for the Reconstruction of Saʿdi's Biography 9
2 From the Fall of Baghdad to the Rise of the Juvaynī Family: the Need for Patronage and the Renewal of Saʿdi's Fame 17
3 After 1270: Political Instability in Fars, Saʿdi's New Travels, and the Construction of a Sufi Lodge 20
4 Chasing the Original Ghazals: Manuscripts, *Mouvances*, and Inimitable Smoothness 25
5 Through the Mirror of the Manuscripts 29
6 Saʿdi's "Inimitable Smoothness" 32
7 Saʿdi through the Eyes of Premodern Manuscripts 33

PART 1
Uncovering the Skin of the Ghazal

Introduction to Part 1 45
1 Tasting the *Punctum* 47
2 The Body of the Bias 53

1 **The Homoerotics of Political Power and the Emergence of Gendered Desires** 56
1 From the Fall of Baghdad to the Gendered Nature of Desire 56
2 Bawdy Portrayals and Homoerotic "Confessions" 61
3 Homoeroticism and Gender (in)Difference 66
4 The Homoerotic Hermeneutics of the Medieval Body 69
5 The Lyric Threshold of Saʿdi's Encomia 86
6 "God Gave the East and the West to the Ilkhan" 92

2 **Movements and Gazes in the Rose Garden**
Pseudo-Biographical Experience, Political Engagement, and Fictive Sensuality in the Emergence of a Lyric Voice 99
1 "Pluck a Petal from my *Rose Garden* ... / May it Shine Forever!" 100
2 Chasing Saʿdi's "I": between Subjectivity and Biographical Indetermination 104
3 Prince Saʿd II as Saʿdi's "Implied Reader" 109
4 Courting Prince Saʿd II through Narratives of Piety and Desire 114
5 Involving the Atabeg as a Figurative Witness of Erotic Explorations 124
6 Articulating the Ghazal: Lyric Reality and Confessional Fiction 133
7 Accessing the Body of the Lyric 137
8 Flirting in the Friday Mosque of Kashgar: Grammar and Rhetoric as Geographical Forms of Seduction 140

3 **The Obscene Revisited**
From the Sexual Reification of the Body to its Spiritual Fetishization 151
1 Unsullied Are My Eyes 151
2 Interpreting the Obscene 158
3 None of them Can I Say to You: the Obscene as a Cognitive Exploration of the Body 163
4 Persian Pornography as a Lyrical Undertone 172
5 The Euphemism and its Undetermined Flesh 184
6 The Beloved's Body as a Shifting Object of Desire 191
7 Re-Orienting the Experience of Gender: from the Grotesque to Spiritual Epiphany 193

PART 2
Through the Mirror of your Glances: The Sacred Aesthetics of Saʿdi's Lyric Subject

Introduction to Part 2 207
1 Amidst the Mud and the Heart 207
2 "I Behold You Through Your Eyes": for a Lyric Anthropology of Vision 212
3 Saʿdi and the Saints of Shiraz: between Detached Homage and the Cult of Beauty 217

4 *Shāhid-bāzī*: Sufi Eroticism 224
5 Religious and Lyrical Renewals and the Influence of al-Ghazālī and Avicenna 227

4 **The Body as a Divine Sign**
The Hermeneutics of Spiritual Desire 232
1 Prostration, Desire, and Bewilderment 233
2 Seeing God: Introvertive and Contemplative Modalities 236
3 The Body in the Text 245
4 Interpreting the Body of the Text: Spiritual Hermeneutics 250
5 The Body as an Inference: between Lust and Incarnationism 255
6 From Incarnation to Affinity: the Body as a Qibla 261

5 **The *ʿĀrif* as a Beholder**
The Divine Pen Depicting the* Khaṭṭ *of the Beloved 271
1 Beholding the Fashioner through the Depicted 272
2 Spiritual Cognition and Meditation as an Active Theo-Erotic Quest 277

6 **Between the Rational Soul and the Internal Senses**
For a Psychology of the Lyric Subject 301
1 The Avicennian Revolution: from Spiritual Hermeneutics to Sensory Cognition 301
2 Beyond Sufi Normativity: the Sensory Aspect of Saʿdi's Lyricism 307
3 The Philosophical Physiology of Love as an Aesthetic Experience: Avicenna's *Epistle* on *ʿIshq* 312
4 Avicennian Psychology, or the Science of the Soul 318
5 The Internal Senses and the Cognitive Foundations of the Lyric Subject 323
6 Through the Mirror of My Imaginings 333
7 Projecting the Senses Toward the Realm of the Unseen 338
8 The Visible World and the Realm of the Supernal 348

7 **Spiritual Cardiology**
The Heart as a Mirror Reflecting the Unseen 352
1 Imagining the Limits of the Imagination 353
2 The Practical Intellect as a Bridge between *Mulk* and *Malakūt* 354
3 The Intoxicating Fragrance of the Unseen 358

4 *Mukāshafa* and *Mushāhada*: from the Science of Unveiling to Spiritual Vision 362
5 Spiritual Cardiology 366
6 The Cosmology of the Heart, Between Philosophy and Poetry 374
7 From the Rational-Inferential Modality to the Imaginal-Cosmological Approach 384

8 **Beholding Beauty**
The Flesh, the Forms, and the* Meanings *of the Visionary Experience 390
1 Painting and Polishing: the Competition Between the Greek and the Chinese Artists 392
2 *Majāz* and *Ḥaqīqat*: Embodying the Images 397
3 The Five Stages of the Visionary Experience 401
4 The Preliminary Contact, between Physiology, Experience, and Lyricism 412
5 Phases Three and Four: Spiritual Frustration and Soothing Retrieval of the Experience 422
6 Transgressing the Boundaries of Lust and Incarnationism 430
7 Beyond the Chinese and Greek Paintings, and toward the Performative Boundaries of the Lyric 435

PART 3
The Lyrical Ritual* (Samāʿ) *as the Performative Space of Sacred Eroticism

Introduction to Part 3 443
1 Experiencing *almost* the Same Thing 443

9 **"Where is This Singer From? He Shouted the Name of the Beloved!"**
Toward a Chronological and Psycho-Physiological Approach to* Samāʿ *in Saʿdi's Ghazals 450
1 The *Ṭayyibāt* as the Enactment of the Ethics of Eroticism 451
2 The *Badāyiʿ* and the *Khavātīm*: toward a Deeper Erotic Awareness 458
3 The Aesthetic Grounds of the "Sublime Sensation" 468
4 The Psycho-Physiological of the Lyrical Ritual 475
5 Saʿdi's Ethics of *Samāʿ* 480
6 Poetry as a Controlled Form of Sexual Desire: *Samāʿ* and *Shāhid-bāzī* 488

10 **The Ghazal as Description of Performance, Ritualized Script, and "Performative" Analogue of *Samāʿ*** 499
1 From Descriptive Locution to Scripted Performance 508
2 Transfiguring the Text into a Performative Experience 513

Epilogue: Poetry as a Mirror for Experience 519

Appendix: Original Texts 525
Bibliography 642
Index 688

Acknowledgments

Although I am still relatively young, more than half of my adult life has been occupied by the preparation of this book, and I am aware that I will likely need one or two more decades to perfect my limited understanding of Saʿdi's poetry. Time is ruthless, they say, but it is also an enchanting flow of words and images that urge us to be pronounced and visualized. Poets like Saʿdi and his predecessors knew that only words can save us from the spiraling destiny of death and oblivion that constitutes the human condition.

With this brief note, in the middle of a pandemic that has disrupted the lives of so many of us, I wish to immortalize the names of all the people—friends, relatives, students, colleagues—who have gifted me with the grace of their presence and affection during the years leading to the publication of this book. These pages would not exist without the existence of these beloved ones, so dear to me, and I would not even recognize myself if it were not for the way their lives offered light and breath to my own life.

Reader from our time or any future time, listen: in one way or another (and some of them in multiple ways), these people have contributed to the birth of this book. All merit is theirs, and any inconsistencies or mistakes are exclusively mine.

Please, thank them on my behalf while reading their names with me:

> Azi Ahmadi, Amr Taher Ahmed, Sari Almenar Baixauli, Maite Alvarez, Luke Arterburn, Blake Atwood, Marian Austin, Carol Bakhos, Lamia Balafrej, Francesca Bayre, Ali Behdad, Uta Bekaia, Anne Blackstock-Bernstein, Alessandra Bonazzi, Catherine Bonesho, Edward J. Borey, Behzad Borhan, Shane Boris, Catherine Brookman, Dominic Brookshaw, Lia Brozgal, Aaron Burke, Fausto Andre Cardoso, Vittorio Celotto, Antonio del Castello, Christine Chism, Gregory Cohen, Kara Cooney, Michael Cooperson, Camille Cotteverte, Peter Cowe, Rashid Crisostomo, Ahmed al-Dailami, Yorgos Dedes, the Derviso family, Iskandar Ding, Tommaso di Dio, Dinah Diwan, Julie Ershadi, Aria Fani, Shahla Farghadani, Joshua L. Freeman, Carmen Gallo, Isaac Gimenez, Ben Gottlieb, Philip Grant, Megan Rose Greene, Nile Green, Davide Grossi, Latifeh Hagigi, Kamron Jabbari, Sean Hazen, Kaveh Hemmat, Edmund Herzig, David Hirsch, Joana Hurtado i Mateu, Ali Igmen, Nanda Imbimbo, Marcello Ingenito, Fabrizio Ingenito, Gianluca Ingenito, Ahmad Karimi-Hakkak, Ali Karjoo-Ravari, Naz Keynezhad, Hani Khafipour, Mina Khalil, Nina Khoshnudi, Selim Kuru, Justine Landau, Rémi Lécuyer, Frank Lewis,

Paul Losensky, Anahita and Jim Lovelace, Azeem Malik, Amir Mansoori, Louise Marlow, Giovanni Maria Martini, the Mazzone family, Evan Metzger, Jane Mikkelson, Levan Mindiashvili, Shaya Mohajer, Victor Montecinos, Arham Moradi, Abolfazl Moshiri, Maryam Niazadeh, Teresa Orlandini, Michael O'Sullivan, Sarah Parvini, Doug Peck, Cesar Perez, Michele Petrone, Judith Pfeiffer, Shaahin Pishbin, Anne Roberts, Paul Ruseler, Catello Russo, Christine van Ruymbeke, Fatima Sai, Aria Safar, David Schaberg, Bill Schniedewind, Asghar Seyed-Ghorab, Sunil Sharma, Ghazal Sheei, Matt Sobel, Gemma Sonego, Marc Sounigo, Iraj Shahbazi, Jahan Sharif, Sahba Shayani, Rahim Shayegan, Zrinka Stahuljak, Marija Stojanovic, Sandi Tan, Francesco Maria Tipaldi, Kevin Tombarello, Marc Underhill, Sasha Wachtel, Kyle Warren, Willeke Wendrich, Jonathan Winnerman, Mohammad Jafar Yahaghi, Luke Yarbrough, Murat C. Yildiz.

This book is dedicated to my family: Ciro, Dorita, Maria Rosaria, Rita, and Victor, my deldār, who has patiently read every single page of this monograph. As an academic accomplishment, I dedicate this monograph to the two scholars who shaped my passion for learning, teaching, and thinking: Alessandra Bonazzi and Camilla Miglio: two women who, along with my grandmother, Giuseppina, taught me how to see through the nature of things and contemplate their beauty.

Abbreviations

See the bibliography for full references.

Bustān	Saʿdi 1363/1984.
EI^2	*Encyclopaedia of Islam*. New Edition. Edited by P. Bearman, Th. Bianquis, C. E. Bosworth, E. van Donzel and W. P. Heinrichs, 11 vols. Leiden: Brill, 1960–2009.
EI^3	*Encyclopaedia of Islam, Three*. Edited by Gudrun Krämer, Denis Matringe, John Nawas, and Everett K. Rowson. Leiden: Brill, 2007–.
EIr	*Encyclopaedia Iranica*. General ed. Ehsan Yarshater. London: Routledge & Kegan Paul, 1982–. Also online at http://www.iranicaonline.org.
Golestān	Saʿdi 1368/1989.
Kimiyā	al-Ghazāli 1380/2001.
Ms. Tehran 1296	Ms. Majles 900
Ms. Berlin 1306	Or Oct. 3451
Ms. Tehran 1321	Ms. Majles 2569
Ms. Dublin 1320s	Per 109
Ms. Kabul 1325	Ms. 3144
Ms. Paris 1320s	Supplément Persan 1796
Ms. London 1328	Ethé 1117 (Islamic 876)
Ms. Dushanbe 1310s	Ms. 502
Ms. Dublin 1340s	Per 113
Ms. Tehran 1340s	Ms. Majles 2570
Ms. Tehran 1352	Ms. Majles 7773
Ms. Qom 1340s	Ms. 1453
Ms. Mashhad 1364	Ms. 10412
Ms. Paris 1366	Supplément Persan 1778
Ms. Qom 1371	Ms. 11920
Ms. Paris 1384	Supplément Persan 816
Ms. Paris 1390s	Supplément Persan 817
Ms. London 1416	Ethé 1118 (Islamic 287)
Ms. Yale 1432	Ms. Persian 7
Ms. Paris 1461	Supplément Persan 1357
Saʿdi YE	Saʿdi 1385/2006a
Saʿdi KhE	Saʿdi 1386/2007

Note on Dates, Names, and Transliteration

Unless otherwise indicated, all dates given in this book (years and centuries) refer to the Gregorian Calendar ("CE"). In the few instances in which Islamic (Hijri) lunar years are given, they precede the Gregorian date (e.g., 656/1258). In the footnotes and bibliography, references to books and articles published in Iran include the solar Hijri (occasionally lunar) or Persian Imperial date, followed by the Gregorian date.

While I have adopted an approach to the transcription that is capable of accommodating both Persian and Arabic (mainly through the guidelines given by the *International Journal of Middle East Studies*), I have preferred to rely on a simplified method for the transcription of modern publications in Persian. For the sake of readability, I have preferred to transcribe the names of the most common premodern Persian poets among the Anglophone readership (such as Saʿdi, Hafez, Rumi, etc.) according to the simplified method. In the case of cities and dynasties that are familiar to Anglophone specialized audiences, I have not specified the long vowels. For the Mongol names, I have tried to stay close to the conventional forms used by specialists in the field of Mongol and Ilkhanid studies. While the word "ghazal" appears throughout the book as an English word, I have chosen to italicize "*qasida*" without recurring to a full transliteration (*qaṣīda*).

Plates

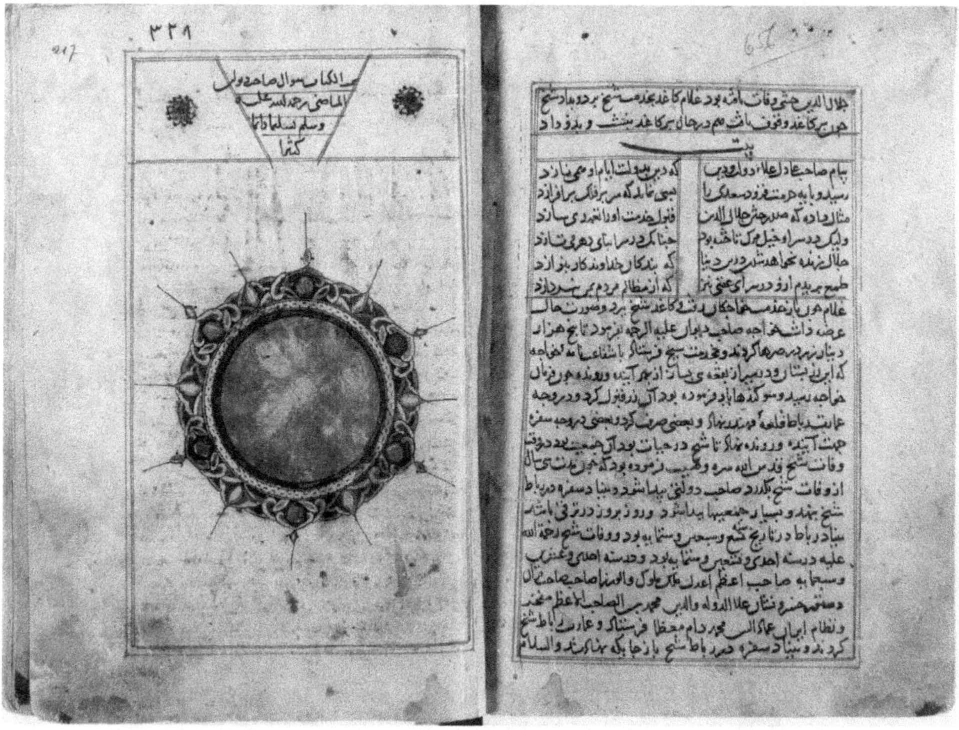

PLATE 1 Folios with colophon and date of Saʿdi's death, construction and restoration of Sufi lodge, Saʿdi's *Kulliyāt*, c. late 1320s.
© BIBLIOTHÈQUE NATIONALE DE FRANCE

PLATE 2 Single-page frontispiece, Saʿdi's *Kulliyāt*, early 14th century

PLATE 3 Left folio of double-page frontispiece, Saʿdi's *Kulliyāt*, mid-14th century

PLATE 4 Folio with heading, Sa'di's *Kulliyāt*, 725/1325, King Muhammad Zahir Shah's Personal Library Collection

Introduction: The Mufti of the Masters of Gazes

As you travel across the horizons
And collect words of wisdom from oceans and opulent lands,
Let me share this fine point with you:
What gift will you bring to your dear ones
If not Saʿdi's *Book of Marvels*, pressed against your chest?
Badāyiʿ 312[1]

•••

Here in the abode of Islam, your countenance is the niche where
I pray:
The Mongols may invade us, but I won't abandon the direction of
my prayer.
Badāyiʿ 384[2]

∴

The image on the cover of this book is from the oldest unstudied manuscript of the complete works (*Kulliyāt*) of Saʿdi of Shiraz (c. 1217–1292). Saʿdi is regarded as one of the most renowned lyric poets of premodern Iran, and his literary masterpieces embody the system of aesthetic and ethical values that dominated the Persianate world for centuries.[3] As one can read in the top cartouche, which is framed by two lotuses emerging from turquoise and azure backdrops, Saʿdi is introduced with the prestigious title of "King of the Poets" (*malik al-shuʿarā*).[4] I have chosen this folio as the cover of this book not only

1 Saʿdi YE, 146 [1.1] Arabic numerals in square brackets refer to the original Persian texts in the Appendix (1.1: Part one, text number one, 1.2, 2.2, etc.). Throughout this book, all translations are my own, unless otherwise noted. Notations at the bottom of each translated poem signal its number and the name of the collection to which it belongs according to Yusofi's edition (Saʿdi YE) or relevant manuscripts.

2 [1.2] Saʿdi YE, 179.

3 Ms. Kabul 1325, 491. The manuscript (see description below) is now kept in the National Archives of Afghanistan in Kabul, and it was copied (presumably in Shiraz) in 1325.

4 Saʿdi is introduced as *malik al-shuʿarā* also in one of the oldest extant manuscripts (copied in 1306) collecting a selection of his poems. See Ms. Berlin 1306, ff. 1b–2a, 76a/b.

 | DOI:10.1163/9789004435902_002

for its rare attestation of a specific literary honorific ascribed to Saʿdi, but also for the compelling lines that the copyist selected to showcase the poet's lyrical art and aesthetic values:

> If you cherish your sanity, do not behold beautiful visages with
> your gaze;
> And if you do behold them, bid farewell to your restful sleep.
>
> I see Zoroastrians, Christians, and Muslims bowing to worship,
> We only worship in the direction of our beloved, as enchanting as a
> painting.
> *Khavātīm* 661[5]

The lines belong to one of Saʿdi's most beautiful exercises in the art of ghazal composition, a poetic form that is comparable to the sonnet of the Western tradition. We may consider Saʿdi's seven hundred ghazals as pieces of minimalist literary architecture that, in the space of six or seven lines, create marvelous poetic intertwinements between courtly, spiritual, and sensual aesthetics.[6] Such formally impeccable miniatures in verse approach the fusion between homoerotic desires and philosophical reflections on the experience of time and the inner space of the beholder with an invisibly intricate levity that one could compare with the masterful verve and the psychological complexity that pervades Dante Alighieri's *sonetti* and Shakespeare's sonnets.

In the broad panorama of world literature, few writers have been as widely celebrated and strictly misunderstood as Saʿdi of Shiraz, who brought the Persian lyric tradition to one of its highest pinnacles of smooth aesthetic elegance and sensual theo-erotic refinement.[7] This book constitutes an attempt

---

5 [1.3] Saʿdi YE, 295.

6 The ghazal, as a poetic genre, can be defined as a relatively short poem (usually between five and ten distiches) whose functions and uses within the Persianate literary polysystem roughly correspond to the tradition of the sonnet in the Western literary tradition. Although the ghazal is a primarily amorous composition, it is often a vehicle—especially after the first half of the 13th century—for expressing spiritual and political content. See Meisami 1987, 237–98, and, for a more in-depth study of the use of the word "ghazal" in the early stages of the gradual establishment of its position within the literary canon and its development as a form and as a genre, Lewis 2006 and the primary and secondary sources discussed therein.

7 It is noteworthy that the 15th-century poet Jāmī, who contributed to the dynamic crystallization of the Timurid and early-Safavid canon of the Persian lyric ghazal (see Lewis 2018a), in one of the paragraphs of his critical survey of the poetic tradition states that "no one composed ghazals before him [Saʿdi]." Jāmi 1385/2006, 105. Jāmi's statement should be interpreted as a piece of evidence attesting to the fact that Persian poets, at least from the 13th

to offer meaningful pathways through the open landscape of Saʿdi's balanced contemplation of the beauty of the world, one which stands at the intersection of imagination and the psycho-physiological dimensions of spirituality and sexual desire.[8] Hopefully, both specialists and readers who approach this treasury of world poetry for the first time will find in this book unexpected reasons to be slowly ravished by Saʿdi's lines. The three parts of this study might be read as three different monographs constantly relating to each other through the multifaceted pathways that Saʿdi's poetry establishes. The first part of the book investigates the flesh of Saʿdi's ghazals through the study of the erotic and political facets of this lyrical corpus as they intersect with some of his other works, such as the *Gulistān* and his obscene output in verse. The second part will endeavor to conjure from the same flesh the most soulful aspects of Saʿdi's poetry through the study of the spiritual and philosophical roots of the ghazals' staging of the "visionary experience." We may think of the third and final part, the final two chapters, along with the Epilogue, as an opportunity to read Saʿdi's ghazals as both traces of historical performances and performative attempts to create experience through poetic language itself. The structure of the book thus reflects the dualistic nature of medieval anthropology, but with the addition of a final spin: the body, the soul, and the movement of images and sounds that mediate between the physical and metaphysical origins of beauty.

Before offering a survey of Saʿdi's life and works within the historical context in which the poet flourished, I wish to present the contents of the chapters of this book through Saʿdi's own words. The text I have chosen for this task, and which I quote in full, is not only one of Saʿdi's most beautiful ghazals, but it also stands out as a poem that incorporates the majority of the key "moods"

century onwards, would recognize the difference between the use of the word "ghazal" as a nonspecific denomination for a lyric mood in poetry (regardless of the genre or the form in which it would appear) and the development of a distinct and formally recognizable genre. For instance, the 14th-century rhetorician Tāj al-Ḥalāvī (1341/1962, 86) mentioned the poetry of Saʿdi as the epitome of the ghazal tradition.

8 The most important monographs, published in English, on Saʿdi's life and works are John Yohannan's *The poet Saʿdi: A Persian Humanist* (Yohannan 1987) and Fatemeh *Keshavarz's Lyrics of Life: Saʿdi on Love, Cosmopolitanism and Care of the Self* (Keshavarz 2015). For the most accurate surveys of the philological, biographical, and literary discussions of Saʿdi's life and oeuvre, see Lewis 2001 ("Golestān-e Saʿdi." *EIr*) and Losensky 2012 ("Saʿdi," *EIr*). The only publication exclusively dedicated to the study of Saʿdi's ghazals is Saʿid Hamidiān's *Saʿdi dar ghazal* (Hamidian 1383/2004). Another indispensable secondary source, mainly as far as Saʿdi's ethics are concerned, is one lengthy chapter of Charles-Henri de Fouchécour's *Moralia: Les notions morales dans la littérature persane du 3e/9e au 7e/13e siècle* (de Fouchécour 1986), 311–48.

and overarching ideas that inhabit the complex and yet evenly elegant literary universe of the author. Moreover, the enchanting articulation of images that the lines are going to deploy before our eyes will hopefully defy the cliché that for decades has reduced the verve of Saʿdi's lyric genius to "an ahistorical, abstracted, and blandly ethical shadow of influence" over the Persian literary canon.[9]

This poem belongs to Saʿdi's second collection of ghazals, known as the *Badāyiʿ* (the "Book of Marvels"), whose poems were probably composed between the end of the 1250s and the mid-1260s. The geographical setting of this specific text is the city of Shiraz, the capital of the southern Iranian region of Fars, at the time of the gradual decline of the ruling family (the Salghurid dynasty) in the 1260s, and only a few years before the Mongol political influence over this semi-independent and wealthy polity reached its apogee. It is possible that the level of self-confidence exuding from the following lines speaks to the poet's grand return from an encounter with Mongol officials of high rank. The encounter may have occurred in Tabriz, the new capital of the Ilkhanid empire, where Saʿdi's future patron, the *ṣāḥib dīvān* Shams al-Dīn Juvaynī, resided.

The poem showcases an excellent intersection between the aesthetic, spiritual, and philosophical values through which Saʿdi presents himself in a political and courtly context and as a source of inspiration for the practitioners of the art of gazing. In the first line, Saʿdi sets the general tone of the poem by introducing himself as the *muftī* (that is, the deliverer of official legal opinions, *fatwās*) in the religion (*millat*) of those who behold beauty:

> Saʿdi left, counting his steps, and here he swiftly returns:
> The mufti of the religion of the Masters of Gazes has returned.
>
> He has returned, with his passion for the "comely boys attesting to sacred beauty" [*shāhid*].
> Nostalgic for the spring breeze, the morning lover of the songs of birds has returned.
>
> He returned for you to believe that his bewilderment did not fade away
> So that you won't say that from intoxication he returned to his senses.

---

9 I owe this evocative metaphor, expressed in a private conversation, to Jane Mikkelson, a true *ṣāḥib naẓar*.

His heart at the mercy of its solitude, distraught are his thoughts,
Stranded he feels, and yet his body to his abode has returned.

For years his intellect left—he thought—to learn tranquility:
What did it learn? As more bewildered than ever it has returned.

Behold how the intellect escapes from the flood of the pain of love:
At large for years across the world, and yet to the whirlpool of danger it has returned.

You shall know that the heart was the firm pivot of his stability,
As it turned like a compass, but to its origin it has returned.

Ah, how thirsty he was to behold the countenance of the dear ones:
And look now how the water of life to his vital organs has returned!

The soil of Shiraz constantly bears the most fragrant roses:
And here a new eloquent nightingale has returned!

Insanity took him away, and passion rushed him back.
His status was gone, but see how loftily it has returned!

He returned from Syria to Shiraz with the passion of Khusraw,
Who gave up Shikar's sweet kisses for Shīrīn's sweeter embrace.

Guilty he is, but, O people, do not blame his deeds, as the Merciful
Does not punish the sinner if through the door he has returned.

So much violence he has faced from the darkest nights of separation
Till today, as the moonlight, shining through the night, has returned.

How wondrous it was for him to reach the day when his desires were fulfilled.
Perhaps the tyrannical celestial spheres withdrew from their cruelty?

The virginal bride of his mind will no longer suffer
From the loneliness of orphanhood: her father has now returned.

But worthless is the handful of cheap marbles that he carries
Now that to the ocean of pearls he has returned.

As he could not secure the kingdom of art [*hunar*], no solution he saw:
Begging at the door of the patrons of masterful virtues [*hunar*], he has returned.

Badāyiʿ 474[10]

What is the exact meaning implied by Saʿdi's grandiloquent self-proclamation that he is the *muftī* in the "religion of the Master of Gazes"? What is the role of religion and spirituality—especially from the jurisprudential angle that the word *muftī* introduces—in a series of lines that discuss the function of erotic and intellectual aesthetics, vision, and poetry in the context of the poet's alleged return to Shiraz? This book will try to respond indirectly to these questions by considering the act of contemplating beauty as the focal point of the aesthetics of vision that circulate within the entirety of Saʿdi's works.

As Saʿdi was never a real *muftī*, we may try to disclose his metaphor by comparing it with an observation that the renowned scholar and theologian al-Ghazālī (d. 1111), one of Saʿdi's sources of inspiration, delivered when asserting that scholars fall into two groups: "those *muftīs* who write official *fatwās* and who are the companions of sultans, and those who have knowledge of divine unity and the actions of the heart and who are the solitary and secluded residents of the Sufi lodges [*zāwiyas*]."[11] Saʿdi experienced spiritual seclusion in the lodges of the Sufis at different stages of his life: not only as a young student in Baghdad and Shiraz, but also later in life, when (according to a key passage that I have recently found in an important manuscript of Saʿdi's collected works) the Juvaynī brothers offered the poet a sum of five thousand gold dinars for the construction of a Sufi lodge (*ribāṭ*), which was completed in 1280–81.[12] Saʿdi also associated with sultans and notables of varying ages, genders, ethnicities, and ethical inclinations. In spite of the modern prejudice that portrays Saʿdi as a poet whose panegyric output is irrelevant in the face of his broader literary production, his works reveal that, after his youthful disaffection toward court poetry, he sought the patronage of rulers throughout his life. In the poem above, the mention of the contrast between the modest worth of his poetic art (compared to modest marbles) and the "ocean of pearls" is an allusion to the wealth of the Salghurid sultanate (with a hint at the Salghurid

10 [1.4] Saʿdi YE, 217–18. The following early 14th-century manuscripts confirm the inclusion on the ghazal in the *Badāyiʿ*: Ms. Kabul 1325, 488; Ms. Tehran 1321, 197. Later manuscripts include the text in the *Khavātīm* collection, which Saʿdi likely composed after the 1270s: Ms. Qom 1340s, 329–30; Ms. Paris 1461, f. 255a.

11 Quoted and translated by Frank Griffel (2009a, 49).

12 See below, p. 22.

monopoly of the pearl trade in the Persian Gulf) and its conspicuous investment in artistic and literary patronage.

Whether for financial gain (pearls in exchange for marbles) or broader political concerns, Saʿdi cultivated the pedagogy of kingship. He wrote a few collections of advice for kings and rulers, mainly for his patrons attached to the Ilkhanate, the portion of the Mongol empire that ruled over Iran and the surrounding lands (including eastern Anatolia, Iraq, the southern Caucasus and the western fringes of Turkistān). Therefore, the metaphorical *fatwās* that Saʿdi composed for his patrons were indeed sources of ethical guidance in verse and prose, but also lyrical intimations inspiring the cultivation of a discourse on the appreciation of beauty as an endeavor directed at fulfilling the spiritual destiny of humankind. In this respect, the allusion to the sacred bodies of beautiful boys in the second line of the ode constitutes no surprise: in Saʿdi's works, the themes of homoeroticism and the celebration of rulers are so pervasive that these two elements have been the object of praise and amusement for centuries, whereas in the past few decades they have often elicited scorn and denial. In partial response to this neglect, the first chapter of this book will explore Saʿdi's peculiar aesthetics of homosocial eroticism and its connection with political power in the context of the courtly foundation of his lyric.

The second chapter figuratively expands on the lines of the ode in which Saʿdi seems to be ascribing his lyrical talent to his peregrinations around the world, in incessant pursuit of objects of sensual and political desire. In one of the lines above, the poet describes Shiraz as a rose garden, which is also the title of the book (*Gulistān*) in which prose and poetry are juxtaposed with each other in a fashion that coats the fiction of his lyricism with a rhetorical veneer of verisimilitude. This chapter will test the limits of Saʿdi's lyric as the appropriation of a genre that frames its obsession with the beauty of the world by questioning the boundaries between historical truth and feigned confessions. Although Saʿdi's poem on his "return" does not defy the boundaries of linguistic decency (as was expected by the standard of courtly lyricism), one may legitimately wonder to what extent the passion for the contemplation of beautiful youths that the poet displays could ever reflect an aesthetic posture that is both spiritual and sexual. Saʿdi's collection of obscene poetry (never published in critical edition) legitimizes this question, and the third chapter reframes this portion of his corpus in an attempt to read the poet's pornographic production as "counter-texts" to the courtly refinement of his ghazals.

While in the third chapter I argue that, from the viewpoint of the relationship between literary language and extratextual reality, Saʿdi's pornography reifies the object of desire (the body and its intimate parts are exposed as they "are," in a sort of hyper-realistic representation), the second part of the book investigates the sacred exposure of the body as a process of fetishization. The body as a spiritual fetish is a body that is elevated through and beyond its flesh, until it turns into or points to something other than itself. The five chapters that constitute this part reframe the misleading concept of "mystical lyric" within a broader horizon that explores how Saʿdi's sacred eroticism (especially in the ghazal in which the presence of a religious afflatus is undeniable) conceives of human beauty as a sign that guides the beholder toward a rational form of awareness concerning the divine. In this context, the act of beholding beauty is filtered through a visionary transcendental experience that never loses touch with the sensory world, while also emerging to the surface of literary creativity as an exercise that incorporates within the aesthetic texture of the ghazal musical performances leading to spiritual forms of cognition.

In the second line of the ode, what I translate as "comely boys attesting to sacred beauty" is a provocative rendition that aims at spelling out the semantic territory covered by the word *shāhid*. Meaning "witness," the term *shāhid* stands for the young man whose beauty is a testimony to the divine splendor. The fourth chapter surveys the tradition of Sufi opinions on the permissibility of amatory poetry and the visual contemplation of human beauty to define the *shāhid* in Saʿdi's ghazals (and in those of his contemporaries, or in the canon upon which they draw) as an interpretive opportunity for the beholder to develop a profound awareness of the beauty of God. I call this approach "rational-inferential," as it expresses the sobriety that is involved in the perusal of beautiful forms when reading them as signs that remind the beholder of a transcendental order of being. This discussion carries on throughout the fifth chapter, in which I will try to make sense of the term *ʿārif* (mystic, Gnostic or, as I shall propose, "spiritual beholder") as an analogue of the concept of "mufti of the Masters of Gazes." The chapter will emphasize the role of optical vision for the development of Saʿdi's representation of the relationship between sensuality and spirituality in the contemplation of beauty.

The series of lines that stresses the role of the heart as a mediator between the poet's peregrinations through the world, the contemplation of beauty, and the interaction between the body and the inner pathways of the imagination motivates my attempt, displayed in the sixth chapter, to reinterpret some aspects of Saʿdi's lyricism through Avicenna's psychological tradition and al-Ghazālī's "spiritual cardiology." In the first part of the chapter I present the role that the five internal senses theorized by Avicenna play within the psychology of Saʿdi's lyric subject. The second part critically questions the traditional "mystical" approaches to the study of Saʿdi's poetry by recognizing the poet's metaphysics of beauty as derivative of the cosmological aspects of Avicenna's psychological system. In particular, I will analyze the problematic question of the "invisible world" (or the "unseen," *ʿālam-i ghayb*) in Saʿdi's poetry from the perspective of the role of imagination in the lyric subject's experience of supernal ideals of beauty.

The seventh and the eighth chapters unearth the Avicennian psychological foundations of al-Ghazālī's approach to the Sufi concepts of *mukāshafa* ("unveiling") and *mushāhada* ("spiritual contemplation") and their reliance on Avicenna's emanationist cosmology. Through these analyses, I relate the most visionary aspects of Saʿdi's lyricism to the "imaginal-cosmological" modality of cognition, which coexists with the rational-inferential approach to the semiotics of beholding human beauty.

The ninth chapter and the tenth, in the third part of the book, consider the performative aspect of Saʿdi's lyricism from the perspective of the practice of *samāʿ*, or "mystical concert," which I translate as "lyrical ritual." By taking into account Saʿdi's approaches to the ethics of both poetry audition and sensual desire in a Sufi context, I explore the chronology of the poet's lyric output from the perspective of a gradual disengagement from the scholastic approach that characterizes his first collection of ghazals. I will follow the poet's trajectory in a fashion that takes into account the transition from Saʿdi's representation of *samāʿ* as a protected environment for the contemplation of the invisible world to his presentation of lyric poetry as the embodiment of the visionary experience itself.

1 New Directions for the Reconstruction of Saʿdi's Biography

Soon after the seizure and subsequent devastation of Baghdad (1258) and the execution of the last Abbasid caliph in that city, al-Mustaʿṣim, the Mongol conquerors established themselves as the new ruling elite controlling a territory that stretched between Central Asia and eastern Anatolia.[13] None of these tragedies directly affected Shiraz, which, during the "short century" between the Mongol destruction of the Central Asian cities of Samarkand and Bukhara (1220) and the downfall of the Abbasid Caliphate, enjoyed some of the most politically and culturally flourishing decades of its premodern history—mostly by virtue of the enlightened government of the atabegs of the Salghurid

13 For a general introduction to the downfall of the Abbasid caliphate and the formation of the Mongol Ilkhanid empire, see Boyle 1968. See in particular Lambton 1988 for an accurate study of the socio-economic and cultural dimensions of the transition from pre-Mongol to Ilkhanid Iran, and the collection of essays edited by Charles Melville and Bruno de Nicola (2016). On the specific events related to the Mongol conquest of Baghdad, see Boyle 1961; Gilli-Elewy 2000; Hassan 2016; and Biran 2016; 2018.

dynasty (wo were local rulers originally affiliated with the Saljuq conquest of Iran). These are the decades when Musharrif al-Dīn Muṣliḥ gained renown as Saʿdi Shīrāzī by attaching himself to the court of the Salghurid Atabeg Abū Bakr b. Saʿd (d. 1260) and his son, Saʿd b. Abī Bakr (d. 1260).[14] The glory of their rule was short-lived, as both the prince and his father died between May and June of 1260, leaving the economically and culturally wealthy province in political turmoil lasting for several decades.[15]

As is the case for most medieval Persian poets, the scattered clues we possess about Saʿdi's life do not constitute a substantial corpus of biographical details capable of providing us with a compelling historical narrative.[16] The little we know about Saʿdi is either gleaned from the semi-fictitious biographical references that he disseminated in his own works, or rooted in scholarly assumptions often made on the basis of unclear demarcations between historiographical veracity and literary creativity. An early 13th-century manuscript of Saʿdi's works, presumably copied in the late 1320s in Shiraz, confirms the consensus reached in the scholarship on the date of Saʿdi's death, which most likely occurred in 1292.[17] Otherwise, the only dates on which one may rely to tentatively outline the chronology of Saʿdi's life and works are the dates of the poet's completion of the *Saʿdī-nāma*, most commonly known as the *Būstān* ("The Orchard," 1257), and the *Gulistān* ("The Rose Garden," 1258). Philological evidence strongly suggests that while the *Gulistān* was dedicated to the

14 For the most recent discussion on Saʿdi's name and patronymic, see Bashari 2020, 45–49.

15 On the history of Shiraz and the region of Fars during the Ilkhanid period, see Aigle 2005. On the economic and political renaissance of Fars during Abū Bakr's reign, see ibid., 100–11. For an unstudied historical source celebrating the first decade of Abū Bakr's military exploits and socio-economic policies, see Shams-e Qays 1388/2009, 31–42.

16 For a romanticized narrative of Saʿdi's life and works, see Zarrinkub 2007. For the most recent developments on the study of Saʿdi's biography on the basis of historiographical and literary sources, see the following pages, as well as Ingenito 2014, Ingenito 2019, and Bashari 2020. Without having consulted my contribution on the study of Saʿdi's panegyrics, Bashari (whose book was published only a few months after my latest article) reaches conclusions similar to mine on some key points. Although I do not agree with many of Bashari's hypotheses (some of which did not take into account specific manuscript sources), his book is by far the most comprehensive monograph on Saʿdi's life and the poet's engagement with the political context of 13th-century Shiraz. Considering the core of overlapping primary sources that both Bashari and I have used for our research, I will often refer to his book to signal the passages in which our findings diverge and/or coincide.

17 Ms. Paris 1320s, f. 337b. The passage in this important manuscript indicates the *hijrī* year 691, which covers most of 1292 in the Gregorian calendar. On the basis of other sources, Saʿid Nafisi suggested that Saʿdi died in the month of Ẕū al-Ḥijja of the same year (November 1292). For a discussion on Nafisi's argument and a comparison with other sources, see Bashari 2020, 304–306.

Salghurid prince Saʿd (son of Abū Bakr, also referred to, in Western scholarship, as Saʿd II), the *Būstān* was offered to prince Muḥammad (Saʿd II's son, who died in November 1262, at the age of fourteen) as a compendium of moral and spiritual teachings.[18] Although the exact derivation of Saʿdi's pen name (*takhalluṣ*) is still contentious among scholars, the close examination of new sources demonstrates that the poet's lyric persona developed mainly through Saʿdi's attachment to prince Saʿd II.[19]

Scholars have proposed that Saʿdi "returned" to Shiraz in 1256 or 1257, after decades spent studying at Baghdad's renowned Niẓāmiyya and travelling throughout Mesopotamia, the Levant, and the Arabian Peninsula.[20] In particular, the conviction that no encomiastic texts were composed before the late 1250s has left room for speculating that Saʿdi's literary activity at the service of (or in proximity to) the Salghurid court did not start before the completion of the earliest recension of the *Būstān* (1257). However, Saʿdi's manifestations of affection toward the Salghurid family and the intimate pedagogical bond that would tie him to the two youngest male members of the family, prince Saʿd II, and his son, Muḥammad, point to the fact that Saʿdi had spent at least two decades in Shiraz before his two major works were completed and presented at court as a token of the poet's reverential acceptance of the ruling dynasty's patronage.

---

18 The analysis of the oldest manuscripts suggests that Saʿdi likely compiled different editions of this book, which he dedicated to Saʿd II and his son Muḥammad at different points in his life. See Ingenito 2019, 127–32, and, for a more detailed analysis, see Chapter 1, p. 87, n. 73.

19 See Qazvini 1377/1998, 34–35. Apart from the internal textual evidence indicated by Qazvini, important 14th-century historical sources confirm the name of prince Saʿd II as the origin of Saʿdi's penname: Ibn al-Fuwaṭī's *Majmaʿ al-ādāb* (completed in 1312, see Ibn al-Fuwati 1416/1995, 5: 248), Mustawfī's *Tārikh-i Guzīda* (1330, see Mostawfi 1364/1985, 734), and Junayd Shīrāzī's *Shadd al-izār* (1389, see Jonayd Shirāzi 1328/1949, 272). Zarrinkub (1386/2007, 65–69) argues that Saʿdi's *takhalluṣ* was related to the Salghurid family as a whole (the "Saʿds"). However, his hypothesis is based on untenable opinions, such as the argument of Saʿdi's return to Shiraz in 1257, the thesis according to which he was in his mid-fifties by that time, the assumption of the historical veracity of his travel to Khʷārazm, and the ostensible lack of encomia dedicated to Abū Bakr during the apogee of his reign. For a partial confutation of these points, see below. For a survey of the diverging opinions on this matter, see Safā 1368/1989, 1.3: 584–614; Losensky 2012.

20 This idea is mainly based on a couple of verses in Saʿdi's introduction to the *Būstān*. In these lines, the poet mentions that the wisdom contained in the book is the result of the experiences acquired in the course of his peregrinations (*Bustān*, 37, vv. 98–105; see also Zarrinkub 1386/2007, 65). For a critique of the historical veracity of Saʿdi's peregrinations, see Yāhaqi 1379/2000; Dehqāni 1393/2014; 2016.

A further point of contention is Saʿdi's age at the time of the completion of the *Gulistān*. On the basis of a line from Saʿdi's introduction to the book, most scholars posit that the author had turned fifty in 1258:

> Every moment a breath of life passes. When I look, not much remains.
> O you who sleep as fifty years pass, can you seize these five days?[21]

As noted by Paul Losensky, fifty "is a conventional age at which to reflect on life's transience and one's life's work."[22] As a potentially rhetorical stratagem, this number does not establish any biographical point of certainty, especially considering that the "you" that the line addresses may be read as a rhetorical "thou" which, as an interlocutory didactic exemplum, does not necessarily coincide with Saʿdi's biographical persona.[23] On the contrary, if we accept ʿAbbās Eqbāl Ashtiyāni's theory that situates Saʿdi's date of birth between 1213 and 1218,[24] we may speculate that the poet was in his late twenties when he attached himself to the Salghurid court in Shiraz in the 1240s, when the atabeg Abū Bakr—"the Heir to Solomon's kingdom" and "Sultan by land and sea"—consolidated his absolute rule over the entirety of Fars, the Persian Gulf, and the islands of Bahrain.[25] In one of the fragments that constitute Saʿdi's collection of political poems known as *Ṣāḥibiyya*, Saʿdi addresses an anonymous patron by declaring that his father "had served him for his entire life." Saʿdi refers to himself as the son who was nurtured by this patron and who has

---

21 [1.5] *Golestān* 52, translated by Paul Losensky (2012).

22 Ibid.

23 A similar rhetorical stratagem is found in a passage from the *Būstān* in which the poet mentions the ages of "seventy" and "fifty." *Bustān*, 182 [1.6].

24 Cf. Losensky's elaboration on Ashtiyāni's argument (2012).

25 Shams-i Qays's *Compendium* on Persian poetics (see Landau 2013) is the oldest historical source (curiously overlooked by modern scholarship on Salghurid historiography) that mentions the official titulature of Abū Bakr in the context of his military exploits (*muḥarriz mamālik al-barr wa al-baḥr*) under the caliphal approval (*Yamīn al-khilāfat*). See Shams-e Qays 1388/2009, 32. Considering that Shams-i Qays refers to Abū Bakr's conquest of both shores of the Persian Gulf, including the Arab port of Qaṭīf (in the spring of 1244, see Vassāf 1259/1852, 178), it can be argued that he dedicated his *Compendium* to the Atabeg sometime in the mid-1240s (and not the late 1230s). Ibid., 39–40. Vaṣṣāf considers Abū Bakr's conquest of Kish (which occurred on May 8, 1229) as a turning point in the glorious destiny of the Salghurid state prior to the Mongol occupation of Baghdad. The Shirazi historian mentions that it was thanks to this achievement that the Atabeg earned the diploma that proclaimed him "Sultan by land and sea" (*Sulṭān al-barr wa al-baḥr*). Vassāf 1259/1852, 178–79. On these events, see Aigle 2005, 101–103. See also Aubin 1953, 82–83; Jackson 2017, 245–46.

offered him his service since the time he was born.[26] Considering the reference to Saʿdi's own upbringing, we may infer that this fragment was composed to address Abū Bakr.[27] If this inference holds true, it is possible that Saʿdi's family (allegedly of scholarly extraction)[28] made good use of Abū Bakr's financial means and connections with the Caliph by sending Saʿdi to the prestigious Niẓāmiyya school in Baghdad, sometime in the 1230s.[29]

The philological foundation of my reappraisal of the chronology of Saʿdi's life lies in a few key manuscripts copied between the late 13th and the early 15th centuries. Some of these manuscripts are the oldest documents recording Saʿdi's collected works (or parts of them), and have been often overlooked by the compilers of the most recent critical editions of the poet's literary output. It is also with the aid of these manuscripts, which prove especially useful whenever *lacunae* appear in the printed editions, that I have formulated a new theory for a chronological approach to Saʿdi's lyric production which will be introduced in the first, the second, and the ninth chapters of this book.[30] Some of the earliest manuscripts of the poet's collected works (*Kulliyāt*) identify the atabeg Abū Bakr as the dedicatee of two poems of praise (*qasida*s) that the editors of Saʿdi's works have usually described as generic praise compositions that lack the mention of specific recipients.[31] These two *qasida*s are the earliest

26 [1.7] Ms. Kabul 1325, 633–34. Cf. Saʿdi KhE, 748.

27 See Bashari 2020, 51–52.

28 All my clan, my people, were religious scholars,
yet falling in love with you taught me how to become a poet.
[1.8] Saʿdi YE, 239.

29 See Shams-e Qays 1388/2009, 35–36. On the relationship between the Salghurids and the Caliph, see Bashari 2020, 109.

30 For a description of the manuscripts, see the end of this introduction.

31 The two *qasida*s open with the following lines:

بزن که قوت بازوی سلطنت داری
که دست همت مردانت می دهد یاری

And:

به نوبت اند ملوک اندرین سپنج سرای
کنون که نوبت توست ای ملک به عدل گرای

Ms. Dushanbe 1310s (ff. 157a, 164b–165a) and Ms. London 1328 (ff. 318a–319b) introduce the two *qasida*s with the heading, "As guidance for the righteous king (*al-malik al-ʿādil*), atabeg Abū Bakr, son of Saʿd." Although in Ms. Kabul 1325 (531) the red ink introducing these two *qasida*s is partially discolored, some legible words (*fī naṣīḥat* … *ʿādil* … *Bakr* …) suggest that the heading reflects that of Mss. Dushanbe 1310s and London 1328. Ms. Tehran 1340s's heading (353, according to the foliation marked with pencil directly on the folios) reads "In praise of the lamented atabeg (*atābag al-marḥūm*) Abū Bakr, son of Saʿd." A similar heading appears in Ms. Tehran 1352 ("In praise of the fortunate atabeg Muẓaffar al-Dīn Abū Bakr b. Saʿd b. Zangī" 440–42). The latter heading is also found in Ms. Yale 1432,

recorded panegyrics ascribed to Saʿdi. As they mention Abū Bakr's ascension to the throne in the context of the consolidation of his rule over the "lands and seas," they were likely composed around the mid-1240s, which most historiographical sources recognize as the time when the Atabeg's rule was formally acknowledged throughout the Persian Gulf and large coastal portions of the Arabian peninsula and Gujarat.[32] The fact that Saʿdi does not mention his own name (a "signature" that is a standard feature characterizing most of his panegyric *qasida*s) in these two encomiastic texts constitutes further proof that the poet must have adopted his pen name (*takhalluṣ*) at a later time, presumably in the early 1250s, when he associated himself with Abū Bakr's son, prince Saʿd II. The two poems reveal a certain degree of familiarity between the Atabeg and the poet. The boldness with which Saʿdi addresses his patron suggests that the composition of these poems was prompted by Abū Bakr himself. Rather than praising the Atabeg with "irrational exaggerations," Saʿdi provides him with pieces of spiritual advice on how to become a righteous ruler.[33] Saʿdi ostensibly conveyed his opinion on the righteous form of government at

---

ff. 190a–91b. Saʿdi's mention of Abū Bakr's ascension to power might seem to refer to the year of the actual commencement of the Atabeg's reign (between 1226 and 1230, according to different sources; see Aigle 2005, 101). As I have recently pointed out (Ingenito 2019, 110–12), my dating of these *qasida*s to the later date of the 1240s finds support in a relatively short encomiastic *ghazal* (*bar angīkht shīrāzam az jūr-i shangī*), in which Saʿdi rhetorically manifests his surprise at how peaceful Shiraz has become since Abū Bakr took up the reins of the Sultanate of Fars (Saʿdi YE, 243; Saʿdi KhE, 696 [with slight variations, arbitrarily included in the *qasida*s section]; Ms. Tehran 1340s, 645; Ms. Tehran 1352, 615–16; Ms. Paris 1366, f. 222a/b; Ms. Yale 1432, ff. 349a–49b). Not only do most manuscripts list this *ghazal* as a later composition, but it is clear from the style of the text, especially in comparison with Saʿdi's manner of addressing Abū Bakr in his early works, that it was not intended to be dedicated to him. While this poem presents clear erotic elements (*khaṭ-i māh-rūyiān chu mushk-i tatārī / sar-i zulf-i khūbān chu dirʿ- i farangī*), Saʿdi's praises of Abū Bakr lack the amatory modality that characterizes the Persian panegyric tradition. Therefore, it is more likely that, in the presence of later representatives of the Salghurid dynasty, Saʿdi composed this ghazal in order to boast of the experiences he had acquired during his travels, or perhaps to convey an idealized image of Abū Bakr's reign to his later patrons. Bashari (2020, 74–76) reads one line of the poem as a reference to the Turkic military presence from Khʷārazm which ravaged Shiraz in 1224: *birūn jastam az tang-i turkān chu dīdam / jahān dar ham uftāda chūn mūy-i zangī*. However, it is more likely that here the word *tang* means "mountain pass" (and not "distress"), thus referring to the pass of Turkān, a locale in the proximity of Kazerun, to which Saʿdi also refers in the *Būstān* (166). Cf. Shabānkāre'i 1363/1984, 184.

32 [1.9] Saʿdi KhE, 693; Ms. Yale 1432, f. 191a. [1.10] Saʿdi KhE, 688; Ms. Yale 1432, f. 190b.

33 I shall not tell you: 'may you live for a thousand years!'
—as this isn't but an exaggeration that you would consider illogical. [1.11] Saʿdi KhE, 693. Ms. Kabul 1325, 532; Ms. Yale 1432, f. 191a.

a time when Abū Bakr had reached the peak of his aggressive policy of military expansionism:

> Do not conquer the East and the West, do not wage war:
> Bring happiness to people's hearts and appease their sorrow.[34]

As I shall illustrate in the first, second, and eighth chapters of this book, it can be argued that the first phase of Saʿdi's poetic activity was characterized by an anti-courtly devotional mood that led him to the cultivation of spiritual practices of seclusion and pious distance from mundane occupations. From the preaching tone of these two *qasida*s we may infer that they were composed during this early period of the poet's literary production. Abū Bakr's religious zeal—in stark contrast with his father's (Saʿd I) and his son's (Saʿd II) courtly engagement—is attested to in a plurality of sources, and it likely informed Saʿdi's initial posture.[35] Modern scholarship has often downplayed Saʿdi's political engagement for a variety of reasons. The fostering of the image of Saʿdi as a national poet embodying the quintessence of the Iranian ethical character has not helped overcome the prejudice that portrays him as a literary and spiritual actor detached from all base worldly affairs. This process of mystification of Saʿdi's persona and works ends up making invisible even the clearest traces of the poet's entanglement with the political affairs of his time. For instance, a lengthy ghazal ending with the expression "*Saʿdī-yi ākhar al-zamānam*" ("I am *the* Saʿdi till the end of time")[36] has been read as a mere

34 [1.12] Saʿdi KhE, 688; Ms. Dushanbe 1310s, f. 157a; Ms. Kabul 1325, 531; Ms. Yale 1432, f. 190b. Cf. Shams-i Qays's opposite wish: "And the hope is that soon all the regions of Iraq, if not the entirety of the horizons […] will be adorned by *khuṭba*s and coins recited and struck in his name, and that the peoples and the inhabitants of those regions, who wholeheartedly obey this ambitious king and yet suffer from injustice and misery, will finally rejoice in the shadow of his affection and the protection of his mercy." Shams-e Qays 1388/2009, 40. See also the lines by the poet Rafīʿ al-Dīn Lunbānī (d. ca. 1235) in which praises Abū Bakr as the "heir to Solomon's kingdom" by lauding his military campaign over land and sea: *girift mamlakat-i baḥr-u barr ba-d-ān khanjar / ki kār-i ʿālam-i shūrīda zū ba sāmān ast.* Lonbāni 1369/1990, 142.

35 As a privileged witness of the transition from Saʿd I's reign to Abū Bakr's takeover, Shams-i Qays offers detailed descriptions of Abū Bakr's religious fervor. See Shams-e Qays 1388/2009. Cf. Vassāf 1259/1852, 155–56; Shabānkāre'i 1363/1984, 184; Bayzāvi 1382/2002, 134; Ebn Zarkub Shirāzi 1389/2010, 150–51. On Abū Bakr's expulsion of prominent scholars who had been accused of teaching rational sciences (including physics and philosophy), see chapter 6, p. 304. See also chap 2, pp. 114vv; Aigle 2005, 107–108.

36 The line is not found in Yusofi's edition (Saʿdi YE, 180). For all the ancient manuscripts that record this line, see ibid., 516.

declaration of the poet's desire for eternal renown.[37] However, the structure of the poem (along with conventional traits, such as its transition from lyrical to encomiastic modality, or its allusion to kingship, etc.) suggests that the text was originally conceived as a panegyric, and the final twist in which the pen name of the poet is converted into an adjective reveals that, in this context, *Saʿd-ī* signifies "belonging to, affiliated with" Saʿd, presumably prince Saʿd II.

The chronology of Saʿdi's collections of ghazals reveals a gradual development of the poet's approach to the sensual aspect of sacred eroticism, evolving from a scholastic posture that often denies the value of sensual experiences to a more nuanced validation of the role of the body in the appreciation of human beauty for spiritual ends.[38] It is my contention that Saʿdi developed his lyrical engagement with the phenomenal dimension of the spiritual experience—through his increasing involvement with the practice of *samāʿ*, the audition of erotic poetry as a form of sacred inspiration—as a result of his proximity to prince Saʿd II.[39] As Saʿdi states in one of the two *qasida*s mentioned above, the "musical sessions" (*samāʿ*) of Abū Bakr's gathering "feature the remembrance of God [*ẕikr*] and Qurʾān recitation / without the voice of minstrels and the melodies of harps and flutes."[40] Saʿdi's juvenile distaste for the circulation and recitation of poetry in a courtly setting may explain both his praise of Abū Bakr's distance from mundane poetry and the poet's apparent encomiastic "silence" between the 1240s and the late 1250s, when he completed the *Būstān* and the *Gulistān*.

During those decades, prince Saʿd II, in his late teens and early twenties, took up a prominent role in the administration of the courtly affairs of the Salghurid sultanate. In 1247 he was in charge of holding court for and receiving the caliphal envoys from Baghdad.[41] Meanwhile, Saʿdi likely took up an active role in the aesthetic and spiritual upbringing of prince Saʿd II. Unlike his father, Saʿd II was keen to welcome lyric poets into his entourage at court, and it is possible that Saʿdi's poetry started circulating in Shiraz during the years of gift exchanges that led to the caliphal diplomatic mission in Fars.[42]

37 Bargneysi 1380/2001, 659; Keshavarz 2015, 6.
38 See chapter 9, pp. 451–68.
39 See chapter 2, pp. 112–20.
40 [1.13] Ms. Kabul 1325, 531. For other variants, cf. Saʿdi KhE, 688; Ms. Yale 1432, 190b.
41 Bashari 2020, 109.
42 For instance, in his praise of Prince Saʿd II, Farīd Iṣfahānī (1381/2002, 12) exclaimed, "Many are your panegyrists (*tu rā maddāḥ bisyār-and*)." While it is evident from the numerous *qasida*s that Farīd composed in praise of Abū Bakr that the atabeg showed little inclination to gatherings featuring the recitation of mundane poetry and wine-drinking, in many of his qasidas praising Prince Saʿd, Farīd emphasizes the drinking habits of his young

The dedication of the *Gulistān* to Saʿd II may be seen as the final consolidation of Saʿdi's proximity to the prince, and the development of the poet's taste for a conflation of the mundane and the spiritual in his renewed approach to the composition of lyric poetry. The final edition of the *Gulistān* was presented at court in the spring of 1258, only a few months after members of the Salghurid family, including Abū Bakr's nephew, Muḥammad-Shāh,[43] had participated in the Mongol sack of Baghdad, and a few months before Saʿd II met Hülegü Khān (the grandson of Genghis Khān and, de facto, the founder of the Ilkhanid dynasty) in Maragha.[44] In 1259, at the peak of Saʿdi's ascent in the Salghurid entourage, Hülegü nominated Saʿd II heir-apparent of Fars.[45] Although both Abū Bakr and Saʿd II died in the spring of 1260, the prestige that the Salghurid family acquired in the eyes of the Mongols solidified Saʿdi's transregional fame throughout the following decades, in spite of the turbulent political destiny of Fars.[46]

2 From the Fall of Baghdad to the Rise of the Juvaynī Family: the Need for Patronage and the Renewal of Saʿdi's Fame

Saʿdi mourned the sudden deaths of Abū Bakr and prince Saʿd II with the same pathos he displayed when lamenting the fall of the Abbasid caliphate and the execution of the Caliph.[47] The poet crafted these moving elegies in a fashion that reveals Saʿdi's interest in promoting dynastic continuity within the Salghurid family. In spite of Saʿdi's call for continuity, conspiracies, dynastic vendettas, and seditions dominated the political landscape of Shiraz throughout the years leading to the final demise of the dynasty. The new atabeg, Muḥammad, Saʿd II's son, ruled for less than three years, and his position was

---

patron's entourage: "Your festive gathering equals paradise, and one may legally drink wine therein / Because drinking wine is by no means illegal in paradise!" (Ibid., 32).

43 Vassāf 1259/1852, 183.

44 Banākati 1348/1969, 419.

45 Shabānkāre'i 1363/1984, 185.

46 Most sources agree upon 658/1260 as the date of Abū Bakr's and Saʿd II's deaths: either April 18 (5 Jumadā I, Shabānkāre'i 1363/1984, 184; Mostawfi 1364/1985, 506; Ebn Zarkub Shirāzi 1389/2010, 154), or May 17 (Jumadā II, Rashid al-Din 1389/2011, 15). See Aigle 2005, 101, n. 241; Ingenito 2019; Bashari 2020, 107. Peter Jackson (2017, 146) mentions that the death of Abū Bakr occurred in 659/1261 on the sole basis of Vaṣṣāf's account. Qazvini points out that the *hijrī* date 659 is a mistake that is found in some lithographic editions of Vaṣṣāf's *History*, whereas other manuscripts report the year 658. See Bashari 2020, 107, n. 1.

47 See Ingenito 2019, 118.

overshadowed by the political dexterity of his mother, Terken Khātūn (d. 1263), who subsumed the guardianship of the Salghurid sultanate and had the influential vizier Fakhr al-Dīn Abū Bakr executed.[48] Soon after the ilkhan Hülegü bestowed the official investiture (*yarligh*) upon Muḥammad, the fourteen-year-old prince passed away either as a consequence of an accidental fall from a rooftop or from being kicked to death by his mother.[49] An attentive perusal of the manuscript tradition suggests that Saʿdi addressed Fakhr al-Dīn (who was also one of the dedicatees of the *Gulistān*), Terken, and Muḥammad in several panegyrics, and dedicated to the latter prince his latest recension of the *Būstān* and his first collection of poems.[50]

After the death of prince Muḥammad, his uncle, Muḥammad-Shāh, one of the sons of Abū Bakr's brother (Salghūr-Shāh, poisoned by Abū Bakr sometime between the 1230s and the 1240s),[51] ruled for only six to nine months—in debauchery and insouciance, according to the sources.[52] Upon Terken Khātūn's instigation, Hülegü had him executed in the summer of 1263. As soon as Saljūq-Shāh, Muḥammad-Shāh's elder brother, took over as the new atabeg of Fars, Saʿdi composed a number of panegyrics to celebrate his enthronement.[53] Considering the extent to which historical chronicles extolled the exceeding beauty of his complexion, Saljūq-Shāh was likely the dedicatee of a number of Saʿdi's erotic ghazals.[54] In fact, in a panegyric lyric dedicated to Saljūq-Shāh,

48 The two oldest complete manuscripts of Saʿdi's *Kulliyāt* (Ms. Kabul 1325, 530–31; Ms. London 1328, f. 318a) recognize the minister Fakhr al-Dīn Abū Bakr as the dedicatee of one of Saʿdi's most moving *qasida*s on the transient nature of worldly experiences:
The world stands on water, and life in the wind:
I admire the wise man whose heart is free from them.
[1.14] See Saʿdi KhE, 655. On the basis of later manuscripts, Both Qazvini (73) and Bashari (2020, 292–93) erroneously stress that the text was dedicated to Majd al-Dīn Rūmī (d. 1289). Although the *qasida* might have repurposed during the last years of Saʿdi's life to praise other patrons, its references to the sack of Baghdad and the death of a young prince (presumably Saʿd II) confirm that Fakhr al-Dīn was the original recipient of the poem.

49 Vassāf 1259/1852, 182; Ebn Zarkub Shirāzi 1389/2010, 155; Shabānkāre'i 1363/1984, 185; Mostawfi 1364/1985, 506.

50 See below, and chapter 1, pp. 87–88.

51 Vassāf 1259/1852, 168–69.

52 Bayzāvi 1382/2002, 126; Vassāf 1259/1852, 181–86; Aigle 2005, 114–15.

53 See Ingenito 2019, 133–34; Bashari 2020, 173–83.

54 Both Vaṣṣāf (*manẓarī rāyiʿ va jamālī bī maṣāl dāsht*, Vassāf 1259/1852, 186) and Bayżāvī (*mardī ba ghāyat nīkū-ṣūrat būd, va mādarash az nizhād-i salāṭīn-i āl-i saljūq būd*, Bayzavi 1382/2003, 126) emphasize Saljūq-Shāh's beauty and Turkic maternal origins. Cf. the wording that Saʿdi chose to extoll the Atabeg's physical appearance:
Not even one's imagination could ever conjure up the frame of his body,
No eloquent tongues could ever mention all his splendid features....
A king whose countenance illuminates the world

Saʿdi displays one of his most elegant transitions from the erotic prelude to the encomium proper. This "transition" is a two-fold progression of images through which, from the beginning of the ghazal, the portrayal of an ideal prince and the praise of an imaginary beloved reach a perfect conflation.[55] In spite of both Saʿdi's and the populace of Shiraz's enthusiasm for the newly enthroned prince, Fars was far from regaining the political stability that it had enjoyed during Abū Bakr's reign. Saljūq-Shāh's decision to first marry Terken Khātūn for political convenience, then have her decapitated at a banquet, triggered months of unrest that culminated with the execution of the Atabeg and the ilkhan Hülegü's threat to move his army into Fars to besiege Shiraz.[56]

Textual evidence suggests that Saʿdi was among the dignitaries, notables, and scholars (led by Amīr Muqarrab al-Dīn Masʿūd, one of Abū Bakr's ministers) who, in the fall of 1264,[57] interceded before the Ilkhanid commander Altājū to avert the massacre of the entire population that Hülegü had ordered.[58] Soon after the execution of Saljūq-Shāh, once the crisis was appeased, some of the notables paid visit to Hülegü (either in Maragha or Tabriz) to confirm the allegiance of Fars to the Ilkhanid rule.[59] It was probably on this occasion that Saʿdi composed his first and only panegyric in praise of Hülegü (or indeed of any Ilkhan). The poem, which most manuscripts introduce as "the transfer of fortune from the Salghurids to another dynasty" opens with the depiction of Mongol occupation as a God-bestowed grace that blesses the entire world.[60] Upon describing his own poetic talent as a musky gift carried from Shiraz to Mongolia, Saʿdi introduces a new political actor: Shams al-Dīn Juvaynī (d. 1284), the minister of finances (*ṣāḥib dīvān*) of the Ilkhanid state who, along with his brother, the renowned historian and governor of Baghdad, ʿAṭā' Malik, set a new course for the socio-political history of Mongol Iran in the second half of the 13th century.[61]

With the same radiance of the moon amidst the sky.

[1.15] Ms. Kabul 1325, 534. In this manuscript, the heading that introduces this *qasida* specifies that the text was composed on the occasion of Saljūq-Shāh's enthronement.

55 For a critical edition of the original text, see Ingenito 2019, 158–59.

56 See Bayzāvi 1382/2002, 126–27; Vassāf 1259/1852, 183–89; Aigle 2005, 115–17.

57 In his *Tārīkh-i guzīda*, Mustawfī mentions the month of Ṣafar, 663 (November–December 1264), whereas Vaṣṣāf places these events "at the end of the year 662" (August–September 1264). See Mostawfi 1364/1985, 507; Vassāf 1259/1852, 189.

58 See Aigle 2005, 166; Bashari 2020, 172–73.

59 Aigle 2005, 117.

60 KhE 2007, 678. See Ingenito 2019, 134–35.

61 On the Juvaynī family, see *EIr*, s.v. "Jovayni Family" [H. Rajabzadeh]; Gilli-Elewy 2011; and Ravalde 2016.

Sa'di's evolving engagement with the ruling elites of his age acted as a catalyst for the development of his own literary prestige outside the boundaries of Fars. We may recognize the Juvaynī brothers as the main political protagonists of this expansion in the scale of Sa'di's renown:

> The benevolence that you two offered to me [*qabūl-i shumā*] spread my name across the world.
> Thanks to the *Ṣāḥib Dīvān* my collection of poems [*dīvān*] became precious.
>
> Today your family is the refuge for all the "people of the heart"; [*ahl-i dil*]
> May its glory flourish until the time of resurrection.[62]

Through these panegyrics, Sa'di signaled his election of the Juvaynī family, and in particular Shams al-Dīn, as his new intercessors between Fars, now losing its position as an independent or semi-independent polity, and Tabriz, the new capital of the Ilkhanate.[63] With the support of Shams al-Dīn, Sa'di hoped to transcend his precarious situation in Fars (which he had already expressed in a *qasida* addressing Saljūq-Shāh)[64] and, furthermore, extend his literary prestige beyond the boundaries of Shiraz.[65]

3 After 1270: Political Instability in Fars, Sa'di's New Travels, and the Construction of a Sufi Lodge

While the Juvaynī brothers consolidated their power in the Ilkhanid administration, five-year old Abish Khātūn, one of the two daughters of Sa'd II and Terken Khātūn, was nominally enthroned Atabeg of Fars in the fall of 1264.[66]

62 Sa'di KhE, 682; Ms. Kabul 1325, 550 (the manuscript signals that the addressee of this *qasida* was Shams al-Dīn).

63 See Ingenito 2019, 134–44. See also chapter 1, pp. 56–60, 92–98.

64 Whoever fell in disgrace was raised by your glory
As evaporating dew that sunshine takes to the sky.
Will this grace embrace Sa'di too, your foremost servant
Who sees no gain, and yet his striving surpasses everyone else's?
[1.16] Sa'di KhE, 676; Ms. Dushanbe 1310s, f. 164b; Ms. Kabul 1325, 534.

65 In one of his most famous *qasidas*, Sa'di lyrically expresses his eagerness to leave Shiraz to join Shams al-Dīn's entourage through a lengthy amatory prelude (*nasīb*) in which the lyric voice declares that no lover should be bound to one single land or object of desire. See Ingenito 2019, 141–44.

66 Bayzāvi 1382/2002, 127; Mostawfi 1364/1985, 527.

Hülegü died shortly after, on February 8, 1265, and he was succeeded by Abaqa (d. 1282), who ascended to the Ilkhanid throne on June 19 of the same year. The political impasse caused by the constant friction between local administrations and the Mongol envoys during the period of reorganization of the Ilkhanid approach to the feudal control of the Iranian provinces was among the causes that fostered Saʿdi's intention to leave Fars and seek refuge in the bosom of the Juvaynī family, in Baghdad or Tabriz.[67] While it is not clear whether Saʿdi actually left his hometown during this decade, Amīr Inkiyānū, the trustworthy governor that Abaqa sent to Shiraz in 1268, soon became the dedicatee of some of his most articulate and politically daring panegyrics.[68] The boldness of Saʿdi's tone when addressing Inkiyānū (probably after being urged by one of the most important court poets of the Salghurid entourage, Majd-i Hamgar)[69] reveals the level of protection that the poet enjoyed through his intimate connection with Shams al-Dīn and ʿAṭāʾ Malik Juvaynī.[70]

Saʿdi's encomiastic liaison with Inkiyānū sheds light on the intellectual environment that surrounded the poet in this phase of his life. While atabeg Abū Bakr's strict religious policies limited the circulation of scientific and philosophical thought in the scholarly institutions of Shiraz until at least the early 1250s, Inkiyānū (who, according to the sources, was either a Buddhist or a Christian) was moved by a genuine penchant for the rational sciences. Historical accounts describe his engagement with the philosophical, theological, and spiritual circles of the city and highlight his curiosity about the Avicennian approach to matters such as the notion of the "Necessary Being" and the analytical explanation of prophecies. One specific passage from Vaṣṣāf's *History* depicts Inkiyānū's intellectual engagement with Najīb al-Dīn Buzghush, the Sufi who exported to Shiraz the spiritual practices and ideas of the Suhravardiyya order.[71] Inkiyānū and Najīb al-Dīn reportedly discussed matters relating to the relationship between intellectual cognition and spiritual illumination in a fashion that is clearly derivative of Avicenna's and al-Ghazālī's psychological frameworks. This account reinforces the assumption that such

67 Life in Shiraz has sickened my heart,
The time has come for you to find me in Baghdad!
My cry will soon reach that city: will the *Ṣāhib Dīvān*
Honor this plea of mine and save me?
Saʿdi, one certainly ought to love the homeland,
But can you die in dejection only for being born here?
[1.17] Saʿdi YE (*Badāyiʿ* 440), 204–205.

68 On Inkiyānū, see Aigle 2005, 120–21; Bashari 2020, 260–71.

69 See Ingenito 2014, 89–90; 2019, 103–104.

70 See Ahmad 1381/2002.

71 Vassāf 1259/1852, 193.

ideas were not only available in Saʿdi's intellectual environment, but that they also directly or indirectly influenced his own approach to the spiritual aesthetics that emerge from his ghazals.[72]

As soon as Abaqa had Inkiyānū removed from power (1272), the failure of the Ilkhanid administration of Fars started manifesting itself in the full extent of its disastrous effects.[73] We know very little about Saʿdi's activity during the rest of this decade. Between 1272 and 1274, and again between 1279 and 1280, the poet praised local officers who were more or less directly controlled by Shams al-Dīn Juvaynī or one of Abaqa's representatives.[74] In all likelihood, Saʿdi spent the years 1275–1279 travelling between Baghdad, Mecca, Damascus, and finally Tabriz, where he encountered the Juvaynī brothers and the ilkhan Abaqa himself.[75] On the occasion of this encounter, the Juvaynī brothers offered Saʿdi five thousand gold dinars for the construction of a Sufi lodge (*khānaqāh* or *ribāṭ*) in the outskirts of Shiraz. Thanks to a uniquely attested scribal description that appears in an important manuscript of Saʿdi's collected works copied in the 1320s, I have discovered that the construction of the lodge started in 1280 (or, less likely, in 1281) on a hill known as Fahandar.[76] Moreover, the copyist concludes his note by mentioning that in 1321, "thirty years after the death of the sheikh [Saʿdi]," which "occurred in 681 [1291–92]," the ilkhan Abū Saʿīd (d. 1335) sent the vizier ʿAlāʾ al-Dīn Muḥammad Fariyūmadī (1280–1342, son of ʿImād al-Dīn Muḥammad) to Shiraz in order to restore (or rebuild) Saʿdi's *khānaqāh*.[77]

The conspicuous investment that the Juvaynīs made to provide Saʿdi with his own *khānaqāh* reflects the involvement of this family with the major poets and religious elites of the time as a strategy to reinforce networks of regional consensus during the beginning of their political decline. Saʿdi's renown benefitted immensely from this active form of patronage, especially considering how the Juvaynīs's support of other fellow-poets based in Tabriz amplified the circulation of his poetry in mundane and sacred *milieux*. The case of one of

72 See Chapter 6, pp. 302–309. In all the *qasida*s that Saʿdi dedicated to Inkiyānū, the poet emphasizes the role of the intellect (*ʿaql*) for the understanding of religion as a rational practice.

73 Aigle 2005, 123–28, 208–206.

74 See Aigle 2005, 119–31; Bashari 2020, 272–83.

75 On the encounter between Saʿdi and Abaqa, see Saʿdi KhE 844–45.

76 Ms. Paris 1320s, f. 216b. Although Bashari (2020, 295–301) provides insightful analyses of the historical and literary passages referring to Saʿdi's lodge, his lack of access to the manuscript Ms. Paris 1320s has prevented him from ascertaining the date on which the Sufi lodge was erected. On the locale known as Fahandar, see Junayd Shirāzi 1328/1949, 274–76.

77 See Plate 1. ʿAlāʾ al-Dīn Muḥammad b. ʿImād al-Dīn ought not to be confused with ʿAlāʾ al-Dīn Muḥammad "Hinduvī," the homonymous member of the same family of statesmen from Faryūmad. See ʿEqbāl Āshtiyāni 1328/1949, 129–31; Rudgar 1384/2005, 176–78.

Saʿdi's most devoted literary imitators, Humām-i Tabrīzī (d. 1314–15), perfectly exemplifies this process, as he too was the beneficiary of Shams al-Dīn's generous investment in the creation of lodges where the practice of poetry recitation was intimately connected with monastic practices capable of involving broad sectors of the local populace.[78]

The building of Saʿdi's lodge coincided with the brief political revival of the Salghurid power in Fars. In the spring of 1282, Aḥmad Tegüder succeeded his brother Abaqa as the new Ilkhanid ruler. Tegüder, originally a Christian, was the first ilkhan who converted to Islam, and the process that led to his conversion should be read against the effort of the Mongol political elites (including Persian statesmen such as the Juvaynī family) to keep a firm grip on local polities through the constitution of pious foundations and Sufi lodges.[79] Tegüder's decision to restore the Salghurid direct control of Fars through the presence of Saʿd II's daughter, the atabeg Abish Khātūn, constituted an important piece of the Ilkhan's hasty political game and the temporary fulfillment of Saʿdi's political desires in the context of his spiritual and literary aspirations.

Abish, aged twenty-two, returned to Shiraz at the end of 1282 as a triumphant regional ruler who could boast a prestigious marital tie with the Ilkhanid family, as since 1273 she had been the chief wife of Mengü Temür (d. April 1282), one of Hülegü's sons. For an entire month, the populace of Shiraz celebrated Abish's return by decorating gardens and streets, closing markets and playing music from the rooftops of the city.[80] Abish's popularity increased exponentially when she took advantage of Tegüder's poor administrative skills by successfully claiming all the lands and revenues of Fars that, up to that point, the central Ilkhanid government had administered directly.[81] Although Abish's uncontrolled expenditures contributed to the famine that ravaged Shiraz toward the end of her princely appointment, between 1284 and 1285, the existing pious foundations and Sufi lodges benefitted greatly from her propagandistic emphasis on the necessity of protecting dynastic and religious values.[82]

78 Homām-e Tabrizi 1351/1972, xlviii. "From the revenue of Anatolia, [Shams al-Dīn] provided a stipend of an annual one thousand dinars to Humām al-Dīn's *khānaqāh*. By doing so, Juwaynī was attempting to gain the loyalty of Humām al-Dīn, and by extension his followers, by giving them some of the proceeds of taxation. More than simply a just and legitimate use of revenue, this cemented the community's loyalty to Juwaynī and established their dependence upon the Ilkhan taxation system." Ravalde 2016, 60.

79 See Pfeiffer 2006.

80 Vassāf 1259/1852, 211;

81 Aigle 2005, 131–32.

82 Ibid.

In the framework of the attentive benevolence that Tegüder displayed toward Sufism, and thanks to both Shams al-Dīn Juvaynī's generous donation and Abish's patronage, we may regard 1281–84 as the golden period of the last decade of Saʿdi's life. The oldest manuscripts recording Saʿdi's literary corpus suggest that the poet offered his collected works to Abish Khatūn in a fashion that lauded the last Salghurid atabeg in the context of the exalting of the ruling dynasty through the auspicious remembrance of Abish's brother, Muḥammad, and their father, prince Saʿd II.[83]

It was likely during these years that the young prince Khān Malik Sulṭān Muḥammad (d. 1285), governor of Multan and son of the sultan of Delhi, Ghiyās al-Dīn Balban (d. 1287), invited Saʿdi to India and offered to establish a lodge for him in connection with the local Suhravardiyya Sufi order.[84] It is reported that upon respectfully turning down this invitation, Saʿdi sent the prince a selection of his ghazals, which were promptly circulated and performed at the courtly and Sufi establishments of Multan and Delhi through the intervention of the famous poet Amīr Khusraw of Delhi, boon companion (*nadīm*) of Muḥammad and one of the earliest divulgators of Saʿdi's lyric poetry.[85]

The apparent political stability of Fars during the reign of Abish Khātūn was interrupted by the dynastic rivalry between Aḥmad Tegüder and his nephew, Arghun (Abaqa's elder son), who had the former executed on August 10, 1284, and was enthroned as the new ilkhan on the following day. Arghun accused Shams al-Dīn Juvaynī of embezzlement and put him to death in October of the same year. At the beginning of 1285, after bravely defying Arghun's order to leave Shiraz, Abish was escorted to Tabriz, where she died one year later.[86] Saʿdi survived this major crisis by seven years, during which he might have praised local administrators appointed by Arghun and dedicated himself to the spiritual activities of his lodge, welcoming travelers and exalting in verse the mysterious connection between human and divine beauty.

Saʿdi's Sufi lodge remained active for many decades after the death of the poet in 1292. This institution contributed to the increasing circulation

83 It is possible that the arrangement of the ghazals in Saʿdi's first collection (the *Ṭayyibāt*) as it appears in these manuscripts was refashioned as a gift to Abish Khātūn on the basis of a previous dedication to prince Muḥammad and his mother, Terken Khātūn. See below.

84 The Suhravardiyya was one of the most powerful Sufi orders in 13th-century Shiraz, and although it cannot be historically proven that Saʿdi ever joined this order officially (see discussion in the introduction to the second part of the book), it is possible that Saʿdi's renown reached India through the extensive social and mercantile networks on which this order relied.

85 See Astarābādi 1387/2008, 1: 280; Losensky and Sharma 2013, xvii–xix; Bashari 2020, 298–99.

86 Aigle 2005, 133–35.

of Saʿdi's ghazals as sources of spiritual, aesthetic, and political inspiration. An in-depth study of the manuscripts copied during the first decades of the 14th century may shed new light on this decisive phase of the crystallization of Saʿdi's fame during the last decades of the Ilkhanate. Future research could also explain under what circumstances, as reported in the oldest manuscript of Humām's poems, one of Saʿdi's ghazals extolling the sublime beauty of Turkic or Mongolian soldiers[87] moved the ilkhan Ghazan (r. 1295–1304) to tears.[88]

4 Chasing the Original Ghazals: Manuscripts, *Mouvances*, and Inimitable Smoothness

Saʿdi's renown is undoubtedly associated with the *Būstān* and the *Gulistān*, the two masterpieces on which he worked throughout the 1250s and which he regarded as the summit of his literary activity at the Salghurid court. While the *Būstān* (whose original title in the early manuscript tradition was *Saʿdī-nāma*, or *The Book of Saʿdi*, probably in homage to the Salghurid ruling family, and in particular prince Saʿd II) has been considered as the versified reflection of Saʿdi's ideal ethical city,[89] the elegant prosimetrum (i.e., a combination of prose and verse) of the *Gulistān* guides the reader through a cosmopolitan blend of biographical reminiscences and fictive accounts, full of wisdom and irony, and seen through the lens of the poet's fascination with the social complexities of his time.[90]

The thematic breadth, linguistic elegance, and human depth of these two monuments tend to overshadow the rest of Saʿdi's literary output, which offers hidden treasures that modern readers rarely enjoy contemplating and discussing.[91] Saʿdi's quatrains, for instance, along with the fragments of political wisdom and lyricism (known as the *Ṣāḥibiyya* collection) that he offered to Shams al-Dīn Juvaynī, and even his obscene works in prose and verse deserve

87 Were *these* beauties perhaps created by pure mercy? As they
Appease the soul, cherish the heart, and enlighten the eyes!
[1.18] Saʿdi YE, 225–26.

88 Ms. Marʿashi 16509, f. 6a. On this important manuscript, see Haydari-Yasāvoli 1396/2017. It is possible that, prior to Humām al-Dīn's performance, Ghazan was exposed to this poem thanks to the intellectual endeavor of the poet laureate of his court and historian, Abū Sulaymān Banākatī (d. 1329–30), who also happens to be the copyist of the oldest extant collection of Saʿdi's works. See below.

89 *Bustān*, 17–30. Yohannan 1987, 17–55.

90 Ibid., 57–91. On the relationship between Saʿdi's ghazals and the *Gulistān*'s prosimetrum, see Chapter 2.

91 For a comprehensive list of Saʿdi's works, see Losensky 2012.

to be studied, read, and translated as much as his famed masterpieces.[92] Moreover, as the Italian scholar Riccardo Zipoli points out, the scholarly emphasis on the ethical aspects of the *Būstān* and the *Gulistān*, along with the dismissal of peripheral aspects of Sa'di's less-studied compositions, has prevented the development of a sound critical approach to the study of Sa'di's ghazals, which the poet's contemporaries regarded as the true jewel of his literary excellence, and which currently still lack a reliable critical edition.[93]

The most popular edition of Sa'di's ghazals was published in 1941 by Mohammad-'Ali Forughi.[94] Forughi's publication, which has been republished numerous times since its first appearance, does not meet the scholarly standard that would qualify it as a critical edition.[95] Although the editor made use of important manuscripts,[96] he only reported a selection of textual variants, and without ever referring to the specific manuscripts in question. Furthermore, this selection seems to have been dictated by his personal taste rather than comprehensive acknowledgment of all the discrepancies found in the sources. Moreover, in order to protect the moral integrity of younger readers, he arbitrarily subdivided the ghazals into love lyrics (*mughāzala va mu'āshaqa*, to be published separately) and homiletic texts (*muvā'iẓ*), a category in which he also included Sa'di's *qasida*s, along with fragments and quatrains characterized by similar overtones of wisdom and pious preaching.[97]

The 2006 posthumous edition by Gholām-Hoseyn Yusofi (with the collaboration of Parviz Atābaki, who, after Yusofi's demise in 1990, edited the second half of the ghazals)[98] constitutes the first critical edition of Sa'di's lyrics, based on seventeen manuscripts copied between the end of the 13th and the beginning of the 15th century.[99] Unlike Forughi's edition, Yusofi's publication replicates the order and the subdivision of what he describes as the oldest and most comprehensive manuscript of the *Kulliyāt* (see below, note on Ms. Mashhad 1364), and he chooses the allegedly oldest selection of Sa'di's ghazals (Ms. Berlin 1306) as his main textual point of reference.[100] The critical edition features

92 For a preliminary edition of Sa'di's quatrains, see Sa'di KhE, 620–25. The most reliable critical edition of the *Ṣāḥibiyya* is found in Minovi 1353/1974.

93 Zipoli 1364/1985, 231–32.

94 See Sa'di KhE, 351–58.

95 See Hasanli 1388/2009, 96–97.

96 Ms. Luqmān-Adham 1318; Ms. Tehran 1321; Ms. London 1328; Ms. Paris 1366; etc.

97 Sa'di KhE, 351.

98 Sa'di YE, xiii–ixx.

99 The most important of which are Ms. Tehran 1321; Ms. Dushanbe 1310s; Ms. London 1328; Ms. Dublin 1320s; Ms. Paris 1320s; Ms. Mashhad 1364; and Ms. Paris 1366.

100 Partially motivated by the fact that Ms. Berlin 1306 contains only 336 ghazals, Yusofi and Atabāki have not been particularly consistent with this choice, as they often arbitrarily

715 ghazals, 23 stanzas of Saʿdi's *tarjīʿāt*, and 17 ghazals that Yusofi flagged as potentially spurious.[101]

Although Yusofi and Atābaki's endeavor offers an exceedingly substantial philological tool that will hopefully revitalize the study of Saʿdi's poetry in the coming years, their edition suffers from numerous oversights and arbitrary editorial choices.[102] Occasional mistakes and inconsistencies aside, one wishes that the editors had adopted a more flexible approach to the critical reconstruction of the ghazals—an approach capable of taking into account the volatile nature of the texts belonging to this genre, which were often the object of multiple authorial variations that circulated through various chains of written and oral transmission. Especially considering the variety of Saʿdi's audiences and the different social settings and occasions in which and on which his ghazals were performed and circulated, both during his life and in the years immediately following his death, even the earliest manuscripts often contain collections of lyrics whose single lines attest to textual stratifications rather than copies of *the* original poem as the author had composed it.[103] To account for the validity of the full range of textual variants that are found in the manuscript tradition, we could consider Saʿdi's ghazals from the perspective of Paul Zumthor's concept of *mouvance*, which he applied to the study of medieval French poetry to account for the mobility of texts generated by "intervocal" and intertextual networks of transmission.[104] Medieval lyric texts are pieces of mobile linguistic craftsmanship whose existence is the result of multiple variations based on semantic and formal negotiations that can often be arbitrary, unpredictable, and impossible to extract from their historical process of stratification.

---

select other manuscripts for the reconstruction of specific ghazals without explaining the motivations behind their decisions.

101 Yusofi's choices for the group of ghazals that he considered spurious seems arbitrary and does not match the doubts that Forughi had expressed before him. See Laiyān 1394/2015, 145–49.

102 On the limits of this edition, see Hasanli 1388/2009, and, for a thorough survey of its major shortcomings, see Laiyān 1394/2015.

103 For a preliminary assessment of this problem in the field of Persian literary philology, see Māyel Heravi 1379/2000, 451–65.

104 See Zumthor 2000, 84–96; 1987, 160–168. See also Cerquiglini (1989) and his focus on the concept of "variance," which emphasizes the role of multiple written renditions of a text for our deconstruction of the quest for philological authenticity. On the overlaps between Zumthor's and Cerquiglini's positions, see Nagy 1996, 9–10. For a comparison with the same kind of textual problems in the troubadour tradition, see Gaunt 1999. For applications of the concept of *mouvance* to medieval Persian literature, see Davidson 1998; Omidsalar 2002; Lewis 2018b, 90–91.

From this viewpoint, the real problem of any critical edition of a collection of ghazals lies in the ambiguous nature of the concept of "original text." Does the text that we ought to reconstruct correspond to the very first poem that Saʿdi composed and set in writing? What if the author had circulated the text orally (during a *samāʿ* session, for instance) and then reworked the order of the lines later on, while the participants memorized (and likely circulated) the ghazal as it was first performed? Given the complexity of the socio-political context in which Saʿdi introduced his ghazals, the kind textual transmission described above could have taken place with a number of different variations, i.e. *mouvances*, as legitimate alternatives.[105] Specific cases aside, one might argue that even the discovery of an authorized recension of the ghazals which Saʿdi might have compiled at the end of his life would not solve the problem of the historical and aesthetic relevance of textual *mouvances* and their impact on the communities of readers and families of texts surrounding the literary activity of the poet. We should therefore think of each ghazal as a conglomeration of textual possibilities as reflected by the variations found in the manuscript tradition.

Approaches similar to Salim Neysāri's in his edition of Hafez's ghazals, for instance, by showing the textual variants of a given ghazal in a chart that keeps track of how different manuscripts can relate to each other as textual families, consider all variants as *mouvances* equally worthy of consideration as virtual possibilities of the poem's existence in different contexts of authorial composition, and social circulation and transmission.[106] In this book, in order to account for the necessity of reassessing the limits of Yusofi's approach (and meanwhile recognizing the limits of my own reappraisal of the original sources), I have decided to refer to both the critical edition of the ghazals and the evidence emerging from other manuscripts, which will be soon introduced.

---

105 Cf. Franklin Lewis's (1995, 1: 103) remark on *mouvance* and the quest for an "original" as a misplaced effort: "Paul Zumthor's concept of *mouvance* […] as applied to troubadour poetry can also be applied to Persian poetry, particularly in the case of *ghazals*, which were frequently not tied to a specific court or ritual occasion by subject matter, and were short and popular enough to be repeated many times by the poet himself as well as his reciters and other performers who heard and liked a particular rendition. Therefore, multiple authorial renditions would be normative, as would variations arising from multiple performances by reciters and singers. The search for an *Urtext* in the *ghazal* context may, therefore, be somewhat misplaced."

106 Hāfez 1386/2007, 1: ii–xv. See also Ingenito 2009, 164–67.

5 Through the Mirror of the Manuscripts

Saʿdi composed most of his works at different stages of his life and on specific occasions, often dictated by socio-political and spiritual circumstances, as was frequently the case with medieval Persian poets. This means that, at least initially, he did not conceive his collections in prose and verse as organic parts belonging to a planned literary architecture. It is possible, however, that the thought of compiling a comprehensive collection of his literary corpus surfaced upon the appearance of the first signs of the Salghurid dynasty's decline, after the death of the young prince Muḥammad (in 1262), when Saʿdi might have realized the necessity of expanding the trans-regional boundaries of his renown within Fars under the Ilkhanid political influence for the survival of his literary activity. Scattered references indicate that Saʿdi offered selections of his poetry to the Juvaynī brothers, who likely interceded for him by presenting his collections to the Ilkhans themselves, possibly Hülegü, and most certainly Abaqa. If we trust the claims of some copyists who present their manuscripts as copies of Saʿdi's autographs,[107] we can certainly assume that, in spite of their discrepancies in terms of textual variants and structure, the oldest extant specimens of the *Kulliyāt* must reflect an editorial plan that the poet orchestrated during the last years of his life.[108]

The idea of a masterplan for Saʿdi's collections (not as an authoritative entity but as a negotiated *vulgata*) is absolutely evident in what in this book I refer to as the "Bīsutūn" recensions of the *Kulliyāt*, which ʿAlī Bīsutūn, a Sufi practitioner and intimate connoisseur and collector of Saʿdi's poetry, compiled more or less thirty years after the death of the author, first in 1326 and again in 1334.[109] The "pre-Bīsutūn" recensions, however, seem to reflect a slightly different structure, the index of which was displayed through elegant illuminations

107 The oldest of the extant manuscripts of the *Kulliyāt* whose copyists claimed to have had direct access to Saʿdi's autograph was copied in 1318. This manuscript, which Foroughi used for his edition of Saʿdi's works, belonged to the private collection of Mohammad Hoseyn Loqmān-Adham (d. 1951). See Safā 1368/1989, 3.1: 587. The document seemed to be untraceable for decades, until it resurfaced recently in the context of Christie's auction sale number 1557, "Art of the Islamic and Indian Worlds," lot 30, 9 October 2014. The manuscript was sold for 30,000 GBP, and one hopes that in the near future scholars will have the chance to access and study such a precious document. The second oldest document reportedly copied on the basis of one of Saʿdi's autographs is Ms. London 1328, in which we read, "*manqūl min khaṭṭ al-shaykh al-ʿārif, al-Saʿdī.*" (f. 310a).

108 See also Safā 1368/1989, 3.1: 607.

109 On the connection between performativity, *samāʿ*, and the context in which Bīsutūn was reportedly inspired to systematize Saʿdi's *Kulliyāt*, see the introduction to the third part of this book.

in the frontispieces of manuscripts copied during the late Ilkhanid and early Injuid periods, between the 1290s and the 1320s. The single-page frontispieces containing the index of Saʿdi's works are in most cases lost, and one of the few specimens attesting to this tradition is found in the Dushanbe manuscript (copied circa in the 1290s–1310s), whose extremely bright gold and blue palette (and bands of gold strapwork) attests to the Ilkhanid techniques of illumination.[110] In this illuminated index (see Plate 2), the titles of Saʿdi's books emerge from golden medallions that, alongside each other, mimic the rotation of the celestial spheres.

This grand visual plan for the illustration of the *Kulliyāt*, along with the relatively impressive number of extant manuscripts from this period, speaks to the popularity of Saʿdi's collected works, regarded as a literary architecture to be copied and circulated over and over in courtly and Sufi circles alike. The manuscript architecture of Saʿdi's *Kulliyāt* was soon to be metaphorically reflected in the rebuilding of his Sufi lodge at the behest of the Ilkhanid minister ʿAlāʾ al-Dīn Muḥammad Faryūmadī, in 1321. The association between the manuscript circulation of the *Kulliyāt* and the revamping of its spiritual and aesthetic legacy in its architectural form will seem less far-fetched if we consider that it was in the context of a Sufi gathering that, five years later, ʿAlī Bīsutūn, upon witnessing the ravishment that Saʿdi's poetry caused during a *samāʿ* session (i.e., a session of music and poetry aimed at producing an ecstatic response in its participants), decided to rearrange the *Kulliyāt* and provide an alphabetical index for the ghazals and the *qasida*s of the poet (according to the first letter of the first hemistich, *miṣrāʿ*, of each poem) in order to facilitate the retrieval of specific texts.

While Bīsutūn described the experience of the musical gathering only in his second introduction to the *Kulliyāt*, composed in 1334, his first brief presentation of his philological endeavor refers to the wide circulation of Saʿdi's works and the necessity to make use of a reliable index in order to confirm whether a given poem is mistakenly attributed to Saʿdi.[111] One of the first attestations of this first introduction is found in a precious manuscript (likely copied in the 1330s or 1340s) kept in the Chester Beatty Library in Dublin. As in the single frontispiece of the Dushanbe manuscript, the double-page frontispiece of this document features the titles of Saʿdi's works (in the order established by Bīsutūn) at the center of polychromatic medallions (in the late Injuid style), in this case rotating around a golden lotus that opens to the gaze of the reader (see Plate 3).

110 Ms. Dushanbe 1310a, f. 1a. See also Wright 2012, 14–19.

111 Ms. Dublin 1340s, f. 3b.

Like celestial spheres delicately rotating around the cultural life of Fars during the 14th century, throughout the Muzaffarid period that saw the emergence of the elegant *nastaʿlīq* script, and continuing beyond the dazzling revolution in the arena of book illumination that the Timurids brought about, the titles of Saʿdi's works and their attribution to the poet remained fairly stable, mainly thanks to the conservative standard that Bīsutūn had set. The contents of these works, on the other hand, have undergone variations, which to date no critical edition has been capable of accounting for. As mentioned above, the number of ghazals and even ghazal collections, for instance, is a problem that still baffles the critical attention of modern philologists. The pre-Bīsutūn manuscripts make little or no mention at all of the so-called *Ghazalhā-yi qadīm*.[112] This "old collection" is featured prominently in the manuscripts of the Bīsutūn tradition, and Yusofi decided to honor the early phase of the manuscript tradition by publishing the texts under the labels of the only three collections that the pre-Bīsutūn documents recognize: the *Ṭayyibāt*, the *Badāyiʿ*, and the *Khavātīm*.

The discovery of additional, important manuscripts calls for a new critical edition of Saʿdi's ghazals, which will have to address the issue of the "old ghazals" with a different critical eye. However, even though Yusofi's decision not to recognize this old *dīvān* as a legitimate collection seems arbitrary, its absence from the pre-Bīsutūn tradition warrants more accurate scrutiny.[113] A series of internal pieces of evidence suggests that Saʿdi compiled different selections of ghazals throughout his life and in light of his intended or historical audiences: while the *Ṭayyibāt* seem to have been offered or composed during the peak of the Salghurid rule (not later than the death of prince Muḥammad), the *Badāyiʿ* and the *Khavātīm* must belong to the years following the ascension of the Juvaynī family. The analysis of the ghazal arrangement in the pre-Bīsutūn manuscripts suggests that Saʿdi, in the early 1280s, dedicated a mature recension of his collected works to the last Salghurid ruler, Abish Khātūn. It is possible that on that occasion Saʿdi polished his collections of poems and dismissed his early lyric experiments (or the texts that did not meet his mature literary taste) as juvenilia that he did not deem worthy of being included in a recension meant to celebrate the return of the newly enthroned princess to Shiraz. It is also possible that these old ghazals resurfaced as soon as Saʿdi's poetry reconquered Fars during the early Injuid period, possibly as wandering texts that

112 A singular exception is found in Ms. Kabul 1325. See below.

113 While new critical editions will have to clarify the origins and scope of the *ghazalhā-yi qadīm*, I follow Yusofi in regarding the pre-Bīsutūn recensions as the preferred source of categorization for Saʿdi's *dīvāns*.

had not been included in earlier recensions, or as newly discovered documents dating back to the early stages of the poet's literary activity.

6 Saʿdi's "Inimitable Smoothness"

According to premodern critics, the main characteristic of Saʿdi's ghazals lies in a stylistic feature that describes the ineffable beauty of his lines and at the same time explains the perseverance with which major and minor poets, from the end of the 13th and throughout the 14th centuries, obsessively imitated his lyric voice.[114] The key word for this sort of literary magic is the oxymoronic expression *sahl-i mumtaniʿ*, which we could translate as "inaccessible simplicity," or "inimitable smoothness." The definition of Saʿdi's inimitable smoothness has challenged generations of scholars, who often declare that the perfection of Saʿdi's style cannot be fully grasped through the language of literary criticism.[115] While dismissing the opinion of the premodern critics on this subject as ridiculous tautology (I will soon reassess the value of these authors' approaches), Saʿid Hamidiyān has offered a definition of *sahl-i mumtaniʿ* that is worth taking into account. According to the Iranian scholar, the only way to disentangle the paradox of such an oxymoronic expression is to ascribe to it the essential quality of Saʿdi's style, which Hamidiyān defines as a total form of harmony (*taʿādol*) between all the semantic, rhetorical, and musical elements of a poem. In Saʿdi, this kind of absolute equilibrium resounds through each aspect of the poem, in a fashion that causes specific forms of harmony to bleed into each other without offering the reader the opportunity to recognize clearly how all of the balanced aspects are capable of influencing each other.[116]

Although Hamidiyān's recognition of balance and equilibrium as a total poetic effect offers a fine lens to scrutinize an essential quality of Saʿdi's poetry, the analysis misses the value of the implied dialogical and anti-essentialist nature of the concept of *sahl-i mumtaniʿ* as theorized by the medieval critics. In their definitions, this otherwise indescribable "inimitable smoothness" appears as a property relating to specific texts rather than an overarching stylistic trait: according to Rashīd al-Dīn Vaṭvāṭ (d. 1182) and Vāʿiẓ-i Kāshifī (d. 1504–05), a poem is to be considered *sahl-i mumtaniʿ* when one cannot

114 See Ingenito 2014.
115 Sabur 1384/2005, 370.
116 Hamidiyān 1383/2004 , 295–96.

write anything "similar to it," even though it seemed "easy" at first.[117] While Vaṭvāṭ identifies the 11th-century Ghazanvid poet Farrukhī Sīstānī as a model for this kind of poetic excellence, Kāshifī declared that the majority of Sa'di's ghazals are *sahl-i mumtani'*.

This definition qualifies the inimitable smoothness of Sa'di's ghazals as a form of poetic excellence that stems from the creative challenges posed by the practice of literary imitation. It involves the pragmatics of reading and writing in a fashion that describes lyric value as a contextual quality. Therefore, while we may agree with Hamidiyān's identification of balance as a key aspect of Sa'di's lyric quality, the mystery of the smooth beauty that inhabits his verses relates also to the movement of the texts among the communities of readers and fellow-poets who were moved by his ghazals and strove to repeat them though the acts of reading and rewriting. Paradoxically, the so-called *mouvances*, or the variations that vibrate throughout the manuscript tradition and prevent scholars from establishing an authoritative edition of the ghazals, attest to the success of Sa'di's lyrical innovation, which, like in Rothko's paintings, is made of delicate simplicity, balanced contrasts of mood, and gradual variations across the spectrum of the sensory experience that the images depict. The manuscripts described below offer one more lens to admire the breadth of the reception of Sa'di's ghazals, and the breath of his words through the most ancient documents that allow his voice to survive.

7 Sa'di through the Eyes of Premodern Manuscripts

The manuscripts below are presented in chronological order and listed according to the abbreviations used throughout the text. To help the reader keep track of the chronology of the early material circulation of Sa'di's works, I have listed the manuscripts according to the year/decade CE in which they were copied or presumably copied, immediately following the cities in which they are kept today. See Bibliography for a list that reflects the official reference numbers found in the published catalogues.

1. *Ms. Tehran 1296*. Majles Library, 900. *Taẕkira-yi shu'arā*. This undated selection from the works of a large number of poets was probably copied

117 "Sahl dar lughat āsān bāshad va mumtani' dushvār, va sahl-i mumtani' ba iṣṭilāḥ shi'r-ī rā gūyand ki miṣl-i ān guftan dushvār bāshad agar chi āsān namāyad, va akṣar-i ash'ār-i shaykh Muṣliḥ al-Dīn Sa'dī az īn qabīl ast." Vā'ez Kāshefi 1369/1990, 77. Vatvāt 1339/1960, 707.

during the first two decades of the 14th century.[118] It has been speculated that the selection of texts by the anonymous collector might have been based on a manuscript copied presumably in 695/1296 by a certain Manṣūr b. Kamāl al-Dīn Ḥusaynī, and whose existence is only attested to by a manuscript fabricated many decades later.[119] It is one of the oldest documents recording a selection of Saʿdi's poems (among which are 38 ghazals, a few *qasida*s selections from the *Būstān*, and fifteen obscene pieces that present uniquely attested variants).[120] The introduction contains an eloquent praise of poetry and, most remarkably, an exaltation of the physiological advantages of reading facetious compositions (*hazl*, in the style of Saʿdi's obscene works in verse, the *Khabīṣāt*).[121]

To my knowledge, this manuscript has never been used for any of the published critical editions of Saʿdi's works. The illuminated rosette (*shamsa*) that contains the name of the poet reads *min kalām Musharrif Muṣliḥ al-Saʿdī*. This old attestation of the poet's name confirms Bashari's observation on this subject (based on manuscripts copied at least one decade after this one) and establishes the form "Musharrif al-Dīn Muṣliḥ" as Saʿdi's complete name.[122]

2. *Ms. Berlin 1306*. Berlin State Library, Or. Oct. 3451. Saʿdi, *Dīvān*. This manuscript was copied in 1306 (Muḥarram 706) by the famous historian Abū Sulaymān Banākatī, who claimed to be Ghazan Khān's *malik al-shuʿarā*.[123] It comprises 336 ghazals, along with a selection of Saʿdi's *qasida*s, the *Ṣāḥibiyya*, and some of Saʿdi's epistles. The document has been referred to as the "Tübingen" or the "Marburg" manuscript as it was transferred between these two cities before and after World War II, eventually being relocated to the Berlin State Library.[124] It is also the oldest document that refers to Saʿdi as "king of the poets" (*malik al-shuʿarā*).[125]
3. *Ms. Luqmān-Adham 1318*. Unknown collection. Among the extant manuscripts of the *Kulliyāt*, this is the oldest dated document. The copyist claimed to have had direct access to Saʿdi's autograph. This manuscript,

118 See Sharifi-Sahi 1392/2013.

119 The fake manuscript, whose fabrication has been demonstrated by Māyel-Heravi (1390/2011), is known as *Muntakhab-i ashʿār-i hifdah shāʿir* (Ms. Majles 87844). See also Ziyā' 1390/2010. I thank Arham Moradi for bringing these publications to my attention.

120 Ms. Tehran 1296, 409–73.

121 Ms. Tehran 1296, 2–3.

122 See Bashari 2020, 43–49.

123 See *supra*.

124 See Shariʿat 1987, 2: 309–19; Saʿdi YE, xxv–xxvi; Derāyati 2012, 26: 214 (where the manuscript is mistakenly described as Or. Oct. 345); Bashari 2020, 33–34.

125 See *supra*.

which Foroughi used for his edition of the *Būstān*, belonged to the private collection of Mohammad Hoseyn Loqmān-Adham (d. 1951).[126] Reportedly, its 153 folios record portions of the *Būstān*, the ghazals, and a few of Saʿdi's epistles. The document seemed to be untraceable for decades, until it resurfaced recently as part of Christie's auction sale number 1557, "Art of the Islamic and Indian Worlds," lot 30, 9 October 2014. The manuscript was sold for 30,000 GBP, and one hopes that in the near future scholars will have the chance to access and study such a precious document.

4. *Ms. Tehran 1321*. Majles Library, 2569. Saʿdi, *Kulliyāt*. Scholars have proven that this document is the second half of a larger manuscript that was copied between 1320 and March 1321 by ʿAbd al-Ṣamad Bayżāvī and which comprised the entirety of Saʿdi's collected works.[127] The first part of the original manuscript, completed in 1320, is now kept in the Bodmer foundation in Geneva (Ms. Bodmer 529). It contains Saʿdi's *Būstān* and *Gulistān*, and it was the main manuscript used by Yusofi for his critical editions of these two works.[128] The second half of the manuscript, kept in the Majles Library in Tehran, comprises Saʿdi's three *dīvāns* (524 poems),[129] his *qasidas* (whose dedicatees are often mentioned in rubrics preceding the texts),[130] and, among other minor works, an extremely important selection of the poet's obscene output.[131]

5. *Ms. Dublin 1320s*. Chester Beatty Library, Per 109. Saʿdi, *Kulliyāt*. Mojtabā Minovi has recognized at least five different hands in this undated manuscript, ranging between the years immediately following Saʿdi's death and the 18th century.[132] According to Minovi, the two oldest portions of the manuscript were copied in the 1290s[133] and in the 1320s–30s,[134] and include 390 ghazals from the *Ṭayyibāt* and the *Badāyiʿ*. On the basis of a comparison of the second portion of this manuscript with Ms. Kabul 1325 (see below), it may be suggested that the two documents were copied by the same hand, or belonged to the same atelier. This correspondence would confirm Minovi's intuition, and establishes the 1320s as the decade in which these specific sections of the manuscript were most plausibly

126 Saʿdi KhE, 183; See Yaghmāʾi 1316/1937, plates between pages 120 and 123.
127 See Saʿdi YE, xxvi; Bashari 2020, 34–36.
128 *Bustān*, 13; Golestān, 19.
129 The *Ṭayyibāt*, 1–131; the *Badāyiʿ*, 133–260; and the *Khavātīm*, 259–326.
130 Ibid. 261–294.
131 Ibid., 361–378.
132 Wilkinson 1959, 22–23; Minovi 1338/1959; Bashari 2020, 37–38.
133 Ff. 25b–31a; 86b–105a; 170a–94; 198a–238a; 240a–50a; 264a–81a.
134 Ff. 7a–17a; 25a; 32a–55a; 57a–86a; 106a–69a; 251a–63a; 282a–88a.

copied. The Bīsutūn introduction with which the manuscript opens was added centuries later, as the internal organization of Sa'di's works herein predates Bīsutūn's recension.

The manuscript is a key source of evidence for the claim that Sa'di composed early versions of the *Būstān* and the *Gulistān* that predate their final recensions (1257 and 1258, respectively) by several years, if not at least a decade.[135] Minovi relied on this manuscript for the publication of an important critical edition of Sa'di's *Ṣāḥibiyya*.[136] The stylistic discrepancies between the two oldest portions of the manuscript shed light on the difference between Ilkhanid and early Injuid illuminations, and can be used to further the study of the early circulation of Sa'di's ghazals.[137]

6. *Ms. Kabul 1325*. National Archives, 3144. Sa'di, *Kulliyāt*.
This is one of the oldest and finest manuscripts containing almost the totality of Sa'di's works (pre-Bīsutūn recension), and it is an indispensable source for any future critical edition of the *Kulliyāt* (especially as far as Sa'di's *qasidas*[138] and obscene poems[139] are concerned, which still lack a critical edition). The selection of ghazals (505 texts, including six ghazals grouped as *Ghazal-i qadīm*, which is an *unicum* in the pre-Bīsutūn recensions)[140] showcases unique variants, which should be taken into account in future editions. The manuscript was copied in 1325 (Muḥarram 726) by a certain 'Abd Allāh b. Muḥammad b. Maḥmūd b. Abī Bakr, known as Dāvar (and not "Dāvūd," as erroneously indicated by de Beaurecueil in his note).[141] As mentioned above, preliminary evidence suggests that this copyist is the same person who reworked Ms. Dublin 1320s sometime during the same decade. In any case, the similarities between this manuscript and the second oldest rearrangement of Ms. Dublin 1320s are such that the two documents must have been copied at the same Injuid atelier in Shiraz.
7. *Ms. Paris 1320s*. Bibliothèque Nationale de France, Supplément Persan 1796. Sa'di, *Kulliyāt*.

135 See Chapter 2.
136 Minovi 1353/1974.
137 See Wright 2012, 10–14; 332, n. 4.
138 Ms. Kabul 1235, 522–94
139 Ibid., 666–90.
140 Moreover, the manuscripts belonging to the tradition of the Bīsutūn recension (which, unlike the pre-Bīsutūn documents, always feature the collection known as *Ghazalhā-yi qadīm*) include these poems in other collections, and not among the "old ghazals."
141 De Beaurecueil 1964, 34; Afshār 1385/2006, 90; Bashari 2020, 37.

This substantial manuscript of a pre-Bīsutūn recension of Sa'di's *Kulliyāt* (414 folios) comprises an excellent selection of the ghazals (463 poems). It is an undated document, and Francis Richard estimates that it was copied between the 1330s and the 1360s.[142] However, the comparison of its style of illuminations (mainly *shamsas*, headings, and floral decorations) with similarly illuminated manuscripts (such as Ms. Luqmān-Adham 1318, Ms. Kabul 1325; Ms. Dublin 1320s; Ms. London 1328; etc.) suggests a probable date of composition in the mid- to late 1320s.[143]

Extraordinary details from Sa'di's biography can be gleaned from specific passages in this manuscript. Specifically, in my reassessment of his biography, I have relied on a short digression inserted by the copyist of the manuscript, one which has not captured the attention of the scholars who have either studied this document or used it for their critical editions of Sa'di's works.[144] The copyist's note closes the little-studied prose epistle on a spiritual conversation between Sa'di and his major patron, Shams al-Dīn Juvaynī, and it confirms that Sa'di died between 1291 and 1292. Most importantly, the passage clarifies that Shams al-Dīn Juvaynī offered Sa'di a considerable amount of money (allegedly, five thousand gold dinars) for the erection of a Sufi lodge (*ribāṭ*, or *khānaqāh*) on the Fahandar hill in Shiraz. This is the only document that explicitly reports that the lodge was built in 679/1280–81.[145]

8. *Ms. London 1328*. British Library, India Office, Islamic 876 (Ethé 1117). Sa'di, *Kulliyāt*.

This pre-Bīsutūn collection of Sa'di's works was reportedly copied from one of the autographs of the author (f. 310a) on Rajab 1, 728 (May 12, 1328), by Abū Bakr b. 'Alī b. Muḥammad.[146] Its double-page text-frontispiece

142 Richard 1997, 50. See also Blochet 1928, 125–27. Both Blochet (ibid.) and Yusofi (*Golestān*, 14; Sa'di YE, xxvii) take at face value a note added by a modern hand (ff. 245a; 273a), in which it is claimed that the manuscript was copied in 664/1265. This claim is clearly an absurdity, as the 14th-century copyist mentions events that took place decades after that date.

143 In a 1937 letter addressing Mohammad-'Ali Foroughi, Mohammad Qazvini argued that the later hand that added the date 664 (1265 CE) covers a preexisting date, that he deciphered as 764 (1362–63 CE). See Motallebi-Kāshāni 1389/2011, 211–13. However, upon close inspection of the folio in question, I have the impression that the deleted text too is a later addition. Furthermore, the style of the illuminations and the script is not consistent with the style of manuscripts of Sa'di's *Kulliyāt* produced during the second half of the 14th century.

144 Blochet, Yusofi, Richard, Bashari, etc.

145 See supra, pp. 22–23.

146 See Ethé 1903, 1: 655–60; *Bustān*, 13; *Golestān*, 19; Sa'di YE, xxvi–xxvii.

is consistent with the early Injuid style (especially the upper and lower panels featuring gold lotus motifs against a blue ground). The manuscript contains the oldest amongst the largest collections of Sa'di's ghazals (656 poems) and, among other texts, *qasida*s whose dedicatee is always carefully signaled, and a precious selection of Sa'di's obscene works (ff. 356b–366a).

9. *Ms. Dushanbe 1310s*. Academy of Sciences of the Republic of Tajikistan, 503. This fine pre-Bīsutūn recension of the *Kulliyāt* contains 538 ghazals. It has been suggested that the manuscript was copied between the end of the 13th century and the 1310s.[147] This document features one of the few extant illuminated frontispieces of Sa'di's *Kulliyāt* to appear in any of the pre-Bīsutūn manuscripts (see Plate 2). This manuscript, along with Mss. Kabul 1325 and London 1328, features one of the oldest and most important selections of Sa'di's *qasida*s.

10. *Ms. Dublin 1340s*. Chester Beatty Library, Per 113. Sa'di, *Kulliyāt*. This is the oldest extant example of Bīsutūn's rare first recension of Sa'di's *Kulliyāt*, compiled in 1326 (ff. 2b–3b, see Plate 3).[148] In spite of the numerous lacunae, this manuscript is particularly important for the accuracy with which Sa'di's *qasida*s are recorded and presented. While the manuscript is undated, Minovi speculated that it was copied in the 1380s. However, Elaine Wright's stylistic analysis established that it most likely belongs to the late Injuid period, i.e., the fifth decade of the 14th century.[149]

11. *Ms. Tehran 1340s*. Majles Library, 2570. Sa'di, *Kulliyāt*. This undated manuscript appears to have been copied during the late Injuid period (see, for instance, the color palette of the index panel at f. 42), probably in the 1340s. It contains numerous *lacunae* completed by early modern and recent hands (1–30; 34; 43–58; 455–72; 477–80). While the frontispiece is lost, the original copyist appears to have appended the older introduction to Sa'di's epistles, known as *taqrīr-i dībācha*, to the beginning of the manuscript. Only the last paragraphs, in faded ink, of this introduction remain, however, and in the *lacuna*, the later hand has added Bīsutūn's second introduction.[150] Of all the late Injuid manuscripts featuring Bīsutūn's arrangement, this manuscript records the largest number of ghazals (371 texts in the *Ṭayyibāt*, 137 in the *Badāyi'*, 76 in the *Khavātīm*, and 31 in the *Ghazalhā-yi qadīm*, for a total of

147 *Golestān*, 19–20; Sa'di YE, xxvii.
148 See *supra*.
149 Wright 2012, 23.
150 See Derāyati 2012, 26: 615.

615 poems). Future editions of Saʿdi's ghazals would greatly benefit from this rich pool of texts collected at such an early stage. The Persian *qasidas* too constitute an excellent resource for the study of Saʿdi's political involvement, especially for the clarity with which the headings specify the contents and the dedicatees of the texts (308–63).

12. *Ms. Tehran 1352*. Majles Library, 7773, 1352/753. Saʿdi, *Kulliyāt*.
This manuscript, copied in 1352, opens with one of the oldest specimens of Bīsutūn's second introduction to his recension, which he composed in 1334.[151] In spite of major lacunae in the section of the ghazals (the *Badāyiʿ* and the *Ghazalhā-yi qadīm* are missing), the lyric texts offer interesting variants that are useful for the reassessment of printed critical editions. The obscene fragments are presented with insightful titles (661–78).[152]

13. *Ms. Qom 1340s*. Marʿashi Library, 14503. Saʿdi, *Kulliyāt*.
This manuscript has been erroneously catalogued (on the basis of a note added by Mahmud Marʿashi-Najafi in 2005, without any indication of the rationale for this claim) as a 13th-century document.[153] However, even though the first part of the manuscript lacks a considerable number of folios, the alphabetical order of all poems follows Bīsutūn's second recension. The style of the surviving original illuminations is consistent with that of the late Injuid period.[154] In spite of the numerous lacunae, reference to this manuscript's extensive collection of Saʿdi's ghazals should be part of any future critical edition of the collected *dīvān*s of the poet. As the copyist mentions the name of the dedicatees of most of Saʿdi's panegyrical ghazals, one could argue that this feature (which progressively disappeared from the manuscript tradition after the 1350s) was already found in some copies of Bīsutūn's recension.

14. *Ms. Mashhad 1364*. Āstān-e Qods-e Razavi Library, 10412. Saʿdi, *Kulliyāt*.
Among 14th-century manuscripts, this document, copied by Muḥammad [b.] Muḥammad ʿAbd al-Laṭīf ʿAqāqīrī in 1364 (Ṣafar 766), contains the most extensive collection of Saʿdi's ghazals (737 poems).[155] The exceedingly elegant hand of the calligrapher (who, in the following year, copied an important manuscript of Niẓāmī's *Khamsa*)[156] attests to the early development of the *nastʿaliq* style that characterized the book culture

151 See above, p. 30; Introduction to Part 3, pp. 443vv.
152 See Derāyati 2012, 26: 615.
153 Derāyati 2012, 26: 614
154 Bashari (2020, 39), on the other hand, argues that the manuscript must have been copied in Central Asia.
155 Derāyati 2012, 26: 615; *Bustān*, 14; *Golestān*, 16; Saʿdi YE, xxiii–xxiv, xxvii.
156 Richard 1997, 66.

of the Muzaffarid period in Shiraz.[157] As the manuscript lacks Bīsutūn's introduction (as well as his index and alphabetical arrangement, along with the section of the *Ghazalhā-yi qadīm*) and contains ghazals that are not found in other manuscripts, it is likely that it was copied on the basis of documents circulating in Shiraz before the 1320s. Yusofi made use of this manuscript (which he labelled as the "oldest, most comprehensive" manuscript of Sa'di's works) for the arrangement of the ghazals in his edition.

15. *Ms. Paris 1366*. Bibliothèque Nationale de France, Supplément Persan 1778. Sa'di, *Kulliyāt*.
This manuscript, featuring Bīsutūn's second recension of the *Kulliyāt*, is one of the most studied documents in the field of modern *Sa'di-shenāsi*.[158] It comprises 473 ghazals, a reliable collection of Sa'di's Persian *qasida*s (ff. 121a–40a), and a valuable selection of the *Khabīṣāt* (248a–53b).
16. *Ms. Qom 1371*. Mar'ashi Library, 11920. Sa'di, *Kulliyāt*.
The Mar'ashi library in Qom acquired this manuscript of the *Kulliyāt* in 1998. It includes a comprehensive selection of Sa'di's ghazals (organized according to Bīsutūn's second recension), the *qasida*s, and the *Khabīṣāt* (523–33).[159]
17. *Ms. Paris 1384*. Bibliothèque Nationale de France, Supplément Persan 816. Anthology.
This anthology constitutes an extraordinary resource for the study of the circulation of Sa'di's poetry during the late Muzaffarid and early Timurid periods. The section of Sa'di's *Kulliyāt* (ff. 1v–512v, Bīsutūn's recension) features an elegant example of early "Muzaffarid" *nasta'līq* and includes a large number of ghazals (681 texts), whereas the last part of the document was copied by a second hand. It has been speculated that the name of the dedicatee mentioned in the almond-shaped *shamsa* in the first folio refers to the Muzaffarid prince Shiblī (Shāh Shujā''s son), who was deported to Samarkand in 1393, upon the execution of the entire Muzaffarid family.[160] Blochet and Francis Richard have read the number "86" that appears in the same *shamsa* as [7]86 and 8[0]6 respectively (i.e., 1384 and 1403–4 CE).[161] Elaine Wright ascribes the style of the

157 On the role of Shiraz as the center of the transition from *naskh* to *nast'alīq*, see Wright 2012, 231–54.
158 See Bashari 2020, 39. See also Blochet 1928, 132.
159 See Bashari 2020, 40.
160 Richard 2013, 2: 1107.
161 Blochet 1927, 131; Richard 2013, 2: 1107.

illuminations to the late Muzaffarid period, and suggests that the copying of the manuscript was completed in 1409 (which is the date reported at f. 523a).[162] Mohamaṃd Qazvini, in a recently published letter (dated February 1937) addressing Mohammad ʿAli Forughi, argues that the stylistic discrepancies between the two hands justify the different dates appearing at the beginning and at the end of the manuscript. The Iranian scholar was confident that the original manuscript was copied in 786/1384.[163]

18. *Ms. Paris 1390s*. Bibliothèque Nationale de France, Supplément Persan 817. Saʿdi, *Kulliyāt*.
This anonymous and undated manuscript of the *Kulliyāt* was presumably copied at the end of the 14th century.[164] The titles of subsections of the *Būstān* contain details that provide new insights onto the genealogy of the book.[165]

19. *Ms. London 1416*. British Library, India Office, Islamic 287 (Ethé 1118). Saʿdi, *Kulliyāt*.
This manuscript was copied at the end of Muḥarram 919, March 1416, by Firūzbakht b. Iṣfahānshāh.[166] Lavishly illuminated, it attests to the legacy of the atelier of the Timurid prince Iskandar Sulṭān (d. 1415) in Shiraz.[167]

20. *Ms. Yale 1432*. Beinecke Library, Persian 7. Saʿdi, *Kulliyāt*. This manuscript, dated 5 Rajab 835 (17 March 1432), was copied by Niẓām al-Dīn Iqlīdī, likely to have been associated with Ibrāhīm Sultān's atelier in Shiraz. The copyist's transcription of post-vocalic *dāl* (usually transcribed as ذ until the mid-13th century) strongly suggests that this manuscript was produced from the oldest manuscript tradition preserving Bīsutūn's recension.[168]

21. *Ms. Paris 1461*, Bibliothèque Nationale de France, Supplément Persan 1357. Saʿdi, *Kulliyāt*. This is a lavishly illuminated manuscript, copied by the famous Timurid calligrapher ʿAbd-Allāh Haravī Tabbākh.[169] Shahāb al-Dīn ʿAbd-Allāh Tabbākh worked first at Shāh-Rokh's royal library in

162 Wright 2012, 128.
163 Motallebi-Kāshāni 1389/2011, 210–11.
164 See Richard 2013, 2: 1109–11.
165 See Chapter 1.
166 See Ethé 1903, 1: 660–62.
167 See Wright 2012, 347, n. 219.
168 Ms. Yale 1432, f. 202a. Cf. Ms. 1352, 438. On the historical and regional developments of the post-vocalic *dāl*, see Orsatti 2019, 47–50.
169 *EIr*, s.v. "ʿAbdallāh Heravī" (P. P. Soucek).

Herat, then for Abū Saʿid, and later for Sultān Ḥusayn Bāyqarā.[170] It is possible that this manuscript was copied for Abū Saʿid (d. 1469) in Herat. Preliminary inspection of the document reveals variants not attested to by the manuscripts of the *Kulliyāt* copied during the same period. Comparison with other manuscripts will possibly unveil the copyist's philological effort in producing a "proto-critical" edition of Saʿdi's works.

170 Richard 1997, 98.

PART 1

Uncovering the Skin of the Ghazal

Introduction to Part 1

We used to tell each other that the difference
Between the experienced prospector and us
Is that he can discern gold
From the reflection of the waters;
Whereas we pursue it
Amidst the labyrinths of stone:
Astray we go, and yet we graze it.

JOAN VINYOLI[1]

•••

Listen, so seductive is the sorcery of your eyes,
In awe the eyes of the deer stare at your eyes.

You are in my eyes, yet hidden from the eye,
Hence my eyes wander in all directions.

Your eyes, your lips, your neck, your ears:
May they never be touched by anyone's arms or evil eye!

The moon shines in people's eyes, but you
Are more beautiful, for your eyebrows and eyes!

The dark night is dotted with stars like eyes:
Its Indian magic enslaved to your black eyes.

One hundred springs will flow from these eyes,
When I set my eye upon that countenance of yours.

You closed my eyes with your enchanting locks,
You stole my senses with the sorcery of your eyes.

---

1 "Ens dèiem l'un a l'altre: / La diferència entre nosaltres i el buscador sapient / està en el fet que ell sap conèixer l'or / en el reflex de le aïgues / i nosaltres el perseguim pels laberints de la pedra. / Però perdent-nos ens hi acostem." Vinyoli 1979, 92.

 | DOI:10.1163/9789004435902_003

Every night I turn my eyes into lamps
Seeking through darkness the lamp and light of my eyes.

I swear by your eyes! Saʿdi is here
With his two eyes, shedding thousands of pearls.
SAʿDI, *Badāyiʿ* 523[2]

∴

Persian poetry has inspired generations of Western readers, scholars, poets, and translators with an incessant source of images and rhythms that have exerted an enormous influence on the formation of some of the most important currents of the European and American literary canons.[3] The creation of aesthetic bonds between a certain premodern author and the taste of modern readership is determined by a sequence of factors that are often hardly discernible, sometimes aleatory, and in most cases related to temporary appreciation of a kind that is diverted to other objects of contemplation in the space of a few decades. Our vociferous postmodernity probably constitutes the right time for the full appreciation of the ecstatic poems of Rumi and their disheveled forms of visionary intoxication. Even Hafez's sensual bacchanalia, with his philosophical and spiritual depths and kaleidoscopic charisma, is now more than ever ready to capture millennial audiences accustomed to the absorption of constant flows of images. But what kind of space do we need to create to appreciatively welcome the delicate prettiness of Saʿdi's ghazals and protect them from the turbulent noise of our times?

Saʿdi's reputation for didacticism, however, has driven many scholars and readers to associate his ghazals with the moralistic overtone that pervades certain sections of his non-lyrical work, such as *The Rose Garden* (*Gulistān*) and

2 [1.19] Saʿdi YE, 239. Edited on the basis of Ms. Tehran 1296, 413.

3 For a general appraisal of the influence of Persian literature on the formation of specific aspects of European and American modern literary canons, see Yohannan 1977; 1998; Ingenito and Miglio 2013. See also (on the influence of Persian literature on American authors) the collection of essays edited by Mehdi Aminrazavi (2014). On the influence of Saʿdi in the European literatures of the 17th, 18th, and 19th centuries, see Lewis 2001a; Yohannan 1987, 128–33. See also ibid., 123–27, for echoes of Saʿdi in "the East." For in-depth analyses of the influence of Saʿdi on Ralph Waldo Emerson's literary activity, see Loloi 2014, and Jahanpour 2014.

The Orchard (*Būstān*).[4] Although clearing one's mind of the cultural biases that superpose pre-acquired meanings and purposes onto poetic artifacts requires remarkable efforts of detachment and critical suspension, it also takes a little while to go past the first line of any of Saʿdi's ghazals to witness the disarming, crystalline beauty of the rivulets of images constituting his masterly crafted miniatures in verse. "Minimalism" is probably the attribute that best suits the alluring charm of his compositions, which—unlike Hafez's kaleidoscopic fireworks of intoxicated flesh and empyreal metaphysics—require the dedication of the attentive prospectors who set their eyes on the stream, and discern gold from the reflections in the water.

1 Tasting the *Punctum*

Saʿdi's ghazals depict and explore the essence of love in some of the most elegant, balanced, and inspiring forms ever conceived in Persian poetry. But if the judgment of the ancients and the moderns about the incomparable excellence of Saʿdi's lyric art is almost unanimous, very little effort has been poured into the direction of determining the nature, the scope, and the anthropological, historical, and psychological specificities of the ardent passion—or, etymologically speaking, "eroticism"—displayed in his verses.

The polymorphic nature of passion, along with its related literary implications, is one of the main vectors informing my approach to Saʿdi's poetry in general, and this part of the book in particular. After all, passion, ardent desire, and love are the pivotal themes that enable the classification of the classical Persian ghazal as a lyric genre. Confusion arises, however, when we notice the profound difference between medieval conceptions of love and modern perceptions of eroticism that inform both our amorous practices, habits, and norms and also the understanding that we have of sensuality and sexuality. The nature of the love that Saʿdi describes in his poems is indeed a legitimate point of interrogation. Love is clearly the main topic of the (more or less) 700 ghazals that constitute his three collections of poems, but the author

4 See, for instance, Massé (1919) and de Fouchécour (1986, 311–48) who, albeit with different analytical approaches and philological methodologies, assess the ethical landscape of Saʿdi's literary personae almost exclusively on the basis of the *Būstān* and the *Gulistān*. "It is, then, hardly surprising that Emerson should have been attracted to the most explicit moralist amongst the poets of Persian literature." Loloi 2014, 95.

offers no clear analytical explanation to clarify the nature of the passion that, line after line, he praises, evokes, and celebrates.[5]

Throughout his three *dīvāns* (the collection of poems that he himself or his contemporaries arranged in allegedly chronological order), Saʿdi stages the effects of love on human behavior and its psycho-physiological condition. He often highlights the emotional energies triggered by this experience, as well as the disastrous and pleasurable consequences associated with the encounter with the beloved: the perils that this presence, the desire *for him*, scatters on the path of the honest person, the believer, the wise man. But his collected poems offer no precise description of what love is and, above all, towards whom or what it is directed.

The sensation of a certain degree of indetermination with respect to the "true" nature of love and of the beloved haunts many of the studies that have tried to tackle the meaning of the amorous verses composed by other premodern Persian poets, especially Hafez of Shiraz, who flourished a century after Saʿdi and whose apparently intrinsic ambiguity has been identified as one of the main characteristic traits of his poetry.[6] Nevertheless, what we may perceive as indeterminacy might more appropriately be identified as the result of unwritten but powerful conventions that shaped the historical development of the ghazal as a lyric genre. These conventions allowed for disconnection between the text and its implied horizon of signification. The effect of such indetermination, far from being inherent to the texts themselves, results from a critical reading of them, when scholarly analyses privilege internal evidence without considering diachronic developments in the social, intertextual, political, and historical contexts.

---

5 See Rypka 1968, 252–53; Meisami 1987, 277–78; Yohannan 1987, 93–107; Manoukian 1991, 14–41, and ibid., 245–61.

6 For a general overview of Hafez's style, imagery, and historical context, see the various articles published under the entry "Hafez" of the Encyclopaedia Iranica, especially "Hafez ii. Hafez's Life and Times" [B. Khorramshahi. EIr]; "Hafez iii. Hafez's Poetic Art" [J. T. P. de Bruijn]; "Hafez viii. Hafez and Rendi" [F. Lewis 2002]. Many are the translations (either complete or partial) of Hafez's *Dīvān* that are available in English (for a survey, see Loloi 2004) although choosing the "best" one among them is a matter of personal sensibility, I would recommend Gertrude Bell's versions (Bell 1897), as well as those of Peter Avery (2007), and Dick Davis's (2013), belonging respectively to a Victorian, mid-century, and contemporary literary and interpretive taste. I would also urge the reader to peruse Geoffrey Squires's lyric rewritings of Hafez's ghazals, probably among the most successful creative renditions ever published in English. See Squires 2014. For the most comprehensive annotated translation ever published in a Western language, see de Fouchécour 2006. For an introductory survey to the imagery of Hafez's poetry compared with that of his contemporaries, see Brookshaw 2019. See also, in Persian, Khorramshāhi 1366/1987; Mortazavi 1344/1965; Purnāmdāryān 1382/2003.

This is true, in particular, with regard to the perception and practices of desire, which informed the composition and circulation of the ghazals in the first place. For instance, cogitations on the difference between love and lust are as old as Western philosophy (and lyric poetry), but when we approach literary texts that belong to different epochs and regions of the world we are often puzzled by how divergent those representations (along with their anthropological reverberations) can be from the text and practices to which we are accustomed.[7]

In spite of such differences, and notwithstanding the fluidity of social and literary experiences of eroticism, evident even within the space of a few decades, some currents of modern critical discussions of Persian literature often display a tendency to interpret the multifaceted nature of the poetic experience of desire according to binary oppositions whose rigidity can tell us very little about the often non-polarized richness of poetic texts on love and sexuality. Nevertheless, one of the prerogatives of most premodern love poetry is to confront us with ambivalences that can lead to the dismantling of our perception of a substantial hiatus between, for example, the representation of romantic love and what today we would consider as pornographic. An investigation of the obscene and the sexually explicit, besides highlighting to what extent passionate love and sexual desire are in fact mutually constituted through literary speculation, also highlights the often neglected intersection of history, literary fiction, and the poetic projections of gender, political, ethnic, and social identities that constitute one of the most fascinating and uncanny aspects of premodern Persian poetry.

We may regard the following ghazal as a taste of the lyrical oscillations that lie in the interstices of Saʿdi's poetry, along with the interpretive problems constituted by their multiplicity of allusions:

7 See, for example, Irving Singer's theorization of the contraposition of idealized and mundane approaches to the relationship between passionate love and sexual desire: "As in the ancient world eros soared upward with the idealists and then returned to earth with the realists, so too were there two traditions of courtly love in twelfth-century France. The earlier one, represented by the troubadour poets of Provence, reveals the unmistakable influence of Moorish and Mediterranean Neoplatonism. […] The latter version, mainly in Northern France, believed in sexual completion as a part of courtly love, even at the expense of adultery, and sometimes for the sake of it." Singer 1984, 1:124–25. See also ibid., 150–55. Cf. El-Rouayheb's (2005, 85–95) meditations on this dichotomy in the context of the early modern Islamic world. As I will expand upon in later chapters, such bipolar theorizations should be taken with a gain of theoretical salt when it comes to projecting them onto lyric traditions (as in the case of ghazal poetry) in which the meaning of a given text is usually collaboratively constructed by the audiences that use its verses as socio-political and spiritual instruments.

1 O moon-faced beauty, do not turn your comely countenance from me.
What merit do you see in killing the innocent?

2 **Last night I was asleep [*khʷāb*] when you joined my embrace.**
How could I ever envision such pleasures but in my dreams [*khʷāb*]?

3 I burn inside and moist are my weeping eyes:
Half of me engulfed in flames, and half submerged in water.

4 "Here he is!" I think, of anyone who enters the door.
Poor is the thirsty one: water he sees in the mirage.

5 **The life of the poor mystics [*darvīsh*] is the target of his darts.**
The blood of the indigent is the dye of his nails.

6 Whenever he speaks, he takes away your heart:
Tasteful spells that ensnare and burn people's hearts.

7 **Regrettable is a shirt on such a body!**
A veil covering such a face would be cruelty!

8 **Imbue your sleeves with the sweat of his neck**
So that the scent of rosewater may impregnate your clothes.

9 **Uproar and commotion if those who reflect God's beauty [*shāhid*]**
Half-asleep hold a candle, intoxicated from wine.

10 For one day, from dawn to dusk, do not cover your face,
So that you may veil the radiant face of the sun.

11 **O Saʿdi, if you want to press him against your chest like a lyre**
You ought to be plucked and tweaked like a lute string.

Ṭayyibāt 194[8]

As is typical of Saʿdi's style, the apparent levity of this poem hides a complex poetic mechanism that intertwines the linguistic, rhetorical, and visual elements into a texture of balances and oppositions. Their concomitant fluidity

8 [1. 20] Saʿdi YE, 91; Cf. Ms. Yale 1432, f. 210a. I have followed Yusofi's edition.

creates the effect of a *real presence* that can also be seen as an intuitive first approach to the quintessence of the lyric.

In Saʿdi's text, the initial invocation of the beloved, a bewildered lingering between the observation of the world and the projections of the poetic voice's innermost desires, as well as the oscillation between enchantment and disenchantment, hope and despair, are all elements that perfectly accommodate this ghazal within the perimeter of the most recent theoretical attempts to define the lyrical both as a genre and as a literary modality.[9] In my translation, I have highlighted six couplets whose images and stylistic features contain five interpretive knots that I will try to disentangle in this first part, and whose literary implications correspond to some of the most salient elements characterizing Saʿdi's lyric uniqueness:

1. The suspension of desire between reality and imagination (line 2: "Last night I was asleep [*khʷāb*] when you joined my embrace / How could I ever envision such pleasures but in my dreams [*khʷāb*] ?"). The two-fold meaning of the word *khʷāb* used here both as "sleep" and "dream" creates an oscillation between the possibility of a physical encounter with the beloved and frustration deriving from a sensuality that took place only in a nocturnal reverie, dream, or bewildered fantasy. Is the poet talking about the real experience of either a physical encounter with an object of desire or an unfulfilled longing, or is this line only projecting onto the space of the literary subjectivity a fictitious variation dictated by the lyric tradition? Why does the poet, in the second hemistich, confess that such an encounter is only possible in his dreams?
2. Technical versus plain uses of the poetic language. What does the *darvīsh* of the fifth line stand for? Is this word used in its original meaning to represent a figurative indigence as a euphemism for the desperate lover, or is Saʿdi, as in many of his works, alluding to the technical meaning of an actual mystic belonging to a Sufi circle?[10] If the latter is more likely than the former, why should a man devoted to spirituality be interested in cultivating an earthly amorous passion? Or maybe it is a higher, purer desire that is at stake in this poem?
3. Nudity and bodily fluids. The desire of contemplating the flesh of the beloved's body, as well as the splendor of her or his face, followed by the

9 See Jackson and Prins 2014, 1–16; Culler 2015, 34–38. For a critical appraisal of the theoretical approaches to the ghazal as a lyric genre, see Meisami 1987, 237–46; and, in particular, Lewis 1996, 1–14; 2006.

10 "Though 'darvish' often designates a stock Sufi character, Saʿdi sometimes uses it to refer more generally to the poor or meek." EIr, s.v. "Golestān-e Saʿdi" [F. Lewis]

invitation to touch his neck and smell his sweat are all elements that sharply deny the plausibility of any spiritual interpretation. This beloved is touchable, fragrant, embraceable. Is this a man or a woman? What kind of veil is the poet trying to describe? How does this physical proximity interact with the oneiric mood of the second line?

4. Tangibility or spirituality of the beloved's presence. Is the body of the beloved believed to reflect God's beauty? In the second part of the book I will dwell at length on the implications of the term *shāhid* (lit. "witness"), which usually refers to a young man whose beauty attests to the magnificence of God's "face." Islamic theologians, philosophers, and mystics have dealt for centuries with the problem of the relationship between God and the beauty of the human body. Is Sa'di envisaging the possibility of an incarnation, a mere reflection, or an allegorical sensuality that reconciles the concupiscence of the flesh with the aspirations of the soul?
5. To press the beloved's body against your chest, as if he were an instrument. This is probably one of the most erotically charged images that readers will ever find in Sa'di's non-obscene ghazals. Is the poet sexualizing the act of playing an instrument, or is this image purely sexual, as it urges its audience to imagine the presence of a human beloved "pressed" against the lover's chest and manipulated as a lyre? Why should the lover (Sa'di himself in his real life? His literary projection?) sigh like a lute in order to possess (at least "musically") his beloved? And to what extent is this image permissible from an Islamic ethical perspective? Does the poet allude to a musical performance as an analogue of an amorous encounter?

The constellation of questions generated by these five critical points constitutes the network of significations around which Sa'di's ghazals organize the complexity of their discourse on desire and the nature of the presence(s) they stage in his texts—their oscillation between reality, fiction, and a hallucinated *terra di mezzo* that can correspond both to the experience of dreaming and the territory of illusions, reveries, and tangible imaginations.

There are of course other elements at work in his *dīvāns*, but they all derive from this archipelago of topics and images. A rigorous approach to his lyrical work does not need to find (or rather impose) a well-defined answer to these questions. The ambivalences of Sa'di's poetry need to be embraced as if we were to navigate through a cluster of islands without the aid of maps—an experience of the literary territory that is rhizomatic rather than cartographical. Reading his ghazals is an experience that does not reach its final point through linear, line-by-line, analyses of his verses. Rather, their meaning emerges through the contemplation of what Walter Benjamin called the "aura" of the work of art, the sacred distance that conjures up the ritualistic value of the aesthetic experience.

The study of Persian poetry, once most of the philological stumbling blocks are overcome, has often been confined to the production of tautologies and self-explanatory truths, to analytical discourses that limit themselves to a paraphrasis of the poetic text that ends up missing its aesthetic target—its "punctum," if we are allowed to use Roland Barthes' theorization of what, in a photograph, is "the element which rises from the scene and unintentionally fills the whole image, [...] that accident which pricks, bruises me."[11] The fact that Saʿdi's ghazals poetically cover the experience of "love," "passion," and "desire" is a self-evident tautology dictated by the genre itself and presented in a form whose limpidity prevents us from easily accessing the secret chambers of its "punctum." This is why, on the one hand, critics have often hastily agreed on the amorous nature of Saʿdi's ghazals without reaching the spaces that lie behind their surface, and, on the other hand, his poems have been scantly studied and translated.

We only needed to slightly break through the surface of Saʿdi's ghazal, "O moon-faced beauty," to discover that, in spite of a linguistic fluency that creates an immediate effect of amorous empathy with the feelings of the poetic persona, the hiatus between the configuration of desire emerging from this poem and our contemporary perceptions of love and sexuality is almost unbridgeable. It is across this gap that the right questions need to be formulated in order to grant these texts their partial alterity with respect to us and our categories. And we might discover how the concept of "love" and "passion" celebrated by Saʿdi through his poems is much more unsettling, disturbing, and confusing than we would have ever imagined. But also more alluring, modern, cosmopolitan, and overarching.

2 The Body of the Bias

Both the idea of a certain ahistorical universality of love, and the relative fluency and grammatical accessibility of Saʿdi's language have allowed many readers and scholars to interpret his ghazals according to value systems that belong to either the deterministic heteronormativity of Western Orientalism, or to the hypertrophic (and often superficial) spiritualization that often characterizes the dominant cultural frameworks of the Islamic Republic of Iran. At the confluence of these two value systems we find the two main paradigms

---

11 Barthes 2010b, 26.

that are today available to the interpreter of Sa'di's ghazals: (1) romantic postures embraced by those who posit that the love celebrated by Sa'di is inherently physical, heteronormative, and based on the biographical experiences of the author; (2) mystical readings, according to which God is the only object of desire in Sa'di's verse, and all traces of carnal desire are but symbols that require to be deciphered through spiritual interpretation.[12]

It is precisely for historical and socio-anthropological reasons (which, as I shall argue, are also linguistic, spiritual, political, and juridical) that the poetry of Sa'di cannot be fully understood without exploring the complex landscape of homoerotic passions and tensions emerging from both his ghazals and his other works in verse and prose. Denying, glossing over, or paternalistically attempting to "absolve" the relevance of homoeroticism in Sa'di's poetry is not only an ethnocentric bias, but also a philological mistake that reduces the text to an abstract and shallow linguistic material.

This book thus opens with a chapter on the homoerotics of political power and desire, which are the two least studied aspects of Sa'di's poetry, and which should be analyzed simultaneously, as they are both ingrained in the very origins of the lyric and encomiastic tradition to which Sa'di belongs. Therefore, the main goal of this chapter is to take advantage of the lacunae of the scholarly discourse on Sa'di's homoerotics of power to revisit the tradition of the early Persian panegyric from the perspective of the multiple significations of homosocial lyric interactions.

In Sa'di's works, homoeroticism oscillates between the platonic contemplation of the angelic beloved and lewd brutality imbued with social scorn and moral condemnation; between unfulfilled physical desires projected onto a superior degree of spiritual satisfaction and the coarse representation of lascivious pleasures. If we consider the entire collected works of Sa'di, it would be hard to ascertain that the poet had adopted a coherent and well-defined approach to sexuality and desire. A foray into the relationship between praise poetry and lyricism, as dimensions that offer a secure grip on the connection between history and literary creation, will prepare the groundwork to address the problem of the identity of the beloved in Sa'di's ghazals—in all his ghazals, and in particular in the text that I have quoted in this introduction: a fleeting presence, a sweaty neck, or a plucked instrument that is suspended between morning reveries, nightly dreams, and nocturnal visits. But how does this partially imaginary and partially bodily presence fluctuate between the multiplication of lyric images and the historical performativity of the text, especially

12 I will often return to the discrepancies between these hermeneutical postures. For now, see Yohannan 1987, 96–103, and Keshavarz 2015, 35–44.

with respect to the biographical contours of Saʿdi's movements in the times and spaces of his poetic activity?

This problem is related to the question of the real presence as an effect that emerges from the lyric text, which demands multiple analytical tools for it to be broken down into a network of devices that put the text in *motion*, between the tangible realm of history and the symbolic arena of artistic invention. This motion cannot be fully understood without addressing the notion of the real presence as an artifact that stems from the literary persona and the identity of the linguistic instances that breathe through a poem. The second chapter will delve into this field by recontextualizing the bodily dimension of Saʿdi's ghazals through the lens of their relationship with his major prose work, the *Gulistān* (*The Rose Garden*), which constitutes a unique corpus of narrations whose intersections with the lyric and the biographical offer outstanding opportunities for a deeper understanding of the poet's stratified representations of desire.

The third and last chapter of Part 1 reconsiders the value of Saʿdi's obscene texts, along with their often parodic, burlesque, brutally explicit, and ambiguously alluring representations of carnal desire. Both these texts and the political odes count among the most understudied and misinterpreted passages of Saʿdi's literary output. By virtue of this reappraisal, the second and third parts of the book will open as a space in which the dichotomy between obscenity and transcendence can be put into conversation with the question of realism and the correspondence of poetic texts to socio-historical reality.

CHAPTER 1

The Homoerotics of Political Power and the Emergence of Gendered Desires

> Sa'di seemed to have a melancholic disposition: he only enjoyed the company of comely and beardless youths, otherwise he would not associate with anyone.[1]

•••

> Marvelous are the brides of my talent, my virginal poems,
> But shameful they turn when facing that gorgeous boy!
>
> *Khavātīm* 712[2]

•••

> The spiritual wayfarers do not care about the vest you wear:
> Fasten your belt at the service of a sultan, and be a Sufi!
>
> *Ṭayyibāt* 42[3]

1 From the Fall of Baghdad to the Gendered Nature of Desire

Between 1263 and 1265, less than a decade after the Mongol conquest of Iraq and the dissolution of the Abbasid caliphate in Baghdad, Sa'di hailed the young minister of the Ilkhanid finances, the *ṣāḥib dīvān* Shams al-Dīn Juvaynī, with a series of panegyrics celebrating the new course that Islamdom on the Iranian plateau was to take after years of social unrest and political instability.[4]

1 Ibn Bazzāz 1373/1994, 104.
2 [1.21] Sa'di YE, 319.
3 [1.22] Ibid., 23.
4 For an appraisal of the Muslim historiographical reactions to the destruction of the Abbasid caliphate in Baghdad, see Hassan 2016, 20–65. Sa'di mourned the death of the last Caliph

 | DOI:10.1163/9789004435902_004

Saʿdi hyperbolically declared that his poetry "would graze the Pleiades / once it reaches the *ṣāḥib dīvān*," who was in his late twenties when he took up this appointment. The poems of praise with which Saʿdi lauded Shams al-Dīn's ascension to the highest office of the Ilkhanid administrative machinery are interjected with lyric excerpts whose homoerotic overtones mirror the relationship between courtly sensuality, spirituality, and political dynamics at work in 13th-century Shiraz.[5] Passages like the following, in spite of their undeniable aesthetic value, have seldom been the object of literary investigation within the framework of Saʿdi's lyric corpus. Saʿdi opens his lyrical exordium with the metaphorical praise of Shams al-Dīn's political attractiveness through the depiction of an ideal male beloved:

1 Where is this beautiful boy [*shāhid*] going? So sweet are his words!
What a divine beauty, why doesn't he appear before my two eyes?

2 For one reason he resembles the sun in the sky:
Whenever you contemplate him, your gaze dazzles ecstatically.

3 A mirror is his countenance that kindles the world
Beholding him cleanses the mirror of the heart from all impurities.

4 The royal diploma of beauty and the edict of grace and pulchritude
Are marked on his rosy face with the golden script of his downy beard,

5 Which resembles pure musk molten in fragrant liqueur,
Masterly painted on silk with the finest brush.

6 How can I describe his countenance and lips?
A scarlet flame, and pomegranate grains!

7 And when he utters words from his sweet mouth
Where are the refined spectators who can sweetly honor him?

8 The morning breeze has left to graze his delicate limbs:
Upon its return to the garden, the leaves of spring have dropped.

---

in Baghdad, al-Mustaʿṣim, with poignant elegies in both Arabic and Persian (Saʿdi KhE, 703–708).

5 See Introduction, pp. 17–25. For an in-depth analysis of the correlation between power and eroticism in Saʿdi's political and spiritual liaison with Shams al-Dīn, see Ingenito 2019, 32–42.

9 Let me be your subject, O my dear, if no shame you feel.
May I be your servant, if your honor is not compromised?

10 Will I ever make you mine? What a glorious destiny!
Would I ever turn away from you? How could I dare?

11 I cannot tell anyone the truth about my love for you
As I am too jealous for strangers to listen.

12 Anyone in the past would come and go from my heart:
There has been no room for others since you made your appearance.

13 You are more precious than my head and life:
A covetous fool I am if I didn't scatter them away for you.

14 Passion is not permissible, but lawful may it be
To those who, like Saʿdi, bring love to the threshold of resurrection.[6]

The lines describing the fine beard of the virtual beloved as a symbolic mirror of the presence of Shams al-Dīn are one of the most beautiful Persian renditions and reinventions of a motif that recurs virtually in all the premodern court poets of Iran and Central Asia.[7] In Saʿdi's poetry, the predominance of these images, along with the languid lingering with which the poet indulges every time that he conjures up depictions of juvenile virility, converts this literary topos into the main cypher of the aesthetic experience that the author conveys through his ghazals.

Why did Saʿdi insert this homoerotic interlude into the praise of the new minister of the Ilkhanid state, and what is the function of such sensual images within the general economy of the text? Above all, how should the reader account for the juxtaposition of delicate homoerotic courtship with the references to kingship ("the royal diploma"), mutual domination ("will I ever make you mine?"; "let me be your subject"), and metaphysical projections ("the divine beauty"; "the threshold of resurrection")? These questions highlight the notion that literary representation of male homoerotic passion is not only a

6 [1.23] Saʿdi KhE, 666. Cf. Ms. Kabul 1325, 544; Ms. Tehran 1321, 401–10; and Ms. Yale 1432, f. 178a, which, apart from few discrepancies, align with Forughi and Khorramshāhi's edition.

7 For a preliminary study of the symbolic connections between the fictive eroticism of the lyric exordium of the Persian panegyric *qasida* and the historical relationship between poets and young patrons, see Meisami 1990a. I shall elaborate on this form of implied political eroticism in the second part of this chapter.

recurrent theme in Saʿdi's texts, but also a socio-aesthetic pivot that articulates the lyric within the spheres of political power and spirituality. The multilayered representation of male homoerotic desire is remarkably more present in Saʿdi's works than in the literary output of any other premodern Persian poet.[8] In fact, the sensuality of his depictions of male youths as the focus of both the loins' appetite and the soul's limpid contemplations exudes from all the different genres in which he exerted his literary talent.

Nevertheless, a Victorian hermeneutical posture manifests itself whenever critics emphasize the importance of romantic love in Saʿdi's poetry, while denying the centrality of the body as a primary locus of physical desire for other bodies.[9] The fact that Saʿdi's ghazals—as well as most of the premodern Persian lyric tradition—stage same-sex desires constituted a primary source for the prudery that still haunts the field of Persian literature, particularly in Iran, but also among the old guard of otherwise respectable scholars of

8 Ironically enough, the modern popularizing receptions of the theopathic association between Rumi and his spiritual guide Shams-i Tabrīzī often present the liaison between these two Sufi masters as a paradigm of the social acceptance of homosexuality in medieval Iran. See for instance Barzan 1995. Apart from the anachronism of using a modern Western category in order to classify premodern sexual habits in an essentialist manner, Rumi's and Shams's writings leave very little room for a homoerotic interpretation of their passion. Franklin Lewis's critique of popular approaches of this sort is particularly informative: "Here may be said to originate the claim which some modern homosexual authors and translators have made about the relationship between Rumi and Shams; though Dowlatshâh does not specify that their relationship was physical, this passage is suggestive." Lewis 2000, 265–66; "The suggestion that the relationship between Shams and Rumi was a physical and homosexual one entirely misunderstands the context. Rumi, as a forty-year-old man engaged in ascetic practices and teaching Islamic law, to say nothing of his obsession with following the example of the Prophet, would not have submitted to the penetration of the sixty-year-old Shams, who was, in any case, like Rumi, committed to following the Prophet and opposed to the worship of God through human beauty. Rumi did employ the symbolism of homoerotic, or more properly, androgynous love, in his poems addressed to Shams as the divine beloved, but this merely adopts an already 300-year-old convention of the poetry of praise in Persian literature." Ibid., 324. On the harshness of their positions on the Sufi aesthetics of homosociality, which places them on the conservative side of the spectrum of Sunni approaches to spiritual perception of the body and its sensual experiences, see Shamisa 1381/2002, 122–26. On Shams-i Tabrīzī's criticism of the practice of homoeroticism in the context of the allegedly promiscuous practices of Awḥad al-Dīn Kirmānī, see Ridgeon 2017, 69–72.

9 This is, for instance, the assumption of Saʿid Hamidiyān (1383/2004), the author of the only substantial monograph on Saʿdi's ghazals ever published in Persian. The Iranian scholar assumes that even though the sensorial experiences of the poet in the contemplation of the world play a key role in the shaping of Saʿdi's lyricism, the beloved he portrays in the large majority of his ghazals corresponds to the manifestation of God, and as such his physical dimension should be dismissed. For references to and analyses of Hamidiyān's approach to Saʿdi's alleged mysticism, see the second part of this book.

Sa'di's works.[10] To some modern readers, especially from the perspective of the perception of same-sex desire as a binary opposition (homosexuality versus heterosexuality), Sa'di's postures, ethics, and ideals with respect to homoeroticism may seem ambiguous, inconsistent, and ultimately hypocritical. Such ambiguities, however, should be read as culture-specific ambivalences whose anthropological background is closer to the homoerotic discourse of ancient Greece and Rome than to the sexual landscape of contemporary Iran.[11] Sa'di's variety of representations, rather than being the expression of double moral standards or ambiguous exaltation and repression of personal desires, reflects an articulate juxtaposition of ambivalent passions whose coexistence could be at times harmonious and at times conflicting.

The peculiar traits of the homoeroticism that surfaces from texts similar to the panegyric dedicated to Shams al-Dīn undermine not only the notion of a quintessential coincidence between modern homosexual identities and premodern male-to-male eroticism, but also the concept of a static binary opposition between activity and passivity as ontic roles that define the sexual schemes of the Islamicate societies of the past. This chapter offers a preliminary attempt to outline the presence of homoeroticism in Sa'di's poetry as a key to access the complexity of his manipulation of both the literary canon and the construction of the lyric subject as a category that emanates from fluid perceptions of gender and sexuality. Forays into the Foucault-inspired theories of sexuality which, in the past four decades, have highlighted the sociocultural construction of both gender and the perception of the body will offer the opportunity to revisit the depiction of the beloved by premodern Persian poets as a persona suspended between linguistic abstraction and historical concreteness. It is precisely in light of this fluidity that the poetic text enables us to read the relationship between literary fiction and bio-historiographical reality as a function of the mechanisms of power that inhabit literature and its social uses.

---

10 See Davidson 2007 (101–105) for a concise presentation of the biases and preconceptions that have haunted for decades the scholarly approach to "Greek love." See, in particular, Halperin 2003 for a critical approach to ancient Greek male-to-male sex and desire from a perspective not too different from the theoretical approaches to which I refer as ways to tackle the same kind of problems in Sa'di's ghazals.

11 I particularly recommend the works of James Davidson (2007) and Craig Williams (2010) on respectively Greek and Roman same-sex eroticism. Throughout this book, I have refrained from sharing with the reader the many similarities between Iranian and Greco-Roman conceptions, practices, and poetic representations of man-to-man love. While this is a fascinating subject, it is one that deserves to be the object of a separate study. On Qajar and contemporary Iran, see Najmabadi 2005, and Afary 2009 respectively.

2 Bawdy Portrayals and Homoerotic "Confessions"

Portions of the collected works of early-14th-century poet and satirist ʿUbayd Zākānī constitute a useful source for the understanding of the bodily dimension of Saʿdi's poetry as it was perceived among the first communities of readers who inherited his lyric legacy a few decades after his death.[12] ʿUbayd's burlesque vignettes would often interpret Saʿdi's manifestation of his appreciation of human beauty as if they were originally conceived as a lustful commitment of the flesh. In some passages, ʿUbayd creates hilarious literary pastiches as a strategy to highlight the carnal side of Saʿdi's contemplation of youthful bodies and their signs of sexual maturation:

> I shall therefore invoke the unsullied soul of Shaykh Saʿdi to put him in conversation with a boy:
>
> Last year you moved as gently as a gazelle,
> This year you're fierce, a panther poised to attack.
> "Bring sweets and almonds," last year you commanded;
> By God, today your favors don't amount to jack.
> Yes, Saʿdi likes a row of green now and then,
> But not the common fibres of a gunnysack.[13]

In this excerpt from ʿUbayd's burlesque prose work *The Book of the Beard* (*Rīsh-nāma*), the speaker is the personification of the beard, who quotes Saʿdi (from the poet's collection of obscene fragments, the *Khabīṣāt*) in order to vilify the haughtiness of an imaginary beautiful young man by reminding him

---

12 For a general introduction to ʿUbayd Zākānī's life and works, see Haidari 1986; Ḥalabi 1998; *EIr*, s.v. "ʿObayd Zākānī" [D. Meneghini]; and Sprachman 2012. On the geo-ethnic aspect of Zākānī's satires, see Brookshaw 2012. The two main editions to which I will refer throughout this book are those published respectively by Atābaki (ʿObayd Zākāni 1384/2005), and Mahjub (ʿObayd Zākāni 1999); for two authoritative critical appraisals of this edition, see Purjavādi 1389/2000; Meneghini 2003. ʿObayd Zākāni 1374/1995 comprises the richest annotated edition of ʿUbayd's major prose works. Some of the most ingenious English translations of Zākānī's prose and verse have been published by Paul Sprachman (1984, 44–75), and Dick Davis (2013). See also D'Erme (2005) for a hilarious and accurately annotated Italian translation of ʿUbayd's facetiae.

13 ʿObayd Zākāni 1999, 335. English Translation by Paul Sprachman (1984, 66–67). The first hemistich of the last line appears in one of Saʿdi's ghazals, whereas the second hemistich belongs to one of Saʿdi's obscene fragments. See Saʿdi 1385/2006b, 983. For the oldest variants, cf. Ms. Kabul 1325, 685; Ms. Paris 1320s., f. 256b. See below for the context of the ghazal in which the first hemistich appears.

of how uncomely his face turns when it is overcome by dark hairs. The term "unsullied soul of Sa'di" hints at both the recent death of the poet (which happened no more than half a century before the composition of this satirical treatise) and the aura of ethical incorruptibility that surrounded Sa'di's saintly persona—which had been very much venerated since the first decades of the 14th century, as Ibn Baṭṭūṭa reported in his *Travels*.[14] I will elucidate in the next two chapters what role the aesthetics of facial hair would play in the amorous anthropology of the Persian ghazal, but these lines suffice to signal that the perception that 'Ubayd had of the inclinations of Sa'di's poetic persona were particularly centered on the cult of male beauty in transition from adolescence to adulthood.

Sa'di's renown as a worshipper of male youthful beauty started circulating beyond the perimeter of Shiraz when the poet was still alive. And if 'Ubayd's burlesque vignettes do not seem to pass moral judgment on the poet's inclinations (apart from the comment on the "unsullied soul of Sa'di," which is readable as a euphemism), Ṣafī al-Dīn Ardabīlī (d. 1334), the founder of the Safavid order, as reported by his disciple Ibn Bazzāz in his hagiographic work *Ṣafvat al-ṣafā*, found Sa'di "to be a man with a melancholic disposition: he only enjoyed the company of comely and beardless youths, otherwise he would not associate with anyone."[15] It is unclear whether such comments derive from direct experience or from elaborations on Sa'di's own literary confessions of his passion for male downy cheeks. These confessions appear very often in his works. They not only serve as one of the main pieces of evidence attesting to the homoerotic content of his lyricism, but also show what details would leave an indelible trace on the sensitivity of later authors:

> Everyone knows that I love the youthful greeneries of the beard:
> Unlike other animals, who only appreciate the verdures of the countryside.[16]
>
> *Badāyi'* 427

14 "Among the sanctuaries outside Shiraz is the grave of the pious shaykh known as Sa'di, who was the greatest poet of his time in the Persian language, and sometimes introduced Arabic verses into his compositions. There is a fine hospice which he built in this place having a beautiful garden within it, close by the source of the great river known as Rukn Abad. The Shaykh [Sa'di] had constructed some small cisterns in marble there to wash clothes in. The citizens of Shiraz go out to visit his tomb, and they eat from his table [i.e. eat food prepared at the convent] and wash their clothes in the river. I did the same thing there—may God have mercy upon him." Gibb 2011, 96–97.

15 Ibn Bazzāz 1373/1994, 104.

16 [1.24] Sa'di YE, 198.

In this line Saʿdi opposes himself, and, by extension, humans in general, to the other species of animals (or human beings unable to appreciate the fine distinction that he is tracing) who cannot distinguish the difference between the beauty of a young man's fuzzy face from the greeneries that the wind broadcasts across the steppe. The pun (*jinās-i tāmm*, in Persian) is based on the repetition of the word *sabza* which, in the first hemistich, refers to the greenish, tender downy beard of the beloved, whereas in the second half of the couplet it designates any vulgar herb that grows in the wilderness. "Everyone knows" is a rather compelling affirmation, as it either reiterates what should already be known by the entirety of Saʿdi's audience, or establishes a rhetorical emphasis on how the reader is expected to interpret the nature and the sex of the object of desire depicted in his poems. In Saʿdi's ghazals, statements of this kind contribute to the formation of an anthropology of eroticism that defines the borders between what is human in its essence and what is nothing but a pale reflection of it:

> Anyone who claims that I do not desire your face
> Is not a human being, but a soulless frame.
> *Badāyiʿ* 431[17]

A second example of the confessional aspects of Saʿdi's appreciation of the freshly sprouted beard of the beloved is found in a ghazal in which the poet presents himself as an old man who lingers in his youthful fantasies for too long:

> Saʿdi loves the tender greeneries of the down
> All around cheeks as rosy as scarlet blossoms.
>
> And look at this old man, how he can
> Hardly forget the days of youth.
> *Ṭayyibāt* 127[18]

The first hemistich of the first line corresponds to a section of Saʿdi's facetious fragment quoted by ʿUbayd. The association between this image and the persistence of sensual homoerotic desires through adulthood can probably explain why ʿUbayd, right before mentioning Saʿdi's poem in *The Book of the Beard*, talks about the "elderly pederasts" (*pīrān-i ghulām-bāra*) and the

17 [1.25] Ibid., 200.
18 [1.26] Ibid., 62.

mocking tones that they use to scorn the youths' beauty ruined by the appearance of a full beard. ʿUbayd Zākānī's parodic descriptions constructed on the basis of Saʿdi's own homoerotic lines constitute a privileged vantage point to problematize the nature of male-to-male eroticism in the context of premodern Persian culture. The aesthetic value of the beard as an anatomical trait capable of heralding a transition between different degrees of attractiveness, or lack thereof, can be considered as a physical frontier that marks specific rules of access to the other's body along with the symbolic implications of intergenerational desire. It seems that ʿUbayd's manipulation of both Saʿdi's lyrical and facetious material to create a literary pastiche entirely devoted to the exploration of the aesthetics and the erotics of the beard stemmed from a deeper meditation on the spectrum of the social manifestations of man-to-man sexual desire.

One of the first pseudo-biographical accounts composed by ʿUbayd a few decades after Saʿdi's death portrays the poet in the light of a scatological phallocentrism that emanates from a burlesque interpretation of the pervasiveness of the homoerotic element in his literary corpus. The anecdote is extracted from *The Heart-Cherishing Epistle* (*Risāla-yi dilgushā*)—a hilarious collection of facetiae that exposes many of the conflicts, anxieties, and parochial tendencies of the Iranian society of the time:

> Mawlānā Quṭb al-Dīn was passing by a lane. He saw sheikh Saʿdi rubbing his cock against a wall after having peed. He said to him: O Master, why do you damage other people's walls? Saʿdi responded: No worries Mawlānā, be certain that now my cock is not as hard as when you experienced it.[19]

This obscene vignette was probably meant to elicit the laughter of ʿUbayd's contemporaries for its attempt to bawdily undermine the aura of charismatic reverence that surrounded not only the towering literary and spiritual persona of Saʿdi, but also that of Quṭb al-Dīn Shīrāzī, who was one of the most influential polymaths of the generation before ʿUbayd, and whose renown reached its peak in Shiraz during the last decades of the 13th and the first half of the 14th century.[20] The representation of Saʿdi as a compulsive penetrator ridicules and demystifies the shadow of his grand legacy with a satirical vein that is much more ambiguous than one would initially imagine. It is true that, considering the obsession of premodern Islamicate societies with an opposition between the inserting and the receiving roles (as categories that transcend sexuality as

19 ʿObayd Zākāni 1999, 291.
20 See Walbridge 1992.

such, and incorporate within themselves broader representations of domination and subjugation), assigning the penetrative role to Saʿdi in this vignette can also be read as a symbolic tribute to his toweringly dominant literary persona. But, at the same time, Saʿdi's figurative sexual domination of a scholar of the caliber of Quṭb al-Dīn could also signify the authority of the phallic pen of poetry over the emasculated fields of philosophy and theology.[21] However brutal and uncompromisingly rudimentary this kind of humor might appear, it reveals a multilayered system of overlapping and often contradicting representations of the body in relation to the literary perception of the personae implied in the satirical interaction. The degrading representation of two mature scholars' potential inclination toward sexual domination of the one by the other underlines the complexity of the mechanism of desire in the framework of the construction of literary fame. The passage incorporates a portion of Saʿdi's lyricism into a pseudo-biography on the basis of the homoerotic elements that exude from his works, and thus manipulates the reception of his persona as a "fictitious author" vis-à-vis a gendered definition of desire. Even though such narratives are far from being reliable as sources of biographic veracity about Saʿdi's life, they offer valuable insights into the patterns that would guide the first communities of Saʿdi's readers in the creation of his authorial persona, especially as a way to make sense of his own statements about his inclinations and aesthetic drives.

As a result of these observations, I would be inclined to read ʿUbayd's scatological account of the poet from Shiraz in light of the broader source of inspiration that Saʿdi's works would constitute for ʿUbayd Zākānī, whose oeuvre is characterized by an anxiety of imitation apparent in his obsessive manipulation of the poetic canon.[22] By taking into account the constant references to Saʿdi's ghazals that can be found in ʿUbayd's "serious" poetic output, one

21 On the distinction between the active and the passive as sexual roles that generate hierarchies of power and domination both in the ancient Greek and in the medieval Islamic social experience of male homoerotic sexuality, see Oberhelman 1997, 55–93. See also Rowson 1991, in particular the following observation: "We may safely assume that the sexual pleasure of penetration was psychologically linked with the emotional gratification of stark domination. […] For a man to seek sexual subordination, on the other hand, was inexplicable, and could only be attributed to pathology. Boys, being not yet men, could be penetrated without losing their potential manliness, so long as they did not register pleasure in the act, which would suggest a pathology liable to continue into adulthood; the quasi-femininity of their appearance, a condition for their desirability as penetratees, was a natural but temporarily condition whose end marked their entry into the world of the dominant adult male." Ibid., 66.

22 I have dealt with ʿUbayd's obscene and serious imitations of Saʿdi's poetry in a forthcoming publication that includes the integral Italian translation of ʿUbayd's ghazals.

could easily argue that this obscene vignette was meant to be a parodic homage to what ʿUbayd probably perceived as the Shirazi poet's remarkable inclination toward the appreciation of human beauty through the transfiguration of homosocial sexual passion.

3 Homoeroticism and Gender (in)Difference

Homoeroticism in premodern Islamicate societies is a complex phenomenon that, although central to the understanding of the premodern and early modern literary aesthetics of the Arabo-Persian world, is too often the object of either moral dismissal or confusion deriving from an ethnocentric and anachronistic sexual essentialism. The moralistic approach that leads to the denial of the centrality of the homoerotic in Islamicate lyric texts can be easily deconstructed by referring the reader to the large amount of philological evidence that highlights the overwhelming predominance of male homoerotic sensual engagement.[23] Nonetheless, the traditional approaches to the study of homoeroticism in Islamicate societies assume the heterosexuality/homosexuality dichotomy as an anthropological constant, a conception that projects models of gender identity and sexual behavior characteristic of Western modernity onto the texts of the past.[24]

One of the few comprehensive academic publications that effectively questions the essentialist approach to the study of homoeroticism in pre-19th-century Islamicate literatures is Khaled El-Rouayheb's *Before Homosexuality in the Arabic-Islamic World, 1500–1800*. El-Rouayheb's study relies on a large variety of literary, historical, and legal texts that offer sufficient evidence for a thorough reappraisal of the centrality of homoeroticism in the literary and belletristic expression of the Islamic cultures during the Ottoman period. In the wake of Foucauldian approaches to the nature of sexuality as a cultural construction, El-Rouayheb's analysis demonstrates that the concepts of heterosexuality and homosexuality are not useful tools for the investigation of sexual identities and inclinations in the premodern and early modern Islamic world. His study also contributes to the understanding of love and sexual desire as

23 See, in particular, Wright and Rowson's (1997) collection of essays on the representation of homoeroticism in classical Arabic literature, and Murray and Roscoe's (1997) approach to Islamic "homosexualities," which analyzes texts and practices from the perspective of cultural studies and social sciences. See Schmidtke 1999 for a comparative appraisal of these two edited volumes. For specific socio-anthropological and literary problems, see below.

24 See Andrews and Kalpaklı 2005, 11–18; Ze'evi 2006, 10–12; Boone 2014, xxviii–xxx.

experiences that are developed along scales of affection that frame the relations between male bodies according to categories that are different from our modern perceptions of physicality and gender identity:

> Recent general histories of homosexuality find a "disparity" between the proclaimed ideals and actual behavior of some Islamic scholars who, on the one hand, condemned 'homosexuality' but, on the other, wrote "strongly homoerotic poetry." What Islamic scholars condemned was not 'homosexuality' but *liwāṭ*, that is, anal intercourse between men. Writing a love poem of a male youth would simply not fall under the juridical concept of *liwāṭ*. What such examples show is that care should be taken before translating as "homosexual" any Arabic term attested in the texts. The possibility at issue is precisely whether pre-nineteenth-century Arab-Islamic culture lacked the concept of homosexuality altogether, and operated instead with a set of concepts (like *ubnah* or *liwāṭ*) each of which pick out some of the acts and actors we might call 'homosexual' but which were simply not seen as instances of one overarching phenomenon. [...] the distinctions not captured by the concept of "homosexuality" were all-important from the perspective of the culture of the period. One such distinction is that between the "active" and the "passive" partner in a homosexual encounter [...]. Another distinction is that between passionate infatuation (*'ishq*) and sexual lust—emphasizing this distinction was important for those who would argue for the religious permissibility of the passionate love for boys. A third distinction centers on exactly what sexual acts were involved—Islamic law prescribed severe corporal or capital punishment for anal intercourse between men, but regarded, say, kissing, fondling, or non-anal intercourse as less serious transgressions.[25]

Whilst I will tackle the problem of love and lust—mainly as Sa'di's lyric reflections are concerned—in the next two chapters, I cannot but agree with El-Rouayheb's emphasis on the fact that, in the study of premodern Middle Eastern sexualities, the modern Western opposition between homosexuality and heterosexuality is not as analytically suitable as the distinction between the role of the penetrator and that of the penetrated, regardless of their biological sex.[26] When it comes to the premodern Persian poetic heritage, El-Rouayheb's observation can be largely supported by the frequent representations of male youths depicted as objects of desire who are equivalent to female recipients of

25 El-Rouayheb 2006, 6.
26 Ibid., 15.

the sexual attentions of dominant virility—which is the case of the apparently manly, yet androgynous depiction of the beloved in the amatory interlude that Saʿdi dedicated to Shams al-Dīn. Nevertheless, in those lines, the juxtaposition between the assertive and accommodating aspects of androgyny and the innuendos to political power demonstrates that the paradigm of demarcated sexual roles (the passive and the active, regardless of their gender) should be integrated with models capable of taking into account the symbolically and ritualistically codified aspects of desire that characterize premodern Persian poetry.

We cannot consider homoerotic desire, as well as its social and literary reflections, as dynamics that relate only to dyadic relationships between individuals, especially in a poetic corpus that is primarily courtly. Through the networks of power relations, we ought to conceive of desire as a source of symbolic transformation that operates between society and the narrative architectures provided by the literary texts. "Passive" and "active" as sexual roles are meaningful structural notions, especially if conceived regardless of the biological sex of the object of desire.[27] However, as "roles," it is necessary to consider their potential fluidity whenever we shift from ethnographic evidence to the complex system of ideals and symbols generated by literary representations.[28] Without

27 "The historical prevalence of male homoeroticism within the nonetheless predominantly heteroerotic cultures of the Middle East has also been attributed to the tendency, in these regions, to measure sexuality in terms of active and passive roles rather than, as in Western societies, in terms of gender. This means, among other variables, that a man may with proper discretion penetrate other males, especially those younger than himself, without compromising his masculinity. In such interpretations, phallic dominance is the cynosure of masculinity, not the gender of the object who submits to domination." Boone 2014, 48.

28 In his study of the homoerotics of Orientalism, Joseph Allen Boone perfectly summarizes the epistemological problem that the perception of a fixed active/passive dichotomy poses to the study of premodern and early modern sexual practices in the Islamicate world: "[…] the tendency among Anglo-European historians to view this ethos of penetrative domination as *the* operative framework legitimating homoerotic relations in Islamicate cultures may impose upon its field of study an overly Westernized idea of phallic masculinity. Even contemporary queer studies, Dina Al-Kassim writes, errs by tending to uphold this so-called 'Mediterranean model' as an absolute marker of the difference 'between the sexual epistemologies of the East and the West and the distinct subjectivities arising along this declivity.' The repeated invocation of this model, Al-Kassim explains, 'serves to simplify rather than explain the play of putative license and prohibition in cultures as complexly diverse as those of the Mediterranean and the Islamicate cultures beyond.' As the scholarship of Ze'evi and Najmabadi similarly suggests, overemphasis on the masculine-biased dichotomy of penetrator/penetrated may miss out on the complex layerings of male erotics being negotiated in what turns out to be a more polyvalent, pliant realm of homoerotic possibility, bodily pleasure, and prohibitions both overt and internalized." Boone 2014, 48. See also Al-Kassim, "Sexual Epistemologies," 302.

these caveats it would be impossible to make sense of the staged interchangeability of the roles of the dominator and the dominated as portrayed in the mature developments of the ghazal—from the eleventh century onwards—and which originally took shape as a result of the symbolic fluidity of tangible relations of power. Thus, the figurative alteration of the sexual schemes that historically set an equivalence between young boys and women as recipients of male lovers' desire is particularly relevant when our attention shifts from the historical mindset that informs social practices to the role of sexuality as a symbolic resource directly involved in the dynamics of political power and aesthetic values.

An anthropologically and historiographically informed approach to sexuality helps us question what Afsaneh Najmabadi defines as the received "modernist" idea according to which "homoerotic practices were what men did in the old days because women were segregated and unavailable."[29] As argued by Everett Rowson, the fact that boys were not women was obviously crucial to the existence of homoerotic desire in the first place; and whatever the psychological basis for this (about which the sources give us few clues), its most common manifestation in the texts, indicating interest in a physical attribute not shared by women, is the delight expressed in the first down on a boy's cheeks.[30] That this down was also the harbinger of the coming full beard which would spell the end of the boy's desirability introduced a tension which took a variety of literary (and presumably psychological) forms—one of which will be explored in the third chapter, through a bawdy fragment in which Sa'di laments the discrepancy between the smooth face of the beloved and his precocious pubic hair growth.

4 The Homoerotic Hermeneutics of the Medieval Body

> *Cheeks divine*, literally the cheek of an angel-(a *Peri*, or *fairy*)-faced *Saki*, or cupbearer. This disgusting object has, in obedience to decorum, been very properly transmuted […] into a *damsel*, fair as a nymph of Paradise, by a licence of which we shall be found to have availed ourselves throughout these poems, and, we trust, for reasons too obvious to need any formal apology on our part.
>
> JOHN HINDLEY, *Persian Lyrics, or Scattered Poems, from The Diwan-e-Hafiz.*[31]

29 El-Rouayheb 2006, 30.
30 Rowson 1991, 58.
31 Hindley 1800, 33.

The contemporary debate on the homoerotics of premodern Persian literature deserves a close scrutiny capable of highlighting the contradictions and the biases with which today we still misread the meaning and functions of the gendered representations of the body and desire in Saʿdi's poetry. While the older generation of scholars, especially those whose primary object of inquiry does not cover the historicized aesthetics of the Persian literary heritage, shows various forms of explicit or implicit reticence with respect to the topic, the current position of the Anglo-American field of premodern Persian poetry is almost unanimous as to the relevance of homoeroticism in this lyric tradition.[32] One of the few Iranian scholars of the old generation who seemed to be consistently in favor of an open-minded approach to the homoerotics of Saʿdi's lyricism was Ehsan Yarshater, who demonstrated in a brief article that, in spite of the lack of grammatical gender in the Persian language, the beloved of the Persian lyric tradition is, as a rule, a young man on the threshold of manhood.[33] Nevertheless, in her discussion of the modern erasure of the homoerotic overtones of Saʿdi's lyricism, Fatemeh Keshavarz brings the

32 "A distinctive component of the Persian *ghazal*, and one that has often proved disconcerting, is its overt homoerotic content. The gender ambiguity characteristic of Persian lyric poetry has traditionally been exploited to permit the critic to construe the beloved as feminine. While this is possible to some extent in the *qaṣīdah*, where explicit descriptions tend to be relatively infrequent and where the analogy between beloved and patron is conventionally predicated on the contrast between the sexes implicit in the complementary relationship between *nasīb* and *madīḥ*, it is less justifiable for the *ghazal*, where the male gender of the beloved, often explicitly indicated, becomes a standard convention of the genre. Critics uneasy with this situation have attempted to rationalize it in various ways, either by allegorizing the male beloved as a neo-Platonic human reflection of divine love, or by invoking such socio-historical factors as the prohibition on the open reference to women in love poems. But while such factors lend a certain verisimilitude to the fictive world of the ghazal, reliance on them to explain away the presence of a male beloved ignores the fact that such love—which might or might not include a carnal dimension—was not only not condemned, but widely tolerated and frequently highly esteemed." Meisami 1987, 245–46. "Homoeroticism pervades medieval Persian poetry. The beloved in most ghazal poetry is androgynous, and often equated with the ruler, decked in armor and slaying those who approach him." Lewis 2000, 321. "For modern readers, the gender of the young male beloved in *The Glorious Epistle* may be more scandalous than that of the courtesan in *The Lover's Confection*. But the opposite was likely the case for Muhtasham's contemporaries, for whom homoeroticism would have been a normative form of romantic love, as it was for the participants in Plato's symposium. The prevalence of homoeroticism in medieval and early modern Near Eastern poetry and society has been amply documented, and Muhtasham's rocky affair with Jalāl holds true to this norm." Losensky 2009, 754. See also Sharma 2004; 2012; Brookshaw 2019, 8–9, and 127–29.

33 Yarshater 2000, 420–39. In the sixth volume of the *Cambridge History of Iran*, in the section devoted to the poetry of the 14th century, Yarshater concludes his survey with a rubric that reads, "The beloved is not a woman," which opens as follows: "Thus far I have

proceedings of a conference held in Shiraz in 1984 (which celebrated the 800th birthday of the poet) to the attention of the reader: no one among the dozens of international scholars who participated in an event that covered all the main details of Sa'di's life, works, and legacy made any reference to homoeroticism.[34] In a paragraph entitled "Two Ways of Absolving Sa'di of Homoerotic Love," Keshavarz calls for a "neutral and open reception" of Sa'di's ghazals, of a kind that she observed among the non-expert, traditional readers when growing up in Shiraz.[35]

As the following chapters will show, the erotic aesthetics that, between the 12th and the 15th centuries, informed the spiritual meditations on the relationship between human and divine forms of passion explicitly represented the object of desire as a male presence. Regardless of the socio-cultural reasons behind the conflation between homoeroticism and spiritual quest, a plurality of medieval texts belonging to various genres and theoretical traditions portray the manifestation of supernal beauty through the physical features of male bodies whose age ranges from late pre-pubescence to early adulthood. Yet, as noted by Matthew Miller in his article on the homoerotic aspects of 13th-century hagiographical accounts, the modern scholarship that engages itself with these texts (as either literary imagery or theoretical expositions and narratives) has so far either blatantly denied the relevance of gender or nonchalantly glossed over—if not expunged or mistranslated—the key words or passages highlighting the homoerotic dimension of spiritual desire.[36] The

---

referred to the beloved as a woman in order to avoid confusion. It should be explained, however, that, as a rule, the beloved is not a woman, but a young man." Yarshater 1986, 973.

34 Keshavarz 2015, 164, n. 21.

35 Keshavarz 2015, 148–55. We may compare Keshavarz's approach to Sa'di's homoeroticism with James E. Miller's criticism of the "homonormative" approaches to Walt Whitman's representation of affection and sexuality: "all readers can share, consciously and/or unconsciously, Whitman's omnisexual vision—omnisexual in the all-encompassing sense of embracing auto-, homo-, and hetero-erotic impulses. Individuals possess these impulses within them by the fact of being human and sexual, assimilated in passing through the stages of growing up. There is much more in their sexuality that brings human beings together than divides them, whatever the nature of their 'sexual preference,' whatever the nature of their sexual experience." Miller 1998, 31. Miller's conception of "omnisexual vision" could be compared with Nasrollāh Purjavādi's argument on "cosmic love" (*'ishq-i kayhānī*) as an overarching erotic value that characterizes the mature phase of premodern Persian mysticism. See Purjavādi 1387/2008, 239–71. However hermeneutically promising these forms of ontologization of love and desire may appear, they risk isolating the texts they analyze from their specific historicity and performativity.

36 See, for instance, Matthew Miller's comment on William Chittick and Peter Wilson's English translation of *Divine Flashes* by 13th-centtury poet and Sufi, Fakhr al-Dīn 'Irāqī: "They bowdlerize the text, completely scrubbing the figure of the beautiful young man

origins of this ideological (if not unscholarly) approach are to be found in the conflation of paradigms and prejudices that belong to both a certain heteronormative academic tradition and the erasure of the relevance of bodily experiences and representations from the study of medieval Persian spirituality in its socio-anthropological context.[37]

---

from their translation. […] They systematically eliminate any homoerotic features of the original text. All of the stories from his hagiography that I will discuss in this study have been excised from their account or substantially altered in order to 'straighten' them. This is clearly not a case of oversight in the process of translation or stylistic editorial intervention. They made a deliberate decision to heteronormatize 'Irāqī's hagiography." Miller 2018, 2–3.

37 See, for instance, the veiled Victorian posture of Leonard Lewisohn's argument in favor of a radically heteronormative reading of Hafez's representation of the beloved: "My own three decades of study of Ḥāfiẓ's *Dīvān* convinces me of the truth of Istiʿlāmī's judgement that 'the term *shāhid* in Ḥāfiẓ's writings simply has the meaning of a person with a fair face [*zībārūʾī*] and a beloved female mistress [*maʿshūq*], and if critics have said or written that it refers to pretty-faced boys, this is wrong.'" Lewisohn 2010, 71 (see Esteʿlāmi 1382/2003, 1: 326–2). "Elsewhere," Lewisohn continues, "[Esteʿlāmi] writes that 'there are more than 15 verses in Ḥāfiẓ's *Dīvān* where this term [*shāhid*] refers to a person with a fair face [*zībārūʾī*], and in most of these instances it cannot be said to refer to the face of a pretty *boy*' [ibid., 1: 98]. He adds that: 'in most of the instances where Ḥāfiẓ employs the word *shāhid*, his regard is for a beautiful woman, or else it remains ambiguous—whether the reference is to a woman or a pretty boy, although it is far more reasonable to assume the former' [ibid., 1: 292]. Istiʿlāmī emphasizes that there is only *one* specific instance in the *Dīvān*, where *shāhid* can be definitively said to be male (*ibid.*, I, p. 345, referring to *Dīvān*, *ghazal* 170: *Dars-i Ḥāfiẓ*, I, p. 477—*zāhid-i khalvat-nishīn*, not in Khānlarī's ed.). I should also add that the prevalence of the mainly female *shāhids* in Shīrāz in 'Ubayd's poetry (*Kulliyāt-i ʿUbayd Zākānī*, pp. 45: *ghazal* 45, v. 4; 113; *ghazal* 114: v. 1, p. 323, lines 5–6) adds greater weight to Istiʿlamī's opinion. This viewpoint of course is contested by some other scholars (cf. Ritter, *Ocean*, p. 481 *infra*; Sīrūs Shamīsā, *Shāhid-bāzī*, pp. 165–70) who largely consider his *shāhid* to be exclusively male, and *shāhidbāzī* simply pederasty." Lewisohn, 2010, 71. Considering the adamant fashion with which Hafez often explicit refers to the beloved as a boy (*pisar*), both Esteʿlāmi's and Lewisohn's heteronormative certitude rely on biased prejudices rather than philological evidence. The "straightening" interpolation of Hafez's representation of the male beloved goes back to the very beginning of the tradition of Persian studies in the West. See Sir Williams Jones' translation of the expression "Shirāzi Turk" as "sweet maid," Jones 1771, 135. Even though most contemporary translators do acknowledge the anachronistic nature of such heteronormative renditions, some authors still force the meaning (and, in some cases, even the letter) of the texts to align them with their heteronormative biases. See, for instance, Giovanni D'Erme's rendition of *shīrīn pisar* ("sweet boy") as "dolce donzella" ("sweet damsel"), discussed in Ingenito 2009, 158. For a critique of the heteronormative agenda undermining the philological relevance of the physical dimension of desire in general, and homoeroticism in particular, see Miller 2018, 4.

In his survey of homoeroticism in Persian literature, *Shāhed-bāzi dar adabiyāt-e fārsi*,[38] Sirus Shamisā is one of the few critics who acknowledges the masculine gender of the beloved lauded by Saʿdi and his contemporaries; nevertheless his book, although presenting for the first time a convincing set of philological proofs on the well-established canonical nature of homoeroticism in Persian poetry, embraces a moralistic approach that prevents him from engaging with the texts at a deeper level of meaning.[39] However, while a certain heteronormative moralistic approach to the study of premodern sexualities is understandable in the case of scholars who were trained within the naive pre-Foucauldian paradigms incapable of analyzing sexuality as a cultural discourse, the ethnocentric resilience of some younger authors is particularly disconcerting. Cyrus Zargar, for instance, in his study of medieval Sufi spiritual aesthetics approaches the medieval practice of *shāhid-bāzī* (i.e., the contemplation of beautiful young men for spiritual and/or sensual ends) from a moralizing perspective that quite naively denounces the medieval intergenerational forms of sacred sensuality as "abusive," "nefarious," "bizarre," and "damaging." He writes that such practices are still "considered bizarre by many of us who research them today," and adds that "while the true extent of *shāhidbāzī* and its abuses in the medieval world perhaps cannot be known, certainly some amount of damage had been done, even if by the few."[40]

It is with the same critical disengagement that, in the only contemporary English translation of a substantial portion of Saʿdi's ghazals, Homa Katouzian dismisses the question of homoeroticism through a series of prejudices that are paradigmatic of a good portion of the contemporary scholarly approaches

38 Shamisā 1381/2002. The Iranian publisher curiously translated the title in English as "Sodomy Based on Persian Literature."

39 Ibid., 134–65.

40 Zargar 2011, 119. In addition, Zargar points out that "it is difficult to deem inculpable such gnostics not only for their lack of foresight, but also for the indifference and even disdain they held and expressed toward the perceptions of other intelligent Muslims," and, as a final gloss, he determines that "[i]n the case of *shāhidbāzī*, one notices that the sober Muslim jurisprudents held what might be considered a more contemporary perspective, if indeed time can serve as a judge." Ibid., 119, 155. It is clear that, in spite of geographical and chronological distances, intergenerational forms of desire constitute a delicate and often perturbing topic, but the lack of anthropological depth with respect to the cultural contexts in which such practices took place risks tainting scholarly investigations with unnecessarily ethnocentric attitudes that project one's personal ethical values onto the social context of the object of study. For a broad anthropological approach to the topic of sexual abuse and the culture-specific perception of intergenerational eroticism, see Donnan and Magowan 2010, 135–56, and Rind 1998. See also Matthew Miller's contextual critique of Zargar's approach (Miller 2018, 18, n. 12).

to Saʿdi's poetry.[41] In the section in which Katouzian discusses the gender of the beloved in Saʿdi's poetry, he argues that in his "lyricism the beloved may be either a woman or a [male] youth." The indicators that he enumerates to highlight the female gender of the beloveds to whom Saʿdi refers (as if they were all to be read as confessional dedications to historical objects of desire) are systematically inaccurate, as they belong to a logic that is both unaware of the development of the Persian literary tradition and ill-informed about the intertextual framework in which some of the images that he mentions took shape.

The discrepancies between these critical postures reveal that the problem of homoeroticism in Saʿdi's poetry (and in general in Persian premodern literature) is twofold: while the sources provide sufficient evidence to safely infer that the ideal beloved of the ghazal is a male youth, poetic texts often show a lack of gender differentiation that entitles some critics either to alter historical evidence in order to "straighten" any evidence of same-sex desire, or to assert that gender in Persian poetry is indeterminable or irrelevant. In fact, in Persian literature, what the reader perceives as a genderless nature of the beloved pertains to a peculiar conception of the eroticization of the bodies that is dissimilar to our modern representation of sex difference in the context of sensual attraction. As I will mention below, this lack of differentiation—which Persian poetry shares with other premodern literary heritages—survived until the mid-19th century, and needs to be taken into serious account when approaching the depiction of the ideal beloved from a critically aware perspective.

Thus, while the failed assessment of the floating nature of the gender of the beloved surely stems from sheer prudery and moralizing distortions of the sources, it is fair to admit that this problem predominantly relates to the necessity of reading the ghazal tradition through the lens of both a more thorough theory of the lyric and an insightful semiotics of the relationship between the poetic persona and the external world. Textual evidence shows that the coexistence of homoerotic depictions and genderless portrayals of the beloved, rather than presenting an unsolvable paradox, pertains to different levels of definition of both the lyric subject and the object of desire: from the maximum abstraction of the linguistic identity of the "I" and "Thou" of the amatory interaction, to the mimetic emulation of historical and biographical characters that correspond to extratextual referents. The dialectic between these two

41 This is not the appropriate venue for me to question the literary merits of these translations, but it will suffice to highlight the limits of Katouzian's approach to gender and Persian poetry by referring to a passage from his collection of Persian articles on Saʿdi in which he points out that "homosexual men have not even the slightest interest in women" (*mard-e hamjens-gerā kuchaktarin tavajohi be zan nadārad*) and, therefore, Saʿdi's poetry cannot be homoerotic, as it addresses women as well. Katouzian 2006a, 267.

poles—the abstraction of the deep structure of the text and the verisimilitude of any reference to external reality—will recur throughout this book, as it represents one of the most vital challenges to the study of the lyric as a suspension between reality and poetic fiction.[42]

A promising point to start an analysis of the gender indetermination of the beloved is the Persian word for "breast" (*pistān*), which can refer to either the male or female chest. This is a case of lack of sexual dimorphism that this poetic heritage shares with, among others, the courtly tradition of Middle High German literature.[43] We occasionally see scholars interpreting the—albeit not particularly frequent—simile of "pomegranate-like breasts" as an incontestable sign attesting to the femininity of the beloved.[44] But, as in German medieval literature, this refers to the more-or-less prominent swelling of the thoracic region regardless of the gender (and, in some cases, "pomegranate" is used synecdochically to refer to the grains of this fruit as a metaphor for the nipples).[45] While it is true that female breasts are occasionally depicted

42 I have addressed the relationship between the gender of the beloved in 14th-century Persian lyric and the connection between literary fiction and historical reality in Ingenito 2018a; 2018b.

43 "In one of his dawn songs, Wolfram can refer to a man and a woman who entwined their mouths, their legs, and *ir bruste* 'their breasts.'" Thus, while courtly writers are aware that women are shaped differently from men, they do not seem to consider the difference to be as significant as we do. We think of women's breasts and men's chests as two different things, while they seem to regard women's breasts and men's breasts as two variations of the same thing. Women's fuller breasts are a gendered inflection of a body that is not sexually dimorphic." Schultz 2006, 42. See also Schultz 1997.

44 "Expressions of heterosexual love are not entirely absent from classical Persian poetry, as shown by occasional descriptions of the breast. The most common conventional metaphorical images for it are the pomegranate, the lemon, and the polo ball." Yarshater 1986, 973.

45 See, for instance, Amīr Khusraw of Delhi's description of a pomegranate-like breast in a ghazal explicitly portraying a boy (*pisar*):
Should that beautiful boy come forth, how will you look at him?
So many pearls in my eyes, for whom will I scatter them?
[…]
He showed his rosy pomegranates and unleashed the lasso of his hair
My heart is frailly bleeding: against whom is this horseman so swiftly galloping?
[1.27] Amir Khosrow Dehlavi 1387/2008, 693. See also Khʷājū of Kerman's description of a princely object of desire, figuratively associated with Khusraw and the Kayanid dynasty:
You are such a renowned beloved (*shuhra yārī*), and such a king (*shahriyārī*)
That you carry the regal signs (*khusraw-nishānī*) and generate princes (*khusraw nishānī*)….
Who are you, who are crushing my heart?
Kayanid [princely] is your nature, who are your ancestors?
The pomegranate of your breast is better than the pomegranate of the orchard:
As you are an orchard from your apple [chin] and citron [doble chin].

in premodern Persian poetry, the peak of their fetishization as an aphrodisiac marker of femininity, as Afsaneh Najmabadi observes, emerged in Iran during the Qajar period. This erotic emphasis was linked to the process that, between the end of the 18th and the first decades of the 20th centuries, contributed to the formation of the aesthetic categories that would turn heteronormativity into the exclusive form of eroticism. Najmabadi convincingly argues that the emergence of female breasts as eroticized aesthetic fixations coincided with the progressive disappearance of the beardless youth from the arena of visual (and literary) representations.[46]

The male/female breast of the beloved is an extreme case that reveals the sexual indetermination that characterizes the literary abstraction of male beloveds. But two of the most frequent signs of such a lack of dimorphism are exemplified by the motif of the "veiled" male beauty and the comparisons between the male beloved and the female characters of the narrative tradition. Interpreting the presence of a veil as a solid proof for the feminine gender of the beloved is one of the most fallacious arguments, as in many lines the Persian and Arabic words for veil that Katouzian mentions appear in association with the noun *pisar*, which unmistakably means "boy."[47] In the broad corpus of Islamicate literatures the "veiled" boy *par excellence* is the Quranic Yūsuf (Joseph), the most beautiful man on earth who was sold to Potiphar ('Azīz) of Egypt, and who soon became the object of desire of his wife—known in the

[1.28] Khwāju 1369/1990, 495–96. However, it is also fair to point out that, in Persian poetry, the eroticized gender differentiation between female and male breasts is more likely to appear in the romance genre, in which the heterosexual forms of desire that its narratives portray are often expressed within the framework of ideals of marital union. See, for instance, Niẓāmī's emphasis on the erotic traits of Shirin's breasts from the perspective of Khusraw as a desiring subject who foresees the chances for procreation in his perusal of the her oine's body:
The key fell from the hands of the garden-keeper:
The pomegranates of her breasts peaking from the garden [of her body].
Any heart who would contemplate such a sweet pomegranate
Like a pomegranate would crack open out of passion.
[1.29] Nezāmi 1392/2013, 185–86. On the symbolism of the pomegranate in Niẓāmī's poetry, see van Ruymbeke 2007, 115–16.

46 See Najmabadi 1998; 2005, 41.

47 Why should we light a candle? The light of your face will suffice!
Lift the veil from that lunar countenance of yours, o boy!
[1.30] 'Attār 1319/1940, 212.
Uncover the cheeks of that beautiful boy
From the veil, and contemplate his countenance!
[1.31] Sayf Farghāni 1341–44/1962–65, 1: 134.

commentaries as Zulaykhā.[48] The "veiled beauty" of Yūsuf as a metaphor for the manifestation of the splendor of the object of desire (regardless of mystical undertones) is a recurrent topic, which from the 11th century onwards became one of the standard images at the disposal of the poets to depict the beloved, as Saʿdi very eloquently penned in this line:

> No market is left for the beauty of the celestial brides
> If your visage reaffirms Yūsuf's proof by lifting its veil.
> *Badāyiʿ* 554[49]

This image resonates particularly well with the passage of the 12th-century *Kashf al-asrār* (*The Disclosure of the Secrets*, one of the most important and extensive Persian exegeses of the Quran, written by Rashīd al-Dīn Maybudī) in which Yūsuf is being held behind a veil in order to show him to a crowd eager to buy this slave about whom so much everyone had heard:

> The merchants and the notables of the city, both on foot and on steeds, gathered along with all the people who, not being able to buy him, had come to admire him. In that moment, a corner of the veil was lifted and the beauty of Yūsuf appeared to them in all its splendor: many of the young girls who were present started menstruating, and innumerous people were cast into turmoil.[50]

If Katouzian had taken into account exegetic passages of this kind, he could have adopted a more nuanced approach to the hermeneutical assessment of lines as the following:

> In this [couplet] the lover says that he will only stop watching the beloved if she puts on a veil:
>
> I have no intention to take my eyes off you
> Unless you stop all this turmoil by covering your face.
> *Ṭayyibāt* 183[51]

48 On the story of Yūsuf and its reception in the Quranic commentaries, see Merguerian and Najmabadi 1997. For an insight on the usage of the character of Yūsuf in Persian homoerotic poetry, see Yaghoobi 2016.
49 [1.32] Saʿdi YE, 250.
50 Maybodi 1382/2003, 5: 32.
51 Katouzian 2016, 19. Original line: [1.33] Saʿdi 1385/2006 YE, 86.

It is clear that Sa'di's line hints at the legendary commotion of the crowd who had gathered to see Yūsuf's unveiled face. This poetic rendition is comparable to the scene that I have quoted from Maybudī's Quranic commentary, especially because both Maybudī and Sa'di talk in terms of *fitna*, "turmoil" (which could be also translated as "temptation") to express the reaction of the beholders. Why then should we deny the relevance of such a pregnant narrative background to arbitrarily assume that the word "veil" automatically applies to a female beloved? The metaphysical connotations that in Persian poetry apply when the beloved is described as a veiled beauty hiding either behind a curtain or concealing his face from the beholder is always a latent interpretive opportunity, and, later on, we shall scrutinize the meaning of such images. But there is no need to transcend the scope of the tangibility of the veil as a physical piece of fabric to understand how central this image is to the visual dimensions of the ghazal and its intimate connection with the story of the unveiling of Yūsuf's face before the most respected women of Egypt, who had happened to criticize Zulaykhā for her lustful approaches to the youth. Although the Quranic *sura* succinctly presents all the main elements that constitute the plot of the story, I wish to refer one more time to Maybudī's commentary. The elegance of his language, as well as the aesthetic conflations that he inoculates into the original tale, were likely a source of inspiration for the ideals of veiled beauty to which later poets would refer when composing their ghazals in total awareness of the images supplied by a shared cultural tradition:

> When the women of Egypt cast their blame on Zulaykhā, she decided that she would summon them in order to display the beauty of Yūsuf so that they could understand that she should be forgiven for her love, and that she was not deserving of blame and reproach. Once the reception was arranged and forty women invited, she [...] had Yūsuf sit close to her. She coiffured his curls with pearls, she dressed him with a green garment, and covered his hair with a black veil of silk. She drew a line of musky fragrances around his face and put a jug and a cup of wine in his hands. She told him: "When I give you the signal, come out from the veil." The women were already seated, and they all had a knife and a bowl full of citrons before them. They spent some time conversing, and they began to cut the citrons. Zulaykhā was sitting on her throne, surrounded by her female servants, as she turned her face towards the women, and said: "You have criticized me and felt compelled to express your blame and scorn because of [me and] Yūsuf?" They said: "Yes, this is true." Zulaykhā said: "O Yūsuf, come out!" Yūsuf lifted the veil and revealed himself. When the women set their eyes upon Yūsuf they were ravished with bewilderment,

> they became unaware of themselves, and started cutting their hands instead of the citrons.[52]

From the perspective of the modern Western heteronormative dichotomy of masculinity as a category radically opposed to femininity, the perceived "effeminacy" of the description of Yūsuf in this lyrical rendition of the Quranic account would be much less disturbing if the veiled, pearl-coiffed, musky-faced protagonist of the scene was a coquettish young woman rather than the epitome of male beauty. In several passages of this same commentary, Zulaykhā's attractive body is portrayed with traits akin to those of Yūsuf. This correspondence provides the evidence that Persian lyric descriptions of ideal human beauty do not offer the reader clear-cut distinctions between the portrayal of male and female bodies. Such a lack of gender dimorphism is also attested to in the visual representations of the aesthetic ideals of Central-Asian Turkic physical beauty, which had started circulating in the Persian-speaking world by the 8th–10th century and eventually imposed themselves as canonical pictorial models until the late Qajar period (end of the 19th century).[53]

In the introduction to his translations of Saʿdi's ghazals, Katouzian argues that in many cases the beloved praised by Saʿdi must have been the reflection of a female presence, as the poet would compare his object of desire to the most famous figures of the romance tradition, such as ʿAẕrā, Laylā, and Shīrīn. But Saʿdi often (as any other poet of his age) addresses a *boy* (*pisar*) by comparing him with one of those female characters: what the male presence of the boy and the image created by the literary reminiscence of the female characters have in common is nothing but their shared function as beloveds. I insist on the importance of the *function*, rather than the outward characterization as such, as the function of the beloved is at times projected onto male characters, such as Ayāz (the historical beloved of Sultan Maḥmūd of Ghazna), or Yūsuf himself. And in these cases the poet's choice of selecting a male or a female character does not depend on external, extratextual, historical, or biographical factors, but is exclusively informed by the interplay between imagery and rhetoric: if the poet wants to emphasize the sweetness of the beloved's lips, he will compare him to princess Shīrīn (which, in Persian, also means "sweet"), whereas if the trope that he wants to develop involves the relationship between slave and king, he will recur to the male figure of Ayāz, etc.

A paradigmatic example of this interchangeability appears in some of the ghazals composed by Jahān Malik Khātūn, a contemporary of Hafez of Shiraz

52 Maybodi 1382/2003, 5: 55–56.

53 See Melikian-Chirvani 1985. See also Schimmel 1975b; Brookshaw 2009.

and one of the most important poet princesses of premodern Iran, who elected Sa'di as her main model for the composition of her poetry.[54] In her verses, the poetic persona of the poetess is by default, and in total disregard of the biological sex of the author, a mature man who celebrates the beauty of a young male beloved. Indeed at times the princess introduces the gender neutrality of the I-Thou lyric interactions by referring to the lovers of the literary tradition in a way that stresses the virtual masculinity of her poetic voice:

> You are Layli! You are Layli! You are the cure for my pain!
> I am Majnun! I am Majnun! I am the wandering madman!
> You are Shirin, seated in the time of Khusraw Parviz
> I am Farhad, the mountain-hacker. My sweet soul has expired.
> You are Shirin! You are Shirin! You are as sweet as the soul in my body.
> I am Khusraw! I am Khusraw! Preoccupied with the night of separation
> You are 'Adhra! You are 'Adhra! I am preoccupied with the pain of your love
> I am Vamiq! I am Vamiq! Provide a cure for my pain!
> You are Gulshah! You are Gulshah! You are rose-scented, just like the moon
> I am Varqah, I am drowning in the endless ocean of separation.
> You are the rose-limbed Vis, because of your soul I am snared in the trap
> I am Ramin, the hem of whose heart burns in grieving for you.
> From my soul I sing the praise of that eternal world ruler
> Who, from his kindness, has given me cares of the soul and of faith.[55]

The word *jahān-dār* (the one who holds the world, the world ruler), which appears in the closing line does not belong to the customary vocabulary of the ghazal, since it refers primarily to a patron rather than an object of amorous desire. In this line, its association with a direct reference to "praise" (*s̱anā*) reveals that the ghazal was originally intended to be a panegyrical piece dedicated to a ruler. The political context in which these lines operate shows yet again how the lover/beloved interaction is a deep structure whose gender

---

54 Jahān Malek Khātun 1374/1995. See also the new poems attributed to Jahān (Bashari 1388/2009). The most comprehensive contributions to the study of her life and works is found in Brookshaw 2005. See also Brookshaw 2008. On the relationship between gender, biography, and lyricism in Jahān's poetry, see Ingenito 2018a. A selection of her poems is available in beautifully crafted English verse. See Davis 2013, 135–193. For an Italian translation, see Ingenito 2010; 2011.

55 [1.34] Jahān Malek Khātun 1374/1995, 404. English translation by Dominic Brookshaw (2019, 229–30).

manipulation belongs to the fictive construction of lyrical images rather than an effective adherence to the body of an external beloved. The gender interchangeability affecting the characters that typify the function of the beloved, as opposed to the lover, stems from exactly the same kind of reciprocity that erases all differentiating anatomical signs between the male and the female embodiments of physical splendor.

Reciprocity is particularly evident in the first chapters of Niẓāmī's 12th-century romance in verse *Khusraw va Shīrīn*, in which the prince and the princess learn about one other and thereby fall in love through the verbal and visual depictions of Shāpūr, prince Khusraw's boon-companion. On Shāpūr's third attempt to show Shīrīn the portrait of the prince, the poet describes the visual depiction of the heroine's future lover as a mirror in which she recognizes herself:

> A sign of herself she saw in that mirror:
> as herself she found, in herself she was lost.[56]

This line hints at a visual analogy that operates on the level of the physical appearance of the two lovers, whose gender differentiation disappears both from the poetic rendition and from the style adopted by later miniaturists to portray this scene in the manuscripts of Niẓāmī's *Five Treasures*. If we apply this lack of gender differentiation of the physical traits of male and female objects of desire to our previous meditations on the abstractedness of the poetic "I" (as a literary projection shared by both the biography of the poet and the poetic tradition), we could safely assert that the poetic "you" of the beloved is an equally abstract linguistic function that, in the deepest structure of the verbal articulation of the text, is essentially ungendered. In spite of the masculinity and femininity of Khusraw and Shīrīn from the perspective of the development of the plot and the personal inclinations to activities and tastes that mark the difference between princehood and princesshood, the physical similarities in the depiction of the two lovers attests to an ideal of love as a mutually reciprocated attraction that does not apply to the dynamics of power embedded in the lyricism of the *qasida* and the ghazal. It is an idyllic situation in which they love each other, they belong to the same generation, and by representing for each other the ideal of the "beloved," they are both depicted as types belonging to this category of physical perfection and inner nobility.

The importance of the role of romance stories similar to *Khusraw and Shīrīn* for the development of the ghazal can be attributed to the fact that this

56 [1.35] Nezāmi Ganjevi 1313/1934, 63.

representation of reciprocity and mutual tension constitutes the very ideal of love at the core of the lyric experience. The lover of the ghazal *hopes* to be reciprocated, *wishes* to be as young and attractive as the beloved, and longs for the interchangeability that turns the two desirous subjects into each other's beloveds. The constant frustration of this ideal of amorous beatitude (or its temporary validity) is what provides the ghazal with its dramatic ethos, which calls for the continuous reiteration of the lamentation.

The genderlessness of the ideal of love expressed in the amatory *maṣnavī* transfers to the deep structure of the lover and the beloved of the ghazal. But the occasional explicit manifestation of the traits of manhood in the beloved's depiction attests to the oscillation taking place in this lyric genre between the abstractness of the ideal of love and the contingency of the passion for real, male bodies. For this reason, contrary to what Katouzian maintains, when poets occasionally define the beloved as a *boy*, or when they compare him to Yūsuf, or allude to his incipient beard, they do not necessarily address a specific same-sex erotic exchange (supposedly opposed to a heterosexual norm): rather, they show the links between the ungendered nature of the abstract "you" and the potential incarnation of that abstraction in a physical body of desire, which, by convention, is a young man. The call for reiteration and the suspension of the epilogue (a ghazal does not rely on a narrative beginning or ending, and it can be read over and over without unfolding any specific narration) are two of the elements that turn the ghazal into a linguistic material that—if not by direct experience—is informed by contact with extratextual reality. Hence, the homoeroticism of the ghazal derives from the gap between an idealized perception of love and the historical reality of the physicality of the passion for beardless boys.[57]

As soon as one approaches the problem of the literary persona from the angle of gender and its fluctuations across genres, poetic functions, and ideals of love and beauty, it becomes clear that what initially might have been perceived as a unitary instance is in fact the result of multifaceted stratifications. The stratified nature of what I called "the horizon of the persona" of the beloved shares many analogies with the paradigm of the "onion" that the anthropologist Clifford Geertz used to describe the multiple layers of what constitutes "cultural identity": we may peel off layer after layer, but as no core can eventually be found, the "essence," the "identity" corresponds with the stratification

57 It is also for this reason that among the most recurrent stories of love that were crystalized in the narrative genre of the *maṣnavī* form, the only one that would be perceived as close to a tangible degree of historicity is the passion of the Ghaznavid Sultan Maḥmūd for Ayāz, his servant, chief cupbearer, and beloved.

itself.[58] However paradoxical it might seem, it is the grammatical genderlessness of the Persian language that highlights the role that gender plays in the construction of the fluid stratification of the persona in the literary texts.

The specificities of the premodern cultural frameworks in which homoeroticism was expressed deserve to be taken into account in order not to fall into the homonormative bias of reading medieval same-sex amatory interactions through the essentialist categories of contemporary sexual identities and orientations. For instance, the use of the term "homosexual" to characterize the relationship displayed in the Persian ghazal denotes a prejudice according to which little difference exists between the male-to-male relationships of the past and the sexual orientations of Western modernity.[59] Just as the deep structure of the persona in a text is a neutral space that awaits characterization as well as a certain degree of interaction with an external world to which it can refer, the biological substratum of human beings can be seen an anatomic "deep structure" whose essence requires a multiplicity of physiological, psychological, and socio-cultural strata to function and to *be*. If, in this light, we look at the meaningfulness of sexuality for the constitution of both the essence of the human being and the historical projection of the literary persona, the difference between sex and gender, as conventionally formulated in the current discourse on sexology, is primarily based on the distinction of bodily vs. non-bodily factors that constitute sex as a "fixed biological substratum or drive (whether genetic, hormonal, anatomical, or psychic)," and gender as "the behavioral and social meanings and power relations attached to sex."[60]

Since the 1980s, in the wake of the Foucauldian revolution in the culture-oriented study of gender and sexuality,[61] many studies have deconstructed the dichotomy of gender, as opposed to sex, through approaches that reconsider the biological substratum of sexuality as a plastic material that modifies and is modified by the gender frameworks of the individual's culture.[62] The existence of such approaches within the contemporary scholarly discourse has

58 Geertz 1973, 37–38.

59 A disarming use of this term, for example, appears in the entry "Homosexuality" of the *Encyclopaedia Iranica*, in which the reader is left with no access to a critical contextualization of homoerotic practices in premodern Iran.

60 Petchesky 2007, 12.

61 According to Michel Foucault, "Sex [...] is the most speculative, most ideal, and most internal element in a deployment of sexuality organized by power in its grip on bodies and their materiality, their forces, energies, sensations, and pleasures." Foucault 1978, 155.

62 "Each individual, thus, manufactures a gender presentation that can feed back on the individual's sex, and is interpreted by others using the specific gender frameworks of an individual's culture. Gender, then, is definitely in the eye of the beholder. Sex and gender presentation are in the body and mind of the presenter." Fausto-Sterling 2012, 8.

facilitated the creation of a "constructivist" paradigm of homoeroticism as a culturally determined set of practices and desires (which may or not correspond with a self-perceived or socially assigned identity) that orient individuals through spheres of sexuality which do not coincide with the fixed gender roles attributed by biological determinism. Essentialism and constructivism are therefore two approaches that explain homoeroticism either through the allegedly fixed biological substratum of human behavior and desire, or by means of culture-fostered dynamics that intervene in the stratified construction of "desiring bodies" as the result of socio-anthropological interactions and mechanisms of power.

To date, no comprehensive studies of the sexual habits of premodern Persian-speaking societies have been published. This lacuna in the scholarship—along with a certain sense of prudery deriving from both a rather nationalistic praise of the ideals of virility and religious or populistic forms of puritanism—has contributed to the creation of the paradigm of "external influence" to explain the origins of homoerotic inclinations and aesthetic values in premodern Iran.[63] Besides its empirical incongruences, the main flaw of this paradigm is that it posits the existence of a natural, healthy, and immutable form of sexuality (the heteronormative discourse) that at some point in history was perverted under the pressure of external influences that caused the emergence of non-native, and very much scorned, sexual habits. Just as Roman homosexuality has long been believed to be an imported inclination stemming from the assimilation of lascivious Greek values,[64] similarly, some Iranian scholars have too often attributed the pre- and early modern homoerotic passion of Persian-speaking city-dwellers for nomadic Central Asian boys to the presence of Turkic slaves—who soon ascended to the role of rulers—whose barbarian promiscuity ostensibly contaminated the incorruptible morals of the Persian.[65] Although ethnocentric biases of this kind can be easily deconstructed with the aid of common sense and rational judgment (why, for example, would the Turks have passed on to the Iranians only their—allegedly *their*—sexual habits and not other equally strong cultural institutions, such as their language or religious beliefs?), any anthropologically informed Foucauldian approach to the study of sexuality would consider the

---

63 Yarshater 2000; Shamisā 1381/2002, 37–39.

64 Ziolkowski 1998, 46.

65 See Shamisā 1381/2002, 38: "pederasty as a 'natural' habit among the Turks." See also Yarshater's argument on the Turkic origins of medieval Iranian homoeroticism, Yarshater 2000. The same interethnic argument is found in Sa'id Hamidiyān's (1383/2004, 276–77) tirade against the sensual and homoerotic aspects of Sa'di's ghazals.

specificities of homoeroticism within a given society as a cultural datum whose practices require neither genealogical explanations nor moral justifications.

Cross-cultural and diachronic anthropological research shows that the formation of culture-specific sexual habits associated with aesthetic ideals that are functional within the symbolic systems of human societies does not take place within the space of a few decades: these are usually centuries-long processes during which complex macro-social structures interact with environmental conditions shaping unique modalities of the interpretation of the so-called "natural" and the "cultural." However "natural" homosexuality might seem today, it is no less culturally negotiated (a process of shaping of identity whose roots can be traced back to early modernity) than the hetero-erotic monogamy found in most Western societies, or the intergenerational practices of ritualistic seminal ingestion that used to be common among the Sambia rites of passage.[66]

Premodern Persian pederasty might have been as local as ancient Graeco-Roman or medieval Japanese homoerotic values and practices, but the Turkish presence was an element that, rather than introducing actual intergenerational homosocial inclinations for the first time, most likely exerted an influence on the aesthetic ideals of pre-existing sexual habits. As attested to by several authors, such ideals—constituting a certain kind of homoerotic "Turcophilia"—were already widespread in early Abbasid Baghdad at a time (9th to 10th centuries) and in a region in which no "Turkic rulers" could have imposed any sexual inclinations whatsoever. However, it became a recurrent literary leitmotiv only under the Samanid and early-Ghaznavid dynasties (10th to 12th centuries), in the eastern fringes of the Persian-speaking world, where the neighboring Turkic tribes could be perceived as a sensually alluring form of somatic and cultural otherness.[67]

---

66 See Herdt 2014.

67 Ethnocentric reflections on the cultural differences between sedentary Persians and nomadic Turks abound in the historiographical sources, and constitute one of the *Leitmotiven* of the lyric representations of the relationship between desire and ethnicity. The case of the Ghaznavids is particularly interesting, as even though they never masked their Turkic ethnic background, their political propaganda and courtly rituals were conceived as the result of a symbolic form of continuity with their "Persian" predecessors, the Samanid dynasty, and the Irano-Islamic ideals of kingship. Many early telling examples from the Ghaznavid period are found in Bayhaqī's *History*, which clearly illustrates the contrast between the Persian refinement adopted by the Ghaznavid Turks and the illiterate, often uncouth demeanor of those Turkic tribes, such as the Oghuz, who had not yet familiarized themselves with Persian customs. See for instance the following passages narrating the awkward fashion in which the Saljuqs, in 1038, temporarily took Nishapur away from the Ghaznavid sphere: "Toghril replied, 'I am willing to carry out your words;

5 The Lyric Threshold of Sa'di's Encomia

In the Persian literary tradition that precedes Sa'di, the homoerotic contents that praise poetry (the *qasida* as an encomiastic form and genre) showcases should not be reduced to a merely reflexive representation of historicized sexual practices.[68] This set of themes reveals an all-encompassing mechanism that regulates the poetic expression of a large variety of social values whose echoes, in spite of radical socio-political changes, were still active in the nature of the homoeroticism displayed by Sa'di in his ghazals.[69] The performative aspect of the panegyric tradition needs to be stressed because, especially in the case of early Ghaznavid praise poetry, it incorporated social functions whose literary representations survived as a latency in the redefinition of the ghazal of the Mongol and post-Mongol periods.[70] Therefore, homoeroticism can be regarded as one of the primary factors of continuity between the function of the lyric embedded in the text of the early *qasida* and the discourse on love—along with its religious and political ramifications—that reached its formal and philosophical pinnacle in 13th-century Shiraz.[71]

---

we are new to this land and as strangers, and unacquainted with the manners and customs of the Persians.'" Beyhaqi 2011, 2: 233. "Ebrahim appeared with two or three hundred horsemen, a banner, two beasts that were being led, and wearing a generally ragged and worn outfit. When the reception committee came up to him, he reined in his horse, and they found him a most handsome young man. [...] The older men were secretly weeping for they had only ever witnessed the troops of Mahmud and Mas'ud parade, and derided the contrast in pomp and retinue." Ibid., 2: 232. The audience hall appeared devoid of all splendour and glitter. A group of riffraff were milling around with no apparent order or sense of decorum, and anyone who wished could go boldly up to Toghril and speak with him." Ibid., 2: 233. On the eroticization of Turkic ethnicity in the Persian literary sources, see Brookshaw 2009.

68 On the ritualistic functions of the pre-Islamic Arabic *qasida* see Stetkevych (Suzanne) 1993. The two volumes on *qasida* poetry as a world literature genre edited by Sperl and Shackle (1996) present an in-depth panoramic view of the origins and uses of this poetic form (especially its encomiastic functions) up to our times, and across a plurality of linguistic and regional contexts in Islamicate societies and beyond. See also Meisami 1987, 40–76; 1990a; 1990b; 1996; 2001.

69 On the *qasida* as a courtly rite of passage in the early new Persian panegyric tradition, see Meisami 1996.

70 On the Ghaznavids, see Bosworth 1963; 1968. A general prejudice on the monotony of the later developments of the *qasida* as a form that would not attract the attention (and the pecuniary resources) of post-Saljuq rulers has prevented scholarship from elaborating a thorough study of praise poetry composed and circulated between the 13th and the 14th centuries. For a preliminary appraisal, see Glünz 1993; 1996.

71 On the connection between politics and eroticism in lyrical openings of Ghaznavid *qasidas*, see van den Berg 1988; Meisami 1990a, 36–38;

In the scholarship, the neglect that affects the homoerotic dimension of Saʿdi's lyric poetry is comparable to the disregard with which generations of scholars have treated the encomiastic aspect of the poet's political activity. Both biases, especially in Iran, belong to the process of modernist purification that Saʿdi has been undergoing for almost a century (from the heteronormative agenda of the constitutional revolution to the anti-monarchic ethos of the Islamic Republic) in order to be elected as the ethically normalized model for cultural excellence and religious piety. The tones of praise that permeate most of his lyric and non-lyric works constitute textual evidence that allows us to safely assert that Saʿdi (at least from his mid-thirties, and until his death) closely gravitated toward the courts of Shiraz and Tabriz, and offered his poetic service to both the Salghurid and the Ilkhanid ruling elites.[72] Unfortunately, the modern editors of the *Būstān* and the *Gulistān* have often omitted the headings that explicitly mention the political recipients of these two books. However, most of the earliest manuscripts reveal that different recensions of the *Būstān* were dedicated to Saʿd II, and then to his son, Muḥammad (aged nine in 1257).[73]

---

72 See Introduction, pp. 9–25.

73 The extant vulgate of the *Bustān* features an introductory laud that lavishes praise on prince Muḥammad, son of prince Saʿd II (*Bustān*, 41–41). Saʿdi might have initially dedicated the book (completed in 1257) to other members of the family before offering it to prince Muḥammad, in the aftermath of his father's and grandfather's deaths. The main piece of evidence corroborating this hypothesis is that most manuscripts introduce the praise of the teenaged prince by referring to him as the *atābag*: "sitāyish-i atābag Muḥammad bin Saʿd bin Abī Bakr bin Saʿd bin Zangī" (Ms. Kabul 1325, 127); Ms. Paris 1320s, f. 17a; "guftār andar madḥ-i atābag Muḥammad bin Saʿd (Ms. Dushanbe 1310s, f. 10a); "dar sitāyish-i atābag Muḥammad b. Saʿd" (Ms. Tehran 1340s, 150); "sitāyish-i atābag Muḥammad shāh, raḥmat Allāh ʿalayhī" (Ms. Tehran 1352, 187; Ms. Yale 1432, fol. 88a). Furthermore, the important "Bodmer" manuscript lacks the lines in which the poet conveys the date of composition of the book. See Ms. Bodmer 529, f. 22a. Cf. *Bustān*, 37, l. 114. However, many manuscripts suggest that the title "atābag" was bestowed upon prince Saʿd II too, long before his two-week-long rule ("ṣanā-yi pādshāh-zāda-yi jahān, atābag Saʿd," Ms. Tehran 1352, 68), probably in 1258, when with an official *yarligh* Hülegü nominated him heir-apparent of Fars. See Shabānkāre'i 1363/1984, 185. Farīd Iṣfahānī too, in many of his *qasidas* dedicated to Prince Saʿd, refers to his young patron as the "atābag," whereas he employs the title *atābag-i aʿẓam* ("the greatest atabeg") to laud his father, Abū Bakr. Therefore, the possibility that the *Būstān* was dedicated to the nine-year old prince Muḥammad should not be ruled out. For a list of Farīd's *qasidas* addressing the Salghurid princes, see Farid Esfahāni, 330. Unfortunately, the editor of Farīd's *dīvān*, Mohsen Kayāni, anachronistically confuses Prince Saʿd II (son of Abū Bakr) with his grandfather, Saʿd I (son of Zangī), who died in 1226, and even identifies prince Muḥammad as Abū Bakr's son, and not Saʿd II's. See ibid., xxxii–xxxviii, 330. Regardless of whether Saʿdi dedicated the *Būstān* to Muḥammad in 1257 or after 1260, I am convinced that an early recension of the text was offered to Saʿd II, possibly even before 1257. I base my conjecture on the final line of Saʿdi's praise of Abū Bakr, which reads as a transition to the laud of the prince in a

The main recipient of the *Gulistān* was prince Saʿd II himself, in his mid- to late twenties by the time the book was presented at court.[74] Moreover, from the oldest manuscripts that were copied before Bīsutūn's recension (and which, for this reason, do not list Saʿdi's poems in alphabetical order) it is possible to infer that the first of Saʿdi's *dīvāns* (*Ṭayyibāt*) was offered, possibly as a literary gift, to the young princes of the ruling family.[75]

In Saʿdi's works, the highest degree of eroticization of the political appears in the praise poems that eulogize young patrons whose physical attractiveness was often confirmed by other contemporary sources.[76] Saʿdi's descriptions of his devotion toward prince Saʿd II are surprisingly similar to the images employed in most of the ghazals in which the poet confesses his longing for the object of desire when his farewell is pending.[77] The pen-name that the poet chose as a

---

fashion that follows the formulaic pattern that is found in most Persian odes that mourn the deceased king (the grandfather of the prince, in this case) and celebrate the new patron: "gar zi Saʿd-i Zangī mānd maṣal-u yād / falak yāvar-i Saʿd-i bū Bakr bād" (*Bustān*, 39). Bashari (2020, 114–15) misleadingly reads the second hemistich as "saʿd bū Bakr" (without the *iżāfa*), in order to prove that the line refers to "the glorious [saʿd] Abū Bakr" and not "[prince] Saʿd, son of Abū Bakr." Saʿdi has used this patronymic *iżāfa* when mentioning Saʿd as the *son* of Abū Bakr (*Saʿd-i Abū Bakr*) at least on three other occasions: in the *Gulistān* ("nām-i Saʿd-i Abū Bakr," *Golestān*, 55), in an encomiastic ghazal in which the entire Salghurid dynastic line is mentioned ("Saʿd-i Abū Bakr-i Saʿd-i Mawdūd," see below) and, most importantly, in an elegy mourning the death of Saʿd II and the enthronement of prince Muḥammad ("omīd-i amn-u salāmat ba gūsh-i dil miguft / baqā-yi Saʿd-i Abū Bakr-i Zangī bād," Saʿdi KhE, 701). Moreover, a late 14th-century manuscript of the *Kulliyāt* kept in the National Library of Paris (Ms. Paris 1390s, f. 37b) opens the section in praise of Muḥammad with the line on Saʿd II ("falak yāvar-i Saʿd-i bū Bakr bād"). As the heading reads "ṣanā-ye shāhzada-yi islām," it is possible that what could otherwise seem a mistake of the copyist may in fact be the trace of a pre-1257 dedication of the book to prince Saʿd II.

74 See chapter 2, pp. 109–14.

75 "In praise of atabeg Saʿd," Ms. Kabul 1325, 297, followed by "In praise of atabeg Muḥammad." Ibid., 298; Ms. Dublin 1320s, f. 87b, ("in praise of atabeg Muḥammad"); and Ms. Dushanbe 1310s, f. 87b, whose *Ṭayyibāt* section opens with a praise of prince Muḥammad and his mother Terken Khātūn, prince Saʿd II's wife. See Introduction, pp. 18, 24.

76 Dominic Brookshaw (2019, 43–44) describes a similar process in the case of the 14th-century lyric praises of the Muzaffarid ruler Shāh Shujāʿ, one of Hafez's most significant patrons. Even the famous "Shirazi Turk" whom Hafez celebrates in one of his well-known ghazals could have been a rhetorical allusion to one of the last Muzaffarid princes, and their charming, "gypsy-like" courtiers. See Ingenito 2018b.

77 Compare, for instance, the imagery of the ghazal with which Saʿdi bade his farewell to prince Saʿd II on the occasion of his departure for the Ilkhanid court (translated and discussed in Ingenito 2019, 118–20) with the following lines:
You left, but how could one forget you?
You return, and I leave, I abandon my senses.
[1.36] Saʿdi YE, 256.

signature for his ghazals, "Saʿdī," most likely derived from the name of prince Saʿd himself, whose patronage of the arts, during the 1250s, attracted to Shiraz a large number of poets who profusely celebrated his virtuous munificence and physical appearance.[78] In a ghazal dedicated to the Salghurid prince, Saʿdi deploys the entire array of associations between eroticism and power that had become customary descriptions during the Ghaznavid period:

1 O minstrel of the gathering, tune up the harmonies of your lute,
O attendant of the royal portico, kindle the odorous aloe.

2 Propitious destiny disclosed the signs of divine mercy:
The beloved has reached the threshold under the auspicious stars.

3 Neither this world nor the hereafter compare with the beloved's worth:
The company of Yūsuf is more valuable than *a handful of dirhams*.

4 How much I enjoy even his violence, his intemperance:
Just as Ayāz's fierce movements would soften Maḥmūd's heart.

5 Why do you sleep today, while springtime is scattering roses?
Stand up, and we might wrap our vest around our innermost desires.

6 The adorned garden shines in the fashion of Solomon's court,
The morning bird is singing Dāvud's melodies.

7 So regal is the heart of the singer, as in the king's banquet
He scatters the rhythmic pearls of Saʿdi's verses.

With one glance he steals a thousand hearts from us:
Behold these fine eyebrows, their market is on fire.
[1.37] Ibid., 252.
Like a sultan he passes by, and a thousand hearts
Following him, like an entire army marching with their sultan.
[1.38] Ibid., 194.
My ears on the path: will I receive news from the beloved?
The herald arrived, and no news I have now of my senses.
[1.39] Ibid., 125.

78 On the correlation between Saʿdi's pen name (*takhalluṣ*) and prince Saʿd II, see Ingenito 2019, 108–109. On the role of prince Saʿd II as patron of the arts and recipient of lyric descriptions highlighting his beautiful appearance (especially in association with the Quranic story of Yūsuf), see ibid., 118–31, as well as chapter 2, pp. 114–23.

8 The heir of the kingdom of Persia, the Great Atabeg:
Sa‘d, the son of Abū Bakr, son of Sa‘d, Mawdūd's descendant.
Badāyi‘ 519[79]

The abrupt transition from a lyric modality to the mention of the prince, first by his title and function, then by his full name, patronymic, and dynastic lineage, suggests that these lines were composed according to the bipartite scheme of the classical Persian *qasida*.[80] If this is the case, either Sa‘di left the poem incomplete by never composing the laudatory section (*madīḥ*), or the first generations of copyists who transmitted this text did not deem it worthy of being preserved and circulated.[81] A similar elision is found in an early

79 [1.40] Sa‘di YE, 236. I accepted the entirety of Yusofi's edition of the ghazal, except for its seventh line, in which I deemed it necessary to replace *ravā-yi* with *rāvī-yi*, a solution that is attested to in a high number of reliable manuscripts. For the manuscript variants, see ibid., 577. Ms. Tehran 1340s (217) and Ms. Yale 1432 (f. 309a) confirm this reading.

80 Persian encomiastic *qasidas* usually open with a short lyric prelude (*nasīb* or *taghazzul*), and, through a brief rhetorical expedient known as the "vanishing point" (*gurizgāh* or *takhalluṣ*), they transition to the praise proper (*madīḥ*). While this model roughly coincides with the *nasīb/madīḥ* structure of the Arabic *qasida* of the Abbasid period (in contrast to the tripartite model of the pre-Islamic *qasida*; see Lewis 2010b, 224), Persian eulogies feature a final "immortalizing prayer" (*du‘ā-yi ta’bīd*) that is not found in their Arabic counterparts, and whose development probably stemmed from political concerns of cosmological nature that were prominent in Iran and Central Asia during the formative period of this genre. On both the lyric exordium and the transition to the praise proper, see Meisami 2003, 144–61, 77–86.

81 Notably, Ms. Berlin 1306, one of the oldest manuscripts preserving a collection of Sa‘di's ghazals, does not include the last line mentioning the name of Prince Sa‘d II (an omission that, lamentably, Yusofi does not signal). Cf. Ms. Kabul 1325, 482–83, where this line is omitted too. As I have discussed elsewhere (Ingenito 2014, 85–86), on many occasions, copyists of Sa‘di's ghazals would suppress occasional encomiastic lines (usually appearing at the end of specific poems) in order to adapt the original texts to the non-courtly *milieux* in which they wished to circulate the poems, whether for spiritual purposes or in relation to local dynastic struggles (see for instance Ms. Tehran 1296, 431–32, where the copyist records only the lyrical exordium of a famous and lengthy *qasida* addressing Shams al-Dīn Juvaynī). Ms. London 1328 (ostensibly copied from an autograph of the author) features this ghazal, along with its final encomiastic line, in the first collection of Sa‘di's ghazals (the *Ṭayyibāt*, which was arguably completed before the 1260s). Many other extant manuscripts belonging to the tradition of Bīsutūn's recension list the poem as part of Sa‘di's later collections (*Badāyi‘* and *Khavātīm*, collected after the 1260s). This discrepancy shows that such ghazals of praise circulated across lines of transmission that would often transgress genre classifications. However, especially considering that poets like Sanā’ī (fl. 12th century) and Hafez (d. 1390), who shared with Sa‘di a similar propensity toward the cultivation of a plurality of audiences, would also compose panegyrics in the form of ghazals, it is not unlikely that a certain degree of familiarity between the poet and

ghazal in which Saʿdi praises the beloved with the overtones characterizing the sacred eroticism that will be discussed in the second part of this study: "he is a divine secret, for he stole the master of gazes' hearts."[82] In some of the oldest manuscripts, the ghazal closes with a line (not included in Yusofi's edition) mentioning the "atabeg." Considering Abū Bakr's distaste for lyric poetry, the atabeg in question could be Saʿd II himself: "people will tell me to let you go and desire someone else. / I won't cultivate two desires, especially in the epoch of the Atabeg!"[83]

Saʿdi was well aware of the Turkic ethnicity of the atabegs of Fars, who traced their descent to the Central Asian clan of the Salghurids. Originally affiliated with the Saljuq sultan Tughrīl (r. 1040–63), the Salghurids had supported his military penetration of Khorasan.[84] In fact, the poet creatively employed the figure of the beautiful Turk in a fashion that corresponds with the ambivalences of amorous warfare and Turkic political power that characterized the Ghaznavid literary expression of the relationship between the encomiastic and the lyrical.[85] The following short ghazal dedicated to prince Saʿd provides a marvelous example of such continuity:

1 No one is more seductive than my beloved Turk:
The chain mail of the crusaders cannot compare with his curly hair.

2 You might not see his comely mouth when he talks
But his lips are not as tight as my broken heart.

3 I happened to hold him strongly in my embrace
But alas not so strong are the hands of destiny.

4 With the sword of your gaze you could defeat an army:
Plunge your sword, as no warrior can compete with you.

---

the young prince allowed the former to praise the latter through short lyric compositions. On the encomiastic value of the premodern ghazal, see Meisami 2005.

82 Saʿdi YE, 74.

83 [1.41] Ms. Kabul 1325, 335.

84 *EIr*, s.v. "Atābakān-e Fārs" [B. Spuler]; Bosworth 1996, 207.

85 It is noteworthy that Saʿdi recounts in the *Būstān* an anecdote in which Toghrīl Beg receives moral admonishment from one of the guardians of his encampment when, engaging in lustful homoerotic pleasure with one of his Turkic slaves, he forgets about the condition of his subjects. See *Bustān*, 175; Wickens 1974, 209.

No one is as gracious as him, but how wondrous that
No one better than Saʿdi can serve prince Saʿd, son of Abū Bakr.
Badāyiʿ 568[86]

In these lines, the eroticization of the beloved's martial capabilities is reminiscent of Farrukhī's and Amīr Muʿizzī's celebrations of Ghaznavid and Saljuq soldiers as models of manliness whose penetrative power could be symbolically tamed through the allegorical shift of the gaze.[87] In the poem above, as in one of Farrukhī's *nasībs*, the phallic value of the sword as a symbol of martial virility is converted into a penetrating gaze that mediates the relationship between Saʿdi and the prince.[88] This figurative flip inverts the power relation of the active dominator versus the passive object of sexual domination and converts it into a rhetorical strategy that allows the poet to engage with his patron on a deeper level of the poetic interaction. Rhetorical strategies of this kind urge us to re-discuss not only the idea of a fixed dichotomy opposing the "active" to the "passive" actors of sexual desire, but also the pertinence of the prefix "homo-" as such. From this perspective, the term "homoeroticism" also ceases to offer secure theoretical grounds: it is the very presence of factors as varied as ethnicity, age, socio-economic status, and the context of ritualized ideals that undermine the value of the essential sameness and identity that the prefix "homo" prescribes merely on the basis of a biological "same-sexness."[89]

6 "God Gave the East and the West to the Ilkhan"

After the unexpected death of Saʿd II (Spring 1260), Saʿdi's rhetorical and stylistic conflation of homoeroticism, lyricism, and political insight as a literary modality to address and symbolically manipulate his young patrons turned into

86 [1.42] Saʿdi YE, 255. Cf. Ms. Tehran 1321, 242; Ms. Kabul 1325, 439.

87 On the encomiastic output of Farrukhī (fl. 11th c.) and Amīr Muʿizzī (fl. 11th–12th c.) in the context of the Turkic ethnicity of their rulers, see Tetley 2009.

88 "O you whose eyelashes are arrows, bow-like eyebrows! What is your arrow for? / Your eyelashes can pierce one's heart more sharply than white-poplar arrows! // So deeply the arrow of your eyelashes pierces the heart and the soul, // That it resembles the spear of the king of the East when passing through iron and stone." See Ingenito 2019, 126–27.

89 "To reformulate, in terms of cultural historicism, the debate about the (hetero)normative 'split' between identification and desire (that they are, and must be, mutually exclusive), we might ask: how does the 'same'—even, or especially, a constructed, adopted, performed 'same'—in the figure of 'same-sex' love and in related modes of analysis, align itself with respect to the deep reserve about the construction of sameness operative elsewhere in cultural studies?" Fradenburg and Freccero 1996, xvi.

a recurrent pattern that survived the gradual collapse of the Salghurid house. Among the ephemeral atabegs who were enthroned after 1260, Saljūq-Shāh (Saʿd II's paternal cousin, r. 1263–64) embodied the aesthetic and political ideals of manly beauty—also widely mentioned by the historical sources—and dynastic pride that would inspire Saʿdi's literary commitment.[90] However, it was only with the Ilkhanid minster Shams al-Dīn, who, after supporting Saʿdi for two decades provided him with the financial resources to build a Sufi lodge (in 1281), that the Shirazi poet fully developed the original combination of erotic and spiritual elements that he had initially cultivated when gravitating around Saʿd II's court.

In most manuscripts, Saʿdi's second collection of poems (*Badāyiʿ*) opens with the praise of the young *ṣāḥib dīvān*, Shams al-Dīn Juvaynī, minister of the finances of the Mongol state. From the closing line of this dedication it is possible to conclude that Saʿdi most likely dispatched a manuscript containing his collection (*safīna*, which also means "boat") in the hope of receiving pecuniary or symbolic compensation:

> People launch their ships in the sea to gain profits
> But not as much as Saʿdi, when he ships his manuscript to an ocean
> like you.
> *Badāyiʿ* 314[91]

Even though no direct link can be traced between the Salghurids and the Ilkhanids, Saʿdi's political commitment shows strong factors of continuity in the transition of his poetic service from the former to the latter dynastic entity. The fourth chapter will show how, in the theophanic eroticism of Persian Sufism, the eyes of the mystics would contemplate the human body as a singular manifestation of God's splendor: any beautiful young man, at a given time and under special contextual conditions, could momentarily function as a metaphor for the manifestation of divine beauty. Similarly, Saʿdi's inclination towards the manifestation of regality in the prime of its attractive youth was not confined to a single political actor, but would shift as soon as a new pole

90 See Introduction, pp. 18–19.

91 [1.43] Saʿdi YE, 147. Ms. Tehran 1296, 441. In a fragment, which appears in some manuscripts in the collection known as the *Ṣāḥibiyya*, Saʿdi shares his frustration for not receiving any response from the *Ṣāḥib Dīvān*, after having dispatched to him "a selection of wise sayings, along with elegant verses and prose writings / which are appropriate for the courts of kings and notables." Saʿdi KhE, 760; Ms. Dushanbe 1310s, f. 177b; Ms. Yale 1432, f. 376a. On the tradition of requesting pecuniary compensation through rhetorical devices, see Losensky 1997.

of power was constituted. It seems that, for instance, he swiftly transferred his representation of prince Saʿd as a reincarnation of Yūsuf to the ideal of enlightened government represented by Shams al-Dīn Juvaynī. Saʿdi's comparisons between Shams al-Dīn and Yūsuf implied the renewal of an underlying correspondence between the Quranic epitome of royal beauty and the young patron whom he ultimately chose as the main addressee of his panegyrics and possibly his lyric compositions.

The appreciation of physical beauty as an embodiment of the new patron's princely qualities transforms the lyric component of the political praise: the body now becomes a venue for the enactment of the performative dimension of poetry, as the text emerges as the embodiment of interpersonal and social dynamics revolving around a sexualized representation of political power. The combination of performativity and actual performance—in the form of recitation and oral transmission of poems in a courtly setting—and aesthetic appreciation of the king's body conjure up a context in which the act of dedicating ghazals turns into a form of erotic communication. The correspondence between poetic homage and implied eroticism clearly emerges in a *qasida* in which Saʿdi praises Shams al-Dīn by celebrating the ineffable beauty of an imaginary boy who equals Yūsuf in comeliness and whose physical perfection causes bewilderment and speechlessness in the heart of the beholder:

1 May God be exalted for converting vulgar liquids into a marvelous painting:
Your splendid countenance, your eyes, your hair, your forehead.

2 No description can honor what the gaze sees in you:
To what end should I describe you? Look at yourself in the mirror!

3 Since God molded Adam's clay and painted humankind,
He has from mud extracted no semen as splendid as your origin.

4 You do not belong to Adam's progeny, as in God's paradise
The beauty of the houris does not reach your perfection....

8 So much do the eyes desire you that bewilderment reigns:
As if watching Yūsuf the knife cuts through the hands and the citrons.

9 The Lords of Gazes [*ahl-i naẓar*] cannot but marvel in silence:
As praise cannot embrace your limitless beauty.

10 No room in my mouth for the laud of your lips
As no mouth, no lips can pronounce the precious treasuries of pearls.

11 And if Ibn Muqla the calligrapher should come back to the world,
In spite of him claiming as miraculous the manifest magic of his pen,

12 He would not be able to paint in gold an *alif* similar to your stature: ا
Nor would he, with molten silver, limn the *sīn* of your smile: س

The allusion to the correspondence between calligraphic elegance and physical beauty suggests that Saʿdi intended to send to Shams al-Din, along with this *qasida*, his collection of poems. Shams al-Dīn had, it seems, solicited his *dīvān* after listening to some of the poet's ghazals during one of his courtly gatherings in Tabriz:

30 God gave the east and the west to the Mongol ruler [the Ilkhan],
You are now the protector and the guardian of all the treasuries in the world....

37 I have dispatched a rose to your gathering of affection
May the turning ages not alter its color and fragrance.

38 My poetic talent [*ṭabʿ-i man*] is a comely bride, do uncover her face!
As she is still virgin and I did not want to give her to impotent husbands.

39 In the grave, I shall cut her off from the progeny of marital union,
As destiny did not honor her beauty with auspicious fortune.

40 Saʿdi, you should not praise your own poetry,
As what is ugly cannot become beautiful with colorful clothes!

41 I thankfully enjoy the indulgence that you bestow upon your servants,
Otherwise, how would I ever dare to offer silk to Byzantium? ...

43 I know that where you are people appreciate the purest musk,
Who introduced you to the fragrance of my humble myrtle?

44 Who circulated my writings in that gathering?
Who has mentioned the name of dust before the skies?

45 How could the flies ever deserve the springtime morning
And broadcast their noise before the nightingales?

46 I am now standing and thanking my high fortune
For the first time it bestows all this grace upon my life.

47 For how long will I be a pawn on the chessboard of Shiraz
Whilst the pawns are all queens in this game?[92]

In these lines Saʿdi compares his ghazals first to a rose, then to a mature bride whom he had offered to various grooms (that is, his patrons), none of whom had been able to consummate the marriage. Saʿdi's praise of his own art as a comely bride offered to Shams al-Dīn implies that the poet regarded his new patron as a connoisseur, able to appreciate truly the quality of his craft and

92 Saʿdi KhE, 684–85; Ms. Kabul 1325, 539–41; Ms. Dushanbe 1310s, ff. 150b–151a; Ms. Tehran 1321, 403–407; Ms. Tehran 1340s, 337–39; Ms. Tehran 1352, 416–18; Ms. Yale 1432, ff. 183b–184b. The perusal of the manuscript variants has led me to prefer certain amendments to the readings that appear in both Forughi's and Khorramshāhi's editions. In l. 38, I have read *bikr* ("virgin") instead of *pīr* ("old"), with Ms. Tehran 1352, 417. On the basis of the variants found in Ms. Dushanbe 1310s (f. 150b), Ms. Kabul 1325 (541), Ms. Tehran 1352 (417), and Ms. Yale 1432 (f. 184b) I have reconstructed two lines that the previous editions of Saʿdi's *qasidas* (both Forughi's and Khorramshāhi's) would render in an awkward fashion:

تو روی دختر دلبند طبع من بگشای
که پیر بود و ندادم به شوهر عنین
به زنده می کنم از ننگ وصلتش در گور
که زشت خوب نگردد به جامهٔ رنگین

38. My poetry [*ṭabʿ-i man*] is a comely bride, do uncover her face!
As she is aging and I do not want to give her to impotent husbands.
39. I should bury her alive and defend my honor,
As what is ugly cannot become beautiful with colorful clothes.

Instead, I have preferred the more meaningful phrasing that appears in the manuscript with the suppression of the first hemistich of line thrity-nine, and the recombination of its second hemistich with a new hemistich that creates an entirely new line (number forty):

38. My poetry [*ṭabʿ-i man*] is a comely bride, do uncover her face!
As she was old and I had given her to impotent husbands.
39. In the grave I shall cut her off from the progeny of marital union,
As destiny did not honor her beauty with auspicious fortune.
40. Saʿdi, you should not praise your own poetry,
As what is ugly cannot become beautiful with colorful clothes!

See [1.44], where I have highlighted my amendments in bold.

provide Sa‘di with the appropriate progeny, namely his renown well beyond his death.

In a short *qasida* which, according to at least one manuscript Sa‘di composed in praise of prince Sa‘d, the poet employs the same metaphor of poetry as a bride whom he offers to the patron for defloration through the act of reading.[93] Sa‘di's repeated use of this image might derive from a *qasida* that Kamāl al-Dīn Iṣfahānī (d. *c.* 1237)[94] had dispatched in the late 1220s to the young Abū Bakr to congratulate his accession to power, and which is crafted with the same meter and rhyme as the ode with which Sa‘di addressed Shams al-Dīn forty years later.[95] In his *qasida*, Kamāl describes his poetry as a bride that he offers to the new Salghurid atabeg as an analogue of his physical presence.[96] The poet crafts a riddle through which he dissects his writing into meanings (*ma‘ānī*) and forms (*ṣuvar*) that he symbolically gifts as comely youths with different qualities.[97] The metaphor of bride-like poetic art offered to a patron as a token of the poet's affection, especially in a context in which defloration and virility are indirectly mentioned, shows that the polymorphic nature of desire is directly implied in what initially seemed to be a straightforward manifestation of political devotion.[98]

In the final part of the *taghazzul* that opens Sa‘di's praise of Shams al-Dīn, the bewilderment that the poet describes as a source of impairment for the beholders' attempt to describe the beloved's beauty ("The Lords of Gazes cannot but marvel in silence: /As praise cannot embrace your limitless beauty") turns into the lover's sexual frustration due to the impossibility of enjoying intercourse with his object of desire. The transition to the encomium of Shams al-Dīn constitutes a pretext through which Sa‘di converts the erotic tension of the *taghazzul* into an act of submission mediated by his own poetry as an analogue of the poet's body:

14 Offer me the nectar of your embrace, as patience is not a syrup
That can appease the palpitations of my heart.…

93 [1.45] Sa‘di KhE, 694. For the identification of prince Sa‘d as the recipient of this panegyric, see Ms. Paris 1390s, f. 174a.

94 [1.46] Kamāl al-Din Esfahāni 1348/1970, 52–53.

95 [1.47] Ibid.

96 [1.48] Ibid., 54.

97 [1.49] Ibid., 54–55.

98 Sa‘di employs the same metaphor of poetry as a bride, offered to the patron for defloration through the act of reading, in another *qasida*, dedicated to either Prince Sa‘d or Shams al-Dīn: "My poetry is a comely bride, do uncover her face! (*tu rūy-i dukhtar-i dilband-i tab‘-i man bigshāy*)." Sa‘di KhE, 694.

18 If no mercy you bestow upon my poor heart
Why should I bear with so much violence and torment?

19 I will bring my plea to the Great Minister of the Ilkhanid court
As his *yasa* [*ayāsa*] are such that forbid violence upon the poor.

Saʿdi's reference to the *yāsās* (the Mongol legal code) in the transition from the *taghazzul* to the *madīḥ* establishes a symbolically powerful overlap between the purely lyrical and the eroticized relation of power. In the context of this conjunction, Saʿdi offers his own body as a poetic object that replaces the virtual beloved of the first part of the poem. As the lyrical portions of these texts show, Saʿdi creates synergy between the erotic and the encomiastic aspects of the devotion with which he embraces Shams al-Dīn's benevolence. This synergy invites comparison with the homoerotics of political affiliation with which Saʿdi had imbued his panegyrics dedicated to the Salghurid princes. In his *taghazzul*s dedicated to Shams al-Dīn, however, the metaphysical undertones that Saʿdi employs to portray the majesty of the beloved seem to reach an unprecedented degree of ineffability.

The sacred dimension of Saʿdi's erotic lyricism reached its mature phase during the decades of his political affiliation with the Juvaynī family. It is difficult to discern whether Saʿdi's attachment to that court was the cause or the result of such a revolution in his poetic path, but it can be safely argued that the members of the Juvaynī family constituted the ideal interlocutors for the development of the conflation between the erotic, the political, and the spiritual layers that characterized the poet's ultimate achievement in the arena of ghazal composition. In order to understand both the origins and the spiritual implications of the form of sacred eroticism that Saʿdi employs when praising the Juvaynīs, we ought to unearth the very roots of Saʿdi's political commitment within the courtly environment that first saw the emergence of his lyrical afflatus.

The next chapter will attempt to unlock the dynamic secret of Saʿdi's lyricism by analyzing the literary activity of the poet at the Salghurid court, between the mid-1240s and the end of the 1250s. It was to these patrons, and in particular to the young prince Saʿd, that Saʿdi dedicated his literary masterpiece, the *Gulistān*. The study of sections of the *Gulistān* and its peculiar alternation between prose and poetry (a literary architecture that scholars refer to as *prosimetrum*) will offer a pretext to access Saʿdi's ghazals from an angle in which the poet's lyricism grazes the delicate relationship between fiction and historical reality in a context dominated by the constant interplay between spirituality and desire.

CHAPTER 2

Movements and Gazes in the Rose Garden

Pseudo-Biographical Experience, Political Engagement, and Fictive Sensuality in the Emergence of a Lyric Voice

Yet Saadi loved the race of men,—
No churl, immured in cave or den;
In bower and hall
He wants them all,
Nor can dispense
With Persia for his audience;
They must give ear,
Grow red with joy and white with fear;
But he has no companion;
Come ten, or come a million,
Good Saadi dwells alone.
Be thou ware where Saadi dwells;
Wisdom of the gods is he,—
Entertain it reverently.
Gladly round that golden lamp
Sylvan deities encamp,
And simple maids and noble youth
Are welcome to the man of truth.

RALPH WALDO EMERSON[1]

•••

An eloquent bird I am: should my form get lost in the soil
The *meaning* of my voice will still resound in the Rose Garden.

Ṭayyibāt 190[2]

∴

1 Emerson 1911, 130–31.
2 [1.50] Saʿdi YE, 90. See ibid., 430 for significant variants of this *maqṭaʿ*.

 | DOI:10.1163/9789004435902_005

1 "Pluck a Petal from my *Rose Garden* … / May it Shine Forever!"[3]

The representation of the world as a resplendent garden is a well-established topos in the Persian lyric tradition.[4] The intoxicating presence of roses mirroring the enchanting nature of the world as a visual landscape of pleasurable forms of longing exudes from the entirety of Saʿdi's literary corpus.[5] In Saʿdi's poetry, in particular, the imagery of the rose garden represents the gamut of phenomenological possibilities of the lyric subject's contemplation of the world as an act of cognition of the self with respect to the creative power of words and images. Few topoi are more apt than the motif of the rose garden to embody the interfusion of artificiality and natural genuineness that characterizes the space of lyric poetry as what we could call a "artificial confessionalism" of the lyric self and its mediated subjectivity. This parallel may shed light on the ghazal as a lyric genre from the perspective of the relationship between language and the external world as a partial projection of the author's experience.[6]

Moreover, in this tradition, the rose epitomizes the courtly ideals of love as an urbane practice of sentimental refinement. In the allegorical gardens of premodern Persian poetry, the rose is the most coveted object of sensory desire. Both the virtuosic care provided by the gardener in the service of the prince and the ephemerality of the rose's blooming season conjure up an ideal of tamed forms of longing that are expected to abide by a specific courtly

3 *Golestān*, 54.

4 On the descriptions of nature in the context of 11th-century Persian poetry and the relationship between princely gardens and bucolic landscapes, see de Fouchécour 1976. See also Meisami 1985; 1995. Many publications have been devoted to the Persian garden from the perspective of its architectonic, cultural and literary aspects. See *EIr*, s.v. "Garden ii. Islamic Period" [L. Golombek]; "Bāḡ iii. In Persian Literature [W. L. Hanaway]. For an articulate overview, see the various essays edited by Elisabeth B. Macdougall and Richard Ettinghausen (1976), especially Hanaway 1976, and Pinder-Wilson 1976. See also Wilber 1979; Moynihan 1979. For a more metaphysical approach to the study of gardens in Islamic Iran, see Rustomji 2009; Schimmel 1976. Particularly interesting is William Hanaway's (1993) description of gardens as one of the main elements that allow us to think in terms of "Persian identity."

5 The representation of nature in Saʿdi's corpus still lacks an in-depth study. For a preliminary survey, see Yazdānparast 1394/2015.

6 While lyric poets often allude to gardens as idealized spaces of intoxicating delight, specific references to their ephemeral architectural dimension in the adjacency of the court open windows into the historicity of the landscape. On the overlaps between idealized allusions and historical descriptions, see Losensky 2003; 2015. For Saʿdi's historical allusion to the *Fīrūzī* (or *Pīrūzī*) Garden of the Salghurid family in Shiraz, see Ingenito 2019, 122, n. 44.

etiquette.[7] The centrality of the rose as a filter through which poetic subjectivity intersects with the courtly ideals of desire emerges in the very title of the most renowned, widely circulated and translated of Saʿdi's works: *The Rose Garden* (*Gulistān*, in Persian), presumably composed between the end of the 1240s and the mid-1250s, and dedicated in 1258 to the Salghurid prince Saʿd in the context of the literary and religious patronage of his father, the atabeg Abū Bakr, ruler of Fars.[8]

The smooth clarity of the *Gulistān*'s rhythmical and ornate prose and the vividness of its humanistic frescoes—depicting personal experiences as well as anecdotes and exempla about kings, saints, and poets from the past—confer on this book an aura of literary excellence with which few other premodern monuments of the Persian literary tradition can compete.[9] The bewilderment with which generations of readers have looked at the *Gulistān* as a mirror of wondrous reflections derives from the coexistence of the particular and the universal aspects of the human experience that Saʿdi intertwines throughout his book. The result is a prismatic literary landscape in which the macrocosmic aspect of social rules and divine edicts contrasts with the most intimate nature of humankind and its psychological refractions. In the book, the ideals of kingship are juxtaposed with the vicissitudes of commoners. The tensions that inhabit the fragility of the human condition are explored against the golden mean of Islamo-Persian virtue. The spiritual dimension of its stories sheds light on the inward path of the heart and its quest for a more profound form of truth, in a fashion that often challenges the tenets of the legalistic aspects of religion and promotes the non-scholastic Islamic wisdom of the piety of

---

7 On the depictions of the rose in Persian culture and literature and the symbolism associated with it, see Schimmel 1992, 169–175; *EIr*, s.v. "Gol" [H. Aʿlam].

8 As argued earlier (p. 36), the textual discrepancies in the manuscript tradition suggest that the book underwent several authorial recensions and was dedicated to different members of the Salghurid family and courtly entourage, including the minister Fakhr al-Dīn Abū Bakr. De Fouchécour (1986, 334–35) has convincingly criticized the opinion of the biographers who, by taking Saʿdi's words at face value, argue that the poet returned to Shiraz in 1256–57 and composed both the *Bustān* and the *Gulistān* in only two years. Considering the evidence that attests to Saʿdi's literary activity in Shiraz as early as the mid-1240s, the composition of the *Gulistān* must have started only a few years later, as a literary endeavor that was meant to solidify the political ties between the poet and the ruling family.

9 Gholām-Hoseyn Yusofi's introduction to his critical edition of the *Gulistān* (*Golestān*, 24–45) counts among the most lucid pages ever written about this masterpiece. See also Arberry 1945, 5–29; Rypka 1968, 250–51; Bausani 1968 521–24; de Fouchécour 1986, 327–48; Lewis 2001a.

the commoners.[10] In its fifth chapter, in particular, the lyricism of the courtly ideals of love and affection reveals the constant interplay between the urges of the flesh and the enchantments that the sensorial perception of the world can offer.[11]

The literary excellence of the *Gulistān* has been praised for centuries, but the study of this prose text (and the annexed verses interspersed as poetic exempla) still lacks a holistic approach capable of assessing how its inner narrative functions within the wider framework of Saʿdi's lyric dimension.[12] I stress the importance of its relationship with Saʿdi's lyricism as the *Gulistān* is far more than a mere collection of moralizing anecdotes.[13] Both its style of enunciation—which relies heavily on rhythmic prose (*sajʿ*) imbued with internal rhymes, consonances and alliterations—and the afflatus of its relentless quest for cohesion between the ethical and the aesthetical aspects of the human experience constitute an exquisite "fourth wall" for a deeper understanding of the dramatic dynamics that animate Saʿdi's ghazals. The *Gulistān*, as a multifaceted inventory of Islamo-Persian reflections on ethics, organizes its contents along multiple narrative threads that comprise a variety of anthropological experiences. Saʿdi's golden mean illustrates the balance between common sense and the hierarchies of power that regulate society as an oscillation between divine will and monarchic order.

From this perspective, we may read the author's approach as providing a compendium of wisdom ready to address and instruct a wide spectrum of ideal interlocutors. However, as Charles-Henry de Fouchécour points out, the primary protagonists of the entire book are kings and "dervishes," a term that

10 "Saʿdi [was] uninterested in the literal or legalistic exegesis of traditional *feqh*, asserting that 'the purpose of the revelation of the Koran is the acquisition of a good character, not the recitation of the written characters [...]. His concerns revolve around pragmatic situational ethics and personal integrity rather than religious law and systematic theology, reflecting the values of the social milieu of the *k̲hānaqāh* and *rebāṭ* more than the madrasa." Lewis 2001a.

11 "Some European commentators found the bawdier passages [of the *Gulistān*] in shocking contrast to the wisdom and moralistic intentions of the work, but generally excused this apparent vulgarity as a difference in occidental and oriental manners." Lewis 2001a. On the "cosmopolitan" dimension of Saʿdi's works, see Keshavarz 2015; Levy 1969, 116.

12 Literary critics define as prosimetrum texts that are composed in alternating segments of prose and verse. For a survey of this form in the premodern Persian tradition, see Meisami 1997. For a preliminary analysis of the prosimetrical aspect of the *Gulistān*, see ibid., 311–16. For an in-depth analysis of the linguistic and rhetorical characteristics of the *Gulistān*, see Bahār 1349/1970, 3: 124–56.

13 See Keshavarz 2015, 18–26.

in Saʿdi's works applies to both the indigent and the Sufis.[14] In the *Gulistān*, the constant reference to kings and dervishes reflects the historical connection between the poet himself and his patrons. From the *Gulistān*'s dramatization of the relationship between kingship and spirituality (as a practice that is both solitary and socially active in its own worldly spaces) we may derive a representation of desire that is twofold: on the one hand the courtly heritage of love as an aristocratic practice of aesthetic and political allegiance, and on the other the spiritual refractions of lyricism as a training ground for the soul of the believer. As a result of this conflation, the entire book exudes a fascinating coexistence of the erotic, the political, and the spiritual. This conflation emerges with particular evidence in the introduction of the book, the lack of analytical study of which remains a major lacuna in Saʿdi scholarship.[15]

In the opening of this introduction, Saʿdi recounts a visionary experience during which a spiritual master attains the visual perception of the "invisible world" in the guise of a rose garden.[16] The bewildering effect of the experience—narrated in a vein that is both ludic and socio-historically abstracted—is akin to the aphasic commotion that Saʿdi exposes in his writings when describing the lover's mental or visual access to the beloved's beauty, either as a manifestation of the divine splendor or as an intoxicating catalyst of sexual desire. In the narrative of the introduction, the solidity of poetic eloquence is reestablished only by virtue of Saʿdi's patron's benevolence and favor (*iltifāt*), which he describes as a gaze that converts the author's "traces" (or "literary works," *āṣār*) into sources of pure radiance.[17] The transition from the vision of the *rose* to the self-laudatory words about the author's poetic excellence serving as a prelude to the mention of the dedicatee of the *Rose Garden* sets a parallel between the eroticism of the metaphysical quest of the invisible world and the verbal expression of a literary work of art offered to the ruling family of the Salghurids.

14 De Fouchécour 1986, 319–25. It is in fact to the illustration of the conduct of these two social groups that the first and the second chapters of the book are devoted, respectively: "Though 'dervish' often designates a stock Sufi character, Saʿdi sometimes uses it to refer more generally to the poor or meek." Lewis 2001a.

15 See Rubanovich 2009 for an excellent point of departure to critically contextualize Saʿdi's *dībācha* within the framework of premodern conceits of authorship.

16 For an in-depth analysis of this specific introductory passage, see chapter 7, pp. 359–61.

17 Muḥammad ʿAwfī expressed a similar idea in his biographical collection on Persian poetry, *Lubāb al-albāb*, composed a few decades before the *Gulistān*. In his note on the Ghaznavid poet ʿUnṣurī, he used the metaphor of the alchemical effect of sunshine to describe how the benevolent favor of royal patrons transmutes the stone-like nature of unknown poets into jewel-like literary excellence. ʿAwfī 1389/2010, 411.

By pursuing the path opened up by the previous chapter, the following pages will track the complexity of the aesthetics and ethics of desire in the *Gulistān* from the perspective of the connection between political patronage and poetic creativity. In order to challenge the common idea that conceives the *Gulistān* as a mere compendium of ethical teachings, this chapter sets out to unearth some of its unexplored sensual subtexts and put them in conversation with Sa'di's lyric production. This comparison will articulate the dialectic between the narrative and the purely lyrical from the perspective of both the autobiographical sketches of the *Gulistān* and the performance contexts of the ghazals that Sa'di incorporated in his prose works.

2 Chasing Sa'di's "I": between Subjectivity and Biographical Indetermination

Sa'di's expression of the multilayered possibilities of desire in a context in which semi-fictional narrations intersect with the circulation of his ghazals reveals the complexity of the relationship between lyric poetry and the boundaries of historical reality. In the medieval Persian lyrical tradition, the poetic "I" of the ghazal constitutes an abstracted self that bears little to no direct connection with the biography of the author.[18] The *Gulistān* shares with the lyric tradition the same lack of clear boundaries between personal confessions and literary convention. Yet the nonchalance with which Sa'di juxtaposes credible accounts of personal experiences with pseudo-biographical depictions of events that could never have happened at the time and place of the fictive narration (Sa'di's travel to Kashgar, for instance) baffles modern readers and critics.[19] De Fouchécour offers a viable solution to the mystery of Sa'di's blurred boundaries between truth and fiction: the *Gulistān* ought to be read as an attempt to persuade its 13th-century readers by means of a web of credible fictive stories that reflect shared sets of values that *seem* to be drawn from quotidian life experiences. Sa'di sketches realistic vignettes (often simple events that anyone, in 13th-century Shiraz, could have witnessed in the streets, markets, gardens, Sufi lodges, mosques, and—through rumors and unofficial accounts—the princely courts and the spaces of the local administration) and

18 See Meisami 1990c.

19 "A more skeptical consensus about Sa'di's historical reliability has been building, [...] and it has been shown that the 'Sa'di' who appears as protagonist in over 40 stories in the *Golestān* should be understood primarily as a poetic persona, rather than as a chronicler of events." Lewis 2001a. See also Dehqāni 1394/2014.

projects them onto the outer horizons of real or fictive travel experiences, historical anecdotes, and teachings from the epic tradition.

But how does the fictitiousness of Saʿdi's lyric language, with its abstract discourse on desire and fascination for human beauty, interact with the peculiar pseudo-autobiographic structure of the narrations in the *Gulistān*? Overall, Saʿdi's juxtaposition of semi-fictive stories and lyric fragments echoing his intimate poetic persona calls for a more compelling theory of the lyric, capable of accounting for the apparently paradoxical coincidence of fiction and truth that surrounds the expression of sensual desire in the *Gulistān* in the historical and political framework in which it was offered to the Salghurid family, and in particular to prince Saʿd II.[20]

Moved by a similar question, in an article on the implied geography of one of Hafez's ghazals, I have attempted to resolve the conundrum of the relationship between the fictive conventionality of ghazal poetry and its potential connections with the external world by theorizing the existence of four levels of abstraction.[21] On the basis of Greimas's model of generative semiotics, I have posited the existence of a deep structure in which the ghazal articulates its narrative functions around abstracted linguistic possibilities. I have called this deep level "deictical abstraction," as it constitutes the grammatical foundation of all kinds of referentiality: personal pronouns ("I," "you," "he/she," "they," etc.); locatives ("here," "there"); and temporals ("now," "tomorrow," "yesterday," etc). The remaining three levels add layers of meaning that coat that deep abstracted structure and provide texts with the imagery that we recognize through the act of reading. So, while the second level ("typological definition") is the stratum in which the grammatical articulation of texts acquires the shape of the types that constitute the genre within its tradition (the "beloved," the "lover," the "garden," etc.), the third level provides texts with "negotiated specifications," such as gender, ethnicity, physical descriptors, and rhetorically dense mentions of locales, regions, and cities (the "Turkish" beloved, "Shiraz" as the city of the amatory encounter, the masculine features of the object of desire, etc.). On the fourth level ("referential possibilities"), texts showcase the possibility of creating direct connections with external reality (be it historical, geographical, biographical, etc.).

The function of referentiality can be explicit and infratextual when a ghazal mentions a person of the real world, a place, a specific date, or historic events. However, in principle, any non-explicitly referential element of a text can potentially signify elements of the external world in their historical setting as a

20 De Fouchécour 1986, 331.
21 Ingenito 2018b, 857–60.

result of the use that authors and audiences make of the texts in question—for instance when a poet refers to specific patrons, or geographical locales, customs, etc., through innuendos that only specific audiences can understand. This model may prove useful in the cases in which the abstract representations of Saʿdi's ghazals are activated by the juxtaposition of fictive narrations with references to specific historical and biographical events. From this perspective, the *Gulistān* represents an excellent ground for the investigation of the complex dynamics that regulate the constant fluctuations between abstraction and historical reality that take place in Saʿdi ghazals when analyzed in their contexts of circulation.

At least since the 1960s, as a consequence of the structuralist turn in literary studies, it has been a common critical practice to recognize a hiatus between the personality of medieval authors and the lyric persona that inhabits their texts.[22] However, over the past few decades, several scholars have reassessed the problem of the "lyric I" in terms of literary subjectivity and the relationship between codified stylistic patterns and the emergence of authorial "selves" whose (albeit loose) connections with the historical authors can and should be the object of further investigation.[23] More recently, in the context of his diachronic study of the lyric, while revisiting mid-century Hegelian perspectives, Jonathan Culler has meditated on the fashion in which the linguistic architecture of lyric poetry imposes upon the reader the constant *perception* of a discourse that stems from the intimate voice of the poet. As de Fouchécour's observations imply, this paradox of the coexistence of abstraction and subjectivity is at work in the *Gulistān* too, where the filter of the pseudo-autobiographical self and its interaction with the courtly environment in which the book was offered as a gift signals an original departure from the

22 See for instance, in the case of Western premodern poetry, Zumthor's meditations on the lack of sincere expression in the amatory poetic tradition: "The subjectivity that formerly inhered in the text, deriving from the presentation of a living subject, has been lost to us. This is probably not the simple result of the obscuring effects of time, but may actually derive from some specific feature of the texts involved." Zumthor 1992, 49. In medieval poetry, "[according to Dragonetti"—as Judith Peraino elaborates on Roger Dragonetti's study of Troubadour poetry (Dragonetti 1960)—"the rhetorical form [...], the parameters of style [...], standard topics [...], and versification [...] provide a ready-made, even ritual-like structure within which the *trouvère* must partially *subordinate* his own voice or self-expression to the desires of his public." Peraino 2011, 15.

23 See Zink 1999; Key 2007; Bond 1995; and Haidu 2004.

Arabic genre of the *maqāmāt*,[24] a term which Michael Cooperson renders as "impostures" in his ingenious translation of al-Ḥarīrī's *Maqāmāt*.[25]

The specific historical setting in which Sa'di explicitly frames the book from the outset of its introduction demands we reconsider the poet's lyricism in light of the content of reality that his ghazals are capable of conveying as mediations between an impersonally abstracted lyric voice and the personal experience of the author. Although the structuralist turn urges us to resist the temptation of indulging in "Romantic" readings of lyric poetry as a form of "lyric of experience" (*Erlebnislyrik*),[26] the emergence of a ghazal from the fictive plot of one of the narrations of the *Gulistān* immediately highlights a discrepancy that takes place at the level of language, prior even to the relationship between the text and the world.[27]

In his exploration of the Western lyric tradition, Jonathan Culler tackles this problem through a reassessment of Käte Hamburger's discussion of "The

24 De Fouchécour 1986, 328–30.

25 "Etymologically, *maqāmah* indicates any occasion when one stands, and by extension a speech made before an audience. As used by al-Ḥarīrī [d. 1122] and al-Hamadhānī [d. 1008], its obvious sense is that of a verbal performance delivered to strangers while standing in a mosque, market, or street, as opposed to one delivered while seated in comfort among friends, as would be the case in a *majlis*." Cooperson 2020, xix. On the *maqāma* as a literary genre, see *EI*², s.v. "Maḳāma" [C. Brockelmann, Ch. Pellat]. Critics have suggested parallels between the style of the *Gulistān* and the *maqāmāt*: "Like the *Maqāmāt*, the stories of the *Golestān* reflect humorously on various social classes and types, are often set in distant locales, and rely upon rhymed parallel prose interspersed with verse." Lewis 2001a. However, "[u]nlike the *Maqāmāt*, the *Golestān* does not follow the framework of a single narrator recounting episodes about a recurring picaresque hero, and, with its generally much shorter stories, does not depend as much on characterization or plot development." Cf. Meisami's observations, presented as a further elaboration of de Fouchécour's comments: "whereas the *maqāmāt* focus on the abuse of language, through the medium of satire, Sa'dī employs his eloquence to convey truth, in the form of advice, especially in those anecdotes in which he himself appears in his persona of the pious sage who has renounced worldly attachments but is elevated above princes by his experience and his power over words." Meisami 1997, 313.

26 Peraino 2011, 14–17.

27 As suggested earlier, the prosimetrum, as a narrative plot expressed in prose along with insets in verse, is a literary form that in the Arabo-Persian tradition predates Sa'di by several centuries. The interplay between Sa'di's own ghazals and the emergence of pseudo-biographical forms of subjectivity is what constitutes the novelty and the critical challenge of the *Gulistān*. Although Meisami is so far the only scholar who has analyzed aspects of the *Gulistān* as part of a Persian prosimetrical tradition, her analyses do not touch upon the problem of the complex relationship between lyric subjectivity and the rhetorical implications of Sa'di's pseudo-autobiographical approach to his narrations. See also Rubanovich 2006.

Lyric Genre" in her provocative *Die Logik der Dichtung*.[28] By recognizing an intrinsic linguistic difference between the fictive logic of a narrative story and the non-mimetic and non-fictive impressions that lyric poetry generates as a genre, Hamburger conceives of the "poetic I" as a "subject of enunciation," whose statements are "real propositions of the experience of an object."[29] The German philosopher hastens to emphasize that the subject of enunciation, far from retrieving the Romantic concept of a direct correspondence between the lyric "I" and the author of a poem, constitutes an "I" that is a linguistic function and, as such, impersonal and non-subjective: "what distinguishes the experience of lyric poetry from that of a novel or a drama is that we do not experience a poem's statements as semblance, as fiction or illusion."[30] This means that, although there is a logical correspondence between the poet and the lyric persona (i.e., the "I" that expresses itself in a poem), the experience that the poem conveys does not necessarily reflect the biographical and psychological identity of the person who composed the text. The result of this approach is that "the relation between the lyric 'I' and the poet is indeterminate"[31] because of the incommensurable nature of the exact link between biographical experience and literary creation.

This perspective implies that, in Saʿdi's ghazals, we may consider the poetic "I" as a linguistic entity that simultaneously *is* and *is not* the literary embodiment Saʿdi's historical presence, as even though the link between the personal experience of the author and fictive lyric creation is incommensurable, the "I" speaks and acts *as if* it were Saʿdi himself uttering the content of the poem. This form of the paradoxical duality of the lyric voice is particularly evident in the ghazal tradition, as it was customary for the poets to have their texts delivered in public by professional reciters. The audience would therefore performatively "acquire" the "I" of the text as a form of aesthetic (or religious, in the case of *samāʿ*, i.e., "the mystical concert," or "lyric ritual") participation capable of turning the ghazal into a linguistic experience that is both personal and collective.[32] If we combine Hamburger's theory of the lyric voice as a dualistic personal/impersonal form of expression with the structural levels of the text that I have mentioned above, we may account for the enormous flexibility of the ghazal as a genre that circulated in multiple contexts of execution and

28 Hamburger 1993, 232–92.
29 Culler 2015, 105.
30 Hamburger 1993, 271.
31 Culler 2015, 107.
32 For the role of the expedient of the *takhalluṣ* (a poet's *nom de plume*) as a link between the text and the historical reality of the poet, see Losensky 1998b; Sharma 2000, 102–106; Lewis 2006; Ingenito 2018a.

created meaning according to its multiple possibilities of adhering to external reality. The biographical experience of the author, along with the historical setting of his physical presence and socio-political engagement, would therefore constitute a latent source of meaning, a meaning that varied according to the different contexts in which the poems were performed and received.

Considering its peculiar intertwinement of fictive, biographical, and pseudo-biographical narrations juxtaposed with lyric insertions, the *Gulistān* constitutes a fertile ground for the study of Saʿdi's development of his own lyric output as a tool to explore and manipulate the historical, political, religious, and aesthetic realities that surrounded his presence at the Salghurid court in Shiraz. In the semi-fictive context of the *Gulistān*, Saʿdi's lyrical exploration of the experience of desire discloses the multiple possibilities of signification that poetic invention can develop through its constant oscillation between literary creativity and the act of beholding beauty as a hermeneutical resource.

3 Prince Saʿd II as Saʿdi's "Implied Reader"

The main recipients of the *Gulistān*—both its intended and primary readers—were the ruling elites of the Salghurid family. From Saʿdi's introduction to his masterpiece one can unequivocally infer that the book was composed in the context of the atabeg Abū Bakr's courtly patronage and explicitly dedicated to his son, prince Saʿd II, whom Saʿdi describes as the primary reader of the text.[33] In the introduction to the book, after the customary exaltation of God's splendor, the poet celebrates his own literary skills by declaring that the good repute of his name (*ẕikr-i jamīl*) circulates among all people, and that "the renown of his poetry has spread across the face of the earth," while "copies of his works are carried about like golden pages."[34] The author adds that the source of such an unmatched literary excellence ought not be attributed "to the perfection of his virtue and of his rhetorical skills." Saʿdi emphasizes that he owes all his

33 Franklin Lewis (2001a) interprets a specific passage from the introduction to the *Gulistān* (in which the concept of praising the notables *in absentia* [*dar ghaybat*], is opposed to the lauds *in praesentia* [*dar ḥużūr*]; *Golestān*, 55) as the manifestation of Saʿdi's reticence to appear at court in person to present the book to the Salghurid family. Lewis's reading is possibly informed by a scholarly tradition that, over the decades, has minimized the relevance of Saʿdi's constant engagement with the political life of Shiraz before and after Abū Bakr's death. For the interpretation of this particular passage, I agree with the opinion of the 16th-century commentator Sūdī, who reads Saʿdi's phrasing as the declaration of a non-hypocritical praise of the ruling elite. Sudi Bosnavi 1349/1970, 99.

34 *Golestān*, 51.

merit to Abū Bakr, "who has looked [upon him] with the eyes of favor, and has eloquently expressed his commendations" in such a way that "both aristocrats and commoners became inclined to show their affection" towards the poet's literary excellence.[35]

Poetic self-praise aiming at creating a bond of courtly affiliation with the ruler was one of the most widespread rhetorical stratagems deployed by Persian courtly poets in pre-Mongol times. By means of this stratagem, authors would create a direct correlation between their own literary excellence and the exaltation of their patrons, who were depicted as sources of poetic legitimation and artistic recognition. This was a mutually consolidating bond, as the king's name, in return, would be further immortalized by the poet's renown for the generations to come.[36] The bold declaration of such an intimate alliance between the poet and the ruler indicated that Sa'di's attachment to the Salghurid court was already an established connection, especially in a courtly environment that was characterized by a high degree of literary competition.[37] Moreover, the reference to Sa'di's prose distributed as illuminated pages could imply that the royal elite had sponsored the composition of the book by offering its author the economic means to produce an illuminated manuscript of the work.[38]

The discrepancies between the oldest manuscripts that contain the text of the *Gulistān* suggest that Sa'di started working on the book much earlier than the years in which the dissolution of the Abbasid caliphate in Baghdad could be foreseen. However, the final recension of the text was brought to completion in 1258 and, in all likelihood, presented at court in the spring of the same year—only a couple of months after the Mongol devastation of Baghdad.

---

35 Ibid.

36 On medieval Persian poetry as source of fame and immortality in the relationship between poets and patrons, see Meisami 1987, 10, 44–5, 47, 291, 305.

37 As argued in the introduction, Abū Bakr developed a taste for panegyric poetry only later in life, as a form of literary propaganda for his military campaigns and in concomitance with his son's propensity to patronize lyric poetry. Sa'di's contemporary, Farīd Iṣfahānī, often mentions the numerous poets who would praise both Abū Bakr and prince Sa'd. See Farid Esfahāni 1381/2002, 12, 200.

38 See, for instance, the following ghazal from the *Ṭayyibāt*, in which Sa'di praises the rhetorical skill of the beloved and concludes the text with an invitation (presumably addressing a patron such as Sa'd II) to invest in golden ink for the circulation of his poems:
The friends do not know about those who are drowning:
In this manuscript they will finally see how drenched my speech is.
It is not poetry that drips from Sa'di's fine elocution, but pearls
If he only had silver in his pockets, he'd write his speech with gold.
[1.51] Sa'di YE, 118.

In this last recension of the text, Saʿdi draws a direct line between the royal legitimation of his poetic talent and the blessing of the Salghurid rule over Fars, which in those dramatic days the poet perceived as the last bastion of political and religious stability given the events rapidly unfolding in Iraq.[39] It was probably this political awareness that elicited the anxiety exuding from Saʿdi's conclusion of the praise of Abū Bakr b. Saʿd I. In this conclusion, Saʿdi lauds both Abū Bakr and his son Saʿd II as sources of stability for the reign. The two lines that he employs are drawn from one of the Arabic eulogies that the poet had composed one or two months earlier, to mourn the death of the caliph al-Mustaʿṣim.[40] Eventually, the poet thus reveals the source of preoccupation that likely motivated the didactic inclinations of the entire book:

> The land of Fars won't suffer from the tragedies of our time [*āsīb-i dahr*]
> So long as you, as the shadow of God, rule over it....
>
> Oh Lord, protect the soil of Fars from the winds of sedition
> As long as in this world the earth and the wind perdure.[41]

In the general introduction to this study, we have shown how historical sources confirm the participation of the Salghurid family in the Mongol conquest of Baghdad. Nevertheless, for mid-13th-century poets, the atabeg Abū Bakr embodied the royal charisma of the Islamic-Iranian ruler who, on the verge of the collapse of the Caliphate, was praised as the last resort for the defense of Islamdom from the evil religious and ethnic otherness constituted by the Mongol threat: "Where is the Solomon in the entire kingdom of the world," asks Majd-i Hamgar rhetorically in the opening of a celebratory poem addressing Abū Bakr—"Who shall not entrust the seal of his heart to Satan's hands?"[42] In this vein, in the introduction to the *Gulistān*, Saʿdi praises the virtues of "the greatest Atabeg (*al-atabag al-aʿẓam*), sultan by land and sea (*sulṭān al-barr va*

39 The fact that this portion of the text is not found in one of the oldest manuscripts of the *Gulistān* (Ms. Bodmer 529—the "Bodmer" manuscript, copied in 1320 and used as main document for Yusofi's edition of the book) suggests that Saʿdi's earliest recensions of his work could have been composed a few years before 1258. See Ibid., ff. 114b–115a. This conjecture is partially supported by Minovi's observations of the lacunae of Ms. Dublin 1320s, from the Chester Beatty collection in Dublin. See Wilkinson 1959, 23.

40 *Golestān*, 51–52; Saʿdi KhE, 707.

41 *Golestān*, 52.

42 Majd Hamgar 1375/1996, 384. We could read Majd-i Hamgar's intimation as an innuendo hinting at Abū Bakr's strategic support of the Mongol conquest of Baghdad, in which members of the Salghurid family (including his son, Saʿd II, and his nephew, Muḥammad-Shāh) participated.

al-baḥr), and heir of the reign of Solomon (*vāriṡ-i mulk-i Sulaymān*)," and lauds him not only as "the shadow of God on Earth," but also as "the pole of the revolving epochs."[43]

Although the political relationship between Sa'di and the Salghurid ruling family still awaits in-depth investigation (especially in light of the Pleiades of poets who offered them their encomiastic services in those years), the wording of the introduction clearly suggests that prince Sa'd II was the book's primary dedicatee. At the end of the excursus where he describes the bucolic context in which his friends induced him to compose the *Gulistān*, Sa'di states that the condition for his work to be brought to completion is prince Sa'd's attentive perusal of the book.[44] "If the lordly favor embellishes this book," Sa'di concludes, "it will turn into a Chinese picture gallery and an album of fine miniatures // as rose gardens are no places of chagrin / one hopes that these pages will not displease anyone // especially because its glorious frontispiece [*'unvān*] / celebrates Sa'd, son of Abū Bakr, son of Zangī."[45] Sa'di wished for the book to reach its completion only through prince Sa'd's act of reading:

---

43 In the history of political Islam, the epithet "shadow of God" initially applied exclusively to the Caliph; see Goldziher 1897, and Darling 2014. At least from the early Ghaznavids, authors would often at their discretion apply this epithet to sultans and notables in non-official communications in order to reinforce the idea of a certain degree of distance, independence, or semi-autonomy from the Caliphate. For an analysis of Mas'ūd of Ghazna's case, see Kozah 2015, 20. On the origins of the association between Fars and Solomon's "throne" as a literary topos, see Brookshaw 2019, 161–67, and the sources therein discussed.

44 *Golestān*, 54.

45 The noun *'unvān*, which here I translate as "frontispiece," can refer to the introduction of a book as well as the heading that introduces a new section or sub-section in a manuscript. Sa'di's emphasis on the fact that the book's *'unvān* is in the "name" of prince Sa'd could suggest that the original manuscript that was offered to the Salghurid court opened with an illuminated medallion (*shamsa*) featuring a blessing addressing the young dedicatee. If we read *'unvān* as "heading," it is noteworthy that most of the oldest manuscripts containing Sa'di's collected works (including those that precede Bīsutūn's recension) introduce the passage above with a heading (often in red ink) that prominently features the name of prince Sa'd ("pādshāh-zāda Sa'd-i Abū Bakr") as the recipient of the poet's praise. See Ms. Tehran 1321, 115 ("ṡanā'-i pādshāh-zāda-yi jahān Sa'd bin Abī Bakr"); Ms. Kabul 1325, 8 ("ṡanā-yi pādshāh-zāda-yi jahān Sa'd bin Abī Bakr bin Sa'd"); Ms. Dushanbe 1310s, 106 ("dar madḥ-i atābag Sa'd bin Abī Bakr bin Sa'd, raḥmahum Allāh"); Ms. Dublin 1320s, f. 28a ("dar madḥ-i pādshāh-zāda-yi jahān Sa'd abī Bakr"); Ms. Tehran 1352, 68. Cf. Ms. Yale 1432, f. 29b; and Ms. Mashhad 1364, f. 12a ("sanā-yi pādshāh-zāda-yi jahān atābag Sa'd"). Some scholars interpret the expression *nām-i Sa'd-i Abī Bakr* as the "felicitous [*Sa'd*] name of Abū Bakr," thus reading *Sa'd* as an adjective and assuming that the *Gulistān* was dedicated to Abū Bakr alone. See Thackston 2008, 8. Sūdī of Bosnia, in his 16th-century grammatical commentary on the *Gulistān*, criticizes readings of this kind. See Sudi Bosnavi 1349/1970, 94.

muṭālaʿa farmūdan is the verb that the author employs: "to read attentively," "to study," "to contemplate and ruminate." This means that the *Gulistān* could only be honored as an accomplished book through the process of reception by the highest princely elite of the Salghurid court. Not only is Saʿd II the primary dedicatee of the book, but he is also Saʿdi's ultimate interlocutor in his effort to rescue Shiraz by offering the future king quintessential wisdom in the art of good governance.

Saʿdi's explicit recognition of prince Saʿd II as the primary recipient of the book ascribes to the young patron the function that the Italian novelist and semiotician Umberto Eco defines as the "ideal reader" of the text. In Eco's theory, the ideal reader is a linguistic function inscribed in the text itself according to the range of meanings and interpretations envisaged by the author. This means that the author, during the act of writing, crafts her or his text in a fashion that generates an ideal possibility of interpretation that is based on specific social and cultural conventions.[46] While the ideal reader is a function of the text as imagined by the author, the act of explicitly specifying a recipient—prince Saʿd II, in the case of the *Gulistān*—offered historical readers the hermeneutical freedom of reading the text according to their own interpretive inclinations. Saʿdi goes even further: by declaring that the *Gulistān* will be completed once prince Saʿd II reads it, he implies not only that the prince is the ideal reader of the text who can freely interpret it according to his disposition, but also that his act of reading partakes in the creative process and defines the ultimate purpose of the book. Therefore, Saʿdi elevates the historical figure of prince Saʿd II to the role of what Wolfgang Iser (possibly on the model of Wayne Booth's concept of the "implied author," formulated in 1961) calls the "implied reader." Just like Eco's "ideal reader," Iser's "implied reader" is a function that is inscribed in the text and orients it in a fashion that converts the act of reading into part of the creative process. According to Iser, the existence of an implied reader turns the act of reading into a process by which the historical reader completes the text in the space of its own making: he imagines settings, events, and characters, fills gaps in the narrative plot, and projects an overall coherent set of meanings onto the fragmented nature of the text.[47] This approach would imply that, among all the meanings that the *Gulistān* can disclose, the specific angle of prince Saʿd II's historical act of reading the book constitutes the preferred point of departure for the analysis of the relationship between the creatively fictive aspects of the text and its connections with the courtly environment in which it was first circulated.

---

46 Eco 1979, 7–11.

47 Iser 1974, 34. See also Compagnon 2004, 109–113.

From this perspective, we may assume that the final goal of the *Gulistān* is to actively inspire the prince by creating direct connections between the narrative plot of the book and the real or imagined experiences constituting the texture of his own life. Through this collection of stories, Saʿdi's "ideal reader," prince Saʿd II, will not learn how to follow compendia of systematic rules and instructions to become a perfect human being, but instead how to gain guidance from a prismatic collection of ideals and thought-provoking contradictions that lead to the path of becoming perfectly human. The quintessentially courtly framework of the *Gulistān* contributes to the development of Saʿdi's lyric voice through a multiplicity of points of view, ideals, and representations of the psycho-physiology of the amorous experience. As mentioned in the previous chapter, Saʿdi interacts with and represents prince Saʿd II as if he were the *manẓūr* of his poetic persona, i.e., the object of the poet's gaze and the recipient of his eroto-political and spiritual influence played out through the performative aspect of poetry composition and recitation. In the *Gulistān* it is possible to witness how the literary reflection of the relationship between the poet and the young prince embodies the courtly ideal of amatory desire as a devotionally refined art that Saʿdi inherits from the previous lyric tradition and combines with tinges of spiritual meditation on the contemplation of human beauty.

4 Courting Prince Saʿd II through Narratives of Piety and Desire

Historiographical accounts consistently depict the atabeg Abū Bakr as a monarch who approached matters of political power, public administration of religious affairs, and courtly entertainment in an idiosyncratic fashion.[48] While for two decades the Atabeg pursued an aggressive military expansion of the Salghurid sultanate's sphere of influence, it seems that his relationship with the public manifestation of faith was guided by a capricious personal admiration for ascetics and religious zealots, regardless of their scholastic competence in the curriculum of the Quranic sciences.[49] A closer inspection of the sources reveals that Abū Bakr's peculiar approach to the religious landscape of Shiraz was first and foremost informed by his obsession with power and the direct control of all public affairs of the Sultanate. After deposing his father, Saʿd b. Zangī (Saʿd I), Abū Bakr conducted several purges aimed at eliminating

48 See General Introduction.

49 See Introduction to the second part of this book. See also Aigle 2005, 107–11; Ingenito 2019, 111–16.

public figures whom he deemed to be loyal to the old regime.[50] Targeting the religious establishment through the dismantlement of powerful figures and semi-institutionalized elites, such as prestigious Shirazi families of *sayyids* (descendants of the Prophet), theologians, and experts of Islamic legal doctrine, was the logical continuation of Abū Bakr's policy of averting the threat posed by concurrent political actors.

By selecting his viziers and chief justices from Sufi circles that would not directly participate in the dynamics of political power or belong to institutionally organized spheres of influence, Abū Bakr fostered the development of the religious life of the region by promoting the constitution of pious foundations and nourishing forms of Sufism disconnected from the most powerful orders of the time.[51] Considering the politics of the religious landscape that Abū Bakr promoted, it is not surprising that Saʿdi makes no reference to institutionalized forms of Sufism in his works, which mention neither specific spiritual orders nor recognizable "scholastic" doctrines. This kind of anti-elitist spirituality exudes from all the stories of the *Gulistān*, and it is indeed tempting to associate Saʿdi's non-scholastic approach to Sufism with the idiosyncratic measures that Abū Bakr endorsed.[52] Therefore, we may regard the *Gulistān* as the literary expression of the system of spiritual values that would best fit the religious pragmatism at work during Abū Bakr's reign. Saʿdi's dedication of the book to prince Saʿd II and his election of him as the ideal reader of the text was part of the poet's effort to engage himself with his young patron in a fashion that would promote the spiritual values that were aligned with the policies of the Atabeg. It was through this continuity that Saʿdi could ensure the protection of his privileges at court and exert his influence over the younger generation of rulers, namely prince Saʿd II and his son Muḥammad. Moreover, taking into account the cultural breadth of some of the religious and administrative figures who belonged to the entourage of Abū Bakr, it is not unlikely that Saʿdi might have secretly hoped one day, after Abū Bakr's death, to become Saʿd II's vizier.

From Vaṣṣāf's accurate description of the social interactions at the Salghurid court, we learn that even though Abū Bakr piously refrained from partaking in drinking sessions featuring the recitation of mundane poetry, he condoned

50 See introduction to Part 2, in which I frame this event within the context of the circulation of philosophical ideas and scientific paradigms in 13th-century Shiraz.

51 We owe to Shams-i Qays-i Rāzī (1388/2009, 33–38) the earliest description of Abū Bakr's investment in the creation of pious foundations, who redistributed among them the material wealth accumulated by his father, Saʿd I.

52 On Saʿdi's possible spiritual affiliations, see the next part of the book.

prince Saʿd II's proclivity toward such activities.[53] Although the historiographical accounts of this prince are scanty, most of Saʿdi's contemporary fellow-poets would celebrate Saʿd II's artistic patronage. On the basis of this complex network of pious ideals and courtly practices in the bosom of the Salghurid family, we may conceive of the *Gulistān* as an exercise of literary pedagogy aimed at capturing prince Saʿd II's benevolent favor toward the non-elitist communities of Shirazi Sufis (the *darvīsh*es celebrated by Saʿdi as a social category) through rhetorical stratagems scattered throughout the book.[54] In fact, the spiritual element that Saʿdi injects into the literary relationship with his young patron interacts with the ideals of courtly love that one may trace back to both the erotics of the panegyric tradition of the Ghaznavids and the *topos* of the lover's chaste devotion to the beloved. This pairing of eroticism and devotion, the latter leading to self-immolation, circulates throughout the entire history of Persian lyric poetry.

One particular story from the fifth chapter of the *Gulistān* epitomizes the overlap between courtly ideals of chaste love, spiritual longing for the divinized object of desire, and the subject-patron relationship. This story, in my reading, represents an allegorical transmutation of the rapport between Saʿdi and prince Saʿd II. The story portrays the misfortunes of a dejected youth who—as we eventually learn—falls in love with a beautiful prince. Saʿdi describes the lover as an eloquent young man with a sophisticated inner disposition and well versed in the art of composing refined poetry through ravishing images. It was a result of this poetic sensibility that, as Saʿdi seems to gloss, "he fell desperately in love and was enraptured by this experience." As soon as the young prince—"the object of the lover's gaze"—receives news of the lover's maddening passion, he decides to pay him a visit and witness in person the effects of so much commotion:

> No matter how the prince tried to allay his discomfiture by asking him where he came from, what his name was, and what trade he plied, he was so sunk into the depths of the ocean of love that he could not even breathe.

---

53 Vaṣṣāf (1259/1852, 165–69) elaborates extensively on the excessive drinking habits of Abū Bakr's brother, Salghūr-Shāh.

54 See Vassāf 1259/1852, 155–56. In the *Būstān*, Saʿdi praises prince Saʿd's son, Muḥammad—who was nine years old at the time of the composition of the book—and describes him as *darvīsh-dūst*, or "companion of the Sufis." For an in-depth discussion of the philological elements that should be taken into account when considering the addressees of the *Būstān*, see the previous chapter.

"Why don't you speak to us?" the prince asked. "I too belong to the circle of Sufis and am devoted to them."

From the midst of the crashing waves of love, he raised his head, and before exhaling his last breath he said:

You are here, and yet I exist—how wondrous!
I can continue to speak while you are speaking.

In a final line, Saʿdi comments:

It's no wonder to be killed on the threshold of the beloved.
Astounding it is to survive: how could one ever stay alive?[55]

Upon a first reading, one may wonder why it is only in this final section, when the story is about to come to a close, that Saʿdi informs the reader that the unattainable object of desire is a prince. And how does the prince come to understand that the person who is in love with him is a mystic? The prince's confession ("I too belong to the circle of Sufis and am devoted to them") provides us with a piece of information that the author had not previously included in the depiction of the character of the young lover. It is possible that what the author wants to suggest is that the prince has inferred from the languid condition of the lover (and the words of love that he utters in verse) that such emotion can only be the result of an experience of desire which the Sufis alone can access.

The young and desperate dervish acts as a projection of Saʿdi's *persona*, portrayed in an allegorical act of amorous devotion towards the prince. The latter's young age, delicate manners, and commitment to the cause and the practices of the Sufis could be read as traits that the poet displays to suggest an association between this fictitious character and prince Saʿd II, the historical dedicatee of the book. Sources do not mention whether prince Saʿd II ever embraced a Sufi order, but the association that Saʿdi outlines through this tale resonates with the introduction of the *Gulistān*, in which the poet underlines the intimate affinity between the Sufis and the notables of the state. This story could therefore be understood as a projection that the poet staged in order to reinforce the potential sympathy that the prince might have cultivated toward the spiritual circles of the time.

The association between the character of the Sufi in love and the literary *persona* of Saʿdi is accentuated by the description of the former as a man of the

55 *Golestān*, 134–35. Thackston 2008, 105–107.

pen.[56] Furthermore, in this anecdote Sa'di inserts a line (the concluding verse) that is originally part of one of his ghazals, and which explores the topic of love as an experience akin to death followed by rebirth through passionate longing. This intertextual expedient allows Sa'di to interject the potentially biographical aspect of his own lyric persona (Hamburger's "subject of enunciation") into the fictive world of the prose narration. The contrast between the fiction of the narrative and the emergence of "real propositions of the experience" through the non-fictive logic of the ghazal provides the experienced reader (as well as prince Sa'd II, as the "implied reader" of the book) with the opportunity of linking the plot of the story to Sa'di's biographical persona:

1 How could your companion's eyes fall asleep tonight?
The beauties of paradise need no sleep in the celestial gardens.

2 The smell of springtime teaches the ground its return to life,
Stone is one whose heart is not revivified by the breeze.

3 The dear one whom I lost! I smell the scent of his shirt
This much I can't say, as they would tell me: *in your old error you fall!*

4 No advice the ears of the lover can ever hear:
Nothing can provide the medical cure for the pain we feel.

5 Repent—they'll tell me—from imagining [*andīsha*] your beloved.
No contrition I see in what is gross sin to me!

6 O companions of my journey, you may leave me alone
As we want to sit, settle, and live by the door of my beloved.

7 O brother, think of the pain of love as the pagan fire of Nimrod:
To me these flames equal Ibrāhīm's fire: a rose garden!

8 The dead will rise from the soil of his tomb and start to dance
If you pass by his bones in the moment they are decaying.

---

56 The dervish is described as "sweet-tongued" (*shīrīn-zabān*), an epithet that Sa'di often utilizes to praise his own poetic art:
O Sa'di, sweet is your tongue, why all this commotion?
Our *shāhid* is a sacred sign [*āyat*], and all this is the exegesis [*tafsīr*] of his presence.
[1.53] Sa'di YE, 271. See also [1.52] *Sa'di* YE, 42; [1.54] *Bustān*, 122.

9 I long for your embrace and yet our farewell I fear:
Nothing else scares me in this world, no other hopes I have.

10 It's no wonder to be killed on the threshold of the beloved:
Astounding it is to survive: how could one ever stay alive?

11 O Sa'di, love and lust cannot bleed into each other:
The demon stays clear of the lauds that the angels chant for the Lord.
Ṭayyibāt 165[57]

The poem showcases an intricate network of connections between the physical aspects of the experience of love and the spiritual overtones provided by the reference to the story of Ibrāhīm, who was cast into fire by the idol-worshipper Nimrod and saw the flames around him transformed into a bed of roses. The Quranic Yūsuf is referred to as the "lost beloved," a description that implies that the lyric *persona* is his father Ya'qūb, who according to the sacred text recovered from his blindness as soon as he smelled the scent of his lost son on a shirt.[58]

These religious references are certainly in line with the metaphysics of the experience of love that affects the Sufi lover in the story of the prince. But the reader may ponder the meaning of the last line of the ghazal. Sa'di classifies love and lust as two separate categories, as distinct from one another as the temptations of Satan and the glorifying chants of the angels. From this distinction it may be inferred that love is the agent that ensures the defeat of lust, just as the angelic glorification of God keeps evil away. Moreover, it should be noticed that Bīsutūn's early 14th-century recension of the *Kulliyāt* includes a line that is not found in Yusofi's edition, and which reinforces the sacred eroticism that links this specific ghazal to the narrative of the story of the dervish from the *Gulistān*:

The beautiful boys attesting to God's beauty [*shāhidān*] do not conceal their faces from the Masters of Gazes;
The nobleman [*mard-i karīm*] may well endure the burden of the dervish.[59]

57 [1.55] Sa'di YE, 79.

58 The expression *żalālī-st qadīm* ("in your old error you fall," l. 3) is a reference to Qur'ān 12:95.

59 [1.56] Ms. Paris 1366, f. 200a; Ms. London 1416, 391b; Ms. Yale 1432, f. 319. Ms. Kabul 1325 (339), as all other "pre-Bīsutūn" manuscripts, does not feature this line in the main body

We may read the "dervish" of this line as the lyrical equivalent of the character of the narration, whereas the figure of the *shāhidān*, who do not prevent the true beholders from perusing their comely countenance, could relate to the young prince of the story, especially considering the generic attribute of nobility that the line assigns to them. If we return to the main plot of the encounter between the dervish and the prince, we may reconfirm the paradigm of sacred eroticism that Saʿdi figuratively incorporates within the ideal of the relationship between himself and prince Saʿd II. Through these parallels, the poet displays the multiple subtexts of the politics of sacred eroticism with which he fulfills his encomiastic agenda within the Salghurid court.

The implied political eroticism exuding from the comparison between the previous ghazal, *Ṭayyibāt* 165, and the story of the dervish deserves to be further explored by comparing these two texts with a similar poem, patterned according to the same meter and rhyme as the previous ghazal. The high number of discrepancies in the manuscript tradition suggests that the this second ghazal was likely one of Saʿdi's later compositions which the poet readapted from a draft of the first ghazal.[60] In this ghazal, several lines refer to the dervish as an ideal lover longing for his object of desire.[61] The association between dervishes and Sufis that appears in the narration from the *Gulistān* and *Ṭayyibāt* 165 is clarified in the second line of this ghazal too, which alludes to the relationship between spiritual imagination and Sufi rituals such as *ẕikr* (the ritualized remembrance of God) and *samāʿ*.[62] Moreover, the closing line of the ghazal makes use of a phrasing similar to that of *Ṭayyibāt* 165 to convey a different closing statement:

---

of the ghazal. However, a later hand (14th–15th centuries) has emended the text by adding the verse to the margin of the folio.

60 [1.57] Saʿdi YE, 301. Ms. Dublin 1320s (f. 104a) includes the ghazal in the *Ṭayyibāt*, whereas in Ms. Berlin 1306 (f. 85a), Ms. Tehran 1321 (245), and Ms. Mashhad 1364 (f. 323a), it appears in the *Badāyiʿ*. In mss Dublin, Mashhad, Dushanbe 1310s, and Ms. Paris 1320s, the first *miṣrāʿ* of the last line replicates the wording of the first *miṣrāʿ* of last line of *Ṭayyibāt* 165 (*pīsh-i taṣbiḥ-i malāyik naravad dīv-i rajīm*). Ms. Paris 1320s also includes l. 10 of *Ṭayyibāt* 165, which is the same line that appears in the story of the dervish and the prince in the *Gulistān*.

61 Ibid., ll. 3, 7.

62 After congregating, they all left the circle [*dāyira*] and followed their path.
We stayed, lingering and contemplating your mental image [*khayāl-i tu*].
See chapter 9, p. 497.

O Saʿdi, love and chastity cannot bleed into each other:
For how long will you hide the resounding drums under the rug?
Khavātīm 674[63]

The emphasis of both variants on the relationship between love, lust, and chastity attests to Saʿdi's attempt to represent carnality as a turbulent subtext to the apparently tame experience of courtly love, understood as a spiritualized and chaste contemplation of the beloved. In Saʿdi's lyric experience, this latent carnal subtext dynamically animates the poet's portrayal of courtly love. To better understand this sensual latency, we may look at a text by Sanāʾī Ghaznavī, whose imagery, meter, and rhyme overlaps with Saʿdi's double rendition of the ghazal inserted in the story of the prince:

1 Yesterday in that quarter of the gold sellers, by the gate of the caravanserai
I saw a boy who was more radiant than a glittering pearl.

2 As marvelous as the moon, the dark eyes of a sorcerer, of an idol:
Peerless beauty, no one could equal him in the seven climes of the earth.

3 I said to my own heart: I wish such a prince of the idols
Could bestow upon my humble presence the graces of his heart.

4 I went and winked at him, and he welcomed my approach:
an intense boy he was, clever, intelligent, and mature.

5 "Where are you from"—I asked him—"and what is your name?"
From Balkh, he told me, and my name is Generous Heart.

6 I said: "O dear son, would you like to be my guest?
"Of course," he said, "why shouldn't I?" And we walked towards the caravanserai.

7 We were swept away by happiness, gaiety, music and wine:
He was the prince, and I his boon-companion.

63 Saʿdi YE, 301.

8 When intoxication overtook him and wine made his head heavy
The temptations of Satan the accursed penetrated my heart.

9 I said to him: "Will you give three kisses to your dear daddy?"
He said: "If you want any, six times must you drop a silver coin from your purse."

10 Ten coins I had left from what my father had given to me
And I donated all of them to that enchanting moon.

11 As he unfastened the belt of his pants I stared at him:
A "pair" he had adorned with all bountiful delights.

12 He put his chest on the ground—O! So comely the waist of that idol
The scent of his silver chest would reach the moon.

13 His stomach and navel were the skin of bright grapes, as fragrant as creamy cheese.
And his buttocks as white as the belly of Jonah's whale.

14 A dome made of whitened silver
His silver dome cut in two halves by a diamond.

15 Satan's oil boiled in my body
And I stuck my *alif* ا into his *mīm* م

16 Underneath me he was trapped like a partridge in the claws of a falcon
And erected I was on that dome, like Moses on Sinai.[64]

The style of the composition, the semantic continuity between the lines, as well as the explicitly obscene vocabulary, are all factors that bestow on this text a halo of realism that could convince many a reader that the poem is a confessional account deriving from the biographical experience of the author. The amatory mood of the description of the encounter reveals an emotional softness that envelops even the explicit depiction of the lovers' intercourse, which is described by means of alphabetic euphemisms (the phallic letter *alif*

64 [1.58] Sanā'i 1389/2010, 484–85. I have preferred Mossafā's edition, as Modarres-e Razavi's (1362/1983, 1083–84) seems grammatically unsatisfactory.

entering the orifice of the *mīm*). These factors place the poem in a gray area that is difficult to classify: the images read as both lyrical and narrative, but also non-satirical and, at the same time, overtly erotic. Furthermore, the sincerity of the description and the emotional involvement that exudes from its lines are in stark contrast to the mood of a couple of passages in which the author refers to the temptations of Satan (in the line where intoxication awakens their senses) and to the evil liquid that starts to boil in his loins as soon as the intercourse is about the begin. The acknowledgment of the sinful nature of the sensual acts that the poem describes creates an oscillation between self-empathic indulgence with respect to the lust stemming from love and the regret of letting the concupiscence of the flesh overcome the purity of the heart's inclination to beauty.

This oscillation creates an appropriate space for us to interpret Saʿdi's ghazal as a spiritual elaboration on Sanāʾī's bittersweet confession, as well as an illustration of the necessity of keeping love and lust as separate categories *precisely* because they do belong to adjacent fields of experience. The awareness of this duality could have informed the dual rendition of the closing line of his twin ghazals, of which one compares lust to evil, and the other describes lustful desires as the sound of a drum naturally pounding under the skin. As I noted in the introduction, it is possible to argue that Saʿdi's approach to the correlation between love and lust can be divided into an early phase, imbued with scholastic condemnations of physical desire, and a later period in which the poet adopts a more relaxed attitude toward the urges of the flesh—which he reads as a deeper form of physical awareness of the majesty of the divine reflections in the material world.

While the context of the composition of the *Gulistān* provides an implied parallel to interpret the prince and the dervish of the story as prince Saʿd II and Saʿdi respectively, the intertextual plot that Saʿdi's lyric insertion generates reveals the role of desire in the manipulation of the relationship between spirituality and political power in the context of the poet's engagement with the Salghurid court. In spite of the representation of unblemished and chaste love as the main ideal characterizing the interaction between the dervish and the prince, the friction between the narrative plot and the ghazal tradition exposes the carnal subtext that regulates the tension between spirituality and courtly commitment. Surprisingly, the role of carnality in the context of the politics of spirituality reflected in the *Gulistān* appears even more strikingly in a story that rhetorically involves the presence of Saʿd's father, the atabeg Abū Bakr, whom Saʿdi represents as the witness to and ultimate judge of the experience of desire in the context of institutionalized spirituality.

5 Involving the Atabeg as a Figurative Witness of Erotic Explorations

In this story too we witness Saʿdi's masterful approach to the creation of a metaphorical representation of the lyric self as a bridge between the erotic horizon of his ghazals and a narrative of desire within a courtly context in which the relationship between spirituality and sexuality faces the trial of the king's prerogative of enforcing Islamic law. The protagonist of the tale is a judge (*qāżī*) from Hamadan who happens to find himself consumed by a passionate infatuation with a young blacksmith. Saʿdi narrates all the events leading to their sexual encounter, which is eventually brought to the moral and legal judgment of the king. The interaction between the enamored judge and the king plays out as a figurative analogue of the relationship between atabeg Abū Bakr and the poetic persona of Saʿdi.[65] At the narrative climax of the sexual exchange between the two characters, the enamored judge recites one of Saʿdi's ghazals. By incorporating the lyric passage into the narrative in this way, just as in the story of the Sufi and the prince that we have previously analyzed, Saʿdi projects his lyric persona onto the fictitious figure of the judge. Once the judge's most loyal associates learn about his passion for the blacksmith, they urge him not to set his sights on him, but rather "to roll up the carpet of inflamed desire." "The office of a judge," they argue, "should be an unassailable position, and you should not sully it with a hideous offense." The judge, who throughout the major part of the narration expresses himself exclusively in verse, rejects his counselors' advice and, by investing a large amount of money to seduce the young man, "manages to achieve one night of intimacy." "All that night," Saʿdi narrates, "the judge had wine in his head and the youth in his embrace." At this point the author portrays the judge in the act of reciting the following ghazal as the lyric manifestation of his erotic rapture:

> Is the rooster crowing ahead of time tonight?
> Lovers wish to further indulge with kisses and embraces.
>
> The nipples of the beloved appear amidst his curly locks
> Like ivory balls in the curve of a polo-stick as dark as ebony.

65 *Gulistān*, 145–48. Most translations (apart from the ghazal below) are adapted from Thackston 2008, 119–23, and compared with Yusofi's critical edition of the book, with a special consideration of major manuscript variants. On the *topos* of prominent religious figures involved in sensual affairs with ephebic beauties, see Lewis 2009, 707–708. Lewis analyzes the tale of the judge of Hamadan in light of the relationship between power relations and religious hypocrisy.

For one night the beloved is a sleeping temptation, beware!
And stay awake, or you'll waste your life in sighs.

Until you hear the call to prayer from the Friday mosque at dawn,
Or the beat of the drums from the gates of the Atabeg's palace,

Dismiss the foolish lamentations of the rooster:
Do not remove your lips from the scarlet lips of the beloved![66]

Before resuming the plot of the tale, I ought to specify that Bīsutūn's recension of the *Kulliyāt* features the text above as an autonomous ghazal, included in Saʿdi's early collection of the *Ṭayyibāt*.[67] Since pre-Bīsutūn manuscripts (i.e., copied either before 1326–34 or according to different lines of transmission) feature the poem, it is possible that it was first recited in the courtly framework of the Salghurid entourage as a lyric praise, and later inserted into the plot of the story from the *Gulistān* as a narrative expedient that deepens the rhetorical structure of the plot. I will return to this point in order to elaborate on the effects of meaning that this lyrical insertion generates.

"That very night"—Saʿdi continues—"the king was informed that such an abomination had been committed in the kingdom." The king, who considered the judge one of the most learned men of the age "and unique in his time," decides to verify the affair in person, in order to ascertain whether detractors have maligned the judge: "I heard," Saʿdi reports,

> that at dawn he went with several of his courtiers to the judge's bedroom. There he saw a candle standing, a beautiful boy sitting [*shāhid*], wine spilled, goblets broken, and the judge in a stupor of intoxication,

66 In the last line, the original text features a pun through the repetition of the word *khorūs* ("rooster"). Saʿdi introduces the word as a simile, to compare the lips of the beloved to the eyes of a rooster (*lab bar lab-i chu chashm-i khurūs*—emended from Ms. Kabul 1325, 83, as Yusofi's choice, *lab bar labī chu …*, is stylistically dubious).

67 [1.59] Saʿdi YE, 289. Yusofi arbitrarily included this ghazal in the *Badāyiʿ*. However, most manuscripts of the Bīsutūn recension include it in the *Ṭayyibāt*. See Ms. Tehran 1340s; 472; Ms. Tehran 1352, 544; Ms. London 1416, ff.112b–113a; Ms. Yale 1432, f. 253a. In the past, colleagues and friends whom I respect profoundly have maintained, in private communications, that this ghazal is the main proof attesting to the fact that the gender of the beloved in Saʿdi's ghazal is feminine. Nevertheless, as argued in the first chapter, the length of the beloved's hair and her or his breasts are in principle ungendered physical features which—as it is the case in the context of the narrative plot in which this specific text is embedded—can also apply to a male object of desire.

> oblivious to the world. Gently he roused him, saying, "Get up! The sun has risen."

The judge, through witty remarks and pleas interwoven with Quranic references, unsuccessfully attempts to gain the king's mercy, who orders for him "to be thrown down from the fortress, so that others may learn a lesson."

> "O lord of the world," the judge said "I have been nourished by the benefaction of this dynasty, and I am not the only one to have committed this crime. Have someone else thrown down so that I may learn a lesson." The king burst out laughing and pardoned his crime, and to the detractors who had insisted that he be killed he said:
>
> "You who admit to your own guilt, do not taunt others for their faults."[68]

The story of the judge of Hamadan and his young male beloved exemplifies how a ghazal that originally belonged to a specific performance context could be incorporated into the texture of the narration to provide the plot with a dynamic articulation between lyricism and historical reality. One of the most appealing effects of the story is the creation of a twofold analogy between the text and the extratextual reality in which the *Gulistān* was circulated and presented at court: while the story implies a correspondence between the king of the narration and the atabeg of Shiraz, Abū Bakr, it also suggests a parallel between the judge from Hamadan and Sa'di's literary persona. The analogy between the king of the story and atabeg Abū Bakr is highlighted by the ideals of righteous government to which Sa'di recurs to depict the former: it is the portrait of a magnanimous king who not only holds the most learned men of his epoch in great esteem, but also relies on the counsel of his attendants and decides to ponder on the available evidence in order to pass his judgment on the cases that require his final sentence.[69] Moreover, I have speculated that the courtly indulgence of his son, prince Sa'd II, diluted Abū Bakr's notoriously strict religiosity and might have mellowed his initial resistance to partaking in sessions of poetry recitation and wine consumption.[70] If this was the case, one could read the narrative association between the king and the Atabeg

68 *Golestān*, 145–8; Thackston 2008, 119–23.

69 Sa'di's portrayal of Abū Bakr as the ideal enlightened ruler (not only in the introduction and in the last chapter of the *Gulistān*, but also in the few extant panegyric excerpts dedicated to the Atabeg) establishes indirect analogies between his historical persona and the ideals of kingship represented throughout the *Gulistān*.

70 See General Introduction, pp. 16–17.

as a playful hint at the development of different sets of ethical ideals within the same family.

The virtual equivalence between the passionate judge and Saʿdi's literary persona is established by the emphasis on the depiction of the former as one of the "most learned men of the age," "unique in his time" (*az fużalā-yi ʿaṣr va bīgāna-yi rūzgār*). These epithets resonate with the literary and scholarly excellence that Saʿdi usually boasts when engaging in the unabashed self-praise of his own qualities as a *litteratus*. The depiction of the judge as an ideal lover (just as the king is represented as an ideal monarch) coincides with the ideal of courtly and spiritual eroticism with which Saʿdi represents his own literary persona both in his ghazals and in the amatory portions of the *Gulistān*.

The poem that Saʿdi interjects into the narration as an amatory lamentation uttered by the protagonist of the story ("Is the rooster singing ahead of time tonight?") is a panegyrical ghazal whose composition predates the *Gulistān*, and which was presumably originally composed to offer a lyrical exordium (in the fashion of the amorous *nasīb*s that open the classical Arabo-Persian *qasida*) that would culminate with the praise of the Salghurid Atabeg, Abū Bakr. In this story, Saʿdi presents the ghazal in the form of direct speech, the judge ecstatically reciting it while enjoying the sexual favors of the son of the blacksmith in debauchery and intoxication. This narrative stratagem produces a remarkable shift in the point of view of the lyric text's poetic persona: once the ghazal is introduced into the narrative frame of the *Gulistān*, its poetic persona attains a perfect correspondence with the protagonist of the prose narration. The I/Saʿdi converts into the "I" of the judge, and the poem partially loses its originally encomiastic function along with the historical framework to which it belonged. From an occasional lyric composition that was originally deeply engrained in the historical relationship between the poet and his patron, the ghazal develops into direct speech enunciated within the plot of the narration in the *Gulistān*. The mention of the Atabeg in the ghazal acts as a point of contact that contextualizes the fourth level of the text (the level of "referential possibilities" in my generative model) within both the historical context of the Salghurid court and the fictive world of the story.

It is within the framework of fictive desires and political interactions that we ought to read the final message of the story: the king urges his subjects not to judge the faults committed by others before meditating on one's own mistakes. But what about the protagonist's moral conduct as far as sexual behavior is concerned? Does the judge truly repent by the end of the narration? And what is the exact nature of the crime that both his detractors and the king are ascribing to him? The only time in which the nature of the offense is disclosed is when the king visits the bedroom of the judge to collect the amount of direct proof that is necessary for the delivery of a judiciary verdict: "There he saw a candle standing, a beautiful boy sitting [*shāhid*], wine spilled, goblets broken, and the judge in a stupor of intoxication, oblivious to the world." The remaining traces (the spilled wine and the broken goblets) provide sufficient evidence for the king to accuse the judge of the crime of contravening the Islamic ban on alcohol. But for the consumption of wine, Islamic Shafiʿi jurisprudence, in principle, does not prescribe punishments harsher than pecuniary exaction or flagellation.[71] Why does the king feel compelled to apply the capital punishment in one of the most severe fashions, i.e., by pushing the offender off a lofty building? The only rationale for the application of such a severe punishment could be the accusation of sodomy (*liwāṭ*), for which, in the case of an active offender who has once consummated a legally valid marriage (*muḥsan*), Shafiʿi law prescribed the death penalty (by stoning or throwing the offender off the highest building in the city) as a consequence of a sub-variant of the crime of fornication (*zinā*ʾ).[72]

The traditional approach of Islamic schools of law to sodomy presents slight variations according to the degree of assimilation that each one of them ascribes to the legal relationship between fornication and sodomy. Considering that fornication is a crime whose chastisement is specified by divine revelation, it is a transgression against a right of God (*ḥaqq Allāh*, as opposed to a transgression against society, *ḥaqq ādamī*) that is liable to *ḥadd* punishment. Schools that treat sodomy as a crime not subsumable under fornication (as in the case of the Hanafis, who argued that the punishment for anal intercourse was prescribed by the companions of the Prophet, and not through revelation) recommended less severe forms of retribution.[73]

Although the posture of the different schools on this matter was consistently and sharply defined, the very perception of a degree of fluidity between the category of *liwāṭ* and *zinā*ʾ would often require the judge to operate within a wide range of discretion. It is precisely within this discretional frame of judicial appeal to Islamic law that the king opts for the maximum degree of punishment to be applied to the judge's case. The king likely makes this decision in view of the gravity of the offender's social status—as an Islamic judge who has committed such a heinous crime—but also as a result of his attempts to win the monarch's absolution through rhetorical tricks. Nevertheless, what is

71 On the premodern opinions of the major Islamic legal school on the matter of alcohol consumption, see Haider 2013. On the relationship between rulers and doctors of Islamic law during the Saljuq period, see Opwis 2011.

72 See El-Rouyaheb 2005, 119; Omar 2012, 227–30.

73 Omar 2012, 230–49.

hardly understandable is the king's sudden decision to commute the death sentence into an absolute pardon once the judge wittily points to the evidence that such a sin could have been committed by anyone else—including his detractors, as we infer through the king's final maxim of wisdom. One way to explain such an unexpected narrative turn is to note that what the king has directly witnessed in the judge's bedroom—at least from what can be inferred from the plot of the story—is not the penetrative act itself, but substantial evidence to presume that an act of sodomy has been committed: the presence of a beautiful boy (*shāhid*), nightly intimacy, and intoxication.

According to most Islamic schools, the legal conviction of sodomy had to be based on direct witness of genital contact between the offenders, unless the act of penetration is attested to by voluntary confession of the convicted.[74] Therefore, in the king's eyes, the destiny of the judge is suspended between the lack of the necessary evidence for the crime of sodomy and a voluntary confession that is imbued with rhetorical twists attempting to gain the favor of the monarch, in such a way that the reader cannot but wonder what exactly has happened in the judge's room during the encounter with the young man. The allegorical equivalence between the judge of the tale and Saʿdi implies that the author of the *Gulistān* turns the whole story into a moral judgment against hypocrisy, while the possibility that an act of sodomy has taken place is considered a minor peccadillo that royal mercy can easily overlook.[75]

If we turn our attention back to the ghazal that has offered us a pretext for a close reading of the story of the judge and its underlying implications concerning sexuality, desire, and the role of its literary personae, we can confidently assert that the implicit nature of the passion that it depicts hosts the possibility of alluding to a male-to-male penetrative intercourse which ultimately,

74 On the mitigating factors that Islamic jurists would take into account when administrating *ḥadd* sentences, see El-Rouyaheb 2005, 123.

75 "The cardinal sin involved here is not so much homoerotic desire and sodomy, as the hypocrisy of one who condemns and punishes others as a profession, while himself not practicing what he preaches." Lewis 2009, 708. Lewis rightly highlights that the judge's "power to oppress," combined with the "pretention to moral probity of the would-be holy man," is what truly constitutes the transgression portrayed in the story. However, if this is valid in light of the recurrent topos of the clerics' hypocrisy, in this case I believe that Saʿdi bestows upon the judge an aura of overwhelming benevolence that points to an allusive correspondence between this character and the literary persona of Saʿdi himself. This argument may be corroborated by the gloss that immediately follows this tale, which describes Saʿdi as the perfect *ʿishq-bāz*, who "knows the path and the customs of love / As well as Arabic is known in Baghdad." *Golestān*, 148.

surprisingly enough, is not abhorred by Sa'di's moralizing approach.[76] The use of the term *shāhid* (literally, "witness") to refer to the beautiful boy with whom the judge from Hamadan is infatuated opens the text to metaphysical speculations on which I will extensively elaborate in the course of the next section of this book. For now, it will suffice to point out that Sa'di and his contemporaries would use the word *shāhid* to designate a young man whose comely physical features, for the eyes of the beholder, *attest* to the undepictable and otherwise unimaginable splendor (*jamāl*) of God. Just as the context of the story projects a latency of homoerotic penetration onto the ghazal of the "Lovers" who "wish to further indulge with kisses and embraces," similarly the word *shāhid* awakens the semantic field of spiritual desire in an apparently purely mundane plot. Furthermore, in this story the word *shāhid*, as a technical term that also pertains to the jargon of Islamic jurisprudence, resonates with both the social position of the main character, who is a well-respected Islamic judge, and the juridical evidence (or lack thereof) gathered by the king for the promulgation of legal conviction. The interplay between the two acceptations of this lexeme is ironically displayed in one of Sa'di's most celebrated quatrains:

> Whoever turns his gaze to everyone
> a wretch he is in the eyes of the Lords of Gazes.
>
> Two witnesses [*shāhid*] sharia prescribes for the judge's fatwa:
> But in the religion of love one witness (of God's beauty) [*shāhid*] is enough.[77]

In the second distich the poet plays with the double meaning of *shāhid*[78] to show the contrast between the legal rules of Islam and the religious school (*maẕhab*) of love, for which only one beautiful object of mundane contemplation is required to satisfy the passionate aspirations of the beholder. Although it is too early in our discussion to dive into the underlying mystical semantics of the whole quatrain, for now the full semantic richness of *shāhid* can be narrowed down to its mundane connotation: a beautiful young man on the verge

76 I say "possibility" because the penetrative act is not explicitly referred to in the text of the ghazal, but it subsists as a latent image provided by the context in which the ghazal is interposed in the plot of the story of the judge as a poetic rendition of an amorous encounter that could *potentially* imply an act of sodomy.

77 [1.60] Sa'di KhE, 615.

78 This kind of pun is commonly defined as *jinās-i tāmm*—of which Sa'di is the ultimate master—that occurs when a word is mentioned twice with a semantic shift in the second occurrence of the term.

of adulthood, which is also the same acceptation it has in the context of the passage from the *Gulistān*. In the quatrain, the allusion to the two witnesses that the judge needs for his religious verdict (*fatwā*) refers to convictions that do not require the application of *ḥadd* punishment. If considered as a *zinā'* (fornication) offense that prescribes four witnesses (expect for the Hanafi school), sodomy is automatically excluded from the gamut of possible infractions. Therefore, the erotic nuances of the poetic excerpt could circumscribe the nature of the judgment (for which two witnesses are needed) to sexual transgressions of a lesser degree of gravity, such as kissing, caressing, or intercrural intercourse.[79] The triangulation between lustful physical desire and the twofold meaning of *shāhid* is also found in a ghazal in which Sa'di elaborates on the difference between passionate love and promiscuous concupiscence:

> Do not seclude yourself in the city of your flesh's lust:
> For urban dogs do not hunt but bones.
>
> Sleeping every night with a different beautiful boy [*shāhid*]
> Will turn the morning of sobriety into a hangover.
>
> We need the judge of the city of the lovers
> Who satisfies himself with only one witness [*shāhid*].
>
> Sa'di's secret is the palace of the Sultan
> Barely anyone can access that threshold.
>
> *Ṭayyibāt* 93[80]

Even though the general content of this poem, along with the secondary meaning of its keywords, is brimful with appetite for the unseen, its close bonds with the nature of sensuality bring us back to the context of the story from the *Gulistān* and the judgment pending on the destiny of the lustful dimension of the experience of passionate love. By comparing the ghazal quoted above with the implied moral indulgence that filters from Sa'di's story of the judge, we notice with surprise that the author, in the larger framework of his literary corpus, is capable of adopting opposing approaches when it comes to applying his judgment to the legitimacy of homoerotic acts.

In the story of the judge, the possibility for sodomy to occur is condoned by both the necessity of abstaining from judging the faults of others and a general

79 El-Rouayheb 2005, 137.

80 [1.61] Sa'di YE, 93.

discourse on love in which a higher spiritual appetite allows the lover to engage in illicit sexual acts. In the ghazal quoted above, what is considered "lustful" is not sexual appetite per se, but the physical inclination towards a multiplicity of objects of desire—i.e., "sleeping every night with a different *shāhid*." In the general framework of the experience of sexuality as reflected in Saʿdi's texts, it is the lack of a specific, exclusive, and open-to-the-spiritual object of desire that traces a sharp difference between love and lustful debauchery. This difference emerges more vigorously when we compare texts that depict actions that are essentially similar, but whose intentions and contexts diverge sensibly. In the story of the judge, the intervention of the king sets the boundaries of the legal flexibility that surrounds the possibilities of meaning in Saʿdi's ghazal poetry vis-à-vis the pure physical enjoyment of the object of desire.

Even though the spiritual subtext of metaphysical aesthetics (what the sources refer to as *ʿirfān*, and which we may for now reductively translate as "mysticism") emerges from the stories of the *Gulistān* only occasionally (as in the tale of the prince and the dervish), the judge from Hamadan's devotion to sensuality reads as an antinomic celebration of the lien between desire and the metaphysical quest of the Sufi tradition. Considering the hometown of the judge of the story, it is tempting to consider the theophanic thinker ʿAyn al-Qużāt Hamadānī (d. 1131) as one of the sources of inspiration for the development of this character. As I shall discuss in the seventh chapter, the role of human beauty as an attestation (*shāhid*) to the divine splendor characterizes the very core of ʿAyn al-Qużāt's meditation on the aesthetics of spiritual desire. This correspondence between the character and the historical "mystic"/judge is particularly significant if we consider that the majority of the chief justices appointed by Abū Bakr during his reign were legal experts who were invested in bridging the gap between Islamic law and the spiritual path of the Sufi orders. Saʿdi kept referring to this peculiar tradition well beyond the demise of Abū Bakr—at least until 1279, when he praised the newly-appointed chief justice (*qāżī al-qużāt*) Rukn al-Dīn abū Yaḥyā by once more lyrically hinting at the correlation between human beauty and the spiritual mastery of one's sensual desire:

> Do not blame the wise man who falls into the trap of desire:
> When love appears in a form, how could wisdom survive? ...
>
> Those who desire the beautiful faces do not recede before the slanderers.
> If such is your desire, come forth and do not mind their disdain....

An idol is your face: if a beauty like you were to walk in every street
I would expect no one to resist their sensual desires, except the Judge….

Rukn al-Dīn, the ornament of the gathering of the Sufis, leads us on the Islamic path:
May the strength of his judgment bring religion back to the epoch of Muḥammad!

Badāyiʿ 382[81]

6 Articulating the Ghazal: Lyric Reality and Confessional Fiction

Some critics have noticed the palpability of the lyric experience in Saʿdi's poetry, as if it were the result of a successful transcription of the texture of the external world.[82] Yet, the world that Saʿdi portrays in his lyrical vignettes does not render the likeness of the external world, as his lines seldom report historically determined locales and events. The sensoriality of his depictions belongs to an effect of real presence that is conveyed by the portrayal of how the lyric subject *perceives* the world through its eyes rather than what it actually *sees*. We may refer to this effect as an aesthetic transfiguration of abstracted physicality. The touch of this inward transfiguration of the external world emerges in those passages in which the poetic rhythm and the prose narrative seem to open the floor to confessions relating to the sensorial expression of the experience of desire. As explored thus far, the *Gulistān* hosts a plurality of fictional narratives in which the courtly and the erotic aspects of desire oscillate between the metaphorical transfiguration of the poet's relationship with his patrons and scattered traces of biographical or pseudo-biographical veracity. Moreover, the book is replete with seemingly confessional passages in which Saʿdi alludes to the sinful bents of both his juvenile past and the fragile nature of the human soul. Such excerpts frame the problem of the experience of desire vis-à-vis the moral and religious ideals surrounding the carnal and metaphysical dimensions of sensuality.

In a short pseudo-autobiographical passage of the second chapter of the *Gulistān* ("On the conduct of the mystics," story number twenty-three), Saʿdi presents himself as an individual who indirectly confesses his allegedly sinful conduct. In the tale, Saʿdi opens his confession by sharing with a Sufi master

81 [1.62] Saʿdi YE, 178.
82 Hamdiyan 1383/2004, 177.

(*yakī az mashāyikh*) that so-and-so has borne witness to his "moral corruption" (*fasād*). In response, the spiritual master urges Saʿdi to cast shame on the slanderer by embracing righteous moral conduct.[83] It is noteworthy that in the *Gulistān* Saʿdi seldom portrays the Sufis in a negative light.[84] On the contrary, one of the explicit purposes of the book is to attract the benevolent attention of the ruling elite towards the poor and the dervishes who embrace the ethics and practices of Sufism as a form of a spiritual and social training of the self. Although the topic of the condemnation of the "false Sufis" and their hypocrisy appears at the very beginning of the Persian spiritual lyric tradition, it seems to have circulated much more frequently in the 14th century than in Saʿdi's time.[85] Therefore, since Saʿdi's indirect critique does not seem to be echoing a literary topos, the confession of his own "corruption" is at odds with the poet's overall favorable portrayal of the Sufis. Even though Saʿdi does not clearly disclose the nature of his corruption, the infratextual and intertextual context of the story suggests that the poet referred to a vice that pertains to the sphere of sexuality. Independently from the moralizing purpose of the confession within the plot of the story, Saʿdi's statement about a sin from which he indirectly repents acts as a normalizing factor for the sin itself. Through this rhetorical stratagem, he represents moral corruption as a natural condition which individuals may repel through actions that reflect their good faith.

The confessional moments scattered throughout Saʿdi's narratives can help us consider the anthropological breadth of the poet's lyricism as a tenuous frontier stretching between the contradictions of the relationship between universal understandings of the world and the particular experiences hiding in the depths of the author's personal life. However, the *Gulistān*'s peculiar mixture of fictive narrations and biographical accuracy has often prompted perplexity, especially if we consider how vividly some of the anecdotes are retold and how much emphasis the author put on the relevance of the specific political horizon in which Saʿdi offered his book to his patrons, the Salghurid rulers of Shiraz, and in particular prince Saʿd II. Most of his learned contemporaries, and especially his patrons, might have often overlooked such blatant discrepancies with historical plausibility. His young patrons, in particular, possibly took at face value the fictional tendency of the narrations that such a respected learned man was offering them. We can even note a certain intentional abuse of the reader's credulity, crafted not through the transmission

83 *Golestān*, 96.

84 One of the few instances of Saʿdi's negative portrayal of a Sufi character is found in the seventeenth story of the first chapter of the *Gulistān* (72–73).

85 Hamidiyān 1383/2004, 111–12; Brookshaw 2019, 10–11.

of verifiable historical accounts, but mainly via the persistent use of a style that dissimulates direct experience. Saʿdi often questions the veracity of his own narrations by warning his audience about the relative nature of truth, especially in the face of what he refers to as "beneficial falsehood."[86] Only a few decades after his death, his Machiavellian definition of "true" as whatever the king determines as such by the force of his power of coercion became the object of parodic commentaries.[87] "Whoever has travelled in the world tells many lies," Saʿdi declares in the conclusion of one of the stories from the first chapter of the *Gulistān* (81). Considering Saʿdi's keen interest in presenting himself as a consummate traveler throughout the *Gulistān* (as well as in the *Būstān*),[88] statements of this kind reveal that the book's peculiar intertwinement of reality and fiction reflects a literary project that transcends the boundaries between creative imagination and the exploration of the visible world.

As suggested so far through Hamburger's approach to the intrinsic linguistic logic of lyric poetry, one solution to explain the coexistence of imaginary narratives and credible autobiographical accounts in the texture of the *Gulistān* lies in the recognition of the difference between the "lyric I" and the "empirical author" in Saʿdi's approach to the narration of his biographical self. In the context of medieval romance literature this distinction was initially formulated by the Austrian philologist Leo Spitzer as a theoretical tool capable of explaining the function of Dante Alighieri's insertion of autobiographical materials into the system of narrative balances of the Divine Comedy.[89] Spitzer describes how Dante, in the *Commedia*, represents his own persona in a fashion that is both abstracted (the "lyric I") and autobiographical (the "empiric I"). Spitzer considers the duality of this representation a necessary strategy for the author to realize a portrayal of a "composite I" capable of transcending the limitations of individuality. The final goal of this deconstruction of the boundaries of autobiographical individuality is to eventually portray a universal experience filtered through the point of view of the author who represents himself in his work.[90] Spitzer argues that "Dante is not interested, poetically, in himself *qua* himself [...] but *qua* an example of the generally human capacity for cognizing the supramundane—which can be cognized only by what is most personal

86 *"Durūghī maṣlaḥat-āmīz bih az rāstī-yi fitna-angīz." Golestān*, 58.

87 ʿObāyd Zākāni 1999, 254.

88 *Bustān*, 37.

89 Spitzer 1946.

90 "For the story that Dante had to tell, both aspects of his composite 'I' were necessary: on the one hand, he must transcend the limitations of individuality in order to gain an experience of universal experience; on the other, an individual eye is necessary to perceive and to fix the matter of experience." Ibid., 416.

in man."[91] If we discard the metaphysical framework that Spitzer envisages for Dante's attempt to represent the universal experience of the unseen in the personification of the individual, this very confluence between individual experience and the representation of the universal can perfectly apply to the apparently idiosyncratic inconsistency of Sa'di's juxtaposition of not only biographical truth and forgery, but also of linguistic verisimilitude and rhetorical fiction.

If traces of metaphysical effort are to be found in Sa'di's *Gulistān*, they belong to the imaginative compromise that has to take place between the physical possibilities of the body of the individual and the intangible body of socio-political, ethical, and spiritual constraints. Thus the simultaneously biographic and universal "I" of the *Gulistān*, though structurally similar to the poetic persona of the *Commedia*, can be compared to the moral realism that characterizes the *Canterbury Tales*. As Donaldson points out, Chaucer's use of the literary persona functions as a device that presents a vision of the social world imposed on the moral world.[92] The pilgrimage that Sa'di undertakes in the *Gulistān* (along his Persian "Canterbury way") is a quest for wisdom that is non-linear in both its geographical and chronological dimensions. Its purpose is to track down the points of contact between the ethical Weltanschauung of his time—in matters as diverse as justice, kingship, morals, and etiquette—and the dazzlingly attractive and multidimensional aspects of the material world, along with the intellectual and physical experiences that one can derive from it.

Sa'di's literary journey does not ask us to believe in the historical accuracy of his travels, as it is the author himself who constantly demystifies his own autobiographical narrations. Through this technique, Sa'di's ultimate goal is to show to the reader that the real voyage that he has undertaken is set in the exquisitely anthropological complexity of the human theater, at whose ends stand the groups that he praises, rebukes, and warns the most: the kings and the poor, who are protagonists of the two first chapters of the *Gulistān*, and the diatribe between the dejected and the aristocrats that the poet stages at the end of the book.[93] For this reason, in the *Gulistān*, desire, sexuality, and love are best understood if we avoid the myopia deriving from the reification of a fixed moral perspective embodied in a flat authorial (and ethically authoritative) subjectivity. Instead, we may follow the iridescence of a plurality of personae in which the author submerges himself to offer a variegated portrait

---

91 Ibid., 417.

92 Donaldson 1954.

93 *Golestān*, 162–68.

of the encounter between morals and real life experiences. The *real*, historical Saʿdi will never be found in this kaleidoscope of subjectivities: as Culler points out when commenting on Hamburger's position, the relationship between the empirical author and the poetic self is incommensurable. What we can retrieve of Saʿdi as the real author behind his writings are the literary traces of physicality deriving from his involvement in the real world, which tend to coincide with the subjective enunciation that generates such a vehement sensation of real presence in his ghazals, notwithstanding the hypertrophic artificiality of the forms and images upon which he draws.

7 Accessing the Body of the Lyric

All the narrations we have perused thus far belong to the fifth chapter of the *Gulistān*, "On Love and Youth," which is arguably the most thought-provoking and aesthetically appealing section of the entire book. "On Love and Youth," strategically positioned in the middle of the *Gulistān*, is the virtual venue in which all the images, mores, and representations of human society—with its hierarchies of power and rules, along with the values that Saʿdi promotes—intersect and conflate to give birth to a dynamic representation of the possibilities of love and desire as overarching anthropological axes. The subjectivity that emerges from the characters of the vignettes of the fifth chapter of the *Gulistān* corresponds to the multilayered and conflicting identity of the lyric subject that animates Saʿdi's ghazals, and it acts in paradigmatic opposition to the stern incorruptibility of the Sufis represented in the second chapter of the book. Saʿdi's portrayal of religious devotion through the lens of his lyric persona is almost never severed from the carnal experience that constitutes the author's peculiar anthropology of passion. The lyric fictionality of his pseudo-historical persona seems to convert the courtly ideals of the metaphorical vignettes portraying his relationship with his Salghurid patrons into the very core of the spiritual psychology of the eroticism exuding from his ghazals.

In the third story of the chapter, Saʿdi remembers his encounter with a pious man (*parsā-yī*) who had fallen deeply in love with an unattainable boy.[94] "What has happened to your keen mind," Saʿdi chides him, "that you let your carnal desires [*nafs*] overtake you?" The response of the pious man, formulated

94 As noted by both Southgate (1984) and Zipoli (1997, 28), any time that Saʿdi mentions genderless objects of passionate desire (regardless of the genre to which the passages belong, be they in the *Gulistān*, the *Būstān*, his lyric poems, or obscene verses), it can be conjectured that the recipient of the lyric subject's inclinations is a male beauty.

as a maxim in verse, appeals to the undefeatable power of the "sultan of love," which will ineluctably defeat the "army of chastity." "How can a miserable man live respectably," he rhetorically asks, "when he has fallen up to his neck in the mud?" The brief account seems to leave Saʿdi speechless when facing the argument so lyrically conveyed by the virtuous man who has fallen into the trap of passionate love. The physical dimension of this ardent desire is underlined by both the character himself (through the image of the mud entrapping his neck) and the author, who associates this passion with *nafs*—carnal desire, or what the Avicennian psychological tradition refers to as the "animal soul."[95] Saʿdi does not seem to personally judge the explanation of the infatuated devout man, as he acquiesces and turns his response into a general rule that overturns the religious imposition of not mixing piety with sensuality. The murky viscosity of the experience of passion finds its allegorical analogue in Saʿdi's utilization of the image of mud—not as a momentary impasse, but as a constitutive soiling that envelops the body of the lover, despite his piety. I stress the inherent nature of this representation of passion as a muddy substance because it constitutes one of the main tenets of Saʿdi's anthropological vision, which is sustained by Islamic ontogenesis and embryology, and occupies an absolute centrality in the poet's physiology of passions:

> My love of you permeated my heart before my water and clay were created:
> I originated from it; it was not me who molded it.
> *Ṭayyibāt* 274[96]

Saʿdi's emphasis on the human body as a base matter that is infused with the experience of desire can be framed through the phylogenetic paradox of the Qurʾān, in which the clay that constitutes Adam's body is despised by Satan, who—as an angel, being a creature of light and fire—considers himself superior to humankind and refuses to bow before God's new creation.[97] But the love that emerges from Saʿdi's illustrations is not as pure as one might be inclined to think when meditating on its spiritual origin: just like the clay described in

95 See how, in the second part of this book (in particular chapters 5 and 6), I frame Saʿdi's representation of the contemplation of beauty within the Avicennian psychological tradition.

96 [1.63] Saʿdi YE, 126. Note the syntactical pun, through which the *-am* at the end of the past tense *āvardam* can be read both as a personal ending ("I brought it with me") or as a pronominal suffix as a marker of the accusative attached to the verb (*bā khʷad āvard-am*, "it brought me with it").

97 See *EIr*, s.v. "Eblīs" [H. Algar].

the introduction to the *Gulistān*, this love revivifies the opaque matter without transmuting it. The dark dimension of flesh coexists—albeit not without dramatic consequences—with the indescribable scent of roses that motivates the quest of the body for other bodies.

In the following pseudo-autobiographical story, Saʿdi resorts to the first person to ingrain the lyric subject's proclivity for sensuality into the allegory of fluids that highlight the luminous aspect of what in the previous vignette was depicted as sullying mud:

> During the days of my youth, I remember that I passed through a lane once at midsummer and spied a face. The heat was drying out my mouth and the hot wind could cause the marrow in one's bones to boil. Because of human weakness [*żaʿf-i bashariyat*] I was unable to endure the heat of the sun and sought refuge in the shade of a wall. I was hoping for someone to bring me cold water to cool down from the heat of the midsummer, when suddenly a light shone from the darkness of the vestibule of a house: a beauty that the tongue of eloquence would be incapable to describe appeared like dawn rising amidst the dark night, or like the water of life sprouting from the heart of darkness. In his hand he held a goblet of ice water into which he had poured sugar and mixed it with fragrant liqueur. I do not know whether it was perfumed with rose water or whether several drops from the rose of his face had fallen into it. In short, I took the drink from his lovely hands, drank it, and felt rejuvenated.
>
> *A thirst in my heart that can scarcely be quenched*
> *By a gush of limpid water, though I were to drink oceans of it.*
>
> Lucky that felicitous ascendant star
> Whose eye falls upon such a face every dawn.
>
> One drunk on wine awakes at midnight
> One drunk on the cup-bearer awakes at the dawn of resurrection day.[98]

One might be tempted to read this story as the literary transmutation of a biographical event *sincerely* retold by Saʿdi as a particularly cheerful remembrance of his youth. However, the flatness of its narrative denouement and the lack of geographical and historical clues capable of setting the story within the framework of a realistic context should make us think of the

98 *Golestān*, 141.

succession of images—presented as a series of frames without an articulated concatenation—that are typical of the line-by-line visual syntax of ghazal poetry. The story reads as a ghazal in prose, or rather one single verse in prose whose image is analyzed through close-ups on details that would not usually be disclosed in a lyric poem: the dryness of the mouth, the bones on fire, or the shade of a wall in the alley of the beloved. The text in prose lacks a proper denouement, and in its final gloss in verse Saʿdi recurs to a line extracted from one of his Arabic *qasida*s to express that it is *not* fresh water that he needs to quench his *thirst*. These two elements permit us to read the story as an allegory—almost presented in the form of a diurnal reverie—of an encounter leading to sexual intercourse. It is precisely this gap that turns the images of the prose excerpt into a poetic accumulation of lustful desires whose climax cannot take place but in the final line in Arabic: "a thirst in my heart that can scarcely be quenched."

The validity of the sexual allegory, along the lines of the correspondence between actual thirst and sexual desire, is reinforced by the curious statement about the weakness of the human condition: *żaʿf-i bashariyat*, which Saʿdi employs as a reference to the fatigue to which the human body is subjected under severe weather conditions. Nevertheless, on an allegorical level, *żaʿf* can also metaphorically denote the natural origins of desire as a weakness of the flesh that affects all human beings. It can also be argued that the image of the sweat dripping from the beautiful boy's face into Saʿdi's cup—"I don't know whether it was perfumed with rose water," Saʿdi hastens to specify—could conjure in the mind of the reader a virtual reference to the exchange of other bodily fluids that constitute one of the physical dimensions of an amorous embrace. This point deserves particular attention, especially in consideration of the direct or indirect allusions to sperm, blood, and saliva as viscous fluids that make up the simultaneously cursed and blessed clay of humankind, to which Saʿdi recurrently refers in the courtly, mystical, and obscene dimensions of his literary output.

8 Flirting in the Friday Mosque of Kashgar: Grammar and Rhetoric as Geographical Forms of Seduction

In this chapter we have explored how the *Gulistān* constitutes a fertile terrain for us to follow the malleable nature of Saʿdi's lyric persona as it floats amidst biographical and fictional representations of the poetic self in a framework that incorporates the complementary rhythm of images of the poet's ghazals. We have seen how such fluctuations between historicity and poetic creativity reflect the complexity of sensual desire as a field where the pull and urges of different ethical orders call into question the boundaries between religious piety and the contemplation of ravishing human beauty. At the intersection of the pseudo-biographical exploration of desire and the emergence of a lyric voice that meditates on the relationship between spirituality and carnality, we have framed sexuality as a dimension that lingers behind all of Saʿdi's courtly representations of the subject's appreciation of human beauty.

The problem of the relationship between chaste contemplation of beauty and the sexual drive that enflames the lyric subject can be better understood through the analysis of a story from the fifth chapter of the *Gulistān* that modern scholars have often avoided taking seriously due to its overt homoerotic content. This allegedly autobiographical account epitomizes Saʿdi's construction of his lyric subjectivity as a development of a sexual awareness around the aesthetic values that reinforce the playfully contemplative dimension of the courtly discourse on love. Saʿdi introduces the account by presenting himself in the Central Asian city of Kashgar, "in the year of Muḥammad Khʷārazmshāh's convenient peace [*ṣulḥ-i maṣlaḥatī*] with Cathay"—an event that took place in 1210, and which caused premodern Islamic historians to hail sultan Muḥammad as "the second Alexander," "sultan Sanjar," and "God's shadow on earth."[99] Scholars have speculated that both the chronological and the geographical trajectory of Saʿdi's travel to Central Asia are highly implausible.[100] This lack of historiographical sincerity should be regarded as what we have called the lyric space of potential veracity, in which the "poetic I" expresses its personal experience as a linguistic possibility rather than through the accurate transcription of biographical events. Saʿdi frames this amatory experience in the congregational mosque of Kashgar, where he allegedly sets his eyes on a student of Arabic grammar[101] of extreme beauty and balanced proportion, and exceeding charm. A beauty about whom one could say:

---

99 For a chronology of the confrontation between Muḥammad Khʷārazmshāh and Tayangu, the Qara Khitan commander of Talas, see Biran 2005, 77–78.

100 Zarrinkub, 1386/2007, 62–64; Dehqāni, 1394/2014

101 Some editions have made use of unreliable (and rather recent) manuscripts to describe the boy of the story as a *naḥvī*, a "grammarian." It is however evident (and also fairly well attested to by the oldest manuscripts of the *Gulistān*) that the student, who barely understands Saʿdi's puns in Arabic, is a teenager and not an adult "grammarian." See Fatemeh Keshavarz's different opinion on this matter, which seems to be an attempt to normalize the form of intergenerational desire that characterizes Saʿdi's homoeroticism: "Here I insist on keeping the adjective 'grammarian' for the man of Saʿdi's desire to highlight the fact that we are dealing with a grown and educated person, not a young beardless boy." Keshavarz 2015, 163, n. 9

Your teacher taught you *sprezzatura* and seduction;
He taught you malice and disdain, arrogance and cruelty.

Whoever learned how to reside in the alley where you live
Neither remembers his homeland, nor desires to travel.

I have never seen a human being with such a countenance, manners,
And frame. Perhaps he learned such fashion from the angels?"[102]

The student is reciting lines from a famed compendium of Arabic grammar when Sa'di intervenes to playfully compare those sentences with events then taking place in Central Asia. The boy laughs and asks Sa'di what his birthplace is. The boy, following Sa'di's response ("the soil of Shiraz") and without recognizing his identity, inquires as to whether he has brought with him any of the poems of Sa'di of Shiraz. In response, Sa'di goes back to their first grammatical interaction in Arabic and converts its content into a flirtatious comparison hinting at his admiration for the student's beauty:

With the arrogance of the genitive he does not lift the head of the nominative:
Can one show so much grammatical affection, and yet treat me like a direct object?[103]

The boy replies that most of Sa'di's poetry circulating in Kashgar is in Persian, and pleas with Sa'di to quote lines in this language in order for him to better understand. Sa'di improvises lines (which do not appear in any of his collections) that reinforce the amatory interplay between romantic disaffection and the study of grammar. The next day, when Sa'di is about to leave the city, the boy is informed of the poet's identity and rushes towards him: "during all this time, why haven't you told me that *you are* Sa'di? I would have offered my homage and the services that one ought to devote to the nobles!" Sa'di responds with a line that reads as a slight adaptation from the opening of one of his most famous ghazals:

How could my voice declare that *I am* when you stand before me?

102 *Golestān*, 141–43.
103 *Golestān*, 142.

The boy naively urges Sa'di to rest longer in that region so that he may benefit from his service. At this point, Sa'di politely declines the boy's invitation by quoting lines intended to explain the moral rationale for the poet's decision to leave Kashgar and not succumb to the temptation of the flesh:

> I saw once a great man in the mountains
> Who lived in a cave after having renounced the world.
> "Why don't you come into town,"—I asked—
> "So that you may find relief from your burden?"
> "Too many are the beautiful boys over there,"—he said—
> "When mud covers the ground, even the elephant risks to slip."
>
> Eventually, they "kissed each other on the forehead and cheeks, and bade each other farewell." Sa'di brings the story to closure with the following lines:
>
> What joy can one derive from kissing the cheek of the beloved
> At the very moment of bidding him farewell?
>
> Look at the pale and the red cheeks of the apple:
> Thus is its color as it abandons the orchard.
>
> *If I do not die of grief on the day of farewell*
> *do not count me as honest in my affection.*[104]

The farewell between Sa'di and the young student is the threshold where all the potential eroticism is reinforced by the implicit necessity of not allowing their mutual attraction to cross the boundaries of physicality. And yet the bodies of the two characters are exposed in the disarming simplicity of their chaste and rueful kiss. The accumulation of this potential eroticism, bound by the mysterious knots of a moral code that the rules of courtly love prevent from breaking, constitutes the primary source of passion in Sa'di's ghazals: a space of carnal longing constantly seeking a meaningfulness beyond the possibility of an immediate fulfillment of desire. It is in the oscillation between such physical compulsions and the opportunity for transcending the unfulfilling frustrations of the flesh that the originality of Sa'di's lyric genius can be discerned.

104 Ibid.

The fact that Sa'di's presence in Kashghar in 1210 is not historically plausible does not prevent the style adopted by the author from conferring an aura of verisimilitude to the story. Multiple narrative strategies contribute to the formation of a fictive architecture that reads as if it were based on real events: the mention of a precise historical occasion ("the year when Muḥammad Khʷārazmshāh ..."); the focus on a specific compendium of the Arabic grammar that could have been used by virtually any Muslim student (Zamakhsharī's *al-Unmūẕaj*); the playful reference to an actual grammatical exercise, along with the complexity of the flirtatious dialogue between the author and the student taking place over the course of two days; and the allusion to the city of Shiraz and a preference for Persian over Arabic in a conversation happening in Central Asia. It goes without saying that, aesthetic reasons aside, Sa'di's main purpose in crafting a story with such a high degree of mimetic plausibility was the opportunity to offer his audience the impression that his poetry would circulate (and be appreciated by schoolboys) even in the north-easternmost fringes of the Persian-speaking world—Kashgar, which is as distant from Shiraz as Tehran is from Istanbul.

As one of the editors of the Brill Studies in Middle Eastern Literatures book series kindly suggested in a private communication, Sa'di's choice of setting this story in Kashgar might have been informed by the literary motif of the renown that this city gained as the abode of beautiful youths. Although this argument might hold true when considering the circulation of this motif in the Ghaznavid and early Saljuq panegyric tradition (especially in connection with poetic reminiscences of the vestiges of Buddhist visual artifacts),[105] late Saljuq and Ilkhanid poets seldom mention Kashgar and, to my knowledge, references to this city are virtually absent in Sa'di's *dīvāns* and those of his contemporaries. This may suggest that, if we follow the fourfold scheme of the relationship between lyric fiction and external reality that I have sketched earlier in this chapter, in the fictitious world of the encounter between Sa'di and the young student, the word Kashgar does not belong to the level of "negotiated specifications" (third level) that make up the imagery of the lyric tradition to which Sa'di's poetry belongs. On the contrary, Sa'di's non-conventional mention of this city relates to what I have called the "referential possibility" of the literary text (fourth level), which, like in the case of the famous "Shirazi Turk"

105 "Like the gardens surrounding Buddhist temples [*bāgh-i Bahār*], your gathering / is full of beautiful youths, resembling elegant pheasants and wild partridges. // Your ears listen to music and your lips seek wine / whereas your eyes admire the cheeks of the idols from Kashgar [*rukhsār-i but-i Kāshgharī*]." Farrokhi 1380/2001, 400. "[These beautiful Turks] come from China, Cathay, Khotan, and Kashgar; / they come from Tibet, Yaghmā, Kharkhīz and Tatār." Sanā'i 1362/1983, 768.

in one of Hafez's ghazals, generates a connection between fictional depictions and extra-textual, historical reality.[106]

As with the stories from the fifth chapter of the *Gulistān* already scrutinized, the porous borders between rhetorical stratagems capable of creating an effect of realism and the construction of fictional representations reveal the complexity of the circuits of desire at play in Saʿdi's ghazals. The juxtaposition of lyric insertion and prose generates a minimalistic approach to the representation of desire in which the poet's scanty allusions to the possibility of physical encounters bleed into the territory of contemplative imagination. In the story of his sojourn in Kashgar, Saʿdi quotes three couplets ("Your teacher taught you *sprezzatura* and seduction …") from one of his own ghazals as a means to describe the beautiful student of Arabic grammar with whom he is about to engage in courtly exchanges. The lines are introduced as if they were composed by a poet other than Saʿdi, and they purportedly describe the "likes of" the Kashgari student. This quotation creates an intertextual echo between the narration offered in the *Gulistān* and the horizon of signification of the ghazal itself. Since most manuscripts include this poem in the *Badāyiʿ* (or *The Marvels*, Saʿdi's second divan, presumably compiled after 1258), it was probably composed only a few years before the final recension of the *Gulistān*, and circulated among the learned elites of Shiraz.

I have often stressed how the beloved of the premodern ghazal (the poetic "thou") is a literary function that does not necessarily correspond to a real human being chosen by the poet as an object of desire.[107] Saʿdi emphasizes this impersonal dimension by first referring to a plurality of charming youths ("about the likes of whom"), and then by de-authorizing himself from the composition of the lines: "it is said," "they have said." By creating an aura of impersonality for both the lyric "I" of the lines and the celebrated object of desire, Saʿdi produces a narrative leap between the fictitiousness of the lyric and the perceived effect of reality of the prose narration describing the encounter with the beautiful student. This literary *trompe l'oeil* enhances the vividness of the ensuing dialogue and, by retroactive juxtaposition, it creates for the reader of Saʿdi's poems a tangible context to conjure up the physical nature of the abstracted beloved by means of the imagination:

> Your teacher taught you *sprezzatura* and seduction;
> He taught you malice and disdain, arrogance and cruelty.

106 For an in-depth exposition of this theory, see Ingenito 2018b, 857–60.

107 See Ingenito 2018a, 857–60; 2018b, 193–94.

I am enslaved to those jesting lips and seditious eyes
that taught spells and sorcery to Żaḥḥāk and Sāmirī….

Where did your teacher learn all this amorous seduction?
Maybe he was instructed elsewhere, and learned the arts of magic? …

You are such an idol, why should you need a teacher?
The Chinese idol-maker learned idolatry from the twists [*chīn*] of
your curls.

Thousands are the singing nightingales who are madly in love.
From you they should learn how to speak regal Persian [*darī*]!

The calamity of loving you uprooted the foundations of piety and
religious devotion
In such a way that the Sufis learned how to practice the path of
debauchery.

Whoever learned how to reside in the alley where you live,
Neither remembers his homeland, nor desires to travel.

I had never seen a human being with such a countenance, manners,
and frame. He learned perhaps such fashion from the angels? …

All my clan, my people, were religious scholars,
yet falling in love with you taught me how to become a poet.

So much I will weep from now on that
One can learn to swim from the rivulets of Saʿdi's tears.
Badāyiʿ 238[108]

The creation of a set of reverberations between the verses within the prose of the *Gulistān* and the independent ghazal from which the verses are quoted magnifies the author's rhetorical scope, and provides the reader with a microcosm of longing and desire in which the interplay between the two texts produces a quasi-realistic effect. Here, the effect of simulated reality—which, according to Roland Barthes, characterizes modern realism through the presence of

108 [1.64] Saʿdi YE, 524; Ms. Tehran 1321, 219; Ms. Yale 1432, f. 305b.

the description of details filling up the interstices of a plain narration—[109] is obtained through the echoes of imagery overlapping between the two texts. The connection with the ghazal creates a lateral text that expands the psychological depth of the apparently linear narration. Once we familiarize ourselves with the verses of the ghazal, their imagery intervenes to create an unspoken voice that marks the difference between what Saʿdi, as an author/character, is actually saying and what he *could* have said, simultaneously thought, or meditated after the farewell. "On the following day," the initiative taken by the beloved/student to run after Saʿdi and ask him why he had not revealed his identity the day before marks the transition from the pure passivity of the beloved as an object of amorous contemplation to a response that creates a new space of erotic possibilities. In the reversibility of the nature of seduction, the young man now initiates a movement that turns himself from an object of desire into a desiring character.[110] Saʿdi's response is extraordinarily revealing, as the utterance "with you standing before me, no voice is left in me to say 'I am'" is the second hemistich of the first line of another of his ghazals. In this case too, since most manuscripts record the text in the *Badāyiʿ* (and, in a couple of instances, in the *Ṭayyibāt*), the ghazal was probably composed before the completion of the last recension of the *Gulistān*, and was already available to Saʿdi's readers at the Salghurid court:

> As long as I am aware of him, I won't be aware of myself:
> **How could my voice declare that *I am* when he stands before me?**
>
> I am tearing my clothes—breath after breath—for my exceeding passion;
> as my presence became him, and I am nothing but this shirt.
>
> O rival, do not be in pain with your belligerence:
> I would rather pull out my eyes than take my eyes away from him....
>
> No gatherings are left in the whole city for which
> my love for him has not made me their legend....

---

109 Barthes 1989.

110 Baudrillard writes (1990, 81–82): "Seduction is immediately reversible, and its reversibility is constituted by the challenge it implies and the secret in which it is absorbed. It is a power of attraction and distraction, of absorption and fascination, a power that causes the collapse of not just sex, but the real in general—a power of defiance."

This burning pain will follow me—this hopeless one!—till the grave:
If you dig into the ground you will find my burned shroud....

As soon as your sweet mouth started speaking
I feared that I would cast bitter seditions throughout the world.

Saʿdi's lips and your lips ... how could they ever ...?
With only this I am satisfied: the mention of your lips brushing my lips.
Badāyiʿ 445[111]

Once his identity is revealed, Saʿdi playfully explains the reticence of the anterior day by reciting a line from one of his Persian ghazals, for which the young student had previously shown so much eagerness. The interplay between the prose text and the ghazal allows Saʿdi to produce an ironic effect centered on the impersonality of a lyric "I" that confesses the inexistence of its identity ("I have no voice to say 'I am,'" which can also be read as "I have no voice to say that this is me") precisely in the moment in which his name emerges before the ravished student/beloved.

With the fusion of the prosaic and the lyrical, the tender irony of this comedic effect is counterbalanced by the dramatic mood of the passion that the poetic persona of the ghazal declares: "I am tearing my clothes breath after breath, for my exceeding passion / as my presence became him, and I am nothing but this shirt." In a typical Saʿdian twist of imagery, the body of the lover brushes up against nothingness in order to show the innermost possibility of physical desire: I tear myself apart, I become you, and you are nothing except me, and I am nothing except both the non-you and the clothes that touch that me-become-you more intimately than anything else. The annihilation of the lover can be seen as an idealized symbolic inversion of the impulse to penetrate the object of desire. It intervenes when the true identity of Saʿdi is revealed, and it introduces a reference to the physical presence of the object of desire: *bā vujūdat*, with your presence, but also "with your body." The accessibility of the body of the student/beloved is reconfirmed by his sudden request that Saʿdi dwell longer in "this region" to enjoy his "service."

Although the nature of the "service" is not specified, its homosocial horizon pertains to the expression of intergenerational devotion rather than alluding to seduction. The naïveté of the youth's unconditional affection appears in stark contrast to Saʿdi's potential sexual inclination, which he neutralizes by

111 [1.65] Saʿdi YE, 206–207. For some minor manuscript variants, see ibid., 541–42.

comparing himself to the "great man" who refuses the allures of urban worldliness for fear that beautiful boys would cause "the elephant to slip on the mud." However, Sa'di's chaste rejection of the youth's hospitality conflicts with the overtly sensual content of the last line of the ghazal. It is through this line that the poet had previously explained to the boy why he could not reveal to him who *he is*: "Sa'di's lips and your lips ... how could they ever ...? / With only this I am satisfied: the mention of your lips brushing my lips." Both the denouement of the story and the final argument used to offer moral advice to the readership collaborate in the creation of a separation between unspoken illegitimate acts (the physical encounter with a beautiful young man, which is alluded to, but never explicitly stated) and the outspoken permissibility of the desire that could potentially inform those acts.

The pseudo-biographical story of Sa'di's encounter in Kashgar brings the dynamics of the lyric construction to their finest and most articulate expression. This story, as well as Sa'di's other amatory plots analyzed in the previous pages, acts as a fictive narrative microcosm that allows its lyric excerpts to attain the full extent of their perfomative meaning. The *Gulistān*, therefore, acts as a resonance chamber that magnifies the abstracted nature of the lyric subject and provides it with a context capable of mimicking the complexity of the world in which Sa'di's ghazals circulated. The more the ideal reader peruses these stories, the more he (in this case, prince Sa'd II) is compelled to read Sa'di's ghazals as vehicles of the lyrical exploration of the world through the eyes of the poet. Through this process of constant re-enactment of the lyric along the patterns of verisimilitude set by the tales, desire stands out as an experience whose value lies in its inability to provide the desiring subject with final forms of fulfillment.

While the internal structure of the story reveals multiple levels of seduction which involve the characters of the tale as well as the poet's playful frustration of the expectation of the readers at every twist of the exchange between Sa'di and the student, its circulation as a portion of the fifth chapter of the *Gulistān* was meant to enact a process of rhetorical seduction of the readers of the book. If we still consider prince Sa'd as the implied reader of this story and the virtual co-author of the book, according to Sa'di's wording, the complex architecture of this narration elevates Sa'di in the eyes of the prince to the rank of a transregional master of "courtly" (*darī*) Persian poetry: in the fictive world of the story, the poet presents himself as the lyric spine of the Persian-speaking world, whose renown stretches from the Chinese frontier with Central Asia to the Persian Gulf. However, during the decade that saw the presumably gradual composition of the *Gulistān*, recension after recension, Sa'di's renown as a lyric poet was far from assured.[112] It is possible that Sa'di's anxiety to acquire literary renown was also informed by the absence of any mention of his lines from the *Compendium* of Persian rhetoric and prosody that Shams-i Qays completed during the last years of Sa'd I's reign and the first decade of the atabeg Abū Bakr's rule, in the 1230s, when Sa'di had not yet returned to Shiraz. Did Sa'di set his pseudo-biographical account within the geopolitical sphere of influence of the Khʷārazmshāh Muḥammad as a form of envious defiance of the position that Shams-i Qays had held decades earlier at the Salghurid court, when he migrated from Khʷārazm to Shiraz?

While Sa'di directed the immediate historical aim of this incessant chain of desire toward the opportunity of carving out a permanent space of learned and political influence over the Salghurid ruling elite, his ghazals would develop a meditation on the lyric subject, exploring the world in the form of a tension with the unspeakable, both as an erotic and as a spiritual category. This space of the erotic unspoken corresponds to the boundaries that Sa'di sets at the end of the story of his encounter in Kashgar. Within these constraints, the poetic persona of his ghazals witnesses the psycho-physiological emergence of aesthetic bents that are both personal and universal. It is precisely within this horizon that, in the following chapter, we will explore the tension between Sa'di's lyricism and the obscene as a linguistic bridge accessing the psychology of the metaphysical contemplation of beauty.

112 "We know that Sa'di's *ğazals* were celebrated in distant parts during his lifetime, though evidently not before the mid-1250s [...], and perhaps not until after 658/1260 [...]. Sa'di himself had complained in 1257 that he was not properly appreciated in Shiraz, but with the appearance of the *Bustān* and *Golestān* that certainly changed." Lewis 2001a. See also *Golestān*, 254–56.

CHAPTER 3

The Obscene Revisited

From the Sexual Reification of the Body to its Spiritual Fetishization

How delightful it is to contemplate that handsome idol of mine:
My cypress, who brings light to my days and cherishes my soul.
I used to travel across the world, but now
My love for his hair keeps me stuck in this city.
Everyone enjoys life with their own companion:
My companion is a hunk as tall as I am....
What I love the most is to stick into his ass
The most cherished limb among the limbs of my body.
I am content with his manners, as his sweat
Is a source that never satisfies my thirst.
Admire the temperance of this mystic [*ʿārif*]:
Won't my erection deserve resurrection?

SAʿDI, *Khabiṯāt*[1]

∵

1 Unsullied Are My Eyes

In his essay *De la séduction*, the French philosopher Jean Baudrillard provocatively defined pornography by opposing it to the technique of *trompe l'oeil* in the context of Baroque visual arts. According to Baudrillard, it is the missing dimension of the *trompe l'oeil*—its enchanting affirmation and simultaneous negation of a correspondence between images and the world—that tricks (*trompe*) the eye (*l'oeil*) and generates seduction:

1 [1.66] Saʿdi 1385/2006b, 981. I have established the text on the basis of Ms. Tehran 1296, 471; Ms. Dushanbe 1310s, 363; Ms. Tehran 1321, 468–69; Ms. Kabul 1325 (678); Ms. Yale 1432 (f. 380a/b). For a discussion of the shortcomings of published editions of Saʿdi's obscene works (which do not seem to have been compiled on the basis of a critical perusal of the manuscript tradition), see below.

 | DOI:10.1163/9789004435902_006

> The *trompe l'oeil* does not seek to confuse itself with the real. Consciously produced by means of play and artifice, it presents itself as a simulacrum. By mimicking the third dimension, it questions the reality of this dimension, and by mimicking and exceeding the effects of the real, it radically questions the reality principle.[2]

The *trompe l'oeil* removes a dimension from real space, and simultaneously magnifies its seductive power. Pornography, on the other hand, adds a dimension to the space of sexual desire and, in turn, it makes sex and the sexualized body "more real than the real." Baudrillard argues that this hypertrophic expression of desire generates the absence of seduction in the mechanism of pornography.[3] Baudrillard's contrastive definition of the *trompe l'oeil* in the visual arts as a perceived truthful representation that simultaneously undermines its own veracity resonates with Culler's and Hamburger's definition of the lyric subject as a linguistic function that simultaneously *is* and *is not* its own empirical author. We have seen how the story of Sa'di's pseudo-biographical encounter with the Kashgari student unmasks the mimetic power of the lyric voice by unearthing the mechanism of desire as a suspension between truth and dissimulation: "how could my voice declare that *I am* when you stand before me?" However, the lyric voice that, just like *trompe l'oeil*, betrays its own ontological falsehood simultaneously exposes its flipside by suggesting that what lies behind the restraints that generate desire is a quest for a hypertrophic representation of reality.

The narrative plots of the *Gulistān* have provided us with the opportunity to discern the tensions animating Sa'di's lyric subject amidst a complex network of contemplative, carnal, and spiritually abstracted desires constantly oscillating between ardent longing and restraint. The stories analyzed in the previous chapter reveal that one of the most prominent dimensions of Sa'di's lyric discourse stems from the symbolic friction between desire and control of the self. The nature of this restraint can vary, as it comprises not only the actual physical satisfaction of the lyric subject within the fictional plot of the texts, but also the narrative control over the explicit linguistic expression of the nature of desire as a fulfillment of the lyric subject's imagination. Lines akin to the couplet quoted below frame the practice of restraint as a courtly value ennobling both the lover and the beloved's chaste contemplative intentions. Yet the very mention of moral restraint underlines the existence of horizons in which the

2 Baudrillard 1990, 63.
3 Ibid., 28.

imagination is potentially free to wildly roam between language and the object of visual perusal:

> This love of ours will not decline:
> Unsullied are our eyes and chaste is your body.
>
> *Ṭayyibāt* 217[4]

In Saʿdi's poetry, the coexistence of a collective persona, *mā*, and an intimate lyric voice generates a space of potential conflict between the perception of physical desire stemming from the self and the ethical expectations of the courtly and religious environments making up the social spaces that surrounded the poet. Just as Dante's sonnets attest to the emergence of lyric subjectivity on the horizon of 13th-century Italian poetry, Saʿdi's ghazals manifest the development of a similar process in the Persian tradition, mainly through his construction of a meditative, individual poetic persona as a means to ponder the boundaries between religious ethics and the aesthetics of desire.[5] The combination of these two aspects—a subjective perspective that strives to reflect the (albeit pseudo-biographical) experience of the poet and a shared "I" that responds to the social values of a community—poises Saʿdi's poetry at the center of a peculiar system of signs on which Christian Kiening relies to define medieval poetry as a liminal space oscillating between body (*Körper*) and writing (*Schrift*).[6] Kiening's position could be seen as an elaboration on Paul Zumthor's approach to medieval poetry as a semi-oral textual practice that, even in its purely written forms, retains the presence of voice and vocalization as constitutive elements.[7] The body follows the text through its voice, and the voice of the text seeks forms of correspondence with the body. Therefore, the courtly ideal of an unsullied gaze upon a chaste body automatically involves the possibility of employing language as a linguistic form of contemplation capable of approaching the body from unexpected angles.

In the second part of this book, I will explore how, in a lyric context similar to the line quoted above, the sacred contemplation of the object of desire may actively mingle with the tensions, the frustrations, and the superior aspirations of the appetites of the body of the lyric subject. This chapter, meanwhile, focuses on the poetic and anthropological foundations of those acts, thoughts, inclinations, and fantasies that in Saʿdi's poetic universe *do* sully the

4 [1.67] Saʿdi YE, 102.
5 See Oppenheimer 1989, 1–40; Picone 2000.
6 Kiening 2003, 7–30.
7 See Zumthor 1987.

eyes of the passionate lover and *do* contaminate the chastity of his object of desire as the hyper-realistic expression of the constraints that define the lyric experience vis-à-vis its pornographic and spiritual counterparts. It is through an approach that considers obscene texts as "counter-texts" of the lyric that I will define the act of erotic contemplation as multi-vocal semiotic operations. In the following line, for instance, extracted from a burlesque text in which Sa'di satirizes anal intercourse among adults by depicting it as a bestial practice, the poet offers a pragmatic rationale for abstaining from indulging in forbidden pleasures:

> Whenever you see a beautiful boy as tall as a cypress tree
> Contemplate his face with your eyes and spit in your fist.
>
> If you tear neither his ass nor his pants,
> No one will kill you with impunity.[8]

When facing the physical manifestation of beauty, the beholder may practice abstention through contemplation, which Sa'di describes as a safe outlet to extinguish desire without denying the aesthetic value of the object of erotic arousal. However, this playful ethical imperative reveals that the space of contemplation acts as an area in which multiple possibilities of approaching the perusal of the physical world coexist.

The obvious point of departure for the study of the role of carnality in Sa'di's poetry is the section of his collected works that, even in some of the oldest manuscripts containing the entirety of the poet's output, appears under the rubric of *Khabīs̱āt*, or "obscenities."[9] The obscene content of the *Khabīs̱āt* is

---

8 [1.68] Sa'di 1385/2006b, 976; Ms. Dushanbe 1310s, f. 362a; Ms. Kabul 1325, 683. Sa'di hints on several occasions at the possibility of enforcing capital punishment for the perpetrators of sodomy (see Chapter 2, pp. 125–29), especially in the case of adults indulging the company of other adults (see *Golestān*, 113–14).

9 The sixty-five poems that constitute the *Khabīs̱āt* belong to a section of Sa'di's works that some of the earliest manuscripts group with a series of obscene texts in prose, referred to as *Majālis-i hazl* and/or *Mażāḥikāt*. On the discrepancies between the earliest manuscripts recording Sa'di's obscene works (especially between the pre-Bīsutūn collections and the later recensions), see the General Introduction. As the compilers of the most reliable editions of Sa'di's oeuvre preferred not to publish his obscene passages, the *Khabīs̱āt* still lack a critical edition. Only after 1989 have a few Iranian publishers decided to incorporate more or less censored versions of these texts into the corpus of pre-existing editions of Sa'di's collected works. For an accurate account of the philological difficulties affecting the study of the *Khabīs̱āt* as well as a preliminary census of the texts, see Zipoli 1997, 183–86. The edition

primarily sexual.[10] Even though variously veiled innuendos to sexuality appear throughout most of Saʿdi's works, the adamant exposure of intimate body parts and lewd actions is what characterizes the content of the *Khabīs̱āt* with respect to the rest of the poet's literary output.[11] Nevertheless, as the French Saʿdi scholar Henri Massé indirectly implied when he classified both the fifth chapter of the *Gulistān* and the *Khabīs̱āt* as disgraceful vulgarities, the boundaries between the poet's overtly obscene works and the rest of his lyric production tend to fade away as soon as we consider them as part of the same literary system.[12] As one might imagine, of all the dimensions of Saʿdi's corpus, the sensual aspect of his prose and poems has received the most scathing criticism since the very beginning of its modern critical reception, both in Iran and in the West. Even though Riccardo Zipoli has called for serious consideration of Saʿdi's licentious works since the 1990s, the scholarship is yet to recognize the intrinsic value of the *Khabīs̱āt* as a valid set of "counter-texts" with which to investigate the broad spectrum of their author's lyricism.[13] In spite of the critical dismissal that Saʿdi's facetiae have encountered throughout the last century of scholarly reception, both the *Khabīs̱āt* and the introduction that Saʿdi purportedly composed to open his irreverent corpus are by no means to be

---

I have consulted for this chapter appears in the final section of Forughi's edition produced by the publishing house Zavvār in 2002 (Saʿdi 1385/2006b). Given that Iranian publications of the *Khabīs̱āt* offer only uncritical editions of the text, I have compared Zavvār's selection with the texts recorded in Ms. Kabul 1325, which offers one of the oldest and most comprehensive collections of Saʿdi's obscene works. I also have occasionally consulted the following manuscripts: Ms. Tehran 1296, 468–72; Ms. Dushanbe 1310s, 360–64; Ms. Tehran 1321, 461–70; Ms. Kabul 1325, 672–90; Ms. Paris 1320s, ff. 249b–56b; Ms. Dublin 1320s, ff. 255a–63a; Ms. London 1328, ff. 360b–66a; Ms. Tehran 1352, 661–76; Ms. Qom 1340s, ff. 229b–34b.; Ms. Mashhad 1364, ff. 362b–67b; Ms. Paris 1366, ff. 248a–53b; Ms. London 1416, ff. 462b–72a; Ms. Yale 1432, ff. 377a–85b; Ms. Paris 1461/865, ff. 283a–88b. While, on the basis of these manuscripts, I am currently preparing a critical edition of Saʿdi's obscene works, the reconstruction of the texts that I quote in the following pages ought to be considered as a preliminary effort to overcome the shortcomings of the published editions of the *Khabīs̱āt*. For a survey of the recent history of the publication of this text in Iran, see Zipoli 1997, 184.

10 Although, among others, the Italian Persianist Alessandro Bausani dismissed the literary value of Saʿdi's obscenities by describing them as repetitive and inelegant representations of dry sexual acts, Zipoli has convincingly highlighted the metaphorical breadth of the *Khabīs̱āt*'s frequent and inventive depictions of the lyric subject's sexual sphere. Zipoli 1997, 205–11.

11 For a general appraisal of topics related to sexuality in Saʿdi's works, see Southgate 1984.

12 Massé 1919, 109.

13 For a critical analysis of the disparaging judgment with which scholars have considered Saʿdi's obscene works, or even denied their authenticity, see Zipoli 1997, 180–81.

considered less authentic than any of Sa'di's non-obscene works.[14] This introduction, in particular, which Massé unfairly exploited to declare the author's senile complaisance towards his Salghurid patrons, is particularly illuminating with regard to the scope, the intertextual tradition, and the intended audience of the *Khabīṣāt*:

> Thus Sa'di says, may God bestow his mercy upon him:
>
> The sons of some kings [*abnā' al-mulūk*] have urged me to compose a book of facetiae [*al-hazl*] for them in the fashion of Sūzanī [of Samarkand, *'alā ṭarīq al-Sūzanī*]. Initially I refused, but facing the threat of being executed I was forced to write these verses—may God forgive me for them! This is indeed a facetious chapter, but the virtuous men should not blame me, as salaciousness in speech is like salt with food. And here goes this jocose book; may God bestow his blessings.[15]

Upon closer analysis, this text discloses some indispensable pieces of information that can help us deepen our reading of Sa'di's manipulation of the obscene register as a specific aspect of his mainstream lyric genres. First and foremost, Sa'di indicates that the works of Sūzanī Samarqandī (ca. 1096–1172) are the original model for these compositions. Sūzanī is probably the crudest of all premodern Iranian satirists, and his spirited collection of poems (apart from his "serious" panegyrics praising the Qarakhanid rulers of Samarkand, as well as the Saljuq sultan Sanjar) includes both invectives *ad personam* (directed at various men of religious and political power) and parodies of a number of dead or living fellow-poets, including Sanā'ī of Ghazna. In spite of his importance to the premodern literary canon, his poetry has received scarce critical attention and the influence he received from poets such as Sanā'ī and Anvarī, along with his impact on Sa'di and the famed satirist 'Ubayd-i Zākānī, remains largely unstudied.[16] Sūzanī's parodic responses to other lyric poets usually transform the courtly language of longing and unrequited love into grotesque depictions of sexual extravaganza revolving around the trickster-like figure of the lyric subject's ravenous phallus. By referring to Sūzanī, and in spite of their

---

14 In his comprehensive analysis of Sa'di's style, Bahār (1349/1970, 3: 123–24) pointed out that his obscene prose cannot be attributed to anyone but Sa'di himself. See also Movahhed, 1391/2012.

15 Sa'di 1385/2006b, 973; Ms. Kabul 1325, 672.

16 On Sūzanī, see Suzani 1338/1959, 1–29; Zipoli 2015, 184–85; and Zipoli 1995. The last of these articles is, to date, the only in-depth study of Sūzanī's obscene works ever published. The poetic output of the poet (including his serious works) remains largely unstudied.

stylistic differences, Saʿdi situates his texts within the scope of a specific genre that belongs to an established licentious tradition in Persian.

The argument of the prince's death threat forcing the poet to compose such lines must be read against the premodern convention of explaining to the reader the reason for the composition of one's book by creating a narrative whose overtones resonate with the content of the text. Therefore, it is possible that Saʿdi spontaneously composed these texts as a literary exercise, but we should not rule out the chance that this specific pretext may reveal the existence of some form of connection between Saʿdi's obscene creativity and the courtly environment in which he circulated these lines. Based solely on the depictions that the historical sources offer when writing about Saʿdi's patrons, the branch of the Salghurid family descending from Abū Bakr's brother, Salghūr-Shāh, seems to have been particularly inclined toward drinking and sexual debauchery.[17] Such accounts could suggest that the "princes" who reportedly commissioned Saʿdi's *Khabīs̱āt* could have been either Muḥammad-Shāh or Saljūq-Shāh, if not their father himself, Salghūr-Shāh.[18] This would constitute a literary pretext that sets these Salghurid princes as the intended recipients and the "ideal readers" of Saʿdi's bawdy works.[19] The final analogy between facetious speech and salt implies the perception of a linguistic affinity between serious poetry and obscene verses, as if the poetic language could not fully express itself without the "salt" of the frivolous modality.[20]

The reference in Saʿdi's introductory note to unnamed princes as the primary audience for the *Khabīs̱āt* resonates with the role of the courtly environment in which, as previously explored, both Saʿdi's panegyrics and the *Gulistān* display the entire phenomenological gamut of erotic possibilities that the poet's lyric voice can embody. This parallel suggests that the obscene is a linguistic territory capable of interacting with the lyric at multiple levels by reason of their symbolic and functional overlaps in the environment of the court.

How do these two modalities interact and inform each other? And how does the obscene belong to a specific linguistic practice capable of reinforcing the

---

17 See Introduction, pp. 18–19.

18 On the basis of one of Saʿdi's obscene lines mentioning a massacre in Baghdad ("He inserted his bronze trumpet into those people / like a sword committing massacres in Baghdad, Saʿdi 1385/2006b, 987) Yazdān-parast (1394/2015, 1: 588–89) suggests that Muḥammad-Shāh must have been the prince who commissioned the composition of the *Khabīs̱āt*. However valid, this argument does not exclude his brother, Saljūq-Shāh, or even his cousin, Saʿd II.

19 On the tradition of adducing rhetorical pretexts to justify the composition of licentious lines, see Zipoli 1994, 258–59.

20 On the topos of salt as a metaphor for salacious overtones, see Zipoli 2015, 25, 65. For a survey of the classical recommendations on the etiquette of alternating salacious and serious modalities, see Zipoli 2001, 178.

aesthetic and erotic values of its non-overtly sexual counterpart, including the ideals of chaste desire along with its spiritual derivations? It goes without saying that Saʿdi did not compose his obscene poems out of an intentional theoretical thrust aimed at creating a conscious correlation between lyricism, ludic jest, and spirituality. After all, it is the literary historian's task to recognize patterns and offer a critical model to better understand the circulation of meaning among the texts from the past and across genres. As I will point out in the introduction to the second part of this book, what should matter to the critic's analytical attention is the tension among texts, rather than the otherwise inscrutable intention of medieval poets (let alone their theoretical postures). And if Saʿdi's underlying ludic intent for the composition of his obscene lines cannot be denied—as a way to playfully conform to a well-established genre—it is this chapter's contention that our critical scrutiny ought to take poetic playfulness seriously, especially in light of its liminal position within the literary mainstream.

2 Interpreting the Obscene

Prudery, a vague reminiscence of Victorian ideals of modesty, and neo-conservative forms of religious puritanism count among the main causes that, for decades, have prevented modern scholarship from approaching the surprisingly large amount of obscene texts composed by an equally conspicuous number of premodern Persian authors.[21] Nevertheless, the real threat posed to the incommensurable importance of this corpus belongs to critical paradigms that posit that only canonized, mainstream "high literature" deserves to be studied, as it allegedly constitutes a spiritually and ethically rewarding reflection of sublime ideals. For this reason, even when the embarrassment is overcome, the obscene, as a genre, is often dismissed as a marginal source of divertissement that offers no substantial resources to further the study of its "serious" counterpart.[22]

Although it has been proposed that pornography is a literary modality that coincides with the emergence of modernity, the first theoretically informed studies of premodern obscene corpora took shape a few decades ago in France,

21 The studies of Paul Sprachman (1981; 1988; 1995), and Riccardo Zipoli (1994; 1995; 1996; 1997; 2001; 2006; 2008; 2010; 2015) constitute a considerable exception to this neglect. See also Halabi 1364/1985.

22 For a thought-provoking meditation on the shifting boundaries of the "obscene," see McDonald 2014, 11–13.

through the creation of new paradigms for the study of the *Fabliaux*—the medieval scatological and sexually explicit vignettes that constituted a conspicuous source of inspiration for both Boccaccio's *Decameron* and Chaucer's *Canterbury Tales*.[23] In spite of the subversive character we may perceive such texts to have today, approaches that attempted a more in-depth understanding of medieval obscenities inaugurated a critical trend that sought a theoretical normalization of the obscene in order to highlight its high degree of functional conventionality. Early studies of the obscene drew upon Bakhtin's reading of grotesque representations of the body as hyperbolic representations aiming to destabilize the balance between the self and the world as such. The Marxist contribution to this approach therefore read the final goal of such symbolic subversions as the destabilization from below of the dominant social hierarchies.[24] Nevertheless, numerous studies have proven that premodern literary and artistic manifestations of the obscene, far from being marginal and alien to the sphere of the sacred, were an integral part of the establishment's moral and aesthetic values.[25] As Emma Dillon points out in her study of the acoustic dimension of the obscene in medieval texts, "sexual or scatological outrage was not intended as a politicized breaking of taboos, but was rather a means of exploring the possibilities of literary representation and narrative."[26]

Literary language, as an exploration of the possibilities of representation, engages the poetic text both at the level of its intrinsic linguistic possibilities (what language can do *within* a text) and in relation to language's power to create bonds between texts and the world that are not only referential (i.e., statements *about* the world), but also performative (i.e., texts as actions *on* the world, following Austin's approach; see Austin 1975). Therefore, in medieval obscenities, subversion as such does not necessarily occur in the social world, but rather within language itself, through its attempt to touch the world from an angle that normative texts fail to access. Following Baudrillard's intuition, pornography, as a modality that adds a hyperrealistic dimension to the space of representation ("more real than the real"),[27] constitutes a desperate attempt

23 See McDonald 2014, 1–16. For an insight into the debate on the conception of obscenity and its participation in the shaping of early modernity, see Hunt 1996.

24 Bakhtin 1984.

25 "Our assumption, following Bakhtin, [is] that the obscene is marginal and other to the sacred [but] so-called 'profane' church art demonstrates instead that obscenity was produced from within the sacred and not always in opposition to it." Camille 2014, 36. For an articulate critique of Bakhtin-inspired readings of the obscene as social criticism, see Thomas 1998.

26 Dillon 2014, 62.

27 Baudrillard 1990, 28

to capture the core of reality through a proliferation of its surfaces. This line of thought, vis-à-vis the various forms and registers through which pornography can appear in medieval poetry, frames the obscene as an opportunity for premodern literary systems to regenerate and innovate the intrinsic and referential possibilities of the language to represent desire in the broad gamut of its contextual meanings and purposes. Especially considering the status of medieval literature as a practice that is poised between the body and writing, obscene materials reopen the formulaic flow of the lyric genre by revitalizing it through unexpected representations of the body.

The acceptation of the term "obscene" to which I refer is primarily concerned with the semantic field of the explicit representation of sexuality, thus roughly corresponding to what today we commonly describe as "pornographic." The specific meaning of pornography varies according to social contexts, but in general it applies to the exhibition of body parts and physical acts that are considered inappropriate in a given arena of communication, and which potentially elicit a variety of responses ranging from disgust, embarrassment, and laughter, to mild enticement and sexual arousal.[28] One may read such responses as the effects that the obscene creates by means of imposing onto language a modality that depicts the world from unexpected angles. It is this frustration of the reader's expectations that, on the one hand, creates an immediate emotional response (disgust, laughter, enticement) and, on the other, enriches the literary system with new semiotic opportunities. In the obscene text, emotionality and novelty are two elements that require a constant correlation: no effective emotional response can be prompted without the renewal of the challenge that the language poses to the reader's expectations in terms of style and imagery. For this precise reason pornography, more than other modalities and genres, risks to generate overexposure, repetition, and invariability in a fashion that saturates the reader's response with boredom.

28 See Peter Wagner's definition: "written or visual presentation in a realistic form of any genital or sexual behaviour with a deliberate violation of existing and widely accepted moral and social taboos." Wagner 1988, 7. In his study of sexuality in *The Canterbury Tales*, Geoffrey Gust warns that pornography "as time-bound linguistic construct" is a "post-medieval label marking a historicized problematic—an inherently ambiguous concept with much cultural baggage attached to it." Gust 2018, 12. While Gust attempts a definition of the difference between obscenity, pornography, and the broad category of "erotica," (ibid., 4–5) he also points out that "it is very difficult [...] to establish a precise and authoritative explanation and definition of such concepts as medieval desire, erotics, obscenity, or pornography, because all of these ideas are etymologically slippier if not problematic in the context of the Middle Ages." Ibid. For a broader discussion on this topic, see Toulalan 2017, 107–108.

This might partially explain why, at least in the Persian medieval tradition, the description of sexualized limbs and acts often appears less formulaic and repetitive than the descriptive patterns that the ghazal's "chaste" depictions of the beloved commonly feature and the manuals prescribe.[29] The texts themselves usually appear less stable than their courtly counterparts, as if the expressive capabilities of the language were nervously vibrating around images that bring a high degree of innovation to the poetic canon. As Leslie Dunton-Downer observes, "the obscenity [...] appears to inveigh against the system itself: it cannot be located squarely on either the referential or the poetic end of the spectrum of language." "Obscene language," she adds, "resides in an unusual poetic space of neither-norness that calls attention, ultimately, to certain (poetic) paradoxes and problems inherent in the language system."[30] This perspective could account for the tendency of medieval Persian obscenities to express vulgar depictions at the intersection of genres, often in the form of pastiches that escape the expectations of the reader and dynamically connect socio-political, burlesque, religious, and courtly images without offering clear boundaries between their realms.

Even though Saʿdi recognized Sūzanī as the main model for his obscene fragments, Sanāʾī of Ghazna (whom Sūzanī imitated extensively) was the real initiator of the obscene tradition as a fully developed convergence of genres that interacts at multiple levels with the relationship between language and the representation of the world. In Saʿdi's output, the absence of insults *ad homimem* breaks a tradition that, up to the early 13th century, would put the genre of the personal invective (*hajv*) at the center of the obscene as a literary practice.[31] Riccardo Zipoli recognizes Sanāʾī as the original architect of this diversification of the obscene modality, and he ascribes to the late-Ghaznavid/Saljuq poet the insertion of socio-political and spiritual dimensions into the bawdy poetic tradition that preceded him.[32] Despite Sanāʾī's emphasis on the pedagogical role of his licentious compositions, the following lines from his spiritual *mas̱navī*, *Ḥadīqat al-ḥaqīqa*, reveal the extent to which the cultivation of the obscene was ingrained in the linguistic texture of the literary system as a social and aesthetic practice:

---

29 See, for instance, the literary inventory of the beloved's anatomy that Sharaf al-Dīn Rāmī (d. 1393) dedicated to the Jalāyrid sultan Shaykh Uvays. Rāmi 1325/1946. See *EIr*, s.v. "Anīs al-ʿOššāq" [G. M. Wickens]. On the lexicographic richness of the Persian obscene tradition, see Zipoli 1996; 2011.

30 Dunton-Downer 1998, 25.

31 Zipoli 2015, 37–50. For the invective in the Arabic literary tradition, see van Gelder 1988.

32 Zipoli 2001, 181.

Although serious poetry is foreign to obscenity [*hazl*]
My obscene are akin to my serious verses.

The beautiful and the unsightly are to be combined
When treasuries are adorned to please the king.

I compose obscenities not just in jest, but to teach:
My lines are not just lines, but a vast territory.

Will you realize what the spiritual teaches
When his intellect crosses these lands?

His serious poetry certainly delights the soul,
But his obscene verse is a magic that bewilders the soul.

So grateful am I for my literary skills, as my obscenities
are more delightful than other poets' serious verse.[33]

If we take at face value Sanā'ī's admission of complementarity between serious and obscene verses, we may regard the obscene as a modality that constantly fluctuates between the language and the objects of the world. It acts as a generative power that establishes pornography and amatory lyric poetry as parts of the same literary macro-system. In this macro-system, we could even regard lyric as a genre that regenerates itself through the subterranean presence of a tension leading to desires whose radical expression coincides with the pornographic. This theory requires to be substantiated by further sources of evidence deriving from other literary systems and through a closer scrutiny of the entire Persian pornographic corpus in the light of the historical development of the ghazal as a lyric genre. It is from these premises that in this chapter I will start sketching an understanding of Sa'di's lyrical representations of desire as a poetic phenomenon that cannot be separated from its underlying inclinations toward the explicit (either imaginary or literary) representation of sexual obscenity.

33 Quoted by Zipoli (2001, 183). Translation is mine, on the basis of Zipoli's rendition and a comparison with the original text.

3 None of them Can I Say to You: the Obscene as a Cognitive Exploration of the Body

Hope is a dream with your intoxicating eyes:
Too restless I am to sleep: sleep well and tight!

How could I be fulfilled by just looking at you?
Other actions I have in mind, but none of them can I say to you.[34]

This is a marvelous fragment from Sa'di's obscene verses which lingers between courtly restraint and an explicit innuendo to the psychological possibilities of desire beyond the boundaries of what the lyric canon would deem appropriate to express. In the first two lines, the poet sketches an amatory narrative that follows the conventional imagery of the lyric tradition faithfully. Nevertheless, the second part of the fragment opens with a rhetorical question that interrupts the enchantment of the lyric, and points to an inclination that transgresses the sexual detachment of the genre: looking at you elicits "actions" and desires in my imagination which I cannot convey through *this language*, i.e., the language of the courtly amatory rules.

The choice of hinting at the sexual dimension of desire without the explicit mention of intimate body parts or actions convinces the reader that this poem is not operating in the realm of the parodic or of the burlesque reversal of courtly ideals. It opens a window into a mental experience capable of bringing the literary projection of the historical author back to the real presence of the body. The lyric subject's mind, like a black box immersed in the sensorial waters of the world, tries to articulate the urges of its flesh without finding words capable of bearing the physical density of such an unsettling contemplative experience. We are left with the blank space where language cannot bring to the surface of linguistic expression a matter that is deeply engrained in the network of feelings, images, and sensorial perceptions that belong to the direct experience of desire. The unfulfilling contemplation of the beloved highlights the act of beholding as the narrative present of the lyric plot. It constitutes the archetypal time of desiring, from which all other action proceeds as the recollection of past events or fantasized possibilities of carnal enactment for the time to come.

In the last line of the fragment, the word that I translate as "actions" reads in Persian as *ḥikāyat*. This term, originally Arabic, means "narration," "story," but, as I will further elaborate in the second part of the book, it also belongs to the

34 [1.69] Sa'di 1385/2006, 976; Ms. Tehran 1352, 675; Ms. Yale 1432, f. 384b.

technical language of medieval Islamic psychology. In the Avicennian psychological tradition, *ḥikāya* (along with the third form, *muḥākāt*) translates the Aristotelian concept of *mimesis* and visual mimicries, and describes the imagination's constant activity in comparing and combining the images perceived by both the external and the internal senses.[35] The imagination turns into a filter mediating between the visual contemplation of beauty and the verbal expression of the carnality of desire ("but none of *them* can I say to you"): it is a space of freedom exuding from the cognitive power of the lyric, and which clashes with the restraints imposed by the linguistic expression of sensuality.

Confessions in which the poetic persona states its incapability of translating its mental images into words are not rare in Sa'di's obscene fragments; and they also appear in his ghazals any time that the degree of eroticization of the utterance increases to such a point that the poet leaves the completion of the image to the reader's imagination.[36] This perception of incommunicability vis-à-vis the contemplation of human beauty in the context of the sensual aspect of its lyrical depiction is a question that involves the concept of the body as a "system of signs" (a *Zeichengefüge*, as Kiening defines it), "in which the tensions between sexuality, gender, and language are played out, where the idioms, the varieties of body as language, the discursive hiding and revealing are on display."[37] The linguistic impairment of Sa'di's lyric subject responds to a matter of etiquette only in the surface of the utterance, as it involves a cognitive pause faced with, on the one hand, sensory exploration of the body and on the other, the courtly ideals of amatory dedication informing lyric as a practice that is bound to a literary tradition. From this point of view, the gap between imagination and the expression of sexual desire is primarily cognitive, and it sets the experience of lyric poetry as a psychological point of departure capable of communicating with both the physiology of desire and its metaphysical elaborations.

---

35 See Vílchez 268–309; Zarqāni 1390/2011.

36 Blind is the eye that sees you and is not
Bewildered by the incomparable Power [that created you].
[1.70] Sa'di YE, 17.
He appeared and left, and I, beside myself:
Was he the beloved, or the mental image of the beloved?
I was senseless, the intellect abandoned me, my language froze:
What a blessing to be annihilated by the perfection of the beloved!
[1.71] Sa'di YE, 218.
I am imprisoned by your snare, subjugated by your hands,
Astounded by sensing you, and bewildered when lauding you.
[1.72] Sa'di YE, 95.

37 See Williams 2016, 102.

If we are to trace the roots of the cognitive dimension of the relationship between obscene poetry and medieval Persian lyricism, we ought to consider works that, albeit not strictly focused on literary criticism, tackle the psychological aspect of the exposure to amatory poetry in its socio-historical context. One of the rare opportunities to gain a certain degree of insight about the hermeneutics accompanying the circulation of lyric poetry in medieval Iran is found in a treatise whose primary purpose is to highlight the path, the practices, and the values that the pious believer ought to embrace on the road towards boundless happiness both in this world and in the next. *The Alchemy of Bliss* (*Kīmiyā-yi saʿādat*) is the Persian masterpiece of Muḥammad al-Ghazālī (d. 1111), one of the most sophisticated thinkers of the premodern Islamic world, whose thought contributed to the illustration of the possible harmony between the legalistic aspects of Islam and the inner path of Sufi spirituality.[38] *The Alchemy*, an Avicennian philosophical and Sufi-oriented abridged compendium in Persian of his Arabic magnum opus *Iḥyāʾ ʿulūm al-dīn* (*The Revival of the Religious Sciences*), is the work in which the spiritual science of the heart, in its balanced interplay with sharia prescriptions, is applied to the anthropological investigation (in its socio-pragmatic sense) of the believer's acts, habits, and intentions as channels of continuity between the self, this world, and the hereafter.[39]

The philosophical and sociological breadth of *The Alchemy*, its meditation on the mundane and spiritual reverberations of the nature of beauty, along with the anthropocentrism of its focus on the quest for the unseen in the traces of this world, make this book an excellent theoretical framework for the contextualization of Persian poetry beyond the strict horizons of its rhetorical specificities.[40] In the chapter dedicated to the illustration of the functions, the permissibility, and the mundane and spiritual uses of music and poetry, al-Ghazālī hints at the intimate bonds that place lyric poetry within the scope of the experience of sexuality and desire:

38 The second part of this study will be based on discussions of al-Ghazālī's approach to the hermeneutics of lyric poetry and the contemplation of human beauty in the tradition that influenced the spiritual dimension of Saʿdi's poetry. For the most recent discussion of the relevance of the *Kīmiyā*, see Hillenbrand 2013.

39 On al-Ghazālī's *Iḥyāʾ*, see *EIr*, s.v. Ġazāli" [W. M. Watt]; and, in particular, Garden 2014.

40 "It is his *Alchemy of Happiness* [...], a Persian work encapsulating the most important aspects of his religious thought, that contains the most valuable statements concerning notions of beauty and aesthetics and their relationship to virtue, and the value of this book has been recognized by scholars of Islamic art as early as Ettinghausen." Elias 2012, 163. On al-Ghazālī's aesthetics, see Ettinghausen 1947, 160–165, Grabar 1977, Necipoğlu 1995 (especially 199–201); Soucek 2000; and, most importantly, Hillenbrand 1994; Vílchez 2017, 737–54.

> Listening to music and poetry is forbidden in the following cases: when a reprehensible characteristic is found in the heart, such as when someone is ravished by desiring a woman, or a young man, and listens to music and poetry either in their presence—in order to increase his [lustful] pleasure—or in their absence—to intensify his passion while longing for a physical encounter. [It is also forbidden] whenever one listens to a poem that contains the description of the hair, beauty marks, and beautiful bodies, and, in one's imagination, these descriptions are applied to specific women or young men.[41]

In this passage, the author draws a direct line between the practice of composition and musical audition of ghazal poetry and a classification of its forbidden sensual effects:

1. The poem (possibly set to music) is enjoyed when an object of desire, regardless of their gender, is visually and physically accessible in order to increase the listener's lustful pleasure.
2. The poem is listened to when the object of desire is not physically accessible. In this case lyric poetry intensifies the passion and the desire of intercourse.
3. The description of physical beauty is presumed to pertain to the realm of abstraction. But the listener might be tempted to apply that abstract description (beauty marks, the hair, etc.) to a specific object of desire whom they know in person.

In another passage al-Ghazālī elaborates on the conditions that make poetry composition and listening unlawful:

> Music is forbidden whenever the poem therein contains inappropriate words [...] or when it describes women who are [personally] known [by the listener; *zanān-i maʿrūf*], as it is not appropriate to describe women before men. Composing and listening to poetry of this sort is forbidden. But it is not forbidden to listen to or compose a poem that features the [generic] description of hair, beauty marks, and physical beauty, or that recounts the vicissitudes of the encounter and the separation, or anything that pertains to the habits of passionate lovers. It is to be considered forbidden when one, by means of imagination [*andīsha*], applies that poem to a woman or a young man with whom he is in love. Then it will be the thought itself that is forbidden. But if one applies it to his wife or concubine, it will not be forbidden. However, the Sufis and the people

41 *Kimiyā*, 1: 477.

> who are immersed in the love of God and listen to music [*samāʿ*] with such passion cannot be damaged by poetry, as they interpret each verse according to their inner condition: they might interpret the black curls of the beloved as the darkness of impiety, or the brightness of the beloved's face as the light of faith [...].[42]

Al-Ghazālī outlines a phenomenology of the lyric in both its performative and interpretative contexts. The Islamic theologian asserts that a lyric poem has a self-standing, independent, and virtually neutral meaning that can only be completed through the intervention of the mental representation of the listener, who is able to "apply" those neutral and abstract images to the "woman or the young man" with whom he is infatuated. Furthermore, al-Ghazālī leaves us with a suggestive reference to the concrete, *ad personam* application of the poetic description of the ghazal: the abstract words of the lyric text are, in the mind of the listener, projected onto a concrete object of desire. What would such an eroticized mental translation read like? Would it constitute the mental representation of a sensual act? Perhaps it would be a merely sensual and blind arousal that focuses on specific parts of the beloved's body?

Considering the flexibility of ghazal poetry as a lyric form that is capable of embodying subjective experiences (as a linguistic construct, according to Hamburger's and Culler's theorizations of the lyric) as well as the shared "I" of a literary community, in al-Ghazālī's pragmatic approach the exposure to amatory poetry entails the possibility of formulating mental representations of sexual appetite that push the meaning of the text beyond the boundaries of its primary signification. And, even more surprisingly, it is not the eroticism of this derivative image that al-Ghazālī considers for his religious ruling, but the status of the object of desire with respect to the individual whose mind hosts the potentially compromising fantasy.

Al-Ghazālī dwells on the characteristics of lustful desire only in a passage in which—still elaborating the risks associated with music and poetry—he qualifies "lust" (*shahvat*) as something that "pertains to a natural bent: whenever a beautiful face appears to the eyes, Satan rushes in and encourages sensual desires so that the musical audition [*samāʿ*] will be ruled by lust."[43] It is interesting to see the kind of logical distinctions that the author employs to further his analysis of the permissibility of voice and poetry and the conditions under which lust can be considered as a source of *fitna*, "sinful temptation":

42 *Kimiyā*, 1: 484.

43 *Kimiyā*, 1: 481.

> And when lust does not prevail, it is permissible to listen to music performed by a young man. But it is not permissible with an ugly woman if the listener can see her, as looking at women is forbidden in all situations. But if one listens from behind a curtain, it is forbidden only if there is danger of temptation, otherwise it is permissible. [...] Just as the face of a young man, the voice of a woman does not have *ʿawrat* [i.e., it does not correspond to a "private part" of the body whose exposure would be considered indecent]. It is prohibited to stare lustfully at young men when the fear of temptation is present. The same case applies to a woman's voice. These situations vary according to one's state and nature: some people trust themselves, others are afraid. This is similar to the case of kissing one's legitimate partner [i.e., one's wife or concubine] during the month of Ramadan: it is permissible only for whoever can control his lust, whereas it is prohibited for those who fear that lust would drive them to engage in sexual intercourse, or to ejaculate from only a kiss.[44]

From these parallels we can infer that al-Ghazālī equates lyric poetry with real life situations in which it is the inner disposition of the individual that determines the potential source of sinful temptation: staring at a boy's face, listening to a woman's voice, or kissing one's partner during a timeframe when intercourse and ejaculation are forbidden. The prospect of a lustful reception of a ghazal can therefore be assimilated into the space of mental representation that corresponds with the visual perception of an object of desire (al-Ghazālī distinguishes the sensorial origins of the perceptions according to gender, legal status, and context) whenever the temptation of committing sins of a sexual nature mingles with the individual's imagination. In the sentence, "lyric poetry is forbidden when one, by means of imagination [*andīsha-yi khʷīsh*], applies that poem to a woman or a young man with whom he is in love," al-Ghazālī employs the term *andīsha* as a generic Persian translation for the Arabic *khayāl*, which in the psychology of perception that he embraces corresponds to the mental representation that the imaginative faculty creates on the basis of external perceptions.[45] In another chapter of *The Alchemy of Bliss*, al-Ghazālī argues that an object can be perceived either through direct visual experience or through imagination (or recollection) via the mental

44 Ibid., 382.

45 Al-Ghazālī takes at face value the physiological foundations of Avicenna's theory of the internal senses not only in the *Kīmiyā* (1: 19, 21), but even in his renowned confutation of the some of the metaphysical claims of the philosophers, (al-Ghazāli 2000, 178–79), the *Tahāfut al-falāsifa*. On al-Ghazālī and the Avicennian approaches to cognition and the internal senses, see Chapter 5.

image that the *khayāl* provides. The only discrepancy between the two pertains to a qualitative difference that does not affect their essence. This means that the visual perception of an object and its mental representation are essentially the same thing, with the only difference being that the former is "more complete." Interestingly enough, al-Ghazālī illustrates this analogy through an amatory example, by comparing the different degrees of pleasure that derive from directly looking at one's object of sensual desire and contemplating him or her through imagination: the former is more pleasurable than the latter "not because the direct vision offers an image that is either different or more beautiful than the imagined one—as it is the same, but brighter, clearer."[46]

In his final comparison, he assimilates the mental image to the contemplation of the beloved early in the morning, when the light is dim, as opposed to the full vision of the beloved at noon—a condition that he associates with the heart's experience of unveiling (*mukāshafa*) the metaphysical truths in the hereafter. Such correlation probably derived from the ideas on the nature of vision circulating in the Islamic world after the composition of Ibn al-Haytham's treatise on optics, *Kitāb al-manāẓir*, which theorized an almost perfect correspondence between the nature of the perceived objects and the images created in the mind of the onlooker. As noted by Jamal Elias, al-Haytham's theory provided mental representations with an ontological authenticity that would have been otherwise inconceivable.[47] The paradigm of this automatic correspondence, which takes place by immediate contact between the visual source and the mental perception of it, presents a striking parallel with al-Ghazālī's emphasis on the identity between the direct view of an object and its mental representation, along with the assumption of a correspondence between linguistic descriptions and sensorial perceptions.

According to this semiotic system,[48] the abstract description of the body of a generic human being that is communicated through the lines of a ghazal is a verbal sign that elicits in the mind of the listener the formation of an image that concupiscence naturally (*aṣl-i khilqat*) interprets as a source of sexual pleasure. Following al-Ghazālī's wording, this process seems to work as a form of

46 *Kimiyā*, 2: 586.

47 Elias 2012, 195–96.

48 "Al-Ghazālī defines an image (*mithāl*) as something in the physical realm that accurately conveys the meaning or signification (*maʿnī*) of what it represents. In the semiotic relationship of a metaphysical entity and its physical image, it is the process of dream interpretation (*taʿbīr*) that connects a visual image to its referent. In claiming that 'Prophets only speak to the people by striking images' (*bi-darb al-amthāl*, what is normally translated as 'in allegories'), al-Ghazālī is arguing that physical images serve as essential signifiers of divine truths." Elias 2012, 222.

embodiment moving from the abstract to the concrete, and it is made possible on the basis of past experiences—either physical or imagined—with actual human beings. This scheme closely follows the Avicennian background of al-Haytham's optical theory, according to which visual recognition can take place only through the process of recalling and comparing the past perceptions that are stored in the mind.[49] Similarly, al-Ghazālī suggests that "in the mind" of the listener the abstract description can be applied to either one's legitimate partner (wife or concubine) or an illegitimate object of desire, i.e. a boy or an illicit woman. In either case, the believer always has the opportunity to reconvert the images (*miṣālhā*) deriving from those abstract descriptions into subtle meanings (*maʿānī*) applied to the spiritual knowledge of God. But for whomever this spiritual transition cannot take place, as in the case of youths who are overcome by lust and have no notion of the love of God, listening to lyric poetry should be forbidden. In the specific case of young listeners, al-Ghazālī argues that "it is very likely that when they listen to the description of the hair, the mole, and the beautiful face, Satan approaches them and inflames their lust in such a way that their hearts develop a passion for the infatuation for the beautiful ones: as soon as they hear about the vicissitudes of the lovers, they will derive pleasure from it and decide to seek the same emotions on the path of passionate love."[50] When the recollection of past direct experiences or the focus of one's desire are not available to the mind of the listener, lyric poetry, according to al-Ghazālī, elicits an active quest, as if the lyric subject were to seek a physical object of desire capable of embodying the abstracted "you" of the lyric description.

What is particularly fascinating in this psychology of the aesthetic experience is the possibility for the subject to automatically switch from the courtly, virtually non-sexual, and per se licit modality embedded in the register of the ghazal as a genre, to the conversion of the abstracted actors of the amatory text into lustful images. The fact that al-Ghazālī does not disclose the actual content of the images that elicit lust in the mind of the listener suggests that their verbal translation would trespass the limits of decency; a kind of decency whose lawfulness from an Islamic perspective depends on the boundaries between the private and the public spheres. The linguistic transition from the abstractness of the non-sexual amorous content of the ghazal to an embodied and lustful verbal rendition of the desires elicited by the poetic text implies a shift from the lyrical to the obscene register. The gap between these two sides of the watershed of modesty, and the lack of verbal access that affects the

---

49 See Chapter 6, pp. 324–25.
50 *Kimiyā*, 1: 486.

ghazal as a genre when it tries to express the other side of lyric reception of the discourse on love, is easier to conceive if we take into account the following poem by Hafez, which exquisitely expresses the accumulation of lustful desires that follows the contemplation of the beloved:

> For God's sake, wipe those drops of wine off your lips,
> As thousands are the sins that are tempting my mind.[51]

The ghazal is a genre whose language cannot express anything beyond the limits of the moral decency to which al-Ghazālī refers. But its proximity to the mental translation of its abstract imagery into lustful depictions suggests that its potentially sexual allusiveness is always active and ready to be unpacked according to the interpretive inclinations of the listener. It is in this direction that, in the line above, Hafez tests the limits of this potential by alluding to imaginings that cannot be expressed, and whose indetermination feeds the mind of the listeners with images that only their active participation can complete. As in Hafez's line, the gray area of the erotic imagination that grazes the boundaries between the courtly and the obscene appears in the line from Saʿdi's *Khabīṯāt* analyzed earlier:

> How could I be fulfilled by just looking at you?
> Other actions I imagine, but none of them can I say to you.

Any specification of that fertile area of the unspoken—any expression of these "other actions"—would mark a transition from the genre of courtly poetry to the register of obscene verse; or, if we recur to modern categories, from eroticism to pornography. I introduce this modern distinction because eroticism may be described as a modality of representation that alludes to physical intimacy without exposing the exact contours of the limbs and the actions that are able to trigger sexual desire. Pornography, on the contrary, corresponds to the full representation of the anatomy of sexuality with the purpose (which is always socially negotiable) of eliciting sexual arousal.[52] By following

51 Hāfez 1362/1983, 1: 342.

52 As I shall soon clarify, my restricted working acceptation of the concept of pornography in medieval Persian poetry applies to the explicit mention of body parts and acts that transgress the boundaries of an idea of decency that is based on the shifting notion of "private body" parts. While part of the current philosophical debates on the boundaries of pornography in the arts defines this category as an explicit sexual representation, Hans Maes (2012) has argued that issues such as the moral status of the representations, their intrinsic artistic quality, and the prescribed responses of the audience are factors that

al-Ghazālī's notes on the phenomenology of amatory poetry in its context of cognitive reception, I reframe the discourse on the obscene as an overarching linguistic possibility that includes pornography as a subcategory, and which departs from the lyric subject's realization of the boundaries separating imagination from experience. The gap between imagination and experience, with respect to the ideals of courtly restraint that form the lyric discourse, ultimately relates to language as a tool capable of defining the boundaries of the obscene to creatively manipulate them.

4 Persian Pornography as a Lyrical Undertone

What in Persian literature can be defined as "obscene" falls within the category of any speech that explicitly refers to the "intimate" regions of the body that in an Islamic context are referred to as *ʿawrat*, i.e., an individual's "private parts."[53] *ʿAwrat*, which is to be kept hidden from public display, is circumscribed by boundaries that vary according to one's gender, social status, and socio-cultural contexts. In the case of men, *ʿawrat* stretches between the navel and the knees, whereas for women it corresponds to the totality of the body, with the exception of the face and hands. For this reason, Islamic jurists would recommend that any mention of private body parts (male and female genitals, as well as the pubic and anal regions) should be made through euphemisms, neutral terms, and figurative speech.[54] The Basran jurisprudent and literary scholar Aḥmad b. Muḥammad al-Jūrjānī (d. 1089) specifies that "the need to conceal terms [referring to private body parts and sexual acts] is like the need to conceal the acts they denote, and thus using a euphemism (*kināya*) for them is a curtain [extended] for their meanings, behind which their fault is hidden, and

undermine all attempts to outline a clear-cut distinction between the pornographic and the "artistic."

53 See *EI*^{3}, s.v. "Body, in law" [B. Krawietz]; Sprachman 1995, ix–xii.

54 Sprachman 1995, ix–xv. On the socio-rhetorical development of euphemistic approaches to the mention of taboos in premodern Arabic literature, see Naaman 2013. In the *Kitāb al-ināya wa al-taʿrīż*, composed in 1009 in Nishapur, the anthologist Abū Manṣūr al-Thaʿālibī (d. 1039) provides a specific list that covers the scope of the taboo topics that writers should mention through euphemisms. The part of the list that covers the *ʿawrat* includes both women ("their sex organs, sexual intercourse with them, defloration, menstruation," etc.) and men ("male sex organs, attainment of puberty in male youths, circumcision, young passive homosexuals, homosexual intercourse with them, pederasts, the appearance of beard on the face of youths, passive homosexuality in male adults, fornication," etc.). Ibid., 475.

their disgrace is veiled from the ears."[55] As Paul Sprachman points out while commenting on al-Ghazālī's recommendations on the euphemistic approach to obscene language, it is this "*ʿawrat*-centric" conception of the body (and its actions as an agent or patient) that defines the boundaries between the appropriate and the inappropriate through intermediate levels of acceptability that the use of euphemisms implies.[56] The direct mention of body parts—the "unveiling" of the *ʿawrat*—is what characterizes two of the main categories of the Persian repertoire of obscenities: the invective (*hajv*), and *hazl*, translatable as "indecorous jest," "burlesque literature," or "bawdy poetry."[57]

When defining *hajv* and *hazl* one may agree with Riccardo Zipoli's emphasis on the fact that the boundaries between these two categories are so loose—often depending on contexts and specific cases—that they should be treated as subdivisions of a single category.[58] However, if we narrow down the scope of their applicability to the binary oppositions that the classical authors have traced with respect to their non-obscene counterparts, we can show the kind of contiguity that their literary function presents with respect to the genres of the panegyric and lyric poetry. In light of the relevance of the princely framework in which Saʿdi's lyricism developed, the analysis of the obscene as a function of courtly poetry of praise may assist us in showing how its mechanism bleeds into the dynamics at work in the amatory ghazal. When the early Ghaznavid poet Manūchihrī praises the literary preeminence of the "poet laureate" ʿUnṣurī, he highlights that:

> In his poetry and prose, in his panegyrics [*madḥ*], and in his invectives [*hajv*],
> In his serious poetry [*jidd*] and his obscene texts [*hazl*], when he writes and when he drinks....[59]

While classical authors and critics distinctly define the opposition between poetry of praise and invective, the difference between *jidd* (serious register) and *hazl* (obscene compositions) is not as clear-cut. It requires interpretation, especially if compared with the parallel position of *madḥ*/*hajv*. Praises and invectives, as literary performances deriving from the socio-political function of celebrating the ruler and undermining the symbolic power or the credibility

55 Quoted in Naaman 2013, 474.
56 Sprachman 1995, xii–xv.
57 Ibid., xxvii–xxxii. For an extensive discussion on the difference between *hazl* and *hajv*, see Zipoli 2015, 12–28. On *hajv* in Arabic literature, see van Gelder 1988.
58 Zipoli 2015, 11–12.
59 Quoted in Zipoli 2015, 21.

of his enemies, require specific addressees or objects of poetic attention: the *mamdūḥ* (i.e., the praised one) in the case of *madḥ*, and the *mahjū* (the despised one), in the case of *hajv*. Conversely, the "serious" and the "obscene" (especially given how they are usually described and juxtaposed to each other) can be seen as literary modalities detached from historical contingencies (as they lack specific targets), and which belong to the realm of learned or entertaining literature.

The main difference between the *madḥ/hajv* and *jidd/hazl* opposition is that the former strictly relates to literary genres (namely the panegyric and the invective), whereas the latter defines two registers that can apply to any genre. This means that, if we consider praise poetry and invectives as object-oriented genres supported by the *qasida*-form, it is implied that the former's (*madḥ*) register is serious (*jidd*), whereas the latter's (*hajv*) is based on obscene elements. Just as the sacrality of the king's body requires a "serious" register in order to fully respect his *ʿawrat*, the derision of the enemy is based on the "unveiling" of his *ʿawrat*. The private parts of the enemy's body are revealed in an attempt to reduce his physical presence to mere bodily functions. By following these parallels, we could argue that the celebratory representations of the king (and, by extension, all notables and courtiers, ministers, commanders of the army, etc.) find expression through the description of his body as a presence standing beyond his flesh: the luminous beauty of his countenance is matched by the generosity of his hands, his head is enlightened by a crown similar to the divine aura, but no other limbs are ever mentioned. On the contrary, the enemy's body is converted into pure flesh through the process of "scatological reductionism": emasculated, passivized, and unveiled, he is the sum of his limbs associated with naked genitalia and excretive functions.[60] When it comes to the representation of the human body, *madḥ* and *hajv* operate within two registers that are respectively idealized and hyper-realistic. On the one hand, the dignity of the prince overcomes the boundaries of the body and presents the few mentioned limbs as signs of eternalization and apotheosis; on the other hand, the body of the enemy is represented as if it were an anatomical table showcasing the unveiled carnality of its secretive and reproductive dimensions.

A comprehensive study should be devoted to the reciprocity of *jidd* and *hazl* with respect to the courtly ideals reflected in the wide spectrum of sociohistorical occasions that can be found in the premodern Persian panegyrics and invectives. For now, considering that classical manuals usually define *hajv* as the mechanical reversal of the panegyric's poetic diction, it is necessary to bear in mind that the symmetry between these two registers implies a high

60 See Bentley 1970, 64.

degree of reversibility, which many poets have often boldly stated as a means to threaten their ungenerous patrons.[61] The reciprocity between praise and invective emerges from the *dīvān*s of almost all classical courtly poets. It is precisely this kind of reversibility between celebration and slander that, if applied to the representation of the human body in the transition from the panegyric to lyric poetry, can cast new light on the relationship between obscenity and courtly love with respect to the discourse on desire.

Even though the interplay between praise and vituperation in the origins of Persian poetry is yet to be fully explored, I propose to use this correlation as a paradigm for the study of the reciprocity between lustful and courtly representations of desire in the symbolic horizons of Saʿdi's ghazals. We can conceive of the amatory affection expressed in the ghazal as the canonized and idealized "high" reflection of desire whose existence depends on the category of the obscene as a non-canonic possibility that focuses on the naked limbs of the object of passion—his/her *ʿawrat*.

The *ʿawrat* of the object of desire is the taboo-zone which, as a social prohibition, determines not only the boundaries between illicit and permissible gazes and actions, but also the difference between acceptable and unacceptable linguistic descriptions generating the formal constitution of genres. As a taboo concerning the body, the *ʿawrat* can be seen as the touchstone of all amorous discourses that engage with the physical presence of the beloved: from the hyper-realistic representation of genitalia to the metaphysical sublimation of the conception of the object of desire as a reflection of God's beauty. As observed when analyzing the role of restraint vis-à-vis the expression of sexuality in the narratives of desire in the *Gulistān*, the courtly celebration of the beloved's beauty may be seen as a euphemistic shift that operates in a regime of reciprocity with the sensual bent that informs the modalities of explicitness characterizing obscene poetry. I ought to underline that what I define as "reciprocal" by no means implies that the courtly and "chaste" descriptions of the beloved—which are typical of the ghazal as a lyric register—derive from their obscene counterpart: what is "chaste," "pure," and "unsullied" in the courtly ideal of love is such as a result of the application of a regimented taboo whose focus is the *ʿawrat* of the beloved (his "forbidden" parts), based on which obscene texts organize their unveiled depictions. This means that both the unexpressed erotic tension of the lyric ghazal and the explicit hyper-realism of its obscene counterpart are linguistic manipulations revolving around the lyric object's posture with respect to the beloved's *ʿawrat*—not only as a direct

61 Sprachman 1995, xxv–xxix. See, for instance, Anvarī's invective against Ḥamīd al-Dīn: "Remember, I'm a poet, I write both *madh* and *hejā*." Zipoli 2015, 53.

object of contemplation but also as imagined desires. According to this model, and regardless of the diachronic development of both lyric poetry and obscene texts before the constitution of Early New Persian poetry as a literary system, Islamic norms and ethics, by reinforcing pre-existing societal prescriptions on desire and the representation of the human body, contributed to the reinforcement of the normative delegitimization of the obscene and the canonization of the non-obscene depiction of amorous desire as the mainstream approach to the representation of passion.[62]

Therefore, we may see obscene poems and courtly ghazals as the two opposite poles of an *ʿawrat*-centric spectrum in which the lyrical representation of the body corresponds to a process of euphemization of the mere mention of the beloved's private body parts. The further we move away from the depiction of the *ʿawrat*, the more the non-*ʿawrat* parts of the body undergo a process of eroticization that culminates with the *fetishization* of the beloved's face, finally reaching the point in which all possibility of sensuality is sublimated into the manifestation of divine beauty. In the obscene spectrum of amatory compositions, the "ʿawratic" private parts of the beloved's body are subject to a process of *reification*: they are exposed as they are, and as nothing else but themselves. Conversely, the spiritualized description of the non-ʿawratic body parts of the beloved (his countenance, eyes, neck, etc.) turn into fetishes, i.e., something other than themselves, through a process of sacred sublimation that—as we will analyze in the next part of the book—projects the traces of the divine onto the human body. Non-obscene amorous poems can present different degrees of euphemistic or metaphorical eroticism according to how closely their depiction of the human body can approach the *ʿawrat*. If we look at the history of the Persian ghazal and consider the lyrical opening of the early Persian *qasida*s (the section known as *nasīb*, or *taghazzul*) as part of the development of the lyric discourse towards the formation of an established technical form (the *ghazal-i iṣṭilāḥī*, or technical ghazal, as opposed to lyric texts that do not present the standard features of the later developments of the genre),[63] we will notice that the amorous excerpts of the early period

62 For general introductions to the complexity of Islamic sexualities in their socio-cultural context, see Boudhiba 2008; Babayan and Najmabadi 2008. On the discrepancy between social norms and sexual practices in medieval Islamic societies, see Szombathy 2013, 1–34. On religion as a pervasive element of the medieval Muslim Arab world and, therefore, as a primary source of inspiration for the development of Arabic obscene literature (*mujūn*), see ibid., 43–112.

63 Lewis 2006.

display a higher degree of eroticism, mainly as a result of the proximity of their representation of the body of the beloved to the boundaries of *ʿawrat*.[64]

The process of canonization and crystallization of the Persian lyric discourse in the ghazal form involved a shift toward idealized representations of desire and the parallel development of burlesque and parodic modalities whose counter-textual nature would prevent them from taking on a fixed form, but would not preclude the formation of a separate genre, with its own conventions and motifs. It is not totally fortuitous then if the first well-established samples of obscene texts not based on *ad personam* invectives are to be found in Sanāʾī's *dīvān*, which is also the collection of poems that presents the first substantial number of technically fully developed ghazals in the history of Persian poetry.[65] It was probably the awareness of the formation of a technically codified lyric genre capable of adapting itself to a plurality of audiences and registers that promoted the written circulation of burlesque verses that would address the forbidden representation of the flesh in its desirous contortions.

The subversive value of the obscene that tends towards the burlesque—along with the humoristic effect that it may trigger—rests in the opportunity it offers of unmasking the subtext of an originally intimate connection with the *ʿawrat* that the courtly poetic discourse strives to hide and transmute through the use of figurative speech. Both Zipoli (in his study of Persian medieval depictions of masturbation) and Henderson (in his pioneering analysis of obscene language in Attic comedy) strongly advocate for an analytical distinction between pornography and obscene literature. They justify this dichotomy by defining pornography as an aesthetic experience aiming at replacing "real" sexual encounters. They both argue that pornography's primary function is to induce a proxy sexual pleasure intended for private enjoyment. The obscene, on the contrary, purportedly intends to repel desire through its ludicrous caricatures of sexuality based on the linguistic denigration of the body.[66] This latter point may apply to the grotesque and the satirical as sub-registers of the obscene. However, the linguistic exhibition of private body parts and libidinous

64 On the explicit sensual depictions found in the lyrical exordia of Samanid and Ghaznavid poetry, see Shamisā 1381/2002, 36–70. See also van den Berg 1998; Sabur 1384/2005, 176–78.

65 Zipoli 2001.

66 "[P]ornography plays upon our sexual fantasies by constructing dream worlds in which our longings for sexual gratification are satisfied with no effort on our part. We are allowed to look at and enjoy the object of our sexual desire; they [are] rendered passive and gratify us automatically. […] thus pornography is introverted; its target is autoeroticism and private imaginings." Henderson 1991, 6. See Zipoli 1994, 262–63.

acts may generate symbolic experiences of desire that do not envisage the fulfilment of subversive or satirical agendas.[67]

In the medieval Persian tradition, within the macro-category of depictions of the obscene, one may distinguish several sub-registers in which, for instance, more nuanced expressions of explicit intimacy coexist with or even prevail over the scatological or grotesque exposure of the body. For instance, while 12th-century panegyrists Sūzanī and Anvarī were more concerned with burlesque or vindictive compositions mentioning the private parts of the body through monstrous representations, authors such as Sanāʾī (fl. 11th–12th centuries) and ʿUbayd Zākānī (fl. 14th century) emphasized the sociopolitical and religious aspects of their licentious endeavors. In this context, Saʿdi's treatment of the obscene stands out as a register that avoids the scatological and grotesque components that characterized the preferred imagery of his predecessors. On the contrary, his licentious fragments showcase rhetorical and stylistic features that keep the poet's obscene language close to the lyricism of his serious ghazals.[68] Part of the origin of the structural proximity between Persian lyric amatory poetry and the obscene dates back to the development of licentious poetry (*mujūn*) in the Arabic tradition of the Abbasid period.[69] Scholars have timidly described the development of *mujūn* poetry as a parodic response to the conventions of the chaste depictions of love that characterize the Arabic *ghazal* canon.[70] However, positing that the obscene derived from its serious counterpart as a diachronic development undermines the possibility of recognizing the potential interdependence of the two genres, as attested in other literary traditions.

For instance, the study of the relationship between troubadour lyric poetry and its obscene "counter-texts" offers a partial solution to this impasse. As argued by Pierre Bec, the deep formal relationship between the canonic lyric compositions and the obscene texts that abound in the troubadour tradition relies on strategies of mimicry and manipulation of the courtly canon. He refers to these obscene counterparts as *contre-textes*, as their structure and

67 Moreover, public as opposed to private consumption of the obscene and the pornographic respectively may apply to Attic comedies, but not to Persian medieval poetry and its oscillation between private and social spaces.

68 See Zipoli 1997, 205–12.

69 For a comprehensive study of *mujūn* poetry in its medieval context, see Szombathy 2013. For a discussion on the scope of *mujūn* as a genre, see ibid., 34–42. Cf. Kraemer 1986, 15; Rowson 1998, 546.

70 Rowson suggests a reciprocity between the chaste *ʿUdhrī* school of love poetry of Umayyad Arabia and the *mujūn* obscene stances that fully developed in Abbasid Baghdad. Rowson 1998. See Meisami 1993; Balda-Tillier 2014.

imagery heavily depend on the formal modalities that are constitutive of the 12th-century Provençal lyric genre.[71] Discussing the chronological connections between medieval texts and counter-texts, Bec points out that the first known Occitan poet, Guilhèm de Peitieus (William IX, d. 1127) composed texts of purified love (*amour épuré*) as well as "truculent, subversif et iconoclaste" counter-texts.[72] The close intertextual ties between serious and obscene texts constitute further evidence for the condition of inter-dependence that allows the poetic system to develop across a plurality of approaches to the depiction of desire.

In the Persian tradition, the interdependence of the lyric and the obscene is reflected in the widespread practice of burlesque intertextual responses through which bawdy poets would parody the compositions of their predecessors or contemporaries. In one of his most renowned lyric *qasida*s, Sanā'ī opens a lengthy description of the canonical ideals of courtly love by addressing the beloved in this fashion: "If the lovers come to you to offer their souls as their most precious gift …"[73] In the opening of his parodic response (which closes with the direct quotation of Sanā'ī's first hemistich), Sūzanī brings the figure of the ideal lovers to the mundane level of explicit sexual desire:

> When the fuckers bring you their cocks as an offer,
> As soon as you look elsewhere, they pound your ass deep and hard.[74]

While on the rhetorical level of the text the mention of the "fuckers" (*tāz—bāzān*) introduces counter-characters that elicit laughter by reversing the idealized depiction of the "lovers" (*ʿāshiqān*), the inversion of courtly values suggests a meditation on the interstitial spaces of desire that inhabit the gap between the body of the lover and that of the beloved.

This interstitial exploration taking place between the body and the writing (between *Körper* and *Schrift*, as theorized by Kiening) is particularly interesting when one considers the performative aspect (in Austin's sense of "doing things with words") of the Persian panegyrical *qasida* as a text that would be staged and circulated in order to elicit a response in the audience, along the lines of the intentions of the poets and the kinds of socio-political negotiations taking place at court. The practice of subverting the imagery of a given *qasida* through obscene rewriting reveals the performative aspect of the contiguity

71 Bec 1984, 11–13.
72 Ibid, 7.
73 Sanā'i, 1362/1983, 142–43 (*ʿāshiqān pīsh-i tu gar tuḥfa hama jān ārand*).
74 Suzani 1338/1959, 386–87.

between genres approaching the physical effects of praise poetry (as an illocution generating "perlocutionary" responses, in Austin's categorization) according to different authorial intentions. The creative regeneration of the literary tradition directly participates in this process, as the imitation and repetition of the performative across the boundaries of different genres reinvents the possibilities of redirecting the representation of the body toward new meanings. This is the case, for instance, of Rūdakī's famous *qasida*, *Buy-i jūy-i Mūliyān* ("the fragrance of Muliyān river is coming"), which the poet composed in the first half of the 10th century to convince the Samanid prince Naṣr II (d. 943) to return to Bukhara after he and his army had spent four summers in Herat.[75] In the *qasida*, the poet portrays the prince and the city of Bukhara as two lovers who long to embrace each other after a long separation ("the memory of the dear beloved [i.e., Naṣr II] is coming"). The perlocutory felicity of the text (the prince reportedly headed back to Bukhara—leaving his boots and leggings behind—before Rūdakī could even end his performance, and the poet was profusely rewarded by the commanders who had commissioned the text) inspired generations of poets to imitate the *qasida*, often under their patrons' solicitations.[76]

In spite of the performative felicity of the text (also on its aesthetic grounds, Jonathan Culler would argue, based on the record of literary imitation), 15th-century literary historian Dawlatshāh Samarqandī questioned the literary value of the poem, by stating that if a court poet of his time were to perform such a rhetorically insipid *qasida*, it would not gain the favor of a princely audience.[77] Therefore, it is not surprising if, one century before Dawlatshāh, Rūdakī's passionate geopoetic *qasida* was re-contextualized by both Hafez, as an innuendo to Tamerlane's political hegemony in Iran and Central Asia,[78] and by his contemporary, ʿUbayd Zākānī, in the fashion of an erotic *tenso* between the intimate geographies of the lover and the beloved:

> Last night my dick smelled the stench of pussy and said:
> *The sweet fragrance of the Mūliyān river is coming!*
> a fart came out from the ass, and my dick said:
> *the scent of the dear beloved is coming!*[79]

75 For a comprehensive analysis of this account and the psychology of the emotional impact of medieval Persian poetry on the soul of the listener, see Landau 2012; 2013, 255–59

76 Nafisi 1341/1962, 375–88.

77 Dawlatshāh Samarqandi 1385/2007, 58–59.

78 See Ingenito 2018b, 873–74.

79 ʿObayd Zākāni 1999, 229.

Sūzanī's and 'Ubayd's burlesque intertextual imitations could be compared to some of the most famous parodic counter-texts of the troubadour tradition. Parallels could be found in this renowned lyric *canso* by the prominent troubadour Bernart de Ventadorn (fr. 12th c.):

> When the cold wind blows/ from your land,/ it seems to me that I feel/ a wind coming from paradise/ because of the sweet lady before whom I bow,/ in whom I have placed my faith/ and with whom I have lodged my heart,/ for I would leave all others/ for her, so much does she please me.[80]

The idealized depiction of the beloved—which is not entirely dissimilar from the courtly descriptions characterizing the Persian ghazals of the same period—was later parodied by an anonymous author who, in a short *cobla*, thus responded to Bernart:

> When the fart blows from the arse/ from which my lady shits and has the runs/ it seems to me as if I can smell/ the aroma of piss [...][81]

Pierre Levron argues that the scatological reduction of the lady, *midònz*, to the physical source malodorous fluids can be read as a symbolic representation of the traumatic perception of the melancholic experience of love in a language that, rather than subverting the ideal of courtly longing, accesses it from a vantage point that offers a different perception of the world and the body.[82]

Following Levron's suggestion, we could argue that Sūzanī's and 'Ubayd's bawdy parodies constitute not only comical reappraisal of the lyric conventions, but also creative re-contextualizations of the performativity of the literary tool with respect to the exploration of the body and desire within the canon itself. A similar process could be recognized in 'Ubayd's hilarious reconfiguration of a ghazal in which Sa'di meditates on the discrepancy between the desire of seeing the beloved in person and the sorrow caused by the act of imagination as the only visual contact that can take place:

> Last night, far from your countenance, fire rose to my head,
> Water was flowing from my eyes and dampened the ground.

80 Translated and analyzed by Simon Gaunt (2014, 89).

81 Ibid.

82 "La proximité dynamique de ces textes avec des pièces beaucoup plus classiques est un principe essentiel définissant le « contre-texte » qui reposerait alors sur une mise en scène de tensions entre les aspirations et les craintes d'une manière beaucoup plus violente que dans la lyrique courtoise." Levron 2010, 88.

> I don't want my life to slip away in sighs, hence
> I mentioned your name over and over, all night long....
>
> My gaze roamed around, and before my eyes
> Your image was depicted on all doors and walls around me....
>
> Your face never appeared, and my senses were coming and going,
> But the mental image of you never left me alone....
>
> *Ṭayyibāt* 207[83]

In ʿUbayd's pornographic parody, the lyric persona of Saʿdi's poetry splits into a two-fold lyric actor: the phallus and the vagina meditating on their anatomical differences and the longing caused by the physiological discrepancy between anal and vaginal intercourse:

> The dick said to the cunt: "O beloved idol of mine,
> *Last night, far from your countenance, fire rose to my head.*"
>
> The cunt replied: "I swear by your life, tonight the asshole and *I*
> *mentioned your name over and over, all night long*";
>
> *My gaze roamed around, and before my eyes*
> *Your image was depicted on all doors and walls around me*;
>
> Longing for your body and stature, till the break of dawn
> *Water was flowing from my eyes and dampened the ground.*[84]

Saʿdi's discourse on the difference between direct vision and imagination is here converted into an exploration of the physiology of longing through the lower anatomical parts that the lyric tradition bars from its linguistic realm, and yet which ʿUbayd displays as subtexts of the lyric modality itself. The semiotic accomplishment of obscene parodies derives from the contiguity of the lyrical with its explicitly sexual counter-text as a possibility that can inhabit the mind of the listener. In "Obscene Hermeneutics in Troubadour Lyric," Simon Gaunt argues that both the parodic responses and prose texts that manipulate the biographical data of prominent authors through scatological and sexual inflections attest to the existence of a tradition of reading courtly

---

83 [1.74] Saʿdi YE, 97.
84 [1.75] ʿObayd Zākāni 1999, 224.

language through obscene metaphors. ʿUbayd's obscene parody (which, from a feminist perspective—through the establishment of the vagina as a preferred point of view—could also be seen as a subversion of the phallo-logocentric nature of the traditionally masculine lyric) indicates that the "high" lyric register adopted by Saʿdi implicitly contains potentially pornographic developments freely accessible to the medieval readers of his ghazals.

Moreover, the erotic interpolations into the troubadour poets' prosaic biographies (*vidas*), interventions which created a narrative context for the occasions behind the composition of their lyrics, resonate with the pseudo-biographical accounts of Saʿdi's sensual inclinations, ranging between homiletic distaste, amatory imagination, and injurious slander, written by Ṣafī al-Dīn Ardabīlī and Zākānī.[85] The proliferation of metaphorical images that lyric poetry deploys to depict the idealized body of the beloved is, according to Gaunt, a sign of their intrinsically obscene undertone, which is otherwise "sublimated discursively into spiritual quests."[86] However radical this position might seem, it actually proves meaningful in the context of the carnal/spiritual dichotomy that al-Ghazālī suggests as an interpretive framework for ghazal poetry, taking into account both the essential nature of human appetites and the personal disposition and experiences of the listener.

In al-Ghazālī's classification, what entices the mind of the young man who has had no taste of divine love is not the experience of sexuality as such, but the linguistic titillation that derives from the interplay between the amorous words to which he has been exposed and the bodily experience of the world. Obscenity, as the textual rendition of the desires substantiated by love poetry, operates exactly in the gap between linguistic representations and their imperfect adherence to the surface of physical experiences. The obscene may trigger laughter because it reveals the gap between the ideal and the instinctual, but it often arouses the reader's mind as it displays the writhing body of language moving between the world and its signs.

Howard Bloch, in his study of the obscene content of medieval French *fabliaux*, stresses that, in the explicit mention of private body parts, "the preoccupation with sexual members is at once the product of and a fascination with narrative and not its referent."[87] The obscene entails an analytic, object-oriented referentiality in which the *ʿawrat* is explicitly mentioned as if the intimate body parts were to be brought to life by simply pronouncing them. In opposition, as the amatory narratives of the *Gulistān* show through their

85 See chapter 1, p. 62.
86 Gaunt 2014, 104.
87 Bloch 1986, 90.

depiction of erotic restraint, the courtly eroticism that characterizes the ghazal is a register that approaches desire without pronouncing its primary anatomy, metaphorically alluding to its presence, but without visualizing its forbidden protuberances and cavities.[88] The friction between these two modalities, along with their referentiality or lack thereof, is what creates interdependence between the lyric and the obscene from the perspective of the medieval readers who perused the ghazal and sought a meaningful reflection in their tangible world—as an active quest of meaning, rather than mere passive enjoyment of poetic entertainment.

5 The Euphemism and its Undetermined Flesh

The texts whose language and imagery euphemistically graze the limits of the exposition of the private parts of the ʿ*awrat* constitute the most interesting area for accessing the points of contact between the lyrical and the obscene. This is usually made possible through the use of euphemisms that allow the reader to intervene in the interpretation of the poem and to stage it in a visual mindscape that is broader than the strict perimeter of the canon. As noted by Simon Gaunt, the fact that sensual metaphors can tell us more about the mechanisms of pleasure and desire derives from their specific focus on language rather than the body:

> [...] as Jacques Lacan and others have argued [...] desire and indeed the social manifestations of our sexual drives are generated and driven by our being caught up in the signifying chain, in other words, desire is generated and driven in and by language.[89]

It is due to this meta-linguistic origin of desire that the most obvious form of literary indeterminacy can be found in those texts that produce riddle-like allegories and whose location with respect to the opposition between the courtly and the obscene is hard to detect: the liminality of their nature with respect to genre opens a space of indetermination that creates contradictory responses in the mind of the reader.[90] As Glenn Davis points out in his study of sexual

88 See Brookshaw 2019, 145–54.

89 Gaunt 2014, 95.

90 "Although the listener is invited to recognize the playful transition from one semantic field to another, the riddler's aim is to gain power by confounding and deceiving his adversary, whose role consists precisely in allowing himself to be deceived. The double voicedness of the riddle is based on a metaphorical deception, the riddler's careful feeding of details

riddles in Old English literature, the mention of non-intimate body parts with a high degree of metaphorical flexibility (such as heads and hands) "makes them prime candidates for sexual euphemism," as they can easily "skate the territory between the erotic and the mundane."[91]

In the following fragment, Saʿdi asks his ideal audience to read each word as a polite euphemism for sexual content lurking behind the surface of the standard lyricism of the verses:

> When I think of you my pen does not fit in my hand:
> Too long it's been since I plunged my hope into the ink-holder.
>
> The days have turned you as black as ink, and yet [or, "for this reason," *hanūz*]
> White drips the ink from the eye of my pen.[92]

If we were to read this fragment in a non-obscene section of Saʿdi's poems, along with his purely amorous compositions, we would define these lines as an attempt to represent the writer's block as a result of the unattractive appearance of the downy beard on the face of the beloved.[93] But if the reader interprets "my pen" in light of the pen-phallus analogy that is a common motif in premodern Arabic and Persian literature, the whole imagery of the fragment is turned into a masturbatory form of amatory longing.[94] Since the connector *hanūz* can be translated as "yet," the obscene reading turns the unfruitful blankness of the pen—which initially signified lack of inspiration—into the spermatic ejaculation resulting from the sexual appreciation of the beloved's body, whose beard still entices the senses of the lover. The more the reader shifts back and forth between the lyrical and the obscene modalities of this fragment, the closer the two fields will appear. And once we familiarize ourselves with the possibility of a pornographic representation floating under the skin of the courtly, we can reread many of Saʿdi's ghazals through the lens of the semiotic possibility of an opening towards the senses:

> No one can improve my art and your pulchritude,
> As you and I set the very limits of beauty and poetry.

to the listener, which give a false gestalt encouraging the 'wrong' solution, often a sexual one, while the official answer is innocuous." Vasvári 1998, 113.

91 Davis 2014, 44. For an introduction to obscene riddles and double entendre in the context of *mujūn* Arab literature, see Szombathy 2013, 140–44.

92 [1.76] Ms. Kabul 1325, 686; Ms. Dushanbe 1310s, 362; Ms. Yale 1432, f. 382a.

93 See van Gelder 2003.

94 See Glünz 1995.

O Sa'di, tonight no one has struck the drums of dawn
Or maybe no morning follows the night of solitude?
Badāyi' 427[95]

This is the conclusion of the ghazal that, in the first chapter, was analyzed to showcase the lines in which Sa'di confesses his wholehearted admiration for young men's downy beards. The declaration concerning the utmost beauty reached by both Sa'di's eloquence and the body of the beloved ends abruptly with the insertion of a concluding line that enacts the suffering deriving from the endless night of solitude. The images of the poet's inspiration, along with his phallus and masturbatory endeavor provided by the allegorically obscene fragment, furnish linking material for a reading of the previous ghazal as a courtly space in which desire can, virtually at any moment, activate the latent possibility of libidinous thoughts.

Memory and imagination as spaces for the unspoken expression of desire in the interstitial loci of lyric poetry emerge whenever the poet employs similar locutions in different registers. For instance, the association between the recollection of the beloved (*ba yād-i tu*) and the concept of the pen/phallus fitting (*namī gunjad*, "it doesn't fit") in the hand of the poet/lover may act as latent subtext in the lyric passages in which Sa'di employs a similar phrasing:

When remembering you [*bā yād-i tu*] Sa'di's name does not fit in the verse:
When unique is the beloved, I cannot associate with the stranger.
Badāyi' 607[96]

In this ghazal, the virtual sexual subtext is highlighted by the fact that the poem opens with a declaration on the compelling nature of physical desire, followed by a meditation on repentance (*tawba*) and restraint (*parhīz*):

One day out of crazed passion I shall embrace you and caress your curls:
I'll set your sweet lips ablaze with the ardor of my fiery kisses....

Loving you nullified all my repentance and restraint,
and this is now my resolution: I shall refrain from all repentance![97]

95 [1.77] Sa'di YE, 198.
96 [1.78] Sa'di YE, 272.
97 [1.79] Ibid.

Sa'di's pornographic fragments fill the gap between the expression of uncontainable desire expressed in the lines above and the imaginings that guide the lyric subject when caressing with its eyes the body of the object of desire. The motif of repentance and restraint acts as a powerful catalyst for the creative enactment of the discrepancy between the lyric register and the obscene twist that often appears in the *Khabīṯāt*:

> Last night I said to myself that I would repent from love
> As the time has come for me to leave this world.
>
> But then I repented of those words,
> As the memory of that seductive beloved came to my mind:
>
> The mention ["name," *nām*] of his ass I brought to my tongue
> And water emerged from my cock's mouth.[98]

The act of mentioning the body of the beloved exposes itself as a constant form of embodiment of those desires that can find no legitimate expression within the boundaries of the lyric etiquette. In the following quatrain, the lyric quality of the sexual innuendo ("to shed water" as a periphrasis for ejaculation) defies the boundaries of the obscene and points to the latency of sexual desire as a subtext for the amatory modality of ghazal poetry:

> O eyes, do not shed in vain your purest pearls,
> Do not shed shining mercury on my golden cheeks:
>
> It is after pleasure that water ought to be shed:
> You saw no pleasure, do not shed your water![99]

Such latency is even more evident in those ghazals whose language does not seem to transgress the courtly genre's scope of decency and restraint, but whose metaphors create a system of allusive implications that cast multiple doubts on the genre to which they are supposed to belong. What follows is

98 [1.80] Sa'di 1385/2006b, 976; Ms. Yale 1432, f. 384b.

99 [1.81] For this quatrain I preferred to follow Ms. Kabul 1325 (687) rather than the published edition (Sa'di 1385/2006b, 978–79), as the manuscript records *sīmāb* ("mercury") instead of *khūnāb* ("tears mixed with blood"), which figuratively interplays with the spermatic innuendo of the text.

one of the most perplexing ghazals of those adorning the *dīvān* of the poet of Shiraz with disturbing and yet alluring allegories:

> O smiling doll, who has tasted your ruby lips?
> O garden of tenderness, who took a bite from the quince of your face?
>
> No fruit has he ever eaten more fragrant than this
> No watermelon sweeter than this must he have ever tasted!
>
> O verdant Khiżr, may the water of life be always forbidden to you!
> So that you may understand how painful was Alexander's quest.
>
> Is that someone's blood or scarlet wine that you spilled?
> Or maybe it is black mulberry that is dripping on your clothes?
>
> You mingle with everyone, and yet you avoid us:
> The fault is not yours: it is our fortune that abandoned us.
>
> It is better for the wall to collapse all at once
> So that you may not say that no one has ever seen your garden!
>
> When the crowds realize that it is ripe and sweet
> Not for long can the juicy fruit dwell on the branch.
>
> Last week the rose bud could not even disclose its lips
> But now the morning breeze is tearing apart its veils.
>
> The fearful ducks would never approach the Tigris's shores
> But now that the Mongols have cut off the bridge, even the boats can pass through.
>
> Farewell to the old times when we used to share with you the wine:
> Enough with this jar from which all the strangers have been drinking.
>
> Sa'di you need fresh air: knock at the door of a different garden
> Abandon this field, for the cattle has already grazed in it.
>
> *Badāyiʿ* 252[100]

100 [1.82] Saʿdi YE, 116. I have compared Yusofi's edition with Ms. Kabul 1325, 398; Ms. Paris 1320s, f. 156b.

As I have already remarked, the rigid conventions of the classical ghazal would prevent authors from the use of distasteful, vulgar, or sexually explicit vocabulary. Although its language befits the courtly refinement of the ghazal tradition, the peculiarity of this poem lies in the fact that it metaphorically alludes to sexual intercourse and its physiological consequences.[101] In the lines above, Sa'di creates a cartography of sexuality whose allegorical indetermination enhances the eroticism of its metaphors and metonymical associations by only mentioning the lips and the countenance of the object of desire. The beloved's lips and face are described through the use of a special kind of simile—*iżāfa-yi tashbīhī*, or the "genitive simile"—which juxtaposes the comparandum (i.e., the body parts) to its comparatum (i.e., the ruby and the quince). Although this ghazal conjures up images of defloration that could apply to a female object of desire, Sa'di usually recurs to the metaphor of the quince (as opposed to the smoothness of an apple's skin) to describe the downy beard of the young male beloved in contexts in which his gender is unequivocally spelled out.[102]

In spite of the connotation of masculinity that the image of the quince elicits, all the other metaphors that Sa'di deploys within this text partake of the same anatomic ambiguity that I explored in the first chapter when determining the ungendered structure of Persian lyric poetry. Here gender indetermination is coupled with a lack of metaphoric specification obtained through the mention of fruits for which codified stock imagery cannot provide direct correspondences. What metaphor can we grasp from the "fruit" of the second couplet, defined only by its "beauty" and edibility? In any given textual context, Persian authors refer to specific fruits and plants as metaphors of equally specific parts of the body, but here "fruit" exposes a form of fleshly nudity that does not offer the eye the opportunity to visualize any specific image.[103]

The more we unfold the allegories that follow the first mention of the beloved's body, the more we encounter metaphors whose lack of standard associations expose limbs and bodily tissues that are at the same time exceedingly vivid *and* unspecified. An intensification of this process appears in the second part of the couplet, in which Sa'di employs the uncodified image of the "watermelon." Even though the lyric tradition does not provide the reader with a stable set of metaphorical correspondences capable of translating the bodily

101 The large number of discrepancies found in the manuscripts suggests that even 14th-century copyists (and readers) were baffled by the unusual sexual innuendos found in this text. See Sa'di YE, 456–57. Hamidiyān (1383/2004, 101–102), qualifies the text as "pornographic."

102 See *Golestān*, 138–39.

103 See Zipoli 2009.

allusion of the watermelon, we do *see* the redness of a bleeding limb or organic tissue associated with the pleasure taken by whoever has cut (or, as in some manuscripts, tasted) *it*. In such cases, in spite of the metaphorical veil covering the explicit presence of the *ʿawrat*, the lack of determination in the depiction collaborates with the reification of the body and the consequent emergence of an obscene aura whose blank space on the linguistic page is filled by the imagination of the reader. At the center of the poem, Saʿdi describes the presence of a red liquid that, through the rhetorical artifice of *tajāhul al-ʿārif* (rhetorical ignorance), figuratively corresponds to the blood of the lovers spilled by the beloved: red wine, or black mulberry that has stained his or her clothes.

The lover's blood spilled by the object of desire is a codified topos that draws upon the tradition of celebrating the martial capabilities of the beloved/soldier who symbolically tortures the lover's unrequited passion.[104] The transition to black mulberries (which, unlike blackberries, immediately release their dark red juice upon touch) brings us back to the use of uncodified metaphors that expose various unspecified parts of the body of the beloved to unsettling associations. This shift generates a symbolic inversion in which the beloved's role transitions from a proud blood-shedder to a bleeding subject. The exposure of the beloved's body, unprotected by a figurative language codified by the poetic tradition, assigns this ghazal to an intermediate area between the courtly and the obscene. While courtly images of amorous encounters represent the lover as being symbolically penetrated by the intervention of the beloved's weapons (arrow-like eyelashes and gazes deriving from the martial tradition), obscene texts focus on the penetration of the object of desire through the violence of the lover/desiring subject's hypertrophic masculinity. This symbolic reversal is thus a particularly suitable base for comparing Saʿdi's lyricism with the dynamics of political power and sexual domination that we have seen at work in the Ghaznavid panegyrics as patterns of sub-textual communication between the poet and the offspring of the Turkic ruling élites.

It is possible that this ghazal was composed on the occasion of a specific event (probably after 1260, as it belongs to the *Badāyiʿ* collection), as in the ghazal tradition the incorporation of geographic landmarks and historical events is usually a marker of the text's strong adherence to a historical and biographical context.[105] But if we look at it from a more abstract perspective, the reference to Baghdad and to the Mongols' destruction of the bridge over the Tigris also suggests a reading that presents the sack of the Abbasid capital (which occurred in 1258, at the peak of Saʿdi's literary activity) as a profanation

104 See Bürgel 2005.
105 See Ingenito 2018b.

that is comparable to the violent defloration of the object of desire. We know that Saʿdi, notwithstanding his prompt involvement in the political affairs of the Ilkhanid state during the post-1260 decline of the Salghurids in Shiraz, bitterly mourned the traumatic fall of Baghdad with two elegies in Arabic and Persian. The short Persian mourning elegy describes both the Tigris and Baghdad with words of inconsolable sorrow that depict the entire world as inundated by rivers of blood. The poet employs blood-related images in almost half of the text, which opens with the concession offered to the sky to bring down rains of blood, and follows with the description of the Tigris turned into a river of bloody tears.[106] It is however likely that the correspondence between the profaned city of Baghdad and the deflowered beloved is only a secondary association that turns around the lover's ambiguous attitude with regard to the beloved.

6 The Beloved's Body as a Shifting Object of Desire

The non-normative nature of Saʿdi's ghazal on the defloration of the beloved helps us understand the multiplicity of layers that are interposed into the structure of the lyric genre as an autonomous development from its original contiguity with political praise. Its metaphorical brutality highlights the psychological complexity of the lyric subject vis-à-vis the turbulent ramification of his desire across the looseness of the roles traditionally assigned to the lover and to the beloved.[107] Metaphorically undetermined ghazals, oscillating between the lyric and the obscene in a way that defies the norms of both genres, are rare in Saʿdi's works, and yet they successfully test the porosity of his idealized representations of the beloved. The existence of such texts demonstrates that the opposition between the obscene reification and the idealized fetishization of the beloved's body does not belong to a dichotomous polarization. It rather highlights the fluidity of the lyric subject's gaze upon his object of desire, regardless of the genre-watershed that the ʿawratic vs. non-ʿawratic registers of poetic diction generate. We may therefore think of the body of the beloved as a shifting object of desire, which the senses perceive and interpret from different angles variously related to real or imagined experiences that inform both the fictitious plot of the lyric and the real-life events

106 Saʿdi KhE, 703–704.

107 For a theory of the self-reflexivity of the courtly experience of desire as a misogynist projection in the medieval courtly tradition of Europe, see Bloch 1991, 162–63.

that constitute part of a poet's source of inspiration, often filtered by the exposure to cross-genre intertextuality.

An extraordinary example of Sa'di's use of bawdy images as a means to explore the linguistic possibilities of the lyric beyond the formulaic restraint of the courtly tradition is a fragment that challenges the relationship between the ideals of canonic beauty and the role of imagination in perusing the surface of bodies in transition. The main topic of the following lines is the indeterminacy of the difference between the prepubescent traits of the desired body and the signs of physical maturity. By irreverently addressing such a delicate physiological and psychological transition for the beloved and the lover respectively, Sa'di alludes to the subtle coexistence of revulsion and desire through which the lyric subject meditates on the physical traits of masculinity:

> Too long it takes for your beard to appear
> And it's down there that your hair is appearing, not from your chin.
>
> Nevertheless, every time that I think of your ass
> Water appears from the mouth of my cock.[108]

In premodern Persian poetry, as highlighted in the first chapter, the appearance of the first downy beard on the countenance of the beloved marks an aesthetic transition that elicits contrasting feelings in the psychological response of the lover, ranging between sexual arousal, regret, nostalgia, repulsion, and self-disdain.[109] The commotion accompanying the physiological development of the downy beard (*khaṭṭ*) finds its full extent of symbolic reflections in the spiritual dimensions of the lyric tradition. Sa'di, in particular, often compares the beard of the young beloved to a scripture attesting to the perfection of the divine creation embodied in the physical presence of the beautiful *shāhid*.[110] The obscene images of the lines above unpack the very turbulent core of the desire that the courtly tradition reframes in tame forms of chaste longing. They depict for us a delay in the appearance of the beard on the beloved's face that does not correspond to the same degree of tardiness affecting hair growth in an unspecified "lower" region of his body, which could roughly correspond with the lumbar area. The third hemistich clarifies that the lower area in which the appearance of pubescent hair precedes the growth of the beloved's beard corresponds to his buttocks, as the lover describes them as the primary object of

108 [1.83] Sa'di 1385/2006b, 978; Ms. Kabul, 1325, 687; Ms. Yale 1432, f. 382b.

109 See Shamisā 1381/2002, 51–53.

110 See second part of this book.

his fantasies. By "nevertheless" (lit. *bā īn hama*, "with all this considered"), with which the line opens, the lover elucidates that the hairiness of the beloved's bottom is in principle supposed to halt his desire. But such a disturbing physical maturation (perceived as a defect that jeopardizes the pristine beauty of the beloved's body) does not avert the lover's sexual imagination when he confesses that he ejaculates (seemingly unwillingly, in the form of a nocturnal or pre-seminal emission) "every time" that he fantasizes about the lower parts of the beloved's body.

The turbulent impatience of the lover ("*too long* it takes for your beard to appear") suggests his bittersweet desire to witness the growth of the first traces of down on the beloved's face. But it also highlights the uneven signs of biological maturity that relegate the beloved to an unsettling intermediate state: a limbo between adolescence and adulthood, which poses a threat to both the permissibility of the lover's passion and the beloved's sexual appeal in the eyes of his beholder. The memory of the beloved's body that triggers the lover's sexual arousal corresponds to the prepubescent condition of the former, as an earlier stage whose remembrance can work as a mental analogue making up for the present unattainability of the sexual encounter. This fragment offers the opportunity to grasp the poetic representation of the transition from sexuality as an act to the mental landscape of desire. Fragments of this sort confirm that the obscene, other than subverting the mainstream rules of courtly decency and scandalizing its audience with grotesque and hyper-realistic descriptions of genitalia, may actually portray strong erotic tensions that expand upon the linguistic horizons of the lyric.[111]

7 Re-Orienting the Experience of Gender: from the Grotesque to Spiritual Epiphany

Among all Persian obscene texts, Saʿdi's *Khabīṣāt* may be regarded as the finest example of the erotic tensions inhabiting lewd portrayals of sexuality. The literary quality of his licentious material derives from the contiguity between his obscene discourse and the "higher" dimensions of his lyric poetry. This contiguity, especially as far as the depiction of the body of the object of sensual desire is concerned, stands out when comparing Saʿdi's literary pornography with the work of authors whose obscene register explicitly subverts the conventions of the lyric genre.

111 Zipoli 1997, 208.

In one of his most explicitly irreverent *qasida*s, Sūzanī of Samarkand (whom Saʿdi indicates as the direct model for his *Khabīṣāt*) engages with the homoerotic courtly tradition (here embodied through a response to a ghazal by the early-Saljuq poet laureate Amīr Muʿizzī) in a fashion that perfectly reveals the strategies that Saʿdi inherited for the development of his own portrayal of the linguistic and cognitive possibilities of the obscene as a complex meditation on the gendered connotations of desire with respect to the fluidity of the body of the beloved.[112] In this text, Sūzanī specifies the gender of the object of desire by recurring to a qualifier (*qaḥbakak*, "little whore") that is unequivocally feminine. However, the poet introduces this gender specification only in the second couplet of the poem. This temporary deferment produces a creative frustration of the expectations of the reader, who might interpret the first laudatory attributes of the object of desire as masculine or neutral:

> Yesterday I ran into an idol in the street:
> A gait as shining as the moon glittered in my eyes.
>
> Provocative, as sweet as sugar, as tall as a cypress
> That graceful little whore: she was much more splendid than the sun!
>
> I stopped her and tried to stand in her way,
> So the heartbreaker had to walk by me.

Apart from the derogatory term *qaḥbakak*, the first part of the poem describes the encounter between the poetic persona and the object of desire according to the standard topoi of the lyric genre:

> In short, I took that moon home with me,
> A moon that was an ornament to every star….
>
> She eventually took up the harp,
> And played a series of melodies:
>
> She sang a ghazal in the style of Nawruz songs,
> With a rhythm typical of victories and triumphs.
>
> In my passion for her, my eyes dried up and my heart melted.
> I was upset: I wept silver tears and my face yellowed like gold.

112 Suzani, 28–30. Translated by Zipoli (2015, 156–59).

"Little whore" is therefore a key word used to create a temporary disruption in the lyric description as a pretext to orient the attention of the reader both towards the facetious modality that he has to expect from the continuation of the poem, and the femininity of a character that would have been otherwise perceived as a male, beardless presence. Under the intoxicating effects produced by the consumption of wine and after a failed vaginal intercourse, the lover confesses the reason for his sexual unease:

> Greatly embarrassed, I said: "O dear moon,
> The desire for a boy has come to my cock.
>
> It is not accustomed to being in the company of women,
> It always keeps away from cunts and only looks for asses."

The poet portrays the transition to anal intercourse by restoring the lyric register that characterizes the first part of the text:

> She turned round and showed something similar to an arch,
> As high as the stars, which cast a bright light into my eyes:
>
> Roses mixed with jasmine appeared,
> Two tulips wide open round a bud.

However, the accommodating offering of the beloved does not satisfy the lover's desire for male bodies. Upon the lover's second sexual failure, the young woman humiliates his virility through a scatological exploit that Sūzanī portrays rather graphically. While describing the abrupt farewell of the woman, the poet discloses the intertextual origin of his composition. In the concluding line, Sūzanī reveals that this *qasida*, rather than narrating an actual biographical encounter, was composed as a parodic response to his contemporary fellow-poet Amīr Muʿizzī (d. ca. 1125–27), who opened one of his ghazals by overtly praising a comely boy's moon-like countenance that shines from his downy beard:

> She put her chador back on her head, did up her dress,
> And left. This is what I wanted to tell you in poetry,
>
> Replying to the poem by Amir Muʿizzī which begins with these words:
> "Look at the moon newly risen amidst the downy beard of that beautiful boy!"

As a parody, the *qasida* should be interpreted as a bawdy exploration of the boundaries between the implied masculinity of the beloved praised in lyric compositions and the availability of female objects of desire. The grotesque depiction of the lyric I's distaste for both of the woman's anatomical offerings is particularly interesting, as it deviates from the widespread classical (and often playfully crafted) disputation over the difference between boys and girls as preferred objects of desire according to one's intimate penchant for the anus or the vagina.[113] Although the young prostitute offers her back to the lover in the hope of satisfying his "phallus's inclination toward boys," her anus—in spite of a brief yet theatrical rapture of enthusiasm shown by her partner—does not elicit the sexual response that she was hoping to trigger. The logic behind the tragicomic scene is that a young man's physical presence can metonymically be reduced to his anus, regardless of his gender, as the primary modality of man-to-boy penetrative intercourse is anal. The lover's final debacle contradicts the presumed analogy of male and female orifices from the physiological perspective of penetrative sex. This discrepancy is further stressed by the scatological irritation of the woman, who eventually classifies the protagonist as a *ma'būn*—which designates a man affected by *ubna*, or sexual passivity and laxity, perceived as a pathological condition.[114] The semiotic discrepancy is clear: even though the anus is first proposed as an anatomic part capable of signifying a boy's body as a whole, the narration disrupts this analogy and establishes a gender difference whose signification requires physical signs other than the anus in order to re-semanticize the body within the framework of the physical traits of masculinity.

This case of renegotiation of the genitalia as signs that collaborate with the notion of gender can be compared with a text by the Roman poet Martial (d. 104 CE), in which the author stages himself as being discovered by his wife while penetrating a boy. The poet, after adducing exempla and arguments to prove the superiority of anal intercourse with boys, salaciously reprimands his wife's suggestion of being herself able to offer him the same kind of pleasure by reminding her that she should stop giving masculine names to her "affairs" and think of herself as someone who has "two cunts" (*teque puta cunnos, uxor, habere duos*).[115] In Sūzanī's poem, the staged impotence of the poet/lover/lyric

---

113 On the anatomical details of such differences in the poetry of Abū Nuwās, see Schoeler 2014, 74. For an appraisal of the classical Arabic authors—among whom al-Jāḥiẓ is an illustrious presence—see Rowson 1991, 59. For a survey of the Islamicate tradition on the discussions concerning the merits of female or male objects of desire, see Lewis 2009, 703–706, and Kennedy 2008. See also Szombathy 2013, 138, n. 68.

114 On the *ma'būn* and *ubna* as a pathology, see El-Rouayheb 2005, 19–23.

115 Williams 2010, 25. See also Richlin 1992, 34–56, and Obermayer 1998, 20–25.

I, apart from the comic effect that it intends to convey, acts as a meditation on the taste for the homoerotic that overshadows the possibility of heteroerotic intercourse even when both vaginal and anal penetration is made available. This means that, in spite of the complementarity of the depiction of the male and female bodies as objects of desire (and regardless of the anatomical details of the insertive opportunities) the masculinity of the beloved constitutes a potentially preferred quality that the feminine cannot match.

Sūzanī's obscene reversal of the amatory modality of the courtly genre through his parody of Amīr Muʿizzī's ghazal generates a playful meditation on the relationship between gender abstraction and gender specification that characterizes Persian lyric poetry. As pointed out in the first chapter of this book, the conflicting opinions that modern scholars express on the gender of the beloved in Persian poetry are not derived exclusively from prudery and biased ethnocentrism. Analytical confusion is justified by the fact that while the sex of the beloved is predominantly unspecified in order to address a potentially ungendered ideal of beauty, poets occasionally introduce elements that explicitly (when the beloved is mentioned as a "boy") or indirectly (the beloved's *khaṭṭ*, for instance—his "downy beard") point at the male homosociality of the erotic tensions inhabiting the world in which their poetry circulated. As I have tried to theorize in the second chapter of this book as well as in an article on Hafez's "Shirazi Turk," we may account for this apparent discrepancy by considering the ghazal as a generative semiotic structure; the deep levels of abstraction that constitute the main feature of the genre do not specify gender difference.[116] The closer poets bring those abstracted levels to the surface of the external world, the clearer the gendered nature of the beloved appears. Given the subversive nature of the obscene with respect to the language that regulates the relationship between the conventional ideals of a genre and the extra-textual world as a non-conventional horizon of experiences, it is not surprising that obscene Persian texts tend to target the very core of the issue of gender in the lyric.

The subversive aspect of the obscene as a modality that explores the boundaries of gender as it is conventionally portrayed in lyric poetry is particularly evident in Saʿdi's *Khabīs̱āt* and their tendency to constantly juxtapose ungendered courtly ideals of beauty with explicit depictions of the gendered body of the male object of desire. In one of his most erotic "non-obscene" ghazals (which was probably crafted on the basis of a lyric text by Kamāl al-Dīn Ismāʿīl, d. ca. 1238),[117] Saʿdi suggests that "a beauty standing like a cypress in the middle

116 Ingenito 2018b.
117 Kamāl al-Dīn Esfahāni 1348/1970, 736.

of a gathering / is better than seventy cypresses amidst a meadow." In spite of the emphasis on the mundane nature of the object of desire and the sensuality of the descriptions, the beloved appears as an ungendered and evanescent presence:

When your body is covered by a shirt
It resembles a soul inhabiting a body;

And whoever admires your bare limbs
Will say that your shirt is filled with roses.
Badāyiʿ 232[118]

Surprisingly, Saʿdi repurposed most of the imagery from the ghazal above (as well as its meter and rhyme) in an obscene text that describes the object of desire as a presence in which masculine and feminine social roles conflate. In these lines, the obscene register offers the opportunity to visualize the contrast between ungendered ideals of beauty and the spaces of literary representation that the lyric does not usually cover:

How delightful it is to indulge in pleasure with a sugar-lipped beauty:
Scarlet cheeks like cherries, a body as white as jasmine.

Night and day, companions in the alcove and in the market:
A man when in public, but like a wife when at home.

At times politely contemplating each other while composed
Like the cypress trees standing amidst the meadows.

Other times so passionately lying in each other's embrace
As if only one shirt were needed for our bare bodies.

The brush so tightly stuck into the makeup case
Like a candle firmly pressed into the lantern.

A rod sliding entirely up to his navel,
With our sperm running down my thighs.

118 [1.84] Saʿdi YE, 155.

> The golden throne of the king does not shine as gracefully
> as the back of a boy whose body is as white as silver.
>
> Will I be satisfied by just one kiss? God forbid!
> Someone like me would never utter these words!
>
> A strike in the middle of two buttocks
> Is much better than seventy kisses on one's lips.
>
> Tell my enemies that these are my truthful words
> So that they may not make up their own stories.[119]

Contrary to the Persianate traditional depiction of idealized male beauty in the form of prepubescent bodies whose traits of masculinity are yet to appear, in many of his obscene texts Saʿdi seems to defy the rule that, in medieval Islamicate societies, confined homoerotic appreciation to intergenerational exchanges. In these texts, Saʿdi often describes the boy as a strong man[120] who has long since crossed the threshold of manhood,[121] and who could break the teeth of the lover.[122] These young men may wear a turban,[123] and while in some rare cases Saʿdi even alludes to the virility of their sexual physiology,[124] the lyric subject often declares that the kind of "moon-faced

119 [1.85] Saʿdi 1385/2006b, 983. I have reconstructed the text on the basis of Ms. Kabul 1325 (679); Ms. Dushanbe 1310s (361); Ms. Yale 1432 (f. 380b).

120 [1.86] Saʿdi 1385/2006b, 976. I prefer the variant found in Ms. Dushanbe 1310s, 362; Ms. Kabul 1325, 682; Ms. Yale 1432 (f. 381a): *kung-i durusht*, rather than *kung-u durusht*.

121 Are you a thirty-year old beardless boy? Never seen
Such a thing in the lands of Islam: maybe a marvel from the end of time?
Should they tie your hands for a week behind your neck,
A week later your beard would reach your waist!
[1.87] Ms. Kabul 1325, 670.

122 "At times a strong boy would break my teeth."
Saʿdi 1385/2006b, 981.

123 Veiled brides are countless,
Lie down with a bride who has a turban:
A bride with pants, which you can take off
And you'll see a turnip as thick as a donkey's.
[1.88] Ms. Tehran 1296, 469; Ms. Kabul 1325; 667.

124 His *cypress*—and I don't mean his height or stature—
Is hard and straight for everyone, but not for us.
[1.89] Ms. Kabul 1325, 683.

beauties" whom he appreciates the most are solid boys who are as tall as him (*kungī-st ham-bālā-yi man*).[125]

The allusions to a non-normative representation of the object of desire show that Sa'di's approach to the counter-textualization of the courtly amatory tradition is informed by the quest for an erotic tension that keeps the aesthetic values of the lyric discourse alive precisely within the context of the contact between literary invention and real experience. In the following text, Sa'di opens the lyric description of an imaginary beloved by shifting registers in just the way we have witnessed in Sūzanī's poem. Subsequently, he keeps grazing the liminal space between the obscene and the courtly by creating an erotic effect that abruptly comes to an end—along with the composition itself—as soon as the limits of decorum are overcome:

> How beautiful it is to offer one's heart to a beloved:
> A moon-faced beauty, so graciously noble and elegant!
>
> His delicate feet wearing manly sandals
> On his head a coarse hat, in the fashion of muleteers.
>
> A beardless boy whose chest is wrapped in a woolen cloth
> Is much more handsome than a girl covered by the veil.
>
> Girls need gold, fine garments, and ornaments
> To entice the passion of their husbands.
>
> Many ornaments are needed to beautify their bodies:
> a musky mole, a fine and dark downy beard won't suffice!
>
> The brides of paradise cover their head with veils:
> I love hemp garments on a beauty's chest.
>
> Better than me no one can describe how that tunic
> closes and opens from behind the neck:
>
> when a boy lays his silver chin on the ground
> the bed is an ornament in full display.

125 See *supra*, n. 1

Comely young men [*shāhid*] are all that a city needs:
No more than one sun ought to shine upon a country.

The kings sleep on verandas [*manẓar*] that overlook beautiful vistas
The veranda of the mystics [*ʿārifān*] is the back of a beautiful boy
[*zībā-manẓarī*].

This staff that we have between our thighs
Can break a door, even if it's of iron.

More than this I cannot write down
An entire anthology is required for these stories.[126]

From these lines one could infer that the physical differentiation between boys and girls as objects of desire does not lie in their somatic characteristics, but rather in the accessories that culturally mark the difference between the masculine and the feminine: rugged tunics and woolen clothes versus veils, musk as a light make-up for the downy beard versus ornaments and golden jewels, etc. Apart from these superficial differences, the somatic traits of the two categories that Saʿdi describes are sexually indistinguishable. In the first couplet, in fact, the poet describes the ungendered beloved in the same fashion that Sūzanī introduces the "little whore" without gendering her body until he makes an outspoken reference to her vagina. It is the adjective *mardāna* ("manly") that, at the beginning of the second couplet, characterizes the gender of the sandals worn by the "delicate" (*laṭīf*) feet of the beloved. This means that even though the obscene belongs to a codified genre whose set of stock images and motifs is as standardized as the ghazal's depictions of passionate love, it constitutes a modality that touches upon the gap between the abstract and imaginary presence of the literary persona and the physical substance of the experience of desire as it is witnessed in the real life of both the poets and their audiences.

The obscene, therefore, rather than opposing a realistic depiction of the idealized abstraction of the amatory ghazal, is a codified fiction that points at the discrepancy between the literary representations of desire and the materiality of the experience of it in the real world. An example of the catalyzing effect of the obscene with respect to this contrast can be seen in the line in which Saʿdi opposes kings and mystics on the basis of their nocturnal inclinations: on the one hand, the visual pleasure of the garden contemplated from a high portico,

126 [1.90] Ms. Kabul 1325, 684.

on the other, the enticement deriving from anal intercourse with boys whose faces are a witness (*shāhid*) to God's splendor. Sa'di outlines this impudent parallel through a pun on the meanings of the word *manẓar*, which literally means "the space in which the gaze (*naẓar*) is set." If in the first instance, *manẓar* is employed with the acceptation of "view," "landscape," or "portico" (overlooking a beautiful landscape), in the second hemistich it means "countenance," and refers to the beautiful countenance that is the object of the mystics' contemplation. The pun that the word *manẓar* introduces reveals how, in Sa'di's poetry, visual contemplation as an aestheticized approach to the relationship between the subject and the world transcends the boundaries between genres and modalities.

As explored in the chapter on the *Gulistān*, kings and Sufis (often referred to as "the poor," "the mystic," or "the indigent") constitute the two poles of the overarching ethical system on which Sa'di has built his literary corpus. The portrayal of their words and deeds, along with the depiction of the discrepancies between the ideals of political and spiritual superiority and the baseness of the reality in which they operate, is one of the most illuminating thematic obsessions recurring in Sa'di's works. The line describing the *manẓar* addresses exactly this relationship, and its parodic effect emerges from the subversion of the ideal of chastity that is supposed to sustain the mystic's gaze upon the face of beautiful boys. The ideal of contemplation upon which Sa'di relies is the face-to-face position that would enable the mystic to look at the boy and transfer his desire towards the exaltation of God's magnificence in a way that is very similar to the suggestions that al-Ghazālī offers in his chapter on poetry and music audition. However, in order to represent the sexual impulses of the desirous mystic, by turning the boy's body on an imaginary axis of a hundred and eighty degrees, Sa'di turns the static depiction of an ideal act of contemplation into a full range of experiential possibilities in which sexual and spiritual appetites can potentially coexist.

In these pages, what I have preliminary referred to as the "mystic" translates the word *'ārif*. In most manuscripts, Sa'di's *Khabīsāt* open with a short *masnavī* that narrates the passion that an *'ārif* develops for a strong young wrestler (*pisarī zūrmand-i kushtīgīr*).[127] After a series of erotic vicissitudes parodying the path that young initiates undertake when embracing a Sufi order, the boy eventually wears the Sufi cloak (*zhanda pūshīd*) and the growth of a full beard marks his transition to manhood and "spiritual realization."[128] Sa'di's use of the word *'ārif* in this context is undoubtedly parodic, but it partially resonates with

127 Sa'di 1385/2006b, 984–85; Ms. Kabul 1325; 665–66; Ms. Yale 1432, ff. 377a–377b.
128 Ms. Kabul 1325, 666; Ms. Yale 1432, f. 377b.

the fashion in which, in his serious output, the poet ascribes to this figure the role of beholding human beauty as an exercise of spiritual eroticism.

As highlighted throughout this chapter, the coexistence of the sexual and the spiritual aspects of Saʿdi's lyric output is a constant in the relationship between the texts themselves and the overlaps between the courtly and spiritual environments in which the poet's lyrics circulated. We have now fully explored the multiple semantic refractions of Saʿdi's expression of desire as the result of an oscillation between a critical meditation on the body and the limits of courtly language. The groundwork has been laid for the study of the spiritual dimensions of the lyric subject's contemplation of human beauty through the cognition and recognition of signs pointing to a reality other than what the senses can access, yet which cannot be "cognized" without the aid of the internal and the external senses. Paradoxically, then, it is through the senses that the *ʿārif*—which from now on I will translate as the "spiritual beholder"—can peruse how the "invisible" may grow out of the flesh of the erotic.

PART 2

Through the Mirror of your Glances: The Sacred Aesthetics of Saʿdi's Lyric Subject

Introduction to Part 2

> They paint splendid countenances on brocades and silk,
> But the eyebrows they depict are no manifest sorcery [*siḥr-i mubīn*].
>
> *Badāyiʿ* 577[1]

•••

> But when Our signs came to them visibly, they said, "This is a manifest sorcery."
>
> *Qurʾān*, 27:13

∴

1 Amidst the Mud and the Heart

The study of sacred eroticism in Saʿdi's ghazals involves philological and theoretical problems that relate to the relationship between poetic creativity, literary influence, and the role of historical "discourses" on the nature of beauty in the shaping of the poet's view of the world, both in its physical manifestations and invisible origin. On what textual, intertextual, experiential, and ideological bases did Saʿdi shape his personal approach to the lyrical exploration of desire as a spiritual and aesthetic practice? In the context of the formulaic, impersonally homogeneous, and abstracted nature of premodern Persian lyric poetry, what texts, historical events, personal experiences, and lines of thought should we take into account in order to explore Saʿdi's contribution to the spiritual dimension of the history of ghazal poetry? Should we still follow the structuralist paradigm of New Criticism by relying on literary texts alone to account for the "meaning" of the sacred contents of Saʿdi's ghazals? Or could we accept a more nuanced approach, closer to the critical practices set by New Historicism, and conceive of Saʿdi's ghazals as texts that are partially influenced by the literary tradition and partially capable of embodying, in a discursive way, historical practices and beliefs?

As it has been illustrated in the previous chapters, Saʿdi was particularly eager to be recognized by his contemporary and future audiences as the most

1 [2.1] Saʿdi YE, 259.

 | DOI:10.1163/9789004435902_007

skillful literary master of his age. Therefore, it is not surprising that he carefully avoided any implicit or explicit references (except for Sūzanī, his licentious model) to the oeuvres of his predecessors. Nevertheless, far from the "anxiety of influence" characterizing post-Romantic ideals of originality, in the eyes of medieval and early modern Persian authors, poetic creativity stemmed from an author's personal re-appropriation of the literary tradition through the orchestration of skillful repetitions and creative variations that were based on a shared repertoire of images, themes, and forms.[2]

On the basis of this peculiar aspect of Persian literary creativity, conceived as the byproduct of repetition and mindful imitation, one of the rewarding pathways to uncover a poet's literary identity lies in the scrutiny of a technique, known as *istiqbāl*, or *javāb*, by which authors would imitate other poets by readopting the formal features of their compositions. In his seminal book on *istiqbāl* in the ghazals of Babā Fighānī (d. 1516 or 1519), Paul Losensky suggests that the study of "response poems," i.e., "the explicit imitations of earlier works," is one of the best forums for studying how a specific author would craft his personal poetic voice by interpreting and recreating the literary tradition.[3]

While the majority of critical studies of the practice of *istiqbāl* have been conducted on the basis of Timurid and Safavid poetry, textual evidence suggests that this technique characterized the development of the Persian ghazal from the early days of its formative period. In spite of the lack of in-depth comparative analyses, Saʿdi's collections of ghazals constitute no exception, and one of the authors that future investigations should take into account for a better understanding of the emergence of Saʿdi's lyric style is the 12th-century poet Sanāʾī of Ghazna.

The following lines, for instance, belong to a short ghazal in which Sanāʾī focuses on the theme of the relationship between sensual desire, love, reason, and religious ethics:

> So arduous is love when the intellect guides it,
> For this path belongs to the heart, not to forms and experiences....
>
> In spiritual semantics [*rāh-i maʿnī*], find the fine line between the heart [*dil*] and mud [*gil*],
> For what you practice, my boy, is nothing but muddy affairs.[4]

2 Losensky 1998, 100–104.

3 Ibid., 100.

4 [2.2] Sanāʾi 1362/1983, 814; Sanāʾi 1389/2010, 381.

In a ghazal showcasing the same meter (*ramal*), rhyme (*-il*) and refrain (*ast*), Saʿdi repurposes all the formal elements of Sanāʾī's ghazal in a lyric that, by elaborating on the imagery offered by his predecessor, offers a new, personal meditation on the value of sensuality as a window opening into the realm of the sacred:

So hard it is to keep one's eyes off beautiful countenances:
The advice of anyone who urges us against it is pointless....

In the past I would declare my claim of self-restraint
Now this much I know: all claims, all efforts were vain....

I shall not step away from the alley where the beloved resides:
I beg your pardon my friends, as my feet are stuck in the mud....

Those who declare sinful gazing upon the beautiful ones
Only see the forms, for they are bereft of their spiritual meanings
[*zi maʿnī ghāfil ast*]....

O camel-driver, proceed slowly: my beloved sits in your palanquin.
The beasts carry loads on their backs, and heavy is the load that burdens
my heart.

SAʿDI, *Khavātīm* 683[5]

When we are faced with a similarity between two texts, as Paul Losensky points out, one ought to decide whether formal correspondences constitute an intentional allusion to a specific subtext or a conventional repetition of well-established topoi that belong to the literary tradition. The study of *istiqbāl* demonstrates that strict formal convergence usually implies the presence of an intentional act of creative imitation. Following this logic, we may read Saʿdi's ghazal as a direct response (*javāb*) to Sanāʾī, in which the reshaping of images through the repetition of forms generates the reinvention of ideas, values, beliefs. This entanglement of form, images, and thought analyzed through patterns of intertextual influence allows us to meditate on the philosophical thickness of Saʿdi's poetry well beyond the strict scope of the exercise of rhetorical playfulness that poetic imitation involves.

When reading Saʿdi's ghazal, how should one account for the ethical disengagement with which he reframed the form and the imagery of the text that

5 [2.3] Saʿdi YE, 305–306.

Sanāʾī had composed almost two centuries before him? How does the "mud" of sensual experiences influence the contemplation of beauty in a context that is spiritual, albeit not normatively religious, and aesthetic, without being scholastically enclosed in a prescriptive theoretical framework? How does Sanāʾī's quest for a form of purity far from sensory experiences reemerge in Saʿdi's devotion to the world of physical possibilities, cognitive perusals, and spiritual meanings? I opened this introduction with a diachronic conversation between these two lyric poets in order to facilitate the transition to the second part of the book. While the previous chapters offered a study of the dynamics of physical desire in the construction of Saʿdi's lyric subject, the next section prepares the groundwork for a more integrated foray into the flesh of Saʿdi's sacred eroticism and anthropology of vision.

In the context of 13th-century lyric poetry, the link between form and thought that emerges from the parallels between Saʿnāʾī's and Saʿdi's ghazals urges us to rethink the problem of influence and imitation beyond the question of the poet's "intentionality" as a clear-cut distinction. In the Timurid and Safavid periods, active imitation was at the forefront of the poets' overt conversations on poetic creativity. In that historical framework (but also during the second half of the 14th century), the active practice of *istiqbāl* took shape through the constant quotation of lines from other poets and, in some cases, even the mention of the names of literary rivals or models of imitatio. In the case of the formative period of the ghazal as an independent genre, between the 11th and the 13th centuries, the emergence of poetic subjectivity was still in the making, and the circulation of a shared lyric "I" reflected a constant overlap between a collective poetic experience and the necessity for the poets to establish their individual authorial and authoritative voices. This means that while intentional processes of intertextual imitation can be often recognized in Saʿdi's *dīvān*s, the tensions stemming from two similar texts are more relevant than the actual (and often inscrutable) intentions of the poet. By shifting our attention to the formal tensions between texts, we may partially overcome the indeterminacy that arises from any discourse on intentionality and, at the same time, we may allow intertextual affinity to speak for the images and thoughts that constitute a poet's individual style when analyzed against his predecessors. From this perspective, we may conceive of influence and imitation as forms of dynamic affinity among ghazals, rather than intentional and personal responses.

When comparing Saʿdi's ghazals with those of his predecessors, especially on the basis of formal variations, it is striking to witness the emergence of a new lyric paradigm of thought for which intertextual interplays across centuries cannot account alone. The questions raised by the comparison between

Sa'di's ghazal and its intertextual tension with Sanā'ī's subtext pertain to a broader meditation on the nature of Sa'di's erotic spirituality. This comparison, along with other analyses that will follow, urges us to read the so-called "mystical" dimension of Sa'di's works as the product of a conflation of specific strands of a "sober" Persian Sufi tradition with psychological and epistemological approaches that, by percolating through literary and non-literary texts that circulated between Baghdad and Fars in the early 13th century, indirectly influenced the novelty of the poet's lyric voice.[6]

The chapters that constitute this second part of the book will highlight forms of intellectual affinity (rather than direct influence) between Sa'di's poetry and a tradition of Sufi thought that goes back to al-Ghazālī's spiritual and aesthetic interpretation of the Avicennian epistemological legacy in the context of the relationship between the perusal of the visible world and the quest for supernal beauty and truth.

When these indirect influences are taken into account, an important caveat is in order: in spite of the high degree of systematization that both Avicenna and the major Sufi scholars who shaped Iranian spiritual thought in its post-formative and classical periods brought about, Sa'di's approach to philosophy and spirituality was primarily informed by his lyrical aesthetics, and as such it remained non-scholastic and non-systematic.[7] For this reason, the theological, Sufi, and philosophical forays that I will tackle in the next chapters should be considered as intellectual infiltrations and sources of both aesthetic and epistemological inspirations that contributed to the constitution of Sa'di's original phenomenology of vision. In this context, what I shall discuss is not the direct influence of Islamic philosophy and theology on the poet's ghazals, but, rather, forms of intellectual and aesthetic affinity that caused al-Ghazālī's spiritual epistemology and Avicenna's theory of the internal senses to filter throughout Sa'di's poetic endeavor.

---

6 On the contrast between intoxication and sobriety (*sukr* vs. *sawh*), see Schimmel 1975, 58, 129; and Wilcox 2011, 103. Ernst (1985, 49–52) highlights the artificiality of the distinction between intoxication and sobriety in the Sufi tradition.

7 On the non-scholastic nature of the Sufi aesthetics embraced by Sa'di in his ghazals, see Hamidiyān 1383/2004, 151–52. See also the passages in which the Iranian scholar compares Sa'di with the Sufi lyric tradition of 'Aṭṭār, Rumi, and 'Irāqī, and concludes that the main difference between his poetry and the latter authors rests in Sa'di's emphasis on the sensory exploration of the external world in a non-prescriptive and non-technical fashion. Ibid., 185–88.

2 "I Behold You through Your Eyes": for a Lyric Anthropology of Vision

In spite of the long-lasting effects that Sa'di's style exerted on the development of Persian literature after the demise of the Ilkhanid empire, the influence of his lyric innovations on the subsequent legacy of the late medieval and early modern ghazal has yet to be studied. While the intertextual relationships between Sa'di's ghazals and his predecessors often do not offer clear patterns of intentional and explicit imitations, the establishment of Sa'di's voice as a lyric *auctoritas* introduced to the historical development of the Persian ghazal the practice of *istiqbāl* as an active manipulation of the past based on the recognition of poetic subjectivity. A preliminary survey of the very first generation of authors whose ghazals manifest explicit signs of Sa'di's influence reveals that the problem of the relationship between spirituality and physical desire from the perspective of the practice of visual contemplation constituted a predominant aesthetic agenda that accompanied Persian lyricism until its early modern evolution, which corresponded with the late-15th-century transition from the Timurid to the Safavid period.

One of the least studied of these "minor" authors is a Central Asian poet, Sayf of Fergana (d. after 1305), who, as a consequence of the socio-political unrest caused by the Mongol invasion, established himself in the Anatolian city of Aqsaray, from which he ostensibly engaged in an epistolary exchange with Sa'di:

> When the nightingale of his [Sa'di's] poetic talent started singing,
> The *Rose Garden* [*Gulistān*] seized all the horizons....
>
> When his poems reached my ears,
> So profound was the passion I felt for them,
>
> That my heart was marked by his seal
> Just like wax being impressed by a ring.[8]

Many of the ghazals by Sayf-i Farghānī are an extraordinary example of how Sa'di's imitators transported his psychology of theo-erotic vision well beyond the boundaries he had set in his own lifetime.[9] In this specific case, the ghazal

8 Sayf Farghāni 1341–44/1962–65, 1: 114.

9 On the impact of Sa'di's work on his contemporaries, including Sayf-i Farghāni, see Ingenito 2014.

is a direct response to Sa'di through the technique of *istiqbāl*, which, as clarified earlier, designates the composition of a ghazal that is strictly based on the meter, rhyme, and refrain of a ghazal authored by a different poet.[10] Sa'di's original text (which we may define as a "hypotext" serving as a subtext for subsequent "hypertexts" imitating its form and imagery) reads as a smooth amatory laud of the object of desire conveyed through the lyric subject's longing for a visual encounter. The poem opens with a statement through which the lyric subject confesses the spiritual ends of its act of beholding:

> O idol, if the moon of your countenance I do behold:
> In truth I behold to seek the signs of God's grace.
>
> I peruse your entire figure over and over every time I see you
> So that my eyes may glean a Sign from your face.
>
> In disdain you look down on my miserable life:
> So faithfully I admire the soil on which you step.
>
> You are the sun, and I am nothing: a weak, dejected particle.
> So far above me, how could I ever behold you?
>
> Your hair is the realm of darkness, your lips the water of life:
> Erratically my gaze wanders amidst your black curls.
>
> My Indian black eyes shall no longer see your Turkic cheeks
> If by mistake I behold the Chinese locks of your hair.
>
> Strenuous is the path of loving you, but like Sa'di
> I walk and look back, filled with nostalgia.
>
> *Badāyi'* 564[11]

This short, thematically compact ghazal reads as a geopoetic map through which the lyric subject contemplates the object of desire within the framework of an intimate practice of careful perusal. Even though the initial declaration of the quest for the signs of divine grace as a rationale for the act of beholding may seem unwarranted within the purely erotic imagery of the poem, the

10 On the practice of *istiqbāl* (also referred to as *javāb*, or *tatabu'*), see Losensky 1998a; Zipoli 1993.

11 [2.4] Sa'di YA, 253–54.

reader feels compelled to naively follow the cartographic object of desire as it is delicately portrayed through the lover's eyes. The penultimate line enhances the geographical aspect of the intimate recital by relying on a strategic use of the "observance of the similar" (*murāʿāt-i naẓīr*), through which the poet uses words belonging to the same semantic field within one single couplet (in this case, geographical entities: India, Turkistan, and China).[12] All lingering questions regarding the real purpose of the initial statement involving God's grace dissolve with the line that brings the ghazal to a close: it is a real, human presence that the lyric subject has been contemplating, and the space of intimacy eventually bleeds into the nostalgia of the farewell, as if the memory of the encounter were to constitute the only token left by the evanescent object of desire.

And yet, if we bypass the naiveté of an inexperienced reading, one question remains: how does the intimate space of eroticism displayed in this ghazal meaningfully interplay with the unwarranted justification expressed in the first line? Why does the lyric subject feel compelled to express that the only reason guiding its gaze is the quest for the traces of divine grace? How does the physical presence of the object of desire relate to the spiritual framework with which the poet seems to stage the overarching meaning of the text since its very outset? I suggest seeking the preliminary response to this broad question by considering how Sayf-i Farghānī's imitation reads as a theoretical gloss to the invisible conflation of carnality and spirituality that inhabits Saʿdi's hypotext. In order to better clarify the emergence of a quasi-theoretical approach in Sayf's gloss upon Saʿdi's ghazal, I have highlighted specific passages of the text in bold:

1 People might **frown upon my beholding you:**
It is not your face that I behold, but the creation of God.

---

12 Although this device had already been employed by Arab critics and poets, it was fully developed by Iranian poets in their quest for that harmony and balance (*tanāsub*) that can be considered one of the dominant aesthetic values of Persian classical poetry. Even though *murāʿāt-i naẓīr*, as a rhetorical device, was first described by Radūyānī, we owe to Vāʿiẓ-e Kāshifī one of its most compelling descriptions: "*Murāʿāt*'s first meaning is to respect someone's right, and *naẓīr* means 'similar'; whilst technically, 'the observance of the similar' refers to the act of the poet when he intervenes on the class of terms belonging to the same semantic field in such a way that, for the sake of giving an order to his verse, similar words such as the names of the stars, plants, weapons, ethnic groups, and parts of the body are juxtaposed within the same space." Vāʿez-e Kāshefi 1369/1990 [1977], 115–16. See also Homāʾi, 1374/1995, 257–60; Chalisova 2009, 146; Ingenito 2018b, 868–73. For a discussion of this device in Hafez's poetry, see Purnāmdāriyān 1382/2003, 125–32.

2 I belong to you: anything that is mine, shall be yours.
Hence this is clear: **I behold you through your eyes.**

3 The enemy says that forbidden is my gaze upon him:
It might be licit or illicit. I will behold!

4 Thirst consumes me, no wonder if I seek the water of life!
It is because of my malady that I seek the cure!

5 **I see the light of divine beauty in that face**—well aware I am:
Purity is what I seek when I behold that mirror.

6 Your beautiful face deprived me of balance and peace:
Why am I here again beholding that complexion?

7 **I look around in all directions so that I may behold your face:**
Yet in my soul you dwell, where is my gaze roaming?

8 My life? No hopes are left to me, alas
If I meditate upon my days, and behold your justice.

9 **For long you have not shown your face to me:**
It is a flaw of destiny, how could I blame you?

10 **Sayf-i Farghānī, till when will you be setting your eyes on others?**
—My hands did not grasp the rose: hence I behold vulgar plants.

11 What should I do if I did not succeed in beholding your face?
"I walk and look back, filled with nostalgia."[13]

We may notice how Sayf, by reworking the last hemistich of Saʿdi's ghazal into his own text (a technique referred to as *tażmīn*), establishes a directly hypertextual connection between the two poems, already bound together by their identical rhyme, *radīf*, and meter. Through a further exploration of the refrain "I behold" (*mī-nigaram*), Sayf converts the intimacy of the erotic encounter into a lyrical gloss that elaborates Saʿdi's allusive imagery and recontextualizes the text around the experience of vision both as an optical endeavor and as an intellectual and psychological effort. We may regard the following

13 [2.5] Sayf-e Farghāni 1341–44/1962–65, 2: 308–309.

observations and questions as the overarching themes of the problem of the psychology of spirituality and desire in Saʿdi's ghazal, which we shall gradually disclose throughout the five chapters constituting the second part of the book:

1. Ethical imperatives against the contemplation of human beauty: the first line of the poem reiterates the purpose of Saʿdi's lyric subject's perusal of the beloved's countenance. Whereas the act of contemplation is frowned upon by other people, the lyric subject exposes the recognition of worldly beauty not only as a function of the divine grace, but also as a justification for the potentially sensual implications of the act of beholding.
2. Undetermined permissibility of the experience of gazing: the third line hints at a space of indetermination in which the permissibility of the gaze upon the beloved's body may be questioned according to different legal and ethical approaches to the problem. The lyric subject, however, peremptorily declares its resolution: "I shall behold!"
3. The face of the beloved as a mirror that cathartically reflects divine beauty: the fifth line clarifies that the ultimate purpose of the contemplation of the human beloved is the perception of a glimpse of divine beauty. The face of the object of desire is represented as a mirror capable of cleansing the beholder from all impurities.
4. Contemplation causes bewilderment and confusion: in spite of the idealized depiction of the metaphysical aspects of the contemplation of human beauty, the sixth line introduces the turbulent dimension of the experience of beholding. Gazing emerges as an obsessive practice, whose effects, depending on its psycho-physiological and social variables, may cause an unsettling state of disquiet in the lyric subject's quest for the divine archetype of beauty.
5. Discrepancy between sensory perception and mental representation of an invisible presence: lines seven, nine, and ten highlight a gap in the apparently straightforward narrative of the perception of divine beauty as a reflection on the face of the beloved. The carnal presence of the object of desire seems to fade away, while the lyric subject seeks signs of his presence in its own soul/heart. This discrepancy highlights the psychological context (in terms of mental processes) of a connection between the visible things of the world and certain kinds of mental content signifying some sort of presence or truth that lies beyond the realm of visual perceptions. In the final lines of the ghazal, Sayf shows the frustration of the lyric subject vis-à-vis the failed retrieval of a mental content capable of providing the visible world with metaphysical meaning. The line before the last reveals a deeper connection with the spiritual aesthetics that characterize Saʿdi's theo-erotic ethos. The contemplation

of vulgar plants as a visual rebound for the failed perception of the rose reminds us of the introductory anecdote of the *Gulistān*—mentioned in the second chapter of this book—in which a spiritual master compares his vision of the invisible world to the intoxicating contemplation of a bush of roses.[14]

These five points raised by the analysis of Sayf's response constitute the very core of Saʿdi's lyric anthropology of vision. In spite of the apparent lack of an overarching theory of the visionary experience in Saʿdi's hypotext, Sayf's Anatolian response brings to the surface of the poem all the hidden tensions and critical knots latently embedded within the smooth surface of the original ghazal. Moreover, Saʿdi's geographical allusions and Sayf's attempt to cover the physical distance between Fars and Anatolia through the practice of literary response present the link between eroticism and spirituality as a lyrical urgency that characterized the circulation of ideas, values, and practices in the historical and regional settings in which both poets lived.

3 Saʿdi and the Saints of Shiraz: between Detached Homage and the Cult of Beauty

The few poems of praise in which Saʿdi announces his alleged "return" to Shiraz offer key vantage points on the official voice with which Saʿdi declares the space of ideas, symbols, and traditions that he wishes to embrace in the public arena. The following poem, for instance, offers us a pretext to meditate on the historicity of the spiritual field in which Saʿdi introduces the literary agency of his persona in connection with the geopoetics of the city of Shiraz in its political setting:

Joyous is the vision of the pure morning when I see myself
Approaching Shiraz again from the Pass of *Allāhu Akbar*!

My eyes again filled with this paradise on earth
Loaded with happiness, no dearth I see, nor violence.

O God, may this region never suffer from tyranny,
As it was Solomon's throne and the outpost to Mecca.

14 I will illustrate in chapter six the cognitive and psychological underpinnings of this anecdote, especially from the perspective of Sayf's allusion to the discrepancy between the vulgarity of the soulless objects of desire and the ideal of beauty represented by the rose.

More than a thousand masters of faith it hosts
And the Ka'ba floats above their heads.

For the litanies and meditations of the Great Sheikh [Ibn Khafīf]
For the honor of Rūzbihān and for the five daily prayers

I beseech you to protect this city of holy men
From the hands of impious infidels and from the vicious barbarians.

I beseech you by the Ka'ba and by the honor of he who built it
For the people of Shiraz to thrive in prosperity and rejoicing.

And anyone who shall covet to threaten this city, the Dome of Islam
May his head like silver and gold be cut by a maul.

As Sa'di in concern for Shiraz night and day used to say:
"all the cities are sparrows, and a royal falcon is our kingdom."
Ṭayyibāt 5[15]

These lines were composed sometime between the mid-1240s and the early 1250s, and they attest to the poet's effort to build a solid groundwork for the legitimacy of his status at the Salghurid court after claiming to have travelled for years in Asia Minor.[16] In what appears as a transparent declaration of affection for the city of Shiraz, it is possible to detect the specific agenda that Sa'di had, namely to penetrate the circles of power of the Salghurid dynasty, at the time facing the imminent threat of the Mongol invasion (in spite of the assistance that Abū Bakr provided, through his son and nephew, to the Mongol conquest of Baghdad). Such a rhetorical blend of royal pride and spirituality seems to be directed at Abū Bakr and his particular favor towards pious men and

15 [2.6] Sa'di YE, 6, and Sa'di KhE 669. I followed Ms. Yale 1432 (f. 179a) in reading the fourth line as *'ibādathā-yi shaykh-i kabīr* instead of the printed editions' implied juxtaposition: *'ibādat, bi rūḥ-i shaykh-i kabīr*. In the manuscript, this short *qasida* opens with a misplaced line that is not found in any of the printed editions of Sa'di's works: *qażā* [*bi*] *gardish-i gardūn-i dūn-i sufla-navāz / bi tīgh-i hijr burūn kard sa'dī az shīrāz* ("Destiny had taken away Sa'di from Shiraz, with the blade of separation / with the revolution of the vile, base-loving spheres"). On the geopoetics of Sa'di's and Hafez's poetry, especially from the angle of the city of Shiraz's transformation as a literary sign, see Ingenito 2018b; Brookshaw 2019, 32–38.

16 See General Introduction, pp. 4–16.

Islamic scholars.[17] In this respect, we may compare the rhetoric of the poem with the section of the introduction to the *Gulistān* in which Saʿdi addresses Abū Bakr and the Salghurid family by praising Fars as the stronghold of the Islamic faith in the face of the Mongol threat.[18] By mentioning the names of Ibn Khafīf ("the Great Sheikh," d. 982) and Rūzbihān-i Baqlī (d. 1209), Saʿdi collocates the official horizon of his spiritual lineage to a tradition of Shirazi Sufism that emphasizes the role of human beauty as the locus of manifestation of the divine splendor.[19]

Saʿdi's allusion to the Shirazi Sufi scholar and saint Rūzbihān is particularly revealing. His works (especially *Abhar al-ʿāshiqīn*, *The Jasmin of the Lovers*) stand out as the highest point in the maturation of a tradition of Sufi reflections on the nature of love, one that conceived mundane passion for beauty as a ladder capable of taking the believer to a higher degree of passion for the divine presence.[20] The system of theophanic aesthetics constituting Rūzbihān's approach to divine beauty can provide a meaningful context for the discourse on amatory contemplation dominating Shiraz in the age of Saʿdi. This potential source of influence is even more meaningful if we consider the devotion with which the Salghurid family came to regard Rūzbihān's

---

17 See Introduction, pp. 10–14. As pointed out in the first chapter, textual evidence suggests that Saʿdi would rely on theo-erotic imagery to exert his influence on young patrons, such as the Salghurid prince Saʿd II and the Ilkhanid minister, Shams al-Dīn Juvaynī. This form of literary eroticism, imbuing praise poetry as part of a lyrical princely upbringing that would directly involve the poets working at court, can be traced back to the relationship between Farrukhī Sīstānī (fl. 11th c.) and his young patrons, Muḥammad and Masʿūd, the successors of Maḥmūd of Ghazna (see Chapter 1, pp. 92–93). As for the origins of the influence of the spiritual discourse on this pedagogical eroticism, the courtly relationship between Sanāʾī and Bahrāmshāh deserves to be further explored: "More difficult to assess are a number of poems written by Sanāʾī for the Ghaznavid Sultan Bahrāmshāh (reigned 1118–ca. 1152). They are really ghazals, mostly describing a Beloved in terms which, though not explicitly mystical, are evidently referring to transcendent Beauty." De Bruijn 1997, 57. De Bruijn ascribes the most accomplished form of panegyrical theo-eroticism to the poetry of Hafez (d. 1390). Following Yohannan's intuition ("There is a possibility that a number of Saʿdi's ghazals are best read neither as religious nor as secular love poetry, but rather as eulogies addressed to a patron." Yohannan 1987, 103, see also ibid., 104–5), I have elsewhere formulated the hypothesis that many of Saʿdi's ghazals could have been originally composed to address his rulers. See Ingenito 2014, 85–86; 2019; Lewis 1995, 1: 171–87.

18 See Chaper 2, pp. 110–12.

19 It is noteworthy that the atabeg Zangī b. Mawdūd (Abū Bakr's grandfather) had the mausoleum of Ibn Khafīf rebuilt and converted into a *ribāṭ*. See Ebn Zarkub Shirāzi 1389/2010, 142. For a survey of all the historiographical sources tracking the presence of Ibn Khafīf in Shiraz, see al-Daylamī 1955, 309–310.

20 On Rūzbihān spiritual aesthetics, see Schimmel 1975, 296–300; Ernst 1994; Murata 2017, 89–93.

pious legacy, especially toward the final years of their control over Shiraz, when Mongol influence on the city started increasing exponentially and Sa'di seemed to be personally involved in the spiritual upbringing of prince Sa'd II, son of Abū Bakr.[21]

However, historical sources suggest that, years later (in 1280–81, according to an important manuscript)[22] the Sufi lodge that the Ilkhanid minister Shams al-Dīn built for Sa'di was loosely connected with the institutional legacy of the order that Rūzbihān founded on the basis of a reciprocal spiritual sympathy that did not involve official affiliations.[23] In fact, one has to bear in mind that the line to which both Ibn Khafīf and Rūzbihān belong partially draws upon the antinomian tradition of the "martyr" Manṣūr al-Ḥallāj and his "theopathic" utterances hinting at the fusion of one's self with the divine presence.[24] Even though we may find in Rūzbihān's writings the development of the aesthetic aspect (in terms of a semiotics of theophanic beauty) of the tradition set by Ḥallāj, the intoxicating and scattered nature of these two authors' intimations on the metaphysics of love can hardly accommodate the rational sobriety of Sa'di's lyric psychology of theo-eroticism.[25] Therefore, we may read Sa'di's single mention of Rūzbihān in his lyric praise of Shiraz as a rhetorical strategy to formally anchor the political landscape of the city to a specific spiritual line

21 See Ebn Zarkub Shirāzi 1389/2010, 222–23. Sa'di might have made this allusion also because, at least until the 1240s, the relationship of the Salghurids with Rūzbihān and his legacy was often turbulent and subjected to recurrent clashes between the spiritual and the temporal power (see Ernst 1996, 132–33). Ibn Zarkūb (1389/2010, 195) interestingly remarks that Rūzbihān and Ibn Khafīf belonged to the same *silsila*, which would also explain why Sa'di mentioned them in the same distich. It is also noteworthy that 'Aṭā'ī (d. early 14th century), in his *'Ushshāq-nāma* (mistakenly attributed to 'Irāqī; see Baldick 1973), stages a conversation between the atabeg Sa'd I (father of Sa'di's patron, Abū Bakr) and Rūzbihān regarding an incident involving the latter's amorous attentions toward a comely youth. See 'Atā'i 1391/2012, 132. For the historical background of this account, see Ernst 1996, 133. Interestingly, in *Tuḥfat ahl al-'irfān*, Rūzbihān's grandson and hagiographer mentions Sa'di in a fashion that bespeaks not only the poet's sympathetic distance from the spiritual order of the Sufi master but also the role of Shams al-Dīn Juvaynī in the political influence that Sa'di would exert over the Ilkhanid religious administration of Shiraz. Ruzbehān-e Sāni 1349/1970, 158.

22 Introduction, pp. 22–23.

23 Ruzbehān-e Sāni 1349/1970, 158.

24 See Ernst 1985,25–45; 63–72; 102–10. Al-Ghazālī, whom I regard as the main theoretical source of Sa'di's approach to Sufi ethics (see below) vehemently criticized Manṣūr al-Ḥallāj's ecstatic pronouncements on the correspondence between self and God. See chapter 4, pp. 263–65.

25 See, for instance, the point made by Mohammad Ghofrāni Jahrami (1366/1987, 100) in his article on the influence of Rūzbihān on Sa'di.

that happened to be particularly concerned with the aesthetics of the visual experience as a hermeneutical tool for the quest of the divine presence.

In this regard, when trying to trace the origins of theories and practices that might have influenced Saʿdi's peculiar and multilayered representation of spiritual aesthetics, one ought to account for the impasses that Saʿdi scholarship has often faced in its attempt to reduce the complexity of the spiritual aspects of Saʿdi's lyricism to a coherent system of thoughts inherited from specific Sufi orders.[26] It is true that scholastic Sufism exerted a great influence on the development of Saʿdi's ethics, but, as I will explore in the last chapter of this book, it can be argued that, as far as the role of the body and desire is concerned, Saʿdi's morals can be divided into two phases, the second of which is characterized by a partial disengagement from his initial adherence to scholastic Sufi doctrines.

As mentioned in the General Introduction, my approach to the chronological classification of Saʿdi's ghazals is based on the difference I have identified between his first divan, the *Ṭayyibāt*, and his later collections, the *Badāyiʿ* and the *Khavātīm*, with respect to the poet's explicit emphasis (or lack thereof, in the case of the later divans) on the morals regulating sensuality in a spiritual context.[27] In this second part too, for each ghazal that I translate and discuss within the framework of the arguments developed within specific chapters, I shall signal which *dīvān* it belongs to, so that the reader may get a sense of the chronological timeline to which specific images and ideas roughly relate. Even though the recognition of the decade of the sixties as the main watershed separating the *Ṭayyibāt* from the maturity of the *Badāyiʿ* and the *Khavātīm* ought to be confirmed by more philologically accurate studies of the genesis of Saʿdi's

26 See, for instance, de Bruijn's opinion on this matter: "Also with Saʿdī, the mystical intention is not in all poems self-evident, but this need not lead to the contrary conclusion. The Czech historian of Persian literature Jan Rypka cautioned: 'It is indeed not advisable to look for Sufism always and everywhere—either in Saʿdī or in other poets.' There can be no doubt, however, that Saʿdī participated fully in the development of the ghazal which made the poem in the first place a vehicle of mystical emotions, or at least of an eroticism which is embedded in an awareness of its transcendental potential. [...] However, there is little reason to doubt the general picture of a man attracted to the life of a dervish, though not to the more extreme aspects of mysticism, and the kind of revered religiously minded person who deserved the nickname 'Sheikh' which the tradition has given to him." De Bruijn 1997, 59–60.

27 The so-called "old ghazals" (*ghazalhā-yi qadīm*), which the oldest manuscripts collect in a separate section of Saʿdi's *Kulliyāt*, deserve an in-depth study capable of taking into account the enormous discrepancies among the most reliable sources. A preliminary study can be found in Haydari 1392/2013, in which the author compares the late ghazals of the *Khavātīm* with the old ghazals. However, Haydari's loose definition of "spiritual afflatus" does not provide his arguments with strong sources of evidence.

divāns, the perspective of a twofold periodization enables us to reappraise the persistent notion of Saʿdi's adherence to specific Sufi orders whose beliefs and practices would have stimulated the development of the poet's scholastic approach to spirituality.

Some critics, on the basis of textual evidence that eventually proved to be spurious, regard Shahāb al-Dīn Abū Ḥafṣ Suhravardī (d. 1234) as the spiritual master whom Saʿdi allegedly met in Baghdad and chose to follow as one of his disciples.[28] As a prominent preacher, diplomat, and author of one of the most celebrated manuals of Sufi etiquette of the 13th century, the *ʿAwārif al-maʿārif*,[29] Suhravardī's influence on the spiritual landscape of Baghdad should not be underestimated. After the caliph al-Nāṣir bestowed upon Suhrawardī the title of *shaykh al-shuyūkh* (Grand Sheikh), the Sufi master acquired the stewardship (*mashāyakha*) of at least five *ribāṭ*s, including the prestigious *Marzubāniyya*, which the Caliph had built specifically for him.[30] The last years of his life coincided with Saʿdi's formative period, as it was presumably in the 1230s that the poet from Shiraz studied in the Abbasid capital. The likelihood of an encounter between the two ought not to be ruled out, and one should also consider how influential the Suhravardiyya order was in Shiraz, especially through Najīb al-Dīn ʿAlī Buzghush, whom Suhravardī urged to establish himself in the city in order to spread the teachings contained in the *ʿAwārif*.[31] It is also worth speculating that both Suhravardī's attempt to create a fusion between Sufism and spiritual chivalry (*futuwwa*) and his political engagement in defense of the Caliphate might have inspired Saʿdi's pedagogical interest in the political events affecting Salghurid rule over Fars.[32] In an article on the common grounds between Saʿdi and the Sufi master, the Iranian scholar Foruzānfar points out that an intellectual affinity between the poet's system of ethics and

---

28 "Manfully hear the party-recitations of true men: / Hear them from Suhrawardī, not from Saʿdī: / That learned *shaikh*, my guide Shihāb, / Vouchsafed two counsels while upon the water […]." Wickens 1974, 75. The only piece of philological evidence on which this assumption rested were two couplets from the *Būstān*, which, as later insertions, eventually proved to be spurious. In his most recent edition of the *Būstān*, Yusofi remarks that the lines mentioning Suhravardī's name are not found in the oldest manuscripts that he has reviewed. See *Būstān*, 449. See Losensky 2012 for the passages in question. See also Māyel Heravi 1364/1985, 35. All the oldest manuscripts I have consulted, including early Timurid documents such as Ms. Yale 1432 (f. 110a), lack the lines describing the encounter between the Sufi master and the poet.

29 See *EIr*, s.v. "ʿAwāref al-Maʿāref" [W. C. Chittick].

30 Ohlander 2008, 107–12.

31 Ebn Zarkub Shirāzi 1389/2010, 237–38. Ohlander 2008, 306, n.2. See Shams 1383/2004, 89–91; *EI*[2], s.v. "Suhrawardiyya" [F. Sobieroj].

32 Ridgeon 2014, 63–74.

Suhravardī's Sufi ideals cannot be denied, especially when considering Sa'di's pragmatical approach to piety in a social context.[33]

Nevertheless, Foruzānfar hastens to underline that the correspondences that he lists almost exclusively apply to the ethical teachings and beliefs that Sa'di explicitly illustrates in his early works, such as the *Būstān* (or, as I argue, the *Ṭayyibāt*) and not in the rest of his literary and lyric production. Therefore, one cannot but agree with Foruzānfar when he states that the nuances of scholastic Sufism that appear in Sa'di's early works reflect the ethical landscape of the poet's formative period, which coincided with the years he allegedly spent in Baghdad, before his permanent return to Shiraz.[34]

Moreover, in the historical context of the practice of contemplating human beauty as a sign attesting to the divine splendor, Suhravardī stands out for his notoriously uncompromising condemnation of *shāhid-bāzī*, or *naẓar-bāzī*, that is, the act of gazing at beautiful youths for spiritual ends.[35] As it will be discussed in the following chapters, the practice of admiring the *shāhid* (pl. *shuhūd*) as a manifestation of divine beauty had been the object of numerous controversies in the Sufi *milieux* of the eastern Persian-Islamic world at least since the early 11th century. This sort of theo-erotic tendency was often discussed in association with the ambiguous role of amatory poetry in the context of *samāʿ* (the so-called "spiritual audition," or, as I will recontextualize it, "lyrical ritual"), a ritualized performance that would often blur the boundaries between the devotional, the erotic, and the purely aesthetic dimensions of listening to ghazal poetry and music.[36] The moral concerns revolving around the admiration of physical beauty that make their appearance in the *Būstān* and some of the earliest compositions of the *Ṭayyibāt* suggest that Suhravardī's ethical regulations were not foreign to Sa'di's initial stands on this matter. But

---

33 These are the main correspondences that Foruzānfar identifies when comparing Sa'di's spiritual ethics with Suhravardī's Sufi ideals: 1) The masters of Sufism should refrain from divulging matters that should not be shared with the uninitiated; 2) The spiritual path should never diverge from the ethical and legal tenets of shari'a; 3) The Sufi path shall not cease to overlap with mundane practices until the highest stage of spiritual accomplishment is achieved; meanwhile, the Sufis are expected to put their piety at the service of the people; 4) Musical audition (*samāʿ*) should be regarded as a practice capable of catalyzing the believer's love for God. Foruzānfar 1316/1338, 82–86.

34 See also Katouzian 1999 for a preliminary appraisal of the dominant opinions of scholars on the lack of evidence capable of attesting to Sa'di's attachment to specific Sufi orders.

35 Ohlader 2008, 238–39.

36 The author of the mid-13th-century Persian translation of the *'Awārif* elaborated on Suhravardī's labelling of the practice of *shāhidbāzī* as pure libertinism (*ibāḥat-i maḥż*) and mere lust-worshiping (*shavat-parastī-yi ṣirf*). See 'Abd al-Mo'men Esfahāni 1364/1985, 90.

to account for the boldness with which at some point, probably after his return to Shiraz in the 1240s, the poet started turning the visual contemplation of the beloved into one of the main axes of his lyrical innovation, we ought to turn our attention to sources of influence other than Suhravardī's strict denial of the role of the bodily and sensual dimensions for the sciences of the spirit.[37]

4 *Shāhid-bāzī*: Sufi Eroticism

Among the prominent spiritual figures who, in the Persianate Sufi *milieu* of early 13th-century Baghdad, might have influenced the later development of Saʿdi's spiritual eroticism in the context of the contemplation of human beauty, one should mention the name of Awḥad al-Dīn Kirmānī (d. 1238), whom the caliph al-Mustanṣir appointed as the new *shaykh al-shuyūkh*, as well as the steward of the Marzubāniyya *ribāṭ* upon Suhravardī's death.[38] Kirmānī's controversial renown among both his devotees and his detractors is linked to his brazen defense of the practice of *shāhid-bāzī* in a fashion that attracted the criticism of many of his contemporaries (including Shams-i Tabrīzī and Suhravardī himself) and the anathema of later hagiographers.[39] The Sufi master's penchant for the contemplation of comely youths gained renown through a large collection of quatrains that he would compose extemporaneously to communicate his spiritual beliefs to his followers. Considering that Saʿdi was ostensibly the first poet who introduced the expression *shāhid-bāzī* as a new technical term for sacred eroticism in the Persian ghazal, it would not be too far-fetched to infer the existence of a link between his poetry and Kirmānī's literary activity.

However, in this case too, the existence of a formal attachment between Saʿdi and institutionalized forms of spirituality cannot be proven. While some of Kirmānī's quatrains do explore the function of *shāhid-bāzī* on the spiritual path, the Grand Shaykh's overall posture is mainly scholastic and based on the core doctrinal values of the social Sufi context. As Hushang Fati emphasizes in an article that confutes the anachronisms of some of the most widespread preconceptions about Saʿdi's biography, not only do we lack compelling textual and historiographical evidence capable of proving the poet's association

37 Saʿid Hamidiyān (1383/2004, 185) emphasizes the distance of Saʿdi from the use of Sufi technical vocabulary. For a general appraisal of the Western and Iranian critics who have emphasized the difference between Saʿdi's thought and scholastic Sufism, see Katouzian 1999, 191–95.

38 On this important (albeit little studied) figure, see Ridgeon 2012; 2017.

39 See Ridgeon 2017, 61–84.

with any specific Sufi order, but even the most widespread and generic Sufi beliefs concerning intellectual and sensually detached forms of contemplating beauty clash with the profoundly mundane aesthetic system that animates the entirety of Saʿdi's lyric trajectory.[40] Therefore, without denying the importance of Sufi thought in the early development of Saʿdi's literary ethos, we need to reassess the sacred eroticism exuding from his ghazals through a broader aesthetic approach capable of explaining the complex background of his lyric subject's psychology of vision.

As noted above, spirituality and Sufism-inspired ideals are certainly key elements emanating from Saʿdi's lyric poetry and prose works. Many of Saʿdi's ghazals can be surely described as an unceasing meditation on human beauty as a reflection of the divine splendor. This dimension constitutes one of the main axes of his entire poetic thought and, as such, its literary, philosophical, and religious foundations deserve to be archaeologically explored. However, in refraining from employing the term "mysticism" whenever possible, I take into account the polemic of some scholars against the ahistorical and ethnocentric misunderstandings that the uncritical use of this word can generate when applied to the broad variety of socio-historical, political and aesthetic experiences and systems of thought constituting the heritage of Sufism between the 9th and the 13th centuries.[41] One cannot but situate Saʿdi's representation of the beloved as a sign of God's beauty within the context of the Sufi love tradition. The fact that this aspect of his poetry is indebted to Sufi-oriented thinkers such as Muḥammad Ghazālī and his brother, Aḥmad Ghazālī, ʿAyn al-Qużāt Hamadānī, ʿAṭṭār, Rūzbihān-i Baqlī, and Awḥad al-Dīn Kirmānī is undeniable. Nevertheless, the generic qualification of "mystical" (also as an impressionistic translation of the adjective *ʿirfānī*)—along with abstracted theories alleging unspecified forms of correspondence between the figure of the beloved and the divine presence—fails to explain the relationship between mundane desire and the metaphysical élan characterizing Saʿdi's ghazals and the pivotal

40 See Fati 1379/2000. The distance between Saʿdi's aesthetic values and the rules dominating the Sufi scholastic approach to the contemplation of human beauty is also attested to in the 14th-century Sufi manual *Awrād al-aḥbāb va fuṣūṣ al-ādāb*, in which the author, Abū al-Mafākhir Yaḥyā b. Aḥmad Bākharzī (d. 1335–36, grandson of the renowned Kubravī sheikh Sayf al-Dīn Bākharzī of Bukhara, d. 1261), invalidates Rūzbihān's solicitation to the Sufis to gather around reciters of poetry whose countenance is pleasing to the eye; see Bākharzi 1345/1966, 207.

41 See Omid Safi's criticism of the crypto-Protestant background of Annemarie Schimmel's definition of mysticism (Safi 2000, 260–62), and Coppens's note on Hossein Seyyed Nasr's reification of Sufism as a trans-historical mystical experience (Coppens 2018, 27, n. 11). For an overview of this problem, see Coppens 2018, 7–10; Sviri 2012. Cf. Lloyd Ridgeon's (2015) moderate reappraisal of this controversy.

role that he constantly assigns to the mundane setting of the experience of beholding beauty for spiritual ends.

For instance, in the only study focusing on the spiritual aspect of Sa'di's ghazals, Sa'id Hamidiyān claims that the figure of the beloved is a metaphor for the divine presence. In spite of his accurate classification of the poems that manifest clear evidence of a spiritual trajectory, the author does not clarify what semiotic genealogy links the lyric (and often erotic) descriptions of the beloved to the theological problem of the manifestation of God in Islam, the unintelligibility of his essence, and the epistemology of the understanding of his attributes.[42] Is the beloved a microcosmic icon of the divine; a sign pointing at his presence; the incarnation of one of his attributes; or a vaguely theorized form of epiphanic manifestation of his splendor?[43] On the other hand, the proponents of an exclusively amatory reading of Sa'di's ghazals, such as Homa Katouzian and Sirus Shamisā, tend to overlook the indisputable spiritual and often visionary content of most of the poet's lyric output. In their anachronistically biographical approach, they not only read Sa'di as a confessional poet, but they also dismiss the spiritual dimensions of his poetry as rhetorical conventions detached from the aesthetic values and social practices surrounding the composition and circulation of his ghazals in their specific historical contexts.[44]

---

42 Sa'id Hamidiyan (1383/2004, 76–79) attempts an interesting classification of Sa'di's "spiritual" themes by recognizing fifteen markers (the names of God, scriptural references, sayings of saints and Sufi masters, technical terms, etc.) whose presence, according the author, would provide a given ghazal with a "mystical" aura. Hamidiyān concludes that 47% of Sa'di's ghazals contain spiritual markers, 38% are overall "spiritual" but without showcasing any specific markers, and 15% are purely amatory with no spiritual overtones whatsoever. However, by not framing his discussion within the context of the spiritual psychology of the lyric subject, especially with respect to the complex problem of the vision of God through human beauty, Hamidiyān fails to produce convincing proofs of the "mystical" nature of Sa'di's spiritual aesthetics. His approach is mainly dichotomous, as he tries to determine whether the beloved is human or divine without considering the interplay between the semiotics of contemplating human forms as signs of God and the divine as an ultimately unattainable presence. See, for instance, his discussion of Sa'di's ghazal *dānamat āstīn chirā pīsh-i jamāl mībarī* (Sa'di YE, 90) which he elects as the poet's "most mystical" composition (129–30). Furthermore, he does not specify the relationship between the sensual element of the lyric discourse, the psychology of imagination at work in most of the lines of this splendid ghazal, and the technical expressions that undoubtedly create significant overlaps between the divine attributes and the physical incarnation of the supernal archetype of beauty.

43 For a radically "mystical" reading of Sa'di's lyrical afflatus, see Yāsemi 1316/1938, in which the author denies the existence of a sensual aspect in Sa'di's lyric voice.

44 See, for instance, Katouzian 2006b, 35–38.

5 Religious and Lyrical Renewals and the Influence of al-Ghazālī and Avicenna

Saʿdi's ethical horizion is certainly "imbued with Sufism,"[45] but it is characterized by an overall Sufi tendency that cannot be ascribed to a systematic line of thought within the framework of specific schools—hence the dispute between different "factions" in the scholarship. Rather than a *systematic* affiliation to historical Sufi orders, we ought to conceive Saʿdi's pragmatic spirituality as a broad conversation with a plurality of *systems* of thought and values circulating in 13th-century Baghdad and Shiraz. After all, the study of intertextuality and literary influence teaches us that (following critics such as Harold Bloom and Jackson Bate), within every literary framework, poems can be seen as direct or indirect responses to other poems rather than philosophical or theological systems. Why should we regard the theological and philosophical discourses initiated by al-Ghazālī and Avicenna as sources, albeit indirect, of Saʿdi's literary inspiration?

Although it is true that, from a structuralist perspective, poems develop their meaning mainly through their connections with the literary system to which they belong, New Historical approaches to the study of literature look at poetry alongside non-literary cultural productions that include ideologies, theoretical postures, and philosophical or religious orientations that shape subjects and their worldviews. Such cultural productions collaborate to the creation of a peculiar and stratified intellectual discourse, or "ambient availability," an expression that Jane Mikkelson uses to qualify the contextual influence of Avicennianism on Bidel of Delhi's thought."[46] As discussed earlier, although Saʿdi's literary vision of the world is not *essentially* rooted in theological or philosophical systems, many of his ghazals do touch upon philosophical, theological, and aesthetic problems that belong to the intellectual discussions of his time. However incomplete my attempt might seem, the parallels that this book intends to trace constitute an effort to sketch a depiction of the environment in which the sacred and the sensual aspects of Saʿdi's poetry were *historically* rooted.

Considering the flexibility of Saʿdi's moral golden mean, it is not surprising that scholars have forcefully demonstrated the paramount influence that al-Ghazālī's thought exerted on the poet's ethical convictions.[47] After all, the only religious *auctoritas* to whom Saʿdi's refers in his works is al-Ghazālī, whom

45 de Fouchécour 1986, 347.

46 Mikkelson 2019, 43.

47 Ibid., 344–45, 348; and, in particular, Ghafuriyān 1398–2019, 43–140; 201–16; 249–81.

he refers to as the "leading spiritual guide" (*imām-i murshid*).[48] On the surface, from the mere perspective of their respective intellectual fields, Sa'di and al-Ghazālī share few if no common traits at all. What could the 13th-century master of the Persian lyric from Fars have in common with the towering Khorasanian intellectual who, around the turn of the 12th century, sought to transform the religious landscape of his age by "restricting law and theology to their proper and limited role in regulating worldly affairs" and "elevating the science of seeking felicity in the hereafter to the central concern of the Islamic scholarly tradition?"[49] But if we think in terms of intellectual affinity with respect to the circulation of religious postures and aesthetic ideals among the center of learning that characterized the development of Perso-Islamic culture between the 12th and the 13th centuries, a comparison between Sa'di and al-Ghazālī might provide us with insightful considerations. Both thinkers sought knowledge beyond the limits of the blind emulation of orthodox prescriptions and travelled extensively to pursue their intellectual and political goals.[50] They were equally weary of political power without ever distancing themselves from it, always in the quest for a compromise between self-interest and the harmonic wellbeing of Islamdom.[51] In spite of professing their absolute adherence to Islamic orthodoxy, they both creatively applied their personal critical insight (often coated with rational pragmatism and benevolent irony) to the connections they traced between matters of faith and syncretic sources of wisdom.[52] In this vein, both Sa'di and al-Ghazālī developed

48 In the anecdote from the *Gulistān* (184), Sa'di attributes to al-Ghazālī a maxim on the acquisition of knowledge through the exercise of inquisitive rationalism. Al-Ghazālī's rejection of *taqlīd* (i.e., the uncritical acceptance of an opinion, see Frank 1991–92) constitutes one of Sa'di's main epistemological tenets, which he expresses explicitly in the *Būstān*:
Worshipping out of uncritical imitation is a misleading path:
Blessed is the wayfarer who is aware of his steps.
[2.7] *Bustān*, 17.

49 Garden 2014, 103.

50 On al-Ghazālī's life and travels, see Griffel 2009a, 19–59.

51 Garden's observation on al-Ghazālī's compromise with political power perfectly fits Sa'di's biographical circumstances: "Though the customary view of al-Ghazālī (and the one he himself encouraged) is almost entirely otherworldly, his life was enmeshed in politics from beginning to end, and he remained in the orbit of the most powerful men of his age throughout his career […]" Garden 2014, 18. On al-Ghazālī's political dimension, see Laoust 1970; Hillenbrand 1988; and, most recently, on al-Ghazālī's service to the Saljuk regime, Garden 2014, 17–29.

52 "[…] al-Ghazālī's unquestionable appeal should not obscure the fact that he was a rather 'heterodox' thinker by any standard and that he put forth and promoted—both openly and covertly—idiosyncratic ideas that boldly synthesized Sufism, Ash'arite *kalām*,

a complex relationship with peripatetic philosophy and Sufism. As we shall see in the sixth chapter, Avicennianism was likely part of Saʿdi's intellectual upbringing, and, contrary to a centuries-old prejudice, al-Ghazāli's religious thought was profoundly influenced by philosophical speculations.[53] Although they both recognized, at least theoretically, the spiritual advantages of reclusion, their approach to Sufism was informed by the pragmatics of an active social life, far from scholastic dogmatism.[54]

If it is true that Saʿdi studied in Baghdad at the famed Niẓāmiyya institution (in which al-Ghazālī himself had taught, between 1091 and 1095),[55] he most likely had access to a number of works by al-Ghazālī which were commonly taught at the prestigious school between the end of the 12th century and the 1230s.[56] Saʿdi's intellectual and ethical reverence for the wisdom and the breadth of al-Ghazālī's teachings could explain the peculiar theo-erotic aesthetics exuding from his ghazals. Following this connection, in this second part I set out to read aspects of Saʿdi's lyricism in light of al-Ghazālī's original combination of Aristotelian cosmology, Avicennian psychology, Ashʿarite theology, Shafiʿi jurisprudence, and Khorasanian Sufi practices, influences that he conflated into an original "science of the hereafter" (*ʿilm al-ākhira*), which he illustrated both in his *Revival of the Religious Sciences* (*Iḥyāʾ ʿulūm al-dīn*) and, most importantly, in the his Persian masterpiece, *The Alchemy of Bliss* (*Kīmiyā-yi saʿādat*).

As I shall argue, in the wake of this non-systematic affinity with al-Ghazālī's spiritual epistemology and aesthetics, Saʿdi never envisages a direct correspondence between the beloved and the divine presence. On the contrary, the poet clearly stages the sensory beauty of the beloved as a sign that acts as a focal point for the recognition of the divine source of all mundane splendor. Al-Ghazālī's speculations on inspired forms of knowledge, spiritual cardiology,

Islamic philosophy (particularly that of Avicenna, al-Rāghib al-Iṣfahānī, and the 'Brethren of Purity'), and Ismaʿili cosmological speculations and methods of allegorical Quran exegesis (*taʾwīl*)." Treiger 2020, 384.

53 On the pervasive influence of Avicenna's writings on al-Ghazālī's thought, see Frank 1992; 1994; Janssens 1986; 2001; 2003; Griffel 2009a; Treiger 2012.

54 "Al-Ghazālī did not retire to a life of obscure devotion, as many of his contemporaries did and as he, too, could surely have done. Rather, he embarked on a campaign to transform the religious landscape of his age. […] Al-Ghazālī's famous spiritual crisis of 488/1095 had a very worldly context. It must be understood at least partially as a response to the political events of his age, both because he felt morally compromised by his political involvement, as his vows demonstrate, and because he despaired of the role of the regime in establishing a stable and just worldly order." Garden 2014, 28–29.

55 Griffel 2009a, 34–35.

56 See Gutas 2011, 16–17.

and teleological aesthetics offer an excellent framework to interpret the intellectual aspects of Sa'di's quest for a heuristic and non-scholastic golden mean to the lyric exploration of beauty as a link between the world of sense and the realm of the unseen. The foundations of this rational approach are quintessentially philosophical, as a direct connection can be traced between al-Ghazālī's theorization of the cognitive process involved by the act of contemplation of the world (*tafakkur*, or *fikra*) and the syllogistic system that characterizes Avicenna's epistemology.

Forays into the Avicennian foundations of al-Ghazālī's science of the hereafter have allowed me to better recognize the relevance of the role of the internal senses, imagination, and cogitation in Sa'di's representation of the visual contemplation of beauty that he stages in his ghazals. Even though other scholars have already highlighted the dominance of the visual in Sa'di's ghazals, I believe my approach constitutes the first attempt to trace the psychology of his lyric subject back to the medieval theories of sensory perception and intellectual cogitation. It is my contention that the Avicennian background is a key element in understanding the sober rationalism with which Sa'di reinterprets the tradition of Sufi hermeneutics and combines it with the lyrical exploration of physical desire. When exploring the "ambient availability" of the Avicennain epistemological discourse that shaped aspects of Sa'di's intellectual environment, it is important to emphasize how this very system of thought was re-elaborated by al-Ghazālī and elevated to a widespread scientific paradigm between the 12th and the 13th centuries. Under the influence of contemporary Sufi thinkers and fellow-poets, Sa'di combined al-Ghazālī's speculative heritage with a unique erotic element, not as a blindingly intoxicating bewilderment, but as a rational sobriety that unifies the tensions of the flesh with the intellectual recognition of the divine creation behind the balanced spectacle of the world.

In particular, the following chapters will analyze how the Avicennian theorization of the internal senses emerges in key passages of Sa'di's works and highlights the poet's high degree of awareness of the scientific and philosophical debates taking place between the 12th and 13th centuries in the Persianate world, and in particular in Shiraz. The comparison between the psychology of Sa'di's lyric subject and the Avicennian-Ghazalian epistemological legacy has allowed me to develop a holistic approach to the theme of contemplating beauty in the Persian ghazal as a constant oscillation between the sensory perusal of the external world and the role of the internal senses in the conversion of the supernal meanings (*ma'ānī*) provided by the realm of the "unseen" into mental images (*ṣuvar*) representing the archetypes of beauty.

Within this complex psycho-physiological system, I have recognized two key modalities that inform both the rational approach of the lyric subject to the recognition of the supernal sources of beauty and the visionary experience generated by what Avicenna and al-Ghazālī describe as the conjunction of the rational soul/heart with the supernal realm (the soul of the fixed stars in Avicennian terms, referred to, in Quranic terms, as the Preserved Tablet, *lawḥ maḥfūẓ*, by al-Ghazālī). On the one hand stands what I have called the "rational-inferential" modality and, on the other, the "imaginal-cosmological" experience. The recognition of these two modalities stems from the Ghazalian epistemological classification of human cogitation on the divine as either informed by the rational contemplation of the world (*fikra*) or by the visionary experience (*mushāhada*) induced through techniques of sensory deprivation, repetition of formulae, and controlled manipulation of one's breath. By comparing al-Ghazālī's exposition of these two modalities with their Avicennian psychological foundation, I have striven to outline a general aesthetic theory capable of explaining the dynamics that inform the lyric subject's processes of imagination at the intersection between the physical and metaphysical worlds, between carnal desires and imaginal perceptions. The recognition of a spiritual psychology focused on medieval theories of perception and cogitation through the interaction between the internal senses and the rational soul has helped me reframe Saʿdi's alleged mysticism within an overarching theory capable of bridging the gap between the courtly, the obscene, and the metaphysical aspects of his poetry.

As a final introductory note, it should be mentioned that there are no traces of any anti-philosophical stances in Saʿdi's works. Non-specialist readers often interpret this couplet from the *Būstān* as an attestation to Saʿdi's distance from peripatetic philosophy: "Not even the philosophers of ancient Greece and Anatolia / Would be capable of extracting honey from bitter cacti." In its original context, the line speaks to the poet's confidence in the scientific dexterity of Hellenistic philosophers, to whom he refers as examples of the highest level of human intellection. Moreover, in the sixth chapter of the *Gulistān*, Saʿdi recounts a pseudo-biographical anecdote set in a mosque in Damascus. While he was debating with a group of scholars, someone asked him to translate into Arabic the words of an old Persophone man. After a brief exchange, Saʿdi reportedly told the old man: "Stop picturing [*taṣavvur*] death in your imagination [*khayāl*], and do not let your futile estimations [*wahm*] overwhelm your nature [*ṭabīʿat*], for the Greek philosophers [*fīlsūfān-i yūnānī*] have said that, regardless of how healthy one's constitution may be, one cannot count on living forever [...]." Hopefully, the next five chapters will help us contextualize this anecdote in the context of the "ambient availability" of philosophical conversations in Saʿdi's intellectual environment. We will see how Saʿdi's juxtaposition of key words such as *taṣavvūr*, *khayāl*, *vahm*, and *ṭabīʿat* alongside his reference to the thought of the "Greek philosophers" reveals the influence of the rational sciences on the poet's cultural upbringing.

CHAPTER 4

The Body as a Divine Sign

The Hermeneutics of Spiritual Desire

This is how I am: I cannot resist the allure of beautiful faces.
I sell hypocrisy to no one, and I don't pretend to be a pious ascetic.

You see the countenances and refrain from contemplating:
I admire your strength, as I don't have such endurance.

It is virtuous to reject the sin that the Turkic beauties may pose
But what remedy for this sinful gazer, who has no control over his carnal soul?

No more will I admire the valleys adorned with beauty,
For not all fragrant gardens display a rose as beautiful as your cheek.

I see a fairy in your visage, an angel in your countenance and good manners,
Listen: anyone who cultivates no affection for you cannot be human!

So many people are blind, even with their eyes wide open:
They resemble soulless paintings depicted on walls.

O brother, the wayfarer on the path won't have to share the pain
Of his heart, for this is a pain that is not concealed from you.

I know no creature who is not bewildered by the One
Whose powerful Pen bewilders my senses in awe.

O Saʿdi, your precious life has now come to its end,
But the story of your melancholic desire is truly endless.

Khavātīm 668[1]

•••

1 [2.8] Saʿdi YE, 668.

 | DOI:10.1163/9789004435902_008

> If Love were not to resort to the trick of depiction [*tamaṣṣul*], all the wayfarers of the path would turn into infidels, as one grows weary of dwelling for too long contemplating an object in one single form and condition. Nevertheless, when its beauty increases in multiple forms every moment or day by day, love surges and the desire of the beholder is amplified. [...] Hence, in this station, the lover beholds the beloved in a different form of beauty, and sees the perfection of his love increasing.
>
> ʿAYN AL-QUŻĀT HAMADĀNĪ[2]

∴

1 Prostration, Desire, and Bewilderment

The widespread conception of the human beloved portrayed in premodern Persian lyric poetry as a manifestation of God entails complex epistemological and hermeneutical problems with which the scholarship has dealt by relying on approaches that oscillate between mystical enthusiasm and the denial of any transcendental discourse whatsoever.[3] The majority of the scholars advocating for a mystical interpretation of Saʿdi's poetry—in terms of the possibility of either seeing God in the form of the beloved, or accessing the divine through the contemplation of human beauty, or even conceiving the beloved as a metaphor standing for the divine—fail to link their transcendental approach to the historical development of the theoretical and phenomenological trends

---

2 ʿAyn al-Qozāt Hamadāni 1373/1994, 124–25.

3 Ehsan Yarshater is particularly adamant with his critique of the radically mystical readings of the premodern Persian ghazal: "If one were to believe such interpretations, poets like Sanāʾi, ʿAṭṭār, ʿErāqi, Rumi, and particularly Hafez, never wrote anything in a direct manner but always in codes, and the reader needs to carefully decode every single word, find their symbolic interpretations, and combine them in order to make sense of the poem. In short, Sufi poets wrote puzzles and riddles, not poems to be read and enjoyed by ordinary mortals. It is rather surprising that the lucid, transparent, and straightforward lyrics of these poets and their like, expressed in the normal, literary language of each period—a language that most Persians, even those with a low degree of education, can understand and enjoy—should be subjected to the mystifying and obfuscating interpretations offered by traders of mystical wares." *EIr*, s.v. "Ḡazal ii. Characteristics and Conventions" [E. Yarshater]. For a comprehensive survey of the secondary literature on this topic, especially from the perspective of the ghazal during the 13th and the 14th centuries, see Brookshaw 2019, 9–11.

that between the 9th and the 13th centuries explored the different modalities through which God can be contemplated.[4]

The spiritual aspect of Saʿdi's lyricism is well-documented,[5] and both his scholastic and reclusive formative experience in his youth and the establishment of a Sufi lodge in his name in 1280 (thanks to the financial support of Shams al-Dīn Juvaynī) attest to the relevance of Sufi practices and beliefs throughout his life. What makes his ghazals unique in the landscape of 13th-century Persian poetry is that in his verses, sensuality and the quest for God are never mutually exclusive. The coexistence of these two aspects constitutes one of Saʿdi's main innovations, which deeply influenced the style and the intellectual concerns of poets such as Amīr-i Khusraw, Khʷājū of Kerman, Hafez, and Jāmi, in the 14th and the 15th centuries.

Humām of Tabriz (d. 1314–15), belongs to the first generation of poets who inherited Saʿdi's lyrical innovations in the field of spiritual eroticism. As one of his younger contemporaries and fervent imitators, he was later known as the "Saʿdi of Azarbayjan."[6] We may consider the following line by Humām as a statement epitomizing the form of spiritual quest exuding from the relationship between the senses and the divine that characterizes a fundamental part of Saʿdi's oeuvre:

> One's head should graze the ground when admiring your face:
> Prostration is what the mirror of God deserves.
>
> A painting is your countenance, contemplate yourself in the mirror,
> So that you may understand the power of your Painter.[7]

As an imitator and a popularizer of Saʿdi's poetry (both in his Sufi lodge, also patronized by Shams al-Dīn Juvaynī, and before the ilkhan Ghazan, for whom he would recite Saʿdi's ghazals with his mellifluous voice), Humām expands upon the innovations that his source of imitation brought to the practice of lyric composition in a religious and courtly context. As we shall see, the two

4 Apart from the dated mystical readings of Yāsemi, Nicholson, and Arberry, see, for instance, Hamidiyān's generic use of the term *ʿirfān* (Hamidiyān 1383/2004, 148) without further contextualizing the specific and historically situated conglomeration of spiritual ideals and practices that the use of this term have entailed during Saʿdi's lifetime.

5 Sirus Shamisā (1370/1991, 88) has offered one of the most succinctly eloquent expressions of this characteristic of Saʿdi's style and imagery.

6 *EIr*, s.v. "Homām al-Din" [W.L. Hanaway, L. Lewisohn]. On Homām's life and works, see Ingenito 2014; *EI*³, s.v. "Humām al-Dīn Tabrīzī" [L. Lewisohn]. Cf. General Introduction, pp. 23–25.

7 [2.9] Homām al-Din Tabrizi 1351/1972, 58.

couplets above convey with adamant clarity concepts that constitute the primary message of Saʿdi's sacred eroticism: the beloved emerges to the surface of the text as a mirror reflecting divine beauty.

But what is the actual nature of this connection? Does the beloved act as an embodiment of the divine? If this is the case, is it the divine essence or the image of God that appears in his mirror-like countenance? If it is an image, is it a faithful representation of some kind of supernal form or an analogue that *stands for* the divine? How does the human object of desire act as a vessel of the divine presence? Is his face a form of immanent attestation to transcendental perfection? And, furthermore, how are the senses of the beholder involved in the contemplation of this manifestation?

The sense of indetermination that a hasty reading of Humām's lines may deliver, far from revealing logical or doctrinal inconsistencies in the texture of the poet's statements, attests to the fluidity of the problem of the relationship between human and divine beauty in a cultural context in which lyric practice reflects the complexity of the philosophical, theological, and spiritual discourses on this matter. The seed of this apparent, yet powerful sense of ambivalence may be discerned in the following line by Saʿdi:

> You appear in the morning and no one bows down to worship your face.
> Why? People fear God, whereas I am too bewildered to prostrate.
> *Badāyiʿ* 465[8]

By juxtaposing Humām's lines with this couplet, it becomes clear that both poets imagine the transcendental source of beauty on the basis of the contrast between the doctrinal conviction according to which God does not directly manifest himself in a human form and the sensation that the divine presence *seems* to appear in the flesh of a comely young man. The reader of Saʿdi's obscene fragments (the *Khabīṣāt*, discussed in the third chapter), may compare the line above with the bawdy quatrain in which the poet describes how a beautiful youth once invalidated the ritual worship of pious Muslims and instilled in the imam the desire of prostrating "behind" the boy.[9] Both the line from Saʿdi's "serious" ghazal and his facetious quatrain approach the

8 [2.10] This line is only found in Forughi's and Yaghmā'i's editions. See Saʿdi YE, 549. As noted by Yusofi (ibid.), this ghazal seems to be derived from a conflation of two distinct texts.

9 That pagan idol came to the mosque
And invalidated the prayer of pious men and Sufis.
The imam, intoxicated by love, kept saying:
I wish I were behind him, and he before me!
[2.11] Ms. Kabul 1325, 689.

problem of the relationship between carnality and the topic of the "vision of God" (*ru'yat Allāh*) which, in the medieval Islamic context, relates to the porosity of the synchronic and diachronic boundaries between this world (*dunyā*) and the otherworld (*ākhira*).[10] This new juxtaposition brings new layers of complexity to our discussion on Humām's and Sa'di's lines. Where does the flesh end and the vision of the divine begin?

2 Seeing God: Introvertive and Contemplative Modalities

The possibility of seeing God, either in this world or in the hereafter, constitutes the pinnacle of most theistic religious experiences and, by necessity, of any overarching aesthetic framework that investigates the origins of beauty within the relationship between human cognition and the narrative of a supernal system of unintelligible causes.[11] As early as the 9th century, on the basis of Quranic evidence, scriptural exegesis, and dialectical reasoning, theologians and Sufi commentators discussed the possibility and the modality of the vision of God from a perspective that is chiefly eschatological and originally informed by the rationalistic approach of the Mu'tazilis and the literalism of the Ash'ari theological school.[12] Pieter Coppens has tried to adapt Elliot Wolfson's typology of visionary experiences in the context of Jewish mysticism to the theoretical tendencies characterizing the historical development of Sufi thought. In the case of Sufism, Coppens argues that the general trend shifted from an initial traditionalist leaning, which considers the vision of God as a physical phenomenon that may take place in this world or in the afterlife, to a "contemplative" modality, which the sources usually referred to as a vision of the heart

10 See Coppens 2018, 1–6, 13–16. On the links between *dunyā* and *ākhira* as diachronic or synchronic modalities, see Lange 2016, 11. Both Lange (ibid., 11–12) and Coppens (2018, 33) are critical of the forced diachrony that the translation of *ākhira* as "hereafter" or "afterlife" imposes upon a concept that is fundamentally based on an atemporal eschatological representation. The translation upon which both Lange and Coppens agree (albeit for different reasons) is "the otherworld," which they locate in what Lange refers to as the "everywhen": "In the case of Sufism, I propose a combination of these two modes: while a linear understanding of history and eschatology remains integral to Sufi theories, the otherworld may also be synchronically immanent in this world, most poignantly in the form of certain Sufi stations and states." Coppens 2018, 14. See also Böwering 1980, 145–46.

11 See Baffioni 1998.

12 For an introduction to the theological discussions of the vision of God in Islam and their impact on the development of early Sufi eschatology, see Tuft 1983; Coppens 2018, 177–184.

(or *mushāhada*), involving an intellectual or spiritual form of vision that is not limited by spatio-temporal boundaries.[13]

From the 10th century onwards, the contemplative modality emerged as the mainstream overarching approach for theorizing upon and making sense of the experience of "seeing" God. On the basis of the different possibilities of describing the spiritual vision of God, Wolfson divides the contemplative modality into an introvertive and a cognitive type of visualization. The introvertive type, mainly informed by Muʿtazilite rationalism, "finds its roots in Neoplatonism and considers the vision of God to be purely intellectual, beyond image and form, rejecting the idea that senses or sensory imagery play any meaningful role in how the vision is experienced and described."[14] On the other side of the spectrum, the cognitive type relies on the "phenomenological parameters" of human experience and translates the vision into an "image and a form that is derived from the images and symbols present in one's own religious tradition, and mediated by the senses."[15]

Following Wolfson's and Coppen's classification, Saʿdi's approach to the vision of God within the world is primarily introvertive and, as such, it rejects all possibilities of "cognizing" the divine presence by means of forms and images:

> O [God], you are above imagination [*khayāl*], syllogisms [*qiyās*], thought [*gamān*], and estimation [*vahm*],
> Beyond whatever was said, whatever we heard, whatever we studied.[16]

Rather than through an intellectual image, Saʿdi seeks the contemplation of the divine through an introvertive and inferential point of view: while God

13 "In early Sufism, generally speaking the idea of an otherworldly ocular vision of God as being the ultimate reward in the hereafter was widely accepted as both possible and existent. This vision was thus considered to be physical, not only contemplative. This wide acceptance can be explained by the fact that the Muʿtazilī and Jahmī creeds were historically insignificant among Sufis. Most Sufis from the formative period had either Ashʿarī or traditionist leanings. The concept of this-worldly vision led to more discord. Some Sufi authorities rejected the idea completely, while others formulated theories of a vision of the heart (*ruʾya biʾl-qalb*) that allowed an abstract, contemplative, non-anthropomorphic and non-indwelling vision of God, often referred to as *mushāhada* (witnessing)." Coppens 2018, 178.

14 Ibid., 175–76.

15 Ibid., 175, Wolfson 1997, 60–1.

16 [2.12] *Golestān*, 50–51. I translate *vahm* as "estimation," (and not with a generic reference to "imagination") because I read this line within the framework of Avicenna's theory of the internal senses. See Chapter 6.

can manifest Himself in the soul of the believer as a spiritual "tasting" (*ẕawq*, a supernal sensation felt in the inner chambers of the heart), the believer can infer his presence through the worldly manifestations of his acts of creation and his attributes of splendor and majesty. Therefore, the contemplation of created forms of beauty (and in particular, for obvious anthropocentric reasons, human beauty) reminds the believer of the divine presence—the supreme source whose acts generate those traces of immanent aesthetic perfection—in a fashion that brings God to his innermost metaphysical "tasting" without him recurring to imaginary representations.

What are the sources of Saʿdi's approach to the vision of God? His "inferential" approach to the mundane manifestation of divine beauty could be ascribed to Rūzbihān's concept of *iltibās*, i.e., the "clothing" of human beauty with divine attributes (rather than his essence, which is deemed unknowable) stemming from his act of creation.[17] On multiple occasions, Rūzbihān insisted on the divine manifestation (*tajallī*) as cognitive vision that translates God into a symbolic human form.[18] In spite of his deference towards the Shirazi Sufi master, Saʿdi's rationalistic approach automatically discards this possibility, to

17 "These attributes and acts become apparent in creation through visual divine manifestations of majesty (*jalāl*) and beauty (*jamāl*), in a process that Ernst has defined as 'an endless game of hide and seek'. Rūzbihān connects this mode of vision of God to *iltibās* (lit. 'clothing'), a term typical for his mystical thought that signifies a bestowal of divine qualities on humanity or creation, a clothing with divinity." Coppens 2018, 189–90. On *iltibās* and the approaches that scholars have adopted to translate this term, see Ibid., 199, n. 78. See also Murata 2017, 90–91, 109–10.

18 See Ruzbehān 1958, 58. For a rather uncritical appraisal of patterns of spiritual continuity in the Shirazi Sufi tradition, see Takeshita 1987. Coppens adds interesting remarks on the shift in the paradigm of the vision of God in the context surrounding the emergence of Rūzbihān's meditations on the divine manifestation (*tajallī*, which, however, is featured much more frequently in the lyric practice of the 14th century than in Saʿdi's sacred eroticism): "A century after al-Muḥāsibī, Sufis indeed proposed a vision of God with the heart by the manifestation (*tajallī*) of God's light on it, or a vision of God through creation rather than in creation, thus differing from the understanding of the early *ḥulūliyya* [i.e., the proponents of incarnationism]. While these early understandings still had a physical idea of the vision, later interpretations took it to be a strictly contemplative vision through the ocular contemplation of creation. Al-Hujwīrī's *Kashf al-maḥjūb* explains manifestation (*tajallī*) as follows: The blessed effect of Divine illumination on the hearts of the blest, whereby they are made capable of seeing God with their hearts. The difference between spiritual vision (*ruʾyat ba-dil*) and actual vision (*ruʾyat-i ʿiyān*) is this, that those who experience *tajallī* (manifestation of God) see or do not see, according as they wish, or see at one time and do not see at another time, while those who experience actual vision in Paradise cannot but see, even though they wish not to see; for it is possible that *tajallī* should be hidden, whereas *ruʾyat* (vision) cannot possibly be veiled." Coppens 2018, 182–83.

which he does not even allude in his most compelling praises of the divine and the reflection of its beauty reverberating through the entire world.

As emphasized in the introduction to this second part, the golden mean of al-Ghazālī's pragmatic approach to the quest for the divine presence offers a generative framework for the investigation of Saʿdi's positions on this matter. We may compare Saʿdi's reluctance toward the act of visualizing God through imaginary symbols to al-Ghazālī's rejection of the Ashʿari theory of the optical vision of God in the hereafter. In fact, in his compromise with the Ashʿari orthodox position, al-Ghazālī accepted the possibility of seeing God only with the the eyes of the heart, in the hereafter, and only after having admired and internalized the aesthetic cognition of the signs of divine beauty in this world as a spiritual exercise.[19]

Following these preliminary observations, this chapter will explore at length the implications of the affinity between al-Ghazālī's and Saʿdi's inferential and introvertive approaches to the contemplation of divine beauty. However, from the perspective of the problem of accessing God's beauty, the issue of sensual desire as a driving force behind Saʿdi's lyricism is of paramount importance, especially for better understanding the poet's peculiar articulation of the connection between the visible world and the realm of the unseen. What I referred to in the third chapter as the relationship between the spiritual fetishization of the beloved and its reified obscene counterpart pertains to a dichotomy that intimately binds the spiritual and the carnal aspect of Saʿdi's lyricism throughout the courtly imagery that he showcases in his ghazals.

Considering the preeminently mundane dimension of Saʿdi's poetic articulation of his lyric subject, the idea of a divine manifestation as a semiotic possibility of the bodies represented by his texts does not reduce his representations to a purely spiritual discourse. On the contrary, the reference to the divine not only magnifies the possibilities of signification of the texts as such, but it also expands the scope of their relationships with the external world. Therefore, the depth that the spiritual dimension adds to the texts involves first and foremost the complexity of both the lyric subject and that of the object of desire, especially in the texts in which the sensual and the divine aspects of the lyric subject are conflated in a way that often baffles the modern reader.

On many occasions the gap between the mundane (and often politicized) sensuality of Saʿdi's imagery and his spiritual afflatus seems irreconcilable. The

19 "It is significant that al-Ghazālī's interpretation of the vision of God in the afterlife as (a perfection of) intellection runs contrary to the Ashʿarite tradition of dogmatic theology, with which al-Ghazālī was formally affiliated, and reflects, instead, a clear philosophical bias." Treiger 2012, 59. See also Ibid., 90–91; Abrahamov 1993; Tuft 1979, 167–74.

two ghazals of the "return" to Shiraz with which I opened the introductions to the three parts of this book, provide one such example, but they also highlight the multiplicity of audiences which Saʿdi would address according to different sets of ideals, as well as the development and the integration of the Sufi and philosophical traditions within the theoretical and performative facets of his lyricism.[20] In the staged anthropology of his early ghazals, the appetites of the soul and those of the flesh seem to deny each other's legitimacy. It is a certain philosophical dimension of his work—especially in a later stage and through *milieux* whose ideals resonate with such speculative aesthetics—that intervenes to bridge this gap in the constant quest for a visual and cognitive mediation between physical matter and the spirit.

Among the multiple themes that radiate through Saʿdi's work, the motif of the control of the carnal soul's instinct is particularly recurrent. Nonetheless, as I argued in the chapter on Saʿdi's obscene works, the aesthetic value of the desires of the flesh cannot be denied, as it is part of the complex epistemological path that illuminates the movements of Saʿdi's lyric subject. When scholars (such as Hamidiyān) reduce the nature of the beloved in Saʿdi's poetry to an entity that is *either* an analogue of the divine presence *or* a mundane object of desire, the complexity of the theo-erotic discourse exuding from the ghazals is flattened in order to accommodate a simplistic discourse on the lyric genealogy of chastity in the courtly tradition.[21] From this perspective, all signs of ethical caution with respect to physical desire are interpreted as part of a tradition stemming from the phenomenon of *ʿudhrī* love and the courtly lyric ideals of chaste forms of passion that developed during the Abbasid period and were later integrated into the Sufi debate on mundane love as a ladder towards the divine.[22]

This flattening emphasis on chastity as the mainstream value of the desire portrayed in Saʿdi's ghazals hides the conflicting tensions animating the poet's depictions of the relationship between the realm of the senses and the quest for the invisible world. Ghazals similar to the following, for instance, clearly show how the normativity of the discourse on "chaste love" as a validating interpretation for the scholastic reading of Saʿdi's "beloved" cannot account for

20 See General Introduction, and Introduction to Part 2.

21 See Hamidiyān 1383/2004, 129–30.

22 Hamidiyān extolls Saʿdi's love by comparing it with the *ʿudhrī* tradition, and qualifies it as "the purest, most terse, immaculate form of love." Ibid., 283. On the *ʿudhrī* tradition, see Vadet 1968, 363–78; Jacobi 1992, 1999; *EI*², s.v. "ʿUdhrī" [R. Jacobi]. For a valid criticism of the genetic relationship between Arab *ʿudhrī* poetry and the courtly spirit or the Persian lyric tradition, see Meisami 1987, 20–22.

the poet's investigation of the meaning of the flesh appearing before the eyes of the lyric subject:

1 Not just anyone deserves the title of "Master of Gazes":
The practice of love differs so much from worshiping the flesh.

2 Most eyes are black and white and well recognize
Whiteness from blackness, but not all of them truly *see*.

3 Anyone who cannot endure the burning pain when set ablaze by love
Should never get too close: the moth's wings will catch fire.

4 My breath is not sincere if I complain about the beloved:
Nothing I know about him, if I am aware of myself.

5 Anyone who has human forms and defeats lustful desires
Will acquire human nature in full: we're nothing but animals otherwise!

6 The beverage that your soothing hands offer may be sweet or sour:
It doesn't matter, as nothing can quench the desperately athirst.

7 Such is my passion for your lips that no words do I understand:
Your words may turn bitter and bitter, yet so sweet you will sound to me.

8 You may slay me with your sword, no animosity shall I harbor:
The enemy is the one who would shield me from the blade.

9 I shan't free myself from these ties all my life long: a crown
on my head is the string around my feet that you hold with your hands.

10 In spite of his cruelty, Sa'di will never detach his hand from the beloved's waist:
Would one even abandon the pearls out of fear for the ocean?

Ṭayyibāt 263[23]

23 [2.13] Saʿdi YE, 121–22.

The opening of these lines resonates with the Sufi ethical tradition that portrays the carnal soul as a hostile presence that the believer ought to subdue.[24] It is a motif that completes the courtly lyricism of the last lines of the poem, in which the lover conceives of his body as his own enemy— an impediment that prevents him from reaching the true essence of the beloved. However, the very fact that Saʿdi deems it necessary to open the ghazal with the problem of the physical nature of the gaze and its adjacency to the perils of the desiring nature of the body reveals dynamics for which the system of ethical values of scholastic Sufism cannot account alone. In this ghazal, the ethics regulating the control of one's lust for the sake of achieving "full" human nature clash with the sensual overtone of the poem. Considering this discrepancy, especially in light of the theo-erotic relation through which Saʿdi connects the issue of the vision of God with attraction toward physical beauty, what does the body of the beloved stand for, and how should the onlooker behold it?

Such questions urge us to reconsider the legalistic and ethical aspects of the problem of the physical presence of the beloved in light of the hermeneutical, and ultimately epistemological, aspects of the lyric representation as a continuing meditation on the relationship between the text and the world that it depicts. Furthermore, keeping our focus on the meaning of the body and of its literary representation helps us account for the rational sobriety with which Saʿdi conceives love: a movement of the soul that is engrained in the ontogenesis of the human and which expresses itself through the interaction between the internal and external senses and the worldly signs of the unseen. Therefore, love, in Saʿdi's ghazals, rather than stemming from an ecstatic intoxication solely concentrating on the quest for the divine, constitutes an aesthetic foundation that is intimately related to the physical manifestation of beauty and the human capability of reading and contextualizing it as part of a supreme plan of cosmic perfection. In a number of ghazals, Saʿdi's juxtaposition of physical and spiritual desires generates a visible rift between the ethical and the carnal aspects of the representation of the beloved. Through such juxtapositions, the nature of the beloved's body shifts from an ostensibly mimetic depiction to a paradigmatic taxonomy in which his limbs are exposed as hermeneutical possibilities that transcend their own flesh. The body of the beloved turns into a space of semiotic conflict, in which multiple desires and possibilities converge—especially with respect to the fictional world of the text and its points of contact with external reality.

In the following ghazal, Saʿdi recognizes the aphrodisiac value of body parts such as the downy beard, the beauty mark, and the hair of the beloved, and

---

24 See, for instance, Suhravardī's criticism of Awḥad al-Dīn Kirmānī's practice of *shāhid-bāzī* (Introduction to Part 2, pp. 490–91).

declares the body a hazardous territory in which the religious prohibition of physical contact coexists with the desire that guides the lover's gaze across the map of the beloved's skin:

1 My restorative sleep is at the mercy of your image, O boy:
Desiring our embrace, I scattered away the hopes of my lifetime like coins....

3 No wonder if I was forbidden to hold you tight
Wondrous is the verdict that made my blood licit to you.

4 The sun shines and converts the crescent into the full moon:
Why did my gaze upon you turn the full moon of my life into a crescent?

5 How befitting the conquest of the mighty kingdom of the heart would be
For he whose mole and status enslave a thousand Yūsufs.

6 Do not marvel if I suddenly shouted a senseless cry from my heart:
No patience was left in it when the flames inside were set ablaze.

7 If Saʿdi sets his eyes on you, do not count it as a sin,
As he is not caught in the yoke of the hair and the mole in the fashion of the others.

Badāyiʿ 544[25]

In spite of the opening invocation ("O boy"), the body of the beloved remains elusive throughout the entire ghazal: the poet seems to be focusing exclusively on the effect of love on the inner condition of the lyric persona and its sorrowful heart. Nevertheless, Saʿdi briefly alludes to the beloved's physical beauty in the fifth line, through a hyperbolic comparison with Yūsuf's mole (*khāl*)—which metonymically applies the properties of one single part of his face to his entire body. This line is not devoid of ambiguities, as the parallel might imply that only divine beauty is capable of overshadowing "a thousand Yūsufs." In Saʿdi's ghazals such allusions to divine beauty are often juxtaposed with images in which the material depiction of the beloved prevents the reader

25 [2.14] Saʿdi YE, 245–46. For the second hemistich of the fourth line, I have chosen the variant given by four of the oldest manuscripts (*badr-i vujūd*), whereas I deem arbitrary the variant chosen by Yusofi (*badr-i nishāṭ*). See ibid., 588. The variant I have preferred is also found in Ms. Kabul 1325, 510; Yale 1432, f. 313a.

from interpreting the verses along the lines of scholastic transcendentalism.[26] In this case, the initial invocation to the beloved as a *boy* anchors the text to a level of lyric intimacy for which it is necessary to account whenever a metaphysical level intervenes to expand the dimensions of the representation. The most striking piece of evidence appears in the last line, when Saʿdi produces a metatextual excuse that deserves closer inspection. The body of the "lyric Thou"—ostensibly the *pisar* of the first line—reemerges through a meta-visual observation: "if Saʿdi sets his eyes on you, do not count it as a sin [*khaṭā*]." The conditionality of the event ("if Saʿdi does this," also implying "should Saʿdi do such and such") brings the physicality of the beloved's presence to a level of abstraction in which the lyrical experience generates theory. In fact, the theoretical aspect of this discursive shift finds its final clarification in the second part of the couplet, in which Saʿdi justifies his gazing activities by declaring that he "is not caught in the yoke of the hair and the mole in the fashion of the others." The line is syntactically ambiguous, as it can be read as "Saʿdi, unlike the others, is not caught in the yoke of the hair and the mole," meaning that the external beauty that other people worship is not the same as the object of Saʿdi's passion.[27]

My interpretation slightly diverges from this reading, as I believe that the clause "not in the fashion of the others" (*na ba rasm-i dīgarān*) implies that Saʿdi *is* caught in the yoke of beautiful hair and fragrant moles, but not in the *same fashion* that other people *are*.[28] Saʿdi does not deny the relevance of the physical aspect of his contemplation of beauty, but suggests that different modalities can apply when an attractive human being enters the visual

---

26 See for instance the opening line of the ghazal featured in the cover of this book (*vah ki gar man bāz bīnam rūy-i yār-i khʷīsh / tā qiyāmat shukr gūyam kirdigār-i khʷīsh*), or the first line of a ghazal quoted below (*yār-i man ān ki luṭf-i khudāvand yār-i ū-st*, p. 257). Although this text refers to religious elements (such as the direction of one's prayer, the visionary experience of the unseen, etc.), the mention of God as an external element demonstrates the fact that the beloved and the divine presence do not correspond to each other. On the other hand, Hamidiyān (1383/2004, 274), in a rather week argument, maintains that even in such cases (even when God is addressed through interjection used to call the beloved's attention or to perform a promise) Saʿdi establishes this discrepancy only for the sake of a rhetorical effect.

27 It is worth signaling that Ms. Tehran 1321 (78) only records this line and the penultimate verse of the poem. The omission of the rest of the ghazal could suggest that these lines might have been circulating as wandering verses in Sufi circles that were particularly sensitive to the topic of the permissibility of the practice of gazing at mundane beauty as a spiritual practice. For a more comprehensive discussion on this topic, see chapter eight.

28 In spite of this syntactical ambiguity, modern commentators tend to read the line from an exclusively moralizing perspective. See Khatib-Rahbar 1367/1988, 1:310; Niyāzkār 1390/2012, 601; Barzegar-Khāleqi and ʿAqdā'i 1386/2008, 1: 468.

field of the beholder. In this text, Sa‘di's reduction of the lyric discourse into theory is reflected by the choice of exposing the body of the beloved through the mention of physical details that are presented as an abstracted anatomical topography. This is an anti-mimetic representation, as it shows the beloved's body as a literary code whose relationship with extratextual reality depends on the modality of the beholder's gaze and the interpretation that the reader produces on the basis of the text. Therefore, in this case, the difference between the unlawfulness of the embrace with the beloved and the permissibility of the gaze upon his body revolves around the ontological status of that same body, and the hermeneutical possibilities of the text that describes it.

Any time that Sa‘di's representation of the object of desire oscillates between a mimetic representation of an external tangible reality and the spiritualization of the lyric subject's desires, the hermeneutical problem splits into two interdependent questions. Firstly, from the perspective of the lyric subject, what does the body described in the text stand for? Secondly, what does its external referent (i.e., the physical body to which the poem may allude) signify with respect to the semiotic values of the text? As mentioned in the introduction to this second part, even though Sa‘di—as a poet and not as a religious polymath—drew upon a plurality of sources for the original elaboration of his own approach to the spiritual dimension of the lyric, Avicenna and al-Ghazālī are the authors who deserve to be looked at the most closely for a better understanding of Sa‘di's broader philosophical and theological framework. While I will explore the epistemological aspect of the influence of the Avicennian legacy in the next chapter, this chapter focuses on the authors whose contribution to the discourse on the spiritual aspects of the experience of desire help us provide a solid background for a deeper understanding of the theophanic lyricism that exudes from Sa‘di's ghazals. This survey will unpack the complexity of the relationship between the text and the physical presence of the beloved by first analyzing the basis of Sufi hermeneutics with respect to the "open" (and, as such, "non-scholastic") reception of erotic texts. The discussion will then shift from the spiritual hermeneutics of the textual body of the beloved to the ontological problem of the beloved's body as a possibility of either a divine indwelling or an indexical reference to the divine presence.

3 The Body in the Text

In medieval Iran, discussion of the conditions that made permissible the act of listening to music in general, and to amatory ghazal poetry in particular, pertained to a debate that involved issues far beyond the scope of merely ethical imperatives.[29] This debate resonates with Saʿdi's textualization of the body of the beloved and the ethical, hermeneutical, and ultimately epistemological questions that stem from the modality with which his lyric subject gazes upon the limbs of the object of desire. What is the meaning of the limbs of the beloved to which a ghazal refers, and how does the textualization of this aphrodisiac flesh intersect with the hermeneutical disposition of the listener? In the previous chapter, I have discussed some of the caveats that al-Ghazālī specifies in *The Alchemy of Bliss* (*Kīmiyā-yi saʿādat*) when arguing in favor of the lawfulness of the audition of poems describing the hair of the beloved and the beauty marks of his countenance.[30] The first condition that al-Ghazālī analyzes applies to all Muslims and, as previously discussed, his verdict on the permissibility of listening to amatory poetry rests on the imagination of the listener and their ability to find an appropriate imaginary embodiment for the lines that describe an abstracted object of desire whose physicality is reduced to the stylized mention of specific body parts.

In the second part of that discussion, al-Ghazālī concedes a further level of reception, which, in this case, applies not to any believer, but to "anyone, like the Sufis, who is immersed in the love of God." When such theo-erotically driven individuals listen to ghazal poetry and interpret it through their passion for the divine, "erotic verses do not affect them, as they make sense of each line according to their inner condition."[31] Here, al-Ghazālī's argument shifts from the initial ethical principles opposed to lustful desires to a spiritual hermeneutic that justifies amatory poetry on a radically different level:

> They might interpret the hair [*zulf*] as the darkness of disbelief, or interpret the radiance of the beloved's face as the light of faith, or they could interpret the hair as the chain of impediments from the divine presence.[32]

The goal of al-Ghazālī's literary hermeneutic is to offer the listener an open interpretive opportunity to bind abstracted visual imagery to the spiritual possibilities of texts whose primary horizon of meaning is purely mundane. I have shown in the third chapter how we may see the linguistic representation of the body of the beloved in obscene texts as tending to be reified, meaning that the object of desire is reduced to its bodily form and functions. Al-Ghazālī's invitation to project a process of spiritual fetishization onto the body of the beloved

29 For a general introduction to the legal status of music in premodern Islam, see Gribetz 1991, Lewisohn 1997; Shiloah 1995, 31–44. Part 3 will be entirely dedicated to this topic.

30 Chapter 3, pp. 165–71.

31 *Kīmiyā*, 1: 484.

32 Ibid.

stands on the opposite side of the spectrum of euphemistic representation of the body.[33] The territory in which he guides his reader strictly adheres to the duality of the courtly models of lyric representations. His approach implies that, whatever source of obscene imagination may come forth, a set of spiritualized correspondences prevents the believer from sensual temptations. It is worthwhile noting that whereas al-Ghazālī's open hermeneutical approach to the possibility of interpreting amatory texts in a spiritual sense stemmed from what he deemed a practical necessity, his suggestions generated a "closed" symbolist tradition (which reached its peak between the 14th and 15th century) that posited that all descriptions of the body of the beloved should be read as "cyphers" belonging to a strict paradigm of codified Sufi concepts.[34]

The circulation of post-13th-century manuals containing lists of symbolic correspondences that Sufi practitioners could consult in order to "decipher" the meaning of a given ghazal offered a number of modern scholars the opportunity to interpret the entirety of the premodern corpus of spiritually-informed premodern Persian poetry as a static collection of symbols constantly deviating from the literal meaning of the texts.[35] Even though this approach may offer

33 For further discussion of this topic, see Ingenito 2014, 108–9; Purjavādi 2008, 142–45. We owe to ʿAyn al-Qużāt of Hamadan (1097–1131, the spiritual pupil of al-Ghazālī's brother, Aḥmad Ghazālī) the development of al-Ghazālī's "open" approach to the hermeneutics of amatory poetry. ʿAyn al-Qużāt developed his interpretative posture around the idea that poetry is like a mirror: just as the images appearing in a mirror vary according to the person who faces it, poetry too has no fixed meaning as such, and any reader interprets it according to their spiritual inner condition. See ʿAyn al-Qozāt Hamadāni 1348–50/1969–71, 1: 216. On this topic see Purjavādi 1991, 245–66; 2008, 146–49; Feuillebois-Pierunek 2002, 121–22.

34 Within the context of Sufi manuals, Yaḥyā Bākharzī's *Awrād al-aḥbāb va fuṣūs al-ādāb* (completed at Bukhara in 1324) is one of the first texts sketching a preliminary spiritual codification of the symbolic meaning of specific terms that are found in lyric poetry (such as *maḥabbat*, "love"; *sharāb*, "wine"; *durd*, "wine dregs"; *dayr* "monastery"; *zunnār*, "Christian belt"; *tarsā bachcha* "Christian youth"; *but*, "idol"; *zulf*, "hair," etc.): "here follows the illustration of the symbolic meaning of some words that the [spiritual] companions and the masters of the heart use in their poetry; even though the experienced masters [...] understand these words according to the level of their spiritual intuition and not on the basis of the intention of the author, the initiates ought to understand that their meaning is different from what the literalists can grasp [....]." Bākharzi 1345/1966, 239–53. Other renowned authors of such catalogues of spiritual symbols are Ulfatī Tabrīzī (fl. 14th century) and Maḥmūd Shabistarī (d. 1318–21), the author of the famous *Gulshan-i rāz* (*The Garden of the Mystery*), see Olfati Tabrizi 1362/1983, and Shabestari 1371/1992. For a critical approach to the hermeneutical validity of these treatises, especially in the case of the poetry of ʿIrāqī, see Feuillebois-Pierunek 2002, 122–28.

35 The poetry of Hafez has suffered from this anachronistic approach more than any other premodern Persian author. While it is true that specific communities of readers would read his poetry in exclusively mystical terms (especially after the 15th century), such hermeneutical stands constituted only one fraction of the multiple approaches that Hafez's

valuable contributions to the understanding of specific and socio-historically circumscribed hermeneutical movements within the medieval and early modern reception of Persian poetry, its mostly dehistoricized and uncritical postures fail to account for the semantic complexity of such complex bodies of work within the contexts of their geo-historical circulation and interaction with external reality.[36]

Al-Ghazālī's transition from the ethical regulation of the exposure to amatory poetry to the interpretive freedom of the listener as a means to overcome the sensuality of the text in the direction of spiritual intuitions shows that the problem of textual hermeneutics is intimately connected with the interpretation of the physical presence of the human body as a source of sensual attraction. This open interpretative modality with respect to the poetic mention of

---

readers developed over time. For an excellent, historically informed and philologically impeccable analysis of this problem, see Fotuhi and Vafā'i 1388/2009. For an acute criticism of the first mystical interpretive translation of Hafez's divan into English, see Thiesen 2003.

36 In a seminal article on the "aesthetics and hermeneutics of Sufi poetry," Leonard Lewisohn (1989, 175) argues that the field of classical Persian literary criticism of the "Sufi *ghazal* (amatory elegy)" is divided between scholars who treat Persian lyric poetry "from primarily an aesthetic and literary standpoint" and those who approach this poetic genre "as a communication derived from the imaginal world [...]" and "understand it as an expression of precise symbolic meanings working systematically at a supraconscious associative level." Lewisohn's comments on the Sufi lyric hermeneutics exposed by Shabistarī in his *Gulshan-i rāz* and expanded upon by Lāhījī (d. 1507) are extremely useful for understanding specific currents of thought circulating in Iran during the post-classical phase of Persian literary history. Nevertheless, Lewisohn's tendency to flatten the entirety of the Persian lyric tradition directly or indirectly influenced by Sufi values and aesthetics into one single macro-category of "Sufi poetry" that requires a constant act of spiritual decoding is particularly disarming. Such an unwarranted and radically symbolic critical approach ceases to offer viable hermeneutical solutions when it reduces all poetic texts to a historically undetermined and aesthetically vague chain of correspondences between lyric imagery and spiritual meanings. One of the unscholarly results of this approach is the publication of contemporary dictionaries that extract ahistorical guidelines for the deciphering of medieval Persian poetry from the aforementioned lists of symbolic correspondences, whose scope should be strictly kept within the boundaries of their contexts of composition and circulation. One such example is Nurbakhsh's *Dictionary of Sufi Technical Terms* (see Nurbakhsh 1984 for the first volume of the series, translated into English and published by Lewisohn), whose interpretation of specific lines by authors such as Sa'di and Hafez reduces their celebration of the beauty of the human body in the context of spiritual aesthetics to a dry collection of metaphysical cyphers that do not take into account the multilayered complexity of the texts. For a more comprehensive study of the spiritual symbolism of Shabistarī and Lāhījī in their historical context (and yet, with little proof of how their hermeneutics may apply to the lyric tradition of the 13th and the 14th centuries), see Lewisohn 1995. For a firm rebuttal of the mystically symbolic reading of Persian lyric poetry, see Meisami 1987, 239–41.

the body parts of the beloved resonates with the ethical condition Saʿdi stipulates in the last line of the ghazal quoted earlier: "If Saʿdi sets his eyes on you, do not count it as a sin/ As he is not caught in the yoke of the hair and the mole in the fashion of the others." The textualization of the body that Saʿdi implies through the different "fashion" of his lyric subject's gaze entails a hermeneutical approach whose origins could be connected with the open set of meanings that al-Ghazālī suggests for the spiritually-informed reception of erotic poetry. The body and the poem correspond to each other as reciprocal analogues ready to be interpreted by the listener, the reader, and the beholder. Nevertheless, the morally acceptable fashion to which Saʿdi refers to boast of his gaze on the beloved's body implies an unacceptable counterpart, which Saʿdi fully explores in his obscene works. The potential duality of the gaze keeps the courtly register in constant communication with both the metaphysics of desire and the exposure of the concupiscence of the loins.

Al-Ghazāli's defense of erotic poetry through hermeneutical expedients focusing on the limbs of the textual beloved highlights the fact that the problem of the interpretation of ghazal poetry does not relate to texts alone, but involves the relationship between the circulation of *both* poetic texts *and* bodies of desire in the social spaces influenced by Sufi norms, ideals, and practices. We may recognize a pseudo-historical precedent for this sort of mimetic erotic correspondence in a spiritual context in an anecdote, later reported by the author of the 12th century hagiographic work *Asrār al-tawḥīd*, in which the author, Muḥammad bin Munavvar, describes the reaction of the famed 10th-century Khorasani Sufi Abū Saʿīd b. Abī al-Khayr when listening to the following line recited by a *qavvāl*:

> I will hide myself inside my own ghazal
> so that I can kiss your lips when you read it.[37]

> Abū Saʿīd asked the singer about the identity of the author of the line. He replied "It's by ʿAmmāra." Abu Saʿīd stood up and with a group of Sufi disciples set off to visit the grave of ʿAmmāra."[38]

37 [2.15]

38 Mohammad b. Monavvar 1366/1987, 2: 267. ʿAmmāra is the *takhalluṣ* (or pen name) of the late Samanid/early Ghaznavid court poet Abū Manṣūr ʿAmmāra bin Muḥammad Marvāzī. See De Blois 2004, 76. I suggest to look at this word, *ʿAmmāra*, as a linguistic sign bridging the gap between the abstracted lyric I of the text and the historical author who flourished and died in a specific space and time. On this anecdote, see also Utas 2007, 298.

In the line quoted by the reciter, a lover is talking to a presumably distant beloved, and he suggests that this *ghazal* can act as medium and analogue of his physical presence: the poet turns himself into the text, and the act of reciting taken up by the imaginary beloved becomes a transfigured form of carnal union. But who are the I and the you of this line? The only specification given about the "you" is the act of reading; therefore, potentially *any* reader of this line can correspond to the you to whom the poet is talking. And such an abstracted you turns the "I" of the poem into an abstracted self whose presence transcends the identity of the author. Within the account related by the author of *Asrār al-tawḥīd*, the mechanism of abstraction of the I/you relationship displayed by this line triggers Abū Saʿid's aesthetic appreciation. But, once the sheikh has learned the name of the poet, why does he want to visit his grave? When the reciter reveals ʿAmmāra's name, we become witnesses to a transition from the total abstraction of the poetic persona of the text to the homage paid to his physical presence through the pilgrimage performed by Abū Saʿid to ʿAmmāra's grave in Marv.

The fluidity of the analogy between the bodies and the texts involved in the theo-erotic experience of poetry and desire in the spiritual context of the 11th and 12th centuries sheds an interesting light on al-Ghazālī's vehement defense of lyric poetry. From his defense, later reflected in Saʿdi's careful emphasis on the "fashion" of the lyric subject's gaze, it is possible to infer that both erotic poetry and homoerotic desires were widespread practices and tendencies that required ethical regulations whose origins were primarily hermeneutical. Therefore, it is at the crossroads of sexual ethics, heresiography, and hermeneutics that one ought to trace the origins of the debate on the permissibility of amatory poetry audition as a source of spiritual validation.

4 Interpreting the Body of the Text: Spiritual Hermeneutics

The *Kashf al-maḥjūb* (*The Unveiling of the Concealed Mystery*)—one of the oldest and most authoritative manuals of Sufism composed in Persian (1058)—offers valuable glimpses into the background of such debates, especially from the perspective of the prohibition of ghazal audition prior to al-Ghazālī's hermeneutical approach. In the chapter dedicated to music, the author, Abū al-Ḥasan Hujvīrī (d. 1071–72), questions the legal permissibility of erotic poetry during the *samāʿ* sessions (which we may translate as "spiritual concert," or "lyrical ritual"), a practice that constituted the key performative context for the circulation of lyric poetry in medieval Iran.[39] By doing so, Hujvīrī traces a

39 See Part 3, Chapter 9, pp. 445–48.

parallel between the unlawfulness of sensual desire towards young men and the illegal status of the texts that describe a physical presence capable of eliciting the sexual arousal of the audience:

> [...] Some declare that it is unlawful to listen to any poetry whatever, and pass their lives in defaming their brother Muslims. Some, on the contrary, hold that all poetry is lawful, and spend their time in listening to love-songs and descriptions of the face and hair and mole of the beloved. [...] Just as it is unlawful and forbidden to look at and touch an attractive youth who might be a cause of temptation, listening to the description of his attributes is similarly forbidden; if someone considers listening to such texts permissible, then touching and staring at youths should be lawful too—but upholding such ideas is heresy [*zandaqa*].[40]

Hujvīrī introduces the process of spiritual inference in order to invalidate the arguments promoting the circulation of erotic poetry as a source of divine inspiration:

> [...] Through [the mention] of the eyes, the countenance, the cheeks, the mole, and the hair [of the beloved], I feel [the presence of] God and I seek Him through these body parts because our eyes and ears are the locus [*maḥall*] of inference [*ʿibrat*] and the source of [spiritual] knowledge [*ʿilm*].

His confutation of the argument above revolves around a specific analogy between texts and bodies:

> At this point a third person could say that "I will touch and kiss that person because so-and-so said that it is permitted to listen to the description of his attributes," and might also conclude that "By doing so, I seek God, since one sense is no better than another for the perception of spiritual meaning [*maʿnī*]." In that case, the religious path [*sharīʿat*] is entirely nullified, and the Apostle's saying "*the eyes commit fornication*" loses all its force, the blame of touching persons with whom marriage may legally be

40 Hojviri 1387/2008, 581–82. My translations from Hujvīrī are partially based on Nicholson's renditions, which I have often modified for the sake of terminological consistency and to accommodate the variants published in ʿĀbedi's critical edition of the book. For Nicholson's translation of this passage, see Nicholson 1976, 397–98.

> contracted [*nāmaḥramān*] is removed, and the ordinances of religion fall to the ground.[41]

According to Hujvīrī, the logic behind using the supposed lawfulness of listening to erotic poetry as a way to legitimize sensual experiences with illicit objects of desire falls into the category of heresy (*zandaqa*).[42] The reason for the application of this specific heresiographic judgment has to be traced back to the correspondence that Hujvīrī establishes between the audition of erotic poetry and the physical contact with a human object of desire. The parallel that Hujvīrī categorically criticizes rests on the justification of reading both poetic texts and beautiful bodies as a "source" (*manbaʿ*) for the knowledge of God (*ḥaqq*, the True, in text) and an inference (*ʿibrat*) that gleans the divine presence. The epistemic correspondence between texts and bodies as sources

41 Ibid., 582; Nicholson 1976, 398.

42 As noticed earlier, Hujvīrī uses the expression *zandaqa* to define the heresy of the logic behind the argument that legitimizes sexual contact with an illegal object of desire as a means to seek the divine presence. In one of the first passages of his book, Hujvīrī defines *zandaqa* as the quest for inner truth without abiding by the external sharia rules. Ibid., 21. In another passage, the author further contextualizes the concept of *zandaqa* by emphasizing the role of spiritual hermeneutics in connection with music and sensual desire: "Ẕū'l Nun the Egyptian says: [...] 'Audition is a Divine influence [*vārid*] which stirs the heart to seek God: those who listen to it spiritually [*bi ḥaqq*] attain unto God, and those who listen to it sensually [*bi nafs*] fall into heresy [*zandaqa*]. This does not imply that audition is the cause of attaining unto God, but it means that the auditor ought to hear the spiritual meaning [*maʿnī*], not the form [*ṣūrat*], as his heart is the locus of the Divine influence. Whenever this spiritual meaning attains the heart, it stirs it up. Who in that audition follows the truth will experience a revelation, whereas one who follows his carnal soul (*nafs*) will be veiled and will have recourse to interpretation [*taʾvīl*]. *Zandaqa* is a Persian word which has been Arabicized. In the Persian language *zand* means interpretation, hence [the Persians] call the commentary on their Book *Zand-u pāzand*. The philologists [*ahl-i lughat*], wishing to give a name to the descendants of the Magians [*majūs*], Bābak and Afshīn, called them *zindīq*, on the ground of their assertion that everything stated by the Muslims has an [esoteric] interpretation, which nullifies its external sense. Ẕū'l Nūn, by using this term, intended to declare that, in audition, spiritually inspired people [*ahl-i taḥqīq*] penetrate the supernal reality [*muḥaqqiq shavand*], whereas sensualists [*ahl-i havā*] become unorthodox interpreters [*muʾavvil*] who make far-fetched interpretations [*taʾvīl-i baʿīd konand*] and thereby fall into wickedness." Ibid, 589–90; Nicholson 1976, 404. For further bibliography on this passage and Ẕū'l Nūn's saying, see Hojviri 1387/2008, 921. See also Ebstein 2014. On the negative connotation of *taʾvīl* as an unorthodox approach to scriptural exegesis, see Abdul-Raof 2010, 104–106. On the relationship between *taʾvīl* and *zandaqa* in al-Ghazālī's hermeneutics, especially in the context of *Fayṣal al-tafriqa bayna al-islām wa al-zandaqa* (*The Decisive Criterion for Distinguishing Between Islam and Heresy*), see Whittingham 2007, 13–27.

of knowledge of the divine is reinforced by positing that the senses equal each other in the perception (*idrāk*) of meaning (*maʿnī*).

In his view, this correlation entails two unacceptable consequences that are legally sanctionable both from the perspective of Islamic law and from the point of view of heresiology: on the one hand, the erotic text and the aphrodisiac body encourage fornication, and on the other, this correlation implies a cognitive correspondence between the human body and the divine that requires attentive scrutiny in order to be considered acceptable. Hujvīrī's harsh prohibition of erotic poetry ostensibly derives from a pragmatic approach to the confusion that inexperienced practitioners of Sufism may develop by justifying lustful actions as a form of spiritual epistemology. The fact that this prohibition does not extend to the expert masters of Sufism is proven by a passage in which the author seems to indirectly imply that erotic poetry is actually performed in the contingencies in which the ignorant reads the ecstatic rapture of the mature participants in the spiritual audition as an analogue of sensual pleasure:

> When ignorant fools who pretend to be Sufis [*mustaṣavvuf*] see the ecstatic reaction of those who listen to poetry with a spiritual commitment [*ba ḥāl*], they think that they are driven by sensual desire. Hence, by observing them, they say: it [lust] is allowed [*halāl*], and if it was not, they would not have done it.' They eventually imitated them, but only took the external aspect [of that practice] and discarded its truthful essence [*ḥaqīqat*]. By doing so they undertook the path of perdition, and led astray other groups of ignorant fools. This is one of the calamities of our time [...].[43]

The passage above highlights once more the duality of lyric as a ground for the potential development of both spiritual and obscene mental representations. In this case, the author approaches the duplicity of the lyric from the phenomenology of a mixed audience's response to the affect manifested in the disposition of the body of the Sufi masters when carried away by the exposure to a

43 Hojviri 1387/2008, 582. Seeking God and being absorbed with the divine presence is the condition (predetermined, according to Hujvīrī, as he make clear in the account of Ẕū'l Nūn) for using the intimation provided by any erotic text and convert it into a source of spiritual inspiration: "when a man has audition of this kind, whatever he hears is lawful to him." Ibid., 588. "This is the condition of the "Unitarians" (*muvaḥidān*) who, when perusing a poem, they regard the poet, and they see the creator of the poet's creative nature, and the disposer of his thought, and they draw an intimation therefrom, seeing in the act an evidence of the Agent." Ibid.

poetic performance. The inexperienced practitioners, or those who embrace Sufism for mundane purposes, do not recognize the difference between lust and spiritual ecstasy in the physical response of whoever is moved by the amatory poetic performance.

In spite of such misleading readings of the effects of ecstatic raptures, the Sufi masters who commit to a spiritual reception of ghazal poetry grasp a level of truth that stems from the interpretative modality that Hujvīrī, in the previous passage, has defined as *ʿibrat*, or *iʿtibār*, "inference." The author stresses the twofold value of *ʿibra* through a maxim ascribed to Shiblī: "the exterior form of listening [to erotic poetry] generates carnal temptation [*fitna*], whereas its inner dimension [*bāṭin*] offers an inference [*ʿibrat*]; therefore, he who recognizes the *sign* [*ishāra*] may lawfully hear the inference, otherwise he seeks temptation and will be exposed to calamity."[44] The word *ʿibra* is a first-form noun of the root *ʿbr*, a verb whose eighth form generates the noun *iʿtibār*. I translate both *ʿibra* (or *ʿibrat*) and *iʿtibār* as "inference," although they could also be rendered as "deduction," "allusion," "suggestion," or even "teaching."[45] The first meaning of the root is "to cross," "to pass through," or "to pass along a way." These two nouns, by extension, refer to the transition from one meaning to another, or from what is known and accessible to the senses to the unknown and invisible, but discernible through an inferential process: "from this meaning of the eight form of the verb, the noun *iʿtibār* is coined as a philosophical term: to take what one sees as an indication or evidence of the concealed; to compare what is non-apparent with what is apparent.[46] This passage clarifies that the solution proposed by Hujvīrī and later incorporated by al-Ghazālī is inferential but not exegetical: the intimation resulting from the inferential

44 See ibid., 590 for a historical survey of the texts in which this maxim appears.

45 For all the possible translations of this term, see de Callataÿ 2014, 280: "a word which [...] scholars and translators have variously translated, each one according to his/her own interpretative preference, with the words 'reflexión' (Tornero; Ramón Guerrero), 'interpretación' (Garrido Clemente), 'transposition symbolique' (Gril), 'inference' (Brown) or 'contemplation' (Stroumsa and Sviri)." See also ibid., 280–83, on the correspondence between Masarra and the Ikhwān al-Ṣafā on this concept. On Masarra's theory of *iʿtibār*, see Stroumsa and Sviri 2009, 204–7.

46 For a comprehensive analysis of the etymological, philological, and theological origins and implications of *iʿtibār*, see Lobel 2007, 119–22. The author recognizes the Quranic origins of the concept and refers to David Z. Baneth (Baneth 1938, 23–30) for the recognition of Pseudo-Jāḥiẓ's *Kitāb al-dalāʾil wa al-iʿtibār ʿalāʾ al-khalq wa al-tadbīr* (*The Book of Proofs and Inference Regarding Creation and Divine Governance*) as the source for al-Ghazālī's teleological speculations on *iʿtibār* appearing in his brief treatise *Kitāb al-ḥikma fī makhlūqāt Allāh* (*The Book of Wisdom on God's Creations*). See also El Shamsy 2016, in which al-Ghazālī's empirical teleology (in particular his *Kitāb al-ḥikma*) is contextualized within the framework of a series of texts discussing the concept of *iʿtibār*.

process brings the reader of the ghazal to a different level of intellectual awareness, which does not require an analytical process of interpretation. It is precisely for this reason that al-Ghazālī—unlike the 14th-century radically symbolistic tradition of the likes of Shabistarī—abstains from suggesting a fixed codification for the meaning of the body parts mentioned in a poem.

From these observations it is possible to deduce that the role of the act of inferring is twofold: its primary role is to divert the intervention of lustful temptations (what both al-Ghazālī and Hujvīrī refer to as *fitna*), but it also converts the desirous yearning of the listener into an intellectual meditation on uncodified possibilities of signification. It is therefore a process that establishes a contemplative modality that disconnects the erotic text from its immediate meaning and prepares the ground for the re-semantization of both the verses and the physical bodies that they portray.

5 The Body as an Inference: between Lust and Incarnationism

Hujvīrī and al-Ghazālī present the inferential modality as a technique for correcting the possibility of lustful thoughts upon the audition of ghazal poetry. Their justification rests on an assumption that Hujvīrī states very clearly: as far as the effects on the listener and the beholder are concerned, erotic descriptions in verse act as the analogues of the physical presence of a potential object of desire, and vice versa. This correspondence entails the possibility of projecting the inferential modality upon physical bodies, as if they were texts whose perceptible presence points at semiotic possibilities that are not immediately accessible to the senses. The transition of the inferential process from the textual representation of the body to an extratextual physical presence implies a switch from a hermeneutical modality to an epistemological approach in which the senses of the beholder are directly implied as a source of cognition of the invisible.[47]

The inferential modality of *iʿtibār* constitutes one of the key approaches that characterize Saʿdi's aesthetics. In a *qasida* that in many manuscripts opens the collection of the *Ṭayyibāt*, Saʿdi expresses one of his most charming lauds of the divine agency as the source of all splendor on earth. The world is a text that opens to the eyes of the beholder, providing one with the opportunity to engage in an intelligent act of perusal in the form of an aesthetic experience:

47 From a logical point of view, it corresponds to the inferential process (*istidlāl*) of gleaning the invisible from the visible manifestation of the world (*istidlāl bi shāhid ʿalā al-ghayb*). See van Ess 1970, 34–35.

1 Who could ever count the supreme virtues of God?
Who could fully thank Him for one out of a thousand of them?

2 That insightful [*laṭīf*] Creator who, upon the fabric of creation
Painted thousands of iridescent forms.

3 It was for the inferring gaze [*ʿibrat-i naẓar*] of the intelligent [*hushiyār*]
That He designed the spheres and made the stars shine.

4 He created the oceans and the lands, the trees and the human beings
He created the sun and the moon, the stars, the night and the day.

5 He hammered the mountains as pins on the edges of the earth
And firmly unfolded the carpet of the ground over the sea.

6 Through the irradiation of the sun, he converted the specks of the soil
Into orchards of fruits, verdant meadows, and valleys of poppies.

7 He gave water to the clouds and to the thirsty roots of the trees,
He turned the bare branches into the ornament of the springtime.

8 He bore the fruit from the dry branch, poured sugar into the cane,
And from the raindrop he solidified pearls inside the oyster.

9 All signs of a mercy that conquered all the corners of the world
All providential burdens that He entrusted to the celestial spheres.

10 He created all these thousands of beautiful countenances
For those eyes capable of inferring [*iʿtibār*] through their gaze.[48]

48 [2.16] Saʿdi YE, 4–5; Saʿdi KhE, 656. Considering the many notable variants found in the manuscripts, Saʿdi likely redrafted and repurposed this text several times. Cf. Ms. Kabul 1325, 294–96. In the second line (first *miṣrāʿ*), most manuscripts record *laṭīf*, instead of *qadīm* as the attribute of God that Saʿdi associates with the act of creation. I prefer *laṭīf* (which I translate as "insightful"), as it is a divine attribute that al-Ghazālī associates with the providential wisdom of God that penetrates the hidden knots that bind the world together. See, for instance, the following passages from *The Ninety-Nine Beautiful Names of God*, in which al-Ghazālī explains the mysterious perfection of the natural world (including the human body) as the result of God's "benevolent insight" (*luṭf*): "For the perfect

If compared with other such celebrations of the divine power penned by previous authors, Saʿdi's poem exalts the role of vision as the primary faculty for the production of a spiritual inference.[49] Beautiful faces appear as signs poised among the marvels of creation: bodies that open to the eyes as texts within the texture of the world. Therefore, the vision of the body of the beloved reads as an aesthetic experience that belongs to an inferential process proceeding from an act of cognition:

1 My beloved is he who is beloved by the divine grace:
At his disposal, justice and injustice, denial and consent....

5 No Masters of the Heart are left now that spring has arrived,
Except for the lovers of the rose, wounded by its thorns.

6 Do not believe that it's his form that bewilders my mind
My intellect is taken away by the Fashioner of his shape [*ṣūrat-nigār-i ū*].

7 The others behold the beautiful countenance with their gaze
But what we gaze upon is the power of his Creator....

Badāyiʿ/Ṭayyibāt 404[50]

---

meaning of 'insightful' combines benevolence [*luṭf*] in action with a delicacy of perception [*idrāk*]. [...] The production of pure milk out of distasted food and blood, as well as the production of precious gems from hard stone, of honey from the bee, silk from the worm, and pearls from the oyster—are all part of His benevolent insight. But even more amazing than that is His creating from impure semen one who is a vessel for His knowledge, bears His trust and witnesses to His heavenly kingdoms—this too is impossible to reckon." Al-Ghazāli 1971, 110–11. My translation is a slight adaptation from Burrell and Daher's version (1992, 97–98). In the last line, I translate *manẓar* as "countenance" because this is the primary acceptation of the term (which could also mean "landscape," "vista" or, more generically, "locus where one's gaze sets") as Saʿdi employs it in his works. Dehkhodā confirms my reading, as he uses this same line to attest to the acceptation that I have preferred. Cf. the sexual connotation of the same term in one of Saʿdi's obscene fragments analyzed in Chapter 3 (pp. 200–201).

49 In one of his most beautiful *qasidas*, ʿAṭṭār praises God through the celebration of the wonders of the cosmos. Whereas Saʿdi adds a sensory dimension to his praise (as if the reader were to perceive the wonders of the world through the eyes of the lyric persona in the text), ʿAṭṭār's lengthy ode resonates with the uncannily powerful intimations that characterize the 55th *sura* of the Qur'ān (*al-Raḥmān*):
Your threshold encircles the seven heavens—*Glory to Him!*
The two worlds are full of you and empty of you—*Glory to Him!*
[2.17] ʿAttār 1392/2013, 862–63.

50 [2.18] Saʿdi YE, 188. The oldest manuscripts record this ghazal among the *Ṭayyibāt* (see, for instance, Ms. Berlin 1306, f. 100a/b), which confirms the theory that Saʿdi's emphasis on *iʿtibār* as an ethical-teleological screen to protect the lyric subject from sensual desires

In a fashion similar to the verses about the modality of the beholder's worship of the beloved's body parts (his hair, his mole, etc.), Saʿdi shows in these lines too that the ethical separation between lust and spiritual inspiration is only the outward aspect of an intellectual process. In fact, rather than the object of physical desire per se, it is the logical recognition of a link between the form of the beloved and the divine painter of those forms that bewilders the intellect of the beholder. From the very first line of the ghazal, Saʿdi stresses the presence of a sharp distinction between divine agency and the result of its actions on visible forms. The difference upon which the poet construes the beholder's inferential logic is obtained through the repetition of the word "beloved" (*yār*) as a means to distinguish the status of the human beloved from the divine attribute of merciful affection toward the proportioned nature of the forms that were shaped by his "grace" (*luṭf*). It is noteworthy that the inferential link that Saʿdi traces between the human object of desire and God corresponds to what Wolfson calls an "introvertive" modality of contemplation of the divine, whose presence is here evoked by recurring to the Persian translation (*ṣūrat-nigār*) of the Quranic epithet *al-Muṣawwir*, the "Fashioner."[51] On the basis of the identification of the role of the intellect in the cognition of the divine presence exuding from the human shape, lustful desires move from belonging exclusively to the realm of ethical normativity to become a problem whose nature is primarily cognitive. The reception of the textualized body ultimately depends on the orientation of the listener's senses with respect to the circulation of bodies of desire in the social spaces in which he is immersed. It is in fact in the social context of intergenerational

belongs to an early stage of the poet's literary development. See General Introduction, and introduction to Part 3.

51 *Al-Muṣawwir* appears only once in the Qur'ān: "He is God, the Creator, the Maker, the Shaper. To Him belong the Names Most Beautiful. All that is in the heavens and the hearth magnifies Him. He is the All-mighty, the All-wise." Qur'ān, 59: 24, translated by Arberry. See al-Ghazāli's inspiring observations on the anthropological, psychological, and teleological implication of this epithet: "Now this is man's share in this name: acquisition of the cognitive form corresponding to the existential form. For knowledge consists in a form in the soul corresponding to the things known. The knowledge which God—great and glorious—has of the form is the cause of the form's existing in individuals, while the form existing in individuals is the cause of the cognitive form's being realized in the heart of man. In that way man benefits by knowing the meaning of the name *al-Muṣawwir* among the names of God—may He be praised and exalted—for by acquiring the form in his soul he also becomes a fashioner, as it were, even if that be put metaphorically. For in point of fact, these cognitive forms only occur within him by the creation of God the most high, and by His invention, not by one's own activity, but rather by one's striving to be exposed to the outpouring mercy of God the most high upon him." Burrel and Daher 1992, 71. For the original text, see al-Ghazāli 1971, 83.

interactions that this problem is raised as an issue that is simultaneously ethical and cognitive.

Intergenerational sensual contacts between Sufi initiates and young men warranted explicit disclaimers in many of the manuals on Sufism composed between the 10th and the early 11th centuries. Al-Qushayrī, whose *Risāla* deeply influenced Khorasanian Sufism, dwells at length on this issue, which he describes as "one of the worst disasters" that threatens the novice on the spiritual path. "Some people," he states, "advance association with youths beyond simple immoral behavior." Therefore, he urges his audience to "let the student beware of sitting with youths and mixing with them, for the mildest consequence of this habit is the opening of the door of spiritual failure and the initiation of the state of abandonment by God."[52]

In this same passage, Qushayrī cautiously suggests that the major risk of this practice is posed by its threat of generating *shirk*, "associationism," or polytheism. He uses the word *shāhid*, "witness of God's beauty" to denounce what seems to have been a semi-institutionalized practice among some Sufi circles, and he adds that as there is no indication of this habit in the *ḥadīth*s, it is not admissible even in the case of those who embrace spiritual chastity (*shuhadā*ʾ). The error to which Qushayrī elliptically alludes is predominantly epistemological, as it belongs to the sphere of the possibility of "interpreting" young men's attractive appearance as an analogue of God's beauty—thereby leading to the peril of polytheism. Hujvīrī elaborates on the risk of this threatening hermeneutical possibility and defines what Qushayrī was alluding to as *ḥulūl*, or "incarnationism," infusion, and more specifically God's indwelling in a human body:

> On the whole, staring [*naẓra kardan*] at youths [*aḥdāṣ*] and associating with them is unlawful and those who legitimize it [*mujavviz-i ān*] are unbelievers [*kāfir*]; any argument [*aṣar*] they allege [for it] derives from

52 Qushayri 1988, 627–28, English translation, in Qushayri 2007, 482–82. As I shall discuss in the ninth chapter, the twelfth century anti-Sufi treatise *Talbīs iblīs* (*Satan's Deception*) by the Hanbali traditionalist Ibn al-Jawzī contains a valuable (especially from a socio-anthropological point of view) collection of anecdotes attesting to widespread intergenerational erotic exchanges in the context of Sufi circles. As noted by Matthew Miller, the arguments that Ibn al-Jawzī adduces to criticize such practices attest to the dominant homoerotic aesthetics of the time, perceived as natural tendencies belonging to the base appetites of the carnal soul (*nafs*). See Miller 2018, 14–16. For a detailed analysis of Ibn al-Jawzī's social and theological criticism of the practice of gazing at comely youths in the Sufi context, see Ridgeon 2018, 86–96. Furthermore, it would be interesting to compare the language of the Hanbali traditionalist on this topic with the lyric portrayals of the beloved in Saʿdi's poetry and in the prose passages of the *Gulistān*.

> falsity and ignorance. I have seen ignorant persons who suspected the Sufis of the crime in question and regarded them with abhorrence, and I observed that some have turned this practice into a religious path. But all the masters of Sufism have recognized the wickedness of such practices, which belong to the legacy of the incarnationists [*ḥulūliyān*]—*may God curse them*—and which have left a stigma on the saints and the Sufis.[53]

In this passage, Hujvīrī shows that unlawful sensual desire and incarnationism constitute the two correlated poles of the experience of interpreting human beauty as an immanent manifestation of God. The author further clarifies that the error does not derive from the observation of the human body as such, but—as in the ghazal of Saʿdi discussed at the beginning of this chapter—from the modality of the observation and the focus of the beholder's attention.[54] In fact, in a paragraph dedicated to the 8th-century traditionist Muḥammad b. Vāsiʿ and the impact of his teachings on the early developments of Sufism, Hujvīrī analyzes one of his most renowned statements, which was widely commented on by later Sufi circles: *I never saw anything* [*in the world*] *without seeing God therein*. Hujvīrī clarifies that this utterance "corresponds to the rank of the manifestation [*mushāhadat*] where the believer is ravished by the passion for the Agent [*fāʿil*] and thereby reaches a level in which he sees the Agent and not the action [*fiʿlī*] caused by Him, just like someone who sees the painter [*muṣavvir*] in the painting [*ṣūrat*]." Hujvīrī stresses the correspondence between the vision of the Agent (*fāʿil*) instead of the object (of vision, *mafʿūl*), and the perception of the presence of the Creator (*khāliq*) as opposed to the creature (*makhlūq*). He then argues that the confusion between the

53 Hojviri 13 7/2008, 606.

54 Cf. ʿAṭṭār's meditations on the problem of incarnationism with respect to the contemplation of beauty in the phenomenal world:
Here both unification and incarnationism are blasphemy
As *this* is oneness [*vaḥdat*] that repeats itself:
One Creator, but more than thousands of creations
All surfacing as exempla offered to the test of *science*.
[2.19] ʿAttār 1392/2013, 714;
From your lips and grain of beauty you brought to knowledge
Both darkness and the water of life.
No one ever saw in Yūsufs of Egypt
The same comeliness I see in you this year.
I pronounce these words with all discretion
As I fear they may stir up the incarnationists.
Here where I am, no incarnationism is at work:
Only sacred drowning and the revelation of spiritual states.
[2.20] Ibid., 419.

creator and the creature as a focus of the believer's attention is what perverts the original meaning of Muḥammad b. Vāsiʿ's statement and converts it into a validation of the heresy of incarnationism:

> But there is a group of people whose error is to think that Muḥammad b. Vāsiʿ's utterance *I have seen God therein* involves the generation of space [*makān*], fragmentation [*tajziyat*] and incarnation [*ḥulūl*]. This is mere blasphemy, because space and what resides in it [*mutimakkin*] are associated with each other, and if we suppose that the space has been created then also what resides in it has been created, and if we postulate that what resides is eternal ["pre-existent," *qadīm*] then the space too will be uncreated. Two blasphemies derive from this argument: either creatures must be defined as uncreated, or the Creator has to be created [*muḥdaṣ*]. It is impiety in both cases. Therefore this vision [*ruʾyat*] of Him in the things [of the world] must be [solely] seen as a sign, proof, and demonstration of His existence.[55]

In the section where Hujvīrī lists all the sects belonging to the path of Sufism, he devotes a paragraph to those whom he recognizes as the historical forebears of incarnationism and states that Abū Ḥulmān (fl. 3rd/9th century), who was originally from Fars and started preaching his doctrine in Damascus, is the most prominent representative of this group.[56] His followers, organised as a sect called the *Ḥūlmāniyya*, used to prostrate themselves before any beautiful young man they would encounter on their path; a practice which, in spite of kindling fiery debates on the heretical nature of its implications, constitutes the primary axis of the theo-erotic aesthetics informing the cognitive phenomenology of Saʿdi's lyric subject.[57]

6 From Incarnation to Affinity: the Body as a Qibla

Al-Ghazālī's position on the relationship between ghazal poetry and the experience of divine love constitutes a radical hermeneutical revolution in the context of the religious reception of amatory poetry, its lawfulness, and the

---

55 Hojviri 1387/2008, 142.
56 Ibid., 382.
57 On Abū Ḥūlmān, see Karamustafa 2007, 105–106; Ernst 1985, 121–23; Ritter 2003, 466–67. See also Ghani 1356/1977, 458; Foruzānfar 1347/1968, 30. On *ḥulūl*, see Ritter 2003, 464; *EI*², s.v. "Ḥulūl" [L. Massignon, G. C. Anawati].

interpretive stratagems capable of converting it into a powerful tool for the exploration of spiritual practices. It was certainly not the impact of his writings alone that made possible a moderate approach to ghazal poetry. However, as a major Islamic authority whose works widely circulated in the context of Shafiʿi law and Ashʿari theology, his legacy strengthened a line of thought that not only did not forbid the composition, circulation, and recitation of mundane lyric poetry, but even encouraged it as a resource in the believer's quest for God.

It is in the context of the discussion of music as a sensorial stimulation for the metaphysical inclinations of the human heart that al-Ghazālī presents the amatory versified description of human beauty as a magnifier of the believer's love for God. Even though al-Ghazālī, as we have seen in the previous chapter, condemns any sensual experience connected with the practice of beholding beautiful bodies as a means to visualize the divine beauty through the senses, his anti-ecstatic approach to amatory poetry resonates with his strenuous defense of the spiritual necessity of loving God.[58] Just as Hujvīrī's *Kashf* and other Sufi treatises had emphasized before him, a total immersion in the love of God is the fundamental prerequisite to legitimize the exposure to erotic poetry without allowing the soul of the believer to be subjugated by the sensual impulses of the carnal self.[59] But, as we have discussed earlier, once the threat of lustful desires is eluded, the intellectualization of the hermeneutical approach to both erotic texts and the contemplation of beautiful bodies is the only approach that enables both the reader and the onlooker to avoid the blasphemy of the incarnationists.

Al-Ghazālī's original contribution to this problem is particularly interesting, as it brings together ontological arguments that—even when not explicitly stated—produce fruitful elaborations of the transcendence of God's essence as a subtext for the mystery of the genesis of human nature. This tenuous connection emerges with stronger evidence in the passages in which—both in the *Iḥyāʾ ʿulūm al-dīn*, and in the *Kīmiyā-yi saʿādat*—the Iranian theologian elusively mentions the possibility of a fifth argument for the love of human beings

58 For two detailed surveys of the problem of love in the Islamicate spiritual tradition, see Abrahamov 2003; Chittick 2013. Whereas Chittick's approach is predominantly based on the Sufi tradition, Abrahamov contextualizes medieval spiritual eroticism within a broad interconfessional and philosophical framework. For a valuable contribution to the topic of love in the development of Iranian Sufism and its influence on premodern Persian poetry, see Purjavādi 1387/2008, in particular 179–208. For a more specific analysis of the development of the ideal of spiritual love in early Sufism, see Lumbard 2007.

59 See Abrahamov 2003, 25–41.

towards God, which is based in their alleged "secret affinity" (*al-munāsaba al-khafiyya*) and "similarity" (*mushākala*, or "conformity") with the divine:

> The idea of the affinity between the form of man and the divine presence has been partially mentioned in the preface of this book,[60] but the remaining truth about it cannot be illustrated in books, as the understanding of common people cannot sustain it. This concept caused even intelligent men to go astray: some of them slipped into anthropomorphism [*tashbīh*], as they thought that "form" [*ṣūrat*] only refers to external forms, whereas others resorted to incarnationism or unification.[61]

Al-Ghazālī is well aware of the slippery terrain into which he ventures with this passage, and he closes his remarks on the affinity and the spiritual similarity between man and God by quoting the *ḥadīth* in which the Prophet states that "God created Adam in His form," which he interprets as an esoteric hint at the secret of the inner forms that do not correspond to their outer counterpart.[62] The Iranian theologian traces a fine line between incarnationism and the secret affinity between mankind and God. In the passage above, he alludes to the ecstatic utterances of Sufis such as Manṣūr al-Ḥallāj and Abū Yazīd

60 In the introduction of the *Kīmiyā*, al-Ghazālī underlines the essential affinity between the human heart and the angels, not the divine essence ("az jins-i gawhar-i farishtagān ast"). *Kimiyā*, 1: 15.

61 Ibid., 2: 581. On the five reasons that explain love between God and mankind, see Abrahamov 2003, 50–59. See also Lumbard 2016, 140–49.

62 On the controversial anthropomorphism implied by this *ḥadīth*, see Watt 1959–60; Abrahamov 1995. Abrahamov (2003, 58–62) points out that al-Ghazālī does not specify the exact meaning of the inner formal affinity between man and God, and speculates that knowledge could be considered as the common element between the two: "Al-Ghazālī expresses here an Aristotelian notion: Aristotle regards the highest activity as being of a contemplative nature since this activity is akin to God's activity, and is therefore God-like. It seems to me that the fact that this notion directly follows the fifth cause of love (affinity) alludes to the possibility that al-Ghazālī regards knowledge as the link which connects man to God." Ibid., 62. A philosophical antecedent of al-Ghazālī's theory of a similarity between man and God can be found in Avicenna's *Treatise on Love*, whose last section affirms a potential "similarity" (*tashabbuh*) between human (and angelic) souls and the "essence of the Absolute Good": "The perfection of both human and angelic souls lies in two things: 1) the conception of those intelligible beings to which they have a possible relation,—each according to its capacity; this is in an effort to become assimilated to the essence of the Absolute Good—, and (2) in the consequent emanation from them of such actions as are in harmony with their nature, and as are just in relation to the latter." Fackenheim 1945, 224. The term *tashabbuh* is also found in al-Ghazāli's *Mīzān al-ʿamal*. See al-Ghazālī 1964, 403–4. Joseph Bell (1986, 84) translates the term as "imitation."

al-Bisṭāmī,[63] whom he directly or indirectly criticizes in many of his works.[64] In his Neoplatonizing treatise *The Niche of Lights* (*Mishkāt al-anwār*)[65] al-Ghazālī reiterates his criticism by remarking that those mystics uttered such words as a consequence of their spiritual ecstasy, which hindered their intellectual faculties.[66] In highlighting that "the speech of lovers in the state of intoxication should be concealed and not spread about," al-Ghazālī does not deny the validity of their spiritual experience as such. Rather, what he rejects is the logic with which they express it: "When this intoxication subsides [...] they come to know that what they experienced was not the reality of unification [*ḥaqīqat al-ittiḥād*] but that it was similar to unification."[67] Al-Ghazālī stresses that the mystics react to the spiritual experience "as if" they were united with the divine, without any actual unification or indwelling ever having taken place.[68]

---

63 See Ernst 1985.

64 For a list of the passages, see Treiger 2011, 699–700, n. 7. Cf. this passage, translated by Treiger (ibid., 701): "The 'correspondence,' [*munāsaba*, between God and man] is a point where one is required to hold fast the pen's reins, for people are split over it into those who are deficient (*qāṣṣir*), inclined to blatant anthropomorphism (*tashbīh ẓāhir*), and those who are extreme and go too far (*ghālin musrif*), transgressing the limit of [what is meant by] correspondence by [claiming actual] union and believing in indwelling. One of them [i.e. al-Ḥallāj] went as far as to say: 'I am the Real.' [...] As for those to whom it has been disclosed that anthropomorphism and similarity [between God and man] on the one hand, and union and indwelling on the other are equally impossible, and to whom in addition the true meaning of this mystery has been revealed, they are exceedingly few."

65 On the philosophical, hermeneutical, and theological problems that this book raises, see Griffel 2009a, 224–74. For the Avicennian influence on the composition of this treatise, see Davidson 1992, 127; Abrahamov 1993, 141–68. For a philologically accurate response to Abrahamov and Davidson's claim of an exclusively empirical approach in al-Ghazālī's appropriation of Avicennian epistemology and cosmology in the *Mishkāt*, see Whittingham 2007, 101–24.

66 Buchman 1998, 16–17.

67 Ibid. "Significantly, al-Ghazālī does not question al-Ḥallāj's and al-Bisṭāmī's mystical experience—in his view, their experience was valid [...]. He takes issue only with their interpretation of this experience. Al-Ghazālī's position is, thus, a partial defense of al-Ḥallāj and al-Bisṭāmī insofar as he concedes that they did have a powerful and authentic experience which easily lends itself—if one is not firmly grounded in intellectual matters—to being misinterpreted as union or indwelling." Treiger 2011, 703.

68 See for instance this passage from the *Maqṣad al-asnā*, translated by Alexander Treiger (2011, 702–703): "When nothing but God's sublimity and beauty (*jalāl Allāh wa-jamāluhū*) indwells the heart, so it is immersed in Him [alone], it becomes as if (*ka-anna*) it is He, not that it is He in reality. There is a difference between saying 'as if it is He' and 'it is He' [...]. This is a stumbling block (*mazallat qadam*). A person who is not firmly grounded in intellectual matters may not distinguish between the two. So he may see the perfection of his own essence (*kamāl dhāti-hī*), which is due to the plain truth that has shone therein (*mā talaʿlaʿa fī-hi min jalīyat al-ḥaqq*) adorning it, and may think that is He and say 'I am the Real.'"

As we shall see in the contexts in which al-Ghazālī recurs to the metaphor of the heart as a mirror in order to explain both the physiology and the spiritual psychology of this perceived unification with the divine, what the mystic perceives during his ecstatic rapture is not God or his essence, but a glimpse of the supernal world, the so-called "realm of the unseen" (*ʿālam-i ghayb*).[69]

Al-Ghazālī's move of partially minimizing the "error" of the mystics by ascribing it to an obfuscation of their rational faculties addresses this issue from an aesthetic and erotic dimension, too. In *The Niche of Lights*, he provides the example of "the furthest Turks," who prostrate themselves whenever they see a human possessing the utmost degree of beauty and recognize him as their lord. "These people," al-Ghazālī comments, "are veiled by the light of beauty, along with the darkness of the senses." Nevertheless, "they are more able to enter into observing light than the worshippers of idols, because they worship beauty that is not limited to a specific individual."[70] The non-specificity of this kind of idolatry causes al-Ghazālī to apply a certain degree of intellectual indulgence with respect to such practices.[71] The partially positive light with which al-Ghazālī addresses the act of worshiping human beauty highlights the critical contradiction through which, in all his metaphysical works, he represents the clash between the veiling nature of the senses and the necessity for the believer of perusing the signs of God in this world. As we shall explore in the next chapters, the solution that al-Ghazālī outlines to overcome such a contradiction belongs to the problem of the relationship between the perception of the external world through the external senses and the epistemological capabilities of the internal senses.

Nevertheless, his timidly critical reappraisal of idolatry, especially if paired with his moderate approach to the permissibility of amatory poetry in the context of the quest of God, opens the door to the legitimization of the gaze upon the human body for spiritual ends—as a perusal of the signs of God's scripture, but also as an instrument for accessing divine love. Al-Ghazālī's balanced

69 See Chapter 7, pp. 368–71.

70 Buchman 1998, 48. David Buchman's translation is based on ʿAfīfī's edition, published in 1964, which the translator reproduces with "minor changes" (see ibid., xxxv). See also Ritter 2003, 469.

71 Zahener's theory on the emergence of some notion of incarnationism in al-Ghazālī's later teachings should be discarded (Zahener 1969). As will become clear both at the end of this chapter and in the subsequent discussions, al-Ghazālī's epistemological approach was based on a faithful (albeit often critical) observance of the Ashʿari theological positions, and any statement involving the possibility of perusing the supernal through the sensible forms belongs to an "introvertive" form of contemplation whose approach is primarily inferential. For a survey of the scholarly and philological debates on the idiosyncratic nature of the *Mishkāt* in al-Ghazālī's thought, see Griffel 2009a, 245–74.

approach to the anthropological aspects of the experience of divine love through meditation on the link between the human figure and God belongs to a rationalizing framework that offers several points of contact with the overarching phenomenology of love in Saʿdi's ghazals. Nevertheless, the idea of the human figure as a primary focus for the experience of divine love is to be found in its most crystalline and influential expression in a treatise composed by Muḥammad al-Ghazālī's brother, Aḥmad Ghazālī. This work, titled *Savāniḥ*, is which is regarded as the first treatise on love composed in Persian.[72]

The *Savāniḥ*, far from being a well-structured scholastic treatise, is a book whose juxtaposition of allusions and poetic remarks provided a solid metaphysical ground for the erotic experience that laid the foundations of the poetic discourse elaborated by the poets of the following centuries. The book is credited with having exerted a profound influence on Saʿdi's entire literary output, and its anthropology of vision is a key turning point for the understanding of his representation of the epistemological value of gazing.[73] It is in this treatise that one can find the full development (albeit without reaching an organically cohesive form) of an idea whose main elements had already been outlined by Muḥammad al-Ghazālī. In the first of the short chapters of the book, Aḥmad Ghazālī describes the appearance of love as an essence whose external point of concentration is, in Aristotelian terms, accidental: "Any distinction in the *qibla* of love is accidental [*ʿāriżī*]: in its true quintessence it is exempt from directions, and as long as it is love, it does not need to be oriented towards a specific direction. But I do not know to what soil the hand of the instant will bring its water."[74] Love is ontologically self-sufficient and per se independent from any specific physical manifestation of beauty. This means that any physical manifestation of love—that is, its *qibla*, the direction of one's

72 For a comprehensive introduction to Aḥmad Ghazālī and his works (and, in particular, the *Savāniḥ*) see Lumbard 2016, 1–50. Various critical editions are available, and I follow Lumbard (ibid., 193, n.2, where the author presents all the other printed editions) in considering that the one published by Hellmut Ritter (along with Purjavādi's integration, see Ahmad Ghazāli 1359/1980) is the most reliable text (Ahmad Ghazāli 1368/1989). Even though the *Savāniḥ* has been translated into the major Western languages (English: Pourjavady 1986; German: Gramlich 1976; Wendt 1978), the most elegant and philologically accurate version is probably the Italian rendition by Carlo Saccone, translated as *Delle Occasioni Amorose* (Saccone 2007), which is based on Purjavādi's and Ritter's editions (Ahmad Ghazali 1359/1980). Between the 12th and the 14th centuries, Aḥmad Ghazālī was at the center of a number of pseudo-biographical accounts describing his passionate indulgence in the practice of contemplating youths for spiritual ends. See Pourjavady 2005; Lumbard 2016, 29–31, 106–107.

73 See Purjavādi 1378/1999.

74 Ahmad Ghazāli 1368/1989, 5.

prayer, and, by extension, its object—is accidental and does not belong to its essence. It is time, however, that brings about love in objects of desire whose manifestation cannot be foreseen. The author further illustrates this concept in one of the last chapters of the book:

> In the first chapter we have said that love, in order to be love, does not require a determined direction [*qibla-yi muʿayyan*]. But now notice that *God is beautiful and He loves beauty* [*Allāh jamīl wa yuḥībb al-jamāl*]. The lover ought to be in love with that beauty, not with his beloved, and this is an immense secret. The lovers must only see, recognize, and desire the locus of the gaze, the sign of beauty, and the locus where the love for him takes place. [...] And it is possible that the lover does not know about all this, but his heart will seek the locus of that gaze and beauty.[75]

The variability of the material object of desire produces a fracture between the ontological self-sufficiency of love and the unpredictability of its accidental manifestation. While in other passages of his book Aḥmad Ghazālī describes this discrepancy as a "secret," Saʿdi makes use of this idea to represent the inner struggle of the believer before the notion of the singularity of the supreme object of love and the multiplicity of the physical reflections of its manifestation:

> This is what idolatry brings: a new *qibla* every hour
> Show us what oneness is, so that we may break the idols!
>
> Drinking wine with the youngsters is all that I desire
> So that the young lads may follow the steps of this old drunkard! ...
>
> On its wooden legs the cypress elegantly sways in the orchard:
> So I want to bring to dance that cypress whose chest is as white as silver!
> *Ṭayyibāt* 286[76]

These lines appear in a ghazal in which Saʿdi disavows the institutional aspect of scholastic Sufism in order to engage in a profound investigation of the relationship between the idolatrous nature of the manifestation of desire and the urge to recognize God as the origin of all attraction. In another ghazal, the expression "spiritual form" (*ṣūrat-i rūḥānī*) can be compared with al-Ghazālī's

75 Ibid., 78.
76 [2.21] Saʿdi YE, 131–32.

statement on the secret of the affinity between man and God, which rests on the level of "inner forms" rather than an outer formal similarity:

> O spiritual form [*ṣūrat-i rūḥānī*], if such is your body [*vujūd*]
> May my existence [*vujūd*] before you fade into inexistence.
>
> If the appearance of all idols were to resemble your form [*ṣūrat*],
> It would have been appropriate for Muslims to elect an idol as their *qibla*.
>
> *Badāyi*ʿ 618[77]

If it were not for the theoretical framework offered by the Ghazālī brothers on the issue of the role of the human body in the exercise of loving God, these lines could be interpreted as mere theopathic utterances very much in line with both the *malāmatī* current of thought and the antinomies that characterize the metaphysics of scholastic Sufism. On the contrary, the point that Saʿdi makes contains no paradox: rather it expresses the bewilderment of the lyric subject before the meaning of the forms and their imperfect connection with their metaphysical source.

Furthermore, what the lines allow the reader to infer is that the mutability of the external form of the physical object of desire is a reflection of an inner form that transiently inhabits the body of the beloved (as an *ʿāriż*, an accident) and attests to an otherwise unimaginable, unthinkable, and overall unattainable divine essence. The emphasis on the spiritual form that inhabits the body of the beloved as a witness to the divine presents the soulless form of the idols as meaningless surfaces of beauty. Therefore, the difference between their form and the physical form of the beloved does not derive from their degree of external beauty, but from the suitability of their comparable beauty to bear witness to God:

> So far is the *qibla*, and the wayfarer won't venture into the desert,
> if he holds the beloved and turns his face towards the *qibla* of meaning [*maʿnī*].
>
> *Ṭāyyibāt* 130[78]

The repetition of a word whose second occurrence bears a different meaning from the first (*jinās-i tāmm*) is one of the most distinctive characteristics

77 [2.22] Saʿdi YE, 277.
78 [2.23] Saʿdi YE, 63.

of Saʿdi's style. In this line, the first instance of the word *qibla* metonymically refers to Mecca, whereas in the second hemistich it signifies what Aḥmad Ghazālī described as "the qibla of love," or the physical object in which the lover fetishizes the presence of the divine. It is my contention that the use that Saʿdi makes of the word *maʿnī* ("meaning," "inner characteristics," "spirit," etc.) is influenced by the Avicennian concept of *maʿānī al-maḥsūsāt*, which are described as "properties [that] are not essentially material, but which nonetheless adhere or attach to sensible forms and can be perceived through them."[79]

In the context of 13th-century Islamicate poetry, the word *maʿnī* could certainly be conflated with the concept of *rūḥ*, "spirit," and it is from the point of view of this conflation that this line ought to be read: if the eyes of the lover are capable of perceiving the divine in the sensible form of the physical beloved, the practice of visual contemplation is comparable with the spiritual quality of the ritual prayer and that of the journey to Mecca. In this line, the mention of the beloved—and the continued references to his physical beauty—is a factor that highlights the projection of *maʿnī* onto what the eyes of the lover detect as the physical manifestation of supernal beauty. This recognition between the physical form of the carnal beloved and the metaphysical *maʿnī* constitutes an epistemological and spiritual awareness of the unseen perceived through the observation of the sensible forms. Only the double articulation of *maʿnī*—as the invisible component of a visible sign—can help us account for the many poems in which Saʿdi clearly hints at the beloved as a tangible presence, especially in the texts in which the separation between the human object of desire and God is unequivocally declared:

> If I could only see again the face of my beloved
> Until doomsday I would be grateful to my Lord! …
>
> Zoroastrians, Christians, and Muslims: in their religion
> They all have a *qibla*, and ours is our beloved, as beautiful as a painting.
>
> *Khavātīm* 661[80]

The idea of the beloved as a painting or a statue had become a recurrent motif from the very beginning of the development of the New Persian literary tradition in Central Asia.[81] Saʿdi's comparisons between the body of the object of

79 Black 1993, 222.
80 [2.24] Saʿdi YE, 295.
81 On the description of idols (*but*) in Early New Persian literature, see Melikian-Chirvani 1974; *EIr*, s.v. "Bot" [W. L. Hanaway]; Pellò 2013.

desire and visual crafts draws upon this very tradition, which the poet reinforces with the idea of the human figure as an artifact that attests to the divine power of representation through the inner "meaning" that vivifies the body as a connection with the divine. By following this idea, in the next chapter we will see how, with Saʿdi, the intellectualized perception of a formal and unspeakable correspondence between the divine and man turns the inferential resource of *iʿtibār* into an active quest. The ghazals will therefore represent the cognitive and aesthetic experience of contemplating the human body as the recognition of a trace limned by the supreme Painter.

CHAPTER 5

The *ʿĀrif* as a Beholder

The Divine Pen Depicting the Khaṭṭ of the Beloved

Behold! A new image of him appears somewhere depicted:
More beautiful day by day the *plan* of His image to our eyes....

From Saʿdi's eyes tears of passion drip upon his hands and scripts:
That's why his eloquence appears so juicy when poetry takes shape.

Ṭayyibāt 53[1]

∵

The concept of the *ʿārif* is one of the key words for understanding the visual dimension of Saʿdi's representation of beauty in the context of the spiritual aesthetics that characterize one of the main aspects of his lyricism. The following lines show the extent to which in Saʿdi's poetry the figure of the *ʿārif* (which is commonly translated as "knower," or "Gnostic") pertains to the realm of visual experiences rather than abstracted metaphysical discourse. On the basis of this emphasis on the visual, I shall explain why, at least as far as Saʿdi's vocabulary is concerned, I prefer to translate *ʿārif* as "the beholder," or the "spiritual beholder":

The ascetics derive their joy from prayers and pious obedience,
The spiritual beholders gain purity by looking at the eyebrows of the beautiful ones.

Badāyiʿ 491[2]

This visual predominance with which Saʿdi presents the figure of the *ʿārif* belongs to the exercise of an active quest for experiences that belong to the eyes and, as we shall see, to the possibility of depicting sublime beauty by means of the imagination. The connection between this figure and Saʿdi's approach

1 [2.25] Saʿdi YE, 28.
2 [2.26] Saʿdi YE, 224.

DOI:10.1163/9789004435902_009

to vision is particularly relevant if we consider how the poet tends to represent himself as a *ʿārif*, at times indirectly and, on some occasions, explicitly: "O Saʿdi, should you bid farewell to your life / in this quest, you shall become a *ʿārif* who is truly alive."[3] Moreover, Saʿdi's contemporaries and fellow-poets, at least after the 1260s, as well as the first copyists of the extant manuscripts of his works, referred to him as the *ʿārif*-poet, or the sheykh-*ʿārif* (*al-shāʿir al-ʿārif*; *al-shaykh al-ʿārif*).[4] In the *bayt* below, while the field of vision is conjured up by the term *muṣavvar* ("depicted"), Saʿdi specifies neither the source from which the visual experience derives nor the surface that displays it:

> Even if paradise were depicted [*muṣavvar*] for the spiritual beholder [*ʿārif*],
> He ought to set his eye on nothing except the beloved.
> *Badāyiʿ* 502[5]

This chapter will try to define the role of Saʿdi's *ʿārif* in connection with the preceding reflection on *ʿibrat* as an inferential process leading one's eyes from material manifestations of beauty to intellectual realization of its divine origin. We will soon discover how the focal point of this connection lies in the correlation between instances of beauty "depicted" (*muṣawwar*) before the eyes of the spiritual beholder and the One who depicts, the "Fashioner" (*al-muṣawwir*).

1 Beholding the Fashioner through the Depicted

In the wake of Muḥammad al-Ghazālī and Aḥmad Ghazālī's intuition on the relationship between the divine and human nature, ʿAyn al-Qużāt Hamadānī—Aḥmad Ghazālī's most renowned pupil—analyzed the concept of the physical manifestation of God as an analogy revolving around a pun based on the possibility of reading the active participle *al-muṣawwir*, "the Fashioner," as the passive form *al-muṣawwar*, "the depicted one":

> Alas, *on the night of the ascension I saw my Lord in the most beautiful form*, this "most beautiful form" [*aḥsan ṣūrat*] is an analogical depiction [*tamas̱s̱ul*], and if it is not an analogy, what is it? *Verily God created Adam and his descendants according to the image of the Merciful*, and this too

3 [2.27] Saʿdi YA, 158–59.
4 See Bashari 2020, 29, n. 1; Ms. Dushanbe 1310s, f. 1a; Ms. London 1328, f. 310a.
5 [2.28] Saʿdi YE, 229–30.

> is a kind of analogy. Alas the names! He is the *muṣavvir* [مصوِر], which means "the Fashioner"; but I also say that he is the *musavvar* [مصوَر], i.e., "the depicted one."[6]

It is worth noticing that, in the same theopathic treatise, ʿAyn al-Qużāt expresses a concept similar to al-Ghazālī's allusion to the fifth reason for loving God as a mysterious imaginal affinity between the divine and humankind. ʿAyn al-Qużāt elaborates on the same concept by presenting three kinds of love: the major (*ʿishq-i kabīr*), the minor (*ʿishq-i ṣaghīr*), and the intermediate form (*ʿishq-i miyāna*), which, in a fashion similar to al-Ghazālī's reticence, he allusively ascribes to the possibility of perceiving signs of the divine presence through the contemplation of human beauty.[7] In another passage, ʿAyn al-Qużāt finally links this mysterious kind of love to the difference between the divine and the mundane reflections of the divine, by explicitly denying that such correspondence implies incarnationism, and implicitly reconnecting his discussion to the problem of the visual representation of the divine presence as a depicting/depicted entity through the image of a human beloved, the *shāhid*.[8]

In the following ghazal, Saʿdi makes no mention of the divine presence, but the link between the mental representation of the beloved and the "spirit" or "meaning" (*maʿnī*) that differentiates it from any other natural form of beauty

---

6 ʿAyn al-Qozāt Hamadāni 1373/1994, 296. This excerpts follows a passage in which ʿAyn al-Qużāt reports a *ḥadīth* attesting to Muḥammad's vision of God in the form of a beardless boy with luxuriant hair. According to Christopher Melchert (2015), this tradition, which circulated in a number of variants (cf. Ritter 2003, 559–60), originated in Basra around the 8th century CE.

7 "O dear, I do not know whether I address the love of the Creator or the love of the creatures. Love appears in three forms, but all love manifests itself in different degrees: the major love, the minor love, and the intermediate love. The minor love is our love for God Almighty, the major love is the love of God for his servants, and alas for the intermediate love, about which I cannot speak, as our understanding is so limited. Nevertheless—God willing—we shall expose a taste of it through allusions." ʿAyn al-Qozāt Hamadāni 1373/1994, 101–102.

8 "O dear, do you know who our 'beautiful youth attesting to God's beauty' [*shāhid*] is? And whose *shāhid* we have happened to be? Listen to the illustration of [the difference between] the major love and the intermediate love, as the 'witness and the witnessed' [*shāhid* wa *mashhūd*, Qur'ān, 83:3] explains what these two witnesses are. In the intermediate love it is still possible to discern the difference between the *shāhid* and the 'witnessed' [*mashhūd*, i.e., God]. But the pinnacle of love implies that no distinction can be made between the two. When the terminal lover turns into love, and when the love of the witness and of the witnessed becomes one, the witness becomes the witnessed, and the witnessed turns into the witness. You may consider this as incarnationism [*ḥulūl*], but it is not! It is the perfection of unity and oneness." Ibid., 115.

reiterates the possibility of a convergence between the flesh depicted in the eyes of the beholder and its metaphysical origins:

> Oh amorous young boy, my lovely moon
> I can dismiss everyone, but I have no choice but you.
>
> As soon as you became depicted [*muṣavvar*] in my devoted heart [*dil-i yaktā-yi man*]
> in my mind there is no more space left for imagination [*taṣavvur*].
>
> *Badāyiʿ* 367[9]

ʿAyn al-Qużāt's emphasis on the visual arena in which the signs of the divine emerge to the gaze of the beholder can be traced back to al-Ghazālī's discussion of the intimate correspondence between man and God. Al-Ghazālī's establishes this affinity—which he describes as the utmost rationale for loving God—through a paradigm that is both intellectual and visual. The idea of recognizing the pen of God by contemplating beautiful human faces on the boundary that separates sexual desire from the cognition of the divine is the aesthetic aspect of a spiritual ideal that al-Ghazāli clearly expresses in the second chapter of *The Niche of Lights*:

> God showed beneficence to Adam. He gave him an abridged form that brings together every sort of thing found in the cosmos [*al-ʿālam*]. It is as if Adam is everything in the cosmos, or an abridged transcription [*nuskha*] of the cosmos. The form of Adam [*ṣūrat ādam*]—I mean *this* form [italics mine]—is written in God's handwriting [*bikhaṭṭ Allāh*]. It is a divine handwriting [*al-khaṭṭ al-ilāhī*] that is not written with letters, since God's handwriting is incomparable with writing and letters […].[10]

Through the image of man as an abridged transcription of the cosmos, al-Ghazāli filters and converts into Islamic scriptural *logos* the Hellenistic idea of the human figure as a microcosm, which establishes a cosmological correspondence between the divine and the human presence as a whole, whose external appearance is a visual translation of a more intimate connection between incomparable natures. The expedient of handwriting as a sign that is simultaneously pictorial (one can see a script without being able to understand its content) and conventionally decipherable creates an interplay between

9 [2.29] Saʿdi YE, 171.
10 Buchman 1998, 31

the visible and invisible aspects of the human figure (the *ṣūrat* proper, and its *maʿnī*) that appears before the eyes of the beholder.

From the perspective of the theo-erotic dimension of Saʿdi's poetry, al-Ghazālī's twofold articulation is capable of bearing a further level of spiritual anthropology of desire: the noun *khaṭṭ* signifies both the concept of handwriting, scripture, or written sign, on the one hand, and on the other, the downy beard of the beloved, which medieval Persian poets described as the most seductive element to the eyes of the lover.[11] The representation of *khaṭṭ* as a physical characteristic that embodies the pinnacle of the lover's attraction for the beloved as well as the societal scorn for an amatory relation that is no longer intergenerational is ubiquitous in Saʿdi's works.[12] In his ghazals, Saʿdi often converts the mundane (and even licentious) imagery associated with *khaṭṭ* into a system of signs inscribed onto the face of the beloved:

> Look at the rhythmical words your *khaṭṭ* writes on your face:
> They resemble traces of black musk covering a scarlet rose.
> *Badāyiʿ* 482[13]

The ghazal to which the line above belongs closes with a ravishingly erotic supplication focusing on the contemplating activity of the lovers, described as "Masters of Gazes." In the following lines, through the deployment of an ingenious pun, Saʿdi bridges the gap between the metaphysics of the traces of the divine emerging from the surface of the human body and the eroticized scripture-like signs of the beloved's downy-beard:

> On the page-like cheek of the beautiful ones they see the downy-beard [*khaṭ*],[14]
> Short is their sight! But the beholder [*ʿārif*] contemplates the pen of God's creation.
>
> Everyone's eyes peruse your face with so much passion, but
> The self-worshippers discern no difference between Truth and lust.
> *Ṭayyibāt* 68[15]

11 See Chapter 3, pp. 185–97.

12 For the socio-psychological implications of Saʿdi's distaste for the development of the beloved's *khaṭṭ* into a full beard, see *Golestān*, 138–39.

13 [2.30] Saʿdi YE, 221.

14 Here *khaṭ*, instead of *khaṭṭ*, for metrical reasons.

15 [2.31] Saʿdi YE, 35.

These two lines offer one of the main interpretive gateways to the complexity of Saʿdi's representation of the relationship between the physical dimension of desire and its metaphysical counterpart. As is typical of Saʿdi's style, the couplets display a magisterial use of simple rhetorical devices whose semantic overlaps contribute to the creation of a manifold representation of the connection between sexual desire and the realm of the unseen. The first striking piece of evidence is provided by the undoubtedly carnal dimension of the object of desire: "the face of the beautiful ones" is a statement that converts the particularity of the lyrical experience into a generalized mundane status. This means that, regardless of the degree of referentiality of the poetic representation of the beloved with respect to historical and biographical events, the horizon of signification on which Saʿdi relies strongly underlines the physical dimension of the objects of desire. The onlookers of such beautiful human bodies are divided into two classes that Saʿdi represents as constantly engaging with a physical act of vision: on one side, the "short-sighted ones," who cannot see anything but the surface of their object of desire; on the other side, the *ʿārif*, a word commonly translated as the "gnostic" or "mystic," but which here takes the sense of "cognizer," "knower," as it displays properties that slightly diverge from the conventions of the Christian mystical tradition.

Given the dominance of the visual in Saʿdi's approach to the spiritual recognition of the divine presence in the sensible world (as I shall soon suggest when analyzing the meaning of *maʿrifa* in the Sufi tradition as well in Avicenna's epistemology), I prefer to translate the noun *ʿārif* as "beholder." By playing with the literal and figurative meanings of *kūtah-naẓar*, as respectively "short-sighted" and "narrow-minded," Saʿdi anchors the multiple semantic levels of his verse to the field of optical vision. Both categories of onlookers—the "narrow-minded ones" and the "cognizers/beholders," or the "recognizers," operate on an optical level with respect to the physical presence of a beautiful face. The difference between them stands in the modality, the "fashion," of their beholding: the former see nothing but the downy beard (*khaṭṭ*), which represented the climax of a young man's desirability, whereas the latter inductively interpret those beautiful traits as signs of the pen of God's creation. Saʿdi, in order to hold together these two modalities—that is, the purely physical vision on the one hand, and the cogitative contemplation of God's signs, on the other—applies the rhetorical device known as *īhām-i tanāsub* (amphibological equivalence) through the twofold meaning of *khaṭṭ*, which means "scripture," or "writing," and is used here in its secondary meaning of downy beard, while it creates a balanced congruence (*tanāsub*) with the semantic field of writing that is expressed by the words "page" (*varaq*) and "pen" (*qalam*). The second couplet elaborates on the meaning of the previous lines, and it furthers the representation of the inferior quality of the gaze of the short-sighted ones, who are now referred to as the "self-worshippers" [*khʷad-parastān*]. In this compound noun, the meaning of "self" is undoubtedly reflexive, but it also extends to the conception of the "self" as the *nafs*, or the carnal soul, which in the Sufi literature is a conflation of the vegetative and animal qualities of the Avicennian categorization of the human soul.

Consistent with the role of sexual desire in Saʿdi's works as an active component of the lyric subject, these lines do not deny lust as such. On the contrary, Saʿdi emphasizes the act of "recognition" of the difference between lustful desires and "truth" that motivates the *ʿārifān*, the "knowers, the "cognizers"—by beholding through and beyond the flesh—as opposed to the short-sighted "self-worshippers." Moreover, the verb *shinākhtan*, "to know, to recognize," echoes the etymology of the noun *ʿārif*, from the Arabic *ʿarafa*, "to know," and resets the allegedly mystical meaning along the semantic lines of intellectual cognition through the perusal of the visible world. The pun around which Saʿdi's entire meditation on sensuality and spirituality revolves confirms the idea that the lyrical mention of a body part—*khaṭṭ*, the downy beard, in this case—pushes the boundaries of signification both in the direction of obscene reification of the object of desire and towards the sublimating experience of reading the body beyond its inherent flesh.

In either case, the twofold contemplation of the *khaṭṭ* that Saʿdi portrays belongs to an emotional and intellectual reaction that pertains to the realm of an active engagement with the field of vision and an interaction with the sensible world. This activity, far from being a passive accident of the beholder's rapport with the object of contemplation, draws a brand new horizon of possibilities for the quest for the divine through the appreciation of beauty. In this new context, *ʿibrat* is no longer a key tool to the quest, but merely a strategy to convert the accidental emergence of visual pleasure into a constant meditative practice.

2 Spiritual Cognition and Meditation as an Active Theo-Erotic Quest

While *ʿibrat* is an inferential modality that protects the believer from the pitfalls of both lust and incarnationism when deciphering the text of the aphrodisiac body, the figure of the *ʿārif*/cognizer in the lines about the "short-sighted ones" contemplating the page-like countenance of the beloved reframes the act of beholding beauty as an active theo-erotic cognitive undertaking. We may compare *ʿibrat*, or the spiritual inferences hitherto discussed, to metaphors, which, as rhetorical devices, enrich a literary text through figurative parallels that temporarily project meanings beyond their literal senses. *Maʿrifa*, on the contrary, is a symbolic, dynamic, and positive habit, that certainly relies on the inferential possibilities of meaning, but which also orients the lyric subject towards a radically different experience of the world: by dismissing the material existence of the world, *maʿrifa* simultaneously exalts its mundane horizons as transient heralds of the Truth. As one may infer from Saʿdi's lines, *maʿrifat*—along with the figure of the *ʿārif*—is a key concept that allows us to access the visual dimension of Saʿdi's theo-erotic lyricism from the perspective of the debate on loving God through the forms of the perceptible world.

In principle, the prominence of the visual dimension contradicts the common definitions of *maʿrifa*, which, for instance, Annemarie Schimmel describes as "a knowledge that is not reached by discursive reason, but is a higher understanding of the divine mystery."[16] The contrast that medieval Sufi masters would perceive as a difference between *maʿrifa* and *ʿilm* ("knowledge" or "acquired science") determines that the realm of empirical acquisition of knowledge substantially diverges from the inspired form of cognition that characterizes *maʿrifa*.[17] This very distinction between acquired knowledge and

16 Schimmel 1975, 130. See, for instance, Qushayrī's definition (translated by Rapoport, 2018, 259, which I slightly modified): "According to those people [sc. Sufis], *maʿrifa* is an attribute of whomever has knowledge of God's names and attributes, and who then entrusts God in his activities [*muʿāmalāt*, which can also be rendered as "mundane religious practices and obligations"] ridding [all that is] bad and harmful from his moral traits. He then remains at the door while his heart abides devoted [to God]. [This person] then gains from God the beauty of drawing near to Him. He entrusts all of his states to God Most High and is cut off from the evil temptations [*hawājis*] of his carnal soul [*nafs*], all the while not bending his heart toward [any] thought that would call him to something other than Him. When he becomes a stranger among his kind, free of the harms of his carnal soul, rid of living with and heeding others, and his intimate conversation with God remains in his innermost self [lit. "secret," *sirr*], and in every moment his return to Him is realized, and through the power of the Truth he begins to speak of making known His secrets concerning the dispensation of His decrees, he is [then] called an *ʿārif*, and his state is called *maʿrifa*." For the original text, see Qushayri 1988, 311–12. For a published English translation, cf. Qushayri 2007, 320. For further considerations on Hujvīrī's criticism of *ʿilm*, see Abrahamov 2015, 37–38.

17 On the difference between *maʿrifa* and *ʿilm*, see Shah-Kazemi 2002, 9, and Jabre 1959. See also Frank 1994, 105–106. Cf. Hujvīrī's remarks on this distinction: "Theologians have made no distinction between *ʿilm* and *maʿrifat*, and consider them as the same, except when they say: 'God Almighty may be called *ʿālim* ["knower"] but not *ʿārif* ["cognizer"] as the latter [term, i.e., *ʿārif*] lacks [scriptural] support [*tawqīf*].' But the Sufis [*mashāyikh-i īn ṭarīqat*] call *maʿrifa* any science [*ʿilm*] that is associated with religious practices [*muʿāmalat*] and [inspired] state[s] [*ḥāl*], and which the knower [*ʿālim*] mentions [*ʿibārat kunad*] as one of his states. [Hence], they call *ʿārif* the knower of that science. They call *ʿilm*—and the knower of it, *ʿālim*, any knowledge that is bereft of [spiritual] meaning [*maʿnī*] and devoid

inspired cognition represents the primary paradox of *maʿrifa*, which is "the highest knowledge to which the individual has access," but at the same time its ultimate content "radically transcends the individual, [so] that it overlaps with ignorance."[18]

The paradox of *maʿrifa* as blinding ignorance stemming from the highest degree of awareness that nothing exists but God implies that the limited horizon of mundane knowledge is not abolished, but relativized in the face of the Absolute.[19] It is therefore this epistemological relativization determined by *maʿrifa* that informs the aesthetic framework in which Saʿdi exposes the figure of the *ʿārif* as a legitimate beholder of the beloved's body as a function of the divine presence. While I retain the noun "cognizer" to render the general meaning of *ʿārif* as the practitioner of the form of deep spiritual awareness hitherto discussed, I deem the agent noun "beholder" more appropriate for conveying the metaphysical visual intensity that Saʿdi projects onto *maʿrifa* as a connection between the eyes of the onlooker and a deep form of understanding that takes shape in the heart/soul of the believer.[20]

In Saʿdi's work, in fact, the relativistic cognitive aspect of *maʿrifat* vis-à-vis the world shifts the focus of the issue of the visual contact with the beloved from a spiritual and ethical discourse to a problem whose nature is predominantly aesthetic and epistemological:

> If you embrace spiritual cognition [*ahl-i maʿrifatī*], beautiful is anything you see
> As anything that the Beloved creates is as charming as the beloved.

---

of religious practices. Therefore, they call *ʿālim* anyone who only knows the verbal expressions and memorizes them without their spiritual meaning [*maʿnī*], whereas they call *ʿārif* anyone who knows the meaning and the reality of that thing. This is why, whenever these people [sc. the Sufis] intend to disparage one of their peers, they call him a learned person [*dānishmand*]. To the commoners this seems questionable, but the Sufis do not blame him for the acquisition of knowledge, as they blame him for having neglected the religious practice, as *the knower depends on himself, whereas the cognizer depends on his Lord*." Hojviri 1387/2008, 558. Cf. Nicholson's rendition (1976 [1911], 382–83), which misunderstands key syntactical features of this passage, partially because of the unreliability of the edition that he consulted.

18 Shah-Kazemi 2002, 1.

19 Ibid., 9.

20 The English verb "to behold" derives from Old English *bihaldan*, and originally conveys the sense of "give regard to, hold in view," but also "keep hold of; belong to." The Oxford English Dictionary thus defines the modern meaning of the transitive verb: "To hold or keep in view, to watch; to regard or contemplate with the eyes; to look upon, look at (implying active voluntary exercise of the faculty of vision)."

Contemplate the trees! Will you ever find a leaf
Upon which the secret of the divine creation is not inscribed?[21]

In Sa'di's collections of poems, as in the lines above, almost all the occurrences of the concept of *ma'rifa* speak to a level of acquisition of insightful knowledge through the visual observation of the world.[22] The following ghazal is an excellent example of how the aesthetic dimension of *ma'rifa* diverges from the theological and doctrinal implications of the term:

No light shines in the onlooker's lamp of destiny
If his gaze does not set upon an object of glances [*manẓūrī*].

What pleasure will the pretentious enjoy in paradise
If no inclination he has today for these paradisiacal beauties?

What delight from the ritual remembrance [*ẕikr*] for the one
Who experiences no secret passion for a praised one [*maẕkūrī*]?

The beholders [*'ārifān*] do not regard as master of gazes the one
Whose mind does not contemplate an object of glances [*manẓūrī*]....

Ever since Sa'di recognized the honey
No longer does he fear the sting of the bee.
Badāyi' 596[23]

In the context of Sa'di's praise of the sensorial experience of the world, one may read the threat of the hornet's sting as a metaphor for the lustful snare that the seductive appearance of the world is capable of placing on the path of the God-seeker. But the act of "recognizing" the taste of honey (*'asal bishnākht*) highlights the relevance of the sensorial experience to the understanding of what the physical presence conveys in terms of access to a superior degree of awareness of the divine presence. From this perspective, the ghazal grounds

21 [2.32] Sa'di KhE, 748.

22 Cf. Avicenna's emphasis on the aesthetic penchant of the *'ārif* as described in the ninth chapter of the *Ishārāt*: "Similarly, at times the knower [*'ārif*] has an inclination for ornamentation, loves the best of all things, and detests what is in complete and what is worthless. He seeks beauty in all things, since beauty is a virtue of the good favor of the First Providence and is close to the kind of thing that he wants to devote himself to." Rapoport 2018, 160–61.

23 [2.33] Sa'di YE, 268.

the entirety of the spiritual experience of beholding in the necessity for the lyric subject of letting the phenomenal world engulf its senses so that superior forms of meaning may emerge from the contemplation of physical phenomena.

The very credibility of the spiritual wayfarer is at stake, as no magisterial understanding of the divine can take place in the heart of the believer without having mastered the process of a profound aesthetic appreciation for the forms of the world. The aesthetic commitment that Saʿdi's proposes in the entirety of his works produces a constant overlap between the experience of the visible world and the intellectual perception of the invisible. The sensible and the suprasensible blend into each other in such a way that the more the lyric subject plunges into the beautiful mud of earthly experiences, the more its heart resounds with supernal meanings. In the following lines, for instance, the reference to both the lyric Thou and God emphasizes the mundane nature of the former, even in a symbolic context in which the beloved is read as a sign of the divine presence:

> May God set His eyes upon you, O marvelous bodily form:
> My beloved, the candle of the gathering, the king of all peoples.
>
> Gorgeous when you leave, then you come back:
> I never saw a cypress swaying with such elegance.
>
> All attributes [*har ṣifatī*] attest to a deep cognition [*maʿrifatī*]:
> On your face the proofs of the divine power shine! …
>
> Your name was being mentioned, and the beholders [*ʿārifān*] overheard:
> Both the listeners and the singers started to dance.
>
> *Ṭayyibāt* 279[24]

In Persian lyric poetry, the noun *ṣifat* refers to the physical attributes of the object of desire: his body parts, the traits of his countenance, or any characteristic that can be perceived by the senses and recounted through the abstract descriptions of the poet. But *ṣifat* can also refer to the "attributes" of God. From a theological perspective, the acquaintance with such attributes constitutes one of the first steps of the believer on the path of *maʿrifat*. The non-theological layer of signification is therefore stressed by the pun in which *ṣifat*

24 [2.34] Saʿdi YE, 128.

as theological "proof" of the divine existence is juxtaposed with the aesthetic perception of the beloved's face as a sign attesting to His power.[25]

Some of the sources of the aesthetic dimension of *maʿrifa* in Saʿdi's lyricism are to be found in al-Ghazālī's empirical approach to this form of spiritual *awareness* proceeding from an active quest that commences through the perusal of the visible world. If the concept of *maʿrifa* in al-Ghazālī is tackled from the perspective of the *Kīmiyā*'s underlying psychology, this term supports an aesthetic dimension that profoundly informs the visual cognition with which Saʿdi's lyric subject is concerned. In this context, *maʿrifa* refers to the individual's all-encompassing awareness that nothing of what he perceives with his internal and external senses exists, except for God. In the introduction to the *Kīmiyā*, in one of the most poetic passages of the entire book, al-Ghazālī thus expresses this concept:

> [...] no heart may remain unaware of the marvels of the divine creation! [...] Hence the heart will necessarily recognize that all the existing things are the signs of His power, everything is the lights of His greatness, everything is the wonders and the marvels of His wisdom, everything is the reflection of His supreme beauty, everything is from Him, everything belongs to Him, everything, actually, *is* Him, as nothing verily exists but He, and the existence of everything is the reflection of the light of His Existence.[26]

Al-Ghazālī's relativistic approach turns the absolutely transcendental projection of the Sufi tradition prior to him (see, *supra*, Qushayrī's and Hujvīrī's definition of *maʿrifa*) into an invitation to the appreciation of the visible world and the human body as a stage for the contemplation of God's attributes and actions. The origin of this idea is based on the Avicennian (but originally Hellenistic, probably reaffirmed through the doctrines of the Brethren of Purity) representation of the human body as a microcosmic version of the macrocosm, which informs al-Ghazālī's contextualization of his concept of *maʿrifa* within the framework of the Islamic reinterpretation of the Delphic maxim "know thyself."[27] The following passage perfectly exemplifies the conflation between

25 For a general survey of the problem of the attributes of God in Islamic theology, see *EI*³, s. v. "Attributes of God" [C. Gilliot]. As for al-Ghazālī's peculiar recontextualization of the topic, see Abrahamov 1995.

26 *Kīmiyā*, 1: 4.

27 See Altmann 1969. On the same topic, see Abrahamov 2003, 57–58. For a brief survey of al-Ghazālī's reiteration of the same concept in works other than the *Kīmiyā*, see Goodman 2005, 171–72. See also Griffel 2009a, 269–70.

the multiple origins of the Delphic maxim and the theological aesthetics of al-Ghazālī's teleology:

> Know that in the books of the Prophets from the past, this maxim is well attested: *know thyself so that you may know your Lord.* And it is known in the [collections of] traditions and in the scriptures that *he who knows himself knows his Lord.* These statements prove that the soul/self of man resembles a mirror, and whoever looks into it sees God. However, most people look into themselves and do not recognize God. Therefore, its knowledge [of the self] is necessary, as it is the mirror of *maʿrifa*. And this [knowledge] pertains to two aspects: one is mysterious [*ghāmiz*], and, as most intellects cannot sustain it, it is not possible to illustrate it to the commoners, and it is not recommendable to discuss it. But this is the aspect that everyone can grasp: man cognizes the existence of God's essence through his own essence, and from his attributes he cognizes God's attributes [*ṣifāt-i ḥaqq*], and through the control over his own kingdom—which is his body and organs—he cognizes the control of God over the entire world.[28]

Al-Ghazālī's suggestion of grasping knowledge of the divine from an epistemological path that relies on the wisdom of "the prophets of the past" (probably a euphemism to disguise its philosophical foundations as ancient sacred wisdom) and the "collections of traditions" (as well as scriptural evidence) generates a conflation between Greek philosophy and Islamic theology whose result is an originally anthropocentric conception of *maʿrifa*. Faithful to the anatomic investigative context in which the Delphic intimation appears in the early Islamicate philosophical tradition (such as in al-Kindī and in the Epistles of the Brethren of Purity), al-Ghazālī's illustration of the necessity of knowing oneself culminates with an extraordinary exploration of the physiological perfection of the human body and its functions.[29] Eventually he states that "[one] shall witness the existence of God Almighty's essence in the appearance of one's essence, and may attest to the perfection of his science in the wonders, the wisdoms, and the bounties [*manāfiʿ*] surrounding him, and in the concurrence of all that is needed by means of necessity, requirement, or beauty and ornament [...], he will see the grace and mercy of God Almighty." "Therefore,"

---

28 *Kīmiyā*, 1: 47.

29 Ibid., 48–49. On the anatomic origin of the Islamicate philosophical meditation on this maxim, see Goodman and McGregor 2009, 289.

al-Ghazālī concludes, "by doing so, knowledge of the self [*maʿrifat-i nafs*] shall turn into the mirror of and the key to knowledge of God [*maʿrifat-i ḥaqq*]."[30]

The focus on the visible world (epitomized by the perfection of the human anatomy) provides al-Ghazālī with an approach to *maʿrifa* that develops compelling aesthetic implications: in spite of the relative inexistence of the world, the primary access to the realization of God as the only necessary existent requires the contemplation of the splendor exuding from the relative existence of the world. By doing so, al-Ghazālī opens his chapter on the denigrating nature of the world with the celebration of its epistemic beauty:

> Know that the world is one of the stations on the religious path, a crossroad for the wayfarer to reach the divine presence, or a market adorned in the middle of the desert for the travelers to collect provisions for their journey. [...] The purpose of this world is [precisely] the provisions for the supernal realm [*ākhirat*]. Even though man, in his original ontogenesis, is a simple and unfinished creation, he is worthy of acquiring perfection by turning the form of the supernal realm [*ṣūrat-i malakūt*] into the picture of his own heart—so that he may deserve the [access to] the divine presence—and eventually find his path towards the contemplation of divine beauty. This is man's ultimate bliss, his paradise, and it for this that he was created. He shan't enjoy such contemplation unless he opens his eyes to capture that Beauty by means of acquiring spiritual cognition [*maʿrifat*]. And the key to the spiritual cognition of divine beauty [*maʿrifat-i jamāl-i ilāhiyyat*] is the cognition upon the wonders of the divine creation [*maʿrifat-i ʿajāyib-i ṣunʿ-i ilāhī*]. Man's [external and internal] senses are the key to access the divine creation, and the [use of the] senses would be impossible without this composite body [*kalbud-i murakkab*] made from water and clay. It is for this reason that [man] fell into this world of water and clay, in order to gather his provisions and to grasp the cognition of God Almighty through the key of the cognition of his own self and the cognition of all the [mundane] horizons as they are perceived by the senses.[31]

Al-Ghazāli's ecstatic celebration of the world as a resplendent reflection of the divine beauty finds an equally compelling echo in one of Saʿdi's most ravishing poetic lauds of God, in which the divine is represented as the only pivot of the relationship between the immanence and the transcendence of being:

30 *Kimiyā*, 1: 50.
31 Ibid., 1: 70–71.

1 Joy fills me in this world, because joyful is the world for Him.
In love I am with the whole world, because the whole world is from Him.

2 O friend, enjoy the Jesus-like breath of the breeze blowing in the morning:
It may bring the dead heart back to life, as that breath comes from Him.

3 No right the stars may claim upon what the angels truly covet:
The secret of humankind's passionate heart is bestowed by Him.

4 The poison I'll swallow is nectar, if that sacred body [*shāhid*] pours it:
Devotedly I shall bear the pain, as its cure too comes from Him.

5 May it never stop bleeding this laceration of mine, how joyful!
Blessed is the wound when a constant balm is provided by Him.

6 What difference between sorrow and joy to the beholder of the Truth [*ʿārif*]?
Pour wine O cup-bearer! Cheers to this sorrow that joyfully we suffer from Him!

7 Beggars and kings equal each other to our eyes:
Before this threshold everyone's back is bowed for Him.

8 O Saʿdi, the flood of inexistence may uproot the house of your heart:
Firmly hold your heart, as the foundations of eternity are solid, thanks to Him!

Badāyiʿ 558[32]

Both in al-Ghazālī's passage and in the ghazal above, the believer's interiorization of the notion of an aesthetic unity of God constitutes the main axis of the cognitive aspect of *maʿrifa*. This attestation to a negative assertion of God's existence, which derives from the denial of the veridical existence of anything else, is balanced by the positive value of the recognition of the world as the place of manifestation for divine majesty. The paradoxical epistemology of this attestation, as al-Ghazālī explains in the paragraph immediately preceding the

32 [2.35] Saʿdi YE, 251.

passage on "nothing verily exists, but Him," stems from the acknowledgment that God cannot be known but through the contemplation of the divine creation: "the profit of all intellects from the gaze (*naẓar*) upon the marvels of His creation is the necessary *maʿrifat*."[33] In this sentence the author mentions the "intellects" (*ʿaqlhā*) as the agent of the contemplation of God's creation—a contemplation that generates the "necessary *maʿrifat*." This means that the process that al-Ghazālī describes is both intellectual and sensorial, as he ascribes the faculty of casting one's gaze upon the perceptible world to the intellect as well as to the internal and external senses.[34] This idea of the contemplation of the world as an intellectual function can be better understood if we consider that al-Ghazālī specifies on multiple occasions that *maʿrifat* has to be regarded as the spiritual emergence of what he calls *tafakkur*, or *fikrat*—a syllogistic cogitative act that he declares a perfect synonym of *iʿtibār*, "inference" and *taʾammul*, "contemplation."[35]

Tafakkur is often translated as "cogitation," or "meditation," but in the chapters that al-Ghazālī dedicates to this practice, it acquires the sense of "contemplation," as it refers to the cogitative observation of the visible world. This active form of cogitation is not new to the lexicon of the Sufi tradition, which draws upon the Quranic use of the fifth verbal form of the root *fkr* (*yatafakkaru*, "to ponder," "to consider") in the contexts of the intimations urging humankind to ponder upon creation as a sign attesting to divine power.[36] Sufi manuals composed in the 10th and 11th centuries present *tafakkur* as a meditation on the signs of God that is subordinate to act of "remembrance" (*taẕakkur*), and which delivers no particular spiritual yield besides a rational—and, as such, quintessentially limited—attestation to the power of God.[37]

---

33 *Kimiyā*, 1: 3.

34 Al-Ghazālī's use of the word *ʿaql* in this context betrays the peripatetic origins of his spiritual epistemology. In the following chapters we will explore how his "spiritual cardiology" is derivative of Avicennian noetics.

35 *Kimiyā*, 2: 598. On al-Ghazālī's usage of *iʿtibār*, *taʾammul*, and *tafakkur* as synonyms, see Jabre 1970, 225.

36 This verbal form is used seventeen times in the Qurʾān. See the verses in which the intimation involves the visual perusal of the world: 2: 219: "[…] So God makes clear His signs to you; haply you will reflect"; 3: 191: "[…] and reflect upon the creation of the heavens and the earth […]; 13: 3: "It is He who stretched out the earth and set therein firm mountains and rivers, and of every fruit He placed there two kinds, covering the day with the night. Surely in that are signs for a people who reflect"; 45:13: "And He has subjected to you what is in the heavens and what is in the earth, all together, from Him. Surely, in that are signs for a people who reflect."

37 "I heard Shaykh Abū ʿAbd al-Raḥmān al-Sulamī ask the master Abu ʿAlī al-Daqqāq: 'What is more perfect: remembrance or [rational] contemplation (*fikr*)?' The master, in turn, asked him: 'And what do you think about this?' Shaykh Abū ʿAbd al-Raḥmān al-Sulamī

Al-Ghazālī, on the contrary, combines the spiritual aspect of the Sufi approach to the scriptural significance of *tafakkur* as a pondering act with Avicenna's epistemic conception of *tafakkur* (and *fikra*) as a syllogistic form of thinking. In both the *Iḥyāʾ* and in the *Kimiyā*, in the chapters dedicated to *tafakkur* (which Abrahamov straightforwardly translates as "syllogistic thinking"), al-Ghazālī equates this practice with syllogistic reasoning by describing a procedure through which two pieces of knowledge (premises) lead to a third piece of knowledge (conclusion).[38] The epistemological reappraisal of *tafakkur* through the filter of the Avicennian syllogistic model of knowledge acquisition enables a rational processing of the sense of awe (*ʿajab, taʿajjub*) that derives from the observation of the world's beauty. Both in the *Iḥyāʾ* and, even more so in the *Kīmiyā*, the pages that guide the reader toward the process of *tafakkur* are undoubtedly some of the most poetic moments of al-Ghazālī's entire corpus.

Al-Ghazālī, by declaring the unfathomable nature of the divine, argues that even saints and prophets have no access to the direct vision of God. Just as the naked eye cannot endure staring at the sun, the believer must peruse the wonders of the world as if they were the reflection of the divine sunshine upon earth: "Therefore the grandness of God must be sought in the wonders of His creation [*ʿajāyib-i ṣunʿ-i vay*]. […] Know that anything that exists is His creation, and everything is marvelous and wondrous, and there is no particle among the particles of the sky and of earth that does not silently laud and glorify its Creator."[39] In the subsequent pages al-Ghazālī methodically describes all the *visibilia* that he mentions in this paragraph: a map for the human gaze to aesthetically recognize the physical reverberation of the otherwise unknowable divine presence. By dividing the divine creation between what is accessible to the senses and the things that are concealed (such as the divine throne, angels, demons, fairies, etc.), al-Ghazālī, through one of his empirical thrusts,

said: 'In my view, remembrance is more perfect than contemplation, for God—praise be to Him—attributed remembrance to Himself, while He never did the same for contemplation. And anything that is attributed to God—praise be to Him—is always better than that which is attributed to His creatures.'" Qushayrī 2007, 234 (cfr. original text, Qushayrī 1988, 298). See also Abrahamov's remarks: "An examination of the Sufi stations (*maqāmāt*) appearing in al-Kharrāz (d. 899 or 900/286–287), as-Sarrāj (d. 988/377), al-Kalābādhī (d. 990/380 or 994/384), al-Makkī (d. 996/386) and al-Qushayrī (d. 1074/466) reveals that the concept of *tafakkur*, whether meaning 'thinking' or 'contemplating in a syllogistic manner,' never occurs." Abrahamov 2015, 36–37.

38 *Kimiyā*, 2: 504. For references to *tafakkur* and *fikra* in other works by al-Ghazāli—especially in the *Iḥyāʾ*'s 39th book—see Abrahamov 2015, 43–46; 1993, 161–62.

39 *Kimiyā*, 2: 511

declares that only what is known to us and attainable by our eyes should be the appropriate object of *tafakkur*:

> Therefore, we shall limit ourselves to [observing] what is visible [*dīdanī*]: the sky, the sun, the moon and the stars, the earth and anything that it contains, such as the mountains and the seas, the deserts and the cities, all the jewels and the minerals that are found on the mountains, and all the species of plants and animals on earth. And, above all, [the contemplation of] humankind, as man is the most wondrous of all things.[40]

The empirical afflatus of al-Ghazālī's passages on *tafakkur* mirrors the passages from other works of his in which aesthetics and scriptural hermeneutics collaborate in the emergence of a teleological theory of the relationship between divine creation and the world: "by observing phenomena in creation, whether within the human body or in the cosmos as a whole, one can discern an order in which parts cooperate to form a whole that achieves specific, recognizable aims."[41]

Al-Ghazālī's exploration of *tafakkur* as an empirical epistemological tool to approach the divine reintroduced a strong teleological approach to the transcendental path that Ash'arism had taken with respect to its speculations upon the unknowable and unpredictable relationship between God and creation.[42] In these passages, incredulity, speechlessness, and awe before the contemplation of the world and the perfection of the human body stem from aesthetic pleasure in the cogitative rationalization that all existing things are a reflection of the divine beauty. The aesthetic élan of al-Ghazālī's exemplification of *tafakkur* reaches its climax when, at the end of the chapter in the *Kīmiyā*, he urges his reader to marvel at the beauty of creation as much as one marvels

40 Ibid.

41 El Shamsy 2016, 93. One such work is *al-Ḥikma fī makhlūqāt Allāh* (*The Wisdom in God's Creations*), which El Shamsy reads against both the passages on *tafakkur* from the *Iḥyā'* and the Galenic origins of the empirical approach that al-Ghazālī outlines therein: "Although al-Ghazālī admits that the objects of contemplation in creation are for all intents and purposes countless, he proceeds to outline, on about fifteen pages in the printed edition, the wisdom and benefits inherent in the sun, moon, plants, and animals, as well as the organs of the human body. *Al-Ḥikma fī makhlūqāt Allāh* is structured by the various areas of creation that al-Ghazālī addresses: the heavens, the sun, and the planets (twelve pages in the printed edition); the sea (three pages); water (two pages); air (four pages); fire (four pages); birds (eight pages); beasts of burden (one page); insects and spiders (eight pages); fish (four pages); and the human body (twenty-six pages)." Ibid., 96–97.

42 Ibid., 109–10.

when contemplating the elegance of a princely palace and its luxurious stuccos, statues, and paintings.[43]

Echoes of al-Ghazālī's conflation of teleological and hierarchical aesthetics involving the "architectural" order of the visible world are attested to in many of Saʿdi's poems. The following lines provide one such example. They read as the aesthetic reverse of the Quranic intimation with which al-Ghazāli opens *al-Ḥikma* ("Say: 'Behold what is in the heavens and in the earth,'" 10: 101).[44] In Saʿdi's *qasida*, al-Ghazālī's empirical response to the divine command turns into a lyrical observation of nature during springtime:

> At dawn, when one can discern no difference between day and night,
> How beautiful appear the edges of the valleys and the vision of springtime.
>
> Tell the Sufi to leave the monastery and settle amidst the garden of roses
> As this is not the time for one to sit idle at home!
>
> The time has come for the nightingales to sing out of passion
> You are not less eloquent than an intoxicated nightingale: sing, o sober!
>
> The entire creation is an intimation from the Lord of the heart:
> Heartless is he who does not attest to the Lord!
>
> Behold all these marvelous paintings decorating the walls of the palace of existence:
> Nothing but frescoes on a wall are those who do not ponder [*fikrat*] upon these wonders.
>
> The mountains, the oceans, the rivers: they all laud the Lord!
> Not all fine listeners can verily understand the chants of these secrets!
>
> Are you aware of what the morning birds are saying to you?
> 'So much have you slept, raise your head from the sleep of ignorance!'

---

43 The aesthetic afflatus of al-Ghazālī's teleology is also reflected in his comparison between the divine creation and the arts: "The more you know about the virtuosic marvels of poetry, narrations, and visual arts, the more your appreciation for the greatness of the poet, the writer, and the artist will conquer your heart. Similarly, the wonders of divine creation provide you with the key to access the science of [recognizing] the greatness of the Creator." *Kimiyā*, 1: 44.

44 El Shamsy 2016, 106.

Anyone who does not see today **the signs of His power** [*aṯar-i qudrat-i ū*]
Certainly shall not enjoy the **Vision** of Him in tomorrow's hereafter! …

The time has come for the rose to appear from **the alcove of the unseen**:
It may appear now, as all the trees are scattering their homages.[45]

Considering that one of the final lines of this long *qasida* mentions the possibility for the virtuous men righteous to grasp the "prize of Bliss" (*gūy-i saʿādat*), one cannot but contextualize the entire text within the framework of the aesthetic teleology of salvation that dominates the passages on *tafakkur* in the *Kīmiyā-yi saʿādat*.[46] In particular, as I shall explore further soon, the idea of the manifestation of sensory beauty as the reflection of the divine power exuding from the realm of the unseen constitutes the cosmological background of al-Ghazālī's theorization of *tafakkur* as the intellectual recognition of a correspondence between the visible and invisible. The penultimate line, in particular (Anyone who does not see today **the signs of His power** / Certainly shall not enjoy the **Vision** of Him in tomorrow's hereafter!), translates al-Ghazālī's technical term *mushāhada* with the Persian verbal noun *dīdār*. By doing so, Saʿdi alludes to al-Ghazālī's theory of the vision of God in the hereafter, which can only be attained through the acquisition of *maʿrifa* in this world, by recognizing the divine signs of beauty. This teleological discourse can also be found in the preamble of the *Būstān*, in which Saʿdi applies a subtle aesthetic twist to the praise of God, which he fashions in a way that should be compared with al-Ghazāli's combination of scriptural portrayals of human ontogenesis and the Galenian and Avicennian teleology attested to in the passages on *tafakkur*, as well as in the *Maqṣad al-asnā*, and *al-Ḥikma*:

Pre-eternal, Good-doer and Celebrator of beauty,
Limner with the brush of Destiny within the womb.[47]

From east to west, the moon and the sun
He set in motion, and cast the world upon the waters:

And when the earth by shaking-fever was harassed,
He hammered mountain-pins around its edges and ridges.

45 [2.36] Saʿdi KhE, 662–63. See Ms. Yale 1432, ff. 175a–176a.
46 [2.37] Saʿdi KhE, 664.
47 "[…] and We establish in the wombs what We will" (Qurʾān, 22: 5).

He gives angelic form to the sperm-drop:
Who else has ever painted upon liquids?

He casts ruby and turquoise into the loins of the stone
And ruby roses on turquoise-colored stems.

He scatters drops from the clouds to the abyss
And thrusts sperm-drops from the loins into the womb:

He scatters gleaming pearls from the drops,
And from the sperm, human forms like cypress trees.[48]

Saʿdi elevates al-Ghazālī's rational teleology to an aesthetic discourse that celebrates human beauty as the focal pivot of the lyrical exaltation of creation. The scriptural foundation of this process can be found in the 23rd Sura of the Qurʾān, whose lexical features and rhythmical imagery fully resonate with the marvel that Saʿdi expresses when contemplating the fetal development originating humankind's angelic beauty: "We created man of an extraction of clay, then We set him, a drop, in a receptacle secure, then We created of the drop a clot, then We created of the clot a tissue, then We created of the tissue bones, then We garmented the bones in flesh; thereafter We produced him as another creature. So blessed be God, the fairest of creators!"[49]

The empirical aesthetics of Saʿdi's lyrical teleology pervades most of the odes that the poet dedicated to those eminent political figures he deemed capable of defending Islamic values during the formative phase of Ilkhanid sovereignty, following the conquest of Baghdad. As pointed out in the first chapter, during the upheavals affecting the Salghurid dynasty after the deaths of the atabeg Abū Bakr and prince Saʿd II, the Juvaynī family became primary recipients of Saʿdi's theo-erotic praises. The following ode, dedicated to the renowned historian ʿAlāʾ al-Dīn ʿAṭā Malik, governor of Baghdad and Iraq, and elder brother of Shams al-Dīn, showcases a fine example of Saʿdi's teleological discourse:

If anyone wants to contemplate lofty paradise
They should come forth and peruse the world in springtime.

48 [2.38] (*Būstān*, 34). See Wickens' translation (4–5), which I have adopted as a subtext for my own freer rendition.

49 23:12–14.

It's no wonder if He who fashioned human forms from extracted clay
From clay too extracted roses amidst gardens and valleys.

God Almighty, whose wisdom fashions the smiling rose
Within its blossom, just like a fetus in its placenta.

It is appropriate for people to prostrate before his will:
A Fashioner [*muṣavvir*] who can shape such paintings!

Bountiful is Shiraz, paradisiacal its youths, behold!
From all windows you shall see houris and springs of fresh water![50]

It is by now clear that the so called "mystical" dimension of Sa'di's poetry is in reality a spiritual approach to an inquisitive posture whose background is undeniably epistemological, rational, and ultimately aesthetic. We may suggest that Sa'di's spiritual aesthetics are imbued with a set of mundane practices and ideals that combine the hermeneutics of certain strands of sober Sufi thought with meditations on temporal power, physical desire, and the deterministic mechanics that explain the origins of beauty through scriptural evidence and epistemological questing. In the subsequent chapters, following the observations outlined thus far, I shall refer to this aspect of Sa'di's teleological aesthetics as the **rational-inferential** approach to the experience of contemplating beauty in a sacred context.

Nevertheless, a number of ghazals by Sa'di (along with specific prose or verse passages drawn from other works of his) contain allusions to realities which the lyric subject's rational perusal of the world in its quest for the divine origins of beauty fails to grasp. In such passages, the poet alludes to mysteries that, while transcending the contemplation of the world as it is grasped by the external senses, cause the human intellect to connect with a supernal level of experience, in which imagination mediates between mental representations and ineffable source of inspiration. Glimpses of this second contemplative modality (which, in the following chapter I shall refer to as the "imaginal-cosmological" approach) are attested to in ghazals similar to the following:

3 O temptation [*fitna*] freshly risen from the world of divine power [*'ālam-i qudrat*]:
Engrained you are in the heart, do not hide from the eyes! …

50 [2.39] Sa'di KhE, 650. Ms. Yale 1432, f. 170a. Cf. the opening of the *qasida* dedicated to Shams al-Dīn Juvaynī, quoted in Chapter 1 (p. 94).

7 I promised I would pronounce a few words about your countenance:
You showed your face, and shut the door of my linguistic reason [*dar-i nuṭq*]....

9 Saʿdi, a jewel-box is the body, created for the divine signs:
you contain a hundred balances, yet did not peruse a single one.

10 The Painter of existence fashioned all these forms so that
You may contemplate the painting and worship the Fashioner [*muṣavvir*].

Ṭayyibāt 221[51]

The last two lines of this ghazal draw a compelling parallel between the self-reflection of the lyric persona upon its own body—which is revealed as the fictitious author's meditation on himself as a result of teleological intimations similar to those presented by al-Ghazāli—and the exterior world as an aesthetic trace of the divine Painter. However, the first line quoted line introduces the topic of sensual temptation along with the apparently mysterious concept of "the world of divine power" (*ʿālam-i qudrat*).[52] Samirā Qayyumi has convincingly demonstrated that, in the theological vocabulary of the 13th century, this expression is a synonym of the concept of "the world of command" (*ʿālam-i amr*), one of the key loci of the cosmo-theosophical representation that al-Ghazālī inherited from the Islamic philosophical tradition.[53]

In general Neoplatonic terms, on the basis of al-Fārābī and Avicenna's cosmology, the "world of command" stands for the intelligible world of the celestial intellects. As Wensick and Griffel observe, al-Ghazālī's use of the term is a synonym for the supernal realm (*malakūt*), or the invisible world (*ghayb*) which is opposed to the material world (*mulk*).[54] For cosmological and theological reasons that I shall illustrate in the next chapters, the supernal realm

51 [2.40] Saʿdi YE, 104.

52 Other manuscripts (Ms. Kabul 1325, 368; Paris 1366, f. 197a; Ms. Paris 1384, f. 388a; Ms. Yale 1432, f. 293b) record a slightly different variant for the first *miṣrāʿ* of l. 3: "shād āmadī ay fitna-yi naw-khāsta az ghayb" ("So welcome you are, of temptation freshly risen from the invisible world"). This variant is a further attestation to the correspondence between the concept of the "world of divine power" and the "unseen" as two expressions alluding to the supernal realm of *malakūt*. On this point, see comments below.

53 Qayyumi 1386/2007.

54 "The world of command is the set of universals—or for Avicenna, the quiddities (*māhiyyāt*)—that function as the blueprint for all individual and material creation and that are accessible to the human intellect. 'Command' refers to the full set of the classes of beings that make up creation." Griffel 2009, 101. As noted earlier (see supra, footnote

is the locus in which the blueprint of the physical world—its past, future, and present events and particulars—is kept in a spiritual form that the human soul (also referred to as the "intellect," or "rational soul" in the Avicennian philosophical tradition) can access through the mediation of the imaginative faculties. Saʿdi's line will become more intelligible if we consider that, from al-Ghazālī onwards—especially in the spiritual and lyrical tradition—the heart is the organ that subsumes all the functions of what in the philosophical tradition is referred to as the "intellect" or the "rational soul." Therefore, what Saʿdi alludes to is the occurrence of a mental contact between the heart/rational soul of the lyric subject and an archetypal form of beauty descending from the supernal realm. This imaginal translation, Saʿdi declares, occupies the visual memory of the "beholder." The mental representation of beauty turns into a source of bewilderment, as it appears as a form that belongs to the physical world and may constitute a source of sensual temptation (*fitna*).

While the exact genealogy of the expression "world of power" as a synonym of "world of command" or "supernal world" is yet to be determined, it is remarkable that its usage is attested to in both *The Jasmine of the Lovers* and the *Illustration of the Theopathic Utterances* by Rūzbihān Baqlī, the Sufi author from Shiraz whom Saʿdi mentions in his *shīrāziyya* ghazal analyzed earlier and whose order was somehow connected to the establishment of Saʿdi's Sufi lodge.[55] In the chapter from *The Jasmine of the Lovers* on the "pretention" of carnal love, Rūzbihān presents the physiology of the human body as a latrine collecting humors whose composition hosts the base soul of concupiscence and lust. As a consequence of this physiology, he argues, the only form of affection that the commoners can experience belongs to sexual desire, as their souls are exclusively prone to engage themselves in idolatry (*ṣanam-parastī*). Their desire is excited by lust:

> Whenever they contemplate the form of beautiful people [*ṣūrat-i nīkuvān*], their eyes fixate on the external forms. Being removed from the beauty of the [divine] actions [*ḥusn-i afʿālī*], the color of the [divine] attributes [*rang-i sifatī*] and the epiphany of the Essence [*tajallī-yi ẕātī*] that is found in the prisons of the bodily frames [*aqfāṣ-i ashbāḥ*], they are deprived of the effluence of the bird-like celestial soul, and cannot see the Sublime Bounties [*ḥuẓūẓ-i jalālī*] encircling the human body.[56]

---

to the second line of the ghazal most recently analyzed) *ghayb* (the unseen) appears as a variant for *ʿālam-i qudrat* in some important manuscripts.

55 See Introduction to Part 2.

56 Ruzbehān Baqli 1958, 94–95.

Whenever the "commoners" contemplate their object of desire, their carnal souls develop an affection toward the "attributeless forms." These forms, bereft of connections with the divine presence, are incapable of reflecting the supernal archetypes of beauty in the guise of divine attributes. On the contrary, they foster mental images that lead the individual towards lustful actions. They eventually perform idolatry in their imagination, without recognizing the difference between "idols" (*ṣanam*) and the "Supreme Provider" (*ṣamad*), claiming that: "we are the Theosophists [*ṭāmātiyān*] of the age, as we dwell in the "world of power" [*ʿālam-i qudrat*].[57]

Saʿdi's mention of the supernal realm of power as the mental abode of the appearance of an object of sensual temptation relates to Rūzbihān's considerations on the psychology and the ethics of such manifestations of beauty. The reference to the teleological aesthetics of the last lines ("The Painter of existence fashioned All these forms") reiterates the necessity of reading the object of desire—as a tangible presence or as an imagined form—through a correct inferential modality that guides the onlooker through risks that both incarnationism (see, for instance, Rūzbihān's insistence on the threat of idolatry) and concupiscence may pose. It is also remarkable that the passage of one other work by Rūzbihān in which the expression "*ʿālam-i qudrat*" is mentioned—the renowned *Illustration of the Theopathic Utterances*—comments on the visionary experience of the 9th-century Sufi master Shiblī and his spiritual capability of seeing supernal beauty from the "world of power" through the coat of mundane reality, including in the hair of one of the little toes of his feet.[58] Rūzbihān eventually quotes the Quranic verse on the divine signs scattered through the horizons, and states that "whatever he had seen in the supernal realm of the spirit, he had found in the spiritual microcosm, and whatever he had seen within the supernal realm of pre-eternal Power and Might [*qudrat-u quvvat-i qidam*] he saw it in the created presence of one of his hairs, as the form of man is the mirror of both worlds, and anything that was poised into those two realms is found in the form of mankind."[59]

Saʿdi's reflection on the contemplation of one's body as a source of spiritual insight informing the supernal origins of human beauty ought to be read within the framework offered by Rūzbihān, which could be regarded as the late 12th-century development of a discourse that al-Ghazālī formulated on

57 Ibid., 95.

58 Ruzbehān Baqli 1981, 245–46.

59 See Chapter 9 (pp. 473–75) for a survey of the correspondences between these passages by Rūzbihān and al-Ghazālī's erotic subtext of the visionary experience.

the basis of Avicenna's psychological and epistemological system.[60] From this standpoint, the meditation on idolatry pertains to an epistemological level that cannot be fully understood without letting a broader psychological system account for its mundane, imaginal, and supernal reflections. In the following lines, for instance, Saʿdi emphasizes the difference between the access of one's imagination to forms descending from the supernal and the vulgarity of all forms of beauty that do not derive from that contact:

4 Your gaze shines like the sun, does it matter if one day
You will illuminate the walls and doors around us?

5 Offer your benevolent glance by looking at us, in this direction:
By your alchemy—a true magic!—our copper shall turn into gold….

9 Since the image of the beloved was not engraved in our heart's imagination,
We shall break all imaginings, as if they were idols.

10 It is true that the sunshine of love shines upon everyone, however
Not all stones share the same nature: not everyone turns into a gem! …

Badāyiʿ 612[61]

In the next chapters we shall explore how the friction between the teleological contemplative modality and the idiosyncratic duality of the human condition (as matter that is simultaneously ephemerally base and blessed by the divine design) is the terrain in which the psychology of Saʿdi's lyric subject explores the extent of the paradoxes of the relationship between the soul and the senses. In particular, the following analyses will help us redefine the meaning of the intersection of the sensual horizon of the lyric subject and the scope of its investigation of the "supernal" through a cognitive-inspirational approach that is derivative of the Avicennian psychological system. In one lengthy homiletic

60 In the next chapters, I shall extensively explore the role of the metaphor of the mirror in al-Ghazālī's spiritual epistemology, which pervades the entirety of Saʿdi's "visionary" lyricism. For now, compare Rūzbihān's statements on the human forms mirroring the visible and in invisible world with al-Ghazāli's formulation of the same concept in the *Kīmiyā* (1: 47).

61 [2.41] Saʿdi YE, 274–75. In Yusofi's edition (ibid., 275), the second *miṣrāʿ* of l. 9 reads as *mutaṣavvar shavad*, which is metrically incorrect. I have edited the line (*mutaṣavvar nabūd*) on the basis of the consistent solutions offered by most manuscripts.

ghazal, for instance, Saʿdi defines the figure of the *ʿārif* on the margins where the practice of contemplation clashes with its ethical and sensual dimensions:

O people, the world offers no rest to the body:
What a shame it is to withhold the learned men in this world!

How can the melody of the morning birds reach those who sleep?
Unaware are the animals of the world of mankind.

Seek the medicine of education from the master of the Path:
No disease worse than ignorance can affect human beings.

However angelically beautiful a countenance may be
It may only be contemplated in a bright mirror.

The night of the men of God is world-illuminating morning:
No truly dark night do the enlightened ones ever witness.

Defeat the demon's assault with the arm of spiritual training [*riyāżat*],
As this strength does not belong to outward physicality.

Do not limit your pious obedience to grazing the ground with your forehead [*pīshānī*]:
Practice sincerity, as spiritual abandonment does not stem from blind imitation [*pīshānī*]....

The jurist, the ascetic, and the Sufi are but infants on the path:
A real man is the beholder of the divine realities [*ʿārif-i rabbānī*].

I am afraid the spiritual reflection of the boy attesting to God's beauty [*shāhid-i rūhānī*] won't show his face to you,
As your desires are engulfed with lustful pleasures.[62]

From these lines it is possible to ascertain the peculiar role that Saʿdi assigns to the figure of the *ʿārif* vis-à-vis the practice of contemplating beauty and the hermeneutics informing such experiences from a point of view that is not only ethical, but also psychological. In particular, the opposition between the *ʿārif* and the representatives of normative approaches to the ethical tenets of Islam

62 [2.42] Ms. London 1328, f. 313a/b. Cf. Saʿdi KhE, 653; Ms. Yale 1432, ff. 170b–71a.

(the jurists, the ascetics, and the Sufis) is reminiscent of Avicenna's description of the *ʿārif*'s epistemological posture vis-à-vis the practices of the ascetics and the worshipers:

> One who abandons the possessions and pleasures of this world is distinguished by the name "ascetic" [*al-zāhid*]. One who devotes himself to the supererogatory performance of acts of worship, such as nocturnal devotions, fasting, and the like, is distinguished by the name "worshiper" [*al-ʿābid*]. One who turns his thinking [*fikr*] towards the Sanctity of the Supernal Realm, continuously awaiting the illumination of the light of the Truth in his secret [*sirr*] is distinguished by the name "cognizer" [*al-ʿārif*].[63]

One could hardly understand the exact meaning of Saʿdi's celebration of the figure of the *ʿārif* as opposed to the jurist, the Sufi, and the ascetic without taking into account the spiritual epistemology in which Avicenna situates the "cognizer"'s intellectual connection with the supernal realm.[64] Both Avicenna and Saʿdi, far from belittling the spiritual value of normative religious practices embodied by the figures that they mention, highlight the higher status of the *ʿārif* from the perspective of his intellectual capabilities with respect to the exploration of the supernal; through spiritual and physical training, he orients his body toward the higher aspirations of his rational soul.[65]

63 Quoted and translated by Rapoport 2018, 119. I have slightly modified Rapoport's and Gutas' translations (for the latter's rendition, see Gutas 2006a, 353), especially to retain the literal meaning of *sirr* ("secret"), which Gutas convincingly translates as "innermost self" and interprets as a reference to the Rational Soul. For a more in-depth demonstration of the connection between the lexeme *sirr* and Avicennian noetics, see Rapoport 2018, 279–80.

64 See Rapoport 2018, 119–22 for a discussion on the role of non-mystical intellectual cognition in Avicenna's passages describing the contact between the rational soul and the supernal realm.

65 "The knower is not concerned with prayer and fasting *per se*, but rather with the purely intellectual activity of focusing one's thought on the Sanctity of Dominion (the supernal realm, where the celestial intellects reside) in order to prepare one's innermost self (the rational soul) to receive intellectual illumination." Ibid, 121. It is worth underlining that Avicenna's main critique of the ascetic's and the worshiper's approach to spiritual practices is their non-cognitive transactional nature, as they "perform activities in this world in exchange for a reward from God in the next world." Rapoport 122–23. Whereas for the *ʿārif* all acts of worship constitute a form of training (*riyāżа*) whereby he submits his bodily functions (including his internal senses) to the perusal of the Truth. See ibid., 123–24. On *riyāża*, see also Rapoport 2018, 274. Saʿdi expresses exactly the same concept by mentioning both the need for spiritual training though the regulation of one's body

The cognitive-sapiential subtext of Saʿdi's depiction of the ideal *ʿārif* manifests itself from the opening of the poem, in which the poetic persona praises the centrality of knowledge and wisdom as tools that the learned man can employ to peruse the world in order to seek the enlightening effluence of the celestial world. Saʿdi's emphasis on the value of spiritual and intellectual radiance reflects Avicenna's constant reference to illumination and optics as metaphorical analogues for the process of intellection.[66] Therefore, Saʿdi's discourse on illumination, rather than stemming from the alleged influence of Suhravardī's illuminationist school,[67] is derivative of Avicenna's model of emanationist intellection, whose optical foundation involved a cutting-edge reformulation of the Aristotelian theory of vision, one presenting multiple overlaps with the contemporary innovations of Ibn al-Haytham further west in the Islamic world.[68]

---

towards metaphysical ends (in the line on the demon's assault) and the vacuity of blind religious imitation (*pīshānī*), which both Avicenna and al-Ghazālī theorize from the point of view of their critique of *taqlīd*'s confessional normativity and the obstacle it poses to the cognitive connection between the rational soul and the Active Intellect. On this topic, see Frank 1991; Gutas 2014a, 217–19.

66 Davidson 1992, 91–93, Hasse 2000, 183. For an acute rebuttal of the esoteric readings of Avicenna's deployment of the metaphor of light in his noetic system, see Rapoport 2018, 120–22. While Rapoport explains Avicenna's usage of the metaphor of light as a way to take "recourse to common concepts and language widely used within his intellectual milieu" (ibid., 122), McGinnis has demonstrated that "virtually every feature in Avicenna's account of intellectual understanding has its analogue in his optics." McGinnis 2013, 53.

67 See Zibāʾi-Nezhād 1385/2006. The few attempts at demonstrating the influence of Suhravardī's illuminationism on the Persian lyric imagery of the 13th and 14th centuries constitute a fascinating approach to the influence of philosophical thought on the mature phase of the premodern literary canon of Iran. While I do not find Zibāʾi-Nezhād's findings on the influence of illuminationism on Saʿdi's ghazals satisfying, Hossein Ziai's meditations on the role of light in the poetry of Hafez deserve to be carefully taken into account and compared with the intellectual yield of the Avicennian psychological and optical tradition. See Ziai 1995.

68 See McGinnis's acute observations on the similarities between Ibn al-Haytham's optics and Avicenna's theory of perception: "It is certainly worth noting that Ibn al-Haytham (965–1039), an immediate contemporary of Avicenna who lived in Cairo, also distinguished two types of light nearly corresponding with Avicenna's division here: light that radiates from self-luminous bodies and accidental light that is acquired by bodies that are not self-luminous. [...] The similarities become even greater when compared with Avicenna's subsequent comments about rays radiating from the illuminated object so as to form a visual cone that falls upon the eye and projects a sensible image of the visible objects to the visual system of the perceiver." McGinnis 2013a, 56, n. 13. And also: "It is certainly worth mentioning here that virtually all of the new features appearing in Avicenna's optics find their counterparts in the more fully developed optics of Ibn al-Haytham, the Alhazen of Latin fame [...]. I shall not speculate whether what Avicenna presented here

In Sa'di's ode to the role of the *'ārif*, the coexistence of a non-lyrical discourse on the ethical training of the body-soul conjuncture with the invitation to contemplate human beauty as a mirror of the supernal world attests to the general cognitive framework of the poet's spiritual aesthetics, in which the role of intellectual illumination is both metaphysical and physiological. It is through the complexity of this psychology, mainly from the perspective of its Avicennian heritage in the form in which it would circulate in 13th-century Shiraz, that the next chapter will explore how Sa'di's ideal of an imaginal-cosmological approach to the visionary experience clashes with the phantasmagoric visions that engulf the internal and external senses of the poetic self as a desiring subject.

in mere outline, Ibn al-Haytham would pick up and expand upon, or whether Avicenna derived his optical model from the works of Ibn al-Haytham, or if even in fact both men were drawing upon some incipient mathematical model of the intromission theory current at the time." Ibid., 52.

CHAPTER 6

Between the Rational Soul and the Internal Senses

For a Psychology of the Lyric Subject

I thought that, while not seeing you, my love would fall into oblivion:
You leave, and yet you stand before me: hidden and yet depicted in the imagination.

Ṭayyibāt 192[1]

•••

O idol, so beautiful you appear inside my gaze
That you inhabit my sight everywhere I look.

Ṭayyibāt 281[2]

•••

The soil of your door is a balm that causes my vision to shine:
I am a man of insight, and I know the value of your soil.

The cypress of your stature stands in the garden of my imagination,
Shame on me, if I were to admire the slender form of the pine trees.

Badāyiʿ 473[3]

1 The Avicennian Revolution: from Spiritual Hermeneutics to Sensory Cognition

In the previous two chapters, we have reassessed the problem of the so-called "mystical" dimension of specific aspects of Saʿdi's ghazals from the point of

1 [2.43] Saʿdi YE, 90.
2 [2.44] Ibid., 129.
3 [2.45] Ibid., 217.

 | DOI:10.1163/9789004435902_010

view of the spiritual hermeneutics involved in the relationship between human beauty and the earthly reflections of the divine splendor. We have seen how this interpretive issue relates to both "extratextual" objects of desire (i.e., the real bodies circulating in the social spaces of intellectual, religious, and artistic activity) and the literary representation of bodies in the lyric tradition to which Saʿdi's belongs. The recognition of a rational-inferential modality has helped us deconstruct the dichotomy that some critics posit when discussing the difference between the physical and the metaphysical nature of the object of desire.

Starting with this chapter, and continuing until the conclusion of the second part of this book, I will develop the discussion of the aesthetic aspects of cognition that I have introduced at the end of the previous chapter in connection with the discussion of the theo-erotic aspects of *maʿrifa* in Saʿdi's lyricism. In the following pages, I will endeavor to transition from the hermeneutics of Persian lyric poetry to a paradigm that is primarily epistemological and cognitive. In order to do so, I will investigate the psycho-physiological grounds that regulate the sensory experience of the lyric subject within the texts themselves. Therefore, our question now shifts from, "what is the nature of the beloved?," to "how does the lyric subject think, how does it perceive and cognize the world and the visual or imagined presence of the beloved?" Furthermore: how can we account for the relationship between the descriptions of visionary experiences, tangible visual encounters, dreams, and imagined ideals of beauty? In order to follow this new path, especially if we are to account for Saʿdi's obsession with the nature of visual contemplation and its relationship with imagination, memory, and cognition in a perspective that oscillates between mundane desires and supernal projections, we ought to take into serious consideration the attention that Avicenna's thought received during the 13th century as an authoritative source of inspiration not only for the study of metaphysics, but also for the development of epistemological debates on the relationship between optical vision and intellection.[4]

Avicenna's systematization of the late-antique and classical-Islamic curriculum of sciences (mainly through logic, psychology, and metaphysics) sparked broad interest both in the Latin Christendom and in the Islamic world. As shown by Robert Wisnovsky, Avicenna's final summa philosophica, *al-Ishārāt wa al-tanbīhāt*, was widely copied, circulated, and commented upon, especially by reason of its comprehensive approach to the theological implications

4 Wisnovsky 2013, 196–7. On the circulation of Avicenna's works in the scholarly environment of the medieval madrasas, see Endress 2006.

of the difference between essence and existence.[5] Although Avicenna's *Shifāʾ* received scholarly attention only a few decades after the author's death (1037), in the 12th and the 13th centuries commentators focused almost exclusively on the *Ishārāt*. This work, whose "opaque style of composition allowed commentators to tease out philosophical implications in ways they wanted,"[6] received its first instance of critical attention by the end of the 12th century (through al-Masʿūdī's *Shukūk wa shubah*)[7] and was further commented upon on at least six different occasions during Saʿdi's lifetime.[8] Overall, scholars have seen Avicennism as "one of the major ideological evolutions of human history," which imposed itself as a mainstream intellectual framework not only for the field of philosophical speculations but also for the development of contexts as different as the natural sciences, Sufi thought and practices, theories of mind, theology, and cosmology.[9] The religious scholars who attempted to reject the systems of thought stemming from the Avicennian tradition "largely responded to the philosophical agenda he had set, either decades or centuries earlier."[10]

From historical accounts describing the vehemence with which, during the first half of the 13th century, illustrious spiritual and political figures attempted to ban the circulation of Avicenna's works in Baghdad and Shiraz, we learn that the scholarly and courtly environments in which Saʿdi's studied and composed poetry were exposed to constant debates on the validity of the core tenets of Avicennian thought. Abū Ḥafṣ Suhravardī's campaign against Avicennism started as early as 1207, when he declared that he would personally destroy every copy of Avicenna's *Shifāʾ* in all the libraries of Baghdad.[11] This reaction

5 Wisnowsky 2013, 194. See also McGinnis 2013b.

6 Wisnowsky 2013, 199

7 Al-Masʿūdī, whom Wisnovsky defines as a "problem-commentator," raised in his commentary fifteen philosophical problems addressing both psychological and metaphysical issues. For the purposes of our investigation, al-Masʿūdī's rebuttal of Avicenna's theory of the internal senses as a filter between extra-mental reality and the rational soul is particularly relevant. See Shihade 2015, 63–66. In order to confute Avicenna's intromissive theory of vision in favor of an extramissive paradigm, al-Masʿūdī partially criticizes the Avicennian model of perception, which he describes as a system that "was accepted by the majority (*al-aktharūn, al-jumhūr*) of his contemporaries." Ibid., 64.

8 The most renowned 13th-century commentaries, which might have been accessible to Saʿdi at different stages of his life and during different phases of the scholarly debates on the main tenets of the *Ishārāt*, are Fakhr al-Dīn Rāzī's (d. 1210) *Sharḥ al-ishārāt wa al-tanbīhāt* and Naṣīr al-Dīn Ṭūsī's (d. 1274) *Ḥall mushkilāt al-ishārāt*. On the former, see Shihadeh 2016, and, on the latter, see McGinnis 2016.

9 Michot 1993, 292–93.

10 Wisnovsky 2013, 206.

11 Ohlander 2008, 291–92.

was probably motivated by the intellectual antinomianism which, according to ʿAbd al-Laṭīf al-Baghdādī (d. 1231), Avicennianism caused to spread in Baghdad, especially in the environment of the Niẓāmiyya.[12]

The Salghurid atabeg Abū Bakr pursued a similar policy when, at the beginning of his rule, he exiled prominent scholars who had been accused of teaching rational sciences (*ʿulūm-i ʿaqlī*), including physics (*ṭabīʿiyyāt*) and philosophy (*ḥikmat*).[13] Among the scholars affected by Abū Bakr's ideological ostracism, it is worth mentioning the name of one of the followers of Rūzbihān-i Baqlī's teachings, Ṣadr al-Dīn Muḥammad Ushnuhī (d. ca. 1257–67), who composed a manual on *samāʿ* entitled *Tuḥfat al-vuṣūl fī ʿilm al-fuṣūl*, and who met Suhravardī in Baghdad after having left Shiraz.[14] The epistles of Ṣadr al-Dīn Muḥammad and those of his father, Tāj al-Dīn Muḥammad, along with the work of Shahāb al-Dīn Fażlallāh Tūrapushtī (*al-Muʿtamad fī al-muʿtaqad*), another scholar whom Abū Bakr exiled, even without directly mentioning Avicenna or Avicennian texts, base their spiritual cosmology and psychology on paradigms whose derivation is clearly peripatetic.[15]

With the death of Abū Bakr and the progressive transition of the socio-political life of Fars toward the Ilkhanid sphere of influence, Shiraz regained its position as a center of learning in which philosophical conversations would kindle debates among a variety of religious circles. The discussions on philosophical issues of clear Avicennian provenance that reportedly took place between the Ilkhanid governor Amīr Inkiyānū (appointed by Abaqa in 1268) and the powerful representative of the Suhravardiyya order in Fars, Najīb al-Dīn Buzghush, attest to the intellectual renewal of the city and the vibrancy of the philosophical debates that it hosted.[16] In all the *qasida*s with which Saʿdi addressed Inkiyānū, the poet emphasizes the role of the intellect (*ʿaql*) as a primary source of refinement of the self.[17] Similarly, in a brief prose text redacted as a response to a question that a certain Saʿd al-Dīn Naṭanzī posed in verse, Saʿdi offers a comparison between love and the intellect as two paths leading to the knowledge of God.[18] Although the discrepancies among the published editions warrant an accurate critical edition, the text reveals theoretical

---

12 Gutas 2011, 20–21.

13 See Zarkub Shirāzi 1389/2010, 150–51; Vassāf 1259/1852, 159; Aigle 2005, 110. Cf. Māyel Heravi's comment on this event: Tāj al-Din Oshnovi 1368/1989, 11–13.

14 Tāj al-Dīn Oshnovi 1368/1989, 11–15.

15 For an analysis of Suhravardī's crypto-peripateticism in his anti-philosophical polemics, see Ohlander 2008, 298–303.

16 On Inkiyānū and Buzghush, see Introduction, pp. 21–22.

17 Saʿdi KhE, 667–68, 696–97.

18 Ibid., 817–20.

foundations that are undoubtedly Avicennian, and whose wording often seems to paraphrase passages from al-Ghazālī's *Kīmiyā-yi sa'ādat.*[19]

References to Avicenna and his philosophical system abound in the poetic tradition, and direct mentions of the *Ishārāt* are found in the poetic corpus of some of Sa'di's contemporaries, such as his devoted imitator, Sayf-i Farghānī, and the famous Sufi poet Fakhr al-Dīn 'Irāqī.[20] Furthermore, as I shall often point out in this chapter, even without direct references to the books of the philosopher, the terminology and the imagery of the Avicennian psychological system often emerge in many passages of Sa'di's works, in verse and prose alike. In the line below, for instance, the poet introduces the concept of the "rational soul" and its connection with the "aperture" of the heart, de facto juxtaposing in the same lyric excerpt (as it will become clear in the next chapters) Avicennian noetics with the exact vocabulary of the spiritual cardiology that al-Ghazālī describes in the *Kīmiyā-yi sa'ādat*:

> From the aperture [*darīcha*] of my thinking [*fikrat*], my heart
> Showed to the rational soul [*nafs-i nāṭiqa*] the signs of my increasingly desperate condition.
>
> *Badāyi'* 539[21]

19 For a brief survey of this *risāla* and a biographical note on Naṭanzī, see Bashari 2020, 301–303.

20 See for instance, Sayf-i Farghānī's pun with the titles of Avicenna's major works, *The Cure, The Canon,* and, above all, *The Pointers* (*al-Ishārāt*):
O polemist, arrange your Cure [*shifā*] out of this Canon [*qānūn*],
As not even Avicenna [*pisar-i Sīnā*] possesses these Pointers [*ishārāt*].
[2.46] Sayf Farghāni 1341–44/1962–65, 2: 309. As for Fakhr al-Dīn 'Irāqī, the anonymous compiler of his theo-erotic hagiography states that at the age of seventeen he had reached the completion of the study of all sciences, rational and scriptural ('Erāqī 1375/1996, 49). The hagiographer adds that once a group of wandering mystics cast an ecstatic spell on him through the presences of their disheveled demeanors and the company of a youth of exceeding beauty, 'Irāqī promptly threw away all of his books on religious and rational sciences, including Fakhr al-Dīn Rāzī's *Tafsīr-i kabīr*, and Avicenna's *Ishārāt* (*The Pointers*), which he dismissively renamed *Fushārāt* (*The Idiocies*). Ibid., 49–50. The anecdote, regardless of its historical veracity, attests to the fact that by the end of the 13th century (or almost one century earlier, if the account is accurate) Avicenna's *Ishārāt* was considered as part of the mainstream curriculum of sciences. See also Rumi:
No other medicine we have apart from you, to cure our sorrow.
O Galen of my soul, you, my Avicenna!
[2.47] Rumi 1376/1997, 738.

21 [2.48] Sa'di YE, 244.

In other cases, Saʿdi recurs to the description of the internal senses in order to illustrate the role of the process of cognition in the mental representation of the object of desire. Ultimately, as I shall show in the next chapter, the metaphor of the mirror as a speculum of the invisible world is so pervasive in Saʿdi's ghazals that one cannot but relate it to its Avicennian and Ghazalian origins.[22]

It is not surprising that when ʿAzīz al-Dīn Nasafī, one of Saʿdi's contemporaries who travelled extensively between Transoxiana, Khorasan, and western Iran (including Fars), was asked to compose a treatise on all the sciences that would constitute the necessary curriculum for the wayfarer, he devoted the first epistle of his *Kitāb al-insān al-kāmil* to a lucid illustration of Avicennian psychology that included a clear explanation of the physiology of the internal senses and their role in the contact between the human intellect and the supernal realm.[23] Following the historical interactions between Sufi thought and peripatetic philosophy, we may succeed in extending to other 13th-century thinkers and literati what Damian Janos has observed in his contribution on the influence of Avicenna and al-Ghazālī on the thought of Fakhr al-Dīn Rāzī (d. 1210): "in other words, it seems that al-Rāzī deploys mystical terminology to

---

22 See, for instance, how Avicenna, in the *Epistle on Love*, compares the connection between the soul and the supernal world through the exemplum of the mirror in a fashion that accommodates Saʿdi's sober sacred eroticism: "[The First Cause] never manifests Itself except in Its pure unmingled essence. It is Its noble essence itself which manifests itself, and for that reason the philosophers have called it 'the Form of the Intellect.' The first recipient of this manifestation is that divine angel who is called the 'universal intellect.' His substance receives His manifestation in the fashion of a form reflected in a mirror so that the individual of which it is an image becomes manifested. Related to this concept is what has been said with regard to the agent intellect being an image of It. And one must be careful to say that it is Its image, i.e., of the Necessary and True. Everything that is brought into being by some immediate cause comes into being through the mediation of an image occurring in the universal intellect under Its influence. This is proven by induction." Mehren 1894, 23; Fackenheim 1945, 226.

23 ʿAziz al-Din Nasafi 1341/1962, 21–22. For a detailed overview of the influence of Avicennian epistemology on Nasafi's thought, see Ridgeon 1998, 90–96. As I shall show in this chapter and in the next, in these epistles Nasafi illustrates the theory of the human heart as a mirror reflecting the supernal meanings (*maʿānī*) contained in the celestial realm (*malakūt*, or *lawḥ-i maḥfūẓ*) with a wording that reproduces verbatim al-Ghazālī's arguments on this topic. The pragmatism with which, both in *al-Insān al-kāmil* and in *Kashf al-ḥaqāyiq*, the author presents his arguments as a conflation of scriptural, philosophical (with Avicenna being mentioned several times), and spiritual lines of thought speaks to the interdisciplinary nature of the cultural environments in which Saʿdi flourished. Moreover, considering the striking emphasis of Nasafi on the optical dimension of the visionary experience within the context of spiritual (albeit rational) aesthetics, the points of contact between this author and Saʿdi's visual lyricism deserve to be the object of a separate study.

describe a cognitive phenomenon that is perfectly accountable on Avicennian psychological grounds."[24] Future studies may be capable of unearthing thicker textual connections by analyzing the circulation of manuscripts within the boundaries of the early Ilkhanid cultural networks. However, the pervasive circulation of ideas reformulating the main tenets of the Avicennian psychological paradigm during the 13th century constitutes alone one of the main overarching frameworks capable of assisting us in the task of reading the mechanics of Sa'di's representations of imagination as a link between physical beauty and the perusal of the unseen.

2 Beyond Sufi Normativity: the Sensory Aspect of Sa'di's Lyricism

Al-Ghazālī's adoption of a variety of major tenets of Avicenna's philosophical paradigms constituted only the beginning of the pervasive circulation of Avicennism during the Saljuq period, which, at that time, detractors provocatively compared to a pandemic affecting all strands of the intellectual elites.[25] In spite of this cultural revolution, there is still no systematic discussion of the impact of Avicennian philosophy on the development of post-11th-century Persian poetry.[26] The prejudice that has for long depicted al-Ghazālī as an anti-philosophical Sufi intellectual has indirectly obstructed the development of critical approaches capable of unearthing the peripatetic roots of some aspects of Persian Sufi thought and their influence on literary genres and practices. The judgment on al-Ghazālī's apparent disregard for peripatetic philosophy has been successfully reassessed and subverted in the light of the multifaceted intellectual environment of Khorasan during his lifetime. A similar approach should be adopted to reread Sufi-inspired Khorasanian poetry between the end of the 11th and the beginning of the 12th century in light of our new picture of al-Ghazālī's debt to philosophy.

Sanā'ī of Ghazna (d. ca. 1130), for instance, in spite of his contextual disdain for *falsafa* as a rational science, should be regarded as the first Persian homiletic and lyric poet who combined certain aspects of Islamic philosophy (in

24 Janos 2016, 202.

25 Michot 1993, 293–97.

26 For a preliminary survey of the influence of Greek thought on the early stages of Persian literature, see Christine van Ruymbeke 2007. The Ismaili poet Nāṣir-i Khusraw (d. 1072) is the obvious point of reference to gauge the effects of peripatetic philosophy on the later end of Persian literature's formative period. However, see de Bruijn's remarks on the limits of his influence on the subsequent poetic tradition in Sunni Sufi *milieux* (de Bruijn 1997, 34–35).

the guise of a generic category of sapiential wisdom, to which he referred as *ḥikma*) with Sufi ideals and beliefs.[27] Sanāʾī is unanimously regarded as the first poet of the Persian literary tradition who elevated the ghazal to a well-established and autonomous lyric genre. His role in the development of the spiritual dimension of amatory poetry is pivotal, especially considering that he flourished in eastern Khorasan at the time when the Ghazālī brothers were bringing about their philosophy-infused syncretic spiritual innovations, and the debate on the relationship between poetry recitation and Sufism was at the center of several religious and courtly circles.[28] Furthermore, considering that "his ghazals [...] best exemplify the blend of courtly elements and spirituality"[29] that characterizes the ghazal as a genre, his influence on the development of Saʿdi's lyric persona deserves in-depth investigation in future Persian literary studies. By studying how later poets, including Saʿdi, elaborated on the complex discourses at work in Sanāʾi's poetry, we may better visualize different degrees of receptivity to the philosophical veins crossing the body of the intellectual postures that we ascribe to the development of Sufi thought in connection with the amatory discourse.[30]

In some of Sanāʾī's ghazals, the term "contemplation" (*tamāshā*) echoes al-Ghazālī's concept of *tafakkur* as an active meditation on the wonders of the world, constituting one of the intellectual strategies that lead the believer to the acquisition of *maʿrifa*—the ultimate cognition of God's unique existence. In the text below, by employing the term "imagination" (*khayāl*) at the very beginning of the poem, Sanāʾī grounds the contemplative modality of the text within the horizon of the cognitive dimension of the act of beholding:

---

27 In this regard, especially as far as the philosophical contents of Sanāʾī's *maṣnavīs* are concerned, see de Bruijn 1997, 90–93, and, for a more extensive analysis, see Mozaffari 1392/2013. See for instance:
O God, offer Sanāʾī some glimmers of philosophy,
So that the soul of Avicenna may envy him!
[2.49] Sanāʾi 1362/1983, 57; 1389/2010, 30.

28 On Sanāʾī's life and poetry, see the seminal studies of J. T. P. de Bruijn (1983) and Franklin Lewis (1995). See also Zipoli 2001 (on Sanāʾī's obscene works); Virani 2019.

29 Meisami 1987, 152.

30 For a preliminary survey of the similarities and differences between the poetic style of the two poets, see Hoseyni 1391/2012. As I will emphasize in the last part of this study, Franklin Lewis's philological and historiographical reconstruction of the "varied audiences of Sanāʾī" offers an excellent point of departure for contrastively formulating a theory of Saʿdi's readership in its historical context; especially for a comparison of the Sufi overtones in Sanāʾi's panegyrics dedicated to the late Ghaznavid ruler Bahrāmshāh and Saʿdi's praise of both Saʿd II (the son of the Salghurid atabeg Abū Bakr) and Shams al-Dīn Juvaynī. Lewis 1995, 1: 171–87.

So long as the beloved's form resides in our imagination
Our entire life will be nothing but contemplation.[31]

In the tradition to which al-Ghazālī belongs, as noted in the previous chapter, the doctrinal aspect of *maʿrifa* asserts the relative existence of the world vis-à-vis God as the only ontological presence, from which the entire universe derives as a reflection. This contrast clearly emerges in the remainder of Sanāʾī's ghazal, whose mundane overtone offers a thematic background for the spiritualization of erotic discourse:

Even though the air is as fragrant as musk,
And even though silk is the garment of the ground,

Even though the blossoms perching from the trees
Shine with constellations of stars like the beloved's smile,

Even though the anemones amidst the mountains
Resemble the eyes on the paradisiacal beauties' faces,

Once the glory of loving [*ʿāshiqī*] takes over
All these marvels fade away and disappear.[32]

The idea of love as a final stage of the lover's dismissal of all enchantment but God's beauty resonates with the sacred eroticism of *maʿrifa*, which al-Ghazālī theorizes as a prerequisite for the all-encompassing passion of the believer for God, leading to the annihilation of the self.[33] However, as noted in the previous chapter, the acceptation of *maʿrifa* that Saʿdi incorporates into the psychology of his lyric subject derives from an active form of aesthetic contemplation rather than an intoxicating amatory ecstasy. In Saʿdi's ghazals, unlike the ecstatically metaphysical poetry of his mysticism-inclined contemporaries, Rumi and Fakhr al-Dīn ʿIrāqī, the experience of *maʿrifa* revolves around the practice of beholding beauty through a controlled sensory appreciation of the world.

In a ghazal presumably composed at an early stage of his poetic activity, Rumi opens his text with the first couplet of the same ghazal by Sanāʾī ("So long

31 [2.50] Sanāʾi 1362/1983, 805; 1389/2010, 376.
32 [2.51] Ibid.
33 See Lewisohn 2014a, 170–71.

as the beloved's form resides in our imagination …").[34] In his reorganization of the formal material provided by Sanāʾī, Rumi pursues a spiritual afflatus whose scholastic normativity partially erases all traces of lyrical sensuality. After tracing cosmic parallels to express the beauty of the beloved, Rumi reveals the transcendental nature of the object of desire, which annihilates both the value of worldly forms and poetic expression itself:

> What else shall I say? When we even mention
> His name against inexistence, it increases existence.
>
> The truth about our love for Him is more plentiful
> Than stellar embrace of Gemini.
>
> And the instant when love revealed its face
> All of this left and vanished.
>
> Silence now seals my entire being:
> This is the supreme will of God the Almighty.[35]

In a poem crafted with the same formal pattern, ʿIrāqī describes the intoxicating power of love in the metaphorical context of a wine bout:

> Commotion arose from the tavern where wine is served,
> A clamor arose from all directions.

The spiritual bacchanal eventually transposes Sanāʾī's comparison between nature and the incomparable beauty of the beloved through reversed metaphors that reveal the divine nature of the object of desire:

> You are my final goal in this existence,
> As the transparent wine is the purpose of the goblet.
>
> My soul is the mirror of your face:
> The reflection of your visage appears on its surface.

34 For a prolegomenon to a methodology that could consistently guide any future attempt at discerning the chronology of Rumi's ghazals, see Lewis 2014a.

35 [2.52] Rumi 1376/1997, 178.

The rose reflects the color of your face, otherwise
Why would its cheeks be beautiful?

And if the cypress had not seen your stature,
Why would its height push toward the sky?

The world is a garden that mirrors your face
Joyful is the heart that contemplates it.

The beholder sees only your face in the garden
When admiring every single petal of the rose.

From the reflection of your face, ʿIrāqī's heart
Turns into a rose garden blooming in springtime.[36]

ʿIrāqī's reference to the reflection of divine beauty in the natural world suggests that, unlike Rumi, he composed his ghazal not as a response to Sanāʾī but as a metaphysical elaboration of the following poem by Saʿdi. Through comparison of Saʿdi's juvenile ghazal with both its source of inspiration (Sanāʾī's hypotext) and Rumi's and ʿIrāqī's compositions, it is possible to discern the nuanced difference between the normative aspect of *maʿrifa* as an intoxicating religion of love and its aesthetic component, which stresses the role of the human beloved as a physical bridge to experience a taste of divine beauty:

The fragrance of roses and the chants of the birds arose
This is the time for rejoicing while enjoying the valleys.

Winter, as a chamberlain, spread veils of new leaves
The zephyr, as a painter, decorated the meadows.

Yet no desire we have for the gardens and the roses:
As anywhere you are, our enjoyment will be there!

They say that gazing at beautiful youths' faces
Is forbidden. But not the gaze that is ours!

The mystery of the unfathomable secret of creation
Appears on your face like water shining through glass.

---

36 [2.53] ʿErāqi 1375/1996, 148.

I shall pull out my left eye from the socket
So that only a righteous eye may I set upon you.

Anyone who was not conquered by love for your
shining face is not human, but a bare stone.

So much my inner pot of nostalgic desire is burning
That one day my dry bones and moist limbs will catch fire!

They say that Saʿdi's countless lamentations
Poorly fit the demeanor of the wise man;

But what could they know of our abyss
If so serene they sit by the shores of the ocean?

Ṭayyibāt 72[37]

Contrary to the customary idea that depicts Saʿdi as a poet of love par excellence, almost under the spell of Romantic desires, however anachronistically,[38] comparison of the ghazal above with those penned by his contemporaries shows that the true core of his lyrical output is the contemplation of beauty at the intersection of multiple philosophical, physiological, and spiritual experiences of the world. Rather than a mystical annihilation of the self leading to the union with the divine, the emphasis on the contemplative dimension of his lyric subject frames the experience of love as a form of inclination towards the visual and imaginal perusal of beauty. In his poetry, we ought to discern an amatory aesthetic posture rather than forms of ecstatic eroticism.

3 The Philosophical Physiology of Love as an Aesthetic Experience: Avicenna's *Epistle* on *ʿIshq*

Considering the subtle link between Sanāʾī's and Saʿdi's elaborations of the sensory aspects of their lyrical theo-eroticism, Avicenna's *Epistle on Love* can be read as one of the keys to contextualize the psychology of love that influenced the history of ghazal poetry. Given the Sufi influence on the development of lyric poetry, this foray may also help bridge the gap between the normative

37 [2.54] Saʿdi YE, 36–37.

38 "No classical Persian poet was a greater and more passionate lover than Saʿdi. One might even claim that he was the greatest lover." Katouzian 2016, 4.

aspect of *maʿrifa* that understates the surface of the world and the recognition of beauty as the primary object of the soul's desire.[39] Avicenna's *Epistle* is the result of a syncretic conflation of Greco-Islamic and Iranian ideas on the nature of the human soul and the mechanisms lying behind its appetite for beauty.[40] The mark that this short and inspiring treatise has left in the post-formative period of Sufi reflections on beauty is significant: both the spiritual aesthetics of the Ghazālī brothers (along with Aḥmad Ghazālī's disciple, ʿAyn al-Quż̇āt), and the theo-erotic idealization of human beauty formulated by the Shirazi mystic Rūzbihān-i Baqlī partially (and often indirectly) stem from Avicenna's original reappraisal of the sensorial aspect of desire.[41]

On the basis of the Hellenistic influences circulating during the formative period of Islamic philosophy, Avicenna refined a tripartite model that divides the human soul into three levels: the vegetative soul (*al-nafs al-nabātiyya*), the animal soul (*al-nafs al-ḥaywaniyya*), and the rational, or human soul proper (*al-nafs al-nāṭiqa*). While the vegetative and the animal soul manage processes and activities such as growth, reproduction, motion and perception, the rational soul presides over human intellection.[42] By indirectly expanding on the Brethren of Purity's explanation of human attraction toward external beauty as a result of the universal passion for God—the "sheer Existent"—Avicenna conceives the human soul's passion for beauty as a collaborative effort of

---

39 The *Epistle* has been edited twice; see Mehren 1894; Ateş 1953. See Fackenheim 1945 for the only available English translation of the treatise, and, for a more accurate rendition of the first chapter, cf. Rundgren 1978–79, 52–55. For a survey of the philological problems that Mehren's and Ateş's editions raise, see Gutas 2014a, 480–81, and, in particular, Soreth 1964; Rundgren 1978–79, 47–49. For a recent critique of the main flaws of Fackenheim's translation, see Bell 1986, 75–76. For the purpose of our study's emphasis on the influence of the aesthetics of the contemplation of beauty on Saʿdi's poetry, it is worthwhile mentioning the following points raised by Bell in the passages that revisit Fackenheim's rendition: "[…] *ʿishq … li-l-awjuhi ʾl-ḥisān*, 'love … for beautiful faces,' is translated, following Mehren, 'love … for external beauty,' which obscures the relation of the treatise to the Arab *ẓarf* or 'refinement' ideal and conceivably also to the Sufi practice of gazing." Ibid., 75. "Again, 'to covet a beautiful sight' (Mehren 1894, 14; Fackenheim 1945, 220) should be 'to covet a beautiful sight in people (*min al-nās*).'" Ibid., n. 15. See also Bell 1986, 75, n. 22, in which Bell prefers the words "gallant" and "chivalrous" to render the Arabic *fityān* mentioned in the title of the fifth section of the Epistle, which Fackenheim translates as "Those who are noble-minded and young" (Mehren 1894, 11; Fackenheim 1945, 218).

40 See Fackenheim 1945, 208–10; Anwar 2003, 339–44; Rundgren 1978–79, 44–45, 50–52; Abrahamov 2003, 21–24.

41 On the connection between Avicenna's *Epistle* and Islamic theology, see Anwar 2003.

42 On the functions of the vegetative and the animal souls in human beings, see McGinnis 2010, 89–116.

the concupiscence of the animal soul and the rational soul's longing for the First Cause:

> Whenever any of the faculties of the soul is conjoined with another higher in rank, then it enters a close connection with the latter, and the result of this alliance with such excellence will be an increase in nobility and ornament for the lower faculty.[43]

The Aristotelian influence on Avicenna's hierarchical relationship between the body and the rational soul enabled the Iranian philosopher to develop a reappraisal of the lower parts of the soul (i.e., vegetative and animal souls, as opposed to the rational soul), the suppression of which was commonly advocated by the currents of early Sufism influenced by Neoplatonic rejections of the body.[44] The dynamic hierarchical partnership between the body and the multiple strata of the soul bestows upon "refined" men (*fityān*, the "gallant" or the "chivalrous") a natural attraction towards beautiful faces as a result of their rational soul's eagerness to conjoin with the First Object of love.[45] Although Avicenna condemns the immorally unbridled excess of lust, he considers physical desire towards beauty as an ennobling faculty, especially when supported by the rational soul:

> Both the rational and the animal soul—the latter by reason of its proximity to the former—invariably love what has beauty in order, composition and harmony, as for example harmonious sounds, harmonious blended tastes of well-prepared dishes and suchlike. But whereas in the animal soul this is due to natural instinct, in the case of the rational soul it results

43 Mehren 1894, 11; Fackenheim 1945, 218. On the Ikhwān al-Ṣafā's Neoplatonic considerations on beauty, see Chittick 2013, 283.

44 When wondering whether Avicenna's ultimate purpose in writing his *Epistle on Love* was to "erect a philosophical foundation for the Arab counterpart of courtly love," von Grunebaum asserts that "love is not the point of departure of his thinking." "In the larger context of the history of Arab psychology," he adds, "it has been Avicenna's special achievement to uncover a hierarchic harmony of the higher and the lower parts of the soul where his predecessors had been able to view their relationship but in terms of a permanent antagonism. The moral duty for Avicenna is no longer the suppression of the lower parts but rather their integration in the soul's struggle toward perfection. As long as direction remains with the rational part, the animal soul has its legitimate function and man's perfectibility is not identified with its power to crush it. In historical terms—and somewhat overstated—the step taken by Avicenna could be termed a shift from a Platonic to an Aristotelian attitude." Von Grunebaum 1952, 243.

45 Bell 1986, 77. Mehren 1894, 15, 17; Fackenheim 1945, 220, 222.

from its occupation with the conception of the ideas which are higher than nature. It recognizes that the closer a thing is to the First Object of love, the more steadfast is it in its order, and the more beautiful in its harmony, and that what follows it immediately attains a greater degree of unity and of such qualities as result therefrom, *viz.*, harmony and agreement [...]. Whenever the rational soul obtains possession of a thing of beautiful harmony, it watches it with an eager eye. [...] we can now make the statement that it is part of the nature of beings endowed with reason to covet a beautiful sight [in people],[46] and this is sometimes [...] to be considered as refinement [*ẓarāfa*] and manly nobility [*futuwwa*]....[47]

If a man loves a beautiful form with animal desire, he deserves reproof, even condemnation and the charge of sin, as, for instance, those who commit unnatural adultery and in general people who go astray. But whenever he loves a pleasing form with an intellectual consideration, in the manner we have explained, then this is to be considered as an approximation to nobility and an increase in goodness. For he covets something whereby he will come nearer to the influence of That which is the First Source of influence [*al-mu'aṯṯir al-awwal*] and the Pure Object of love [*al-maʿshūq al-maḥż*], and more similar to the exalted and noble beings. [...] For this reason one will never find the wise—those who belong to the refined [*al-ẓurafā*] and learned [*al-ḥukamā*] [...]—to be free from having their hearts occupied with a beautiful human form. Therefore, if a man acquires over and above those perfections which humans have in addition, the excellence of a harmonious form,—which derives from the integrity and harmony of nature and from the manifestation [*ẓuhūr*] of a divine trace [*aṯar ilāhī*]—, then that man has the strongest claim to receive the very kernel of the fruit of the heart and the very essence of the purest kind of love. Therefore the Prophet says: *Seek what you need from those with beautiful faces*, the plain meaning of which is that beauty of form is to be found only where there is a good natural composition, and

46 See supra, note 39.

47 Mehren 1894, 14–15; Fackenheim 1945, 220. See Avicenna's caveat on the psychological foundation informing the ethical judgment on one's attraction to physical beauty: "This disposition is either specific to the animal faculty alone, or it results from a partnership [of the rational and animal faculties]. But if it is specific to the animal faculty alone, the sages do not consider it as a sign of refinement and nobility. For, it is an incontrovertible truth that when a man expresses animal desires in an animal-like fashion, he becomes involved in vice and is harmed in his rational soul." Mehren 1894, 15; Fackenheim 1945, 220–21.

> that this good harmony and composition serve to improve the internal disposition and to sweeten the character....
>
> As for embracing and kissing, the purpose in them is to come near to one another and to become united. The soul of the lover desires to reach the object of his love with his senses of touch and sight, and thus he delights in embracing it. And he longs to have the very essence of his soul-faculty, his heart mingles with that of the object of his love, and thus he desires to kiss it. These actions, then, are not in themselves blameworthy. However, feelings and actions of excessive lust happen to follow them frequently, and this makes it necessary that one should be on guard against them, except if the complete absence of physical appetite and immunity even from suspicion is beyond doubt. [...] Whoever is filled with this type of love is a man of nobility and refinement, and this type of love is an ornament and a source of inner wealth.[48]

Avicenna's analytical approach to the role of the senses and of the intellect to the contemplation of beauty directly involves the problem of desire from its twofold perspective of an appetite oriented toward human forms as either the "manifestation of a divine trace" or objects of a base instinct at the mercy of the blind inclinations of the carnal soul. We may revisit our previous considerations on Saʿdi's representations of desire as either pornographic reificatations of the body (in the case of obscene poetry) or spiritual fetishizations (in the case of the ghazals expressing sacred eroticism) in light of Avicenna's approach to the twofold nature of attraction toward beauty. In his works, Saʿdi stages not only the two poles (the carnal/obscene and the spiritual/intellectual) of Avicenna's complex representation of the soul/intellect's desire for beautiful forms, but also the entire gamut of intermediate possibilities, in which sensuality and spirituality act as two contrasting forces that shape in multiple ways the desires and the actions of the lyric subject. The spiritual framework stemming from the psychological complexity of the Avicennian approach to the contemplation of beauty, especially as far as the intertwinement of sensual desire and supernal contemplation in Saʿdi's poetry is concerned, finds its pragmatic reflection in al-Ghazālī's polemic against the *soi disant* practitioners of spiritual love, whom he mocks while denouncing the sensual (and pederastic) propensities which they disguise as "courtly gallantry" or "spiritual refinement" (*futuwwa* and *ẓarāfa*, just as in Avicenna's notes):

---

48 Mehren 1894, 15–17; Fackenheim 1945, 221–22.

> Many are the men and women who disguise themselves as Sufis and engage themselves in such activities [i.e., unlawful sexual practices with beautiful people following exposure to amatory poetry], and through paradoxical utterances [*ʿibārat va shīva-yi ṭāmāt*] they try to justify their actions by saying such things: "So and so was enraptured by [spiritual] passion and he stumbled on a branch on the path." They also add: "love is God's trap, and he has been caught in the trap!" Or even say: "It is a great deed for one to keep the heart solid and strive in order to see one's Beloved." They rename pimping "spiritual refinement" [*ẓarīfī*] and good morals, and they think they can elevate corruption and sodomy to "passion" and "longing," while justifying themselves by saying: "so-and-so spiritual master of ours set his eyes on so-and-so youth, and this something that has always occurred on the path of great people, as it is not sodomy, but sacred contemplation of comely youths [*shāhid-bāzī*]. And they may even come up with a further explanation: "This [sensual practice] is the source of spiritual engagement [*rūḥ-bāzī*]." And they put together foolish utterances of this kind, so that they cover their turpitude with such nonsensical words.[49]

Considering the influence of both al-Ghazāli's insight on the social facets of contemplating beauty and the aesthetics of Avicennian theo-eroticism that pervade certain aspects of the ghazal tradition, Saʿdi's perception of love and *maʿrifa*—far from corresponding to a mystical ideal of divine epiphany—reveals the sedimentation of multiple (often contrasting or overlapping) sensorial and intellectual experiences: from direct perception to the recollection of a past encounter, from the idealization of a physical desire to be fulfilled in an undetermined future to the recognition of a carnal breakthrough opening onto the manifestation of a metaphysical level.

What all these experiences have in common is the interplay between the representation of a solid sensorial grip on material reality and the mental drift toward oneiric and liminal spaces: dreams, visions, and the psychotic states that medieval physicians would associate with melancholia and near-death conditions. Glimpses of this complex oscillation are clearly seen in al-Ghazālī's

---

49 *Kimiyā*, 1: 486. Cf. Saʿdi's playful critique of the Sufis of his age: "One of the spiritual masters of Syria was once asked about the truth concerning Sufism. He responded that in the past, these people were scattered in the world and looked troubled externally while internally composed. Today they seem composed on the outside, and internally troubled." *Golestān*, 96–97. A similar argument is found in al-Ghazālī's legal ruling on the "endowed wealth" of the Sufi convents (*Amvāl-i khānqāh*): Purjavādi 1381/2002, 90. See also Griffel 2009a, 49–50.

phenomenology of spiritual cognition, and the language that he offers fully resonates with the system of values shared by Saʿdi with respect to the quest for the invisible through mundane practices and the discipline of the self. But it is only through the Avicennian empirical approach to the psycho-physiological nature of perception and cognition that the full extent of the aesthetic potential of al-Ghazālī's epistemology comes to light in Saʿdi's ghazals.[50]

What follows is an analysis of the Avicennian foundations of this psychology of the aesthetic experience and its implied sacred eroticism, which, filtered through al-Ghazālī's spiritual epistemology, shines throughout Saʿdi's depictions of the lyric subject's intellection of sensible reality and imaginary worlds. The Avicennian oscillation between the sensory and intellectual processing of the physical and intelligible worlds is the system that best explains not only al-Ghazālī's spiritual cardiology, but also the psychology of the aesthetics that Saʿdi represents in his lyric poetry.

4 Avicennian Psychology, or the Science of the Soul

The epistemological aspect of Avicenna's psychology constitutes an original amalgam of Galenic, Neoplatonic, and Aristotelian notions that influenced Islamicate as well as Latin Christian theories of mind throughout the Middle Ages.[51] As pointed out earlier, notwithstanding the criticism that Avicenna's

50 "As has become increasingly clear, al-Ghazālī's importance in Islamic intellectual history rests at least as much on the role he played in integrating core elements of Avicenna's metaphysics and psychology into Sunni theology and prophetology as well as into Sufi spirituality, as in appropriating the basic framework of Avicenna's syllogistic into Sunni jurisprudence." Wisnovsky 2013, 206. To date, the two major monographs on the philosophical influence on al-Ghazālī's works are Frank Griffel's *Al-Ghazālī's Philosophical Theology* (Griffel 2009a) and Alexander Treiger's *Inspired Knowledge in Islamic Thought: Al-Ghazālī's Theory of Mystical Cognition and Its Avicennian Foundation* (Treiger 2012). See also Abrahamov 1991; Janssens 2003. On the conflation of Avicennian psychology and Ashʿarite theology in al-Ghazālī, see Griffel 2004, especially 131–33, where the author discusses the passages in which al-Ghazālī quotes almost consistently verbatim from Avicenna's treatise on the soul. For a reappraisal of al-Ghazālī's criticism of Avicenna's psychology, see ibid., 131, n. 104; Gianotti 2001, 95–103.

51 Psychology has been defined as the "spine" of Avicenna's philosophical system, acting as a main axis that holds all the other branches of knowledge together: "Psychological theory extends from noetics down to faculty psychology and to physiological psychology; it connects smoothly with cosmology at one end and physiology at the other. It connects also with astronomy and with a celestial thaumaturgy at the cosmological end; with epistemology and methodology; with anthropology, in the original sense of the theory of the person; with political theory; with dynamics; with chemistry; and with anatomy

works received, the cosmological and psychological models that he defined and systematized soon became the main point of reference for Islamic intellectuals thinking through the connection between the human soul, the senses, and the relationship between man and cosmos. We should regard al-Ghazālī, in this case too, and in spite of widespread prejudice, as the critical popularizer of Avicenna's thought, if not the "Trojan horse" that contributed to the propagation of Avicennism well beyond the strict boundaries of philosophical speculations.[52]

One of the most prominent characteristics of Avicenna's psychology is the stark dualistic conception on which his representation of the relationship between the body and the soul is based. What human beings have in common with other animals is a complex system of external and internal senses and two "bodily" souls, the vegetative and the animal, which allow all animals—including man—to inhabit the material world, flourish, and procreate.[53] What distinguishes man from other animals is what Avicenna calls the Intellect, or rational soul: a created, non-physical, and immortal substance that is not located in the body but is accidentally connected with it (just as divine love, in Aḥmad Ghazālī's passage, as we may recall, accidentally attaches itself to random focal points).[54] In spite of such a radical distinction between the material dimension of the body and the immateriality of the soul, Avicenna conceives of intellectual cognition as a series of intricate interactions between the raw external material provided by the senses and the process of gradual abstraction operated by the rational soul with the aid of what he calls the "Active Intellect" (*al-ʿaql al-faʿʿāl*)—a cosmological entity that generated the material

---

and zoology and botany at the physiological end. Helping to structure and support a very large part of Ibn Sina's philosophy and science, psychological theory is really the spine of the system. Moreover, Ibn Sina seems to find the congruence of other parts of his thought with psychological theory to be a prime means of testing them." Hall 2004, 63. For a useful chart of the tripartite division of the soul and its multiple faculties, see Skellie 2010 [1938], xvii.

52 "[...] al-Ghazālī was, in fact, one of the greatest popularizers of philosophy in medieval Islam, indeed a kind of 'Trojan horse,' which brought Avicenna's philosophy into the heart of Islamic thought." Treiger 2012, 104.

53 As mentioned earlier, a valid terrain for testing the circulation of Avicenna's tripartite representation of the soul in the spiritual circles of 13th-century Transoxiana, Khorasan, and western Iran is ʿAzīz al-Dīn Nasafī's exposition of the ontogeny of the rational soul. ʿAziz al-Din Nasafi, 1341/1962, 21. A similar exposition is found in Rūzbihān's *Risālat al-Quds*, in which the Shirazi spiritual master illustrates the complexities of the human intellect across all the stages that Avicenna describes. Ruzbehān Baqli 1351/1972, 75.

54 See McGinnis 2010, 89–96. See also Rahman's introduction to Avicenna's *Kitāb al-najāt*, Rahman 1952, 2–20, and 24–25.

world and "illuminates" the rational soul for the latter to obtain cognition of the "intelligibles."[55]

One important subdivision that Avicenna envisages for the human intellect with respect to his dualistic body/soul conception rests on the difference that he traces between the theoretical and the practical intellect as two aspects that execute distinct intellectual operations. While the practical intellect (*al-ʿaql al-ʿamalī*) turns toward the body in order to manage the function of the external and internal senses and to process the preliminary abstraction of the particulars, its theoretical counterpart (*al-ʿaql al-naẓarī*) turns towards the "high," as it seeks the intercession of the divine effluence (*fayż*) to visualize the intelligibles that are eternally thought by the Active Intellect.[56]

55 "The Active Intellect (*nous poietikos; al-ʿaql al-faʿʿāl*), that complex idea of the intellect that produces the actual intelligibles (the objects of what we call conceptual thinking), was first presented by Aristotle [...] *De Anima*, III 5. It became, arguably, the most discussed topic in the Aristotelian corpus, and several roles were variously assigned to it over the centuries through the excogitation of Aristotle. According to Ibn Sina, the Active Intellect emanates the human soul, which is essentially the rational soul, to the fetus that becomes its particular body. There it emanates its own suprational (animal, vegetative) faculties. The Active Intellect is responsible thereafter for human intellection-in-act. Ibn Sina considers the human soul an individual substance, and thus it can survive the death of the body. [...] The rational faculty—the human intellect—remains, embedded in an incorporeal and eternal individual substrate, an 'ego,' the ultimate substrate of personal experience. Ibn Sina is a pioneer in arguing for such a substrate, and his basic idea regarding the afterlife is that the intelligibles of the Active Intellect will forever be present to the soul." Hall 2004, 65. See also McGinnis 2010, 95. On the role of the theoretical and the practical intellects in the process of cognition, see ibid., 118–26, and 210–26 respectively. Cf. McGinnis 2007. For an accurate analysis of Avicenna's influence on al-Ghazālī's psychology, see Kukkonen 2012. Cf. Alexander Treiger's intuition (2012, 105) on al-Ghazālī's creative appropriation of the concept of the "Active Intellect." On the cosmological connection between the human soul and the supernal realm, see the Avicennian heritage that imbues ʿAzīz al-Dīn Nasafī's (1391/2012, 127) chapter on the intellect in his *Kashf al-ḥaqāyiq*.

56 See Heath 1992, 63–65; Davidson 1992, 74–102; Sebti 2003; McGinnis 2010, 118–23. Al-Ghazālī fully accepts this division, as he clearly illustrates it in his *Precipitance of the Philosophers* (see Treiger's argument—2012, 108–15—for his criticism of the traditional translation of *tahāfut* as "incoherence"): "Hence the soul has two faculties in relation to two sides: the theoretical faculty in relation to the side of the angels, since through it [the soul] takes from the angels the true sciences—and this faculty ought to be constantly open to reception from the side above; and the practical faculty, which belongs to [the soul] in relation to what is below—namely, the direction of the body to its management and the rectification of moral dispositions. This is a faculty that ought to take control over all the rest of the bodily faculties, whereby the rest of the faculties would be disciplined by its educative action [and be] vanquished by it, so that it is not influenced by [the bodily faculties], but, rather, that these faculties [themselves] are influenced by it." Al-Ghazāli 2000, 181 (translated by Michael Marmura).

As the intelligibles comprise abstract concepts such as universals, axioms, and any sort of "immaterial" truth, they are stored in the celestial world and, in particular, in the "active intellect," which through its contact with the human rational soul offers man the faculty of thinking.[57] I have pointed out earlier that the intellectual operations of the rational soul with respect to the process of abstraction of the particulars of the physical world constitute the foundation of Avicenna's epistemology. The two incorporeal elements required in order for this process of abstraction and cognition to take place are the theoretical aspect of the human rational soul and the Active Intellect, which is an "intelligence" that brings a cosmological dimension to the mechanism of human intellection.

Avicenna's cosmological system—inherited from the conflation of Ptolemaic cosmology with Neoplatonic emanationism—posits that the universe is organized as a hierarchy of intelligences that determine the movement of their respective celestial bodies. All intelligibles are eternally thought by the First Intellect (or First Mover), which passes this celestial cogitation onto the intellects of the subsequent spheres. The tenth and last emanation, referred to as the Active Intellect (*al-ʿaql al-faʿʿāl*), is the intellect of the sublunar world, i.e., the world of matter and forms as man perceives them through the senses.[58] As the Active Intellect is the depository of all universals, it is by means of its interaction with the human rational soul that man can produce rational thought through syllogistic thinking. The consequence of this system is that the syllogistic model describes not only all forms of intellectual knowledge but also the teleological structure of reality.[59]

57 As I shall elucidate later, the possibility of perceiving either the intelligibles or the particulars is determined by the ontological difference between souls and intellects. On determinism and intellection in Avicenna, see Marmura 1985, 86–92.

58 See McGinnis 2010, 178–207. See also Nasr 1993, 177–281. For a study of the Islamic reception of Avicenna's noetics, including al-Ghazālī's complex fascination with the subject, see Davidson 1992, 127–72. On the overall development of astronomy after Avicenna, see Morrison 2009. See also Griffel's (2009b) in-depth analysis of al-Ghazālī's reformulation of Avicenna's cosmology in *Mishkāt al-anwār*.

59 "All understanding that involves syllogistic thinking [...] must include the middle terms which explain a statement. Avicenna repeatedly states in numerous contexts that the intelligibles are thought of and understood by, or 'imprinted' on the human intellect, 'in an order which includes the middle terms.' Now the intelligibles which the human intellect thinks are contained essentially in the intellects of the celestial spheres and in the active intellect [...], and by definition represent the way things are, ontological truth. And since, following the syllogistic process, the human intellect thinks of the intelligibles contained in the active intellect in an order which includes the middle terms and this in accordance with the order of the terms of propositions in a chain of mutually dependent syllogisms, not only do the contents of this knowledge correspond, one-to-one, to

As preliminarily mentioned in the previous chapter, the meditation on the beauty of the mundane forms that al-Ghazālī presents as the first step towards *maʿrifa* is a cognitive process that originates in Avicenna's epistemological approach to the intellectual knowledge of the universals through the sensorial perception of and assiduous meditation on the particulars. In the context of Saʿdi's lyric, this process implies that the attestation to the existence of God as the source of all beauty through the contemplation of the human beloved's body derives from a syllogistic acquisition of knowledge that links the beauty of the particular with the splendor of the One—which is accessible to the senses only through His signs.

From the perspective of the Avicennian epistemological system, what the *ʿārif* of Saʿdi's lines accomplishes by beholding the divine creation upon the face of the beautiful ones[60] is an inferential operation that belongs to the realm of the intellectual experiences rather than to an ineffable horizon of mystical insight: God is the source of all beauty, this body is beautiful, this body's beauty derives from God. Therefore, the meditative approach (*fikra*, or *tafakkur*) to the contemplation of the world that al-Ghazālī posits as a preliminary empirical approximation to spiritual cognition derives from Avicenna's theorization of a voluntary effort of intellection that syllogistically guides the individual towards the acquisition of the middle term (*al-ḥadd al-awsaṭ*).[61] Avicenna defines this meditative cogitation as "a certain motion of the rational soul through the notions [*maʿānī*], conducted usually with the aid of the imagination, whereby the middle term, or what fulfills its function, is sought."[62] This means that—if one follows the philosophical genealogy of the spiritual thought that pervades the aesthetics of Saʿdi's lyricism—even in the moments in which Saʿdi overtly highlights the direct connection between the beloved and the divine, he does so by strictly abiding by the rules of rational cognition:

> If I could only imagine joining your presence
> Nothing would prevent me from throwing my body at your feet.
>
> My cogitations [*fikrat-i man*] do not concern you, but the pen
> Of the power that can create such forms!
>
> *Badāyiʿ* 628[63]

---

ontological reality, but the progression of this knowledge also must correspond to the structure of reality, which is accordingly syllogistic." Gutas 2014a, 371–72.

60 See chapter 5, pp. 255–77.

61 Gutas 2014a, 8–10.

62 Treiger 2012, 148, n. 66

63 [2.55] Saʿdi YE, 280.

Nevertheless, al-Ghazālī's adaptation of Avicennian syllogistic thinking to the spiritual life of the believer constitutes the necessary transition between, on the one hand, the purely philosophical origins of the intellectual aspect of the contemplation of the world and, on the other, the aesthetic articulation of the relationship between the world itself and the internal and external senses of Saʿdi's lyric subject. The contemplative path that Al-Ghazālī describes as a spiritual practice whose instrument of "meditation" produces the light of spiritual cognition (*maʿrifa*) constitutes the practical substratum of the syllogistic cognition of the beloved as a sign of the divine, preparing the spiritual groundwork for the Persian lyric tradition of the Saljuq period to gradually absorb the Avicennian psychological innovations.[64]

5 The Internal Senses and the Cognitive Foundations of the Lyric Subject

In order to investigate the cognitive sphere of Saʿdi's lyric subject, we ought to focus on the mechanisms through which man, according to the Avicennian tradition, perceives, handles, and stores in the brain the "particulars," i.e., the singular or composite objects of the physical world as they appear to the senses and through which the rational soul, with the aid of the Active Intellect, cognizes the "universals."[65] The full understanding of the epistemological, cosmological, and spiritual aspects of cognition that the interaction between the rational soul and the Active Intellect entails requires an in-depth analysis of the physiological aspects of Avicenna's theory of perception and cogitation. It is noteworthy that the sensory aspect of the Avicennian cognitive model did not provoke al-Ghazālī's criticism. On the contrary, the Iranian religious scholar fully embraced this scientific paradigm in his chief works, by either quoting Avicenna's text verbatim (as an Arabic translation of the Persian text of the *Dānish-nāma*), or reworking and readapting its main tenets according

64 It is worth mentioning that in his *Risāla-yi ʿaql va ʿishq*, Saʿdi defends the function of the intellect as a necessary "lamp" (*charāgh*) for the acquisition of spiritual knowledge, which reads as a paraphrase of al-Ghazālī's metaphor. See Chapter 7.

65 "The causal elements in the essences of concrete particulars furnish the content of the universal predicables conceptualized in the mind. It is precisely because one has discovered, for example, that animal body and rationality are the matter and form respectively of the essence of concrete particular humans that the essence of human conceptualized in the mind in terms of the genus 'animal' and the difference 'rationality' provides the scientific definition of 'human' as 'rational animal.'" McGinnis 2010, 43. On the external senses, with a particular emphasis on Avicenna's optics and his rebuttal of the extramissive theory, see ibid., 100–111.

to the variety of audiences he would address.[66] In *The Precipitance of the Philosophers*, after describing in great detail the functions of the external and internal senses and their relationship with the human cogitative faculties, he concedes that "there is nothing in what [the philosophers] have mentioned that must be denied in terms of the religious law […], for these are observed matters which God has ordained to flow according to habit."[67]

By the 12th century, the Avicennian psychological model was so widespread that even a generic encyclopedic compendium like Niẓāmī ʿArūżī's famed *Chahār maqāla* (*The Four Discourses*, whose pragmatic approach to poetry, medicine, astronomy, and statesmanship was informed by empirical sciences rather than rhetorical or belletristic corpora) could describe the physiology of the internal senses with remarkable accuracy.[68] By the 13th century, the theory of the internal senses, as well as their role in the processes of imagination and cogitation as mediators between the visible world and the supernal realm of the celestial intellects, was an integral part of the canonical epistemological models of the time. For instance, Fakhr al-Dīn Rāzī not only accepted and further illustrated Avicenna's models of perception and imagination in his scholastic commentary on the *Ishārāt*, but he also adopted the theory of the inner senses and their mirror-like connection with the celestial world in his pedagogical encyclopedia *Jāmiʿ al-ʿulūm* (*The Compendium of the Sciences*, composed between 1174 and 1185).[69] Naṣīr al-Dīn Ṭūsī too, apart from his encomiastic commentary on the *Ishārāt*, added notions of Avicennian psychology (mainly the tripartite structure of the soul and the functions of the internal senses) to his rewriting/translation of Miskawayh's 11th-century *Tahẕīb al-akhlāq* (*Refinement of Character*), known as *Akhlāq-i nāṣirī* (Nasirean Ethics, completed in 1235).[70]

---

66 Jules Janssens (1986) has convincingly demonstrated that al-Ghazālī's *Maqāṣid al-falāsifa* is a close paraphrase of Avicenna's *Dānish-nāma*. While in this text the treatment of the internal senses reads as a faithful transposition of Avicenna's original compendium, al-Ghazālī's later works, especially the *Iḥyāʾ* and the *Kīmiyā*, partially redefine Avicenna's vocabulary without changing the substance of his psychological paradigm. See Janssens 2003, 40–49. See also Skellie 2010 [1938], xxiii–xxvii; Kukkonen 2012, 545–55.

67 Al-Ghazāli 2000, 181.

68 See Nezāmi ʿAruzi 1336/1957, 13.

69 Rāzi 1382/2003, 261–64. Unlike his commentary to the *Ishārāt* in Arabic, the *Jāmiʿ* was composed in Persian, and its passages explaining the true nature of dreams through the contact between the human soul and the invisible world of the celestial spheres closely follow the wording of the same passages in Avicenna's Persian treatise *Dānish-nāma* (*The Book of Science*). Ibn Sinā 1353/1974.

70 See Nasir al-Din Tusi 1256/1977, 56–58. It is remarkable that, even though Miskawayh's psychology in the *Refinement of Character* is clearly pre-Avicennian, especially from the

The systematization of the notion of the internal senses (*al-ḥawāss al-bāṭina*) constitutes the radical innovation that Avicenna brought about in the field of animal and human cognition. This notion consists of a "hierarchy of five faculties which do not immediately perceive the external world, but instead apprehend *sensibles*, forms abstracted from material entities perceived by the five external senses."[71] The internal senses are physically located in the front, middle, and back ventricles of the brain, adjacent to each other as pairs that fulfill receptive and retentive functions respectively.[72]

The first faculty is the "common sense" (*al-ḥiss al-mushtarak*), which collects and coordinates the sensations received by the five external senses. It is important to note that, according to Avicenna, it is in the common sense that vision physically takes place, and not in the eyes: the sensible perception of an object (*mushāhada*) is a mental experience whose "idealistic" nature implies that direct optical perception and mental vision (deriving from creative imagination, dreams, or visions from the supernal realm) do not essentially differ

---

point of view of his treatment of the imagination as a monolithic faculty rather than a retentive/compositive dyadic system (see, for instance, Miskawayh 1966, 4–6, 9–10, 55–56, 88, and 175; cf. Zurayk's translation of the same passages, Miskawayh 2002 [1968], 6–7, 9–10, 50–51, 79, and 157), Naṣīr al-Dīn works the description of the Avicennian internal senses into his translation. Even though the illuminationist model of Shahāb al-Dīn Suhrawardī (d. 1191) put the spiritual and epistemological role of vision at the center of the philosophical arena of his time, his reduction of Avicenna's five internal senses to one single faculty of representation (working in tandem with the light-soul, "Isfahbad-light" for the retrieval of the universals) does not match the inner, often physiological, complexity that exudes from Sa'di's lyrical descriptions of the experiences of imagination and cognition. On Suhrawardī's post-Avicennian psychology, see Marcotte 2007. See also Walbridge 1992, 105.

71 Heath 1992, 61. Cf. the description of the five internal senses in ʿAzīz al-Dīn Nasafī's *Kashf al-ḥaqāyiq*, in which we can clearly witness his effort to introduce the Avicennian theories of perception and cognition to the Sufi circles of his time. ʿAziz al-Din Nasafi 1391/2012, 131–32.

72 "One of the chief innovations in medieval adaptations of Aristotelian psychology was the expansion of Aristotle's notion of imagination or *phantasia* to include a variety of distinct perceptual powers known collectively as the internal senses (*hawâss bâtinah*)." Black 1993, 219. For a concise description of the internal senses, see Heath 1992, 62–63. See also McGinnis 2010, 113–16; Gonzàlez-Ginocchio 2013. The first seminal work on this subject is Harry Wolfson's "The Internal Senses in Latin, Arabic and Hebrew Philosophic Texts." See Wolfson 1935, in particular 93–97, in which Wolfson clearly illustrates the historical genealogy of Avicenna's theory of the internal senses, originally based on the Ikhwān al-Ṣafā's and al-Fārābī's integration of Aristotelian intuitions and Galenic physiological observations. It is noteworthy that Avicenna's theory of perception was based on the advance in neurology that took place in his time. On this topic, see Hall 2004; Pormann 2013. On the Galenic influences on Avicenna's theory of the internal senses, see also Strohmaier 1988. For a chart of the brain as a locus of the internal senses, see Elamrani-Jamal 1984, 130.

from each other.[73] This explains why, in some ghazals, Saʿdi scrutinizes the imaginal apparition of the beloved and compares it with the memory or the direct witnessing of a real, physical encounter:

> How blessed is the morning when the glances set on the beauty of the beloved:
> Eating the fruit from tree-like hope of embracing the beloved.
>
> My fortune was not asleep when in the morning from sleep
> I awoke under the auspicious star of the constellation of the beloved.

73 "[for Avicenna] la vision inspirée est un phénomène mental, une saisie opérée par la puissance interne qu'est la fantaisie. [...] Avicenne voit dans la perception (*mushāhada*) sensible d'un objet par le sens commun l'unique espèce de sensation qui soit. Ce n'est pas parce que la vision intérieure est mentale que son coefficient de sensibilité serait appauvri : il n'y a de sensation que mentale. [...] Tel est l'idéalisme mental de la sensation." Michot 1986, 156–57. See also Meryem Sebti's notes on the ontological status of mental images in Avicenna's psychology: "Toute forme sentie est conduite au sens commun; c'est là seulement qu'elle est perçue, non selon la modalité selon laquelle elle affecte le sens particulier, mais selon la modalité selon laquelle l'appréhende le sens commun. La forme que se représente le sens commun est donc *une image qu'il constitue et qui ne se trouve pas dans la réalité sensible*. Cette première saisie du sensible est donc une première représentation par l'âme du monde extérieur." Sebti 2005, 115. Cf. McGinnis's rhetorical question with respect to the difference between extra-mental and mental objects in Avicenna's psychology: "For if what is immediately known to us is only mental objects, what justification is there that extra-mental objects correspond with our mental objects, or even more strongly, what justifies that there is anything except the mental?" McGinnis 2010, 261, n. 7. Avicenna's virtual response, McGinnis argues, is that what really matters to the Iranian philosopher is not whether knowledge of the external world is theoretically possible, but the process through which we acquire such knowledge. This problem ultimately relates to the relationship between the particulars as they exist in the extra-mental reality and the process of abstraction by which mental reality is formed through the contact between the senses and the active intellect: "For Avicenna essences exist in either one of two ways: they may exist in concrete particulars, that is to say, extramentally, or they may exist in conceptualization, that is to say, mentally. Although essences always and only exist according to one of these two modes of existence, both modes have something in common, namely, the essence considered in itself, which bridges the gap between the extra-mental and the mental. So, for example, the essence of animal may exist as instantiated in concrete particulars or it may exist as an intelligible in the mind, and yet, despite the difference between these two ways that animal might exist, both modes of existence have in common the essence of animal considered in itself. It is this commonality that guarantees that in salient ways the objects of the intellect map onto things in the world. Logic as a tool used in the sciences is for Avicenna concerned primarily with those accidental features that accrue to essences considered inasmuch as they are conceptualized." Ibid., 35.

Quit my heart, O pain inflicted by the world and the hereafter!
No dreams can reside in the house if it is the abode of the beloved....

He made his appearance, then he left: so bewildered am I that I still
do not know whether in my gaze it was the beloved or his mental image
[*khayāl*].

Senseless I remained, the intellect left me, and my eloquence shut down:
Blessed is the one who vanishes before the beloved's perfection!

There are no veils, Saʿdi, but keep your mirror pure:
How can a rusty surface reflect the beauty of the beloved?
Badāyiʿ 475[74]

The very empirical evidence of experiencing direct visual perception, dreams, and visions—as if they were to belong to the same degree of reality that takes shape in the common sense—generates the bewilderment that Saʿdi expresses. In this ghazal, it is the common sense that acts as a screen in which both the initial "real" presence (or perceived as such) of the beloved and the subsequent apparition as a mental image are equally ontologically valid; hence the confusion of the lyric subject with respect to the level of reality to which the encounter—the embrace (*viṣāl*)—pertains.

As I will elucidate in the next chapter, it is probably the vacillation between the material and the mental perception of the object of desire that, in Saʿdi's poetry, generates a dramatic emphasis on the role of the eyes as a peripheral organ from which the lyric subject desperately seeks the traces of a tangible presence:

You left, but you still linger in my imagination:
It seems that before my eyes you are being depicted!

My cogitations cannot reach the apogee of your beauty
As you are more beautiful than anything my imagination ever conjured.

The moon never walked on earth, no eyes ever apprehended a fairy:
How can I think of you as a fairy, of your face as a moon?

---

74 [2.56] Saʿdi YE, 218. On the basis of the textual discrepancies signaled by Yusofi, I have chosen to include the variants included by Foroughi in his edition. See Saʿdi YE, 555–56.

You are an angel indeed, for not from this clay were you conceived.
Humans are made of water and earth: you from pure musk and
ambergris! ...

Too much weeping for you may ruin my eyes, but who cares?
More precious you are than the eyes with which from my head I see!

Sa'di, as your hands cannot reach the encounter with the beloved,
For once you shall dedicate your time to remembering him.
Badāyi' 329[75]

In spite of the lack of strictly philosophical technical vocabulary, key words such as *khayāl* ("imagination"), *muṣavvar* ("imagined," "depicted"), *fikr* ("cogitation"), *bā dīda bar dāshtan* ("to visually apprehend"), and *ẓann* ("thinking") contextualize the ghazal within a semantic sphere that directly relates to the Avicennian theory of perception and imagination. The reference to the blurred difference between the extra-mental presence of the beloved and his imaginal simulacrum—along with the emphasis on the distinction between the physical eye end the eye of mental vision—relates to the peculiar ontology of mental sensations that we have discussed above. As an elaboration on the function of the common sense, this ghazal illustrates the role of the imagination as a two-fold faculty (retentive and compositive, discussed below) that provides the beholder with mental images whose ontological status does not differ from the perceptions acquired through the external senses.[76]

75 [2.57] Sa'di YE, 153–54.

76 See Avicenna's illustration of this principle in the fourth chapter of the section on psychology in the *Shifā'*: "[The mental form that the imagination projects onto the common sense] appears as if it were existent externally, because the impression perceived from what comes from outside, and what comes from inside, is that which is represented in it, and they are only distinguished by relation. And when the thing sensed exists in reality as it is represented, then its state which is represented is like the state of what has returned from outside. And for this reason, what the madman, and the fearful man, and the weak man, and the sleeping man, see as existent representations are like what is seen in the state of health in reality. And likewise he will hear sounds. So when the discriminative faculty or the intellect perceives any of these things, it wins the imaginative faculty over to itself by admonishing it/alerting it, and so these forms and images will disappear." Rahman 1959, 172–73. Translation by Deborah Black (2009, 3). Cf. Meryem Sebti's comment on this passage: "Cette thèse a une implication importante: la représentation et la sensation requièrent un processus identique qui ne diffère que par le chemin suivi par l'image qui s'imprime dans le sens commun. Ainsi, une image forgée par l'imagination composante à partir des formes et des intentions conservées dans les deux mémoires dont dispose l'homme—dès lors qu'elle est imprimée dans le sens commun—a le même

In the first line, "imagination" (*khayāl*), which Avicenna also calls the "form-bearing" (*al-muṣawwira*) faculty, is the internal sense that enables the lyric subject to store the perception of the beloved as a mental image that is accessible to the intellect independently from the external senses. This "retentive" imaginative faculty is the second of the internal senses theorized by Avicenna, and is located in the back of the front ventricle of the brain. It acts as a sort of storage unit that contains all the forms that the individual collects through sensorial or intellectual experience, via the common sense or the practical intellect respectively.[77]

The imagination should not be confused with what Avicenna terms *takhayyul*, "imaginative faculty" or "compositive imagination," located in the *cerebellar vermis* (*dūda*, in Arabic, the "silk worm"), and which presides over the act of combining and separating parts of sensible objects with other parts. It is the faculty that allows the formation of dreams and visions, and which shapes images that do not correspond to objects that exist in the world of the external senses.[78] One interesting characteristic of the imaginative faculty, on which

statut épistémologique qu'une image forgée par le sens commun à partir des données sensibles reçues des cinq sens; seul diffère le chemin suivi. Dans le cas de la sensation, l'origine de l'image est à l'extérieur et dans le cas de la représentation, la source est une ou plusieurs images conservées dans l'imagination rétentive et dans la puissance remémorative." Sebti 2005, 117–18.

77 As observed in the previous chapter, in the *Kīmiyā-yi sa'ādat* al-Ghazālī often represents the human body as microcosm of the entirety of creation. In one of the most interesting passages in which such parallels are traced, he states that the retentive imagination (lit. "the depository of the imagery," *khazāna-yi khayālāt*) corresponds, on a macro-cosmic level, to the "preserved tablet" (*lawḥ-i maḥfūẓ*), which, as we shall explore extensively in the next chapter, is the scriptural analogue of the Avicennian concept of the soul of the fixed stars. *Kimiyā*, 1: 55.

78 "We know with certainty that it is natural for us to combine and separate parts of sensible objects with other parts, not according to the form that we found in them externally nor even affirming that some of them exist or do not. Thus, in us there must be some faculty by which we do that. This [faculty], when the intellect is using it, is called the 'cogitative [faculty],' while when the animal faculty is using it, it is called the 'compositive imagination.'" Rahman 1959, 165–166. Translated by McGinnis (2010, 115–15). See also the passage, likewise translated by McGinnis, in which Avicenna clearly illustrates the physiology of the *dūda*, which also introduces the third faculty ("estimation"), to be discussed below: "[The estimative faculty] opens up the *cerebellar vermis* (*dūda*) by removing what is between the two porous appendages (which [...] are the *cerebellar vermis*) and [the form that is in the retentive imagination] conjoins with the *pneuma* harboring the estimative faculty by means of the *pneuma* harboring the faculty of the compositive imagination (which in humans is called the cogitative [faculty]). The form that is in the retentive imagination is then imprinted onto the *pneuma* of the estimative faculty, and the faculty of the compositive imagination, which serves the estimative faculty, conveys what is in the retentive imagination to it." Ibid., 110. Original text in Rahman 1959, 153. The

Avicenna often dwells at length, is its pre-intellective status. This derives from the physiological nature of the imaginative faculty's activity of manipulating the images provided by other faculties, which causes it to operate heedlessly in a constant and unbridled activity of combining and dividing images, especially when the rational soul loosens its control over it.[79] One ought to stress that this very fleeting nature of the imaginative faculty determines both the degree of veracity and the level of purity of the solicitations coming from the supernal world during sleep, and its close association with the animal soul often compromises the rational soul's power of intellection. It is worth highlighting that the imaginative faculty is also the bodily core of all artistic activities of the soul and the main "translator" into images of all inspirations, intimations, metaphysical visions, and reveries dictated by all sorts of altered conditions of the individual's body. The internal sense that Avicenna introduces as a regulator of the ceaseless, often subconscious, and potentially haphazard activity of the compositive imagination is called the "estimative" faculty (*wahm*). Avicenna places it in the back of the median ventricle of the brain. It is a retentive faculty in the sense that just as imagination collects the forms (*ṣuwar*) provided by the common sense, the estimative faculty receives and retains the non-sensible, pre-intellectualized "concepts," "ideas," or "meanings" (*maʿānī*, traditionally translated as "intentions," whereas Hasse renders the term as "connotational attributes")[80] that relate to specific objects of visual perception.[81]

The exact dynamics of estimation in Avicenna's psychological system are still an object of debate, but it is worth emphasizing that this faculty represents the highest level that the animal soul can reach, as it plays a vital epistemological role in areas such as "the perception of affective qualities; incidental perception; the creation of fictional ideas; the formation of materialist propositions; the process of mathematical abstraction; apperception; and the formation of ethical beliefs."[82] As Deborah Black proposes, it was probably the radical dualist paradigm based on the opposition of soul/intellect vs. body that informed Avicenna's theorization of the estimative faculty as a bridge between sensible and intellectual cognition. By reason of its grip on the physiological

English translations of the terms "retentive imagination" and "compositive imagination" to translate *khayāl* and *takhayyul* were first introduced by Harry Wolfson (1935).

79 Black 1993, 227–28.

80 Hasse 2000, 132.

81 For a general introduction to the role of *wahm* in Avicenna's psychology, see McGinnis 2010, 110–15. See also Black 1993; Hasse 2000, 127–53 (in which an in-depth analysis of the estimative faculty is followed by a discussion of the influence of this concept in the Latin sources); Hall 2004, 67–69; 2006; Kaukua 2007, 36–69.

82 Black 1993, 244.

functions that support perception and imagination, the estimative faculty subsumes the function of judging the veracity of the images processed by the other internal senses with the risk of extending its "blind" evaluations to nonsensible matters.[83] This is the case of the scenarios in which the estimative faculty processes the intelligibles provided by the intellect as if they were sensible objects. This possibility of error, which is based on the "materialistic" tendencies of estimation, directly concerns the matter discussed in the last chapter à propos of the intellectual recognition of a beautiful object of desire as a sign of God and not as an indwelling of the divine. In several works, Avicenna points out that "since the estimative sense is prone to deny the reality of immaterial beings [...] it is the source for materialist views of God and the afterlife."[84]

I will return later to the implications that this epistemic error entails for the psychological system of the lyric subject in Saʿdi's ghazals, but it is necessary to highlight that this confusion of the immaterial with the material—and, in this case, of the divine with the human as a perceived incarnation—derives from the weakness of the beholder's intellectual faculties and the consequent failure in assisting the rational soul in the recognition of the difference between sensible and intelligible objects of intellection. Therefore, from an Avicennian point of view, we can consider incarnationism (*ḥulūl*) as a logical flaw arising from an intellectual incapability to properly manage the estimative faculty's natural tension toward the sensibles. This is a position that, as explored earlier, was embraced by al-Ghazālī as well, who maintained that whoever's *wahm* is stronger than the intellect may be led "to believe in an anthropomorphic God."[85]

The recognition of the beloved as a sensible form that *signifies* the divine presence as a trace of its Creator can be seen as an intellectual operation that is initially processed by the estimative faculty, then brought to the level of epistemic cognition through the conjunction of the rational soul (mediated by the cogitative dimension of the compositive imagination) with the Active Intellect.[86] Whenever the rational soul is appropriately trained and capable

83 Ibid., 227–28.

84 Ibid., 252–53, n. 58.

85 Griffel 2011, 29. Cf. al-Ghazāli 2000, 23, and 230–31, n. 9. In the *Mishkāt* (Buchman 1988, 18), al-Ghazālī attributes incarnationism to a flaw in the "ruling authority of the intellect." It is clear that what al-Ghazālī refers to is failed control of the intellect over the wrong association between human forms and God that the *wahm* of some individuals happens to establish. See Chapter 4.

86 See, for instance, Avicenna's considerations in *On the Proof of Prophecies* (*Fī iṣbāt al-nubuwwat*): "Indeed, all who have perished have suffered this because they have conformed with the estimative faculty, which is the animal faculty that gives false judgments regarding the abstracted images when the senses are dormant. No wonder, then, that this audacious faculty, calling itself 'the material intellect,' by taking away reason, renders

of managing the internal senses to fulfill its intellectual tasks, it can be argued that it is the estimative faculty that undertakes the preliminary step toward the inferential recognition of the beloved as a "sign" pointing at the divine, by grasping the *maʿnī* of the beloved's sensible form as a non-sensible characteristic of its beauty. At that point, the intellect will be ready to further abstract and inferentially relate *that* particular beauty to its divine source of splendor.

Contrary to what most interpreters would infer, when Saʿdi refers to *maʿnī* (*maʿnā*, or its plural, *maʿānī*) in some of his ghazals, he uses this word not to refer to a generic "spirit" or "soul" of the beloved. In fact, Saʿdi often uses *maʿnī* to refer to the non-sensible concepts that we have been discussing along with the estimative faculty, that is, the *maʿnī al-maḥsūsāt*: "concept or properties that are not essentially material but which nonetheless adhere or attach to sensible forms and can be perceived through them."[87] The following lines clearly show the close relationship that the non-sensible concepts (*maʿānī*) that the lyric subject ascribes to the beloved bear to the sensible dimension of his beauty:

> The vision of you bewilders me, I have no words to describe your *maʿāni*,
> And amazed I am by anyone who has eyes, and yet is not bewildered
> by you.
>
> Would I ever find one single defect in your beautiful form?
> Your seditious, flirtatious gazes are bereft of no magic....
>
> You came from God, O sign of the Merciful upon the people
> And I see shining upon you all the signs of grace that you deserve.
>
> *Badāyiʿ* 438[88]

them to inevitable corruption and future destruction. When thus corrupted with his believed images, such an individual finds that the rational soul, whose activities to some degree correspond to his, is devoid of the noble intellectual forms that actualize it. The soul is then naturally impelled to seek the impending cause in the same way that a stone, raised to its unnatural place and then released, descends seeking its natural place when separated from the impediment. But this happens to the soul when the instruments used to attain the acquired intellect, such as the external and inner senses, estimation, memory, and the faculty of cogitation, have been corrupted. The individual thus remains longing for the soul's natural activity of acquiring the things by which it realizes its essence, at a time when none of the instruments for such an acquisition exists." Marmura 1963, 119. On the limits of *wahm* as an epistemological tool in al-Ghazālī, see Griffel 2011.

87 Black 1993, 220.

88 [2.58] Saʿdi YE, 203.

From the contemplation of the physical aspect of the beloved, the lyric subject perceives a set of non-sensible characteristics whose manifestation, conjoined with the indescribable beauty of his external form, casts him into a state of speechless amazement. The last line confirms that the association implied by the non-sensible characteristics that the lyric subject's estimative faculty retrieves—while the other senses perceive the beloved's sensible forms—ultimately relates to the divine as a source of grace, of which the beloved is a physical sign, a material trace. The mention of the beauty of the beloved as a sign (*āyat*) attesting to the divine mercy provides a rational elaboration on the pre-rational activity of the lyric subject's estimative faculty, which, if left unguided in the retrieval of the *maʿānī*, might run the risk of perceiving the beloved as an indwelling of God and cast the beholder into the blasphemy of incarnationism.

6 Through the Mirror of My Imaginings

References to the inner senses and their role in the perception of the beloved's beauty pervade Saʿdi's entire poetic corpus. Lines similar to the following abound in his ghazals and, in spite of the apparent lack of technicality of the vocabulary, they attest to the poet's awareness of the physiology of visual perception and the role of the inner senses in the intellectualization of the sensorial experience:

> Come back, as your image [*khayāl*] has remained in my eyes
> Sit by me, as a trace of you [*nishānat*] was set in my mind.
>
> *Ṭayyibāt* 222[89]

Modern commentators trivialize this image by describing the second hemistich as a reference to the topos of the burning brand on the heart of the lover.[90] But if we read this line against the background of Avicennian psychology, it will be clear that the second hemistich describes the process of retention of the image of the beloved in both the visual (properly *khayāl*) and the semantic memory. The visual memory of the beloved is presented as if it were to linger in the optical nerve of the beholder, in the effort of reestablishing the visual sensation collected by the common sense. In other lines, the complexity of the relationship between the pure contemplation of the beloved and the

89 [2.59] Saʿdi YE, 104.

90 Khatib-Rahbar 1367/1988, 1: 218–19. Cf. Bargneysi's (1380/2001, 165) visual interpretation.

process of intellection of the intelligibles emerges as a dramatic confrontation between the inner senses and the rational soul:

> So pervasive is the depiction of the beloved in my imagination
> That no intelligibles [*maʿqūl*] are any longer depicted in my mind.
> *Ṭayyibāt* 136[91]

Overall, in Saʿdi's collections of poems, both the frequency and the complexity of the relationship between vision and imagination speak to the shift in the aesthetic paradigm that took place when Persian poets incorporated the Avicennian psychological model into their representation of the effects of the passion for the beloved on the lover's cognitive system. The use of the word *khayāl* for example, which in pre-Islamic Arabic literature was used to describe a ghostly presence troubling the sleep of the lover and reminding him of his longing for his object of desire, appears in early Persian poetry as the mental image of the beloved—constituting, de facto, a continuation of the Abbasid canonical motifs.[92]

In the erotic preludes of Samanid and Ghaznavid panegyrics, between the late 9th and the 11th centuries, the poets do not seem to be interested in exploring the psychological implication of the beloved's image, and this trend—at least as purely amorous poetry is concerned—continued until the late Saljuq period. During the 12th century, Sanāʾī and ʿAṭṭār were among the first poets who displayed a preliminary degree of awareness with respect to contemporary conversations on the psychology informing the mental image of the beloved. Nevertheless, the approach of these two authors is mainly negative, as in the metaphysical quest of the beloved that they portray, the psychological dimension of the lover's mind constantly confesses the impotence of the imagination in the effort of conjuring up the divine presence:

> Step back from all the paintings that may appear to you
> So that amidst those the absolute Painter may appear.
>
> Pleasant or unpleasant, go beyond the painting of the two worlds
> So that imagelessness may offer you the eternal Image!
>
> If you succeed in hiding from your own eyes
> A secret treasure will appear amidst your soul.

91 Saʿdi YE, 66.
92 See Jacobi 1990; Seybold 1994.

Your eyes won't see but phantasies when looking at the world
Go past these images, so that the World may appear to you![93]

As far as the spiritual dimension of their poetry is concerned, what Sanā'ī, 'Aṭṭār, and Sa'di have in common is that the beloved they portray is an abstract literary function that embodies a semiotic possibility for the cognition of the divine presence. But their approach to this process of cognition diverges with respect to the epistemological strategies deployed by their respective lyric subjects: while Sanā'ī's and 'Aṭṭār's spiritual poems mistrust the use of the senses as an active intellectual resource for the cognition of the unseen, Sa'di regards the encounter between sensory perception and abstract intellection as a complex cognitive interplay through which the lyric subject seeks the breath of the divine within the pulsing flesh of the world.

As noted earlier, the estimative faculty mediates between the sensory and the extra-sensorial dimensions of the perceptions provided by the external senses. It should be noted that while in his non-philosophical works al-Ghazālī often employs *wahm* in its popular negative sense (false illusion, conjecture, wrong idea, etc.),[94] influential late 12th- and 13th-century authors such as Fakhr al-Dīn Rāzī, Naṣīr al-Dīn Ṭūsī, and Nasafī faithfully reflected Avicenna's acceptation of the term. Presumably under the influence of contemporary Avicennian trends, and more often than his predecessors, Sa'di tends to link the psychological dramatization of the lyric action to the physiology of the estimative faculty.[95] In the following ghazal, the poet mentions the word *wahm* in its technical sense, as it appears in a line that connects a purely mundane experience with a discourse on the limits of mental representation:

A new thought occupies my mind every night:
I shall bid my farewell, and leave you for elsewhere.

But when in the morning I step outside my abode
My covenant does not allow me to take a further step.

---

93 [2.61] 'Attār 1392/2013, 355

94 Janssens 2003, 47.

95 I shut the door of my cogitation and broke the pen of estimation,
As you are more beautiful than whatever I can describe with my art.
[2.62] Sa'di YE, 187.
So bewildered is the faculty of estimation by you
That it is incapable of tracing a sign of your presence.
[2.63] Sa'di YE, 267.

Everyone seeks something and desires someone
Whereas we covet no other desires but you.

Through the mirror of my imaginings [*vahm*],[96] no other form and limbs
will ever be depicted as beautiful as yours.

A Vāmiq was once desperately in love with a ʿAẕrā
Look at us today: a new Vāmiq, a new ʿAẕrā.

It is time now for roses and hyacinths to cover the plain
The people are out: each one seeking a different valley....

And I say to myself that not many are the days that are left:
Saʿdi, endure this day, and the new day that will follow.
Badāyiʿ 330[97]

By opening the ghazal with a confessional representation of time from the perspective of the lyric subject, and closing it with a metaphysical possibility for the time beyond *this* time—the time beyond "today" and "tomorrow"—, Saʿdi displays the threshold on which the realm of the visible and the invisible meet. In the first and last couplets of the poem, the author addresses this very threshold, and projects it onto the lyric subject's psychological perception of the difference between the contemplation of the external world and the mental representation of the beloved as a form that *estimation* cannot better grasp:

Through the mirror of my "estimation" [*vahm*], no other form and limbs
will ever be depicted as beautiful as yours.

Saʿdi metaphorically represents the estimative faculty as a mirror that—through the aid of the compositive imagination, which *wahm* controls—reflects the beloved in a shape of utmost beauty. No other form of the sensible world could ever match the splendor of this vision. A similar concept is formulated in the following line, in a fashion that conveys the same psychological

96 I could have taken the liberty of translating *wahm* with the more generic noun "fantasies," as the *terminus technicus*, "estimation" does not fit the semantic density of the line. This choice would have reflected the original lack of differentiation characterizing the Aristotelian subtext (*phantasia*) that inspired Avicenna's theory of the internal senses. See Black 1993, 219.

97 [2.64] Saʿdi YE, 154.

apparatus focusing on the role of the internal senses vis-à-vis the contemplation of the world, in which the visual access to the beloved attests to his incomparable beauty:

> My imaginings [*fikram*] do not attain the sublime boundaries of your beauty:
> You are more handsome than anything that could ever cross my imagination!
> *Badāyiʿ* 329[98]

The non-sensible concepts (*maʿānī*) that the estimative faculty collects from the "form and limbs" of the beloved are such that the lyric subject's mental representation reaches a threshold that no other exposure to the external world could approach. In the opening of another ghazal (which the critic Bargneysi regards as expressing a perfect balance between mundane and spiritual love),[99] Saʿdi concludes each line with different synonyms of the noun *sīmā* (face). The role of *wahm* oscillates between an aesthetic sense of awe and the quest for a repeated mental connection with the image of the object of desire:

> Should I say that this stature of yours resembles the cypress?
> Words cannot express the love radiating from your complexion.
>
> When you manifest yourself, I disappear from myself:
> Awe overtakes *wahm* when contemplating your visage.
>
> I wish that my eyes were a hundred times more sleepless
> So that I could gaze upon the scenery of your face over and over.
>
> You took over my heart, now you may occupy my eyes:
> I fear that my inner chamber in ruin may be too tight for your splendor....
> *Khavātīm* 662[100]

In Saʿdi's poetry, estimation is a faculty that prepares the groundwork for the rational soul to intellectually perceive the beloved as a trace of the divine. It can be argued that the lines in which the poet introduces *wahm* as a faculty depict

98 [2.65] Saʿdi YE, 153–54.
99 Bargneysi 1380/2001, 567.
100 [2.66] Saʿdi YE, 296.

the pre-rational encounter of the lyric subject with an external beauty whose formal perfection pushes the internal senses towards a space situated *beyond* the reach of the external senses. This means that even though this ghazal does not offer any mystical underpinning with respect to the contemplation of the beloved, it does project the psychology of the lyric subject's sensorial and intellectual experience toward a metaphysical dimension whose presence is alluded to through a discourse on the cognitive limits of the mental representation of supreme beauty. The bewilderment that Saʿdi describes opens a psychological space situated beyond the contemplative logic of *tafakkur*, as it brushes against the very metaphysical core of the aesthetic experience.

7 Projecting the Senses Toward the Realm of the Unseen

The previous ghazal shows how, in Saʿdi's lyric poetry, the spiritual intensity behind the visual perusal of the beloved's body as an aesthetic reification of the world's splendor can be projected toward a space of intellection that the eyes and the imaginative faculty cannot immediately reach. If it is true that, on the one hand, as pointed out in the previous chapter, the visual perusal of the beloved belongs to a hermeneutical awareness of the divine origin of beauty, on the other hand, the form of his body is often represented as a window opening to an often undefined "invisible" realm. Once more, estimation (*wahm*), by virtue of its suspension between the body and the soul, is the key physiological point of access to a threshold whose potential incommensurability bewilders the intellect of the lyric subject.

As argued earlier, Saʿdi's depiction of the beloved as a sign of the divine responds to an epistemological process that can be originally ascribed to al-Ghazālī's revisitation of Avicenna's syllogistic model of cognition. In the remaining part of this chapter I will turn to the apparently ineffable experiences that constitute a further element of exploration between the sensible world and the realm of the invisible in Saʿdi's poetry. Once more, the shift from the emphasis on how to interpret the presence of the beloved to the study of the cognitive system of the lyric subject offers the opportunity to depolarize the relationship between mundanity and spirituality.

The key word that here I translate as the "unseen" is *ghayb*, a term that appears forty-nine times in the Qur'ān, mainly to describe the invisible realm that belongs to God's absolute knowledge "of the seen and the unseen."[101] Even though the Quranic references to *ghayb* ascribe this knowledge to God alone

---

101 See, for instance, Qur'ān 6: 73; 23: 92; 39: 46; 59: 22.

("the Unseen belongs only to God," *al-ghaybu lillāhi*, 10: 20) "it is not clear whether the *ghayb* is to be equated with the divine realm alone, or if it is a 'thing' that may pertain to other realms as well."[102] It seems that the Quranic allusions to the possibility of grasping the signs of the unseen as terrestrial and heavenly manifestations have allowed both philosophical and Sufi lines of thought (as well as their convergences, as in the case of al-Ghazālī) to conceive *ghayb* as a realm that the soul/intellect of the individual may be able to access under special circumstances.[103]

The conflation of scriptural and philosophical paradigms in the Sufi literature of the 11th century, especially in Khorasan, reveals interesting connections between the concept of the unseen and the psychology of inspired forms of access to supra-sensory epistemological experiences. In the late-11th-century Persian translation of Qushayrī's *Risāla*, for instance, spiritual insight (*firāsat*) is defined as a "light [*rawshanā'ī*] that shines in the hearts, a spiritual cognition [*maʿrifat*] that is well-grounded amidst the secrets [*asrār*], and which leads [the Sufi] from one form of unseen to another [*az ghayb ba ghayb*] so that he may see the things that are revealed by God Almighty in order for him to speak the truth about the quintessence of creation."[104] This wording shows that although *ghayb* does not correspond to the divine presence itself, it belongs to a space of divine omniscience which the believer can grasp through forms of spiritual awareness. Therefore, it would be misleading to reduce this "invisible" (of which spiritual insight is a direct vision, *muʿāyanā*)[105] to a mystical realm, as the latter constitutes only one specific and partial dimension of an experience that is primarily psychological and epistemological.

Qushayrī defines the practitioner of spiritual insight as a *mustanbiṭ*, i.e., one whose mind accesses a fresh form of cognition,[106] and who "constantly peruses the unseen without ever detaching himself from it."[107] Furthermore, Qushayrī adds that one who has insight (*mutafarris*) "sees with the light of God, which corresponds to shining lights that irradiate through the heart, and by which he can perceive [*idrāk kunad*] the 'supernal meanings' [*maʿānī*]."[108]

---

102 Ziai 1994, 455. See Ibid., 454–56 for a survey of the scriptural references to *ghayb* and the interpretations of early Persian Sufi thinkers.

103 Ibid., 450–60. See, for instance, among the Sufi authors predating al-Ghazālī, Qushayrī's comment on the access of the Sufis to the "world of the unseen" (*ʿālam-i ghayb*): "for they have a way into the unseen." Quoted by Ziai, ibid., 459.

104 Qoshayri 1391/2012, 358.

105 Ibid.

106 Ibid., n. 1.

107 Ibid.

108 Ibid., 359.

In the Avicennian cosmological system, the *maʿānī* correspond to the "contents" that are found in the souls of the celestial spheres. In scriptural terms, these contents correspond to the Quranic concept of the "Preserved Tablet," which, as we shall analyze in the next chapter, al-Ghazālī situates at the center of his spiritual epistemology. The space of the supernal, also referred to as *malakūt*, is the supra-sensible region in which such *maʿānī* can be grasped through the contact between the practical intellect and the celestial spheres: "the 'souls' [*arvāḥ*, here clearly referring to the souls of the celestial bodies, and not to human souls] rotate in the supernal realm [*malakūt*] and have cognition [*ishrāf*] of the supernal meanings of the invisible realms [*maʿānī-yi ghuyūb*]: they speak of the secrets of creation by means of direct vision which no doubt can affect."[109] One revealing acceptation of the semantics of *ghayb* from a philosophical perspective that deeply influenced the Sufi approaches analyzed thus far is the definition given by Avicenna in *Provenance and Destination*: "The function of this faculty [i.e., the Imagination of the perfect man] is to warn of [future] events and to indicate unseen [past and present] events. This occurs to most [people] in the state of sleep through dreams."[110]

As I will show shortly, the invisible space—which relates to a metaphysical level of the lyric subject's experience as much as the realm of imagination—emerges in Saʿdi's ghazals in absolute contiguity with the psychological process of intellection. Through this process, the lover understands the beloved as a particular form of beauty that *indicates* the existence of a unique origin of the absolute splendor. Such contiguity is attested to by the continuity that in the Avicennian psychological system bridges the gap between the visible world and the possibility for the human soul to access a metaphysical space. As demonstrated by Dimitri Gutas,[111] anytime that Avicenna discusses the role of *ghayb*, he does so by framing it as the space through which not only God and the angels, but also regular people, under specific conditions, can grasp details concerning past, present, and future events.[112]

Hence, the "mystery" to which Saʿdi often alludes when describing the beloved's beauty derives from the interaction between the cognition of God as an unfathomable presence and the appearance of spaces other than the visible world, which the syllogistic operations of al-Ghazāli's spiritual *fikrat* cannot immediately attain:

---

109 Ibid.

110 Quoted and translated by Rapoport (2018, 172–73, n. 19).

111 By relying on Quranic evidence: 3: 34, and 12: 102.

112 See Gutas 2006a, 9–11.

The mystery of the inexplicable power of God
Shines through your face like a face appears in a mirror.
Ṭayyibāt 81[113]

I shall elaborate later on the cognitive and metaphysical relevance that the image of the mirror acquires within the framework of the Avicennian background of the psychology of Saʿdi's lyric subject, but it is clear how, in the line above, the poet describes the face of the beloved as a screen on which a mysterious (*bī-chūn*, "incomparable") reflection shines. In order to start unpacking the cognitive physiology of the mysterious spaces shining through the face of the beloved and before the senses of the beholder, we may refer to the relationship between contemplation and the access to the invisible world that the following ghazal addresses in a compelling fashion:

No, I don't know what you resemble in this world:
The world and its things are only images, pure soul [*jānī*] you are.

The lovers willingly walk toward your snare
As whomever you catch, he shall be freed from himself.

Do not ask me how I am—however you wish, I am!
Do not ask my name—call my name by the name you prefer.

So swiftly you take one's heart upon his first gaze
That no chance is left for a second glance.

You hid yourself behind a veil, and while longing for your beauty
The hidden mysteries appeared: their veils were torn apart.

We sat upon your fire, set ablaze by passionate longing:
Too briefly you sat among us, to extinguish our fire.

Whenever my mind imagines your beautiful form
What should I tell you about the "mental contents" [*maʿānī*] going adrift?

113 [2.67] Saʿdi YE, 41.

> I commit no sin when I set my gaze upon the young:
> As the old man is aware of how fleeting youth is....
>
> *Badāyiʿ* 189[114]

Although one might be tempted to read the "mystery" (*rāz*, or *sirr*, in the couplet preceding the ghazal above) to which Saʿdi alludes as a drift towards an unspecified mystical aura, the rest of the poem anchors its nature to a process that is cognitive and mundane rather than esoteric and ineffable. This secret pertains to the nature of the relationship between the visual form of the object of desire and what in the Western Avicennian tradition is translated as "intentions" (*maʿānī*), or pre-intellectual concepts, conveyed through the estimative faculty (*wahm*) and causing the bewilderment of the beholder:

> Whenever my mind imagines your beautiful form
> What should I tell you about the "mental contents" [*maʿānī*] going adrift?

The state of confusion of the beholder ("what should I tell you," "how can I express?") is magnified by the difference that Saʿdi implies between the beloved as a sensible object, physically accessible through optical vision, and his mental image (his *khayāl*) as retained by the internal senses. This gap generates a discrepancy between the "meanings" or "intentions" (*maʿānī*) of the beloved's form as a pre-intellectual perception (via the faculty of estimation) and as an intellectualized vision (through the rational soul). The mystery lies precisely in the hiatus between the possibilities of "meaning" that the object of desire elicits as a pre-rational connection with the divine (along with the implied cognitive error of incarnationism) and the appearance of an imaginal form in the imaginative system of the lover through the intervention of the intellect. The brevity of the experience ("too briefly you sat among us") suggests that the poet is trying to depict a cognitive condition that lies beyond the hermeneutics of inference (*iʿtibār*) and meditation (*fikrat*, or *tafakkur*): it is in fact through the practice of meditative contemplation of the beloved that a door seems to open for a brief instant to fleetingly disclose a deeper form of visionary awareness that involves the active participation of the senses.

As neither the senses nor the intellect can see or perceive God, any perception of the divine obtained through a spiritual cognition (*maʿrifat*) that is aesthetically informed by spiritual meditation on human beauty is limited to

114 [2.68] Saʿdi YE, 89. Even though Yusofi bases his critical edition of this ghazal on Ms. Berlin 1306 (which includes the text in the *Badāyiʿ*) he chose to follow less reliable manuscripts, and listed it among the *Ṭayyibāt*. See ibid., 430.

the recognition of a sign pointing towards God, rather than representing Him as He is. Therefore, semiotically speaking, if the beloved is a sign of God, it ought to be thought of as an *index* (like an arrow pointing towards a direction) rather than an iconic representation. This means that the bewildering vision experienced by Saʿdi's poetic persona, along with the mystery that inhabits it, does not entail the visual representation of the divine but rather the imaginal translation—a visual analogue—of those *maʿānī* that cause so much bewilderment and whose origin requires further investigation.

As noted earlier, the lover's perusal of the beloved's body for the sake of inferring the divine traces through the meditative process of *fikr*/*tafakkur*—as theorized by al-Ghazālī in his attempt to offer a rationalizing approach to spiritual cognition (*maʿrifat*)—originates from Avicenna's primary model of syllogistic knowledge acquisition, that is, the retrieval of the middle terms through the contact between the rational soul and the Active Intellect. Avicenna states that the process of *tafakkur* is contingent upon the materiality of the individual's mundane experience:

> There is need for Thinking [*fikr*] in this world only because the soul is turbid, or because it has had little training and is impotent to attain the divine effluence, or because of distractions. Were it not for this, the soul would obtain certain knowledge about everything to the farthest reaches of truth.[115]

This and similar statements speak to Avicenna's concern with the relationship between intellection and its material contingencies. They underline the contingent limits of human thought, but they also highlight its ontologically limitless possibilities, which, to meet their fullest potential, need to be analyzed from a metaphysical perspective. However, hitting upon the middle term as a result of meditative cogitation is not the only way that Avicenna envisages the mechanism of acquisition of new knowledge.[116] In most of his writings, Avicenna describes a second modality, *ḥads*—translated by Gutas as "correct guessing"—through which "the middle term presents itself [...] to the mind all at once, either as a result of a search and desire [for it] [...] or without any desire and motion."[117]At its highest degree of manifestation, correct guessing

---

115 Gutas 2014a, 188.

116 Treiger 2012, 75–76.

117 Gutas 2014a, 187. See Gutas's considerations on his choice of translating *ḥads* as "Correct Guessing" rather than "intuition": "[...] in the first edition of this book and in subsequent studies, I used the word 'intuition' to render in English Avicenna's key epistemological concept, *ḥads*. In retrospect, this was rather unfortunate. This convenient one-word

corresponds with a faculty that Avicenna describes as the "sacred intellect." However, while some individuals have a natural ability for it, all humans are potentially capable of reaching some degree of correct guessing, and thereby cognizing the intelligibles with no meditative efforts.[118]

The metaphysical implications of the process of guessing correctly, especially considering the phenomenology of contexts in which such an instantaneous form of cognition can take place, are particularly interesting from the perspective of the aesthetic and lyric aspects of the lover's inferential perception of the divine through the vision of the beloved. In one passage in which the Iranian philosopher defines and exemplifies his theory of *ḥads*, it is possible to trace an analogy between the sun as the source of the moon's brightness and the divine splendor as a paradigm for the beloved's physical beauty:

> Guessing Correctly [*ḥads*] is an accurate and spontaneous movement of this faculty toward tracking down the middle term. For example, when one sees that the moon is bright only on the side that faces the sun (according to its phases), his Mind tracks down the middle term by means of Guessing, and hits upon the fact that the cause of its brightness comes from the sun.[119]

From the perspective of the aesthetics of the lyric subject's act of perusing the physical form of the beloved, the process of "guessing correctly" the trace of transcendental beauty in the particular body perceived by the senses derives from a form of habituation of the intellect to the object of its contemplation. Just as the familiarity of the intellect with the syllogistic meditation on the position of the moon with respect to the sun prepares the intelligent subject with an instantaneous intellectual explanation for lunar brightness, the practice of *tafakkur* upon the beauty of the human body prepares the intellect for

rendering of the Arabic term is serviceable if one understands it—and as I meant it to be understood—exclusively in the narrow sense given to it by Avicenna to mean the ability to hit upon, guess correctly, or 'divine' the middle term of a syllogism. However, the more common meaning of the word, 'sensing without the use of rational processes' [...] tends to mislead—and it has misled even some serious scholars of Avicenna—and create a misunderstanding of this crucial concept as something mystical or extra rational, which is exactly the opposite of what was intended by Avicenna. I have accordingly avoided it in this edition and translated *ḥads* literally as 'guessing correctly,' which necessarily evokes the middle term as the object of the transitive verb in the reader's mind—precisely what Avicenna meant to express." Gutas 2014a, xii–xiii.

118 Ibid., 182. On the influence of Avicenna's distinction between *fikr* and *ḥads* in the epistemological system of Fakhr al-Dīn Rāzī (d. 1210), see Janos 2016.

119 Ibid., 184.

automatic recognition of the beloved as a sign attesting to the divine. It is noteworthy that, in the passages from the *Kīmiyā* analyzed in the previous chapter, when al-Ghazālī describes the process of meditation/*tafakkur* as a means to recognize the perfection of the world as a divine reflection, he does so by methodically applying the syllogistic *modus cogitandi* that he inherits from Avicenna. The partially innate and partially acquired process of familiarization with the intelligibles through "correct guessing" leads the rational soul of the individual toward a peculiar form of habituation with intellection, which Avicenna calls *mushāhada*, translatable as "direct vision," "experience," or "witnessing." *Mushāhada* derives from a ceaseless engagement of the rational soul with syllogistic intellective activities and, by bypassing any obstruction that the senses could bring about, it provides the soul with a certain degree of intimacy with its object of intellection.[120]

In Avicenna's words, this kind of intellection is "accompanied by an emotive state of joy and pleasure," and it constitutes the utmost source of intellectual bliss or felicity that the *ʿārif* can achieve. I have frequently underlined how the word *ʿārif* (whose literal meaning is the "cognizer" or, in Saʿdi's spiritual aesthetics, the "beholder") covers a broad semantic field according to the specific discipline or cultural context in which it is employed. In one key passage of the *Ishārāt*, Avicenna compares the activity of the *ʿārif* against the figure of the ascetic and that of the worshipper: whilst the two pious figures direct their religious zeal at the bounties promised in the afterlife, the *ʿārif* "turns his attention to the sanctity of divine power by means of his thinking, seeking the continuous radiation of the light of Truth in his innermost self," i.e., his rational soul (*sirr*).[121] Avicenna's demystified and non-scholastic representation of *maʿrifa* and *mushāhada* as intellectual practices that orient the individual's rational soul toward both rational cogitation on the visible world and intellectual contemplation of the intelligibles in the quest of their transcendental pure form constitutes the background that informs the broader system of visionary intellection in which Saʿdi staged the interplay between the body of the beloved and the mysteries of the unseen.

120 Gutas 2014a, 372. Avicenna also discussed a facility for habituation with intellection, which he called direct vision or experience (*mushāhada*) of the intelligibles. It comes about after prolonged engagement with intellective techniques through syllogistic means until the human intellect is not obstructed by the internal or external senses and has acquired a certain familiarity or "intimacy" with its object, "without, however, the middle term ceasing to be present." This kind of intellection is accompanied by an "emotive state of joy and pleasure." Gutas 2006b, 365–69.

121 Ibid., 353.

In order to pin down the metaphysics of Sa'di's representation of the contact between the lyric subject and the unseen through meditations on both optical and mental vision, it is again the filter of al-Ghazālī's spiritualization of Avicenna's philosophical doctrine on immanent perception and transcendental intellection that is key. In a revealing passage of the *Kīmiyā*, al-Ghazālī traces a comparison between the intellect and the imagination as modalities of knowledge. He recognizes that both optical and mental vision belong to imagination, the difference being that direct optical vision offers an image of a superior quality if compared with the image retrieved by the internal sense of imagination. This parallel perfectly follows Avicenna's theory of perception, as it is not the eye that "sees" what it perceives, but rather the common sense that "visualizes" the image and stores it in the imagination. Al-Ghazālī stresses that the difference between the former and the latter is qualitative, but not essential. Optical vision is therefore an *entelechia* of imagination.[122] The author exemplifies this difference by arguing that the pleasure that one obtains by seeing one's beloved is superior to the pleasurable effects caused by imagining her or his presence. In this passage he correlates *ma'rifat* to imagination (*khayāl*), and *mushāhadat* to optical vision (*dīdār*), which means that he juxtaposes *ma'rifat* with *mushahādat* just as imagination relates to optical vision.[123]

In the Avicennian theory of perception adopted by al-Ghazālī, imagination is the mental function that allows optical vision to "see" the objects of the world and correlate them to their "meaning" (i.e., both their pre-intellectual concepts, *ma'ānī*, and their intellectualized abstraction, the intelligibles). Similarly, *ma'rifat*—fueled by the physical contemplation of the world that the practice of meditation and inference are capable of providing—prepares the soul for the intellectual vision of God in the hereafter. However, in the following *qasida*, Sa'di establishes a clear mundane context for the aesthetic training of the soul on the path of the ultimate contemplation of the divine, which can only take place in the afterlife:

> At dawn, when one can discern no difference between the day and the night
> How beautiful appear the edges of the valleys and the contemplation of springtime.

122 See Treiger 2012, 49–55.

123 See Lazarus-Yafeh's comments on the multiple meanings of *mushāhada*, encompassing both physical and spiritual forms of vision. Lazarus-Yafeh 1975, 219.

Tell the Sufi to leave the monastery and settle amidst the garden of roses
As this is not the time for one to sit idle at home!

The time has come for the nightingales to sing out of passion
You are not less eloquent than an intoxicated nightingale, so sing,
O sober one!

The entire creation is an intimation from the Lord of the heart:
Heartless is he who does not attest to the Lord!

Behold all these marvelous paintings decorating the walls of the palace
of existence:
Nothing but frescoes on a wall are those who do not ponder [*fikrat*]
upon these wonders.

The mountains, the oceans, the rivers: they all laud the Lord!
Not all fine listeners can verily understand the chants of these secrets!

Are you aware of what the morning birds are saying to you?
'So much you have slept, raise your head from the sleep of ignorance!'

Anyone who does not see today **the signs of His power** [*a<u>s</u>ar-i qudrat-i ū*]
Certainly shall not enjoy the **Vision** of him in tomorrow's hereafter! …

The time has come for the rose to emerge from **the alcove of the unseen**:
She may appear now, as all the trees are scattering their homages.[124]

Although Saʿdi occasionally mentions the possibility of contemplating the "beloved" in the hereafter as a transcendental transfiguration of the human object of desire, the majority of his allusions to the invisible are not concerned with the exclusively metaphysical dimension of *mushāhadat*. On the contrary—also considering the strict adherence of Saʿdi's lyricism to the relationship between the senses and imagination— the spiritual grounds of the invisible that inform his descriptions belong to the realm of *maʿrifat* as a mediation between optical contemplation and the visual translation of what al-Ghazālī calls the "supernal world."[125]

124 [2.69] Saʿdi KhE, 662–63. See Ms. Yale 1432, ff. 175a–76a.

125 See Treiger 2012, 106; Gianotti 2001, 159; Davidson 1992, 133.

8 The Visible World and the Realm of the Supernal

The broader ontological arena that defines the boundaries of the metaphysical aspect of the psychology of Saʿdi's lyric subject derives from al-Ghazālī's opposition between the supernal realm (*malakūt*) and the visible, sensible world (*mulk*, the world of "dominion"). This opposition, directly inherited from Avicennian cosmology and metaphysics, is based on the idea that the material world is a pale reflection, a shadow, of the supernal world, which corresponds to the soul of the fixed stars and represents the blueprint of the divine creation. While the Avicennian model of existence of universals is threefold (the divine mind, concrete existence, and the universal recollection in the human intellect), al-Ghazalī splits the intellectual level of existence into an imaginal and an intellectual level, thus reaching a fourfold scheme:

> There are four levels of existence to the world. [First there is its] existence in the Preserved Tablet, which precedes corporeal existence; this is followed by the world's real existence (*wujūd ḥaqīqī*), just as its real existence is followed by its imaginary existence, by which I mean the existence of its form in the imaginary faculty. Its imaginary existence is then followed by its intelligible existence (*wujūd ʿaqlī*), by which I mean the existence of its form in the heart. Some of these existences are spiritual (*rūḥānī*) while others are corporeal, and of the spiritual some are more spiritual than others: this is one of the finer points issuing from the Divine Wisdom (*al-luṭf min al-ḥikmat al-ilāhiyya*). For when that [Wisdom] created the pupil of your eye, in all its smallness, in it came to be represented by way of impression the form of the world and the heavens and the earth, in all their broad extent. Then [that form's] existence in the senses proceeds to an existence in the imaginary faculty, and from there to an existence in the heart. You can never perceive anything except for that which has reached you, you see: and if He had not placed a likeness of the world in its entirety (*li-l-ʿālam kullī-hi mithāl*) within your essence, you would not have any information of anything other than yourself.[126]

1. Archetypal existence (*malakūt*). In Avicennian cosmology, this corresponds to the soul of the fixed stars. It is the blueprint, or the archetype of creation. In Islamic terms, it corresponds to the Quranic "mother of the book" (*umm al-kitāb*) and the "preserved tablet" (*al-lawḥ al-maḥfūẓ*), which is also the term that al-Ghazālī uses in his spiritual cardiology.

126 Quoted and translated by Taneli Kukkonen (2012, 555).

2. Intelligible existence. This corresponds to reality in its abstracted form, as it appears in the human intellect/rational soul or, in al-Ghazālī's terminology, in the form in which both the visible and invisible are cognized by the spiritual heart.
3. Imaginal existence. This corresponds to reality as it is, when perceived by the internal senses on the basis of the sensations gathered by the external senses.
4. Material reality (*mulk*). This is the lowest stage of the divine creation, perceived by the external senses.

Sa'di's use of the term *ghayb*, along with his direct and indirect references to the realm of the invisible, ought to be ascribed to al-Ghazālī's theorization of this concept as an ontological category. Mainly through the influence of Avicennian cosmology, the category of the invisible belongs to a level of reality that is intimately connected with imagination, the mental visualization of future or past events, and to universal ideas and subtle meanings which the human intellect can only grasp through its interaction with the celestial bodies. All these elements are contained in what al-Ghazālī calls the "Preserved Tablet" (*lawḥ-i maḥfūẓ*), which, as a sort of matrix or blueprint of creation, constitutes the highest point of spiritual intellection for the believer's quest towards the divine presence. Even though Sa'di denies the possibility of a direct knowledge of God, he certainly highlights the cognitive possibility of a contact with the realm of the invisible as the highest intellectual possibility that human beings can attain. The boundaries that al-Ghazālī prescribes for the exploration of the "Preserved Tablet" fall within the cognitive scope of the human heart as an analogue of Avicenna's theorization of the rational soul.

In the following ghazal, Sa'di approaches the aesthetic, spiritual, and psychological aspects of the vision of the beloved by covering all the different levels of reality that al-Ghazālī posits in his diagrammatic representation of intellectual and imaginal existence as intermediate layers between the materiality of *mulk* and the archetypal existence of *malakūt*:

Your face stole its soothing freshness from the paradise above us
Unique beauty is your face in the picture gallery of the world.

Mānī's finger shall never paint an image as beautiful as you are
Even though your face tears apart the glowing portraits of Mānī.

More beautiful you are in my eyes than the rose, the moon, and the angel:
Not the rose or the moon, nor the angel: only your face conquers my heart.

No market is left for the beauty of the celestial brides
If you follow Yūsuf's proof by lifting the veil from your face.

The moon and the Pleiades would timidly cover their radiant bodies
Should your face appear as an epiphanic [*tajallī*] sunshine in the middle of the night.

Should the eyes of the blind men imagine your countenance
Their pupils would tear apart the veils that prevent them from seeing....

My wisdom imposes the rules of devotion upon amatory practices [*ʿishq-bāzī*],
But your face strikes the drums of plunder over the field of my piety.
Badāyiʿ 554[127]

The imagery that Saʿdi deploys in this text combines its undeniable psychological framework with the cosmological ontology that links the realm of the visible world to the ineffable reality of *malakūt*. Considering the correspondence between the angelic bodies and the supernal archetype of creation in the Avicennian ontological system, Saʿdi's mention of Mānī's painting, the rose, the moon, and the angel expresses the entire arc of the levels of reality to which the object of desire pertains: spanning between the visual ideal of painted images, the symbolic carnality of the rose, the cosmic projection of the moon, and the celestial body of the angel, as the highest vault that the human intellect can graze. In this ontologically multilayered territory, the imagination of the lyric subject seeks multiple possibilities of existence for the passionate belonging that draws it to the object of desire.

From the perspective of the Avicennian psychology of the inner senses, the line of the blind man's reacquired vision incorporates the entire spectrum of epistemological possibilities oscillating between the different levels of reality discerned by al-Ghazālī:

127 [2.70] Saʿdi YE, 250. Cf. the variants reported by Yusofi, ibid., 593. This ghazal was probably the object of different authorial renditions, which created a certain degree of confusion in the manuscript tradition. For my translation I have relied on Ms. Yale 1432, f. 324a–324b, adding a line (in bold in the original text quoted herein) that Yusofi has recorded from reliable manuscripts. Considering the discrepancies affecting the seventh line in all the available manuscripts, I have taken the liberty of reading Ms. Yale 1432's *ʿumiyā* with a pluralizing *nūn* (*ʿumiyān*), whose nasalization does not affect the meter and yet provides the line with a more logical meaning.

Should the eyes of the blind men imagine your countenance
Their pupils would tear apart the veils that prevent him from seeing.

We may compare the blind person of this couplet with the "short-sighted" onlookers of the ghazal analyzed in the previous chapter ("On the page-like cheek of the beautiful ones they see the downy-beard [*khaṭ*], / Short is their sight! But the beholder [*ʿārif*] contemplates the pen of God's creation"). In those lines, it was the lack of spiritual awareness, the failure to perform the meditative practice of *fikrat*, that would prevent the onlookers from recognizing the signs of the divine and cause them to develop instead a sensual passion for the beard of the beloved. On the contrary, the line above explores the psychological process that guides the *ʿārif*, the spiritual beholder, even when the physiology of his optical system is compromised. The vision of the invisible world stimulates the depiction of an image of indescribable beauty in the imagination of the blind *ʿārif*, in such a way that his eyes open up to the phenomenal world and restore an ideal correspondence between the supernal, the imaginal, and the material dimensions of the act of beholding.

The "epiphanic" moment that Saʿdi describes, through the extraordinary intuition that posits a spiritually inspired source of imagination as a guide to *seeing* the physical world as a reflection of the invisible, relies on the noetic power of the heart. This is the organ that occupies a central position in the ontological system that al-Ghazālī posits on the basis of Avicenna's psychological cosmology. It is the organ that, as we shall explore in the next chapter, through its conflation with the Avicennian intellect and the Islamic conceptualizations of the soul, takes the lyric subject beyond the rational cogitations of meditation and pushes it towards the uncharted waters of *mukāshafa* and *mushāhada*, the ultimate unveiling and witnessing, or the supreme form of *beholding*.

CHAPTER 7

Spiritual Cardiology

The Heart as a Mirror Reflecting the Unseen

[…] These beauteous forms,
Through a long absence, have not been to me
As is a landscape to a blind man's eye:
But oft, in lonely rooms, and 'mid the din
Of towns and cities, I have owed to them
In hours of weariness, sensations sweet,
Felt in the blood, and felt along the heart;
And passing even into my purer mind,
With tranquil restoration:—feelings too
Of unremembered pleasure: such, perhaps,
As have no slight or trivial influence
On that best portion of a good man's life,
His little, nameless, unremembered, acts
Of kindness and of love. Nor less, I trust,
To them I may have owed another gift,
Of aspect more sublime; that blessed mood,
In which the burthen of the mystery,
In which the heavy and the weary weight
Of all this unintelligible world,
Is lightened:—that serene and blessed mood,
In which the affections gently lead us on,—
Until, the breath of this corporeal frame
And even the motion of our human blood
Almost suspended, we are laid asleep
In body, and become a living soul:
While with an eye made quiet by the power
Of harmony, and the deep power of joy,
We see into the life of things.

WILLIAM WORDSWORTH[1]

• • •

1 Wordsworth 1835, 101.

 | DOI:10.1163/9789004435902_011

The cypress of the garden is grounded in the soil
Our heart is the soil where the roots of *our* cypress spread.
Ṭayyibāt 123[2]

•••

We are scattered and focused:
Our beloved is hidden, but present in our gaze.
The fresh leaf goes dry over time,
The leaf of our eyes is constantly moist.
Khavātīm 680[3]

∴

1 Imagining the Limits of the Imagination

Sa'di is the master of paronomasia (*jinās-i tāmm*), the rhetorical device by which a poet repeats the same word with two different meanings. Sa'di's use of this device is particularly subtle, as the semantic transition between the words that he repeats is highly nuanced, the first meaning repeated with a slightly different acceptation.[4] In the following line, for instance, the repetition of the word *khayāl* is a magisterial example of Sa'di's virtuosic capability to convey complex associations of thoughts through seemingly simple puns:

Everyone's mind imagines [*khayāl*] someone's beautiful face,
But the one I imagine [*khayāl*] is beyond imagination [*khayāl*].
Ṭayyibāt 73[5]

By locating the imaginative passion for an object of desire in one's "head" (*dar sar ast*) rather than the heart, Sa'di ascribes the act of amatory imagination to the cognitive functions of the internal senses, which are located in specific areas of the brain.[6] While the first two instances of the word *khayāl* signify the

2 [2.71] Sa'di YE, 60.
3 [2.72] Ibid., 304.
4 For one of the most eloquent illustrations of how this rhetorical device characterizes Sa'di's style, see Purnāmdāriyān 1382/2003, 464–65, n. 4.
5 [2.73] Sa'di YE, 37.
6 Hence the liberty with which I synecdochally translated *sar* as "mind."

mental image of the beloved stored in what Avicenna identifies as the retentive (or "form-bearing") imagination, the third instance refers to what in the previous chapter we have referred to as *al-mutakhayyila*, or *takhayyul*, the imaginative faculty, or compositive imagination.[7] By rhetorically juxtaposing these two acceptations of the term *khayāl*, Saʿdi describes the cognitive challenge posed to the lover when his mind strives to process images that his imagination cannot form or visualize. The paradox derives from the fact that even though the incapacity of imagination is declared, the line confines the description of this ecstatic anxiety to the horizon of mental cognition, as if the capability of the lyric subject's imagination to represent inspirations from the invisible world were limited by the very physicality of the cognitive system that distinguishes human physiology.

The rational meditation on the body of the beloved as a trace of the divine presence cannot alone account for the aspects of Saʿdi's erotic lyricism that seem to belong to experiences taking place beyond the boundaries of the visible world, and which are intimately connected with the realm of visionary, inspired, and imaginative thinking. In order to account for this aspect of Saʿdi's poetry, this chapter will consider the influence of the cosmological framework of Avicenna's cognitive model on the sciences that al-Ghazālī describes as "unveiling" (*mukāshafa*) and spiritual witnessing (*mushāhada*). We will see how al-Ghazālī's recontextualization of Avicenna's metaphysical psychology conceives of the human heart as a mechanism that accounts for both the processes of analytical thinking and the irrational perceptions of the soul attained under the effect of altered mental conditions. Al-Ghazālī's "spiritual cardiology" will provide us with a flexible set of critical tools to reassess the imaginative dimension of Saʿdi's sacred eroticism.

2 The Practical Intellect as a Bridge between *Mulk* and *Malakūt*

We may obtain a better grasp of the relationship between the materiality of *mulk* (the world of sense) and the metaphysical nature of *malakūt* (the supernal realm) by taking into account Avicenna's theory of the human intellect, or rational soul, as an entity displaying a downward and an upward orientation, respectively corresponding to what he calls the "practical" and the "theoretical" intellect. While the practical intellect presides over the physiological functions

7 Avicenna himself often used the word *khayāl* to refer to both faculties. See Wolfson 1935, 98–101, Gutas 2006b, 339; 2006a, n. 19.

of the body (including one's external and internal senses), the "theoretical" intellect puts us in contact with the Active Intellect (cosmologically, the intellect of the terrestrial realm) for the cogitative intellection proper and the intellectual "vision" of the intelligibles (such as universal concepts, or "the forms of things as they are in themselves").[8] As mentioned in the previous chapter, Avicenna's theory of intellectual cognition is intimately intertwined with the emanative cosmological system with which he explains the existence of the visible world as the final result of a concatenation of emanations. Below God, the series of incorporeal and cosmic intelligences corresponding with the concentric positions of different celestial bodies ends with the tenth intelligence, which is referred to as the Active Intellect and corresponds to the soul of the sublunar world.[9]

As the human intellect can only process the particular things that are present in the physical world and captured by the senses, it needs to conjoin with the universal intelligibles provided by the Active Intellect in order to perform its cognitive activities: we can conceive of the Active Intellect as the storehouse of the intelligibles that the human intellect needs to access in order to think. However, the Active Intellect is not the only cosmic entity with which the human mind connects to retrieve information. In the section entitled "Epistle of the Soul of the Celestial Sphere" from the *Risāla fī aḥwāl al-nafs*, Avicenna clearly illustrates the deterministic cosmological system according to which the particular objects and events of the sublunary world are known to the souls of the celestial spheres (or the "intellects," which proceed from the First Cause by means of emanation) because their own concatenation of movements generates and determines the past, current, and future status of this material world.[10] Since anything that happens on earth (the realm of *mulk*) is causally

8 See previous chapter (pp. 320–21) for a preliminary description of the difference between these two aspects of the rational soul. For a more in-depth analysis, see Gutas 2006b, 342–44; Rapoport 2018, 171–73.

9 See Davidson 1992, 129–53 for an in-depth analysis of al-Ghazālī's permutation of Avicennian noetics and cosmology and his partial rebuttal of some aspects of the inherent logic of Avicenna's theories.

10 Michot 1986, 110–117. See also Michot 1985 for a French translation of the epistle and an accurate critique of its critical editions. On the absolute divine determinism and the absence of any form of contingency whatsoever, see Michot 1986, 60–64. See also Janssens 2003; Belo 2007, 55–89; and, for a different opinion on this issue, Janssens 1996. Avicenna's passages on this topic are particularly interesting because they appear almost verbatim in a minor work attributed to al-Ghazālī, the *Maʿārij al-quds fī madārij maʿrifat al-nafs*. On this work, and the philological and philosophical implications of its attribution to al-Ghazālī, see Vajda 1972, 470–73; Janssens 1993; Griffel 2004, 131–32.

predetermined by the First Principle, the souls of the celestial bodies, in particular those of the fixed stars, contain the reflections of all present, past, and future events taking place on earth. Not only can our intellect (through its theoretical faculty) access the intelligible concepts stored in the Active Intellect (which we constantly do when thinking), but it can also access (through its practical faculty, and under extremely special circumstances, when awake, or normally, when dreaming) the particular events that the soul of the fixed stars constantly reflects.

The subdivision of the human rational soul into a theoretical and a practical intellect, describing the different points of access to the information stored in the celestial spheres, constitutes one of the most striking noetic refinements in Avicenna's epistemological system. According to this paradigm, while the theoretical intellect is concerned with the intelligibles that are contained in the active intellect, the practical intellect deals with the particulars that are stored in the soul of the sphere of the fixed stars and which, by forming the celestial blueprint of the divine creation, correspond to the past, current, and future particulars that are found in the world of matter. Avicenna explains that, as these particulars of past or future events are "ideas" of the things as they are (*maʿānī*), they need to be processed by the practical intellect—through its direct control over the inner senses—in order for them to be translated into images by the compositive imagination.[11]

Avicenna's insistence on the intellect's need for images in order to cognize derives from his attempt to adapt his epistemology to the intromissive optical paradigm that he inherits from the Aristotelian tradition. However, the necessity of aligning the dynamics of intellectual vision with intromissive optics is not the sole reason that compels Avicenna to theorize that the practical intellect requires a visual translation for the reception of the particulars provided by the celestial spheres. As noted by Gutas, it is the fleeting nature of the connection between the human soul and the celestial spheres that compels the former to seek a strategy to stabilize the information issuing from the contact with the supernal realm. And the translation of supernal ideas into images through the internal senses is the most viable way for the soul to incorporate the content of intellection. As the rational soul is deprived of retentive powers, the task of processing and manipulating the material provided by the supernal

11 See Michot 1986, 122–23; Gutas 2006b, 338–42. Even though Davidson accurately describes the cosmological aspect of the connection with the supernal realm (Davidson 1992, 119–23), Gutas points out that he fails to explain the role of the practical intellect in mediating the activity of the internal senses during such contacts. See Gutas 2006b, 341, n. 12.

spheres falls upon the internal senses.[12] The "reflection" of the ideas of these particulars from their supernal abode upon the internal senses through the mediation of the practical intellect implies a process of physical embodiment of the metaphysical that brings any possible ineffable experience (including dreams, visions, and prophecies, but also mental alterations due to illness) back to the horizon of pure mundanity.[13]

This rationalization of the physiological contact between the human intellect and the invisible provides us with a powerful paradigm that, when applied to the study of Persian lyric poetry, allows one to dismiss the generic category of "mysticism" to focus on the psychology of the lyric subject's negotiation between the physical stratification of its mundane experience and the verbal articulation of its mental processes. From this perspective, especially after the incorporation of the Avicennian tradition into the psychological dimension of Sufi thought, we may regard the so-called mystical aspect of the ghazal tradition as a meditation in verse on the lyric subject's psychological disposition toward beauty and desire as a link between the possibilities of the flesh and the experiences that he perceives as ineffable reflections of an invisible realm.

---

12 "These notions [i.e., these perceptions of the supernal world] come about for reasons which arise in the [rational] soul for the most part furtively; they are like stolen intimations which do not stay long enough to be remembered unless the [rational] soul acts quickly with the intent to retain them, and what it does most is to preoccupy the imagination with the sort [of activity] that is unrelated to what it [the imagination] had been doing." Rahman 1959, 171. Translated by Dimitri Gutas (2006b, 350).

13 "What is essential to comprehend here is the extreme variability of the manifestation of this knowledge of past, present, and future events. It can come to prophets, of course, but also to every man, even simpletons and fools—and this fact alone is enough to guarantee that this is not any kind of knowledge of divine or mystical secrets; it can come while one is asleep or awake, or in a state of semi-consciousness; and it can manifest itself in all forms: as dreams that need interpretation and dreams that do not, as visions of individuals talking to one, as simple warnings about events, as poetry, and even as intelligible concepts. This bewildering variety of manifestations is due both to the great complexity of the apparatus of the internal senses that Avicenna describes—the imagination, the estimation, and the imagery and the common sense must all have certain relations to each other and all of them collectively to the rational soul, relations which sometime inhibit and sometime support the process—and to the multiformity of combinations of individual constitutions, strengths of the soul, state of preparedness, and so on. Avicenna, keenly aware as a scientist of the multiformity of psychic and mental experience, tries to account for all these states within a comprehensive theory in a truly scientific spirit. It may not be an exaggeration to suggest that the entire Book IV (of the *Kitab al-Nafs* of the *Shifāʾ*) on the internal senses deserves to be considered as the first modern treatise of psychology." Gutas 2006b, 350.

3 The Intoxicating Fragrance of the Unseen

The Avicennian model of human imaginative faculties as a mediator between the upper and the lower levels of the soul's experience of the world clearly emerges throughout the entirety of Saʿdi's works. In order to see the clear connection between Avicenna's psychological cosmology and Saʿdi's approach to the relationship between imagination and the invisible realm, we ought to consider the role of al-Ghazālī in converting Avicenna's model into a spiritual science, which the Iranian theologian refers to as *mukāshafa*, or the science of "unveiling." Before tackling al-Ghazālī's approach, I wish to return to a specific passage of the introduction to the *Gulistān*, in which Saʿdi concludes his praise of God with a line that declares the impossibility for human intellection to grasp the divine presence:

> O [God], you are above imagination [*khayāl*], syllogisms [*qiyās*], thought [*gamān*], and estimation [*vahm*],
> Beyond whatever was said, whatever we heard, whatever we studied.[14]

The notes of the previous chapter on the philosophical background of Saʿdi's representation of perception, cognition, and intellection vis-à-vis the visible, the imaginal, the intellectual, and the metaphysical levels of reality help us recognize the author's deployment of technical vocabulary that clearly derives from the Avicennian psychological tradition: *khayāl*, *qiyās*, *gamān*, and *vahm*. Saʿdi, by explicitly mentioning these terms, reminds his reader that the human intellect cannot form a mental image of God (*khayāl*), nor can it syllogistically (*qiyās*) cognize (*gamān*) the divine presence, for which the external senses cannot provide veridical intentions or concepts (*maʿāni*) capable of being processed by the faculty of estimation (*wahm*).[15]

The declaration of such unfathomability clarifies not only the intellectual boundaries of the knowledge of the divine, but also the nature of the "supernal world," or *malakūt*, as a space that the human intellect is capable of exploring only on the basis of the categories that the internal senses can provide. As a consequence, whenever Saʿdi represents the lyric subject of his ghazals as an

14 See Chapter 4, pp. 237–38.

15 This line is strikingly similar to a statement that Sanāʾī makes in the opening of the *Ḥadīqat al-ḥaqīqa*: Only the heart of those who seek divine cognition / is above estimation, senses, intellect, and syllogisms (*bartar az vahm-u ḥiss-u ʿaql-u qiyās* / *chīst juz khāṭir-i khudāy-shinās*). Sanāʾi 1382/2003, 1. Yāhaqqi and Zarqāni (Sanāʾi 1397/2018, 2: 904) read Sanāʾī's line within the context of Avicenna's psychological model.

actor that attempts the cognition of the supernal, the divine presence constitutes a cognitive boundary that the intellect can only approach negatively, for it is an area that cognition cannot access. Just as in the case of Avicenna's description of the metaphysical connection with the particulars stored in the realm of the supernal, whatever lies *within* such boundaries constitutes the real metaphysical, non-mystical, and fundamentally imaginal space of the spiritual and intellectual perception of the lyric subject. While the intellect cannot grasp God, it can access this imaginal space that constitutes an approach, or an approximation to the divine presence, which corresponds to what Sufis and poets call the realm of the unseen, *ʿālam-i ghayb*.

In the *Epistle on Love and the Intellect* (*Risāla-yi ʿaql-u ʿishq*), one of Saʿdi's rare theoretical meditations, the poet repurposes the lines above ("you are above imagination …") as a gloss to a passage in which he discusses the limits of the intellection of God. The textual variants that are found in one of the earliest manuscripts recording the epistle show the clear Avicenian derivation of Saʿdi's argument:

> The Sufi may well step into the treasury [of the hidden knowledge of God], however he won't access it without losing his head. You may ask what the tool of spiritual knowledge is [*ālat-i maʿrifat*], and you may respond that it's the intellect [*ʿaql*], syllogistic reasoning [*qiyās*], and the sensory faculties [*quvvat-i ḥavās*]. But to what end when the wayfarer arrives at his destination and, in its first station, the fragrance of springtime arises and it confounds the intellect, perceptions [*idrāk*], syllogisms, the imagination [*khayāl*] and the senses?
>
> I promised I would pronounce a few words about your countenance:
> You showed your face, and shut the door of my linguistic reason
> [*dar-i nuṭq*].[16]
>
> It is indeed bewildering that no unveiling [*mukāshafa*] takes place without ecstatic rapture (*vajd*), and ecstatic rapture bars one's perceptions.[17]

We may regard this passage as the theoretical foundation of the anecdote that opens the introduction to the *Gulistān* (and which immediately precedes the lines on the unimaginable nature of God). The anecdote constitutes an extraordinary statement on the spiritual effort of translating into images the

16 This line belongs to a ghazal analyzed in the previous chapter (pp. 292–93).

17 Ms. Paris 1320s, f. 218b.

supernal realm through the cognitive and epistemological resources that the sensorial experience of the world can offer. The phrasing of the passage, especially if compared with the excerpt from the epistle quoted above, reveals the full extent of the Avicennian background that informs al-Ghazālī's spiritual imagination and its influence on Saʿdi's aesthetics:

> One of the Masters of the Heart [*ṣāḥib-dil*] entered into a state of visionary rapture till drowning in the ocean of unveiling [*mukāshafat*]. As soon as he reemerged from these imaginal transactions [*muʿāmalat*], one of his associates asked him with joyful enthusiasm: "What present are you bringing for us from the *garden* of fragrances [*bustān*] that you visited?" He replied: "I was resolved to fill my vest with gifts for my companions once I reached the rose bush. But as soon as I approached it [and started picking the roses], the fragrance of those roses intoxicated me so deeply that I lost control and dropped all of them."[18]

The "Master of the Heart" (*ṣāḥib-dil*) is a poetic euphemism for the beholder, the *ʿārif*, for whom the ecstatic disclosure of the spiritual experience involves a contact between his internal senses and the *malakūt*, which, in Avicennian cosmological terms, corresponds to the supernal realm of the soul of the fixed stars. The fact that Saʿdi refers to the figure of the *ʿārif* as a master of the heart is extremely important. It is in fact the heart, as we shall see, that al-Ghazālī elects as the organ that, in his spiritual epistemology, subsumes the functions of the intellect/rational soul in the Avicennian model. Given the lines on the inaccessible nature of the divine, the object of spiritual perception during the protagonist's vision is not God himself, but a level of reality that is situated beyond the tangible world and whose presence—under special conditions—is accessible to the intellectual faculties of the beholder.[19] The vision of the roses, rather than being a symbolic presence alluding to an unfathomable mystery, represents the imaginal "translation" of the contents that the master's intellect gathered from its contact with the supernal realm, also referred to as the unseen (*ghayb*) or, especially in al-Ghazālī's terminology, the celestial "Preserved Tablet." We ought to read the roses that the anecdote describes not as a symbolic element, but as an actual mental image perceived by the internal senses of the Sufi master: the presence of the roses directly involves the process of imagination as it is regulated by the intellect (the practical intellect,

---

18 *Golestān*, 50. See also Ms. Dushanbe 1310s, 103 (where *muʿāmalat* is recorded as *ḥālat*); Ms. Kabul 1325, 4; Ms. Yale 1432, f. 27b.

19 Treiger 2012, 58–60.

in Avicennian terms) during the task of impressing the emanations from the unseen in the form of a sensible object of cognition upon the screen of the "common sense."

What one may legitimately interpret as an allegorical representation is the master's failure to bring the roses from the supernal realm to his companions (patiently and playfully waiting for his "return" to the external senses) as a token of his metaphysical experience. This allegory might represent the failure of the intellect's desire to cross the boundaries of the supernal world and thereby experience the direct vision of God.[20] However, in Avicennian terms, the nature of the contact between the rational soul/intellect/heart and the invisible world is ephemeral, and its duration depends on the capability of the internal senses of the subject to manage the visual translation of the *maʿānī* reflected by the celestial bodies. Al-Ghazālī compares this ephemeral contact with the invisible world to a flash of lightning that seldom lasts longer than an instant.[21] While the prior Sufi tradition often recurred to the metaphor of lightning to represent the ephemeral, blinding nature of the contact of the soul with the supernal realm, al-Ghazālī, by relying on Avicenna's psychology and theory of perception, converted the spiritual "state" of the Sufis into a process that is primarily mental and imaginal, and ultimately capable of leaving a visual trace impression in the mind of the beholder.[22]

20 The lines that follow the passage—"O [God], you are above imagination [*khayāl*], syllogisms [*qiyās*], thought [*gamān*], and estimation [*vahm*]"—partially confirm this reading, as they precisely address the unreachable nature of what falls beyond the limits of the intellect and the imagination. For discussions on the possibility (or lack thereof) of seeing God, see chapter 4, pp. 235–40. As for al-Ghazālī's distancing himself from the normative literalism of *kalām*'s theology, see Treiger 2012, 58–60.

21 "Regardless of whether this happens during sleep or in the state of wakefulness, the period of the curtain's removal is usually exceedingly brief, 'as a flash of lightning' (*ka-l-barq al-khāṭif*), and only seldom lasts longer. The curtain between the heart and the Preserved Tabled will be completely removed only after death." Ibid., 69. On similar passages in other works by al-Ghazālī's, see ibid., 145, nn. 35–36, 146, n. 40.

22 See, for instance, Qushayrī's description of *ḥāl*: "Someone asked Dhu 'l-Nun al-Misri about the [...] gnostic [*al-ʿārif*]. He answered: 'He was here [a moment ago], but left.' One Sufi master said: 'States are like [flashes of] lightning. If they persist, they are but self-deception.' The Sufis say: 'States are like their name'—that is, they alight upon the heart only to leave it instantaneously. They recite the following poetic lines: If it [the state] were not changing constantly, it would not be named *ḥāl*. Everything that changes, passes / Look at the shadow: as soon as it has reached its full size / And become long, it begins to wane! Some Sufis have pointed out that the states can last and endure. They say that the states that do not last and continue are but flashes of light (*lawa'ih*) and unexpected appearances (*bawadih*). Those who experience them have not yet arrived at true states. Only when this experience lasts can it be called 'state'." Qushayiri 2007, 78–79. See original

4 *Mukāshafa* and *Mushāhada*: from the Science of Unveiling to Spiritual Vision

Both in his introductory passage and in the *Risāla-yi ʿaql-u ʿishq*, Saʿdi lyrically introduces a technical term, *mukāshafa*, which he connects with the peak of the visionary experience of the spiritual beholder. In Saʿdi's passages, the expression relates to the imaginal connection between the visible world and the unseen. Although *mukāshafa* is of clear Sufi derivation,[23] al-Ghazālī elevates it to a spiritual science, the "science of unveiling," to which he often refers as a secretive corpus of knowledge that is not to be shared with the common folk and which one should refrain from committing to writing.[24] As a consequence of the esoteric nature of this science, al-Ghazālī is often sibylline when addressing this subject, and he refrains from expressing its contents systematically. As it will soon become clearer, among all the categories that Alexander Treiger has recognized as the main theoretical tenets of *mukāshafa*, the following topics directly pertain to the science of unveiling in the context of Saʿdi's sacred eroticism: "God as the only being in existence"; "the human cognition of God"; "the connection between the sensory 'world of manifestation,' *ʿālam al-shahāda*, and the suprasensible, intelligible 'world of dominion'"; "the heart"; and "the adverse influence of bodily desires upon one's proximity to God."[25]

Although, apart from Saʿdi's references, this technical term is not particularly common in the literary tradition, the theo-erotic aspects of the Persian poetic legacy were profoundly influenced by al-Ghazālī's reappraisal of *mukāshafa* as a mediation between Sufi and philosophical thought. In particular, the concept of the "unveiling" as a constant interplay between the visible world and the realm of the invisible, mediated by the relationship between the carnal and the rational soul vis-à-vis the contemplation of the divine creation, would become one of the main intellectual positions of the Sufi literature of the Saljuq and Ilkhanid periods. This specific aspect of *mukāshafa* is found in a saying that ʿAṭṭār, in his *Taẕkirat al-awliyā*ʾ, ascribes to the Sufi ʿAlī Rūdbārī:

---

text, Qushayri 1988, 117. Cf. the same passage in the 11th-century Persian translation of the *risāla*. Qoshayri 1391/2012, 135–3, 78–79.

23 For the first attestations of the term *mukāshafa* in the Sufi tradition (especially in Qushayrī and Sarrāj), see Treiger 2012, 42–44. See also, on Tustarī, Böwering 1980, 211–30.

24 Lazarus-Yafeh 1975, 349–411. Treiger 2020.

25 For a summary of the general categories covered by al-Ghazālī's notion of *mukāshafa*, see Treiger 2012, 40–41. For a selection of the passages of the *Iḥyā*ʾ covering these topics, see ibid., 134.

> And he said: "[A Sufi is the one who] vacates his heart, carnal soul, and spirit from the contingencies around him; wisdom [*ḥikmat*] takes shape in his heart; the carnal soul turns at his service; the spirit discloses the unveiling [*mukāshafat*], then he will contemplate the divine creation and peruse His secrets and his Truths."[26]

One particular passage from al-Ghazālī's *Kīmiyā* bridges the gap between the homiletic nature of 'Aṭṭār's description of *mukāshafa* and Sa'di's aesthetics of the imaginal translation of the invisible world. Al-Ghazālī refers to this form of spiritual vision emerging from the unveiling as "witnessing," *mushāhada*.[27] In the following excerpt, al-Ghazālī provides a phenomenological and psychological framework for Sa'di's anecdote of the *ṣāḥib-dil* by exposing the theoretical background of the imaginal aesthetics informing the Avicennian substratum of Sa'di's lyric subject. Even though al-Ghazālī describes the experience of *mushāhada* within the framework of his project on the revival of the religious sciences, in this passage he clearly frames the visionary experience of the Sufis by strictly abiding by Avicenna's observations on the relationship between the internal senses and the contact of the rational soul with the soul of the fixed stars:

> Those who turn invisible to themselves and to their own perceptions, and—as it is customary in the commencement of the path of Sufism—delve into their own selves and plunge into the remembrance [*ẕikr*] of God, will have a taste of the other world's realities through the [process of] witnessing [*mushāhadat*]. This is because the carnal soul, by going dormant and weakening (even though its physiological equilibrium is not compromised), does not prevent them from accessing the truth of the Essence. Therefore, their condition will be akin to that of the dead. Anything that to the others is unveiled through death, will become accessible to them in this world. In most cases, whenever they come back to themselves and to the perceptible world, they might have no recollection of that experience. [...] And if they recall something, they might talk about it. And if the storage of their imagination [*khazāna-yi khayāl*] depicts their recollections [*muḥākātī karda bāshad*], it will appear as an image, for images can be best stored in the memory, so that they may be retrieved. The Prophet said: "A bunch of grapes from paradise was

26 'Attār 1391/2012, 658–59.

27 On the concept of *mushāhada* in al-Ghazālī, and the Avicennian foundations of this Sufi term, see Treiger 2012, 55–63.

> shown to me, and I wanted to bring it to this world." Do not think that the supernal essence [*ḥaqīqat*] of which the grapes are a [visual] representation can be brought to this world. It is impossible. If it were possible, the Prophet would have brought it here, but what happened to him was a revelation through contemplation.[28]

Al-Ghazālī describes how the visionary experience is induced by a spiritual practice that involves a physiological effect on the carnal soul of the initiate—in this case, a voluntary disconnection from the external sensations and the repetition of a formula (*ẕikr*).[29] The dormancy of the carnal soul (which, as a physiological element of the body, should not be confused with the metaphysical status of the rational soul) causes the rational soul to retrieve its congeneric affinity with the supernal realm.[30] The result of this interaction generates a trace in the soul that the internal sense of imagination represents (*muḥākātī karda bāshad*) as an image made available both to the common sense—which allows the subject to *see* what his soul perceived—and to the imaginal memory

28 *Kimiyā*, 1: 91–92. On the early Islamic accounts describing Muḥammad's "tasting" of paradise, see Lange 232–33.

29 Cf. Fakhr al-Dīn Rāzī's reception of al-Ghazālī's discussion of the techniques inducing spiritual visions: Janos 2016, 208–209.

30 Compare the passage above, from the *Kīmiyā*, with a similar passage from the *Iḥyā*ʾ: "Prophets and saints are acquainted with this. Light illumines their chests not through learning, study, and writing books, but through renouncing the world, severing the ties to it, emptying the heart from its occupations, and turning unswervingly to God. He who is devoted to God, God is devoted to him.... In order to reach this ... a person's heart has to reach a stage when he is indifferent to any particular thing's presence or absence. Then he goes into a place of seclusion, confining himself to observances and acts of devotion. He sits there with an empty heart and focused intention, without distracting himself with reading the Qurʾān, examining its interpretation, consulting books on prophetic traditions, or anything else. Instead, he strives to ensure that nothing but God enters his mind. After sitting like that in seclusion, he keeps uttering with his tongue 'God! God!' over and over again, with presence of heart. Eventually he reaches the stage when he ceases to move the tongue and yet sees the word, as it were, still reverberating upon it. He continues like that until it disappears from the tongue, yet he finds his heart still mentioning (*dhikr*) it. He continues like that until the form and letters of the utterance and the configuration of the word disappear, but its naked meaning remains present in the heart as if it were inseparable from it.... At this point, if his will is strong, intention pure, and perseverance stable, if bodily desires or internal speech do not distract him with ties of this world, then flashes of Truth will shine forth in his heart. At the beginning, they come as a flash of lightning (*ka-l-barq al-khāṭif*), and disappear without remaining. After that, they appear again, possibly after delay. On second appearance, they can stay or disappear immediately. If they stay, they can stay for a longer or a shorter period of time. Similar visions [of other types?] can subsequently occur, or else they can remain confined to one and the same type." Treiger 2012, 70. Cf. Skellie's translation (2010, 54–55).

(*khazāna-yi khayāl*). The verb that al-Ghazālī employs, *muḥākāt kardan*, can be translated as "to imitate," or "to depict"; it is the same verb that Avicenna uses when describing the conversion into images of the inspirations from the celestial souls through the mediation of the compositive imagination and under the guidance of the practical intellect.[31]

In Saʿdi's account, the rose that the "Master of the Heart" beholds—just like the grapes from paradise that al-Ghazālī ascribes to the Prophet's vision—is a visual simulacrum that the internal senses generate under specific conditions: it is the result of the contact between the rational soul (under the function of the practical intellect) and the supernal realm, while the carnal soul (*nafs*) goes into a dormant state. As a further gloss to the exemplum of the Prophet's grapes, al-Ghazālī points out that it would have been impossible for Muḥammad to bring grapes from paradise: he would have certainly done so if he could. The question of the discrepancy between the imaginal and the material levels of existence of the depictions created by the imagination through its rational soul-mediated contact with the unseen is situated at the very core of Saʿdi's anecdote of the Master's vision: the intention of the "Master of the Heart" was to bring tangible proof of the vision of the roses, but also to share with his companions the beatitude of that imaginal contemplation. Interestingly enough, in Saʿdi's passage, it is the intoxicating scent of the imaginal roses that causes the Master to return to his senses with no tangible gift for his companions but the description of his experience. In spite of the theological and philosophical controversies on the nature of the sensorial experience of the soul after the death of the body, the impact of the scent of the imaginal roses on the intellect of the Master attests to the role of the internal senses in the reception and translation of the material descending from the unseen.

---

31 See, for instance, Avicenna's *Epistle of the Sphere*: "Un degré plus puissant que celui-ci consiste à faire se stabiliser ces situations et ces formes (révélées) telles qu'elles sont, en empêchant la puissance imaginative de se mettre à les imiter [*muḥākātihā*] par d'autres choses. Un (degré) plus puissant (encore) que celui-ci, c'est que l'imaginative continue à imiter [*muḥākātihā*] (les formes révélées) et que l'intellect pratique et l'estimative ne soient pas privés de ce qu'ils ont fait se stabiliser. La forme de ce qu'ils ont appréhendé se stabilise alors dans la mémoire, tandis que l'imaginative se tourne vers la fantaisie et y imite ce qu'elle a reçu (de la révélation) par de merveilleuses formes audibles et visibles, chacune de ces (puissances) procédant selon son point de vue." Michot 1985, 519–20. See also a similar description in Avicenna's Persian treatise, the *Dānish-nāma* (Ibn Sinā 1353/1974, 135–39), on which al-Ghazālī relied extensively for the incorporation of philosophical thought into his own works. On al-Fārābī as the precursor of the idea of the internal senses as the faculties that "imitate" (*muḥākāt*) as a form of mental representation, see Davidson 1992, 58. See also Walzer 1998, 210–13; 1957. For a survey of the concept of *muḥākāt* in the Islamic philosophical tradition, see Zarqāni 1390/2011.

In the introduction to the *Gulistān*, the imaginal roses of the Master's experience of *mukāshafa* interplay with the real roses sought by his companions and eventually touched by the literary persona of Saʿdi himself, in his bucolic retreat, after giving up his monastic asceticism. Similarly, the beloved that appears in Saʿdi's ghazal is a presence that is simultaneously tangible, imaginal, ideal, and metaphysical, as a result of the conflations between levels of reality (the world, the internal senses, the intellect, and the supernal realm) produced by the rational soul's mediation between the mundane experience and the quest for the unseen. The overlap between these levels and functions with respect to Saʿdi's lyric subject's intellectual and spiritual cognition of the beloved is often overlooked because of the simplistic reading that is often projected onto the lyric representation of the heart, which, from al-Ghazālī onwards, operates both as a gateway to the external world and as an opening toward the unseen.

5 Spiritual Cardiology

In the Avicennian epistemological model, the rational soul (or practical intellect) is the entity that connects with the supernal realm to retrieve "meanings" from the unseen. By relying on scattered ideas taken from a variety of pre-existing currents of thought, al-Ghazālī ingeniously reinvented the Avicennian model and ascribed the metaphysical functions of the rational soul to the heart.[32] Both in al-Ghazālī's passage from the *Kīmiyā* and in Saʿdi's anecdote from the *Gulistān*, as the expression "Master of the Heart" (*ṣāḥib-dil*) suggests, the heart is the seat of the visionary experience of the beholder who peruses the supernal world and translates its sublime ideas into the mental images of celestial roses. It is therefore mainly to al-Ghazālī that the post-11th-century Persian lyric tradition owes the cohesive relocation of the functions of the Avicennian psychological and noetic system from the rational soul to the heart.[33] Even

32 On the heart as the seat of spiritual knowledge in pre-existing traditions, see Treiger 2020, 389.

33 In the Khorasanian literary tradition, this process took off only after the second half of the 12th century. In Sanāʾī's ghazals, for instance, the heart does not take up a prominent epistemological role. Nevertheless, Sanāʾī's later work, *Ḥadīqat al-ḥaqīqa* (whose materials were collected shortly before his death, presumably in 1131; see Lewis 1995, 134) shows both philosophical and theological influences in the representation of the heart as a mirror of one's deeds. In the first chapter of this renowned *maṣnavī*, even though the cosmology of the contact between the rational intellect and the invisible is not clearly stated, the heart is represented as a screen which the believer ought to polish in order to approach the divine presence:

though al-Ghazālī's spiritual cardiology involved a simplification of Avicenna's complex theorization of the cosmological and epistemological dimensions of the intellect, his rarefied and reified translation of the philosophical system that he inherited offered a flexible set of metaphors that slowly penetrated and revolutionized the psychological imagery of the Persian ghazal. It is through al-Ghazālī's spiritual cardiology that the legacy of Avicennian psychology—in the role ascribed to the rational soul as a filter between the physical world, the imagination, and the invisible—reverberates throughout the entire history of the medieval ghazal in the guise of the representation of the heart as a polyfunctional object of erotic, sensible, and metaphysical perception.[34]

The most compelling definition of the correspondence between the heart and the functions of the Avicennian rational intellect can be found in al-Ghazālī's Persian magnum opus, *The Alchemy of Bliss*.[35] In the introduction,

---

The royal road of the soul and of your breath toward the True
Is nothing but the polishing the mirror of the heart.
[2.74] Sanā'i 1382/2003, 5. Moreover, considering the reference to the rebuttal of incarnationism through the metaphor of the mirror, al-Ghazālī's influence (see Treiger 2012, 33, and, for al-Ghazālī's parable of the Greek and the Chinese painters as a metaphor for the heart, Griffel 2009a, 263–64) over the composition of Sanā'ī's lines can be hardly denied:
Whoever ignores the difference between epiphany and incarnationism
Will utter nothing but nonsense when discussing this portion of the path.
If you want your mirror to reflect Vision,
Do not distort it, and keep bright its surface.
[2.75] Ibid., 6.

34 "Al-Ghazālī uses 'heart' (*qalb*) as a synonym for what in philosophy is called 'soul.' Cf., for instance, the second definition of *qalb* in *Iḥyā' ʿulūm al-dīn*, III, 3 (XXI, 1), or the same definition in *Maʿārij al-quds*, p. 21. In his *al-Risāla al-Laduniyya* (in: *al-Quṣūr al-ʿawālī min rasāʾil Imām al-Ghazālī* [Cairo, 1964], pp. 97–122), p. 101.13–15 al-Ghazālī says that those engaged in Sūfism (*al-mutaṣawwifa*) use '*qalb*' for the substance (*jawhar*) that the philosophers (*al-ḥukamā'*) call '*al-nafs al-nāṭiqa*.' MS Berlin, Spr. 1968 (Ahlwardt 3210), fol. 41b probably has the more complete textual version and says that the *mutaṣawwifa* call this substance 'sometimes the *qalb* and sometimes the *rūḥ*.' Three lines later, both texts have: '*al-qalb* and *al-rūḥ* are for us (*ʿindanā*) names for *al-nafs al-nāṭiqa*.'" Griffel 2004, 142, n. 132. The most comprehensive analysis of al-Ghazālī's projection of the functions of the rational soul onto the image of the heart has been published by Alexander Treiger, who thus explains the rationale that likely informed al-Ghazālī's endeavor: "In calling it heart rather than rational soul or intellect, al-Ghazālī did not intend any radical departure from philosophical noetics in the direction of a more 'emotional' noetics of the heart. He merely intended to defuse the concept's philosophical connotations so as to make it more palatable to the broader circles of religious scholars (*ʿulamā'*), while leaving its content essentially the same." Treiger 2012, 18. See also ibid., 17–21.

35 Although the metaphor of the heart as a mirror pervades the entirety of al-Ghazālī's works, the philosophical underpinnings of this association are particularly evident in the *Kīmiyā*. This could be explained by the Persian-speaking intended audience of the book,

al-Ghazālī clarifies that the heart (*dil*) to which he refers is a subtle and invisible substance that other authors call "spirit" (*rūḥ*) or "soul" (*nafs*). Unlike man's physical body, the external eye (*chashm-i ẓāhir*) cannot see the heart, whereas only inner vision (*baṣīrat-i bātin*) accesses it. Al-Ghazālī argues that this spiritual heart does not correspond to the "chunk of flesh" that lies in the left part of one's chest, but to the subtle spirit that belongs to the body only accidentally and which will survive it after its physical decay.[36]

The metaphor of the heart as a mirror enables al-Ghazālī to synthesize the double articulation of Avicenna's rational soul as an instrument of cognition of both the physical and the metaphysical layers of reality:

> At the outset of its creation, the human heart is like iron from which a bright mirror is made—a mirror in which the entire world appears if it is carefully preserved. Otherwise, it will be entirely covered in rust in such a way that no mirror will ever shine from that iron.[37]

Even though this passage relates to a context in which al-Ghazālī discusses the metaphysical dimension of the heart, the nature of the "world" (*ʿālam*) that appears on its surface is both physical and transcendent. In one of the key paragraphs of the book (*ʿAjāyib-i ʿālamhā-yi dil*, "The Wonders of the Worlds of the Heart"), al-Ghazālī further explores this double articulation of the heart by describing it as an organ that is divided into an outer and an inner side. The outer side of the heart has five gates (*darvāza*), which through the five senses open to the world of sensations (*ʿālam-i maḥsūsāt*), or the physical world (*ʿālam-i jismānī*). By contrast, the inner side of the heart features a small window, or aperture (*rawzanī*), that opens to the supernal world (*malakūt*). In this passage, the perception of the physical world and the vision of the unseen seem to be mutually exclusive, as they depend on the interference of the senses or lack thereof: "During sleep, when the path of the senses is closed, that inner door opens up and the unseen [*ghayb*] starts appearing from the supernal world [*ʿālam-i malakūt*] and the "Preserved Tablet" [*lāwḥ-i maḥfūẓ*]."[38] The heart, at that point, under the inspiration of the Preserved Tablet, "will start knowing and seeing what will happen in the future, either in a clear way, or

---

which must have been particularly familiar with the Avicennian tradition and would have read al-Ghazālī's work within that specific intellectual context. For other key passages in which al-Ghazālī illustrates his spiritual cardiology, see Treiger 2020, 393–96.

36 *Kimiyā*, 1: 15. On al-Ghazālī's recurrent emphasis on the difference between the physical heart and its spiritual counterpart, see Treiger 2012, 123–24, nn. 3–4.

37 *Kimiyā*, 1: 25.

38 Ibid., 1: 28.

in the guise of images that require interpretation." What al-Ghazālī describes as the truth about dreams is only one empirical aspect that he puts forward to illustrate the metaphysics of the heart and its ontological connection with the supernal world:

> […] the heart resembles a mirror, and the Preserved Tablet is akin to a mirror that contains the form of all existing things: just as when the images appearing in a mirror are reflected in another mirror when the latter is held in front of the former, so the images [of all existing things] are reflected from the Preserved Tablet into the heart—but only when it is clear and free from sensations, and it acquires an affinity with the Preserved Tablet. So long as the heart is occupied by sensations, its affinity with the spiritual world will be hindered. But during sleep, the heart is free from [external] sensations, therefore anything that corresponds to its essence will start appearing from its contemplation of the supernal realm. […] Nevertheless, even though the senses are shut down because of sleep, the [compositive] imagination [*khayāl*] will be active. This is why whatever the heart sees during sleep will appear in the guise of an imaginary analogue: it will not be clear or fully manifested […]. But when [the individual] dies, neither the senses nor the imagination will remain. At that point [the heart] will see things without veils.[39]

The scientific explanation of the interference caused by the imagination reveals the extent to which al-Ghazālī's spiritual cardiology directly derives from Avicenna's psychology and his representation of the human intellect, especially with respect to the external world and the cognition of both the intelligibles and the supernal realm.[40] There is a striking similarity between this passage and the texts (especially his Persian *Dānish-nāma*, completed in 1027) in which Avicenna explains the physiology of sleep as an altered state of consciousness that favors the connection between the soul and the supernal world.[41]

Alexander Treiger has convincingly demonstrated that in al-Ghazālī's spiritual epistemology the concept of the "Preserved Tablet" is the functional analogue of Avicenna's soul of the fixed stars, which constantly cogitate and reflect

39 Ibid., 28–29.

40 See, in particular, Kukkonen 2012.

41 See, for instance, the passages from the *Dānish-nāmā* (Ibn Sinā 1353/1974, 131–46) that most likely influenced al-Ghazālī's spiritual cardiology. On the overall influence of this book on al-Ghazālī's thought, see Janssens 1993.

the particulars of past, present, and future events that belong to the material world.[42] The epistemological character of the "Preserved Tablet" derives from the conflation of a notion widespread in Semitic languages, which can be traced back to the Babylonian concept of "tablets of fate,"[43] with a probable syntactical misreading of the Quranic verse 85: 22.[44] Among early Quranic commentators, this conflation generated the idea of a correspondence between the expression *lawḥ maḥfūẓ* and the concept of *umm al-kitāb*, "the matrix of the book," designating the celestial matrix of the Quran, in which the archetypes of all things past, present, and future are inscribed.

Even though the concept of the *lawḥ-i maḥfūẓ* is not a particularly recurrent topos in medieval Persian poetry, sparse occurrences of its usage are found in a number of early texts that do not necessarily belong to the Sufi or spiritual tradition. For instance, in a panegyric dedicated to Sultan Maḥmūd (d. 1030), ʿUnṣurī praises the monarch by inviting him to read the name of his enemies in the "Preserved Tablet," thus implying that Maḥmūd, by means of his psycho-cosmic power, may clearly read the destiny of his kingdom.[45] In one of Amīr

42 Treiger 2012, 105–107, and 158–59, nn. 18–26 for a comprehensive survey of the key passages in which al-Ghazāli discusses the characteristics of the "Preserved Tablet." See also ibid., 169, n. 27 for Treiger's confutation of some scholars' theorization of the "Preserved Tablet" as the analogue to Avicenna's Active Intellect. See also Kukkonen 2012, 554–56. Frank Griffel has pointed out that even though al-Ghazālī, in the *Tahāfut al-falāsifa* (*The Precipitance of the Philosophers*), criticizes the positions of the philosophers on the metaphorical status of the *lawḥ maḥfūẓ*, his "own understanding of [the preserved tablet] in his later writings like *al-Arbaʿīn fī ʾuṣūl al-dīn* is, however, hardly different from the *falāsifa*'s position." Griffel 2004, 116. On this apparent conundrum, see Frank 1992, 45. On the influence of Avicenna on al-Ghazālī's theorization of the Preserved Tablet, see Pines 1987.

43 "The tablet as the record of the decisions of the divine will is also found in the Book of Jubilees. In Jub., v, 13 it is said that the divine judgement on all that exists on earth is written on the tablets in heaven. Enoch prophesies the future from the contents of these tablets (Book of Enoch, xciii, 2; lxxxi; ciii, 2; cvi, 19). The 'scripture of truth' is mentioned as early as Daniel, x, 21, the contents of which Daniel announces in prophetic form." *EI*², s.v. "Lawḥ" [A.J. Wensinck, C.E. Bosworth].

44 "*Al-lawḥ* thus means the tablet kept in heaven, which in sūra LXXXV, 22 is called *lawḥ maḥfūẓ* , usually translated as the 'safely preserved' tablet. But it is not certain whether the words in this passage are really syntactically connected. If we read *maḥfūẓ^{un}*, the word does not go with *lawḥ* in but with the preceding *ḳurʾān^{un}* and the translation is: 'Verily it is a Ḳurʾān, famous, preserved on a tablet' […]; 'safely preserved', i.e., against alteration." Ibid.

45 "Hamī nāmash zi lawḥ-i maḥfūz khʷānī." ʿOnsori Balkhi 1363/1984, 279. Early Saljuq poets too, such as Azraqī of Herat and Amīr Muʿizzī of Nishapur, would emphasize the conflation of psychological and cosmological aspects of the "lawḥ-i maḥfūẓ" as an analogue of their patrons' semi-divine intellect or the macro-cosmic dimension of their rule:

Muʿizzī's panegyrics we can find an apotheosized development of al-Ghazālī's theorization of the retentive imagination (*khayāl*) as the micro-cosmic correspondence of the macro-cosmic nature of the preserved tablet:

> You would say that your mind is a transcription from the Preserved
> Tablet,
> As you may peruse it and foresee with certitude the events to come.[46]

The following lines composed by Sanāʾī attest to some of the earliest literary reflections of al-Ghazālī's epistemic and anatomic reorientation of the concept of *lawḥ-i maḥfūẓ* as a symbolic transition involving the correspondence between the Avicennian rational intellect and the heart:

> The Master of the Intellect brought the magic of creation from the first
> Intelligence,
> From the last Intelligence it brought Sirius and the springtime breeze.
>
> The eyes wonder what the spirit [*rūḥ*] could ever find beyond the Tablet,
> And the carnal soul inquires whether intelligence can retrieve anything
> outside the heart![47]

It was probably as a result of al-Ghazālī's reorientation of the concept of the Preserved Tablet that, from the 12th century onwards, *lawḥ-i maḥfūẓ* embodied the renewal of a sacred epistemic correspondence between the heart and the invisible realm. By the 13th century, the philosophical background of al-Ghazālī's innovation was incorporated within the Sufi tradition in such a way that authors like ʿIrāqī (d. 1289) would defend the epistemological powers of the heart against the fallacy of philosophical inquiry:

No error ever affected your mind, O wonder!
You'd say that the Preserved Tabled hides in your mind!
[2.76] Azraqi Haravi 1336/1957, 80.
Should Destiny compose collections of poems in your praise
It would inscribe the Preserved Tablet in the pages of its *dīvān*!
[2.77] Amir Moʿezzi 1385/2006, 161.

46 [2.78] Amir Moʿezzi 1385/2006, 463. Cf. *Kimiyā*, 1: 56: "*az khazāna-yi khayālāt lawḥ-i maḥfūz-i tu sākht.*"

47 [2.79] Sanāʾi, 1362/1983, 41.

Your heart is the Preserved Tablet, and yet you seek the science of the philosophers?
The sun is in your abode, and you seek a lamp from the dark alley?[48]

The allegorical equation between, on the one side, the heart and the sun, and, on the other, the philosophical science and a lamp, may be read as a judgment that does not lead to the complete dismissal of rational inquiry, but which portrays it as a less effective epistemological path, especially if compared with the training of the heart as a spiritual exercise.

Even though we may regard ʿAṭṭār as the first poet who brought to the territory of the lyric full exploration of the spiritual epistemology of the heart as a mirror reflecting the unseen, Saʿdi's lyricism develops this image within the context of sacred eroticism.[49] Throughout Saʿdi's ghazals, the spiritual heart of the lyric subject shines as a polyfunctional representation of human eroticism at the intersection of physical desire and the metaphysics of the contemplation of the world. In Saʿdi's poetry, the explicit references to the heart as a polished mirror capable of reflecting the unseen are the most self-explanatory pieces of evidence of al-Ghazālī's condensation of the Avicennian epistemological heritage:

The heart is the mirror that reflects the form of the unseen [*ṣūrat-i ghayb*]
Provided that no rust covers its surface.
Ṭayyibāt 132[50]

In some contexts, Saʿdi reveals the Avicennian background of the heart as metaphorical analogue of the rational intellect. The line below is particularly striking, as the poet makes use of al-Ghazālī's image of an aperture or little door (*rawzan, darīcha*) from which the heart may contemplate invisible realities:

48 [2.80] ʿErāqi 1375/1996, 99.

49 See, for instance the following lines by ʿAṭṭār:
The heart is a mirror whose bottom is dark,
If you polish it, its surface will open up.
The heart is nothing but dirt when its bottom is up,
But when the darkness is cleansed, all its radiance will appear.
[2.81] ʿAttār 1392/2013, 226.

50 [2.82] Saʿdi YE, 64. Yusofi's edition does not include the first *miṣrāʿ* of the line above. Nevertheless, it is found in some of the most reliable manuscripts. See ibid., 406.
Cf. this other line, also from the *Ṭayyibāt*:
O Beloved, open a door upon my face from creation
So that no one may be aware of my mysteries.
[2.83] (*Ṭayyibāt* 141). Saʿdi YE, 68.

From the aperture [*darīcha*] of my thinking [*fikrat*], my heart
Showed to the rational soul [*nafs-i nāṭiqa*] the signs of my increasingly desperate condition.[51]

In other lines, the intertextual link implied by the noun *rawzan* ("aperture") reveals the contemplative nature of the lyrical eroticism that the poet displays:

Day and night that hour comes forth: when like the sunshine
You reveal your face, and suddenly shut the aperture behind you.
Ṭayyibāt 211[52]

In many ghazals, Saʿdi converts the simile of the heart as a mirror into a full metaphor, whose flexibility of usage allows the lyric discourse on vision to develop the epistemic background of Avicennian psychology:

So splendidly your face appears in our mirror:
for pure is the mirror and beautiful is your face.

Glittering wine shines through the transparent cup:
thus your beautiful nature shines through your complexion.

Irresistible you are to anyone who has walked with you
or spent a few breaths in your enchanting company....

Saʿdi is a man who contemplates the garden of your beauty:
It is the poor's hands that loot the delicacies of the banquet....
Badāyiʿ 591[53]

The metaphor of the mirror establishes a twofold aesthetic condition that asserts both the objective beauty of the beloved's face and the relative aptitude of the lover's heart to reflect and compare the ideal forms of beauty filtering from the supernal world with the images provided by the external senses. The purity of the mirror introduces the theme of the heart as a reflective surface that the actions, beliefs, and inner disposition of the lyric subject can polish in order to prepare it for the perusal of both the visible and the invisible world. The idea behind the conflation of these two depictions is that the lover's

51 See Chapter 6, pp. 305–306.
52 [2.84] Saʿdi YE, 99.
53 [2.85] Saʿdi YE, 266–67.

heart—"provided that no rust covers its surface"—is a mirror that reflects the perceptions coming from both the external senses and the realm of the supernal, through the mediation of the internal senses: on the one hand, the beloved's face, and, on the other, the "form" of the invisible world (*ghayb*), from which particulars belonging to past, present, and future events are reflected onto the mirror-like intellect of the beholder. This idea constitutes the theoretical and aesthetic backbone of the anthropology of vision that Saʿdi has designated as the keystone of his lyrical innovation. The psychological value of such images is particularly significant if we consider that, in his lines, the heart stands for the rational soul: it operates as a mirror that reflects both the physical form of the beloved and a set of unspecified concepts (*maʿānī*), which filter from the unseen and, by intermediation of the practical intellect, emerge to the internal senses as mental images.

6 The Cosmology of the Heart, Between Philosophy and Poetry

As mentioned earlier, major sources of evidence to test the circulation of al-Ghazālī's spiritual psychology in the Persian-speaking Sufi *milieux* of 13th-century Iran are to be found in the works of ʿAzīz al-Dīn Nasafī (fl. 13th century).[54] Nasafī's epistles (namely the *Kitāb al-insān al-kāmil*, which he started composing in Bukhara in 1261 and completed a few years later in western and southern Iran, and *Kashf al-ḥaqāyiq*) showcase an original conflation of theological, Sufi, and philosophical ideas, although, like Sanāʾī, he refrains from using the word *falsafa* and opts instead for the generic sapiential category of *ḥikma*. Even though Saʿdi's access to Nasafī's texts cannot be philologically proved, his works attest to the intellectual availability of al-Ghazālī's spiritual synthesis of Avicennian psychology and cosmology in the western Persianate world during the 13th century.

Nasafī's comments on the concept of *lawḥ-i maḥfūz* are particularly telling, as in the passages in which he explores the meaning of this concept and its cosmological, psychological, and epistemological functions, he clearly draws upon (often verbatim) both al-Ghazālī's *Kīmiyā* and Avicenna's last works, namely the *Ishārāt* and in particular the *Dānish-nāma*. In one of his last works, *Kashf al-ḥaqāyiq* (completed in 1281 at Abarquh, near Yazd), Nasafī declares that the spiritual curriculum for the attainment of *maʿrifa* involves the gradual acquisition of knowledge of one's soul (*dānistan-i nafs-i khʷad*), knowledge of God (*dānistan-i khudāy*), knowledge of the world (*dunyā*), and

54 For an extensive study of Nasafī's thought and works, see Ridgeon 1998; 2002.

eventually knowledge of the hereafter (*ākhirat*).[55] This sequence closely follows the lengthy introduction with which al-Ghazālī opens the *Kīmiyā* (and which does not appear in the *Iḥyā'*) as a deductive approach to the spiritual sciences that he illustrates therein.[56] While the relationship between cosmology and psychology that Nasafī presents to his audience follows al-Ghazālī's representation of the connection between the heart and the supernal realm, it also overtly retrieves the technical philosophical vocabulary that al-Ghazālī had carefully transposed to a less abstruse register in order to make his arguments more effective among his peers:

> Man possesses a human soul [*nafs-i insānī*], which is the reflection of the soul of the angels [*nafs-i malakī*]. When the carnal soul [*rūḥ-i nafsānī*], which is located in the brain, finds affinity with the essence of the celestial spheres, it becomes capable of reflecting the celestial soul, and the reflection of the celestial soul will appear in it. [...] The carnal soul of some people approaches the substance of the sphere of the fixed stars [*falak al-aflāk*]. Their souls reflect the soul of the fixed stars, which is the universal soul [*nafs-i kull*], and it turns into their own soul.[57]

The association between the heart/rational soul and the supernal realm as two mirrors reflecting each other is another element that clearly derives directly from al-Ghazālī's cosmological noetics:

> When one's carnal soul, through spiritual training and commitment [*riyāżat va mujāhadat*], reaches the balance of the essence of the celestial spheres, the rational soul, in terms of purity and isolation, gains similarity with the celestial soul. Subsequently, through the affinity [*munāsabat*] that comes to exist between the rational soul and the celestial soul, things that proceed from the celestial soul start appearing in the rational soul like two clear mirrors [*āyina-yi ṣāfī*] that are held in front of each other [*dar muqābala-yi yakdīgar*]. Nevertheless, since anything that appears therein [i.e., in the celestial soul] manifests itself in a universal fashion,

55 ʿAziz al-Din Nasafi 1391/2012, 115.

56 On the peculiarity of this epistemic curriculum inserted at the beginning of the *Kīmiyā*, see Hillenbrand 2013, 61–62.

57 ʿAziz al-Din Nasafi 1391/2012, 127. See also ibid. 134–35, in which Nasafī illustrates Avicenna's emanationist cosmology by relating the human soul to the Active Intellect (referred to as the vessel of the soul of the moon) and the chain of emanations that lead it to the contact with the soul of the fixed stars, the Universal Intellect, and eventually the divine light. For a comparison with Avicenna's cosmology, see the chart in Nasr 1978, 204.

> it will appear in the rational soul as a universal which the rational soul mimics [*ḥikāyat*] as a particular through the aid of the imaginative faculty [*mutakhayyila*; i.e., the compositive imagination]. They [the mimicked particulars] will be projected onto the common sense, which allows the subject to perceive them without sensing the difference between what is perceived from outside or from within the common sense—and it is for this reason that they call it "common sense," as it can perceive from both sides. Therefore, the more one's brain is in good health and their imaginative faculty and common sense are free from attachments, the more their perceptions will be veridical and accurate. This applies to dreams too [...], and some prophets experienced their revelations by means of dreams.[58]

While the references to the affinity [*munāsabat*] between the rational soul and the supernal realm as two mirrors held against each other [*dar muqābal-i yakdīgar*], along with the translation (or imitation) [*muḥākāt*] of the celestial universal into particulars processed by the imaginal faculties, follows the Persian wording of the *Kīmiyā*, the vocabulary of the entire passage reestablishes the Avicennian substratum of al-Ghazālī's passages. This operation—with a major emphasis on al-Ghazālī's wording—is even more evident in *The Book of the Perfect Man*, which Nasafī partially composed in Shiraz in the early 1260s, allegedly by the mausoleum of Ibn Khafīf,[59] which had been recently rebuilt by the Salghurid family, and which sources associate with Sa'di's Sufi activity.[60] In the eleventh epistle of this book, Nasafī clarifies that whatever denominations the scholars of different epistemic traditions have given to the visible and the invisible worlds, they all go back to the main distinction between the physical realm, *mulk*, and the supernal, *malakūt*, which is also referred to as "the world of command," "the world of the unseen," or the "intelligible world [*ʿālam-i maʿqūl*]."[61] In the eighteenth *Risāla*, after discussing the physio-psychology of dreams and visions in terms that are both philosophical and scriptural (with wording that reminds us of Avicenna's *Dānish-nāma*), Nasafī reintroduces the topic of the intellect/heart and the celestial souls mirroring each other under the influence of the imagination and the estimation (*wahm*), in a fashion that shows how influential the wording of the *Kīmiyā* had been throughout his oeuvre:

58 ʿAziz al-Din Nasafi 1391/2012, 137.
59 ʿAziz al-Din Nasafi 1341/1962, 118.
60 See Bashari 2020, 285.
61 ʿAziz al-Din Nasafi 1341/1962, 156–57.

> O dervish! Estimation [*vahm*] faces the intellect, and often it subjugates it [...]. The purpose of my discussion is to show that the philosophers [*ḥukamā*] say that these images [appearing in the imagination through contact with the unseen] are not the angels [themselves], as the celestial angels are constantly in their own position and busy with their occupations [...]. Nevertheless, the celestial angels are all pure and clear, and contain all sciences and purities. Anyone who purifies himself through spiritual training and commitment will find an affinity with the celestial angels. Once the affinity is established they [i.e., one's soul and the celestial spheres] will be like two clear mirrors that are held in front of each other, and this encounter is the reason for all inspiration during wakefulness and veridical dreams during sleep. This is what the philosophers say about the meaning of the angels coming into images, the meaning of seeing Khiżr and Iliyās, the "men of the unseen" [*mardān-i ghayb*], and the meaning of the images that the wayfarers see during their spiritual seclusion.[62]

Considering the stylistic restraint with which Saʿdi deploys technical terms in his lyric poetry, explicit references to the celestial tablet are very rare in his ghazals. However, the passages from Nasafī's works quoted above attest to the widespread circulation of the Avicennian subtext of al-Ghazālī's spiritual cardiology within Saʿdi's environment. Overall, the few times Saʿdi explicitly mentions the Preserved Tablet, he confirms the association between the spiritual psychology of the heart and the "meanings" that the invisible world can reflect upon it:

> O Saʿdi, clear the tablet of your heart from anyone but your beloved:
> Any science whose path does not lead to the truth will take you astray.[63]
>
> *Ṭayyibāt* 121

The reference to "science," *ʿilm*, stresses the epistemological framework in which Saʿdi conceives the process of cognizing the quest for the supernal realm through the mirroring properties of the tablet-like heart of the lyric subject. The doubt expressed about the nature of the sciences that might not succeed in leading the beholder to the Truth points to the epistemic complementarity of philosophy and the sacred cognition that *mushāhada* can provide.

62 Ibid., 241.
63 [2.86] Saʿdi YE, 59.

In another ghazal, Saʿdi displays a conflation between the manifestation of divine beauty through the beholder's *qibla* (as analyzed in the fourth chapter, on the basis of Aḥmad Ghazālī's passages from the *Savāniḥ*), the sensorial perception of the object of desire, and the epistemological background of the Preserved Tablet, in which love is portrayed as an experience mediating between the external senses, the internal sensory faculties, and the intellect:

I shall no longer pray in *that* direction
If you show me where the real *qibla* is.

Is that the light radiating from his forehead,
Or does he stand next to his tent, reflecting the sunshine in a mirror?

They may erase the entire world from the tablet of my intellect:
Love shall not disappear, as it is the effigy on a precious stone.
Ṭayyibāt 153[64]

At times, al-Ghazālī's simile of the mirror metaphorically substitutes the heart, by elevating the purity of its surface to a filter capable of associating the perception of the visible world with the meaning of the supernal realm:

To whom shall I attach my heart, if I take it away from desiring you?
No one resembles you in the world, and yet the world is not a narrow alley!

Not all eyes can see our beautiful witness [*shāhid*] as he *is*
A mirror with no rust on it is required to contemplate creation!
Khavātīm 693[65]

The real novelty of al-Ghazālī's approach in transferring the seat of Avicenna's noetics from the intellect to the heart is the opportunity to support the preexisting Sufi homiletic considerations on the spiritual cardiology with a powerful psychological model that accounts for the complexity of the relationship between the world of senses and the invisible realm. A full confluence of these two perspectives appears in a ghazal in which Saʿdi elaborates on both the

64 [2.87] Saʿdi YE, 73. Instead of the genitive simile "the tablet of the intellect" (*lawḥ-i fikr*), some manuscripts record "the intellect *and* the tablet" (*fikr-u lawḥ*), which would imply a direct reference to the preserved tablet and the intellect/soul as mirroring surfaces reflecting each other. See Ibid., 415. Ms. Yale 1432 (f. 216a) confirms Yusofi's edition.

65 [2.88] Saʿdi YE, 310.

imaginal dominant of the heart's "mystery" and the ethical aspect of the epistemological impediment affecting the senses by means of their attachment to the material world through the concupiscence of the carnal soul:

> For an entire life I have concealed in my chest the mysteries of the heart
> But now the pointer of the secret has fallen out of the compass of the heart.
>
> If you are a Muslim, my friend, why would you need Christian monasteries and a Mazdian belt?
> Lust is the fire temple of the soul, and desire is the Mazdian belt of the heart....
>
> Your essence is as pure as a mirror, behold yourself!
> For how long will you conceal the truthful forms under the rust of the heart?
>
> This much you should know: the angel shall not visit the chamber
> of your mind, if the image of the demon appears on the panel of your heart.
>
> You shall not conquer the kingdom of freedom and deliverance from possessions:
> Put the two worlds at your service, by recurring to the assistance of the heart!
>
> In the picture gallery of the world, amidst the images, abandon your carnal soul:
> And you shall explore the supernal world through the tool of your heart.
>
> I fear the charisma of your aspirations won't go past the affairs of this worldly clay:
> Will the possibilities of the heart leave a trace on you?
>
> Sa'di, how wrong it is to discuss the science of music with a deaf person:
> The melodies of the soul are needed to illustrate the mysteries of the heart!
>
> *Badāyiʿ* 535[66]

66 [2.89] Sa'di YE, 242–43.

Before Saʿdi, prominent lyric authors such as Sanāʾī, ʿAṭṭār, and Anvarī had composed ghazals formally similar to the one above, whose refrain-word (*radīf*) appearing at the end of each line is "heart" (*dil*). In spite of the spiritual overtones of a good number of Sanāʾī's and ʿAṭṭār's poems, their compositions centered on the description of the heart do not seem to be informed by al-Ghazālī's spiritual psychology as much as the content of Saʿdi's ghazal.[67]

---

67 Sanāʾī:
The heart received the news of your hair, O beloved:
Forgive me if I am here, following my heart.
Send my heart back to me, O moon-faced idol,
Or at least show me the path leading to my heart.
If you show no affection toward us,
We lose our heart, and find no trace of it.
No one can endure such preoccupation and folly:
Bleeding for the beloved, my liver and heart on fire.
Were we not in love with you, no peril would affect us:
How grave is the peril that threatens the heart, O beloved?
As soon as the heart happily embraced the sorrow of loving you,
We gave up our life, and tightened the pain of love to our heart.
[2.90] Sanāʾi 1362/1983, 919; 1389/2010, 361–62.
Without your hair, O idol, the heart enjoys no peace:
The heart was troubled by your hair, O seduction of the heart's lifetime!
The soul is your servant, the heart drowns in your ocean,
You have caused melancholia to take over all the sections of the heart.
As soon as the soul was enslaved to you heart, it shone from this servitude,
The heart was revived by your name, and the renown of the heart resounded through the two worlds.
O love, my heart senselessly fails to recognize the signs of evil eye:
Did you receive the message from my heart, saying: "O moon, settle our trouble!"
You dismiss the message of the heart: will I ever gain anything?
You are the moon in the sky—from your face; and you are the scarlet wine—from your lips.
Since my heart desires one like you, no satisfaction I will ever receive from the heart.
Everyone enjoys the companionship of joy, whereas I see only pain from you.
For every breath that ʿAṭṭār takes, O love, you are the only peace of his heart.
[2.91] ʿAttār 1392/2013, 800. Anvarī:
With whom shall I share the pain of my heart in this city?
Anyone from the two worlds who can cherish my heart?
My heart is constantly in the company of sorrow
And my sorrow constantly accompanies my heart.
I have no notion of the heart of the world, this is why
I fell straight into the world of the heart.
My heart bleeds with thousands of sighs.
The pain was excessive: farewell to the dead heart!
Will you bless me with your mercy?
All at once I'll unload the pain that burdens my heart.
[2.92] Anvari 1337/1958, 2: 865–66.

Among Sa'di's contemporaries, Rumi does approach heart-centric compositions through a more spiritually-informed posture that does not limit itself to the discussion of lyric emotionality. However, his poems lack the psychological complexity that Sa'di displays in his meditation on the imaginal power of the heart.[68] Hints of Sa'di's psychological appreciation of physical beauty can be found in 'Irāqī's lengthy lyric cardiology, which the poet developed around the twofold reflective characteristic of the heart as a link between the visible world and the celestial realm:

> The painted portico of the heart is more beautiful than the high heaven,
> Especially when the Sultan of the heart holds a magnificent gathering in it.
>
> With His beauty, He manifests the paradisiacal city of the soul,
> With His face, He decorates the picture gallery of the heart.
>
> When the Sultan of the Truth holds court in the palace of the heart,
> The souls of the universe stand in line before the royal patio of the heart.
>
> What is the body? A painted curtain hanging from the threshold of the heart.
> And what is the soul? A chamberlain attending to the gate of the beloved of the heart!
>
> Every instant, the intellect composes a new letter before the soul,
> So that the chancellery of the heart may issue new edicts!
>
> Why does the bird of high aspiration fly from the lofty paradise?
> It seeks a soothing breeze from the garden of delights of the heart.

68 See, for instance, one of Rumi's most beautiful cardiologic ghazals, in which the exploration of the heart is projected toward a cosmological dimension. The internal senses of the beholder, nevertheless, do not seem to be involved in the metaphysical journey of the lyric subject:
I knocked at the door of the heart one night, desiring the heart's greeting:
A shout arose: "Who is this?" I replied: "The servant of the Heart!"
The alley of the heart shone from the waves of light radiating from the face of the heart
The vessels of the sun and the moon turned into the humble goblets of the heart.
Should the Universal Intellect visit the heart, it would offer its service.
The intellect and a thousand of its peers would offer their necks to the lace of the heart....
[2.93] Rumi 1376/1997, 319.

The endless beauty of the heart manifests itself around the world.
Anyone who has eyes will turn like the soul: bewildered by the heart.

The Khiżr of the soul constantly wanders around the imperial garden of the heart,
So that it may drink the water of life from the rejuvenating spring of the heart....

Behold its internal and outer sides, its beginning and its end,
So that it will be clear to you what the four pillars of the heart are.

The arch of its portico is the bow of the eyebrow of my beloved,
The *qibla* of my soul has been only the portico of the heart.

Every moment, the radiant face of the heart kindles a flame
So that it may attune to its colors anything that it finds in the world.

Since my beloved, like a painting, appears every time with different hues,
The colors of my heart radiate different colors with every breath.

In the sea of the soul, the two worlds are nothing but morning dew:
How could droplets of water ever appear in the ocean of the heart?

The world acquires its iridescent appearance from its heavenly decorations,
For that, paradise was adorned by the heavenly climate of the royal garden of the heart.

What a sumptuous table has been offered to this world!
Wouldn't it be a shame if we were unaware of the beauty and the splendor of the heart?

'Irāqī's tongue falls short when praising the heart:
All perfection that he thinks of pales before the heart.[69]

While 'Irāqī's ghazal includes an imaginal component in its celebration of the spiritual exploration of the heart, his representation focuses almost exclusively

69 [2.94] 'Erāqi, 1375/1996, 223–24.

on the metaphysical aspect of the cardiologic perusal of the world. Saʿdi's lyric cardiology, on the contrary, seeks a constant interaction between the sensory possibilities of the mundane experiences of desire and the role of the imagination in the interplay between the heart and the celestial speculum:

> It befits this blessed complexion to herald fortunate destiny:
> May the heart cogitate [*andīsha*] it and the eyes imagine it.
>
> No similar face will ever appear on the horizons
> If a mirror were not to be placed before its beauty.
>
> *Badāyiʿ* 413[70]

The association between the mental rumination (the hearts' "cogitation," *andīsha*) and the visual picturing of the object of desire in the heart and the eyes of the beholder hints at the simultaneous practice of the outwardly meditative (*fikrat*) and inwardly contemplative (*mushāhadat*) approach of the lyric subject to the overlaps between the carnal, the imaginal, and the intellectual movements of the heart. The physio-psychological background of the experience that both al-Ghazālī and Saʿdi describe shows how the processes leading to the so-called *mushāhada*, or metaphysical contemplation, are deeply entangled with the bodily aspect of imagination. In the next chapter I will discuss how even though al-Ghazālī frames death as the ideal condition for the unveiling that leads to the contemplation (*mushāhada*) of the supernal world, he hastens to specify that the heart's contemplative activity can be induced by the exposure to performative acts of aesthetic enjoyment and spiritual concentration.

At this point, for a better understanding of the multilayered functions of the heart of Saʿdi's lyric subject as a tool capable of mediating between the visible world and the realm of supernal imagination, it is worth considering the spiritual contemplative modality of *mushāhada* as an epistemological possibility that can be contrasted with the active meditation (*tafakkur*, or *fikrat*) described in the previous chapters. It is from a synthetic approach to these two apparently compartmentalized modalities of experiencing the physical and the metaphysical aspects of the world that one can further penetrate the psychological complexity of Saʿdi's erotic discourse.

---

70 [2.95] Saʿdi YE, 192.

7 From the Rational-Inferential Modality to the Imaginal-Cosmological Approach

According to al-Ghazālī, the ultimate function of the heart is to turn the physical body into a cognitive instrument capable of receiving the eternal bliss of God's presence—which he describes as the real paradise that man ought to seek.[71] In this argument al-Ghazālī suggests that cognition (*maʿrifa*) of the supernal realm is gleaned through the perception of God's creation by means of the five senses. From this representation, one might be tempted to assume that the perceptible world is the main focus of al-Ghazālī's cognitive psychology. However, its Avicennian background shows that this spiritual epistemology is a system that is quintessentially based on a twofold articulation that reflects a dualistic relationship between the body and the soul: the knowledge of the supernal realm can be obtained either through metaphysical inspiration or through the study and perusal of the earthly dimension of existence. Even though al-Ghazālī does not organize the relationship between these two modalities systematically, it is possible to infer from his writing that these two approaches—the sensorial perusal of God's creation and the path of metaphysical inspiration—correspond to two different stages that can often overlap by reason of the practices and the conduct of the believer.

In a key passage of the *Kīmiyā,* al-Ghazālī warns the reader that the perfection of spiritual cognition [*maʿrifat*] is acquired precisely through the two paths mentioned above, which carve out different approaches to the bodily aspect of sensorial perception and imagination:

> [1.] The path of the Sufis, who are known for their purity and for the spiritual effort that they embrace. [In this path] one ought to keep limpid his inner self through the ceaseless mention of God [*ẕikr*], till forgetting about himself and anything that is not Him, the Truth. At that point, things will start appearing in one's soul which manifest the greatness of God the Almighty in the guise of a contemplative experience [*mushāhada*]. This path is comparable to the act of setting a snare, which may either lead to the capture of a prey or constitute a failed attempt. It might also happen that a rat is caught or a falcon. People experience different degrees of success with this, depending on one's allotted luck and [spiritual] means.
>
> [2.] Another path is the acquisition of the science of spiritual cognition not through speculative theology or other exoteric sciences, but primarily

71 See Treiger 2020.

> through meditation [*tafakkur*] upon the marvels of creation [*ʿajāyib-i ṣunʿ*], just as we have pointed out when discussing the syllogistic process of spiritual cognition. [...] This science is acquired over a long time, but it is possible for the intelligent to attain it through cogitation [especially] whenever he finds a spiritual knower [*ʿārif*] as a teacher. On the contrary, the dense shall not grasp this science. This science is different from setting a snare—which may or may not catch a prey—for it is more akin to cultivating, trading, and acquiring. It is therefore similar to the practice of having a male and a female sheep mating in order to obtain economic gain [...].[72]

On the surface, al-Ghazālī seems to describe these cognitive possibilities—*mushāhada* and *tafakkur*—as two divergent paths that are mutually exclusive. In light of the Avicennian influence on the theorization of these two approaches, we may define the first path as an imaginal-cosmological modality, whereas the second, since it involves a rigorously intellectual approach to the cognition of the divine signs in the world, could be named as rational-inferential.

The relationship that the rational-inferential and the imaginal-cosmological approaches imply between the self and the sensible world also points at their divergent nature. The first model relies almost exclusively on cogitation upon the world, which the intellect syllogistically conducts through its control of the sensorial faculties. Conversely, through the imaginal-cosmological modality spiritual knowledge is acquired through a process of inner cleansing that brings the individual to a state of sensory dormancy leading to contact between the heart and the fixed stars/Preserved Tablet. This apparent dichotomy reflects the influence of both the empiricism of Avicennian noetics and al-Ghazālī's own attempt to formulate a general theory of spiritual cognition that is capable of taking into account the entire gamut of experiences and practices leading to the knowledge of the divine through different paths. What he describes as two opposite strategies is in fact the theoretical result of an ideal polarization whose aim is to cover the various possibilities of the phenomenology of spiritual cognition, along with their potential flaws, limitations, and unpredictable results.

Overall, one could argue that al-Ghazālī's juxtaposition of the imaginal-cosmological and rational-inferential modalities acts as an ideally hierarchical solution aiming at solving the paradox of the body. This paradox, as described earlier, haunts medieval Islamic spirituality's representation of physicality as both a negative cradle of opaque, engrossing temptations, and as a positive

72 *Kimiyā*, 2: 598.

temple from which the signs of the divine ought to be witnessed. In the chapters on *tafakkur*, al-Ghazālī posits that meditative contemplation (in the form of syllogistic observation of the world) constitutes the first step toward the spiritual cognition (*maʿrifat*) that prepares the soul for *mushāhada*. One might be tempted to argue that al-Ghazālī conceives of this form of contemplation, in which the body of the initiate is expected to be actively engaged with the physical observation of the world, as a preliminary step toward what he calls "the path of the Sufis," which corresponds to the stage of intellectual perfection obtained through sensory dormancy and inward meditation. Nevertheless, whenever al-Ghazālī approaches the topic of the contact of the heart with the unseen from the perspective of its psychological implications and the mechanisms that regulate the formation of mental images, the two paths cease to appear as different stages of a spiritual ladder and are conflated into a dynamic interplay between the senses and the intimations provided by the invisible world.

In the *Iḥyāʾ*, at the end of the book on the "Marvels of the Heart," al-Ghazālī elaborates on the quality of the images that the imagination creates on the basis of the inspirations coming from the invisible and their correlation with the images that derive from the external senses:

> For, of necessity, reality must appear in the heart from that side of it which is turned toward the world of spirits. Then its influence shines upon the side which is turned toward the visible material world, for the two sides are connected, the one with the other. We have already explained that the heart has two sides. One of them is turned toward the world of the unseen, which is the place of entrance of inspiration […]. Another side is turned toward the world of sense; and that which appears of this world in the side turned toward the world of sense is only an imagined form, for the world of sense is entirely subject to imaginative reproduction. Sometimes the image comes from looking by means of sight at the exterior of the visible world. It is possible that the form may not correspond to the ideal reality. You may see a person with a beautiful external appearance, while he is abominable in his heart and hideous in his inner life, because the world of sense abounds in deception.
>
> But the form produced in the imagination by the illuminating effect of the world of spirits upon the inner secret hearts cannot but reflect accurately their qualities and correspond to them. For the form in the world of spirits follows the true characteristics and corresponds to it. So it is not strange that the hideous reality is not seen, save in a hideous form. Thus Satan is seen in the form of a dog, a frog, a pig, and so on. The angel is seen

> in a beautiful form, and this form is an indication of the ideal realities and a true reflection of them.[73]

Al-Ghazālī's double articulation of the heart with respect to the images derived from the sensible world and those communicated by the invisible realm reflects Avicenna's theorization of the rational soul as operating according to two aspects: the theoretical and practical intellect, respectively. As noted in the first part of this chapter, Avicenna ascribes to the theoretical intellect all the functions that involve the conjunction with the Active Intellect in order to mentally perceive the intelligibles. On the other hand, man's practical intellect is oriented towards the internal senses, as it presides over their process of initial manipulation and abstraction of the perceptions communicated by the external senses and gathered by the common sense. Al-Ghazālī draws upon this dual formulation for his model of the spiritual heart, but he describes Avicenna's two aspects as two "sides," opening respectively toward the supernal realm and the physical world.

It is noteworthy that, in Avicenna's system, it is the practical intellect—as a result of its direct access to the senses—that conjoins with the realm of the unseen, which, cosmologically, corresponds to the soul of the fixed stars. Al-Ghazālī, by conflating the functions of Avicenna's practical and theoretical intellect within the heart, de facto strategically excludes the role of the relationship between the rational soul and the Active Intellect from his spiritual epistemology. Furthermore, considering the Active Intellect's capacity to permanently store the intelligibles that allow humans to think syllogistically, al-Ghazālī did not deem its function necessary to his spiritual reformulation of the Avicennian noetic system.

The elimination of the aspect of the soul that interacts with the active intellect leaves al-Ghazālī with an accentuated soul/senses dichotomy that is held together by the heart as a source of spiritual projection toward the physical world and the supernal realm through the imaginal activity of the internal senses. Al-Ghazālī's relativization of conceptual abstraction opens the door of spiritual contemplation onto the aesthetic experience of the physical and supernal world as they are either perceived by the external senses or imagined by the internal senses through the unifying functions of the heart. Poetic language soon subsumed this dual epistemological property of the heart by idealizing this organ as the main tool capable of guiding the lyric subject through the experience of the mundane world (including the treacherous paths of desire) and the invisible realities. From Sanā'ī onwards, the opposition

73 Skellie 2010, 114.

between love (*ʿishq*) and intellect (*ʿaql*) that crystallizes in the canonic imagery of the spiritual dimension of ghazal poetry does not derive from a denial of the Avicennian noetic system tout court, but it rather corresponds to a higher degree of awareness with respect to the rationalizing aspect of the rational-inferential approach to reality and the need for the lyric subject to invest in the imaginal-cosmological possibilities of exploration.[74]

In Saʿdi's case, these two aspects seem to emerge in a state of constant conflation, leading to serene portrayals of desire that hide the dramatic conflicts of the lyric subject in its appetite for all the ontological possibilities of being. Ultimately, it is precisely this anxiety for the quest for a universal truth as a redeeming unification of the tragedy of the gap between the soul and the body that informs some of Saʿdi's most compelling meditations on the nature of imaginal-cosmological contemplation:

> Last night I hit the ball of solitude in the valley of spiritual seclusion,
> I pitched my tent above the heights of the highest objects of
> contemplation.
>
> The Sufis of the monastic orders tore apart the duality of their vests
> As soon as I hit the ball of solitude in the alley of oneness.
>
> So often with my experience I hit the glassy vault of the sky
> That the feet of the First Intellect were covered in shiny shatters.
>
> The intellect was my guide, until love held my hand:
> Then, with my hand I shut down my melancholic intellect....
>
> *Badāyiʿ* 600[75]

This ghazal represents the ultimate frontier of Saʿdi's cognitive effort in the exploration of the cosmological origins of the relationship between imagination and the supernal nature of reality, whose experiential dimension is nothing but a pale fragment of the First Intelligence, as the very origin and source of creation. The frustration deriving from the efforts of experience in coveting the truth nestled in the highest vault of the supernal spheres generates the alternation between the guidance offered by the intellect and the inspirational opportunities that love—as a meditative form of passion—can provide for the

74 On Sanāʾī's familiarity with Avicenna's psychological system, see in the introduction to this part of the book, and de Bruijn 1983, 208–20.

75 [2.96] Saʿdi YE, 270.

lyric subject. As I will elaborate in the next chapter, it is the awareness of these clashing modalities that generates the constant dramatic effect that is typical of those ghazals in which Saʿdi's lyric subject wanders between the remembrances and illusions flashing in its heart and openings toward the world of experiences. In those liminal spaces, the human bodies that appear to the senses as objects of contemplation reveal the contiguity of the sensual appetites of the flesh and the redeeming signs of the divine.

CHAPTER 8

Beholding Beauty

The Flesh, the Forms, and the Meanings *of the Visionary Experience*

I suffered injustice, the veil of my desire was torn,
My painful reality: a long journey ahead, and my heart is lost.

Can distance veil one from old recognition [*maʿrifat*]?
You are absent with your body, yet present in my vision.

You are my ultimate purpose, the apogee of my effort and wishes,
I won't abandon the hand of hope, until I finally join you.

Ingrained in my veins, entangled with my joints, how could the
remembrance
Of you slip from my tongue, the thought of you leave my
imagination [*khayāl*]?

I am so occupied by your presence that I am absent to everything,
And my thinking is so focused on you that I'm unaware of all
people.

I beseech you: cast one glance upon me and my endurance will
blossom:
If you won't, what fruit could my frustrated hope ever bear?

Badāyiʿ 339[1]

•••

1 [2.97] Saʿdi YE, 158. Yusofi arbitrarily dismissed the variant "fikr-i tu az khayāl-i man," (replaced by *janān-i man*) which is found in the majority of the manuscripts (ibid., 496) and which emphasizes the role of the internal senses in the psychological drama that the lyric subject experiences.

 | DOI:10.1163/9789004435902_012

The supernal light [*nūr-i ʿulvī*] shines through all apertures:
You saw it in the Sufi lodge, and we admired it the wine tavern.
Badāyiʿ 549[2]

•••

I have loved You piously,
And adored You, furiously.
I profaned You, dilapidated You,
Cursed at You.
You can say anything about me
Except that I avoided You.
Yet you don't speak,
You don't say.
You are the deaf God;
The mute God.
You had to become flesh
In the illusion of letting us
Talk to You.
GIOVANNI TESTORI, *Nel tuo sangue* (*In Your Blood*)[3]

•:

2 Saʿdi YE, 249.

3 T'ho amato con pietà
con furia T'ho adorato.
T'ho violato, sconciato,
bestemmiato.
Tutto puoi dire di me
tranne che T'ho evitato.
Ma Tu non parli,
non dici.
Sei il Dio sordo;
il Dio muto.
Per illuderci di poterTi parlare
Ti sei dovuto incarnare.
Testori 1973, 22.

1 Painting and Polishing: the Competition Between the Greek and the Chinese Artists

Al-Ghazālī's tendency to present the purely intellectual (*mushāhada*) and the purely contemplative (*tafakkur*) paths to spiritual cognition as a phenomenological dichotomy requires interpretation as an attempt to formulate an ideal classification of the relationship between the heart, the body, and the senses. Exploration of the Avicennian background has helped us discern the overlaps between these two modalities, especially in the cases in which imagination draws upon material coming from both the external world and the supernal realm. For a better understanding of the role of the imaginative faculties in Saʿdi's lyrical approach to the vision of the visible world and the realm of the unseen, we ought to refer to an extraordinary figurative rendition of al-Ghazālī's classification of his rational-inferential (*tafakkur*) and imaginal-cosmological (*mushāhada*) methods for the attainment of spiritual cognition (*maʿrifa*).

Al-Ghazālī illustrates the visual aspect of his classification through the parable of the competition between the Greek and the Chinese painters, which several authors have retold in slightly different forms over the centuries according to their personal philosophical, aesthetic, and ethical perspectives.[4] Christine van Ruymbeke has argued that the story circulated through multiple lines of transmission, probably going back to pre-Islamic Hellenistic sources in Central Asia, and in connection with the legendary album of paintings (the *Arzhang*, or *Ardhang*) by Mani, the founder of Manicheism.[5] Although al-Ghazālī's account of the parable constitutes the oldest extant source recording the story of the artistic competition, the version that is found in Niẓāmī Ganjavī's *Iskandar-nāma* (completed in the 1190s) could be seen as the rendition in verse of older texts, which might also have been the original source of inspiration for al-Ghazālī's variant of the story.[6]

In Niẓāmī's account, Alexander the Great is engaged in a dispute with the emperor of China to determine whether it is the Greek or the Chinese

4 For al-Ghazālī's version of the story, see Skellie 2010, 61–63. See also Griffel 2009a, 263–64. On the literary reverberations of this legend, see Piemontese 1995. For a philosophical perspective on Niẓāmī's and Rumi's variants of the account, see van Ruymbeke 2008. On the relationship between the content of the anecdote and the visual arts, see Soucek 1972; Necipoğlu 2015, 45–48.

5 On the relevance of Mani's *Arzhang* in Persian literature, see Pellò 2013.

6 Most scholars assume that Niẓāmī's version of the story was inspired by al-Ghazālī (see, for instance, Griffel 2009a, 355, n. 133). I agree with van Ruymbeke (2008, 290–91) in arguing that the differences between Niẓāmī's version and al-Ghazālī's rendition are too stark to assume that the latter was the main source for the former.

painters who should be considered the most excellent masters in the visual arts.[7] Two teams of Greek and Chinese artists were asked to display their mastery on the two opposite sides of a vaulted room, which had been separated by a curtain hanging from the middle. When the curtain was removed, all the onlookers were surprised to discover that the two images that the artists had limned were identical. After his initial bafflement, and by means of empirical inquiry, Alexander discovered that while the Greek artists had been painting their section of the vault, the Chinese team had turned their wall into a mirror by meticulously polishing its surface. Both groups won the competition, for Alexander judged the Chinese superior in polishing and deemed the Greeks the unrivaled masters of painting.

Nizāmī's final gloss is particularly interesting: polishing and painting are equally necessary for the purposes of vision (*baṣar*). While Priscilla Soucek has analyzed this story from the perspective of Niẓāmī's assimilation of the theories of perception into the literary representations of visual arts,[8] Christine van Ruymbeke has convincingly demonstrated the philosophical underpinnings of the anecdote.[9] As a further elaboration on the perspective of these two scholars, I would be inclined to read Niẓāmī's remark on polishing and painting as a gloss on the different roles of the internal senses in managing the relationship between optical vision and the imaginative faculties. In fact, in the middle of the narration, the author refers to the Greek painting as a "projecting" (*mī-namūd*) image, whereas he qualifies the Chinese counterpart as a "receiving" (*mī-paẕīruft*) depiction. Given Niẓamī's familiarity with Hellenistic philosophy and the Avicennian model of the internal senses, we could look at the "projecting" and "receiving" images as analogues of the faculty of the compositive imagination (which creatively composes and combines images in the mind) and of the common sense (as a screen upon which images are impressed) respectively. Therefore, the story could be reread as Niẓāmī's meditation on the role of the internal senses in the process of intellection and the empirical observation of reality.

This analogy helps us reconsider specific aspects of al-Ghazālī's spiritual approach to the same narration, which he tackles in the context of a discussion on the Preserved Tablet that is included in the twenty-first book of the *Iḥyā'*. In his version, al-Ghazālī compares the Greek artists to the philosophers and the

7 Nezāmi Ganjavi 1316/1937, 401–404. Translating *Chīn* and *Rūm* as "China" and "Greece" is indeed problematic. What premodern Persian authors really meant by *Chīn* is "the Chinese dependencies in Central Asia [i.e.,] Turkistan." De Blois 2006, 60.

8 Soucek 1972.

9 Van Ruymbeke 2008, 273–85.

men of wisdom, who attain spiritual knowledge through study and discursive inquiry. The Chinese painters, on the other hand, stand for the Sufis and the saints, who access the supernal Preserved Tabled by polishing the surface of their hearts to receive the reflection of the unseen.[10] From al-Ghazālī's wording one can detect the paramount relevance of the visual dimension in the effects of these two approaches: one the one hand, we find the "wondrous" colors of the Greeks, whereas the Chinese achieve the same result without applying any color. As in the passage from the *Kīmiyā* analyzed in the previous chapter,[11] in this case too, al-Ghazālī presents the speculative and the contemplative paths as approaches that are equally valid, just as the final result of the Greek and the Chinese painters are equally beautiful.

Interestingly, al-Ghazālī mentions that the reflecting process has bestowed great clarity upon the Chinese image. This concise observation has induced some scholars to assume that the Iranian theologian narrated this parable to defend the supremacy of the contemplative over the speculative, of the Sufi way over the inquisitive path of the philosophers.[12] However, as noticed by Ibn Khaldūn in his commentary on the passage, al-Ghazālī's symbolic juxtaposition functions as an analogue of the two facets of the heart/rational soul, one of which opens to the external world whereas the other peruses the celestial matrix of creation, the Preserved Tablet. We should therefore explain the less clear image rendered by the Greek painters by the veiling effect of the "curtain" of the body, whose material nature tends to obscure the clarity of the images descending from on high.

Among Saʿdi's contemporaries, in the context of the reception of the parable of the painters, Rumi embraced an approach that shifted al-Ghazālī's balanced mediation between the body and the invisible toward an active denial of the value of physical experience and rational observation of reality.[13] This shift can be witnessed in Rumi's reassessment of al-Ghazālī's parable, narrated in the *Maṡnavī-yi maʿnavī*, in which the approach of the Chinese and that of the Greeks are inverted, as the former stand for the philosophers, and the latter

---

10 "In his commentary on al-Ghazālī's passage, Ibn Khaldūn interpreted the Greek and the Chinese artists of the story as the double articulation of the rational soul as theorized by Avicenna: the practical intellect, turned toward the material world, and the theoretical intellect, occupied by cogitative speculations." Necipoğlu 2015, 47–48.

11 See chapter 7, pp. 366–70.

12 Moosa 2005, 254–55; Soucek 1972, 14. For a critique of this perspective, see Griffel 2009a, 355, n. 133.

13 Rumi 1925–40, 1: 213–15; 2: 189–90.

for the Sufis.[14] Apart from this discrepancy, Rumi's lines follow quite closely their original model. However, the final judgment of the king is determined by the vibrancy of the reflection created by the Greek artists, which no eye could sustain. Rumi compares the superior endeavor of the Greek artists to the Sufis who polish the surface of their hearts in such a way that they can access the "formless form" (*ṣūrat-i bī-ṣūrat*) of the unseen without having to rely on speculative sciences. On an aesthetic level, by denying the value of intellectual inquiry, Rumi also downplays the sensorial aspect of spiritual imagination: he describes the "color of colorlessness" as more radiant than the real colors that the senses of the beholder could ever perceive.

Although in Saʿdi's poetry the body is often represented as a veiling presence, it also acts as an indispensable tool for the process of spiritual imagination. From this perspective, Saʿdi's position consistently aligns with al-Ghazālī approach in his parable of the twofold act of visualization, and it was probably influenced by the rationalization of the esoteric aspects of perception and intellection in Niẓāmī's literary works. In the following line, Saʿdi rhetorically stages the difference between external and internal sources of contemplation from the perspective of the lyric subject's spiritual cardiology:

> With the water of devotion, I washed all external images and paintings:
> In the chamber of my heart, I lodge *paintings* and *images*.
>
> *Badāyiʿ* 472[15]

Once more, Saʿdi's magisterial use of paronomasia (the repetition of a word generating a slight semantic shift, *jinās-i tāmm*) revolves around the lyric subject's psychological perception of different levels of reality through the mediation of the internal senses and the heart. In the line above, the repetition of "images and paintings" (*naqsh-u nigār*) in both hemistichs establishes a sensory opposition between the external and the internal aspect of visual representation, as if portraying the opposite approaches of the Greek and the Chinese artists.[16] The reiteration of the formula "images and paintings" highlights the ontological unity of the image in the Avicennian psychological system: the images perceived by the external senses differ from those retrieved

---

14 It is possible that Rumi decided to invert the ethnicity of the painters who symbolize the spiritual path to adapt the text to his Anatolian (*rūmī*) readership, and possibly as a peripheral allusion to the monastic practices of the Christian presence in the region.

15 [2.99] Saʿdi YE, 216–17. See ibid., 552 for the manuscripts containing this line.

16 I have chosen to invert the order of the two words in the second hemistich (*paintings* and *images*) in order to convey the sense of a slight semantic variation taking place through the repetition of the locution.

from the solicitations of the souls of the fixed stars/Preserved Tablet only with respect to their origin, as they both manifest themselves on the screen of the common sense and belong to the same degree of reality. Therefore, the semantic discrepancy that Saʿdi establishes through this repetition relates to the loci producing the forms that the imagination perceives: the external world of senses and the intellectual realm of the unseen. Both levels of image-inducing reality appear on the surface of the heart, which, as shown in the previous chapter, sees the conflation of the functions of Avicenna's practical intellect and those of the internal senses.

In this chapter we will see how both al-Ghazālī and ʿAyn al-Qużāt refer to the imaginal translation (*muhākāt*, or "imitation" of the invisible as "allegorical representation," *mis̱āl*, or *tamas̱s̱ul*), which, by following the insight offered by the Avicennian psychological system, they conceive as an analogue of the images (*shabḥ*, a term which also Rūzbihān employs) that the phenomenal world projects onto the screen-like faculty of common sense. We may follow Meryem Sebti in calling these two ontologically equivalent classes of images "imitation-images" and "vestige-images." While vestige-images derive from a trace left from the impression of forms conveyed by the external senses (the mental vestige of the tree standing before us, which we see as a visual memory after having closed our eyes), imitation-images reflect and translate into mental forms meanings collected from the realm of the unseen.[17] In al-Ghazālī's and Niẓāmī's versions of the story of the painters, the Greek artists' painting appears as an act of creative perception that leaves a vestigial image, whereas the Chinese, by means of reflection, create the "double," the simulacrum to which Sebti refers.

Since the brain is the locus in which imitation-images from the unseen take shape, the degree of "physicality" of their status does not essentially diverge from the vestige-images, which derive directly from the external world. We

17 "L'image produite dans le rêve et la vision prophétique n'est ni vraie ni fausse. Elle renvoie à autre chose, elle est *une représentation allégorique et mimétique* de ce qui a été saisi par les sens ou par l'intellect. Cette détermination de l'image comme doublure mimétique a une incidence forte sur le statut ontologique de l'image. Elle est appréhendée comme ce qui tient lieu de quelque chose, le re-présente et l'imite. Comme l'image-vestige qui fait nécessairement suite à un épisode de perception sensible et tient lieu de ce qui est absent, l'image-imitation n'a de signification que par rapport à un modèle, qu'il soit sensible ou intelligible. Son statut ontologique est donc aussi celui d'un double qui ne peut être appréhendé que par rapport à ce qu'il imite avec plus ou moins de fidélité, et elle est aussi dotée d'une certaine matérialité en ce qu'elle s'imprime dans les puissances-organes. Ces deux sortes d'images qui ne se laissent concevoir que dans la relation à ce qu'elle représentent s'inscrivent bien dans la conception antique et médiévale de l'image comme double." Sebti 2005, 127–28.

shall see how the duality of such representations, by vestigial impression or imitation (*ḥikāya*) of the unseen constitutes a key epistemological tool that, from a purely cognitive point of view, enables Saʿdi's lyric subject to navigate the body/soul structure of reality and provide the rational soul with opportunities to negotiate coping strategies vis-à-vis the sensual aspects of the physical world.[18]

2 *Majāz* and *Ḥaqīqat*: Embodying the Images

The different sources for the mental production of images establish a hierarchy that generates an opposition between the intellectual life of the lyric subject and its experience of the world of senses. For the lyric subject it is a baffling situation, similar to the bewilderment faced by Alexander when beholding the two identical pictures appearing on the two surfaces of the painted vault. From the point of view of the amatory aesthetics of the lyric discourse, on the one side, human beauty is contemplated as it appears in the physical world, whilst on the other, it appears as a trace from a supernal realm. This discrepancy bolsters the dramatic dynamics of Saʿdi's ghazals, in which the real problem is not the level of veracity of the beloved's image, but the way sensory and intellectual sources of imaginal inspiration align or diverge from each other. Mental representations are therefore the unifying form constituting the gamut of possibilities of interplay between what we have defined as the rational-inferential and the imaginal-cosmological approaches to spiritual contemplation that define the difference between *tafakkur* and *mushāhada*. In some of Saʿdi's ghazals these two modalities seem to align in a way that turns the visual representation into an epiphanic moment of pure contemplation, in which the difference between the physical and the intellectual worlds disappears:

> Anyone to whom you show your face in the pure morning
> You open a window from paradise onto his face.
>
> The world is a long night, and your face illuminates the entire universe.
> Fortunate is the morning of he who sees you appearing from the door.
>
> *Badāyiʿ* 420[19]

18 Sebti 2005, 128.

19 [2.100] Saʿdi YE, 195.

While we may read the image of the "window from paradise" in the light of al-Ghazālī's theorization of the heart's aperture onto the celestial mirroring surface of the Preserved Tablet, the origin of the "face" appearing in the morning shifts between internal and external sources of visual cogitation. It is the Avicennian soul-body dualistic paradigm of cognition that turns the forms of the mental images into the only veritable epistemic link between the visible world and the heart.[20] The centrality of the imaginal layer for the lyric subject's spiritual and aesthetic cognition turns the external world into an entity that is indispensable to the quest for what, in the Sufi literature, is referred to as *ḥaqīqat*, or the ultimate truth of the divine presence. Whatever lies in the ultimate truth is pre-imaginal, as it corresponds to a level of reality that the practical intellect is yet to convert into images capable of being processed by the internal senses.

Therefore, the relationship between what Sufi texts refer to as the "metaphorical" (*majāzī*) and "supernal," or "truthful" (*ḥaqīqī*) dimensions of reality corresponds to the role that the sensorial perusal of the world acquires in managing the intellectual translation of the supernal truths into images. The opposition between *ḥaqīqat* and *majāz*, which originates in the rhetorical debates on the relationship between meaning and figurative speech, helps us define the unifying factor of imagination as the point of contact between the rational-inferential and the imaginal-cosmological approaches.[21]

It is on the basis of the necessity for the human soul to know the supernal realm through the production of images that ʿAyn al-Qużāt, the most renowned pupil of Aḥmad Ghazālī, defends the "metaphorical" (*majāzī*) aspect of the aesthetics of the spiritual experience as a necessary bridge to grasp the supernal world through one's grasp of mundane reality:

> Alas, who has spoken of the stage of manifestation [*shuhūd*], and who could ever know about that? You still do not know that the witness [*shāhid*, i.e., the young man attesting to God's beauty] is needed for the Beloved! The hearts have received a foretaste of the Supreme *shāhid-bāzī* [*-yi ḥaqīqī*] through this metaphorical [*majāzī*] witness. That Supreme truth can be metaphorically represented by means of this beautiful face [*ān ḥaqīqat tamas̱s̱ul ba-d-īn ṣūrat-i nīkū tavān kard*].[22] May my soul serve

20 Sebti 2005, 136–40.

21 Heinrichs 1984. See also Key 2018.

22 ʿAyn al-Qozāt Hamadāni, 1373/1994, 297. My translation diverges from that of Ridgeon, who—probably because of the misleading punctuation chosen by the editor of the Persian text—reads an *iżāfa* between *ḥaqīqat* and *tamas̱s̱ul*: "This is the reality of *tamas̱s̱ul*. It can be [manifested] in a fair form." Ridgeon 2011, 10.

> the one who worships the metaphorical *shāhid* [*-i majāzī*], for worshipping the supernal *shāhid* [*-i ḥaqīqī*] is so rare! But do not think that I am speaking of carnal love, which derives from lust; I am talking about the love of the heart.[23]

ʿAyn al-Qużāt describes very clearly the dramatic difference between a supernal form of human beauty and a physical reflection: the "true" young beloved versus the "metaphorical" presence of any handsome lad who captures the sensory attention of the *ʿārif* striving to grasp divine beauty.

From a doctrinal point of view, sometime around the mid-13th century, these meditations became the "pre-text" for ʿIrāqī to reappraise al-Ghazālī's conundrum of incarnationism (*ḥulūl*)—which was one of Hujvīrī's main concerns and, after all, the last theoretical barrier preventing Persian poets from the full development of a non-technical and non-scholastic representation of love in its broadest spectrum of possibilities:

> Know that between the image and the mirror neither unification [*ittiḥād*] nor incarnation [*ḥulūl*] is possible: the only person who on this subject can say something like this is the one who does not distinguish incarnation from epiphany [*tajallī*]. Incarnation and unification can take place only between two [separate] essences [*ẕāt*], and in the eyes of the manifestation [*shuhūd*] all beings are but part of a single essence.
>
> […] The master of the unveiling [*ṣāḥib-i kashf*, i.e., the initiate] sees the multitude [*kas̱rat*] in the *phenomena* [*aḥkām*], not into the essence, and knows that any variation [taking place] in the *phenomena* does not affect the essence, because the essence possesses a perfection that cannot be subject to change and influence. When light filters through colored glass, its color does not change, even though it appears so. […]
> And if you do not understand what I am saying:
>
> Get close to my eyes and look, so that you can see.
> The sun shines through thousands of colored glasses
> and shows the color of each of them.
> All of them are but one single light with several colors,
> what difference is there between this and that?[24]

23 Ibid.
24 Fakhr al-Din ʿErāqi 1371/1992, 81–82.

The legitimation of the representation of the Absolute principle in the form of mundane shapes without compromising the unity of Being is what truly inaugurates the main aesthetic tenets of the sacred eroticism that, thanks to Saʿdi, peaked during the second half of the 13th century. According to Nasrollāh Purjavādi, "the idea according to which mundane love [*ʿishq-i majāzī*] is a ladder leading towards the spiritual love [*ʿishq-i ḥaqīqī*] became widespread mainly thanks to Saʿdi."[25] It was during Saʿdi's lifetime, in fact, that Muḥammad b. Maḥmūd Zangī Bukhārī, in his treatise *Nuzhat al-ʿāshiqīn* declared that, from a Sufi perspective, the experience of mundane love is a necessary condition to experience the divine love and that "the sheikhs of the path and the followers of the Truth do not deem reliable an initiate who has not experienced mundane love."[26] Purjavādi's emphasis on the theory of mundane passions as a ladder towards the "real" and ultimate object of divine love rests on the assumption that—at least as reflected in the theoretical texts analyzed above—physical experiences channelled through the body are hierarchically inferior to the realm of the soul in its quest for the supernal. This hierarchical dichotomy emerges in the theoretical approach by which *majāz*, as a phenomenal level of experience, is thought of as inferior to the "real" object of the spiritual path.

In his study of the sacred eroticism of the hagiographic accounts on ʿIrāqī's life and works, Matthew Miller emphasizes that the category of *majāz* deserves a focus capable of reassessing not only the often negative connotations with which modern scholarship has received this concept, but also the active role of the body that it involves within the aesthetics of the spiritual discourse.[27] Inspired by the necessity of finding new ways to translate *majāz* in a fashion that accounts for the role of the body in the spiritual narratives that either explicitly or implicitly rely on this implied dichotomy, Miller proposes to render the term with the concept of "embodiment" and "embodied" (for the adjective *majāzī*) experiences.[28] This solution effectively shifts the focus of the discourse from the ephemeral perception of the role of corporality to a more holistic representation of the soul/body duality. Among its advantages, it also accounts for the need of conceiving the role of metaphorical and allegorical representations as meaningful enactments that involve the real presence of the senses that participate in the aesthetic dimension of the spiritual experience.

---

25 Purjavādi 1387/2008, 203.

26 Zangi Bokhāri 1372/1993, 140.

27 Miller 2018.

28 Ibid., 5–9.

Nevertheless, we may draw upon the figurative aspect of *majāz*—especially if applied to the context of some sort of visionary experience involving both sides of the inferential and imaginal modalities discussed so far—in order to account for the role of imagination in the spiritual experience of the body (both as the source and the object of vision) as an overarching cognitive phenomenon. In order to do so, I propose to bring the dyad *majāz/ḥaqīqat* back to its rhetorical origins and conceive it as a broad analogue for the opposition between form, *ṣūrat*, and content, *maʿnī*. Considering that the visual aspect of the *majāz* formulation entails the so-called "imaginative metaphor" (*istiʿāra takhyīliyya*), which is the technique of "comprehending the intelligible in the form of what can be sensed" (*tafhīm al-maʿqūl fī ṣūrat al-maḥsūs*),[29] we may think of the "embodying" aspect of *majāz* as a subcategory of a broader imaginal function that involves both the internal and the external senses.

This approach of recognizing *majāz* as an imaginal dimension accounts for the idealistic nature of the Avicennian conception of visual perception and the way by which, as observed thus far, it informs al-Ghazālī's meditations on the role of the external and the internal senses as mediators between the observation of the phenomenal world and the translation of the invisible realm into mental images. Furthermore, the recognition of a unified imaginal framework for the connection between mundane and visionary experiences helps us reframe the soul/body dichotomy according to a more fluid understanding of Saʿdi's lyricism beyond the limits of spirituality and sexuality as separate categories.

3 The Five Stages of the Visionary Experience

Saʿdi's ghazals often stage a dramatized representation of the imaginal overlaps between the physical and the metaphysical dimensions of the lyric subject's experience as a meditation on the visual processes of spiritual cognition. In particular, the language of the amatory courtly rituals, such as the encounter, the embrace, the sorrowful farewell, and the immolation of the lover, can be seen as lyric renditions of the twofold nature of desire, constantly pulling toward both the physical world and the realm of supernal beauty. As we have seen, Sufi authors (such as Aḥmad Ghazālī, ʿAyn al-Qużāt, Ruzbihān, Nasafī, etc.) meditating on the amatory relationship between *majāz* and *ḥaqīqat* often address this issue, mainly through metaphors, allegorical speech, and ecstatic utterances aimed at testing the boundaries of figurative language. Saʿdi too,

29 Heinrichs 2016, 265.

in his rare theoretical passages (and often as a response to specific audiences who solicited discourses crafted according to the mainstream Sufi theopathic tradition), offers explanatory readings of his poetry as a lyrical gloss on the psychology of the sacred embodiment of desire. For instance, in the *Epistle on Love and the Intellect*, Saʿdi compares the sensory and intellectual obfuscation of the seeker of divine truth to the case of a king's confidant, whose head ought to be cut off once he learns about the location of the royal treasury. At the beginning of the path, as soon as the Sufi steps into the secret treasury of contemplation of the divine truth, he loses both his senses and, figuratively, his head.[30] The two lines with which Saʿdi concludes this prose passage happen to be the same lines that introduce the anecdote of the Master of the Heart in the opening of the *Gulistān*.[31] The third hemistich ("the lovers are killed by the Beloved") appears in a short ghazal (crafted as a response to a purely erotic ghazal by Anvarī) that elaborates on the restlessness of the lovers who seek divine beauty through their dreams, the perusal of the signs of the world, and the contemplation of physical objects of desire.[32] In this case too, as we have experienced with the intertextual passages in the *Gulistān*, the juxtaposition of different texts shows that Saʿdi's discourse on love belongs to overlapping levels of reality whose primary tool of exploration lies in the connection between the body and the mental production of images deriving from a variety of physical and metaphysical origins.

The majority of the Sufi theoretical passages attending to this process do not offer a clear explanation of the psychological dynamics of the imaginative pathways of Saʿdi's lyric subject. On the contrary, al-Ghazālī's pragmatic observations on the supernal nature of beauty and its effects on the cognitive system of the beholder's soul constitute a precious source of analytical speculation. In particular, I regard the following excerpt from the *Kīmiyā* as a gold touchstone to test and exemplify not only al-Ghazālī's reception of the aesthetics of Avicenna's psychology, but also the phenomenological conditions that provide Saʿdi with a fertile and solid ground for his lyric subject's imaginal perception of the supernal realm vis-à-vis its experience of the material world. I elevate this passage to a primary source of interpretation for specific aspects of Saʿdi's

30 Ms. Paris 1320s, f. 218b.

31 They'll ask me to describe Him, but
My heart is lost, how could I point to His presence?
The lovers are killed by the Beloved,
No voice comes back from the dead.
[2.101] *Golestān*, 50.

32 Saʿdi YE, 46.

poetry (on the basis of intellectual affinity, rather than direct influence) only because it describes methodically a series of stages that are, directly or indirectly, the object of the majority of the Sufi speculations on the relationship between bodily beauty and supernal ideals of splendor. Therefore, the following considerations ought to be taken as a source of relative guidance, rather than a systematic application of a theory.

To my knowledge, the excerpt in question has received no scholarly attention. The passage appears at the end of the chapter of the *Kīmiyā* that assesses the permissibility of poetry and musical audition (*samāʿ*). This is probably al-Ghazālī's clearest explanation of *mushāhada* as a psychological process, and its methodical illustration acts as a rationalization of the system of signs in which the spiritual beholder is immersed when experiencing physical desire while beholding the imaginal forms of beauty descending from the supernal realm during the contact with the invisible:

> And a further reason [that justifies a spiritual master's gaze upon youths]—although it rarely occurs—takes place whenever there is someone to whom things appear in a way similar to the spiritual inspiration [*ḥālat*] of the Sufis.
>
> [1] It can happen that the essences of the angels and the prophets' souls are revealed to him in the guise of an image [simulacrum, exemplum, *mis̱ālī*]. In such circumstances, the revelation takes place in the form of a human being of utmost beauty. [2] Since images [*mis̱āl*] necessarily correspond to the reality of the supernal meanings [*maʿnī*] they represent, whenever that supernal meaning—among all the supernal meanings of the souls—is absolutely perfect, the image [*mis̱āl*] that corresponds to it in the world of forms [*ʿālam-i ṣūrat*] will also appear as extremely beautiful. Among the Arabs no one was more handsome than Diḥya Kalbī, and it was in his form that the Prophet saw the angel Gabriel.
>
> Therefore, one can receive a mental revelation in the form of a beautiful beardless boy [*amrad*], and will take great pleasure in contemplating him. [3] Whenever the beholder returns from that vision, the supernal meaning [that it represents] will hide again behind the veil, and that person will start longing for the supernal meaning whose image was that form [of the young man]. And it can happen that he might not be able to retrieve again that supernal meaning. [4] At that point, if his external eye [*chashm-i ẓāhir*] falls upon a beautiful form that is similar to that [previous] form [i.e., the beardless boy], the conditions of the previous vision will be refreshed, and the meaning that was lost is now found again, in such a way that he will enjoy an ecstatic pleasure.

> Hence, it is acceptable to show physical desire for a beautiful form in order to attain such an ecstatic contemplation. [5] And whenever the eyes of someone who is not familiar with such mysteries fall upon the individual who experiences this kind of ecstatic contemplation of beauty, he will think that that person is observing the same [external] attributes that he himself is observing, as he has no idea of those other [inner] attributes [i.e., the connection between the form of the young man and the supernal meanings]. Ultimately, the destiny of the Sufis is particularly dangerous and mysterious. No other practice is subject to so many errors on the path.[33]

The passage is less complex than it seems. The influence of Avicenna is such that al-Ghazālī's effort to represent the experience of visualizing the unseen seems to shift from the Sufi set of practices of his chapter on mystical audition to the purely cognitive framework that characterizes his passages on the role of the imagination. From the perspective of the analyses carried out in the previous chapters, al-Ghazālī's description of the visionary experience provides an extraordinary example of how the Iranian theologian represents the phenomenological conflation of the imaginal-cosmological and the rational-inferential modalities (*mushāhada* and *tafakkur*) characterizing his original spiritual appropriation of Avicennian epistemology.

The context of the passage is the portion of the *Kīmiyā*'s chapter on music in which al-Ghazālī lists the specific conditions that render the otherwise permissible practice of listening to music a forbidden activity. Among these, al-Ghazālī deems the exposure of youths to poetic and musical audition particularly pernicious, as it potentially causes the corruption of the young subjects and possibly threatens the moral integrity of the adult participants. The passage above is one lengthy caveat that al-Ghazālī deploys to explain and justify the spiritual context in which the contemplation of a youth's comely features derives from a spiritual aesthetic practice that does not automatically imply moral corruption. The reference to Diḥya Kalbī—whose notoriously beautiful features constituted the angel Gabriel's external aspect when he appeared to Muḥammad—enables us to compare this excerpt with both al-Ghazālī's and Saʿdi's passages in which the beholder psychologically translates the contents received from the unseen into mentally perceptible objects characterized by an overwhelming degree of beauty.[34]

---

33 *Kimiyā*, 1: 487–88.

34 Cf. the passage in the *Tamhīdāt* in which ʿAyn al-Qużāt illustrates the meaning of the imaginal translation (*tamaṣṣul*) by recounting the story of archangel Gabriel appearing

The fact that, in this case, al-Ghazālī applies this psychological pattern to the mental depiction of human beauty and its correlation with physical and intellectual desire sets a solid term of comparison with Sa'di's lyric subject's articulation of desire with respect to the realm of the invisible and the tangible world. What al-Ghazālī describes is the chronology of the contact between the physical world and the invisible realm though a progression that may be divided into five phases, which correspond to stages of habituation to the psychology of contemplating beauty. We will see how each one of these phases can be used as an ideal model to reappraise specific stages that Sa'di describes when dramatizing the sacred eroticism of the lyric subject in his ghazals:

Preliminary contact (*phase one*): a set of different conditions and stimulations, ranging from exercises of sensorial deprivation to a compulsive practice of meditation on the beauty of the visible world, induces a spiritual contact between the heart/intellect of the individual and the invisible world. As will be discussed in the next chapter, Sa'di often tackles the performance context in which contact with the invisible world takes place from the perspective of both inward meditations and outward forms of contemplation involving acts of visual focusing, repetition of formulae, exposure to music, and the mental recollection of past experiences. In the following line, for instance, Sa'di addresses the unexpected manifestation of a form of controlled temptation emerging from the world "of divine power" that aligns itself with the visionary conjunction between the heart and the eyes of the beholder:

> O temptation newly manifested from the world of divine power:
> Engrained you are in the heart, do not hide from the eyes!
>
> *Ṭayyibāt* 221[35]

The image of the "world of power" frames the character of the invisible world as the possible forms of existence that the particulars reflected in the Preserved Tablet impress onto the ontological progression of the visible world. As we shall see, many of the poems in which Sa'di celebrates a preliminary encounter with the beloved can be read as lyric explorations of this contact with the invisible realm.

---

to Muḥammad in the guise of Diḥya Kalbī and associating this spiritual experience with *tafakkur*. 'Ayn al-Qozāt Hamadāni 1373/1994, 293–94.

35 [2.102] Sa'di YE, 104. On the cosmological underpinnings of the expression "world of divine power," in the context of this ghazal, see Chapter 5, pp. 292–95.

Imaginal translation (*phase two*): The perfect *ma'ānī* from the realm of the unseen (or the Preserved Tablet) reach the heart of the spiritual practitioner. His internal senses translate those "ideas" (or "supernal meanings") into images. In the previous chapter, we have seen how both al-Ghazālī and Sa'di often describe the heart as a surface on which these images take shape, according to a physiological process that the Avicennian tradition applies to explain dreams, prophecies, hallucinations, etc. By reason of the correlation between *ma'ānī* and forms, the degree of spiritual perfection of the ideas reflected by the unseen corresponds to the degree of aesthetic perfection of the images that the mind of the spiritual beholder depicts. Even though the internal senses may translate that supernal perfection into any form of idealized visual beauty, al-Ghazālī suggests that the most common form of imaginal manifestation in the mind of the beholder is represented by the figure of an ephebe, an angel, Diḥya Kalbī (the most beautiful of Muḥammad's companions), or any generic beardless boy (*amrad*), comparable with the *shāhid* of the Persian lyric tradition.

In Sa'di's poetry, this imaginal translation corresponds to the realm of the vision proper, and, in many cases, the lyric subject cannot discern the difference between mental representations and concrete experience. The lyric subject approaches the mental vision of the object of desire as a visual translation that represents the climax of its aesthetic and spiritual experience:

> What pleasure [*ẕawq*] does the vision of the invisible beloved [*yār-i ghāyib*] elicit?
> A cloud bringing rain to the thirsty in the middle of the desert.
>
> O fragrance of recognition, I do know where you blew from:
> The message of the beloved's arrival is intimately intertwined with the soul.
>
> Would you like to know why Sa'di sits in the corner of seclusion [*kunj-i khalvat*]?
> He doesn't dare come out, because of the beautiful ones!
>
> *Ṭayyibāt* 87[36]

We may compare the last line of the excerpt above with the remarks with which Sa'di concludes the story of his alleged encounter with a young student in Kashgar. In that context, by quoting lines on the slippery nature of desire,

36 [2.103] Sa'di YE, 43.

Saʿdi rejected the accommodating services of the youth whose physical comeliness had been the object of the poet's melancholic attentions.[37] In the ghazal above, by contextualizing the lines on the visionary experience through the lyric subject's confession of conducting a life of seclusion in order to stay away from the temptations of the flesh, Saʿdi clearly represents the commencement of the pleasurable vision as a purely mental experience.

In terms of al-Ghazālī's spiritual epistemology, these first two phases correspond with the imaginal-comological process of *mushāhada* as a visionary unveiling, as they do not seem to involve any extra-mental perception belonging to the world of sense. This is the same kind of vision that Saʿdi describes in the introduction to the *Gulistān*, in which the "Master of the Heart" visualizes the invisible world in the guise of a rose garden.

Return to the external senses and aesthetic frustration (*phase three*): as the connection with the invisible world comes to an end, the internal senses keep the recollection of the visionary experience, along with the imaginal impression left by the intellectual perception of the supernal *maʿānī*. The subject's return to the sensory world is marked by an aesthetic anxiety that triggers the quest for forms capable of mirroring the perfect images stored in the memory and for access to the *maʿānī* to which they belong. It is noteworthy that al-Ghazālī describes the inaccessibility of the supernal *maʿānī* in this phase as if they were hidden behind a veil, which is an image that is quite common in the Persian lyric tradition describing forms of theo-erotic manifestation.

It is possible to infer that, according to al-Ghazālī, the subject's return to sensory experiences elicits an increased degree of mundane contemplative activity in the physical world. From a phenomenological perspective, this is the most delicate phase of the whole process leading to the practice of inspired vision: the imaginal-cosmological modality of the vision that the beholder experiences shifts to a nostalgic perusal of the world in the form of a rational-inferential form of contemplation that fails to keep the metaphysics of *mushāhada* alive. The bewildering vision provided by the unseen acts as a catalyst that urges the beholder to seek forms of sensual satisfaction in the physical world.

As we shall soon verify, Saʿdi lyrically represents this disconnection from the invisible world through the traditional amatory imagery that relates to the "departure" of the beloved (or, in some cases, the death of the lover).[38] It is the

37 See Chapter 2, p. 143.

38 As discussed earlier with respect to Saʿdi's *Epistle on Love and the Intellect*, the poet is keen to represent the death of the lover as a metaphor for the loss of the beholder's senses

"departure" of the vision of the beloved, or the "veiling" of the supernal *maʿānī*, that generates the dramatic tension exuding from the ghazals portraying such circumstances. In Saʿdi's poetry, this stage represents the anthropological condition that affects the poetic persona as a subject immersed in the world of sense and yet at the mercy of the imagination and its dramatic relationship with the realm of mundane experiences. The nostalgic longing for the original vision triggers the lyric subject's quest for the lost "meaning" capable of projecting supernal signification upon the visual objects of the physical world. In the following ghazal, for instance, the reiteration of the refrain *bāz* (variously translated as "again," "no more," etc.) signifies the lyric subject's compulsive desire to access the *door* of "meaning" of the supernal through the visual manifestation of an imaginal object of desire:

> Grand is the fortune of he who sees you return from the door:
> Do come, do come! Welcome you are, where are you now?
>
> What respite can one imagine after seeing your countenance?
> You disclosed it once, and now won't show it again?
>
> Sliding doors are your enchanting, seductive eyes:
> What have I done that you do not open them to my face anymore? …
>
> In the time before Time my soul tasted the wine of our encounter:
> Over and over again that cup of affinity intoxicates me.
>
> How could I find the heart that I had lost in your alley?
> Only the light of your face will guide my eyes again.…
>
> The crowds of commoners cast their blame upon the Sufi:
> "You should reject these fantasies, and disavow your natural instinct!"
>
> O sober one, if you only knew how sweet intoxication is,
> You won't mention the name of piety for the rest of your life.

---

upon the ecstatic experience of *mushāhada*. See for instance the following line, in which Saʿdi clarifies that the death of the lover in the context of a spiritual concert (*samāʿ*, see the next two chapters) is an invisible event:
They shall see the one who has been killed, but not the murderer:
As this is an arrow made of poplar, which pierces only in secret.
[2.104] Saʿdi YE, 163.

Should you too, like Sa'di, receive a morsel at this *door*
You'll never give up your passion for begging.
Badāyi' 574[39]

These lines stage the full spectrum of the experience of *mushāhada* as illustrated by al-Ghazālī. The commotion that filters through the lines derives from Sa'di's dramatization of the pathos affecting the return of the beholder/lover to a mundane space inhabited by the absence of the supernal vision. The final couplet is particularly suggestive, as it hints at the compulsive nature of the quest after the "door" of the heart is closed, which generates the turmoil that invalidates the "piety" of the beholder and attracts the blame of the "commoners" who deny the value of the imaginal experience. The mention of the lyric subject's begging activity relates to the hope for a renewal of the visionary experience.

Renewal of the Imaginal Contact (*Phase Four*): when the eyes of the beholder meet an object of physical contemplation whose appearance is similar to the forms that had previously constituted the imaginal translation of the supernal *ma'ānī*, the connection with the invisible world is re-established. The heart takes aesthetic and spiritual pleasure from the recognition of a formal correspondence between the mundane object of desire (sensed through the eyes and perceived through the common sense), the remembrance of the imaginal translation of the supernal *ma'ānī* (stored in the retentive imagination, *khayāl*), and the supernal *ma'ānī* themselves, which are newly available through the reopening of the connection with the invisible world caused by the contemplation of a human form of utmost beauty. The jubilant tone with which the lyric subject describes such experiences derives from the fortunate conflation of the imaginal-cosmological and the rational-inferential modalities of the aesthetics of spiritual contemplation:

To the eyes of the Masters of Gazes, among all creatures,
You shine like a gash of light amidst the dark night.
Badāyi' 413[40]

Both in al-Ghazālī's description and in the lyric passages that address this fusion of mental and optical modalities for the perusal of beauty, the subject enjoys some sort of habituation with the supernal *ma'ānī*, which can be immediately

39 [2.105] Sa'di YE, 257–58.
40 [2.106] Sa'di YE, 192.

retrieved through the mere contemplation of physical beauty. This process resonates with the Avicennian concept of "correct guessing" (*ḥads*) that we analyzed in the sixth chapter, and which the Iranian philosopher recognized as the foundational kind of cognition leading to what he calls the "sacred intellect." In the lines below, Saʿdi showcases how this form of spiritual habituation generates an intoxicating relationship with the phenomenal world in which the visible and the invisible aspects of reality are constantly juxtaposed with each other:

> … The tragedy of loving you has left no pious men in Fars
> But me, and yet I do not know how I have been able to pray.
>
> I did pray, but senselessly unaware as to how
> I could perform my religious obligations while imagining you.
>
> Sharia forbids praying while being drunk.
> Who shall accept my prayers, as I am intoxicated night and day?
>
> So much the visual remembrance of you has grabbed my waist …
> If only I could touch your waist with my hands …
>
> *Badāyiʿ* 456[41]

The reference to the praying activity of the lyric subject indicates that the contemplative activity of spiritual rituals (prayers, remembrance of God, and all the practices that "polish" the surface of the heart to prepare for the *mushāhada*) is a habit that generates constant access to the mental perception of the supernal realm. While everyone else's heart in Fars goes astray (probably as a consequence of the sensual thoughts that the contemplation of supernal beauty may generate), the lyric subject emphasizes the purity of its intents in spite of the intoxicating effects of the contemplation of beauty. By constantly keeping the sensual undertone in the forefront of the text, Saʿdi suggests that the beholder's mastery of the art of spiritual contemplation cannot be detached from the physiology of carnal desire. It is in this light that we can read the final line of the ghazal, which shows how the boundaries between the visionary experience and sexual attraction can fade away when the internal senses bring the mental images back to their bodily source.

41 [2.107] Saʿdi YE, 210–11.

Dangers on the Path (*Phase Five*): in the last part of the passage, al-Ghazālī warns the reader about the perils posed by the psychological aesthetics of contemplating human beauty as a narrow path that risks degenerating in lust and incarnationism. In particular, he alludes to the blame that the spiritual beholders (*ʿārifān*) can attract when their appreciation for human beauty is judged by those "commoners" who never experience the "secret" of the imaginal manifestation of the supernal.[42] In the context of the visual perusal of the human figure and the supernal "meanings" (*maʿānī*) to which it is attached, the "secret" to which al-Ghazālī alludes corresponds to the mystery of what he calls the fifth reason for the passion between man and God—their inherent affinity, which we discussed in the fourth chapter. Through this observation, al-Ghazālī bridges the gap between the intellectual modality of the contemplative perusal of human beauty and the inspired form of cosmological understanding of the mysterious correlation between the forms of the world, imagination, and the intimations belonging to the supernal world. In some ghazals, Saʿdi seems to be hinting at this very juxtaposition of the physical and metaphysical aspects of visual contemplation through the filter of the relationship between forms and supernal meanings in a space that lust may comfortably access:

> With their forms [*ṣūrat*] the beautiful boys attesting to God's beauty
> Stole the hearts of the pious beholders. You did it with your forms *and maʿānī*....
>
> O friend, do not urge me not to set my eyes on him
> As you do not know by what secrets we are bound together.
>
> *Ṭayyibāt* 58[43]

The first line, specifically, shows how the beholding activity of the *ʿārif* tends to focus on bodies of beauty at the risk of missing the spiritual connection capable of connecting their metaphorical (*majāzī*) presence with the truthful nature (*ḥaqīqī*) of the *maʿānī* to which their imaginal forms belong. In the first sentence of the passage, al-Ghazālī presents his case by emphasizing that the experience that he is about to describe is *similar* to what the Sufis are capable

42 This critique of the commoners (among whom al-Ghazālī includes most classes of scholars from the religious elites of his time, including experts in Islamic law, theologians, and grammarians who do not see God as the only object of their spiritual dedication) appears in all the passages in the *Kīmiyā* in which al-Ghazālī dismisses the arguments of those who deny the value of admiring natural beauty and the possibility for human beings to love God.

43 [2.108] Saʿdi YE, 30.

of witnessing—which indirectly extends the possibility for such experiences to happen to a broader group of non-Sufi individuals. In spite of the alleged rarity of such events, al-Ghazālī is de facto preparing the ground for an anthropological pattern that describes a psychological process that all humans can experience. The experience that he describes consists in the appearance, in the mind of the individual, of beautiful images whose visual forms translate the manifestation of excellent ideas—angels, or the spirit of the prophets. Al-Ghazālī does not provide details for the causes or the contexts that may trigger this preliminary visionary experience, but from both his other writings and from Avicenna's passages on the interaction between the human intellect and the souls of the stars (which, in al-Ghazālī's Islamic terminology, corresponds to the Preserved Tablet, or the celestial blueprint of creation), this much can be inferred: such visions are peculiar to powerful intellects, but their physiological mechanisms allow them to occur in a variety of situations, spanning from sleep to full wakefulness, and affecting both sharp-minded individuals and the physically impaired or the fool. In Avicennian psychological terms, the intimations that the practical intellect receives from the supernal world are translated ("depicted," "imitated") into images that the common sense converts into sensorial perceptions through imagination and on the basis of the previously-perceived images stored in the retentive imagination (*khayāl*). This means that the sensorial forms of such visions of beauty proceeding from the supernal world are primarily informed by prior experience of the world, just as in this passage al-Ghazālī remarks that the angel Gabriel appeared to Muḥammad in the shape of the most beautiful of his companions, Diḥya al-Kalbī.[44]

4 The Preliminary Contact, between Physiology, Experience, and Lyricism

In his *Ishārāt*, Avicenna offers a tentative list of the possible ways in which, during such visions, the unseen might manifest itself to the senses of the individual:

> The trace [from the unseen] becomes observable and visible, or a cry that calls out, or other things; and sometimes it becomes an image with a perfectly developed form, or speech with a definite metrical structure, and sometimes it is in a state of the greatest beauty.

44 See Bashear 2004, 64–70.

> [...] Sometimes, the fleeting glance of the unseen is a sort of strong opinion; sometimes, it resembles the address of a genie or a call from someone absent; and sometimes it takes place with something coming to view face to face, with the result that we actually observe the form of the unseen.[45]

Out of all these possibilities, al-Ghazālī alights on the prophetic tradition of representing the manifestation of these "ideas" from the unseen in the form of a young male beauty, by using the term *amrad*, which, in the Persian-Islamic tradition—including al-Ghazālī's own writings—is perilously charged with sensual homoerotic overtones. As Avicenna specifies in his treatise on the soul, these perceptions of the supernal world "come about for reasons which arise in the [rational] soul for the most part furtively; they are like stolen intimations which do not stay long enough to be remembered unless the [rational] soul acts quickly with the intent to retain them."[46]

The reason the intimations from the unseen are translated into images is that the intellect is not capable of storing the "ideas" that are provided by the Active Intellect or the celestial soul. For this reason, Avicenna clarifies that, as soon as the contact is established, the meanings grasped by the intellect need to be translated into images for the purpose of storing them in the internal sense known as "retentive imagination" (*khayāl*).[47] Al-Ghazālī confirms Avicenna's theory of the involuntary nature of the visions that shine from the unseen in the human heart/intellect, especially if we consider that he describes very precisely the transition from a passive reception of the supernal intimations to an active search for those radiant concepts. The reason for this haste is that, as soon as the visionary connection with the unseen is interrupted, the soul only retains scattered images of indescribable beauty. Therefore, the individual actively seeks the contemplation of beautiful human beings to fulfill a sort of aesthetic nostalgia for the intellectual appreciation of the supernal ideas.

Al-Ghazālī's extraordinary intuition, formulated as a dynamic interpretation of Avicennian psychology, depends on the possibility that he envisages for the beholder's heart to turn the relationship between the sensible forms of the material world and the spiritual meanings that shine in the Preserved Tablet—the blueprint of God's creation—into an active practice that can be put in the service of the spiritual quest. In al-Ghazālī's description, the preliminary fortuitous connections with the unseen prepare the groundwork for a sort of

---

45 Gutas 2006b, 351. Sa'di uses a similar locution (the "form of the unseen," *ṣūrat-i ghayb*) in one of his ghazals. See *supra*, p. 372).

46 Ibid., 350.

47 Gutas 2006a, 365, n. 35.

flexibility of the individual's cognitive system with respect to the recognition of a correspondence between the supernal forms and the beauty of the bodies that the senses can perceive in the material world. Al-Ghazālī, by recasting Avicenna's noetic system, offers a psychological and cognitive foundation for the spiritual aspects that justify the practice of *naẓar-bāzī*, which, in the case of Saʿdi's lyric poetry, needs to be read within this precise philosophical framework, and not solely in the wake of scholastic Sufi thought.

When both Avicenna and al-Ghazālī describe the phenomenology of the contact between the heart/intellect and the supernal world, their account of the actual content of the stupendous ideas that the Preserved Tablet/soul of the fixed stars projects onto the beholder's internal senses often seems vague. Al-Ghazālī defines those *maʿānī*—whose imaginal translation is in the form of magnificently beautiful human beings— as angelic essences whose nature is the most perfect spiritual content that the human intellect can cognize.

The philosophical background of this idea of vaguely defined perfection that the intellect translates into images derives from the recognition of the fixed stars of Avicenna's cosmology as angelic presences that take on the same function as the metaphysical intelligences constantly engaged in cogitation of the particulars constituting the material world. Therefore, what al-Ghazālī hints at is probably the pure contact between the human soul and the soul of the fixed stars themselves, which, by necessity of the psychological mechanism of imaginal transcription described by Avicenna, emerge to the internal senses as a human form of utmost beauty. I propose to refer to this parallel in order to explain the bewilderment with which Saʿdi's lyric subject fails to recognize the origin of the blinding beauty appearing before his eyes and his imagination:

> Behold! Someone is coming from the garden of paradise!
> A star is crossing the sky, or maybe an angel is coming!
>
> As sweet beauties appear from the invisible world [*ʿālam-i ghayb*]
> The salt of passion opens wounds in the hearts of the intimate masters.
>
> One breath abandons my life and one more breath comes back
> So that for one breath the intimacy with the beloved is bestowed upon me.
>
> O Saʿdi, the sorrow of loving him is a Sultan, and his army
> Shall seize the kingdom of your life: his nightwatch is coming.
>
> *Ṭayyibāt* 634[48]

48 [2.109] Saʿdi YE, 282–83. Yusofi mistakenly inserted this ghazal among the *Badāyiʿ*, even though the oldest manuscripts See ibid., 625. This is confirmed by Ms. Yale 1432, f. 231b.

The explicit reference to the "invisible world" (*ʿālam-i ghayb*) allows us to frame the ghazal within the context of al-Ghazālī's psychological theorization of the spiritual contact with the unseen in the guise of a beautiful human form. The lyric persona rhetorically questions the identity of the object of contemplation: is it a human being, an angel, or a star that appears from the "invisible world"? The conflation of these different specimens attesting to the incomparable beauty of the object of desire speaks to the validity of the Avicennian background that informs Saʿdi's deployment of al-Ghazālī's spiritual aesthetics. The word *ʿazīzān* that Saʿdi employs in the second line of this ghazal—which I render as the "intimate masters"—echoes those "companions" who, in the introduction to the *Gulistān*, witness the spiritual unveiling of the Master of the Heart and inquire about his visionary experience upon his return from the supernal world, which his internal senses had "translated" as a rose garden. The presence of a plurality of spiritual companions implies a social setting akin to the visionary process described by al-Ghazālī in the passage quoted earlier. Rather than an individual experience of ecstatic contemplation, the poet describes an imaginal opening that, as a window engrained in the heart of any trained practitioner of the spiritual path, discloses the "invisible world" for the sake of the intellect's and the internal senses' perusal.

One may note that in this text Saʿdi does not portray the beloved as a tangible presence: unlike most of Saʿdi's lyric compositions, this poem does not linger on the limbs of the beloved as an eroticized focal point. On the contrary, this short ghazal (as it is typical of Saʿdi's first collection of ghazals, the *Ṭayyibāt*) attempts to convey the experience of the spiritual contact with the invisible from a purely mental perspective, precisely along the lines set by the first part of the passage in which al-Ghazālī elaborates on the psychological mechanism of the unveiling, and thus coinciding with what we have designated as the first phase of the visionary experience.[49]

The parallel between a heavenly creature, a star, and an angel as metaphors for the beloved perfectly fits the conflations between Avicennian cosmology and al-Ghazālī's theological reformulation of the contact between the soul/heart of the individual and the soul of the fixed stars, which is referred to as an angelic agent or a reflection of paradise. The heart of the spiritual masters opens up as soon as this conjunction takes place, and the initial uncertainty with respect to the nature of the supernal ideas (*maʿānī*) shifts to the languidly painful bewilderment caused by the imaginal translation of those ideas into perfect human forms.

---

49 See next chapter for a theory of the chronology of Saʿdi's ghazals based on the relationship between ethics, eroticism, and the twofold nature of the imaginal experience.

The physiological backbone of the visionary experience conveyed by the internal senses is supported by the reference to breath, which appears in the third line as a rhythm that sets the imaginal pulse of the metaphysical eroticism: "One breath abandons my life and one more breath comes back / So that for one breath the intimacy with the beloved is bestowed upon me." Overall, this ghazal shows how a lyrical description can accommodate the mental space of the visionary enactment of the ideas filtering from the supernal by containing the experience within the boundaries of the purely psychological, and yet without forsaking the bodily substratum that animates the conjunction between the intellect/soul and the internal senses.

A similar representation focusing on the first phase of the visionary experience appears in another of Saʿdi's ghazals, in which once more the poet stages the rhetorical question addressing the identity of the vision:

> Who is this shining moon who so elegantly walks by?
> The thirsty one is dying, while the purest water flows by.
>
> Even if the cypress were capable of strolling from place to place
> Would it ever be more beautiful than he who is now passing by?
>
> The virgin of paradise is crossing the gaze of the ardent lovers:
> Or is it the moon of the fourteenth night, or the Chinese marionette
> who moves by? …
>
> Beware! Anyone who in the city holds his heart and religion firmly!
> He'll pass by and destroy all hearts, all religions.
>
> His coming and going from the imagery [*khayāl*] through my heart and
> before my eyes
> Is it truly real—I wonder—or does the imagination deceive me?
>
> Whether he decides to appear to us or not, the judgment is his:
> He is a sultan crossing a domain by his right.
>
> Saʿdi, practice asceticism and contemplate the boys who reflect supernal
> beauty [*shāhid-bāzī*]:
> As the beautiful ones reveal the supernal when they appear to the ascetic.
>
> *Ṭayyibāt* 41[50]

50 [2.110] Saʿdi YE, 22.

In this text too, the psychological mechanism of imaginal cognition is directly referred to through the description of visual representations circulating between the imagination (here the term *khayāl* could refer to both the retentive and the compositive faculties of this internal sense), the heart/soul, and the eyes of the beholder.

As noted on several occasions, the lyric subject's confusion with respect to the veracity of the vision rests on the idealistic nature of mental images in the Avicennian psychological system: as the locus of visual perception is the common sense and not the eye, the nature of the images perceived by the subject does not vary by reason of their origin, which can be either external, internal, or, in the case of contact with the supernal realm, metaphysical. The penultimate line emphasizes both the ephemerality and the randomness of the vision, thus suggesting a correlation between divine intervention and the physiological conditions that may trigger the commencement of the contact with the invisible world.

The visionary scope that delimits the horizon of the lyric subject's experience to the mental space of the connection with the invisible world (phase one and two) finds a further confirmation in the paradox of the last line, in which Saʿdi is urged to contemplate beautiful boys and to simultaneously confine himself in the corner of pious asceticism. This tension between the eroticism of beholding beautiful young men and the spiritual piety exuding from ascetic practices of restraint from worldly temptations parallels the nostalgic affection with which Saʿdi, in the story of his encounter with the young grammarian from Kashgar analyzed in the second chapter, bade his farewell by adducing that isolation should be preferred when erotic attraction threatens the rigorous devotion of the spiritual master.

In the lines above, Saʿdi's paradox that presents mundanity and asceticism on the same semiotic level determines that the kind of *shāhid-bāzī* (the practice of gazing upon beautiful youths) that he wishes to embrace relates to the mental contemplation of beauty through the imaginal translation of the *maʿānī* into forms (like the boy) that the devout may encounter in the world of sense. It is by means of such lines that we are offered the opportunity to discover how Saʿdi intertwines the seemingly opposite realms of *majāz* and *ḥaqīqat*, the mundane and the spiritual, through the powerful imaginal resources of the relationship between the visionary heart and the imagination.

Both al-Ghazālī's description of the erotic and cognitive aspects of the unveiling process and Saʿdi's visionary anecdote of the Master of the Heart underline the relevance of the interplay between the spiritual and the physical dimensions of contact with the invisible world. The explicit reference to this interplay, involving the physiological attraction exerted on the subject, is of utmost relevance to understanding the psychological dynamics that animate the implied eroticism of Saʿdi's ghazals, namely the constant oscillation between the mundane aspects of desire and the theosophy induced by the practices of *mushāhada* and *tafakkur*.

In order to appreciate the imaginal metaphysics that Saʿdi blends with the flesh of physical desire, I propose to compare one of his ghazals on the spiritual psychology of the contemplation of the beloved with a poem by Sanāʾī, which likely served as subtext for Saʿdi's rendition. In spite of the carnal triviality of Sanāʾī's mundane depiction of the appearance of the beloved in a public arena (abruptly ending with a private encounter tinged with sexual innuendos), there are formal correspondences between the two ghazals that offer intriguing insights into Saʿdi's visual spiritualization of the object of desire:

> Intoxicated my idol appeared one day at the market
> Suddenly clouds of turmoil rose up from the heart of the lovers.
>
> The light of day faded away for a hundred lovesick hearts:
> Hundreds bewildered by desire, blinded by their pain for him.
>
> Silk and ambergris were his cheek and downy-beard
> He could offer both valuables, and the buyers came forth.
>
> In amorous despair for that fine silk and fresh ambergris
> Commotion arose from the markets and the perfume sellers.
>
> The local comely beauties envy the down of his soft jaw:
> They slander him saying that thorns grew from the rose of his cheek.
>
> How wondrous is the benevolent gaze of God
> Which gave shape to irises and jasmines amidst the rose garden.
>
> And the night that I was granted access to his intimate encounter
> The morning shone from the mountains before my night was over.[51]

Saʿdi's intertextual response recombines the imagery of Sanāʾī's ghazal and turns the homoerotic motif of the urban encounter with the beloved into a natural allegory that blends the aesthetic perception of a mundane presence with the territory of spiritual imagination:

51 [2.111] Sanāʾi 1362/1983, 141; 1389/2010, 429.

1 From the pavilion he appeared in the rose garden, intoxicated,
Tumultuous commotion suddenly arose from the anemone and the rose.

2 I saw the birds of the flower beds turning vociferous, loudly singing
When this blossom surfaced from the corner of the meadow.

3 The waters of the stream reflected the rose of his cheeks
And fire arose from the blossoming pomegranate flowers.

4 The **prayerful** who became the **devoted disciple** [***murīd***] of longing for him
Cast his renown amongst the drunkards of the tavern.

5 When the **ascetic** witnessed the **secret marvels** of his idol-like countenance
He abandoned the cell of pious confinement and embraced the belt of paganism.

6 Anyone **whose gaze saw him manifesting** as a **beauty from paradise**
Was thrown like me on the ground: desperate and deranged by love.

7 The outset of my misery was the day when, from **the shrine of the invisible** [***ḥaram-i ghayb***],
I saw the silk of your beauty arising in the market.

8 My heart's only desire was to throw my soul at your feet
My wishes were fulfilled, and here I am what I have become.

9 On that day Saʿdi cast the blossoming meadow away and let winter plunder it,
When from **his heart's garden the fragrance of the rose of his beloved** arose.

Badāyiʿ 501[52]

In spite of the sensuality of the imagery that Saʿdi constructs as a further elaboration on the mundane atmosphere of Sanāʾī's text, this ghazal features key words that reframe the poem within the psychological horizon of the

52 [2.112] Saʿdi YE, 229.

visionary experiences discussed thus far. In particular, both the description of the beholder as the apprentice of a spiritual order embracing the path of longing for the object of contemplation and the reference to the "shrine of the invisible" (*ḥaram-i ghayb*) place this ghazal at the center of al-Ghazālī's phenomenology of the visionary practice.

Unlike the ghazals so far analyzed in this chapter, which pertain to the first two purely mental phases of al-Ghazālī's phenomenology of the visionary experience, this poem explores the territory lying beyond the strictly imaginal boundaries of inspired connection with the invisible. It tackles the condition of the beholder during the third phase, i.e., the transition that al-Ghazālī qualifies as the return of the subject from the contemplative state and his longing *in the physical world* for the imaginary beauty that the intellect had depicted for him during its contact with the invisible world. The nostalgia deriving from the loss of psychological contact with the beautiful forms descending from the invisible world transpires from the desperation and derangement (sixth line) affecting the lyric subject as well as *anyone* whose internal senses depicted the awe-inspiring ideas from the supernal world as a beauty of paradise. It is the liminality of the contemplative experience that casts the beholders into a state of bewildered confusion, in which the boundaries between the cognitive experience of the vision and the illusion of a real presence directly perceived by the external senses fades away.

If we follow both al-Ghazālī's account and the Avicennian texts informing his spiritual psychology, we see that once the beholder returns from his contemplative state, all contacts between his soul/intellect/heart and the invisible world/soul of the stars/Preserved Tablet are severed. The subject is left alone with the visual memory of the images of utmost human beauty and the emotional exchange that they induce as a result of the interplay between the external senses and the internal imaginal faculties of memory and imagination—estimative, retentive, and compositive alike. The bewildering overlap between the echo of the visionary experience—the tangible trace of its memory as recorded by the internal senses—and the sensorial solicitations of the visible world finds its lyric reflection in Saʿdi's rearrangement of Sanaʾī's metaphor of the beloved's complexion as a precious silk causing turmoil in the market of textiles and luxury goods:

Sanāʾī:

Silk and ambergris were his cheek and downy-beard
He could offer both valuables, and the buyers came forth.

In amorous despair for that fine silk and fresh ambergris
Commotion arose from the markets and the perfume sellers.

Sa‘di:

7 The outset of my misery was the day when, from **the shrine of the invisible [*ḥaram-i ghayb*]**,
I saw the silk of your beauty arising in the market.

Whilst Sanā’ī’s metaphor derives from the market-centric tradition of the so-called "city-enticer" erotic genre (*shahr-āshūb*), Sa‘di redevelops its related imagery into an allegorical representation for the psychology of the transactional transfer from the invisible world to the process of active imagination.[53] The visionary experience as a psychological transaction representing the imaginal translation of the *ma‘ānī* descending from the invisible world brings us back to the opening anecdote of the *Gulistān*, in which Sa‘di describes the master of the heart's return from his mental contemplation as his coming back from a state of *mu‘āmala*, or "spiritual transaction" based on what al-Ghazālī describes as the pious practices leading to the purification of the heart.[54] A further element of comparison between the allegorical dimension of this ghazal and Sa‘di's anecdote in the *Rose Garden* stands out from the closing line:

9 On that day Sa‘di cast the blossoming meadow away and let winter plunder it,
When from **his heart's garden the fragrance of the rose of his beloved** arose.

Once again, in spite of the apparently purely amatory emphasis of this image, the visionary elements of the previous lines help us recognize that the heart that Sa‘di mentions is exactly the same screen reflecting the invisible world, which, in the account from the *Gulistān*, appears in the shape of a rose garden whose intoxicating fragrance prevents the Master of the Heart from further exploring the supernal territory.

In this ghazal, Sa‘di's final correspondence between the heart and an allegorical rose garden from which the rose-like beloved blossoms contextualizes the natural setting described at the opening of the poem. One may read the entire ghazal as an allegorical crescendo that represents spiritual imagination

53 On this genre, see *EI*^{2}, s.v. "Shahrangīz" [J. T. P. de Bruijn]; Sharma 2000; 107–16; 2004.
54 See chapter 7.

as the only context described by Sa‘di. Nevertheless, the idea of a dual level of existence in the portrayal of the garden—one mental, and the other material—is far more compelling. As may be inferred from the last line, once the metaphysical garden discloses the images from the invisible world, the lyric subject is consumed by the frustration of not being capable of finding similar forms in the real world. And no garden of beauty can match the blossoming splendor of the beloved as a mental representation—a silk which no mundane marketplace can provide.

5 Phases Three and Four: Spiritual Frustration and Soothing Retrieval of the Experience

Al-Ghazālī represents the beholder's access to the vision of the supernal *ma‘ānī* and the subsequent interruption of the contact between the internal senses and the Preserved Tablet as the alternation of the *ma‘ānī*'s veiling and unveiling. Both the opening and closing of the heart's aperture onto the invisible world and its mirror-like surface reflecting or veiling the supernal metaphorically explain the spiritual physiology of the beholder's condition once the awareness of a visionary experience is converted into a form of nostalgic longing. This nostalgia corresponds to the third phase of the visionary connection and, as noticed earlier, it marks the transition from a purely mental experience to the poignant juxtaposition of external perceptions and internal remembrance of the visual incarnation of the supernal *ma‘ānī*. In this state of disconcerted wandering among the visual clues inhabiting the mundane world, the lyric subject expresses its longing for the renewal of the epiphany:

> O moon-faced beauty, you are present and yet concealed:
> No day passes without your presence crossing my heart....
>
> Come back, longing and distance have consumed us
> You hide from the gaze, but face the supernal inspiration [*ma‘nī*]....
>
> You hide behind the veil, then you tear a *veil* apart:
> What forms will take shape once the veil is lifted?
>
> *Badāyi‘* 327[55]

55 [2.113] Sa‘di YE, 153.

In the ghazal below, Saʿdi combines the recurrent amatory theme of the beloved's farewell with a more insightful (as well as explicit) approach that delves into the cosmic psychology of a possible reconnection with the invisible:

> Alas, your image does not depart from my imagination!
> What will eventually happen to me in this quest for you?
>
> Louder and louder every time the high and low pitches of my laments:
> This is what I suffer from your departure, while loving you.
>
> The sunshine of your face steals the light from the stars
> While the people point their fingers at the pale crescent of my body.
>
> At every breath the light radiating from your face falls on everyone:
> And I am the only one for whom the *connection* [*iṭṭisāl*] is yet to happen....
>
> The celestial spheres heard my cries and urged Saʿdi not to despair:
> "Your sighs darken the mirror of our supernal beauty."
>
> *Badāyiʿ* 489[56]

The penultimate couplet reintroduces the social setting of the spiritually informed companionship in which the beholders witness the physiological effect of the visionary experience of their fellow initiates. The lyric subject sees its companions illuminated by the radiance of the vision, while the renewal of the connection is yet to be established for it. The technical term used here, *iṭṭiṣāl*, "connection" or "contact," far from representing a mystical idea of a vaguely theorized "union" with the divine, primarily signifies a stellar conjunction and, by extension, in Avicennian terms, the alignment between the inner senses of the beholder and the emergence of the *maʿānī* to the surface of mental forms of exceeding beauty.[57] The last line reinforces the cosmic dimension of this visual experience through the personification of the celestial spheres,

56 [2.114] Saʿdi YE, 223–24.

57 "Avicenna calls this process of acquisition or reception a 'contact' (*ittiṣāl*) between the human and active intellects. In the emanative language which he inherited from the Neoplatonic tradition, and which he incorporated in his own understanding of the cosmology of the concentric spheres of the universe with their intercommunicating intellects and souls, he referred to the flow of knowledge from the supernal world to the human intellect as 'divine effluence' (*al-fayż al-ilāhī*). The reason that this is possible at all is again the consubstantiality of all intellects, human and celestial alike." Gutas 2013, 41.

which intervene in Saʿdi's amatory lamentations (he represents himself in the garb of the lyric subject) and mention their own mirror-like surface capable of reflecting the supernal ideal (*maʿnī*) of pure beauty. The association between the celestial spheres represented as a mirror reflecting beauty and the socio-spiritual pathos of the lyric subject's longing for the "turn" (*nawbat*) of his conjunction with the invisible *maʿānī* is probably one of Saʿdi's most striking lyric elaborations on the Avicennian background of al-Ghazālī's psycho-physiology of the visionary experience of the contemplation of human beauty.

Even though Saʿdi was not the first poet to lyrically address the psychological aspect of the conjunction of the heart with the celestial world, he was the author who, before anyone else, perfectly combined the complexity of this philosophical background with both the Sufi discourse on vision and worldly reflections on the nature of human desire. One of the spiritual subtexts of Saʿdi's undertaking can be found in a ghazal by ʿAṭṭār in which, contrary to the sensual dominant that surfaces from all of Saʿdi's lyric composition, the mention of the connection with the invisible world is almost completely reduced to the quest for the divine presence without the imaginal intercession of the carnal soul and the internal senses:

> The souls and hearts of the Masters are lost in your perfection
> The intellect of all the intimates receives no notice of encountering you.
>
> You are everything, look at yourself and see how incessantly
> Eighteen thousand worlds are the mirror of your beauty.
>
> How can the hearts of those who seek you infer your presence?
> Anything that exists in the world is the image of you.
>
> Mute is the tongue of all the beholders because of you
> No subtle point can be uttered in describing your perfection.
>
> For centuries the turning spheres rush on your path:
> For the impact of your pull, they curve the back of their trajectory....
>
> The creatures of the visible and the invisible are left far from you:
> People lose their existence when they reach a connection [*ittiṣāl*] with you.
>
> So dry we are on earth, lift the veil from your face:
> So that your clear water may moisten the dry lips of the lovers.

Even though poets more eloquent than Farīd [al-Dīn ʿAṭṭār] live in the world,
Do not reject him: speechless turns his speech before you.[58]

While the fusion of the psychological elements of desire and the cosmological projection of the visionary experience is quite rare in the lyric tradition prior to the 13th century, ʿAttār's lines show that the Sufi representations of the theological reconsideration of Avicennian cosmic psychology had already offered a viable poetic paradigm for the development that Saʿdi brought about.[59]

The novelty of Saʿdi's depiction of the visionary experience as a conflation of mundane and supernal sources of aesthetic inspiration left a remarkable trace in the works of authors such as Khʷājū of Kerman or Sayf-i Farghānī, whose poems constitute a transitional phase toward the ingenious intertwinement of metaphysical and sensible experiences that characterizes the poetry of Hafez of Shiraz. The following lines by Khʷājū, for example, reveal the extent of Saʿdi's influence on the lyrical depiction of the third phase of al-Ghazālī's account of the visionary process:

Do not expect me to seek distance from beautiful faces:
Separation from the beloved is no condition of affection....

When the conjunction is supernal between two lovers,
How can the Egyptian Yūsuf remain separated from Yaʿqūb? ...

The broken heart is both the wayfarer and the enlightened beholder:
It grasps the light of supernal meaning from your beautiful forms.[60]

58 [2.115] ʿAttār 1392/2013, 551.

59 Preliminary traces of Saʿdi's psychological innovations with respect to the cosmic conjunction between the internal senses and the First Cause are to be found in some of Khāqānī's ghazals. Such evidence deserves to be studied within the general framework of the development of imagination-related imagery in the history of the Persian ghazal:
No light illuminates the nights but the image of you
No garden adorns the souls but your beauty.
Every day, for the sun of love
What horoscope better than the conjunction with you?
So far off is the hope of seeing your face at noon every day,
Yet no midnight is devoid of your image.
[2.116] Khāqāni Shervāni 1382/2003, 561.

60 [2.117] Khwāju Kermāni 1369/1990, 185.

Because Saʿdi's poem is evidently the subtext of the images that Khʷājū develops, I translate the expression *nūr-i maʿnavī* as "light of supernal meaning," which a less informed approach might render as "spiritual light." In Khʷājū's ghazals too, the phase following the first conjunction with the invisible causes the emotional distress that leads the lyric subject to invoke the angelic presences that constitute the imaginal translation of the supernal while the potential carnality of the gaze is still active:

> [...] Do not gaze with your carnal eyes, as when looking at the beautiful ones
> The purpose of the Masters of the Heart is the spiritual conjunction.
>
> O angelic face, how could I not invoke you night and day?
> No chance is left to the insane but invoking the angels....
>
> Do not cover your face, as from your countenance
> Khʷājū seeks the perusal of the divine secret of creation....[61]

We may read the few ghazals in which Saʿdi represents the lyric subject's enjoyment of the beloved's "return" against the pattern that al-Ghazālī describes as the renewal of the visionary contact through one's exposure to a particularly remarkable aesthetic experience involving the perusal of physical perceptions of beauty. In the guise of a purely lyrical discourse, Saʿdi's most intimate lauds of the beloved expressed through the lyric "thou" contain subtle references to the fourth phase of the visionary experience. In these poems, the object of desire, rather than corresponding to an improbable personification of God or merely addressing a carnal beloved bereft of any metaphysical underpinning, stands out as an earthly presence whose perfect beauty lacerates the veil of the supernal "secret":

> I've never seen a seducer like you
> I've never seen such a fragrant rose petal!
>
> No one similar to you appears in the world:
> I've never seen such an angel!
>
> Not even in the artifices of Sāmirī
> Have I seen such wondrous enchantments.

61 [2.118] Khwāju Kermāni 1369/1990, 214.

I admire the moon, then your face:
I've never seen room for comparison!

No ruby as sweet as your lips
Have I ever seen in the jewelers' workshops

Similar to your perfect teeth, no poetry
Have I ever seen in the pure Persian language....

The veil of the devout master?
I've never seen anyone tearing it as much as you!

I have seen all the beautiful seducers in the world,
I've never seen anyone as inspiring as you.

Grave is the threat that you pose to Islam.
I've never seen all of this in the religion of the heathens.

Too much you suffer for the beautiful faces:
I've never seen anyone like you, O Sa'di!

I have seen all the Sufis in world,
But I've never seen a *qalandar* like you.
Ṭayyibāt 26[62]

The comforting retrieval of the supernal meanings corresponds to what we have labeled as the fourth phase of the visionary experience, in which the lyric subject's cognitive system simultaneously interacts with both the external senses and the forms that the internal senses reconstitute on the basis of the intellectual perception of the supernal realm:

In the hour that my walking cypress returned from the door
You may well say that the soul returned to my dead body.

Decrepit I was from the violence of the stars and the hatred of time
But youthful love has now returned to my old head.

62 [2.119] Sa'di YE, 15. The last two lines are only found in the Khorramshāhi-Foroughi edition. See Sa'di KhE, 500. Yusofi's edition (as well as Ms. Yale 1432, f. 266b.) records this variant: *Sa'dī tu na mard-i khānaqāhī / man pīr-i qalandarī nadīdam.*

My victorious fortune overcame its hostility,
Peaceful it returned this morning from my door.

The beloved has returned, and the enemy recedes.
Notwithstanding the cold winter, the springtime breeze has returned.

Convey the happy news, O carnal soul, that hardship has come to its end.
O body, do not suffer any longer, as the soul has returned.

I cannot believe the fortunate twist of my destiny:
Gracefully that stone-hearted idol, ruthless archer, has returned.

As soon as you retuned from the door of the unseen, O companion of my soul
Everyone dropped the lust they were nurturing in their thoughts.

Loving your face is forbidden, but not to Sa'di:
Who, in your passion, abandoned all worldly things.

O friends, criticize me not, nor blame me:
No return is now possible from these affairs.
Khavātīm 690[63]

Without the context offered by al-Ghazālī's passage, the contradictory elements that constitute the images displayed in this ghazal could hardly provide a coherent aggregation of narratives. How can one explain the revivification of the lyric subject's body that is shown in the first line with the final confession of detachment from the world? Moreover, how does the spiritual level implied by the reference to the "unseen" intersect with the mundanity of the prohibition of desiring the beloved's physical presence? A viable allegorical reading is provided by the possibility of conceiving the "return" of the beloved as the re-establishment of the connection between the vision of the object of desire and the recognition of the forms of the supernal world that metaphysically reflect his bodily presence. What the lyric subject welcomes from the "unseen" is the return of the spiritual meaning that renews the ecstatic pleasure deriving from the contemplation of the divine truth. This re-appropriation of meaning vivifies both the flesh of the subject—whose senses no longer belong to the urges of carnal desire—and the limbs of the beloved, whose presence signifies both

63 [2.120] Sa'di YE, 308–309.

his own carnal beauty and the intellectual commotion that his spiritual form provides to the heart of the beholder. The appellation "companion of the soul" as a way to address the beloved could be seen as a reference to the practical intellect's recognition of an affinity between the soul and the supernal realm.

It is interesting to witness how, in the fifth line, the lyric subject addresses the carnal soul (*nafs*) and the body (*jism*) in its attempt to declare the appeasement of the physical instinct toward the flesh of the beloved, soon replaced by the cognition (properly *maʿrifat*) of the correspondence between the physical and metaphysical aspects of the manifestation of beauty:

> Convey the happy news, O carnal soul, that hardship has come to its end.
> O body, do not suffer any longer, as the soul has returned.

By declaring three times that the beloved has entered from the lover's door, Saʿdi aligns the poem with the traditional lyric motif of the morning encounter with the object of desire.[64] But as soon as the poet specifies that the "door" (*dar*) is not simply the lover's door, but the door of the "unseen" as well, Saʿdi produces a creative twist in his audience's horizon of expectations by overlaying a spiritual/psychological dimension on a classical lyric theme. Even in the ghazals in which Saʿdi does not seem to explicitly express the psychological dominant of the visionary experience, he does recur to the image of the "door" as an aperture through which the supernal meanings are converted into images by the effusive power of the divine mercy:

> With such beauty and your splendid forms, you may appear again from any door:
> A door you shall open onto the people, from the pure mercy of God.
>
> Wherever like Yūsuf you manifest your beauty behind the veil
> The vain blamers won't tell the difference between their hands and the citrons.
>
> Beautiful is their countenance, they often adorn their bodies with jewels.
> Silvery is your candid frame, so beautiful you are that you adorn the jewels.
>
> *Ṭayyibāt* 293[65]

64 See Lewis 2010a.

65 [2.121] Saʿdi YE, 134–35.

In these lines too, as remarked in the first chapter, the door onto the invisible world acting as an imaginal source for the lyric subject's sacred desire helps to explain the semantics of the veil, not as an actual garment but as a symbolic curtain capable of concealing and disclosing the epiphanic manifestation of beauty. The physical presence of the body, along with its carnal weight, which hinders the superior aspirations of the soul, elucidates the physiological aspect of these moments of spiritual disclosure in their relationship with physical desire.

In the ghazal analyzed immediately before the one above, the lustful desire (*havas*) that Sa'di mentions in the second hemistich belongs to the "hardship" of the body and the urges of the soul, in the context of a sensual drive towards a body whose supernal "meaning" is yet to be found:

> As soon as you retuned from the door of the unseen, O companion of
> my soul,
> Everyone dropped the lust they were nurturing in their thoughts.

The return of that "meaning"—the spiritual ideal behind the bodily form of the beloved—relieves the beholders from their carnal desires and allows Sa'di, in the subsequent line, to practice an amorous passion that is, in principle, forbidden (*ḥarām*). The emphasis on the permissibility of the gaze upon the physical body of the beloved speaks to the fact that contact with the supernal meaning of his presence does not imply the dismissal of the role of the senses. Departing from the scholastic approaches to sacred eroticism, Sa'di declares that the mundane experience channeled through both the internal and the external senses is a fundamental component of the spiritual quest, and that contact with the unseen is the missing link that allows the lyric subject to cover with meaning both his own body and the limbs of the beloved. "No return is now possible from these affairs" can be read as the permanent impact that the contact with the unseen has on the psyche of the lover: just as al-Ghazālī theorizes in his passage, once the link with the supernal ideas is established, the imagination of the subject will seek in the world the physical signs of that spiritual beauty, and anytime that he sets his eyes on a beautiful bodily form, that original contact happens to be automatically renewed.

6 Transgressing the Boundaries of Lust and Incarnationism

At the end of the passage on the visionary experience, al-Ghazālī emphasizes that, in spite of the metaphysical dimension the beholder attains when contemplating the visual translations of the supernal forms, his return to the world of senses nonetheless requires submission, once again, to the physio-psychological and ethical imperatives entailed by mundane dwelling. In the lines below, Saʿdi associates the contemplation of pure beauty—its metaphysical "essence"—with the pending risk of seeing one's ritual prayer invalidated by sensual thoughts involving the mental production of erotic images:

> Your countenance is the panacea for all hardship.
> Resisting you exceeds the realm of possibilities:
>
> The prolegomena of your marvelous forms
> Are the epigraph upon the perfection of the essence of beauty....
>
> I never saw a face like yours in the city,
> Capable of invalidating all ritual prayers!
>
> *Ṭayyibāt* 39[66]

As I will further point out in the next chapter, the role of both the downward orientation of the practical intellect and the internal senses' attachment to the carnal soul confer on the visionary experience a window in which the imagination is free to direct the mental images it produces toward sensual tensions. Just as in the case of the oscillations between courtly and obscene poetry, the liminal space of spiritual imagination, by relying on the access to the beholder's bodily functions in order to translate the supernal into images, constantly comes up against the possibility of transgressing the limits imposed on both the imaginary and concrete pleasures of the flesh.

Both al-Ghazālī's analytical wording and Saʿdi's lyrical intimations seem to imply that the beholder may run the risk of this transgression, especially whenever he returns to the world of senses after his imaginal exploration of the metaphysics of desire. As al-Ghazālī points out, the detractors of the visionary experience focus solely on the phenomenal aspect of metaphysical contemplation as a social practice that involves the physical reactions of the initiates. What they judge, he warns, is the association between the spiritual pleasure deriving from the aesthetics of the contemplation of beautiful bodies and the sexual dominant perceived by the eyes of whoever lacks familiarity with such practices. Saʿdi seems to elaborate on this paradox when offering the reader a revealing pun that unpacks the different possibilities of desire:

66 [2.122] Saʿdi YE, 21.

Everyone blames us for indulging in desire,
except the one who is caught in the trap of desire.
Ṭayyibāt 79[67]

The paradoxical repetition of the word "desire" (*havas*) highlights how the beholders may aesthetically mingle with the mundane experiences of life after the first imaginal epiphany and let their gaze linger upon bodies whose presence could differently adhere to the supernal paradigm of perfect beauty. Once the validating presence of the supernal informs the correspondence between the ideal forms and the forms of the world, the consequence of the coexistence of a variety of approaches to the experience of desire is that particular objects of contemplation may coincide with the supernal meanings without other beholders perceiving the spiritual nature of that sensual liaison:

For once in my entire life you'll enter from the door, unannounced
So that the dervish's night might see the dawn amidst darkness....

Why do you blame the enraptured beholder [*ʿārif*]?
The beautiful boy [*shāhid*] is present to us, yet you don't know *which* one he is.
Ṭayyibāt 276[68]

After the fourth phase of the visionary experience, multiple re-conjunctions with the supernal are established through the aesthetic admiration of the phenomenal world. At that point, the mental interplay between visible and invisible forms of presence in the imagination of the beholder during his first connection with the Preserved Tablet converts into a form of visibility/invisibility that relates to the potential meaning that bodily presences may acquire with respect to their metaphysical counterparts. If during the first and second phases the lyric subject's source of pleasure and frustration derives from the access to or inaccessibility of the supernal meanings, the post-fourth phase entirely revolves around the perusal of mundane bodies of beauty and the degree of aesthetic pleasure that their presence is capable of diverting towards the regained visibility of the *maʿānī*:

67 [2.123] Saʿdi YE, 40.
68 [2.124] Saʿdi YE, 127.

Cover your face, otherwise little chance is left
for the spiritual beholders to abstain from gazing at you.[69]

Sa'di's call for abstention playfully hints at the social space of the coexistence of visionary experiences and contemplative approaches to the physical presence of objects of desire, whose beauty constitutes both a source of spiritual elevation in the quest for the lost *ma'ānī* and a sensual snare for the carnal soul. As the following lines point out, it is the retrieval of the *ma'āni* that frames the dubious forms of visual contemplation of carnal beauty within the territory of permissible forms of aesthetic cogitation:

So many times I have implored you not to show your face,
So that the eyes of the spiritually blind won't contemplate you.

Then I think that with the form and "meaning" that you possess
Only the true beholders can really *see* you.
Ṭayyibāt 113[70]

We may remark how the very ethical problem of the permissibility of gazing upon human forms reveals the dual nature of contemplation when the lyric subject enters the final phase of the visionary experience. From this point of view, the twofold ontology of vision in the works of Sa'di—which, as often noted in our analyses, tends to switch between imaginary and optical pathways—clarifies itself by highlighting the conflation of intellectual and mundane forms of sight and the way in which only the true beholders can safely transit between the two dimensions.

Once the visionary practice prevents the beholder from experiencing lustful desires, the peril of incarnationism is the last threat that the individual ought to consider when cogitating upon the epiphany of archetypal beauty as a human manifestation. As highlighted in the previous chapters, Avicenna would recognize the mistaken perception of a divine indwelling inhabiting a human body as an error of the estimative faculty (*wahm*). Al-Ghazālī and the ensuing theosophical tradition discussing the problem of incarnationism and personification—including, as shown at the beginning of this chapter, 'Ayn al-Qużāt's and 'Irāqī's opinions on this matter—underline that this potential form of blasphemy pertains to the semiotics of the subject's gaze on the epiphany of the supernal. Such a reading implies that the beautiful form should

69 [2.125] Sa'di KhE, 443.
70 [2.126] Sa'di YE, 55.

not be read as an icon standing for or representing the divine, but as an index pointing to the metaphysical origins of beauty.

In the ghazal below, Saʿdi addresses the issue of incarnationism (or personification) by playfully comparing the lack of rational agency that affects the astonished lyric subject with the ethical and theological constraints that prevent the commoners from prostrating themselves before the blinding beauty of the beloved:

> Tone down your arrogance, if you are the *shāhid* of the Sufis
> A gentle demon is better than a frowning angel!
>
> I am moved by the desire to walk with you in the orchard
> But any corner will satisfy me, as you are a garden yourself!
>
> Your departure killed me, sit by me for one breath
> So that the spiritual breath may bring me back to life!
>
> You may peruse the horizons, but except for your mirror
> No one will ever find traces of a form similar to yours.
>
> They say that no epoch is devoid of seditions,
> Is perhaps your beauty the seductive sedition of our time?
>
> You appear in the morning and no one bows down to worship your face.
> Why? People fear God, whereas I am too bewildered to prostrate.
>
> You may not appear again through Saʿdi's door,
> But you cannot leave his recollections!
>
> *Badāyiʿ* 465[71]

The ghazal seems to depict the coexistence of a physical *shāhid* with a manifold mental representation. While the physical object of desire inhabits the social space of spiritual practices (the "arrogant" beauty admired by the Sufis, the "sedition" of our time, the reflection in the "mirror," etc.), Saʿdi describes the imaginal *shāhid* as both the mental translation of a contact with the unseen and the trace of a visual memory lodged in the mind of the lyric subject. Furthermore, this memory appears as vestigial echo of both a visual experience with a bodily beloved and the visual recollection of a supernal mental

71 [2.127] Saʿdi YE, 214.

contact with the past. We can almost imagine the *ʿārif*/beholder/lover practicing spiritual cleansing to attain *mushāhada*, and interacting in the social spaces where the physical presence of attractive youths constitutes a source of temptation that is not only carnal, but also doctrinal, as the uninformed or bewildered onlooker may regard them as incarnations of the divine presence. Eventually, Saʿdi's virtuosic juxtaposition of physical perceptions and mental projections conjures up a presence that is both physical and metaphysical.

In the penultimate line, while the risk of incarnationism seems to have been avoided ("people" do not worship what appears—physically perceived or imagined—as divine beauty, for they recognize that you are a sign of God, not the divine itself), the lyric persona declares that its observance of the doctrine stems from the bewildering nature of the vision, which obfuscates the senses and prevents the beholder from bowing down before a physical beloved or his imaginal icon.[72] In the final verse, the reader is left with the nostalgic resolution of the lyric persona in the guise of Saʿdi as the author of the poem: I might not see you again, because I ought to resist lustful thoughts, or because the "door" onto the unseen will not open anymore; yet my remembrance of you is what I cherish the most.

7 Beyond the Chinese and Greek Paintings, and toward the Performative Boundaries of the Lyric

We conclude this chapter with a ghazal in which Saʿdi magisterially combines the earthly and the psychological aspects of the visionary horizon of desire by incorporating the pre-Islamic literary topic of the journey across the desert within the courtly canon that inspires his lyric voice. Moreover, the text will reconnect us with the legend of the Chinese and the Greek painters with which we began our journey across the erotic dimension of the visionary experience of Saʿdi's lyric subject:

> Your limbs shine like silver, stone is your heart: return, O beloved
> and disentangle the rose from its thorns, alleviate my wounds, free me from the mud....

72 Compare this image with this other line from the *Badāyiʿ*, featured in a ghazal that opens the collection:
When I look at your face I fear for everyone's faith:
Will you bring a new heresy to the world?
[2.128] Saʿdi YE, 146.

O morning breeze, do you want to see the day in the middle of the night?
Blow through the curtains of the litter and disclose that wandering sunshine! …

I have companions who deny my intellect and faith:
They grab my hand and ask me to keep it off his waist.

What does the wise man say to those who blame the lover?
"Whoever sleeps ashore knows nothing about those who drown in the ocean."

Let those two delicate hands shed my blood!
I do not want to be killed, but so much I long for the hand of the murderer!

If the camel had **reason**, it would know that no patience is left to Majnūn:
It would let him spend the night wherever Leylī's campsite is found! …

Thoughts stem from **reason**, which cause people to suffer:
O wise man, do fall in love if tranquility is what you seek!

As long as my steps are steady, I seek the path to the encounter.
Do not mind the **intellect** complaining about how sterile the efforts are.

Sit with the beloved for some time, forgetful of this world and the next:
Wondrous images you shall see, more alluring than Chinese and Greek paintings.

For this "meaning" [*maʿnī*], a form is required that only Saʿdi can beautifully craft:
Anything that surfaces from the soul finds its reflection on the surface of the heart.

Ṭayyibāt 109[73]

The theme of the journey across the desert acts as a symbolic analogue of the cathartic process of the soul/heart's quest for its conjunction with the supernal realm. By introducing this theme, Saʿdi traces a parallel between, on the one hand, the conventional motif of the *recherche* for the beloved through a mundane journey and, on the other, the psychological path leading to the retrieval

73 [2.129] Saʿdi YE, 53. Ms. Tehran 1296, 438.

of the "meanings" capable of elevating the spiritual status of the physical bodies to idealized loci of manifestation of the invisible. If we read the ghazal against the Avicennian psychology of the contact with the invisible through the perusal of earthly forms of beauty, the first invocation uttered in the presence of the beloved does not read as a plea for his return as a physical entity: it is rather a supplication directed at the supernal meanings reconnecting with the perfect aesthetics of his body as it is perceived and cognized by the eyes and the intellect of the lover.

While the reference to mud could be read as the "hardship" that the lyric subject undergoes when seduced by the temptations of the carnal soul, we may read Saʿdi's repeated emphasis on intelligence and the intellect throughout the entire ghazal as an attempt to create a multilayered semantic echo between the conventional topic of the struggle between love and rationality and the underlying noetics of the visionary experience. The repeated references to the intellect as a resource that only love can overpower forms a crescendo culminating in the image of the lover sitting next to the beloved in order to engage himself with an imaginal journey capable of overshadowing Greek and Chinese paintings. The association between the noun *ʿajāyib* (which here Saʿdi utilizes as an adjective, "wondrous") and the *Rūmī* and *Chīnī* pictures is a clear reference to the parable of the competition between the Chinese and the Greek painters that al-Ghazālī narrates in the *Iḥyāʾ*.[74] By means of this intertextual stratagem, Saʿdi elevates the act of contemplating the beloved to an aesthetic and spiritual activity that bridges the gap between the rational path (symbolized by the Greek paintings) and the Sufi approach (symbolized by the Chinese act of polishing the surface of the wall). Saʿdi adds an aesthetic level to the story and combines al-Ghazālī's religious teaching with Niẓāmī's meditation on the role of the internal senses and the psychology of artistic creation. The echo of Niẓāmī's rendition of the story (through the reference to Chinese and Greek paintings) emphasizes the philosophical and artistic aspects of contemplating physical beauty and its imaginal counterpart.

Considering the subtext of mud as a metaphor for the perils posed by the carnal soul, the rational impediment that the intellect poses to the lyric subject's correct contemplation of the object of desire could be read as a cognitive error that derives from the interaction between the soul and the body. As observed in the previous chapters, one such cognitive error derives from the internal sense of estimation's tendency to misread the beautiful form standing before the beholder's eyes as an ontological manifestation of God, rather

74 Al-Ghazālī refers to the "wondrous techniques" that characterize both the Greek painting and the Chinese reflection.

than a sign pointing at the divine origin of all beauty. The line portraying the imaginal journey ("wondrous images you shall see") confirms this reading, as it represents the alignment between the world of sense, in which the object of desire appears, and the formation of mental images that correspond to the past experiences of the visionary conjunction between the heart and the supernal realm's "meanings." Therefore, the celebrated "return" of the beloved corresponds to the coexistence of the phenomenal access to the object of desire and the correct psycho-cosmic alignment of mental images and metaphysical intimations.

Without the hermeneutical awareness provided by the psychology of the visionary experience, one could read the reference to *maʿnī* in the last line exclusively from the viewpoint of the codified relationship between content and form as act of literary creation. In such lines, the poet portrays himself in the skillful process of decorating the virginal thoughts stemming from his creative mind with beautiful linguistic garments:

> For this "meaning" [*maʿnī*], a form is required that only Saʿdi can beautifully craft:
> Anything that surfaces from the soul finds its reflection on the surface of the heart.

While the first half of the line confirms this conventional reading, the rest of the verse reorients the concept of *maʿnī* toward the framework of al-Ghazālī's science of the heart and the psychology of the imaginal experience. We could read Saʿdi's reference to *maʿnī* as a pun bridging the gap between the field of poetic creativity and the spiritual recognition of the invisible through the psychological suggestion caused by the exposure to the beloved's formal beauty. The coexistence of these two realms in this verse aligns with Alexander Key's theorization of *maʿnī* (*maʿnā*, in the Arabic diction that he analyses) as "mental content," poised at the epistemological and ontological confluence in which the problem of "meaning" involves an encounter between language, mind, and reality.[75]

Saʿdi's mention of the heart and the soul as two separate entities could be read as an attempt to account for the interaction between the two aspects of the Avicennian practical soul in its mediation between the supernal realm and the visible world; these become the two poles that constitute the imaginal activity of the subject. From this perspective, what Saʿdi refers to as *maʿnī* is

75 Key 2018, 69–70.

the "mental content" constituting the experience described in the penultimate line, in which the poet alludes to the indescribable mental visions coexisting with the physical contemplation of the beloved. Through the allusion to the story of the Chinese and Greek artists, Saʿdi depicts himself as both a consummate spiritual beholder who accesses the *maʿānī* from the unseen, and a careful observer of reality as a source of aesthetic inspiration. Moreover, the literal levels of the story allow him to introduce himself as both a Greek painter and a Chinese polisher: his poetry is both a creative act of imitation of reality and a polished reflection of this imitation, capable of reconnecting the images that his words depict with their supernal meanings.

Therefore, by praising his own literary skills, Saʿdi presents his ghazals as the verbal translation of the imaginal activities deriving from the soul's contemplation of the correspondence between the visible and the supernal worlds. This verbal translation is expected to leave a trace on the heart of the listener, just as the contemplation of beauty leaves the beholder with a formal intuition that resonates with the mental forms deriving from the supernal "meanings." In a similar vein, in the following lines, Saʿdi declares his intention to offer his eyes to the beholder as a privileged lens to peruse the real meaning of physical beauty beyond the surface of the object of desire. Saʿdi seems to enact Alexander's unveiling of the vaults painted by the Chinese and Greek artists, and he sets the orientation of his gaze as the preferred vantage point to understand the point of contact between the visible and the unseen without denying the centrality of the erotic experience:

> I wish the curtain were lifted from that surface of splendor,
> So that everyone may see the gallery of paintings!
>
> Everyone's eyes would be bewildered by your forms
> And no one would judge my own bewilderment anymore.
>
> However, not everyone has the eyes
> To see the image that I see on your face.
>
> I told the doctor about the condition of my crying eyes,
> And he urged me to kiss at least once those smiling lips.
>
> *Badāyiʿ* 409[76]

76 [2.130] Saʿdi YE, 190.

The correspondence between the sensory exposure to beauty and its mimetically lyrical enactment leaves us with one of the most interesting aspects of the spiritual eroticism of Saʿdi's imaginal lyricism. Saʿdi's representation of his own creative act as a form of spiritual investigation of beauty introduces the object of the next and final part of this book: we will soon discover how Saʿdi conceives of lyric poetry as an analogue of the visionary experience, as it incorporates within its own verbal expression the trajectory of the beholder's soul between the world of sense and the supernal realm.

PART 3

The Lyrical Ritual (Samāʿ) *as the Performative Space of Sacred Eroticism*

Introduction to Part 3

In the *lyrical ritual* of *samāʿ*
You seek a taste of *ẕawq*—a *sublime sensation*:
Listen, then, to the poetry crafted in Shiraz!

HUMĀM-I TABRĪZĪ[1]

•••

Language is a skin: I rub my language against the other. It is as if I had words instead of fingers, or fingers at the tip of my words. My language trembles with desire. The emotion derives from a double contact: on the one hand, a whole activity of discourse discreetly, indirectly focuses upon a single signified, which is "I desire you," and releases, nourishes, ramifies it to the point of explosion (language experiences orgasm upon touching itself); on the other hand, I enwrap the other in my words, I caress, brush against, talk up this contact, I extend myself to make the commentary to which I submit the relation endure.

ROLAND BARTHES, *A Lover's Discourse: Fragments*[2]

∴

1 Experiencing *Almost* the Same Thing

Lyric poetry, by means of the aura of artificial intimacy that exudes from its focus on the lyric self, provides the reader with multiple potential points of interaction with the external world, both as an historical presence surrounding the context of composition of a given poem and as a constantly evolving horizon of meaning that circulates among various communities of readers across time. The lyric modality, therefore, if we follow the intuitions of Hamburger and Culler,[3] offers a linguistic experience of the real world that is *almost* the equivalent of the experience of the world as imagined and embodied by the

1 [3.1] Homām-e Tabrizi 1351/1972, 106.
2 Barthes 2010a, 73.
3 See Chapter 2, pp. 107–109.

 | DOI:10.1163/9789004435902_013

historical author of the text. We have seen how Saʿdi's ghazals adhere to their own historicized external reality (as fictive constructs) in multiple fashions, ranging between encomiastic occasions, pseudo-biographical accounts, and the obscene and courtly poles of the lyrical expression of desire. Even when the texts involve the quest for supernal possibilities of meaning, the spiritual psycho-physiology of the lyric cannot be isolated from an active perusal of the physical world.

The invisible is nothing but an evocation of the supernal that *almost* equals the visible realm: through the active use of the imagination, the visible *is* in fact *almost* the invisible. Exploration of the phases of the visionary experience as an elaboration of al-Ghazālī's pragmatic approach to the practice of desiring beauty for spiritual ends shows how the contact of the lyric subject with external reality acts both as a hazardous impediment and a precious contemplative opportunity. Through this experience, the body of the subject acts as the "almost" that separates the visible from the invisible. The aim of these final chapters is to investigate the "almost" of the body through the aesthetics of the performative horizon of Saʿdi's poetry in the spaces of its own "making."

In spite of the common prejudice that invites one to read the spiritual dimensions of Saʿdi's ghazals as a vaguely mystical exercise of observation of the divine detached from any mundane experience of beauty, it is not possible to conceive of the metaphysics of Saʿdi's lyric subject without taking into account its psychological involvement with the phenomenal world. Just as both the introduction and the first two chapters of this book tested the historiographical validity of Saʿdi's attachment to his patrons and their courtly environments in Shiraz and Tabriz, these final chapters bring the poet's spiritual afflatus back to the mundane origins of poetry composition and circulation as practices that relate to the "making" of the ghazals and their historical readership in contexts influenced by the aesthetics of sacred performativity and in the form of ritualistic experiences.[4]

The historical development of the Persian ghazal as a genre cannot be separated from the musical context in which this lyric form originated.[5] Even when

4 "The notion of the *ritualistic* captures first of all the principle of iterability—lyrics are constructed for repetition—along with a certain ceremoniousness, and the possibility that the poem itself may be an event rather than the representation of an event (practitioners of rituals certainly conceive them as events and hope they will be efficacious). The concept of ritual encourages concentration on the formal properties of the lyric utterance, from rhythm and rhyme to other sorts of linguistic patterning, which make lyrics discourse to be repeated." Culler 2017, 37.

5 "Likewise, it is my contention, the genesis of the Persian ghazal as a genre must be understood in terms of its performance before an audience and its purpose within that context."

music is not directly involved in the historical framework of the circulation of specific texts, the forms, contents, and social practices connected to the composition and reception of ghazal poetry are such that the performative dimension is embedded in the very linguistic structure of these poems.[6] This inscribed potential for performance confers on the ghazal a level of hermeneutical flexibility which, at least from the first half of the 11th century, turned this genre into the preferred textual vehicle for the expression of sacred aesthetics in the context of social rituals of theo-erotic meditation.

In the medieval Persianate world, this form of lyrical ritual performed for spiritual ends (regardless of the mundane or more or less secluded Sufi venues in which it would take place) is consistently referred to as *samāʿ*. In an effort to render both its etymological and technical sense, scholars often translate this term as "spiritual audition," or "spiritual concert."[7] Given the limits posed by such qualifications as "concert" or "audition," I suggest referring to *samāʿ* as a "lyrical ritual," thus accounting for the poetic and spiritual "performativity" that this practice usually entailed, both as performance proper and as a "thing"—in Austin's terms—that its words "do."[8]

Lewis 1995, 71. See also Lewis 2018b, 90–94. On the performative and epideictic aspects of the ghazal as a genre emerging from multiple oral traditions, see ibid., 69–111. For a study of the connection between performance and intertextuality, see Ingenito 2018b.

6 "The ghazal, then, should be seen not as a mere text, but through a proscenium arch as a textual representation of a performance occurring in a specific context drawing on a nexus of genres and expectations, themselves in flux." Lewis, 1995, 111.

7 "*Samāʿ* is a difficult word to translate. It has usually been rendered as 'audition,' but this sounds like a musical try-out. 'Spiritual concert' has also been tried, but in the usage of Rumi it is much more than listening. *Samāʿ* ideally involves the use of poems and music to focus the listener's concentration on God and perhaps even induce a trance-like state of contemplative ecstasy (*vajd, hâl*)." Lewis 2000, 309. On *samāʿ* as a spiritual practice, see Schimmel 1975; During 1988, 178–86; Gribetz 1991; Lewisohn 1997; Shiloah 1997; Meier 1999; Lewis 2000, 309–13; Ernst and Lawrence 2002, 34–46; and Avery 2004.

8 I prefer to qualify *samāʿ* as a ritual mainly because most premodern manuals emphasize the ritualistic aspect of this practice by illustrating sets of specific of norms and guidelines that were consistently discussed between the 10th and the 15th centuries. The manuals highlight the lyric aspect of *samāʿ* by referring to the singer as *mughannī* (lit. "lyricist"), and the verses he performs as *ghināʾ* (lit. "lyric"). See Bākharzi 1345/1966, 188. See also the passage from the *Gulistān* (*Golestān*, 94–95) in which Saʿdi mentions the ritualized custom of offering one's turban to the performer, to whom he refers as a *mughannī*. Cf. Jonathan Culler's notes on the characteristics of the ritual that are relevant to the understanding of lyric as a codified action: "The ritualistic is characteristically experienced as (1) external to the actor; (2) involving conspicuous regularity not accounted for by communicative or other ends; (3) its meaning does not depend upon the intention of the actor; and (4) it prompts recognition and offers stimulation more than communication." Culler 2015, 366, n. 26.

In the scholarship, 13th-century authors such as Rumi and Fakhr al-Dīn ʿIrāqī (whom modern critics often define as "mystical" or "ecstatic" poets) are usually presented as representatives of the spiritual gusto that characterizes the practice of *samāʿ* in the context of the circulation of lyric poetry.[9] However, mainly as a consequence of the prejudices that, on the one hand, depict *samāʿ* as an exclusively Sufi practice and, on the other, relegate Saʿdi's lyricism to the category of strictly mundane eroticism, the role of the lyrical ritual (both as a practice and as an embedded textual archetype) in the performative dynamics of Saʿdi's ghazals is yet to receive the attention it deserves.[10] Not only did Saʿdi engage with the Sufi environments of Baghdad during his formative years, but he also promoted the consolidation of the relationship between Sufism and political power in Fars throughout his career as a professional poet. Moreover, a specific note I found in an important manuscript (Ms. Paris 1320s, see plate 1)[11] has shown that in 1280 he became the recipient of a conspicuous donation offered by Shams al-Dīn Juvaynī, which allowed him to build his own Sufi lodge in the outskirts of Shiraz. The document also attests that the renown of the lodge survived Saʿdi's demise, as the ilkhan Abū Saʿīd (d. 1335) had it restored in 1320 through the intervention of his powerful vizier, ʿAlāʾ al-Dīn Muḥammad. One may speculate that this pious foundation was the key locale for the dissemination of Saʿdi's ghazals in the ritualized context of *samāʿ* performances at the intersection of religious piety and political power.

In fact, references to the circulation of Saʿdi's ghazals as being performed during *samāʿ* are attested from the second half of the 13th century.[12] More

9 On the hagiographic and lyric evidence for the role of *sāmāʿ* in Rumi's life and works, see Lewisohn 2014b, especially 62–80. As far as Fakhr al-Dīn ʿIrāqī is concerned, the ritual of *samāʿ* is not featured prominently in his ghazals. One of the three instances in which the poet refers to the lyrical ritual appears in a ghazal that seems to be an intertextual response to one of Saʿdi's ghazals. See Fakhr al-Din ʿErāqi 1375/1996, 145–46 (for Saʿdi's hypotext, see Saʿdi YE, 215). Overall, it seems that the weight that has been historically ascribed to the role of *samāʿ* as a spiritual practice in ʿIrāqī's life and works is based mainly on the hagiographic account that introduces his collected works. See Fakhr al-Din ʿErāqi 1375/1996, 49. On this introduction, see Miller 2018.

10 As will be shown in the next chapter, the practice of *samāʿ* is featured extensively in Saʿdi's works (albeit not as pervasively as in Rumi's *dīvān*). It recurs as often as in the *dīvān*s of his contemporaries and imitators, Humām-i Tabrīzī and Sayf-i Farghānī, and much more prominently than in the *kulliyāt* of Fakhr al-Dīn ʿIrāqī. For a preliminary survey of the representation of *samāʿ* in Saʿdi's poetry, see Niyāzkār 1392/2013.

11 See General Introduction, pp. 22–23.

12 Both Sayf-i Farghānī and Humām-i Tabrīzī directly or indirectly present the ghazals of Saʿdi, their contemporary fellow-poet and source of aesthetic inspiration, as objects of spiritual meditation in a performative context. Humām, in particular, because of his attachment to the court of Shams al-Dīn Juvaynī, is key to understanding the spiritual

importantly, Bīsutūn's second draft of his introduction to Saʿdi's *Kulliyāt*, composed in 1334, offers a rare glimpse into the aesthetics and social dynamics accompanying the circulation of Saʿdi's lyricism in the context of *samāʿ* sessions taking place no later than three decades after the death of the poet. Bīsutūn's introduction describes a lyrical ritual that took place in 1326, presumably in Shiraz, and during which the recitation of Saʿdi's poetry generated waves of spiritual commotion among the audience. This account is an invaluable document attesting to the performative aspect of the spiritual psychology that surrounds the reception of Saʿdi's ghazals in a milieu that witnessed the convergence of political, courtly, and Sufi practices, ideals, and aesthetics in early 14th-century Shiraz. Bīsutūn's narration not only reflects the social context and the specific procedures constituting the practice of *samāʿ* (as it presumably had also taken place during Saʿdi's lifetime), but it also highlights the ritualistic dimension of this practice as described in the Sufi manuals of the time:

> One night, I [...], ʿAlī b. Aḥmad b. Abī Bakr Bīsutūn, happened to be present at a gathering attended by a group of notables of the state, religious leaders, eminent aristocrats, as well as sheikhs who were popular among the commoners. A [poetry] reciter was performing with his mellifluous voice. The resulting spiritual harmony was such that all the participants in that session—masters and amateurs alike—ended up lying senseless, each in his own corner, with their clothes torn apart [by the ecstatic commotion]. Once the session was over, they all unanimously reckoned that they had never experienced such a bewildering lyrical ritual [*samāʿ*] in their entire lives. It happened that during that musical session, the reciter was reading the following hemistich from the ghazals of the greatest sheikh of his epoch, the most noble seeker of the Truth, the most honorable among the spiritual lovers, the most eloquent litteratus, pride of the wayfarers, *sharaf al-millat va al-ḥaqq va al-dīn*, Muṣliḥ al-Islām va al-Muslimīn, sheikh Saʿdi Shirazi:
>
> "Not from lust stems the gaze of God's beholders" [*naẓar-i khudāy-bīnān zi sar-i havā nabāshad*]
>
> He read four more lines from this ghazal, then moved on to another ghazal. After the conclusion of the musical session, one of the attendees asked the reciter to provide him with the entire text of Saʿdi's ghazal, but

usage of Saʿdi's poetry after the 1260s, in the mature phase of the poet's political and literary commitment. On the relationship between Saʿdi and these two authors, see Ingenito 2014.

> he had no recollection of the remaining lines. Therefore, he addressed me in this fashion: "since the *dīvān* of sheikh Saʿdi is in your possession, it would be such a bountiful grace if you could find the remainder of this ghazal! The following day, in order to fulfill his request, I looked into Saʿdi's several collections of poems (*Ṭayyibāt*, *Badāyiʿ*, *Khavātīm*, and the *Ghazalhā-yi qadīm*), and I browsed all of them several times before I could eventually find that specific ghazal.[13]

This historical account situates Saʿdi's poetry at the center of the practice of *samāʿ* and as the performative epitome of the opposition between lust and the contemplation of human beauty. The specific line quoted by Bīsutūn, in fact, ("Not from lust stems the gaze of God's beholders") simultaneously describes and performs the ritual of *samāʿ* as a linguistic action intended to produce an ecstatic response in the audience. The participants were offered the chance of seeing themselves as the beholders of God while meditating on their own visual approach to the contemplation of beauty.

The line which reportedly inflamed the spiritual sensibility of the participants in the *samāʿ* session revolves around the theme of vision and sexual desire from a perspective that reiterates al-Ghazālī's emphasis on the contemplation of human beauty as a reflection of the supernal splendor: those who "see" the trace of divine presence in the world (in the form of a *shāhid*, or a comely "witness" who attests to the divine rather than incarnating it) will not succumb to lustful urges when setting their eyes upon a physical object of desire. The successful enjoyment of this image during a lyrical ritual depicts Saʿdi's poetry as a protected erotic environment capable of guiding the pious beholders through the perils deriving from the sensual contemplation of worldly forms for spiritual ends. It is through the *samāʿ* session that the seekers of God may imagine the signs of beauty through descriptions in verse rather than exposing themselves to the treacherous path of their potentially lustful eyes. We may read this approach as a performative gloss on al-Ghazālī's observations on the caveats that the literalists should take into account when questioning the permissibility of the Sufis' gaze upon comely youths.[14]

Bīsutūn's account opens a windows into the pragmatics of the phases of the visionary experience as described by al-Ghazālī in the *Kīmiyā*: it unearths the historical grounds of the conflation between what we have called the rational-inferential and the imaginal-cosmological aspects of the sacred eroticism at

13 Saʿdi KhE, 847–48; Ms. Yale 1432, ff. 1b–2a. Folio 1b of the manuscript is unfortunately lost, and the first part of Bīsutūn's narration has been copied by a modern hand.

14 See chapters 4 (pp. 246–49), and 8 (pp. 403–405).

work in Sa'di's lyricism. The performative enactment of the lyric through the lyrical ritual constitutes the point of contact between these two aspects, as it allows the participants in the *samāʿ* session to acquire the abstracted physicality of the lyric subject and to make it "their own," as a means of embodying the erotic quest for the supernal realm.

As a form of critical meditation on Bīsutūn's historical attestation, this part of the book will endeavor to discuss Sa'di's approach to the process of embodiment that takes place through *samāʿ* as a performative practice intimately connected with the inner structure of lyric in the context of sacred eroticism. Part three will open with a chapter ("Where is This Singer From? He Shouted the Name of the Beloved!") that investigates the diverging ethics of sensual desire that exude from Sa'di's collections of poems. I will argue that lines similar to the one quoted by Bīsutūn explicitly stress the ethical logic behind Sa'di's justification for the practice of beholding physical beauty. Moreover, I will show how these lines belong to an early stage of the development of the poet's approach to the relationship between sensual desire and spirituality, and how later collections (the *Badāyiʿ* and the *Khavātīm*) attest to Sa'di's deeper and less normative engagement (probably as a consequence of the Juvaynī family's patronage of the arts) with the connection between eroticism and the active perusal of beauty in a performance context. Through an analysis of al-Ghazālī's comments on the practice of listening to music and by comparing them with the evidence provided by Sufi manuals composed between the 13th and the 14th centuries, I will reassess the physio-psychological nature of *samāʿ* and the role that *ẕawq*, which I translate as "sublime sensation," plays in Sa'di's representation of the lyric ritual.

In the tenth and last chapter, the reconstruction of the chronology of the ethics of beholding beauty in an eroticized space of contemplation for spiritual ends will eventually offer a vantage point for the study of Sa'di's ghazals as both linguistic traces of performative experiences and the lyric embodiments of the experience of listening and beholding. I will approach Sa'di's references to *samāʿ* through three interconnected lenses: as transcriptions of historical or literary experiences of ritualized performances, as texts composed for the purpose of being circulated and performed among Sufi circles of the time as scripted rituals, and as literary performativity that substitutes the *samāʿ* performance itself, by offering the reader a linguistic analogue of the lyrical ritual.

CHAPTER 9

"Where is This Singer From? He Shouted the Name of the Beloved!"

Toward a Chronological and Psycho-Physiological Approach to Samāʿ *in Saʿdi's Ghazals*

> Where is this singer from? He shouted the name of the beloved!
> Tell me, and I'll offer my cloak to the message of the beloved!
>
> The heart comes back to life in hope of his loyalty,
> And the soul dances when they perform the words of the beloved.
>
> SAʿDI *Badāyiʿ* 403[1]

•••

> [...] a shudder ran through my whole body, and I stopped, intent upon the extraordinary changes that were taking place. An exquisite pleasure had invaded my senses, but individual, detached, with no suggestion of its origin. And at once the vicissitudes of life had become indifferent to me, its disasters innocuous, its brevity illusory—this new sensation having had on me the effect which love has of filling me with a precious essence; or rather this essence was not in me, it was myself. I had ceased now to feel mediocre, accidental, mortal. Whence could it have come to me, this all-powerful joy? I was conscious that it was connected with the taste of tea and cake, but that it infinitely transcended those savours, could not, indeed, be of the same nature as theirs. Whence did it come? What did it signify? How could I seize upon and define it?
>
> MARCEL PROUST, *Remembrance of Things Past*[2]

1 [3.2] Saʿdi YE, 187–88.

2 Proust 1957, 56.

 DOI:10.1163/9789004435902_014

1 The *Ṭayyibāt* as the Enactment of the Ethics of Eroticism

Both hagiographic literature and some modern critics explain the variations in medieval poets attitudes toward morals as a progressive development from youthful debauchery to conservative forms of pious virtue in old age.[3] In Saʿdi's case, chronological examination of the poet's three collections of ghazals suggests a different trend.[4] In the second chapter, we showed how the explicitly autobiographical materials that appear in the *Gulistān*, rather than reflecting historical events, often function as rhetorical strategies through which Saʿdi attempted to build a courtly relationship (based on a conflation of political, aesthetic, and spiritual forms of influence) with the Salghurid family. If we combine the narratives of the *Gulistān* with the evidence provided by the development of Saʿdi's voice as a panegyrist, it can be argued that, in the years following his religious training at the Nizamiyya school in Baghdad and upon his return to Shiraz (presumably in the mid-1240s), Saʿdi gradually developed a distinct approach to the role of the senses and sensuality in his spiritual quest.

In the introduction to the *Gulistān*, Saʿdi describes his resolution to compose the book by portraying himself in the context of a devotional form of contemplative seclusion that is interrupted by the visit of a companion with whom he had spent his youthful days in spiritual confinement. After a brief exchange, Saʿdi's anonymous friend convinces him to abandon his self-imposed spiritual isolation and join him and other companions at a *locus amoenus* on the outskirts of the city, surrounded by orchards and rose gardens. The following morning, before they head back to the city, while admiring the handful of roses that his friend has collected, Saʿdi meditates on the transient nature of the beauty of springtime and decides to compose the *Gulistān*.

If we compare this pseudo-biographical narration with the visionary account of the *ṣāḥib-dil* with which the *Gulistān* opens,[5] we may read the two stories as a symbolic transition from the rose garden of the spirit to the rose garden of the world. As a metaphorical analogue of Saʿdi's life, the transition

3 See, for a critique of the alleged "mystical conversion" of Sanāʾī, Lewis 1995, 1: 124–25.

4 For a radically different opinion, see Haydari 1392/2013. According to Haydari (ibid., 83), the differences in style and content between Saʿdi's early ghazals and his later output attest to the poet's "natural progression" from the experience of earthly passion to spiritual love. Haydari's analysis is based on the widespread bias according to which spirituality and physical desire belong to opposite poles. Moreover, the author does not recognize the problem raised by the fact that the separation of the "old ghazals" (*ghazaliyāt-i qadīm*) as a comprehensive *dīvān* appears only with the Bīsutūn recension; moreover, many of the texts on which he bases his argument follow the outdated classification of Foroughi's edition.

5 See Chapter 7, pp. 360–61.

could signify the poet's abandonment of scholastic practices of seclusion and his access to a new phase of artistic development marked by the role of sensory engagement as a means to pursue spirituality through the sensory perusal of the world.[6]

The constant quest for a spiritual framework capable of orienting the poet's representations of beauty and moral values constitutes the backbone of Saʿdi's entire body of work. Nevertheless, the form and means of this quest are what really signals a transition in Saʿdi's approach to the psychology and aesthetics of spirituality that roughly corresponds with the composition of the *Gulistān* and which, I speculate, is reflected in the difference between his early collections of ghazals and the mature phase of his lyric output. Determination of the exact chronology and specific audiences of Saʿdi's ghazals during his lifetime is an endeavor that can only be accomplished through a careful study of the oldest manuscripts and analysis of the intertextual interactions between the poet and his contemporaries. Even though attempts to establish a tentative chronology for the lyric output of premodern Persian poets have already yielded fruit, the new critical postures of what we could refer to as the "Chicago and Oxford school" of Persianate studies (mainly through the works of Franklin Lewis, Paul Losensky, Julie Scott Meisami, and Sunil Sharma), which have developed since the 1990s, provide fertile ground for the study of ghazal poetry at the intersection of intertextuality, historicized networks of reception, and geocriticism.[7]

Although future research will have to consider the genetics of stylistic and intertextual variations, my preliminary investigation of the chronological arrangement of Saʿdi's ghazals in his three *dīvān*s primarily takes into account the development of the poet's depiction of sensuality as a function of the spiritual quest for the divine. In Saʿdi's first *dīvān*, the *Ṭayyibāt*, the poet often filters his celebration of the physical beauty of the beloved through an emphasis on the necessity for the beholder to avoid the temptations of the flesh by reading the traits of pulchritude as fetishes pointing toward the supernal world. It is in this early collection of poems that the line quoted by Bīsutūn on the nonlustful gaze of the seekers of God is found. Moreover, in most pre-Bīsutūn manuscripts, the *Ṭayyibāt* close with a ghazal in which the lyric subject declares

6 See Introduction (pp. 16–17).

7 For a chronological approach to the study of Hafez's ghazals, see Lescot 1944. For an important preliminary proposal for the chronological assessment of Rumi's *Dīvān-i Shams*, see Lewis 2014a. On the theoretical turn that the contributions of these scholars brought about, see Ingenito 2018b, 853.

that it is not the form of the beloved that bewilders him, but He who painted him.[8]

Some of these images have made their appearance in the chapters in which we have analyzed Saʿdi's differentiation between a sexualized body of desire and human beauty as an object of spiritual contemplation for the cognitive practice of *ʿibrat*, or spiritual inference:

Do not believe that it's his form that bewilders my mind
My intellect is taken away by the Fashioner of his shape [*ṣūrat-nigār-i ū*].

The others behold the beautiful countenance with their gaze
But what we gaze upon is the power of his Creator.
Ṭayyibāt 404[9]

Even though lines similar to the ones above may occasionally appear in Saʿdi's later collections, their presence peaks in the pseudo-collection of the "old ghazals,"[10] and in the *Ṭayyibāt*, whose composition predates that of the final recension of the *Gulistān* (1258).[11] One may be tempted to read such lines—especially given the moralistic aura that surrounds the modern reception of Saʿdi's works—as ethical intimations that the author inserted in his ghazals as a form of pedagogical reinforcement of the Islamic values concerning

8 Saʿdi YE, 140.

9 [3.3] Saʿdi YE, 188. While Yusofi lists this ghazal in the *Badāyiʿ*, some of the oldest pre-Bīsutūn manuscripts record it in the *Ṭayyibāt*. See Ms. Dushanbe 1310s (182).

10 Considering the intrinsic philological uncertainties with which the "old ghazals" were transmitted in the manuscript tradition, I decided to exclude them (as a collection, not as single ghazals that other manuscripts feature in the pre-Bīsutūn collections) from the scope of the observations shared in this chapter.

11 In some cases, Yusofi includes the ghazals to which such lines belong in the *Badāyiʿ* or the *Khavātīm*. However, the early manuscripts recording pre-Bīsutūn recensions consistently list these lines in the *Ṭayyibāt*. See for instance the following lines:
[3.4] Saʿdi YE, 266. See also:
[3.5] Ibid., 190.
Among the ghazals from the *Ṭayyibāt*, see also the lines below, analyzed in the fourth chapter when discussing *ʿibrat*:
Not just anyone deserves the title of "Master of Gazes":
The practice of love differs so much from worship of the flesh. [3.6] (Ibid., 121);
All these thousands of beautiful countenances He created
For those eyes capable of inferring [*iʿtibār*] through their gaze. [3.7] (Ibid., 4);
Everyone's eyes peruse your face with so much passion, but
The self-worshippers discern no difference between Truth and lust. [3.8] (Ibid., 35)

sexuality.[12] A further explanation may be adduced in the form of the likelihood of the author defending himself from the slander of any detractor who might potentially deem his ghazals excessively sensual.[13]

We may consider both rationales as descriptive of the fluid system of values determining the broad spectrum of ethical attitudes toward the practice of erotic poetry, especially at the intersection of spiritual and courtly ideals—as it was the case for the Salghurid court, where Saʿdi was bound to two young patrons, prince Saʿd II and his son, Muḥammad, whom he would describe as *darvīsh-dūst*.[14] In the lines below, for instance, Saʿdi tackles the sensual potential stemming from the act of staring at the beloved, along with the implied consequence that erotic images might emerge that are capable of invalidating the prayer of the lyric subject:

How interminable is the night for the desperate lovers,
Please come forth at dusk, so that the gates of dawn may open.

Will my peregrinations ever let me leave your hands?
How could the dove flee when the falcon captures it?

I love you too much, I won't gaze upon your face:
The sincere lover ought to be inspired by purity.

Bestow the grace of your eyes upon us: a furtive look!
Out of real necessity stems the plea of those who agonize.

Words come to the surface, I have no chance to conceal them:
Will I ever find a confidant to whom I may entrust the mystery?

---

12 See, for instance, Meisami's reduction of Saʿdi's lyric persona to a "pious" dominant, merely on the basis of the celebration of God with which Saʿdi opens the *Ṭayyibāt*, and in contrast to the "profane" nature of the first line of Hafez's first ghazal. Meisami 2010, 164, n. 6. However, it is noteworthy that even in Saʿdi's opening praise of God, the lyric discourse emphasizes the visual dominant of the appreciation of the world as a formal emanation deriving from God's splendid act of creation from which the "beautiful faces" (*ṣūrat-i khūb*) derive. Saʿdi YE, 3.

13 One rare instance of a lyric poet denouncing the narrow-mindedness of their detractors can be found in the autobiographic introduction that the Injuid princess Jahān Malik Khātūn composed to explain the reasons behind her choice of sharing her poetry with the literati of her age. See Ingenito 2018a.

14 See chapters 1 (pp. 88–92), and 2 (pp. 115–18).

How could the one whose imagination you inhabit pray?
O idol, you offer me no chance to perform my ritual prayer! ...
Ṭayyibāt 289[15]

In this ghazal, the close analysis of the narrative progression that the loose semantic connections between the lines generate points to the same aesthetic frustration that characterizes the second phase of visionary experience analyzed in the previous chapter. The lyric subject lingers between oneiric experiences, imaginings, and the direct vision of the beloved's body without finding words capable of expressing the mystery of the contact with the supernal. The calamity of fostering sexual thoughts thrives amidst such a state of confusion, and it compromises both the purity of the courtly ideal of love ("I love you too much, I won't gaze upon your face: [...]"), and the validity of the ritual prayer ("how could the one whose imagination you inhabit pray?"). Where does Sa'di, as fictitious author, stand vis-à-vis the poignant incertitude of the lyric subject? Once more, it seems that his reservations concerning the visual perusal of the beloved oscillate between the necessity to abide by a certain moral rigor and a veiled self-defense capable of justifying the sensual undertones of the spiritual psychology of desire.

One may compare the validity of both angles with the performative context in which such moralizing or defensive utterances appear. In poems that describe this context, Sa'di's admonitions against the perils of sensual attraction are always paired with the act of beholding human beauty as a collective experience in which some individuals may be capable of offering guidance and an edifying example of righteous moral conduct to other "participants." The collective experience to which Sa'di often alludes includes the presence of "companions," i.e., associates whom he invites to partake in the psychological journey of the metaphysics of mundane eroticism as a bridge toward the "concealed mystery." In such cases too, the sacred aesthetics of the communal gathering involve moralizing pleas with respect to the temptation that the "external forms" may pose:

1 Do not vaunt the beauties of Greece or China before me
As I entrust my heart to someone from this very land.

15 [3.9] Sa'di YE, 133. See the quoted *miṣrāʿ* highlighted in bold. I have preferred the variant found in the majority of the manuscripts, as Yusofi's choice seemed arbitrary. See ibid., 473.

2 Every moment that he surfaces to my memory
No recollection do I have of whatever is existent or inexistent.

3 Enduring pain was allotted to us in this world
No subsistence should one enjoy but the morsel of destiny.

4 Sweet is the date, but out of reach is the palm tree.
Pure water flows around us, and yet we're thirsty.

5 What an irresistible body attesting to the Supernal [*shāhid*] appears in our imagination:
I know no ascetic in the city who unsullied shall perdure.

6 No object of glances resembles his countenance
No delight of the senses compares with his body's scent.

7 Neither with him nor without do I seek a joyful life:
How could we be pearls set on the same string?

8 O companions, close your eyes to external appearances:
Concealed is the mystery that we share with him.

9 Should everyone in the world see these forms of his
No one would understand the real, supernal meaning [*maʿnī*] behind his face.

10 The inexperienced will never feel my scorching fire:
Burning fevers do not touch the vigorous man.

11 You may offer your heart to me, or take my life away:
Inexorable duty is my obedient submission.

12 In these affairs, Saʿdi, I see no salvation for your soul:
Thirsty is the wayfarer, and the nectar so imbued with poison.

13 Not even iron can endure when cast into fire:
Why should wax resist without melting?

Ṭayyibāt 214[16]

16 [3.10] Saʿdi YE, 100–101. See in the Appendix the variants (highlighted in bold) that I have preferred, on the basis of Mss Kabul 1325 (364–65) and Yale 1432 (ff. 268b–269a).

This ghazal is an eloquent example of Saʿdi's lyrical involvement with the relationship between physical experience and spiritual imagination in the early stage of his poetic maturity—presumably corresponding with the fifth decade of the 13th century, upon his alleged "return" to Shiraz. As briefly mentioned earlier, my speculation on the existence of an "early stage" as opposed to an "advanced stage" of the poet's lyric output rests merely on the chronological classification that appears in the earliest manuscripts recording the pre-Bīsutūn recensions of his collections of poems, and exclusively with respect to his different approaches to the ethics of physical desire in its spiritual context.

The overarching motifs of the poem relate to the exploration of the relationship between physical desire and the psychology of spiritual cognition, which—as analyzed in the last part of the previous chapter— al-Ghazālī tackles in the *Kīmiyā*. From the very first line, the ghazal appears as a space in which the poet represents a tangible interaction with the beloved, who is represented as an embodied presence that belongs to the *hic et nunc* of an imaginary geography of desire (from "this land," *īn būm*, as opposed to the beauties of China and Greece). In spite of such an emphatic attestation to the tangible nature of the object of desire, the second *bayt* points to the difference between the existing and the inexistent levels of reality, a juxtaposition that stems from the lover's cogitation upon the nature of the beloved.

The ontological complexity of the amatory intellection of the beloved further develops in the direction of a tangible space through the prominent traits of his perceptible nature. Saʿdi, in the fourth line, compares the beloved to the taste and freshness of juicy dates and pure water: he is the excellent object of vision (*manẓūr*) as well as a unique object of olfaction (*mashmūm*). The prominence of the psychological dimension of the process of intellection that characterizes the experience of beholding starts with the recollection of the beloved's presence (second line), followed by the imaginal representation of his physical appearance (fifth line), and culminates with the process of cognizing a supernal meaning (or concept, idea, *maʿnī*) that corresponds to his sensible form (ninth line). Given the explicit juxtaposition of vividly sensual representations of desire with a clear reference to the physio-psychological dimension of spiritual vision, Saʿdi's expression of an ethical divide between sensuality and metaphysical intellection constitutes no surprise. Nevertheless, the impossibility for the commoners to decipher the spiritual matrix of the physical form that appears before one's eyes ("no one shall understand …") indicates that ascetics, too, are potentially prone to experiencing sexual desire. The "companions," therefore, are urged not to consider the physical dynamics of the amorous affection between the lyric subject and the beloved. Overall, the *Ṭayyibāt*, while showcasing the full extent of the interaction between sensuality and spiritual urges, determines very precisely what boundaries the beholders ought not to cross. The demarcation of this perilous zone of theo-erotic experience overlaps with the construction of "Saʿdi" as a fictitious author who takes on the role of the pedagogic guide of his audience through the inspired path of the eyes and the spiritual hermeneutics of desire.

If we are to individuate the biographical background capable of explaining the origins of Saʿdi's conservative posture in the erotics of the *Ṭayyibāt*, we should probably consider both the influence of Suhravardī's sober spiritual pragmatism on Saʿdi's formative years in Baghdad, and the religious zeal dominating Shiraz during the first decade of the atabeg Abū Bakr's rule in Fars. On the other hand, the contents of Saʿdi's second and third collections, the *Badāyiʿ* and the *Khavātīm*, reflect a biographical phase in which Saʿdi seemed to approach the aesthetics of the spiritual eroticism of authors such as Rūzbihān-i Baqlī and Awḥad al-Dīn Kirmānī. Furthermore, given the interest of the Juvaynī brothers in patronizing the arts (and the socio-political necessity of doing so), we could ascribe the post-1250s positive shift in Saʿdi's stances regarding the ethics of musical performance to the openness with which the Ilkhanid rulers and ministers promoted musical and visual arts.[17]

In the pre-Bīsutūn manuscripts, even the arrangement of the ghazals attests to the sensory eroticism characterizing the new course of Saʿdi's poetic experience. While, as mentioned earlier, the *Ṭayyibāt* closes with lines that highlight the ethical pretext of *ʿibrat* as a rational tool to contain desire within the chaste boundaries of its theo-erotic context, the ghazal that opens the *Badāyiʿ*, and which makes a direct reference to the title of this specific collection, reads as a manifesto of the carnal dimension of Saʿdi's visionary experience:

> So beautiful is your countenance that I fear for the people
> And their piety: will you bring to the world a brand new heresy?
> *Badāyiʿ* 312[18]

2 The *Badāyiʿ* and the *Khavātīm*: toward a Deeper Erotic Awareness

While Saʿdi's scholastic posture early in his life might have steered him away from mundane manifestations of theo-erotic desire, historical and hagiographic reports highlight the unapologetic penchant for human beauty that the poet would manifest during the mature phase of his literary and spiritual

17 See Biran 2016.
18 [3.11] Saʿdi YE, 146.

journey. For instance, sometime in in the 1270s, Ṣafī al-Dīn Ardabīlī (d. 1334), the founder of the Safavid order, visited Shiraz to meet the Suhravardīyya-affiliated Sufi master Najīb al-Dīn Buzghush (d. 1279). Ṣafī al-Dīn, who was in his early twenties at that time, happened to meet with Saʿdi and was reportedly offended by poet's appreciation of beardless youths.[19] As a consequence, the young Sufi rejected the autograph manuscript of one of Saʿdi's *dīvāns* which the poet had offered him.[20] If the account is authentic,[21] the *dīvān* that Saʿdi offered to Ṣafī al-Dīn was presumably his second collection of ghazals, the *Badāyiʿ* which, along with the *Khavātīm*, displays a less guarded approach to the erotic desires of the lyric subject.

In these collections, the lyric "I" appears as a beholding presence that openly peruses human beauty in spite of the anti-sensual prescriptions of ethical imperatives. Unlike the poems from the *Ṭayyibāt* analyzed above, but very much in line with most of the ghazals scrutinized in the previous chapter as examples of Saʿdi's non-scholastic psychology of sacred eroticism, the *Badāyiʿ* and the *Khavātīm* attest to the poet's conversation with a plurality of audiences capable of meaningfully reading the complexity of Saʿdi's discourse on sensuality and the poetics of beholding beauty.[22]

Franklin Lewis has convincingly demonstrated that the range of lyric modalities in Sanāʾī's *dīvān* attests to a broad variety of ideologies and values shared by different groups of readers.[23] In Saʿdi's case too, any attempt at discerning a chronology of his poetic output should take into account the variety of audiences the poet addressed throughout his career. In particular, the increased mundanity of the sacred eroticism that characterizes Saʿdi's later collections of ghazals may also be explained as a consequence of the progressive fragmentation of the Salghurid dynastic order (from the early 1260s onwards), which

19 Ebn Bazzāz Ardabili 1373/1994, 104.

20 Ibid., 107.

21 The story is also reported by Amīnī Haravī in his *Futūḥāt-i shāhī*. See Amini Haravi 1383/2004, 15.

22 The crowds of commoners cast their blame upon the Sufi:
"You should reject these fantasies, and disavow your natural instinct!"
[3.12] Saʿdi YE, 258;
So much the visual remembrance of you has grabbed my waist …
If only I could touch your waist with my hands …
[3.13] Saʿdi YE, 211;
You appear in the morning and no one prostrates before your face:
People fear God, whilst I am too bewildered to bow.
[3.14] Saʿdi YE, 465.

23 Lewis 1995, 1: 151.

pushed Saʿdi toward the active quest for new patrons.[24] Furthermore, the coexistence of purely mundane and spiritually informed ghazals in all of his collections suggests that different audiences might have experienced the same texts according to different interpretive postures.[25]

It is in these texts, which showcase a constant blend of sensuality and spirituality, that one may discern a chronological development. For instance, the sensual boldness that characterizes ghazals similar to the one below attests not only to Saʿdi's indulgent attitude toward the sinful aspects of eroticism, but also to the preparedness of his audiences for following the poet's wandering gaze:

> If anyone ever heard of a cypress walking, here it is!
> What a slender pine tree he is: his neck and chest as bright as silver!
>
> Real height is not what you display with your figure
> As the narrow-minded beholder sees nothing beyond the form.
>
> Midnight has passed, and everyone enjoys their rest,
> But no chance for me and the Pleiades to enjoy restful sleep.
>
> I do reckon that it is blasphemy to set one's eyes on a beautiful face.
> Will I eventually repent? I won't: this is my religion!
>
> This is a day for the crowds to go out and admire the valleys,
> Especially now that springtime has come, with the beginning of *Farvardīn*!
>
> Today the meadow resembles paradise: your presence is so much needed!
> Come and let people believe that the heavenly beauties are here on earth! …
>
> The violence that Saʿdi suffered from your hands, as white as silver,
> No dove would ever suffer from the claws of the falcon.

---

24 See Chapter 1 (pp. 96–97) for the occurrences in which Saʿdi's expresses his frustration with the lack of appreciation for his poetry during the years following the death of Abū Bakr and his son, Saʿd II.

25 For a comparison with the divergent hermeneutical approaches that different communities of readers would adopt when reading or performing Hafez's ghazals during the 15th century, cf. Fotuhi and Vafāʾi 1388/2009.

No more poetry will I compose from now on, you know why?
Flies are such a nuisance, when poetry is so sweet!
Badāyiʿ 354[26]

The beholder's gaze lingers on the anatomic details of the object of desire in such a fashion that his visual appreciation leads him to formulate a profound meditation on the nature of the invisible dimension from which external beauty stems. In spite of the apparent dismissal of external forms, Saʿdi guides the gaze of the beholder toward the relationship between the realm of dreams and the visionary experience that stems from the contemplation of supernal forms of beauty in the shape of imagined bodies. Although the reference to the nocturnal solitude of the lyric subject contemplating the Pleiades (*parvīn*) is not an unusual image in the lyric tradition, the mention of the visionary experience in an erotic context might be read as an indirect allusion to the role of the fixed stars in the psychological background of Avicennian cosmological epistemology.[27] Such nocturnal meditations on the nature of beauty, loneliness, and oneiric contemplation of the ideal of desire lead the lyric subject to the formulation of one of Saʿdi's boldest statements on the act of gazing, herein portrayed as a religious practice. Whilst the poet acknowledges the negative value of the sensuous perusal of beauty within the framework of Islamic law, he eventually hastens to declare such activity a practice that embodies a system of beliefs and rituals akin to a religious path.[28]

The practice of beholding beauty as the mundane aspect of a spiritual and aesthetic path constitutes the main axis of Saʿdi's entire lyric activity, but it is

26 [3.15] Saʿdi YE, 165.

27 See, for instance, Sanāʾī 1362/1983, 1000:
[3.16] The moon and the Pleiades are my companions every night, until dawn:
As I imagine your smile and your countenance, shining like the Pleiades and the moon.

28 In principle, one ought to refrain from considering such blunt invitations to transgress religious norms as part of a broad antinomian discourse centered on the theme of "blame" (*malāmat*), which saturates part of the Sufi poetic tradition. As specified in the introduction to the second part of this book, if we were to locate Saʿdi's approach to Sufism within one of the two poles of the spiritual rhetoric of "intoxication" and "sobriety," the latter would constitute a much more accommodating ideal venue to account for the poet's "golden mean," one which we have frequently associated with al-Ghazālī's spiritual postures. Moreover, the lack of bacchanalia-related imagery (which often accompanies the *malāmatī* tradition in Persian poetry) and the overall light lyrical context of the poem situate the antinomian line of gazing at beauty as a form of religion within the framework of the ironic discourse that emerges even more clearly toward the end of the composition. Overall, the focus on *malāmatiya* (or, more appropriately, *malāmiyya*) as an antinomian rhetorical tool is much more pertinent when analyzing Hafez's poetry. On this topic, see *EIr*, s.v. "Hafez viii. Hafez and Rendi," [F. Lewis].

in his final collection of ghazals, the *Khavātīm* (*The Endings*), that the poet vehemently professes this dimension as an axiom that ought to constitute the very nature of humankind:

> Gazing upon ever-increasing beauty, early in the morning,
> Brings luster to one's lofty fortune: an auspicious horoscope!
>
> Especially those whose temperament is naturally balanced
> How could they not love a well-proportioned frame?
>
> *Khavātīm* 706[29]

During the last decades of his life, Saʿdi further developed his aesthetic endeavor as an anthropological imperative behind the practice of beholding beauty.[30] Even the carnal soul's desire to participate hierarchically in the contemplation of human beauty (in the guise of the reorientation of the lower bodily faculties toward the higher aspirations of the intellect, as framed by Avicenna), which Saʿdi would blame and condemn in the *Ṭayyibāt*, acquires a new source of legitimacy in this last stage of his poetic endeavors.

In the following ghazal, we may visualize the poetic persona as the subject undergoing the final phase of the visionary experience (as described by al-Ghazālī), in which the initial anxiety deriving from the nostalgia of the metaphysical vision finds its point of equilibrium with respect to the mundane solicitations of the flesh. The preliminary astonishment of the quest embraces the powerful pull that derives from the connection with the supernal realm:

1 Behold his face: how could I describe its beauty?
Ask someone else to do so, as bewilderment impairs me.

2 **Everyone sees, but not the same creation that I see!**
Everyone peruses, but not the same painting that I peruse!

3 No wonder if they wander in astonishment when seeking the beloved.
Wondrous is my condition: connected and yet I wander.

---

29 [3.17] Saʿdi YE, 316.

30 Cf. the lines from the *Khavātīm* quoted in the previous chapters:
[1.2] Saʿdi YE, 319. P. 1.
[2.3] Saʿdi YE, 305–306. P. 209.

4 The cypress stands amidst the garden, and you before one's face and eyes:
If you bestow your permission—O walking cypress—I shall be your ground.

5 You may hold me hostage with your arrows and urge me to leave:
Your love holds me hostage. I'd never leave our covenant.

6 Look at my soul, leaving my body in the quest for the beloved.
What better destiny could I ever foresee for my life?

7 O dear companion, I shall listen to all your advice:
But do not ask me to endure far from him, as I can't!

8 **Are you perhaps marveling at my yearning nature, filled with desire?**
What I marvel at is the unnatural condition of those who cannot yearn.

9 My love for the rose of your cheeks is not from today:
For years I have been the nightingale of this garden of fragrances.

10 You asked who Sa'di really *is* in this world.
I am nothing by myself, I shall be anything you pronounce!

11 Bestow upon me the honor of your presence, I shall be an angel;
Or Satan the accursed, if you push me away with your anger.
Khavātīm 709[31]

The disarming restlessness of the lyric subject speaks to the quintessential humanity of the pseudo-biographical self that Sa'di stages in his liveliest accounts of the *Gulistān*. The movement of the theo-erotic quest animating these lines conjures up the very core of Sa'di's representation of human nature as a nostalgic matter poised between the satanic baseness of the flesh and the angelic aspirations of the soul. The balance ensuing from these two poles generates the complex identity of the lyric persona, whose transient nature is staged in an ontological correlation with the proximity to or distance from the object of desire. In spite of the fundamentally negative role of the flesh,

31 [3.18] Sa'di YE, 317–18.

Sa'di ostensibly represents the passions of the carnal soul as a natural component of the process leading to the "re-cognition" of the supernal subtext of the embodied beauty. The poet declares desire—across the gamut of its multiple manifestations—to be a natural condition whose most corrupting effect may be tamed through attaining a balance between mundane bewilderment and "connection" (*vaṣl*) with the supernal realm.

The fusion between a higher appreciation of the role of the senses and the fulfillment of the aspirations of the heart/rational soul characterizes many of the ghazals of the *Khavātīm*. Nevertheless, as pointed out earlier both in the case of the circulation of Sanā'ī's poetry among a variety of audiences and Sa'di's own activity in both Sufi and political circles, the poet could have crafted his imagery around ethical discourses that would best fit the historical occasion of specific compositions, and regardless of the personal evolution of his spiritual trajectory. The following poem, for instance, is a *qasida* that most manuscripts list as a lengthy ghazal from the *Ṭayyibāt*. As a relatively early text, it might have addressed one of the young princes of the Salghurid family, possibly Abū Bakr's son, Sa'd II. Both the princely dimension and the mention of Shiraz as a historical locus contribute to the creation of a more vivid effect of "real presence." This effect highlights the positive value of the sensual aspects of the mundane experience, despite the virtual discrepancy between the maturity of the sacred desire that it portrays and the chronology of its composition:

> No sublime sensation [*ẕawq*] is possible in life without the beloved.
> This hidden fire makes me lightheaded and confused.
>
> Shiraz opens its gates to all caravans, free to leave the city;
> But the doors won't let us go: affection keeps us where we are.
>
> I shall not illustrate the pains I suffer because of you: peruse my face,
> If too long is the book, start from its introductory passage!
>
> The camel enjoys no free will during its journey:
> So powerless it appears when dragging its load.
>
> You are so seductive that you killed a thousand Vāmiqs with your charm
> And you defeated a thousand 'Aẕrās when stealing hearts.
>
> Senselessly astonished remain the Chinese painters
> contemplating your image, whose form is pure meaning [*ma'ānī*]
> beyond all form.

Hordes of lovers flock to the threshold of your palace
Like the wayfarers of the caravans when the water is sweet.

No distress attains you, while you deem our love a playful affair:
Wait for your haystack to catch fire to understand our commotion.

I once used to call you "soul," how foolish my words!
If any essence exists more precious than the soul, it is you!

You are a cypress in the lyrical ritual, a full moon when spoken of,
A morning in the embrace, a candle amidst the gathering.

You were not such before, then the supernal took shape:
You once were my carnal soul's greed, now you fortify my spirit.

Yours is the city, yours is the kingdom, rule according to your wish:
You may bestow upon the unworthy, or exile the virtuous.

The forehead of Sa'di's hope grazes the soil of your threshold:
He shall not behold anyone after you, O *apogee of all desires*.[32]

By comparing this ghazal with other poems in which Sa'di employs similar expressions and rhetorical patterns, it can be argued that the text was composed to praise a patron, possibly Sa'd II in his transition from adolescence to adulthood.[33] If this is the case, Sa'di celebrates the coming of age of the young patron in a fashion that reproduces the rhetorical posture of the eroticism of patronage and courtly upbringing that we have discussed in the first two chapters. Overall, the regal aura of the text offers the poet an opportunity

32 [3.19] Sa'di YE, 52; Ms. Kabul 1325, 311; Ms. Yale 1432, ff. 284b–285a. See variants from the Yale ms. highlighted in bold in the original text.

33 Sa'di often resorts to the expression *ghāyat al-amānī* ("the apogee of desires"), which appears in the closing line of the text, in poems of praise. For instance, Sa'di YE, 320 (*"vaqthā yak dam bar āsūdī tanam," Khavātīm*, 713), which some of the oldest manuscripts classify as a *qasida* (ibid., 657), associates the expression *ghāyat al-amānī* with the mention of *Ḥātim*, the epitome of generosity in the context of Arabic and Persian poetry, whom the poets would often employ as an analogue of their patron (see *EIr*, "Ḥātem Ṭā'ī," [M. Omidsalar]). *Ḥātim* as an epithet for the *mamdūḥ* appears in *qasidas* that Sa'di dedicated to a plurality of patrons, such as 'Aṭā' Malik Juvaynī (Sa'di KhE, 660; Ms. Yale 1432, ff. 174b–175a, "*kudām bāgh ba didār-i dūstān mānad*"), and Terken Khātūn (Sa'di KhE, 686–87; Ms. Yale 1432, ff. 187b–188a, "*ay bīsh az ānkī dar qalam āyad ṣanā-yi tu*").

to combine the ethics of courtly commitment with the spiritual aesthetics of theo-erotic psychology. Sexual desire, rather than meeting the early lyric subject's ethical denial, is sublimated through a hierarchical reorientation that places the carnal soul at the service of the heart's intellectual endeavors with respect to the exploration of the supernal realm. Hence, the poem perfectly attests to how Saʿdi's later ethos can apply to early texts of praise in which eroticism does not constitute an immediate factor of moral concern:

> You were not such before, then the supernal took shape [*ḥaqīqatī shud*]:
> You once were my carnal soul's greed, now you fortify my spirit [*quvvat-i jānī*].

While we can hardly deny the mundane dimension in which the lyric subject weaves the praise of the object of desire, the psychological aspect of the visionary component of the text is officially introduced by the reference to the "supernal meanings" (*maʿānī*) that constitute its visual essence. Such references bridge the gap between the scholastic tones characterizing the didactic dimension of the early production of Saʿdi's *Ṭayyibāt* and the poet's renewed experience of mundanity as a fruitful axis around which his lyrical exploration of the world acquires new, deeper meaning in the context of courtly ideals:

> You are a cypress in the lyrical ritual [*samāʿ*], a full moon when spoken of,
> A morning in the embrace, a candle amidst the gathering.

Saʿdi does not deny the tangible presence of an object of desire (who, as noted above, likely corresponded with the theo-eroticized figure of a young patron), and he also offers a spectrum of phenomenological possibilities surrounding the celebration of the beloved as a sensual manifestation of the invisible. In this case too, just as in some of the non-encomiastic ghazals of the *Ṭayyibāt*, Saʿdi alludes to a ritualistic setting in which the contemplation of the beloved takes place.[34] While in the *Ṭayyibāt* the poet seems to focus on the ethics of

---

34 Although the candle is a recurrent *topos* in Persian lyric poetry (see Seyed-Gohrab 2012), Saʿdi's metaphorical allusion to the beloved as a lamp illuminating the gathering should be read against the early 13th-century Sufi practice of lighting candles during the *samāʿ*. In the case of *samāʿ* sessions held by Awḥad al-Dīn Kirmānī, the candles would often be held by beautiful youths. See Foruzānfar 1347/1969, 40, 149. Cf. Bākharzī's mention of candles in a *samāʿ* session witnessed by an anonymous sheikh. Bākharzi 1345/1966, 193. See also this line by Saʿdi:
Anyone who, like a candle, spends the night admiring a *shāhid*
Won't be afraid of being killed and hung when the morning takes over. [3.20] Saʿdi YE, 280.

his companions' interpretation of the object of desire's nature and ultimate meaning for the spiritual path, the *Badāyiʿ* and the *Khavātīm* directly involve the problem of the psychology of any performative context capable of providing a framework of spiritual aesthetics in which the contact with the invisible world may coexist with the contemplation of the earthly aspect of existence.

We may say that while the spiritual aesthetics of the *Ṭayyibāt* (and, to some extent, the "old ghazals," if the existence of a conspicuous authoritative recension were ever to be proven) are primarily concerned with what we have called the rational-inferential approach to the visual perusal of the world as a sign pointing to the divine Fashioner of earthly beauty, the *Badāyiʿ* and the *Khavātīm* seem to focus on the expression of the dynamics of the imaginal-cosmological dimension of the visionary experience in performative contexts that approach the contemplation of the supernal realm as a form of sensual embodiment. The following ghazal from the *Badāyiʿ*, for instance, affirms the complementarity of external and internal vision not as an accident leading the beholder toward purified forms of spiritual contemplation, but as an essential experience without which no real connection with the supernal is ever possible:

> No light shines in the lamp of fortune
> Of a gazer who no object of gazes holds in sight.
>
> What shall that pretentious moralist seek in paradise
> When no paradisiac beauty he desires today?
>
> What sublime sensation [*z̲awq*] does one derive from the ritual of remembrance [*z̲ikr*]
> Without experiencing any secret passion for a "remembered" one [*maz̲kūr*]?
>
> The beholders [*ʿārifān*] do not regard as master of gazes the one
> Whose mind does not contemplate an object of glances....
>
> Ever since Saʿdi recognized the honey
> No longer does he fear the sting of the hornet.
>
> *Badāyiʿ* 596[35]

35 [2.33] Saʿdi YE, 268.

We find in these lines the mature development of Saʿdi's acquisition of the Ghazalian principle of a functional correspondence between vision and audition as parallel tools capable of providing the heart/rational soul with the forms that are required to process the meanings descending from the supernal realm. The scholastic forms of Sufi poetry preceding Saʿdi approach the phenomenal dimension of experience as transitory states of metaphorical reality whose worth is overlooked in the face of the appreciation of the supernal as the only reality worthy of being explored. Conversely, Saʿdi's final lyric solution affirms the necessity of engaging one's senses in constant perusal of the mundane shapes of the world in order to retrieve the heart's theo-erotic form of cognition and inspiration. It is the mundane that informs the aesthetics of spiritual cognition that Saʿdi embraces, and the lyric experience evolves as an analogue of the theophanic practices inherited from the Sufi tradition.

In the ghazals quoted earlier, Saʿdi mentions the technical word *samāʿ* (along with *ẕikr*) to refer to a ritualized form of sacred contemplation within the context of a psychological point of contact between supernal inspirations of beauty and the allusion to a tangible object of desire conjured up by the lyric performance. In the fourth chapter, we referred to the practice of *samāʿ* as the "lyrical ritual," which Hujvīrī and al-Ghazālī, among other Sufi thinkers, would discuss in the context of their analyses of the sensual aspects of amatory poetry as a possible source of *ʿibrat* for the believer. A close scrutiny of the practice of *samāʿ*, both as a social ritual that fuses spirituality and aesthetics and as an implied textual strategy, enables us to account for the constant oscillations between the ethics and the psychology of the performative aspects of contemplation that appear throughout Saʿdi's various stages of lyrical commitment with respect to the morals of desiring beauty. It is through study of this aspect of the performative component of Saʿdi's lyricism that *samāʿ* will appear as a ritualized tool which, both in the micro-narratives of the lyric texture and in the social trajectories of poetry circulation, is capable of converting sensual desire into controlled forms of spiritual quest.

3 The Aesthetic Grounds of the "Sublime Sensation"

In the ghazal analyzed at the end of the previous paragraph—"no sublime sensation is possible in life without the beloved"—Saʿdi opens the first line with the mention of the word *ẕawq*, a technical term central to the relationship between the sensory and the metaphysical dimensions of his approach to the performative aspects of the psychology of lyricism. *Ẕawq*, which I render as "sublime sensation," is usually translated in the context of Sufi thought as "taste," or "intuition."[36] Although as a technical term it already occurs in the Sufi manuals of the formative period (between the 9th and the 11th centuries), in the tradition of al-Ghazālī's experiential approach to *maʿrifa* it becomes one of the most important concepts expressing the link between sensory experience and the spiritual "perception" of the supernal world.[37]

As is the case in Saʿdi's poetry, whenever the use of *ẕawq* transcends the strict boundaries of Sufi technical acceptations, it describes an aesthetic psycho-physiological experience that ranges between the inexplicable pleasure derived from the contemplation of natural and artistic beauty and the bewilderment that we may describe as the experience of the sublime.[38] In the following lines from the *Ṭayyibāt*, for instance, the aesthetic experience of *ẕawq* pertains to the psycho-physiological space of the spiritual vision in the context of the poet's early discourse on the treacherous seductions of sensuality:

> Show me the one whose mind does not embrace your presence,
> Or the one who does not behold you: no eyes have they for contemplation.

36 "*Dhawq* is the verbal noun […] of the verb *dhāqa* […], meaning 'to taste' literally and figuratively. *Ṭaʿm*, which is often associated with it, has more specifically the sense of the 'flavour' of something. Al-Jāḥiẓ (d. 255/868–9) gives several examples of figurative uses of the verb *dhāqa* in the ancient language, especially in poetry […]. Ibn Manẓūr (d. 711/1311–2) provides other examples taken especially from the Qurʾān and *ḥadīth*, always with the sense of 'to feel' or 'to experience' […]." *EI*³, "Dhawq" [D. Gril].

37 In the Sufi context, *ẕawq* "expresses the ineffable and incommunicable nature of spiritual, amorous, contemplative, and cognitive experience." Ibid. On *ẕawq* as one of the cornerstones of al-Ghazālī's theology, see Ormsby 1991, and Treiger 2012, 48–55. For a recent survey of the various definitions of *ẕawq* given by premodern Sufi manuals, see *EI*³, "Dhawq" [D. Gril].

38 While courtly lyric poets such as Anvarī, Khāqānī, Kamāl-i Iṣfahānī, Majd-i Hamgar, and Farīd-i Iṣfahānī employ the term *ẕawq* in its mundane sense of "taste," "talent," or "aesthetic and sensual enjoyment," in Saʿdi's *dīvān* it almost exclusively relates to the spiritual aesthetics of the Sufi tradition. Ultimately, the semantics of *ẕawq* in Saʿdi's poetry are comparable to Sanāʾī's and ʿAṭṭār's usage of this concept:
What *ẕawq* does the vision of the invisible beloved [*yār-i ghāyib*] elicit?
A cloud bringing rain to the thirsty in the middle of the desert.
[3.21] Saʿdi YE, 43.
Anyone whose innermost purity derives from *ẕawq*,
The candle of his heart will necessarily burn for a beautiful boy [*shāhid*].
[3.22] Ibid., 283.
The lover is he who selflessly, from the *ẕawq* of *samāʿ*,
Will dance while advancing toward the sword of calamity.
[3.23] Ibid., 163.
I beg you: forgive me, O idol:
The *ẕawq* of Presence made me lost to myself.
[3.24] Ibid., 267.

It is not lawful for everyone to look at your countenance,
Forbidden is the gaze to the eyes that are not unsullied.

Perhaps not everyone enjoys the sublime sensation [*ẕawq*] that
I experience:
What *I see* is invisible to the eyes of the others!
Ṭayyibāt 220[39]

The lines below, also extracted from the *Ṭayyibāt*, were likely dedicated to one of the young patrons of the poet, possibly prince Saʿd. The text shows a peculiar consonance with the rhetoric of the return to court after a long journey across the world, a rhetorical strategy that characterizes the depiction of space in both the *Būstān* and the *Gulistān* as a lyric gift to a princely audience:

When the wind shakes a bough from your rose garden
The soul starts dancing within the body, set ablaze by desire.

No need of paintings for the walls of your palace:
No images decorate your portico but your very presence....

May Saʿdi never die in this world, as you know:
He holds you as dearly as the soul, you are more precious than his life.

As much as Alexander has he explored the horizons of the world:
So thirstily he bends, dying by the eternal water of your threshold.
Ṭayyibāt 288[40]

As one may infer from these excerpts, the overarching context in which Saʿdi usually describes the poetry audition as a performative analogue of the contemplation of the object of desire is practice of *samāʿ*, informed by the aesthetic experience of *ẕawq*. Even though *samāʿ* is commonly described as either a plainly mundane experience of musical performance or as a spiritual Sufi ritual, the focus on *ẕawq* allows us to bridge the gap between these two apparently dichotomous aspects and emphasize the psychological dominant of such aesthetic experiences, regardless of the overarching religious agenda that might contextualize a given session.

39 [3.25] Saʿdi YE, 103.
40 [3.26] Saʿdi YE, 132.

One of the most interesting sources for the study of the aesthetic experience of *ẕawq* in the performative psychology of *samāʿ* appears in the kaleidoscopic *Safīna-yi Tabrīz*, copied at the beginning of the 14th century by Abū al-Majd Muḥammad b. Masʿūd Tabrīzī. The passage, reported by Amīn al-Dīn Ḥājī Bulah (d. 1320), describes a *samāʿ* session that took place in Tabriz, in which several poets, including Asīr al-Dīn Akhsīkatī, Ẓahīr Fāryābī, and Khāqānī, allegedly participated by listening to each other's lyric compositions:

> It is said that one night all the poets joined the lyrical ritual [*samāʿ*]. They agreed that whenever they met the poetry reciter [*qavvāl*], he would perform a ghazal by each one of them. Anyone whose ghazal stirred up the *samāʿ* would be considered the master of lyric composition. As they entered the house, the lyrical ritual was taking place in the middle of the portico, by the courtyard. The reciter first performed a ghazal by Khāqānī. The *samāʿ* did not ignite. Then it was the turn of Ẓahīr's ghazal, which did not ignite the session either. Eventually they read a poem of Ashharī, but no sublime sensation [*ẕawq*] was elicited. None of their ghazals were able to trigger an aesthetic response, until they started reciting the following ghazal by Asīr:
>
> A wind I want, filled with my soil, to gently caress your hair.
> On fire I am, for waters as pure and fresh as your limbs.
>
> Suddenly, from the portico, Ẓahīr threw himself in the middle of the space and let out a scream. A remarkable sublime sensation was triggered; they entrusted their cloaks to the reciter, and during the *samāʿ* they did not let him perform any other lines but these two. When the ritual calmed down, Ẓahīr asked whose ghazal that was. Asīr claimed its authorship, and was immediately asked to recite the rest of it. Eventually Ẓahīr proclaimed Asīr as the absolute master of lyric composition.[41]

In spite of differences in terms of settings and social roles of the participants, the *samāʿ* session portrayed in this narration presents many points of contact with the lyrical ritual witnessed and described by ʿAlī Bīsutūn. Both texts emphasize the relevance of specific rituals that Sufi manuals on *samāʿ* etiquette often describe (such as the tearing of one's clothes, which are subsequently entrusted to the singer; or the ecstatic expression of physical movements, etc.). Moreover, the accounts place the aesthetics of ghazal recitation

41 Mohammad Tabrizi 1381/2002, 529–30.

and the connection between single lines and the rest of the poem to which they belong at the center of the pleasure that the participants derive from the performances.[42]

These similarities question the boundaries between what we may ethnocentrically define as strictly religious (or mystical) or mundane. For instance, in his analysis of the passage above, the Iranian scholar Shafi'i-Kadkani qualifies as "non-Sufi" the *samā'* session recounted by Ḥājī Bulah. He argues that the description is of a setting akin to any generically mundane musical performance, which, as such, is bereft of any direct references to a spiritual context.[43] Nonetheless, as in Bīsutūn's account, both the ritualistic aspect of the gathering and the physiological response of the listeners speak to a psychological background that draws upon the fusion of mundane and spiritual aspects that characterizes *samā'* as a tool capable of generating a visionary experience stemming from the contact with the supernal realm.[44]

The psychology of the sacred aesthetics of eroticism that lie behind the musical enjoyment displayed in Bīsutūn's and Ḥājī Bulah's anecdotes can be better understood if we contextualize them within the framework of al-Ghazālī's pragmatical assessment of *samā'* as a physiological *experience* of the invisible that involves the senses and the intellectual faculties of its practitioners. Al-Ghazālī's account of the visionary experience as a psychological alignment between the contemplation of the sensible world and the retrieval of the metaphysical "meanings" reveals the full extent of the aesthetic dimension of the friction between mundanity and spirituality that characterizes the contemplation of beauty. One cogent parallel between the metaphysics of the contemplation of beauty and the sublime dimension of artistic fruition

42 Chronicles and, in particular, hagiographies often emphasize the intrinsic values of specific lyric texts as tools that either trigger an emotional reaction during the *samā'* session or fail to excite the participants in the ritual (see, for instance, the description of how Amīr Khusraw of Delhi, in order to achieve an ecstatic response during *samā'*, would often rely on Sa'di's poetry rather than his own lyric; Amir Khword 1978, 314). I am currently endeavoring to apply Austin's distinction between illocutionary and perlocutionary speech acts to the study of ghazal poetry in the context of its aesthetic reception (see below). What Austin calls the conditions of "felicity" of a given "speech act" fulfill its purpose in a social context, rather than responding to an intrinsic true/false dichotomy. For a meditation on this topic in the context of the Western lyric canon, see Culler 2015, 128.

43 Shafi'i-Kadkani 1382/2003, 164.

44 Cf. the non-scholastic aesthetics of the *samā'* session reported in this account with the anecdote of Abu Sa'īd Abī al-Khayr's first performative experience in a Sufi circle: "chūn qavvāl īn bayt biguft darvīshān rā ḥālatī padīd āmad va īn shab tā rūz bar īn bayt raqṣ kardand va dar ān ḥālat būdand va az bisiyārī ki qavvāl īn bayt biguft shaykh yād kard." Mohammad b. Monavvar 1366/1987, 1: 16.

appears in the opening passage of al-Ghazālī's chapter on music and poetry in the *Kīmiyā*, to which we may turn as an extraordinary term of comparison for a more meaningful appraisal of *samāʿ* as an aesthetic experience that transgresses the boundaries between mundanity and spirituality:

> Know that a divine secret inhabits the heart of man, and it is as concealed in it as fire hides in iron. Just as the secret of fire manifests itself when a rock is struck against iron, pleasing musical performances, mellifluous singing, and poetry shake the essence of the heart in such a way that something appears in it without one having any form of control over it. The reason for this is the affinity between the essence of man and the supernal world, which is also referred to as the spiritual world. The supernal world is the world of beauty and splendor, and all beauty and splendor originates from balance. Hence, all balanced proportions [in this world] attest to the beauty of the supernal world. All beauty, splendor, and proportion that are found in this sensible world derive from the beauty and proportion belonging to that [supernal] world.
>
> Therefore, pleasing, rhythmical, and balanced sounds feature a similarity with the wonders of the supernal world, as they elicit a profound awareness in the heart, and cause a movement and a commotion that man cannot explain within the heart.
>
> All this naturally occurs even in a heart that is simple and bereft of all passions and desires. But when a heart is not free from such passions and something ravishes it, its inner desire produces a movement whose flame grows in intensity like a fire on which one starts blowing.
>
> However, the lyrical ritual is important for anyone whose heart is dominated by the passion for God Almighty, as it stimulates the fire of divine passion. On the contrary, audition is a deadly poison to those whose hearts harbor a superficial form of passion, and, as such, it should be forbidden. The lawfulness or unlawfulness of lyrical rituals is the object of contention among scholars. And those who deem it unlawful are literalists [*ahl-i ẓāhir*] who cannot fathom that the human heart may host love for God.[45]

By relying on his own appropriation of a peripatetic cosmological model, al-Ghazālī identifies a correspondence between the proportions of the visible world and the balanced architecture of the supernal realm as a foreground for his theological judgment on the conditions that make music and poetry

45 *Kimiyā*, 1: 473–74. Cf. a similar description in Bākharzi 1345/1966, 225.

recitation permissible. By doing so, he outlines a theory of aesthetic enjoyment that correlates his phenomenology of the spiritual vision with the effects of artistic beauty on the human heart/soul.[46] This correlation reinforces the reciprocity between *tafakkur* and *mushāhada* as parallel means to attain the visionary experience. From this viewpoint, we may regard all aesthetic experiences as techniques that are capable of catalyzing the beholder's spiritual appreciation of the invisible through sensory exposure to perceptible forms of beauty.[47] The metaphor of the heart as an iron which, if struck by a stone, delivers a mysterious spark signifying a spiritual commotion before the visual or aural contemplation of beauty is also used by al-Ghazālī to represent *tafakkur* and its function vis-à-vis the inherent logic of spiritual meditation: if we imagine *tafakkur* as the act of striking an iron with a rock, the light of spiritual cognition that stems from that friction represents *maʿrifa*.[48]

Given this parallel, we may revisit one of the questions that emerged in the last chapter when analyzing the five phases of the visionary experience: what practices are capable of generating the beholder's visionary connection with the invisible world as a form of initiation into intellectual habituation with the Preserved Tablet? The practice of asceticism is a possibility that al-Ghazālī takes into account as a form of inner purification (*riyāżat*) that eliminates the influence of bodily interference in the cardiological perusal of the invisible. However, the mundane dimension of the aesthetics inherited by Saʿdi points toward al-Ghazālī's election of the visible world as the stage on which the perusal of tangible proportions stirs an emotional response in the heart that can even compete with other spiritual exercises based on abstinence and purification.[49] This aesthetic response deriving from the beholder's meditation on physical beauty leads to a deeper understanding of the invisible balances of the universe. On such bases, as suggested in the second part of this book, we may then reconsider the correlation between performative exposure to amatory poetry and the contemplation of human beauty as two dimensions of an overarching aesthetic paradigm that is directly involved in the development of

46 From both this passage and from the passages analyzed in Chapter 4, it is clear that al-Ghazālī's emphasis on music and rhythm in poetry rather than the semantics of a given poetic text served his purpose in outlining a general psycho-physiological theory of the lyrical ritual. On the contrary, in the case of the *samāʿ* session in Tabriz, the aesthetic ravishment of the poets who participated in the gathering derived primarily from the semantics of the lines that they entrusted to the reciter.

47 Cf. Bākharzi 1345/1966, 181.

48 *Kimiyā*, 2: 505. For a similar discussion of *samāʿ* as a tool to attain *mushāhada*, see Bākharzi 1345/1966, 181.

49 "In some cases, even an excess of spiritual training [*riyāżat*] cannot produce the same results that *samāʿ* can offer." *Kimiyā*, 1: 480.

a form of intellectual and sensory habituation that leads the heart toward the imaginal experience of the invisible.

4 The Psycho-Physiology of the Lyrical Ritual

Manuals on *samāʿ* composed between the 13th and the 14th centuries specifically address an audience of initiates who belong to the socio-spiritual spaces of Sufi orders (*ṭuruq*) and monasteries (*khānaqāh*).[50] While these texts offer an invaluable source of information for a better understanding of the etiquette regulating *samāʿ* as a ritualized gathering, al-Ghazālī's chapters on this practice (especially in the *Kīmiyā*) transcend the social boundaries between the monastery and non-institutionalized spaces and outline a comprehensive system that fuses psychological and theological theory, aesthetic response, and praxis.[51]

---

50 Even though "the spiritual concert does not seem to have been of great importance" to Abū Ḥafṣ Suhravardī's "system" (Ohlander 2008, 242), the discussion of the etiquette of *samāʿ* as a communal ritual features prominently in his manual on Sufi practices and beliefs, *ʿAvārif al-maʿārif* (Suhrawardi 2000, 5–36), with which Saʿdi was most certainly acquainted. The *ʿAvārif*'s chapters on *samāʿ* were likely influenced by passages on the same topic that are found in the *Ādāb al-murīdīn*, composed by Abū Ḥafṣ's uncle, Abū al-Najīb Suhravardī (d. 1168; see Abu al-Najib Suhrawardi 1977, 61–68, and, for the English translation, Abu al-Najib Suhrawardi 1975, 61–66). The *ʿAvārif* was translated numerous times into Persian throughout the 13th century (see Chittick 1997; Māyel Heravi 1364/1985; and ʿAbbāsi 1396/2017), and the broadening of the discussions on *samāʿ* that is found in the works that were either Persian versions of the *Maʿārif* (ʿAbd al-Moʾmen Esfahāni 1364/1985, 90–98), or free elaborations of its contents (*Miṣbāḥ al-ḥidāya*, Kāshāni 1367/1988, 179–202), or a reappraisal of Abū al-Najīb's positions (*Awrād al- aḥbāb*, Bākharzi 1345/1996, 180–253) attest to the growing interest in this practice in the institutionalized settings of *ribāṭs* and *khānaqāhs* in the Persianate world during Saʿdi's lifetime.

51 As often emphasized, what is unique to al-Ghazālī's treatment of the techniques and habits leading to the spiritual quest for the unseen is his non-institutionalized and yet predominantly rational approach to these topics. As far as *samāʿ* is concerned, one might find in Ruzbihān's *Risālat al-quds* (in spite of the author's visionary style) a similar degree of awareness of the psycho-physiology of the lyrical ritual. See Ruzbehān Baqli 1351/1972, 50–54. It is noteworthy that, just as al-Ghazālī highlights that the spiritual yield of *samāʿ* can overshadow even ascetic training (*riyāżat*, *Kimiyā*, 1: 480) and religious orthopraxis (*khayrāt-i rasmī*, ibid., 479), Ruzbihān states that "the *ʿārif* can gain from *samāʿ* a spiritual pleasure that no act of worship [*ʿibādat*] can ever bestow." Ruzbehān 1351/1972, 50. Another important treatise that seems to align with al-Ghazālī's posture is Aḥmad b. Muḥammad al-Ṭūsī's *Bawāriq al-ʿilmāʿ*, composed in 1248. See al-Tusi 1938. For a comparison between al-Tusi's epistle and al-Ghazālī's approach to *samāʿ*, see Lewisohn 1997.

One of al-Ghazālī's most compelling contributions to the analysis of the phenomenology of the aesthetics of *samāʿ* as a sacred lyrical ritual can be identified in his classification of the different levels of psycho-physiological response affecting the participants in such sessions: "awareness" (*fahm*), "ecstasy" (*vajd*), and "rapture" (*ḥarakat*). These three levels of response correspond to ascending degrees of spiritual expertise.[52] Additionally, as I shall soon illustrate, these levels coincide with the transition from an initial semi-rational and aesthetic response (*fahm*) to irrational ecstatic reactions (*vajd*), culminating with the experience of visions and physical raptures (*ḥarakat*).[53] Al-Ghazālī's description of the two degrees of the first stage, "awareness" (*fahm*), is particularly interesting, especially from the perspective of its aesthetic implications:

> [In its first degree] the initiate undergoes a plurality of states [*aḥvāl*], ranging between euphoria and dysphoria, levity and hardship, content and discontent. His heart will be totally occupied by such conflicting emotions. By listening to different emotional states in a poem, he will apply those to his own condition, and anything that is contained in his heart will be set ablaze. Multiple emotions will overtake him, and he will start processing different thoughts. If the foundations of science and his convictions are weak, there is a risk of blasphemy with his thoughts while performing *samāʿ*, such as ideas [from lines of poetry] that he would misleadingly apply to the divine presence:
>
> At first you were inclined toward me, what happened to that inclination?
> And what is the reason for your turning distressed today?
>
> Any initiate who experiences an initially powerful spiritual pull which subsequently weakens might think that God has withdrawn from the providence and inclination that He once would manifest [to the initiate]. He might perceive this change as a variation affecting God, which is blasphemy. He should know that God is not subject to variations and changes, as He is the One who operates variations [*mughayyir*] and is not subject to them [*mutaghayyar*]. He must know that it is his condition [i.e., of the initiate] that has changed as soon as that spiritual content

52 Compare the following observations on al-Ghazālī's approach to *samāʿ* (focused on the *Kīmiyā*) with the points raised by Yaron Klein (2014), mainly on the basis of the *Iḥyāʾ*.

53 On *vajd* in the context of al-Ghazālī and the Sufi tradition, see Lewisohn 1997, 22–25. On the "ontology" of *vajd* "in classical Persian Sufism," see Lewisohn 2014b, 38–52. See Bākharzi 1345/1966, 206, for a discussion on *vajd* as a "secret" that resonates through the heart.

> [*maʿnī*] that had opened up for him has returned under the veil. Whereas from *that* side [i.e., from the side of the divine realm] no impediment or veiling occurs, as that threshold is constantly open. This is similar to the case of the sun radiating its light upon everything but the person who stands in the shade of a wall. In this case too, it is the individual ['s position] that has changed, not that of the sun [...].
>
> As for the second degree, it applies to the experienced wayfarer who has received a taste of what they call "spiritual annihilation" [*fanā*] or "inexistence" [*nīstī*] [...]. For such people, *samāʿ* does not proceed from the [rational] understanding of meaning [*maʿnī*].[54] On the contrary, when he is caught by *samāʿ*, that condition of inexistence and [recognition of God's] unity [*yagānagī*] is renewed for him and he becomes totally invisible to himself, unaware of this world [in such a way] that he may step on fire without even noticing it. However, the *samāʿ* of the initiates [first degree] is mixed with human qualities [*ṣifāt-i bashariyat*], whereas this one [second degree] reflects the state of the women who, after having seen Yūsuf, lost their senses to the point of cutting their own fingers.[55]

If we compare al-Ghazālī's phenomenological approach to the first stage of the effects of music and poetry with the psychological response that the participants of the *samāʿ* session in Tabriz experienced upon the recitation of the "winning" lines, we may trace a comparison between *fahm* and *ẕawq* as terms describing an entrancing aesthetic experience that is in principle detached from any spiritual connotation. Both terms describe a sort of bewilderment that the listener (as well as the beholder) experiences when exposed to a source of intense aesthetic pleasure. The raw degree of this stage (*fahm*'s first degree) corresponds to what al-Ghazālī describes, at the very beginning of his chapter on the lyrical ritual, as the passion stirring the innermost essence of the heart when the senses are exposed to musical and poetic balance.

The second degree describes the spiritual aesthetics of *fahm*/*ẕawq* as the formation (or the striking renewal) of a form of cognitive awareness that leads to spiritual cognition, *maʿrifa*, i.e., the "negative" understanding of the

54 In this case, *maʿnī* refers to the hermeneutics of the lyric poetry performed during the lyrical ritual.

55 *Kīmiyā*, 1: 488–91. For an analysis of this narrative, see chapter 1 (pp. 78–79). Saʿdi alludes to this specific anecdote in one of his most famous ghazals:
Should you see him and make distinction between your hands
and the citrons: you may well cast your blame upon Zulaykhā.
[3.27] Saʿdi YE, 101.

divine as the only real being, opposed to the ephemeral nature of all created things, which partake in the ontological absolute as its pale reflections. This means that *fahm*/*ẕawq* applies to the perception of beauty as an overwhelming aesthetic experience that leaves the individual in a state of psychological bewilderment. Moreover, this stage corresponds to the mature phase of the rationalization that the believer projects onto the sensory world as a semiotic canvas that denies its own ontological value and simultaneously attests to the divine as the only true being:

> You should not deny this "inexistence" [*nīstī*] by saying: "I see him [the enraptured wayfarer], how is it possible that he has become inexistent?" As he is not what you see, as that is the [bodily] *persona* [*shakhṣ*], and when it dies, you'll keep seeing it, even though he has gone away. His truth is that subtle *maʿnī* [the soul] that is the locus of spiritual cognition [*maʿrifat*]. As soon as he loses cognition of all things, everything will have become inexistent to him, including himself, and nothing will remain but the remembrance [*ẕikr*] of God Almighty [...]. Therefore, the meaning of unity is this: he does not see anything but God, and will say: "all things are Him, and I am not." Or, he will say: "I am Him." And some people, when listening to this, have made the mistake of calling it "incarnationism" [*ḥulūl*]. And this happens only to the person who has never seen a mirror, and when he looks at the reflection of his image, he thinks that he has become part of the mirror, or that the reflection is the actual image of the mirror. If one thinks that the reflection is his own form embodied in the mirror, this is called incarnationism [*ḥulūl*]. The belief that the reflection is the actual image of the mirror is called infusion [*ittiḥād*].[56]

Whereas the twofold irrational/rational aspect of *fahm* approaches the individual's aesthetic experience from the perspective of his meditation on the phenomenal world, the second level that al-Ghazālī theorizes to explain the complexity of the human psycho-physiological response to music pertains to the realm of visionary experiences. This level clearly involves the role of the internal senses vis-à-vis the rational soul's conjunction with the supernal world. Just as in the passage (analyzed in the previous chapter) on the visionary experience involving the contemplation of beauty, al-Ghazālī defines the first level of the visionary experience as *aḥvāl*. He describes it as a set of inspirations taking over the initiate's heart—a physiological condition in which the internal senses in the brain are affected and start moving:

56 Ibid., 491.

> When the fire of those inspirations starts burning in the heart, its smoke reaches the brain until obfuscating the senses [...], hence the individual will not see or hear anything, as if he were asleep. And if he sees and hears, his perception of things will be veiled and altered as in a drunken state.

The second stage corresponds to the full extent of the visionary experience proper, which he defines as the "unveilings," *mukāshafāt*:

> Things start to appear—in a fashion similar to what happens to the Sufis—either clearly or in the guise of imaginal analogues [*mis̱āl*]. The influence of the lyrical ritual on this process is such that it purifies the heart, and converts it into a mirror that is cleansed from all the dust that would previously cover its surface. The mirror turns pure again, and images appear on its surface.[57]

Al-Ghazālī's analytical articulation of the lyrical ritual in three stages constitutes an extraordinary attempt to align this practice with the contemplative experience of beauty as a means to access the invisible world. He envisages a transition from an initial form of foggy understanding to an ecstatic rapture that paves the way to the purification of the heart, which is necessary for the perusal of the invisible. We may confidently compare this model with the relationship between any preliminary and uninformed exposure to perceptible beauty and the establishment of a cognitive connection between the forms of the world and the ideal images that the internal senses conjure as analogues of the supernal *maʿānī*.

Both the unexperienced perception of beauty and the third phase of the visionary experience are marked by the coexistence of physiological instincts surrounding the contemplation of physical beauty with the spiritual tension toward the memory of the invisible. Similarly, the twofold stage of *fahm*, or spiritual awareness of aural and poetic stimulations, stands out for its mix of spiritual and mundane forms of sensorial emotionality. Al-Ghazālī's emphasis on the risk of blasphemy (*kufr*) that the inexperienced initiate might face when misunderstanding the interpretive applicability of mundane lyric poetry to the divine presence shows parallels with the error of the beholder's faculty

57 Ibid., 492. Compare this passage with both al-Ghazāli's extensive descriptions of the visionary experience in other sections of the *Kīmiyā* (see Chapter 8, pp. 403–404) and Saʿdi's introduction to the *Gulistān*.

of estimation when reading a human form of utmost beauty as a divine indwelling (*ḥulūl*).

Both the participant in the lyrical ritual and the beholder in the early stage of their initiation into the contemplation of the invisible world experience a poignant confusion as they peruse sensory forms of proportioned beauty. Reading with these in mind, we comprehend the scope of Saʿdi's lyric subject's bewilderment at the interplay between the physical world and imagination, the value of reality stemming from poetic depictions, and the cathartic role of the aesthetic experience.

5 Saʿdi's Ethics of *Samāʿ*

> It is the masters of *maʿnī* that *samāʿ* entrances and enraptures:
> You ought to possess a true kernel before you emerge from your skin.
> *Ṭayyibāt* 172[58]

The study of Saʿdi's pornographic output has shown the complementarity of the obscene and the spiritual as two linguistic discourses that enact the desire of the lyric persona from reifying and fetishizing angles. Since *samāʿ* is the territory in which sexual desire and visual experience graze each other as physiological potential and spiritual purpose, Saʿdi's ethics of the lyrical ritual should be considered as an effort to regulate the psycho-physiological tensions inhabiting the practice of beholding beauty in a performance context.

Before analyzing Saʿdi's peculiar depiction of *samāʿ* in his ghazals, it is worthwhile considering the relationship between the ethics and the aesthetics of the lyrical ritual in the *Būstān* and the *Gulistān*, which respectively open a window onto the author's theoretical-idealistic and narrative-experiential approaches to the complex of values that he embraces and enacts throughout his entire oeuvre.[59] The *Būstān* is regarded as Saʿdi's narrative masterpiece in verse, one that provides its princely readership with a manual of conduct spelled out through short abstracted anecdotes and passages in which the author clearly exposes the theoretical grounds of the values that he wishes to share with his audience.

The passage on *samāʿ* (which I quote below almost in its entirety) is particularly illuminating, as it seems to adhere closely to the articulate set of

58 [3.28] Saʿdi YE, 82.

59 Very few studies have addressed the role of *samāʿ* in Saʿdi's work. For a recent overall assessment of the poet's depiction of the lyrical ritual, see Niyāzkār 1392/2013.

arguments that al-Ghazālī had dedicated to the legal, phenomenological, and spiritual aspects of music and poetry. In spite of Saʿdi's references to the enrapturing effect of *samāʿ*, the tone and the lucid progression of his arguments align with the argumentative sobriety that characterizes al-Ghazālī's rationalizing approach to the spiritual perusal of the invisible world:

> Not the musicians, but the steps of cattle
> Inspire the lyrical ritual in the heart filled with passion and love....
>
> The enraptured cannot tell the difference between bass and treble
> timbres.
> The inspired poor joyfully shout when the birds sing.
>
> The singer may never stop chanting, but
> The ears are not always open to the melodies.
>
> When the inflamed believers start worshiping wine
> They are intoxicated by the pulley resounding through the well,
>
> Like pulleys they twist and whirl around
> And cry while squeaking and dancing.
>
> They submit themselves to pure contemplation,
> If ravishment overcomes them, they tear their cloaks!
>
> Do not blame the dervish's intoxicated bewilderment:
> He drowns! Hence why he flails his hands and feet!
>
> Brother, I shall not tell you what the [legitimate] lyrical ritual is
> Unless I know who the listener is!
>
> If his soul, like a bird, takes off from the tower of inspired meaning
> [*maʿnī*]
> The angels would be astonished by the trajectory of its flight.
>
> But if he is a ludic man devoted to hilarity and amusement,
> The demon in his brain will grow ever stronger.
>
> How can the man of lyrical rituals indulge in lust?
> A beautiful voice wakes up the dormant, not the drunkard!

The breeze of the morning enthralls the rose,
But the firewood, only an axe can split.

The world fully resounds with music, intoxication, and rapture
But what could the blind man ever see in the mirror?

Have you ever seen how a camel reacts to Arab melodies?
How joyful he dances when music pervades him?

Music brings passionate joy to the camel's head
But a donkey is a man who is not moved by it.[60]

The theoretical grounds that Saʿdi deploys in the passages on lyrical rituals in the *Būstān* show parallels with the pragmatics of the golden mean that al-Ghazālī applies to his ruling on the conditions that determine the permissibility of music and poetry both in their playful context and as an aesthetic catalyst for the believer's quest for the supernal realm. One important element pointing to the Ghazalian origin of Saʿdi's theoretical approach to performed music and poetry is the poet's representation of music as an aesthetic experience that is based on anthropological grounds. In other words, for both al-Ghazālī and Saʿdi, *samāʿ*, as a cathartic experience capable of generating an ecstatic response (*vajd*) in the listener, depends on a physiological feature that naturally stirs the innermost essence of human beings.

By recognizing phenomenal reality as a soundscape in which sensitive and passionate hearts may be moved by any natural or artificial rhythm, Saʿdi aligns his position with al-Ghazālī's anthropological approach to the physiological response of the human heart/soul to any balanced melodies, regardless of their source or meaning. Saʿdi reformulates al-Ghazālī's cosmic dimension of music as a spiritual catalyst not only through the comparison between performed music and the sounds of nature (cattle steps), but also by referring to the natural disposition of camels toward the melodies capable of appeasing their senses. The example of the camel's response to Arabic poetry as a source of stimulation that does not depend on the actual understanding of the text derives from al-Ghazālī's reference to the same animal in his final argument in defense of music, in which he declares that the content of any mellifluous

60 [3.29] *Bustān*, 111–12. Translation mine, with occasional adaptations from Wickens's rendition. See Wickens 1978, 117–18.

utterance is capable of opening up the inner chambers of the heart regardless of its meaning.[61]

Sa'di's description of the pathos with which the body of the *samāʿ* practitioners reacts to musical stimulation—by "twisting and whirling around, and crying while squeaking and dancing"—exemplifies al-Ghazālī's definition of the "physical rapture" (*ḥarakat*) that generates spastic movements and may cause the listeners to unwillingly tear their cloaks (*khirqa*) apart.[62] The tearing of cloaks to which Sa'di alludes is featured in both Bīsutūn's and Ḥājī Bulah's descriptions of *samāʿ* rituals.[63] Considering both the unorthodox status and the widespread practice of this habit, Sufi manuals on *samāʿ* elaborate extensively on the permissibility of dancing and tearing one's cloak as a result of a sincere psycho-physiological response to music and according to precise indications that regulate the etiquette of raptures of this kind.[64] Sa'di's explicit reference to the brain of the listener underpins the physiological framework of al-Ghazālī's explanation of the aesthetic and spiritual effects of music as a bodily function that involves the inner senses' manipulation of the stimuli provided by external perceptions. What Sa'di describes as demonic intervention in the brain of the ludic listener corresponds to al-Ghazālī's "blind spot" caused by the obfuscation of the senses brought about by the flames of the heart during the enrapturing phase (*aḥvāl*) of the ecstatic response.[65]

This preliminary obfuscation of the senses, which al-Ghazālī compares to the distorted forms of perception and cognition that characterize intoxication, constitutes a space of indetermination which, on the basis of the purity of the believer's heart, may or may not lead to the unveiling of the invisible

---

61 Sa'di's polemical tone ("a donkey is a man who" unlike camels "is not moved by" music) reflects al-Ghazālī's critique of the "foolish people" (*ablahān*) who do not recognize the parallel between the effect of poetry on camels and the physiological response of the *samāʿ* practitioners. *Kimiyā*, 1: 485.

62 In al-Ghazālī's classification, *ḥarakat* and dance correspond to the third stage of the experience of *samāʿ*. For a comparison with Bākharzi's detailed illustration of the physiological effects of this stage, see Bākharzi 1345/1966, 182–83.

63 Sa'di often alludes to this practice in his ghazals. In the following line, for instance (quoted as part of the above analysis of the visionary experience), the poet frames the habit of tearing one's cloak as an ecstatic reaction to the end of the visionary experience of *mushāhada* in the context of *samāʿ*-induced bewilderment:
Look at them! They start to dance when they see you
And when you leave, they tear their cloaks while seeking you.
[3.30] Sa'di YE, 117.

64 See *Kimiyā*, 1: 495–96. Cf. Bākharzī's extensive discussion on this topic, which summarizes the complexity of the conversations that were likely taking place during Sa'di's lifetime. Bākharzi 1345/1966, 212–21.

65 Cf. Bākharzī's description of how *samāʿ* "floods" the frontal lobe of the brain. Ibid., 182.

world. This is the turning point where the physiological response of the body is offered the chance to overcome the limits of mundanity and convert the intoxicating obfuscation into an opportunity for spiritual contemplation and aesthetic catharsis. It is in this direction that Saʿdi incorporates the parallel between the visionary experience of supernal beauty and the inspired cardiology stemming from the lyrical ritual into the image of the bird-like soul flying from the parapet of *maʿnī*. We now know that, in this case too, what Saʿdi alludes to by referring to *maʿnī* is not a generic discourse on spirituality, but the precise psychological concept of "supernal mental contents" descending from the invisible world upon the heart/practical intellect of the listener/beholder. The reference to the angels confirms this reading, as their presence signifies the allegorical analogue of the soul of the fixed stars, which contains the *maʿānī* that the heart/soul/practical intellect of the individual converts into inspired images through the uncontrollable activity of the internal senses.

A further parallel with the psychology of the visionary experience emerges from the narration that immediately follows Saʿdi's considerations on the spiritual physiology of lyrical ritual. The protagonist of the tale is a young man who night and day strives to teach himself how to play the reed flute. His efforts are constantly frustrated by the anger of his father, who repeatedly reprimands the boy and sets his flute on fire. Eventually, upon careful listening to his son's talent, the father declares that, for the first time, his heart is being set ablaze by the beauty of the boy's musical skills:

> One night, the father listened to his son's melodies.
> He was astonished and bewildered by that melody [*samāʿ*].
>
> With his face covered in sweat, he said:
> "This time it is the flute that has set *me* on fire!"
>
> You do not know why those who are frenzied by intoxication
> Agitate their hands while dancing?
>
> A door opens upon the heart from the inspirations [*az vāridāt*]:
> They cast their heads and hands upon existence.
>
> May dancing for the Beloved be lawful to anyone
> Who sacrifices his entire being to Him.[66]

66 [3.31] *Bustān*, 112.

In this case too, Saʿdi relies on a mundane event—a father's emotional response to the music performed by his son—to reconfirm his observance of al-Ghazālī's spiritual anthropology of music and recitation. The image of a door opening onto the "inspirations" (*vāridāt*) from the invisible world is a clear proof of the Ghazalian framework that the poet embraces in tracing a parallel between the effects of visual contemplation and aural ravishment.[67] Whilst al-Ghazālī confines his defense of the contemplation of comely youths for spiritual purposes to the strict context of the visionary experience, he allows himself greater theoretical flexibility in the arena of music and poetry audition. The subtext of al-Ghazālī's staunch defense of the spiritual aesthetics of the lyrical ritual vis-à-vis the detraction of the "literalists" reverberates through key passages of Saʿdi's lines on *samāʿ*.[68]

As Saʿdi restates it, the lyrical ritual is not legal or illegal per se. The final ruling on its legal status and ethics depends on the listeners and their inner condition ("tell me who the listener is"): music may magnify their feelings and lead them either astray or to a closer proximity to the divine.[69] The defensive tone of Saʿdi's argument attempting to explain the disheveled physiological reaction of the listeners who move their bodies upon the spiritual inspiration provided by the lyrical ritual attests to the permanence of the debate that al-Ghazālī had initiated in the 11th century.[70] Saʿdi seems to have been aware of both the legal

---

67 On the concept of *vārid* in al-Ghazālī, see Klein 2014, 230. Cf. the use of this term in Qushayrī's *Epistle*, Qushayri 1988, 151. Knysh (Qushayri 2007, 108) translates the term as "occurrence," whereas Sells (1996, 145) renders it as "oncoming." Cf. the definition of the term in the 11th-century Persian translation of the *Epistle*, Qoshayri 1391/2012, 173. Cf. Ruzbihān-i Baqlī's (1351/1972, 23) notes on the *vāridāt* in the context of *maʿrifa*, *vajd*, and the perusal of the invisible world. In a passage from the mid-13th-century anonymous hagiography of the Sufi master Awḥad al-Dīn Kirmānī, the term *vārid* is used to describe Kirmānī's visionary experience during a *samāʿ* session. In the account, the loss of consciousness causes Kirmānī to be taken from "that place to another place" (*az ān maqām ba maqāmi dīgar rasānīd*) while his external eyes are closed and his internal senses are engaged (*mashghūl*) with something else. Foruzānfar 1347/1969, 98. The expression *az ān maqām ba maqāmi dīgar* resonates with a line that opens one of Saʿdi's most famous ghazals:
You entered from the door, and I abandoned myself:
You'd say that I moved from this world to another world.
[3.32] Saʿdi YE, 125.

68 *Kimiyā*, 1: 474, 481.

69 "The legal ruling on *samāʿ* [*ḥukm*] ought to be issued by one's heart." *Kimiyā*, 1: 474. For an analysis of al-Ghazālī's overall position on the legal status of *samāʿ*, see Klein 2014, 217–20; and Lewisohn 1997, 17–19. Cf. Bākharzi 1345/1966, 221.

70 See *Kimiyā*, 1: 495–96, where al-Ghazālī defends dance in the context of *samāʿ* on the basis of legal and spiritual grounds. In the *Iḥyāʾ* al-Ghazālī quotes the opinion of the "philosophers" to justify the physiology of the physical movements stemming from "intellectual

aspect of this problem and its social and aesthetic reverberations as issues that the scholars around him had been discussing since his youth.[71] We may regard the dialectic confrontation between the detractors and the upholders of the legitimacy of music and amatory poetry recitation as the main historical link between al-Ghazālī's theoretical framework on this subject and Saʿdi's lyrical enactment of its main tenets.[72]

The Hanbali jurist Ibn al-Jawzī (d. 1200) is the chief historical figure whose writings we must consider in order to assess the theoretical continuity between al-Ghazālī's and Saʿdi's anthropological and psychological approaches to *samāʿ*.[73] In one of his main works, *Talbīs Iblīs* (*The Deceit of Satan*), Ibn al-Jawzī warns his audience against the temptations affecting the path of the Sufis. He crafts his polemical arguments aimed at discrediting *samāʿ* and the spiritual contemplation of youths by applying a severe rationalizing approach to the role of the intellect in one's beliefs and practices.[74] The centrality of rational intelligence leads Ibn al-Jawzī to an approach to the relationship between the heart and the senses that radically diverges from al-Ghazālī's complex spiritual cardiology.

According to the Baghdadi polemist, the heart is an impregnable fortress that only the angels may access. He represents Satan as a bodily fluid capable of engulfing the purity of the heart as soon as the senses are allowed to access its pure surface.[75] By individuating the origin of idolatry in an excessive reliance on the senses,[76] al-Jawzī subverts the Avicennian origins of al-Ghazālī's

love" (*al-ʿishq al-ʿaqlī*). MacDonald 1901b, 721–22. For an analysis of the passages in the *Iḥyāʾ*, see Klein 2014, 237.

71 See Gribetz 1991. On Suhravardī's "strict" legalistic approach, see Ohlander 2008, 239–42. In his mid-13th century Persian translation of the *ʿAvārif*, ʿAbd al-Muʾmin Iṣfahānī (1364/1985, 95) omits with a pretext the chapters of the book (22nd and 23rd) focusing on the prohibitions (*inkār*) regarding the lyrical ritual.

72 Yaḥyā Bākharzī's *Awrād al-aḥbāb* (inspired by the deeds and rules of the 13th-century sheykh Sayf al-Dīn Bākharzī) attests to the complexity of the historical conversations on the permissibility of *samāʿ* that were taking place during Saʿdi's lifetime. In one passage, the author denounces how "nowadays," this practice has become a "meaningless word, and a soulless body," in all the circumstances in which the appropriate etiquette is not followed. Bākharzi 1345/1966, 195. Cf. the conservative opinion—mainly based on hermeneutical grounds—that Sayf al-Dīn Bākharzī upheld when considering lyric poems unfit for the *samāʿ* ritual. Bākharzi 1345/1966, 191–92.

73 On Ibn al-Jawzī, especially from the perspective of the relevance of his criticism for the study of Sufism and theo-aesthetic practices related to *samāʿ*, see Ridgeon 2018, 86–99.

74 Ibn al-Jawzī 1975, 223–26. Cf. Klein 2014, 215–16.

75 Ibn al-Jawzī 1975, 223–265. See ibid., 26–28 on the positive role of the intellect and Satan as a blood flowing in the believers' veins.

76 Ibid., 42.

hierarchical appraisal of the positive functions of the phenomenal experience and recasts the body/soul dichotomy in a way that harks back to the early Islamic Neoplatonic paradigm that conceives of mundanity as an absolutely negative dimension.

While the crux of al-Jawzī's arguments is a hyper-rationalizing approach that is at odds with the irrational anti-worldly tenets of asceticism, the logical result of his speculations overlaps with the literalists' positions that al-Ghazālī had vehemently confuted in both the *Iḥyāʾ* and in the *Kīmiyā*. In his reappraisal of the origins of Sufism as the progressive corruption of the original proximity to the divine presence through ascetic practices informed by religious zeal, Ibn al-Jawzī overtly discredits both the theoretical and the pragmatic dimensions of al-Ghazālī's spiritual cardiology. By doing so, al-Jawzī undermines the very foundation of the Avicennian psychology of spiritual vision, and he deems al-Ghazālī's science of the unveiling (*mukāshafa*) a form of blasphemy supported by unreliable prophetic traditions and which dangerously crosses the boundaries of jurisprudence.[77] We may read al-Jawzī's mocking of al-Ghazālī's statement on the imaginal translation of the angelic presences of the invisible world into mental representations as the main source of invalidation of the latter's inclusive perspective on the spiritual value of music and poetry.

Saʿdi's defensive remarks on the commotion overtaking the listener's movements during the *samāʿ* session act as an indirect response to the inflammatory debate that pushed Ibn al-Jawzī to hold al-Ghazālī's defense of the mundane effects of lyrical rituals responsible for the lustful excesses of the Sufis. On the basis of such counter-arguments expressed in the *Būstān*, it is possible to make better sense of an ambiguous pseudo-biographical anecdote from the second chapter of the *Gulistān*, in which Saʿdi anachronistically refers to Ibn al-Jawzī as his spiritual master. Over the past few decades, uncritical historiographical readings of the *Gulistān* have convinced some scholars to take Saʿdi's anecdote at face value in order to determine the historical veracity behind the link between the poet and the Hanbalite traditionalist. Given that the author of *Talbīs Iblīs* died in 1200—more than a decade before Saʿdi could possibly have been born—it has been suggested that the Ibn al-Jawzi mentioned by Saʿdi is actually the grandson of the renowned conservative scholar, bearing the same name as his grandfather and himself a well-respected Hanbalite preacher who died in Baghdad in 1258.[78] In the anecdote, Saʿdi describes how his "teacher" (*murabbī*) would urge him not to listen to music and poetry and

77 Ibid., 138.

78 For a summary of the controversy regarding the identity of Ibn al-Jawzī in Saʿdi's pseudo-autobiographical account, see, in Persian, Yusofi's comment on the passage from the

to prefer asceticism and spiritual seclusion instead. Nevertheless, often, Saʿdi recalls, "the prime of his youth" would overwhelm his religious resilience, and the prevailing force of his sensual passions would push him to partake in lyrical rituals and pleasurable gatherings. In this tale, Saʿdi's exposure to the inharmonious voice of a performer becomes the pretext for the author to ironically embrace the prohibitions of his "educator" again.[79]

It should be noted that from the wording that Saʿdi uses when referring to Ibn al-Jawzī's sermons, it is not entirely clear whether the author refers to his connection with the preacher from Baghdad as a personal acquaintance directly involved in the religious upbringing of the young poet. I would be inclined to consider the bond between the two a purely literary stratagem, through which Saʿdi brings the historical epitome of the polemic against music to the arena of literary fiction in order to ironically subvert the values upheld by the conservative juriconsults of the age and defend the legitimacy of the lyrical ritual.[80] Through this parodic subversion of values, Saʿdi shifts the conditions for the permissibility of music and poetry from the realm of religious ethics to purely aesthetic grounds.

6 Poetry as a Controlled Form of Sexual Desire: *Samāʿ* and *Shāhid-bāzī*

I have suggested that Saʿdi's progressive detachment from the dry religious zeal that characterized the atabeg Abū Bakr's public display of piety was stimulated by his association with the courtly entourage of prince Saʿd.[81] This shift may partially explain the poet's overall positive attitude toward the sensual aspects of *samāʿ* as a social practice capable of blending the spiritual values of the *khānaqāh* with the aesthetics of the courtly *majlis*. Moreover, as mentioned in the introduction to this third part of our study and from the perspective of the ethics of Sufi practices, we may trace the seeds of Saʿdi's favorable attitude

Gulistān, (339), and, more recently, in English, *EIr*, s.v. "Saʿdi" [P. Losensky]. Cf. Mahmudpur 1395/2016.

79 *Golestān*, 94–95.

80 Cf. Farah Niyāzkār's diverging opinion on this matter. Niyāzkār 1392/2013, 280. Niyāzkār's position on Saʿdi's approach to *samāʿ* is primarily scholastic and dichotomous. As she summarizes by means of a diagram at the end of her article (ibid., 294), she exclusively considers the normative ethics of the lyrical ritual without taking into account the importance of the sensual component in Saʿdi's lyricism and the chronological development of his moral stances with respect to the contemplation of human beauty in courtly and spiritual settings.

81 See Introduction; Ingenito 2019.

back to the theo-erotic legacy that Awḥad al-Dīn Kirmānī left in Baghdad in the 1230s, especially after the demise of Suhravardī and in light of the political impact generated by the protection that the Caliph officially accorded to him.[82]

Both Kirmānī's own literary output and the hagiographical sources from the 13th and the 14th centuries adamantly highlight the Sufi master's appreciation for lyrical rituals attended by comely youths in contexts that would cause most contemporaries to frown.[83] Although we ascribe to Sa'di the creation of a solid association between the lyric subject and the role of the *shāhid-bāz* (i.e., the worshipper of youths as sacred bodies), Kirmānī's quatrains on the practice of *shāhid-bāzī* could be regarded as one of the most significant historical sources of inspiration for Sa'di's literary innovation. Whilst al-Ghazālī employs the expression *shāhid-bāzī* with a sarcastically negative connotation in the *Kīmiyā*,[84] the term gained spiritual relevance through 'Ayn al-Qużāt Hamadānī's illustration of its theo-erotic function.[85] It is in the context of Hamadānī's reformulation of the semantics of *shāhid-bāzī* that we may explain Kirmānī's prideful ascription of the attribute of *shāhid-bāz* to the lyric subject of some of his quatrains:

> I worship the beautiful boys, but beware of those
> Who blame me: they do the same, night and day.

---

82 See introduction to Part 2. Foruzānfar points out that one of the rituals that characterized Kirmānī's spiritual etiquette in his Sufi circle was the custom of shaving the heads of the initiates before entrusting them with the cloak (*khirqa*). Foruzānfar 1347/1969, 41. In one of his early *qasidas*, Sa'di alludes to this very practice:
And if you prefer the surface rather than the core of the Truth
Go ahead: wear the blue cloak and shave your head!
[3.33] Sa'di YE, 23.

83 "When the *samā'* began, they all started dancing. The sheikh [Kirmānī] was enjoying the presence of beautiful youths, and would attain a sublime sensation with them [*bā īshān ẕawq kardī*]. They had brought all the comeliest youths to that gathering, and each one of them was holding a candle. The sheikh was suddenly experiencing entrancing and ecstatic raptures [*ba vajd-u ḥālat-u ẕawq kh^wad mashghūl ast*; I read *kh^wad* as an emphatic term, but it could also be read as a possessive adjective: *ẕawq-i kh^wad*]." Foruzānfar 1347/1969, 40. "Many handsome boys [*shāhid pisarān-i ziyād*] often attend the *samā'* sessions of the sheikh." Ibid., 194. See also ibid., 212–13. The historian "Ḥamdallāh Mustawfī (d. 749/1349) relates that when the *samā'* was in full swing, Kirmānī would rip open the shirts of young men and place his hand upon their breasts." Ridgeon 2018, 79, n. 1. See also Foruzānfar 1347/1969, 39–41; Ridgeon 2018, 70–79.

84 See Introduction to Part 2, p. 224.

85 See chapter 5, p. 273.

They all worship the beautiful boys
And yet no courage they have to confess their love.[86]

The self-indulgent and yet defensive tone with which Kirmānī's lyric persona affirmed its own practice of *shāhid-bāzī* as a positive quality reemerged, years later, in Sa'di's appropriation of this rhetorical pattern in the mature context of the *Badāyiʿ*:

Sa'di's renown as *shāhid-bāz* spread far and wide:
And I say that this is not a sin in our religion, but a virtue!
Badāyiʿ 335[87]

We may read Sa'di's ostentatious defense of *shāhid-bāzī* in a socio-cultural context that associates this practice with the spiritual aesthetics of *samāʿ* as a reaction to the coexistence of diverging ethical stances in the spiritual arena of Shiraz in the 1250s.[88] The juxtaposition of conflicting spiritual values vis-à-vis the role of sensuality for spiritual ends reflects the disdain that Kirmānī allegedly met any time he unabashedly performed lyrical rituals in the presence of comely youths.[89] The ambiguous nature of this practice as depicted in Kirmānī's hagiography helps us regard the emphasis on the problematic nature of desire that characterizes Sa'di's *Ṭayyibāt* as an overarching ethical terrain that includes the poet's cogitations on the practice of *samāʿ* both as aesthetic enjoyment and as a tool for the spiritual improvement of the beholder.[90] Ultimately, it is possible that the scattered instances of criticism

---

86 [3.34] Kermāni 1366/1987, 225, *rubāʿī* no. 1075. See also ibid., 226–27, *rubāʿīs* nos 1086, 1087, 1092, 1093, 1096.

87 [3.35] Sa'di YE, 156.

88 This is reflected also in the context of the Salghurid political arena of the time, in which prince Sa'd II's mundane forms of courtly indulgence coexisted with his father's religious zeal. The poetic sources often celebrate the lavish environment of Sa'd's gatherings, which presumably took place in the same palaces and gardens enjoyed by his grandfather, Sa'd I, and which Abū Bakr, according to Shams-i Qays, had temporarily decommissioned to fund pious foundations, *khānaqāhs* and *ribāṭs*. See General Introduction.

89 See Ridgeon 2012.

90 Bākharzī's recurrent emphasis on the necessity of barring beardless boys from dancing during *samāʿ* or even participating in its rituals speaks to the extent to which their presence was perceived as a source of forbidden desire and spiritual distraction, but also theo-erotic inspiration. See Bākharzi 1345/1966, 201. Rūzbihān-i Baqlī, on the contrary, allegedly stated that the singers animating the *samāʿ* sessions should be chosen on the basis of their external beauty. Ibid., 207. In another passage (ibid. 222), Bākharzī suggests that some *samāʿ* practitioners would fake their spiritual raptures and ecstatic movements only to impress the beautiful participants in the sessions, as a form of *shāhid-bāzī*. In the

that Saʿdi received, especially after the 1260s, could reflect the same kind of scorn experienced by Kirmānī as a consequence of the sensual overtones of his approach to *samāʿ*. For instance, in the *Shirāz-nāma*, the renowned 14th-century biographical collection on Shirazi rulers and Sufis, Ibn Zarkūb inexplicably avoids mentioning Saʿdi's Sufi lodge and literary activity. We might suppose that the hagiographer was among the detractors who, like Ṣafī al-Dīn,[91] did not approve of Saʿdi's erotic ostentations. Ibn Zarkūb was in fact a disciple of the sheikh Amīn al-Dīn Baliyānī (d. 1345), who practiced extreme forms of asceticism and often forbade the practice of *samāʿ*.[92]

Saʿdi's innovative understanding of the *topos* of the *shāhid* as a link between spiritual imagination and eroticized lyrical rituals caused a shift in the literary arena of the second half of the 13th century. For instance, the following lines by Sayf-i Farghānī, Saʿdi's contemporary and devoted imitator of his ghazals, illustrate the scope of this development:

> Every night we slide into our bed and think of the beloved
> While embracing the *shāhid* of the imagination.
>
> During *samāʿ* our cloak tears apart like the petals
> Of the rose, while loving the youths who dance like clothed cypresses.[93]

The fact that Saʿdi seems to be inclined to discuss the problems raised by the lyrical ritual not only in the *Gulistān* and the *Būstān* but also in his early collection of poems confirms that he perceived ethical hostility toward eroticism and the practice of *samāʿ* as intimately correlated discourses. In spite of his defense of lyrical rituals against its detractors, Saʿdi's early ghazals often follow al-Ghazālī's warnings on the subtle line separating lust from the forms of spiritual engagement with the senses that characterize both the practice of *samāʿ* and the contemplation of human beauty. These two aspects clearly conflate in the way the lines below emphasize the separation between mundane sensuality and spiritual hermeneutics:

> A beautifully smooth face whose demeanor is equally pure
> Casts darkness away from existence through its radiance.

---

same passage, the author declares that beardless boys are more dangerous than leopards and lions.

91 See chapter 1, p. 62.

92 See Aigle 1997; *EIr*, s.v. "Balyani, Amin al-Din" [D. Aigle].

93 [3.36] Sayf Farghānī 1341–44/1962–65, 3: 136.

If lust slips away from your brain's imagination,
Anyone you set your eyes upon will appear as a beautiful *shāhid.*

Prevent your carnal nature from hindering your inner soul
And the aesthetic pleasure of the *samāʿ* of affection will resound in your heart.
Ṭayyibāt 219[94]

From both the perspective of al-Ghazālī's theoretical approach to the quest for the supernal forms and Kirmānī's pragmatic illustration of the social eroticism that *samāʿ* involves, we may read the lines above as the lyrical rendition of a performative act that fuses contemplation and poetry recitation as two conflating psycho-physiological tools. While denouncing the perils posed by the lustful contemplation of carnal beauty, Saʿdi elevates *samāʿ* to the function of a protected environment in which the beholder/listener may experience a form of spiritual elevation without the risk of being led astray by lustful thoughts. In other ghazals, Saʿdi playfully alludes to the physical dimension of *samāʿ* as an alternative way of touching the forbidden fruit of the object of desire in connection with the excess of commotion generated by the musical performance:

The minstrel could not tolerate me anymore,
For I was left with no endurance for his music.

When the hand of the desperate cannot reach for his own soul,
Tearing one's cloak is the last resort left....

I said: "O spiritual orchard, why can't I
Take a bite from the apple that I see?"

He responded: "Saʿdi, do not foster futile imaginings [*khayāl-i khīra*]:
The silver apple ought not to be picked!"
Ṭayyibāt 159[95]

94 [3.37] Saʿdi YE, 103. Ms. Kabul 1325, 366–67.

95 [3.38] Saʿdi YE, 76. The variants found in the manuscripts suggest that the text was recorded and circulated on a number of different occasions (ibid., 417). Since Yusofi's reconstruction seems arbitrary, I have followed Ms. Paris 1320s, f. 110b.

The fine line separating spiritual imagination from lust also appears in ghazals in which Saʿdi seems to introduce a pun aiming at the difference between the beloved as a physical presence and the Beloved as the ultimate recipient of the believer's spiritual passion. Moreover, the reference to *mushāhada* in the context of the vision of the garden establishes a parallel with the pattern of the visionary experience as illustrated by al-Ghazālī and Saʿdi himself (in the introduction to the *Gulistān*):

> How wicked is the path of embracing a beloved to feed one's lust:
> We shall kill our lust, for the sake of the Beloved! ...
>
> I heard that my companions headed toward the desert
> Exhausted by the blame of people and the ruthless mood of the beloved.
>
> My path leads nowhere, if not to the alley where he resides:
> My head bows down only at the feet of the beloved....
>
> Seeing the garden without visionary experience [*mushāhada*] is vain striving [*mujāhada*],
> Even if you plant a hundred rose bushes instead of the beloved.
>
> O wind, should you blow in the rose garden of the spiritual beings,
> Entrust the prayer of this companion to the ancient lover....
>
> Everyone joins a gathering whilst Saʿdi sits in a corner:
> Whoever enjoys the beloved's intimacy is estranged to all people.
>
> *Ṭayyibāt* 75[96]

In this case too, the contrast between the "gatherings" and the "corner" of seclusion expresses the difference between the social and psychological dimensions of the visionary experience. The reference to the companions fleeing from blame and lovesickness may be read as an allusion to antithetical ascetic practices. As in the lines below, the experience of training one's psyche to recollect the supernal *maʿānī* on the basis of external forms of beauty interacts with both the exposure to visual and aural forms of inspiration and the *meaning* that poetic creativity can generate:

---

96 [3.39] Saʿdi YE, 38.

Tell the minstrel to keep playing the tune of this ghazal,
As the path he took leads to a *place* imbued with meaning.
Ṭayyibāt 121[97]

The expression *dalālat* which Saʿdi employs in the line above literally means "guidance" and, by extension, "signification," as it describes the "guided" transition from verbal (or formal) expression (*lafẓ*) to mental content (*maʿnī*). The few times premodern Persian poets employ this word, they usually highlight the semantics of the process of signification in a fashion that often conflates the concept of spiritual "guidance" toward the truth with the speculations on the relationship between form and meaning that informed contemporary linguistic debates.[98] It is noteworthy that the closing line of the ghazal places the text at the center of the spiritual cardiology explored thus far:

O Saʿdi, clear the Tablet [*lawḥ*] of your heart of all images that are not of him:
The sciences that cannot pave the way to the Truth only lead to ignorance.[99]

The verse on *dalālat* ("signification") directly involves the aesthetics of the lyrical ritual and relates them to the psychology of the visionary experience

97 [3.40] Saʿdi YE. 59. The Bīsutūn recension lists this text among the "old ghazals."

98 See *EI*², s.v. "Bayān" [G. E. von Grunebaum].
Anyone who is acquainted with these three experiences
Shall recognize the interplay between words and significations.
[3.41] Shabestari 2535/1976, 48.
You are everything, look at yourself, your totality:
Eighteen thousand worlds constantly reflected in the mirror of your beauty.
As soon as the hearts of your seekers reflect intuitions [*dalālati*] of your presence
Anything that exists in the world is entirely the image of you.
[3.42] ʿAttār 1392/2013, 551.
"He said: 'Signification belongs to the intellect, intuitions to wisdom, and witnessing to spiritual cognition.'"
ʿAttār 1391/2012, 573.
[3.43] Rumi (1393/2014 , 1: 190):
Even though meaning appeared in this form
Forms approach the meanings and yet recede from them.
They signify like water and trees:
Reciprocating each other, and yet essentially different.
[3.44] Salmān Sāvaji (1383/2004, 406).
In these words, one rhyme misses the mark of the object
And this signifies nothing but the unease of my poetic art.

99 [3.45] Saʿdi YE. 59.

in its performative context. By comparing this line with both al-Ghazālī's passages on the practice of music as a spiritual practice akin to the contemplation of beauty and the account of the *samāʿ* session in Tabriz, we may read Saʿdi's reference to the ability of the minstrel to produce "signification" (i.e., a correct form of spiritual meaning) in a sense that is both aesthetic—involving the access to *ẕawq/fahm*—and psychologically visionary. The "guidance" that the lyric persona seeks through the tunes performed by the minstrel during the *samāʿ* session is simultaneously aesthetic, psychological, and ethical. It converts the passion triggered within the heart of the believer into a form of controlled rapture, in which the psychological experience of *ẕawq* reaches the ecstatic commotion of *vajd* without leaving the desires of the subject at the mercy of the carnal soul and its base instincts.[100]

In another of his early ghazals, Saʿdi elaborates on the controlled environment of *samāʿ* by referring to the ritual as the "true companion of the soul":

> Saʿdi's most intimate companion is the spiritual *samāʿ*:
> No room is left for the melody of the nightingale and the dove's rhythms.
>
> In *this samāʿ* you may find the countenances of the most beautiful *shāhids*;
> Around *this* wine all the Sufis who enjoy the dark liquors gather.
>
> *Ṭayyibāt* 208[101]

100 One may compare Saʿdi's implied pedagogy of *samāʿ* (as a catalyst for passionate desires that would obfuscate the senses and lead them toward the carnal soul) with Abū Saʿīd Abī al-Khayr's physiological comment on the strategic deployment of *samāʿ* as a means to appease the sexual urges of young initiates: "The carnal soul of the youths is never devoid of lustful desires. Carnal desire overpowers them and flows in all of their limbs. Now, if they wave their hands [while dancing], desire flows away from their hands. Similarly, if they raise their feet, passionate desire decreases in their legs. By doing so, desire deteriorates in their limbs and they are more likely to prevent themselves from practicing capital vices. When all the desires are collected [in the body]—*may God protect us!*—they are prone to cast the youth into major vices, whereas that fire calms down when performing *samāʿ*..." Mohammad b. Monavvar 1366/1987, 1: 207–208.

101 [3.46] Ms. Kabul 1325, 360. Cf. Saʿdi YE, 98. The Bīsutūn recension includes the text among the "old ghazals," see ibid., 437–38. In this case too, the variants point to a context of circulation that involved multiple authorial renditions on the basis of an initial performative occasion. For instance, in some manuscripts the first *miṣrāʿ* of the penultimate line reads as a recrafting of the original scholastic content in a fashion that highlights Saʿdi's poetic excellence: *samāʿ-i ahl-i dil āvāz-i nāla-yi saʿdīst* ("The melody of Saʿdi's voice is the *samāʿ* of the 'masters of the heart.'"). Ibid., 437.

Considering Saʿdi's constant emphasis on wine-related imagery as a metaphor for spiritual and aesthetic intoxication, the image of the Sufis drinking dark liquors (lit. "wine dregs") sets the demonstrative "this" (*īn*) as a modifier that specifies that both the *samāʿ* filled with attractive young men and the wine consumed therein ought to be interpreted as spiritual metaphors.[102] This metaphorical level projects the entire erotic description of the ghazal into the dimension of spiritual imagination in which any *samāʿ* session replaces the beholder's attraction to beauty with the linguistic enjoyment of desire.[103] The practice of an active form of imagination that the lyric experience stages as meditation on the object of desire allows the lyric subject to disengage from the techniques that are supposed to catalyze the imaginal conjunction with the archetypal forms of beauty.

---

102 Saʿdi's representation of real wine and wine-drinking (unlike that of his contemporaries and 14th-century poets such as Hafez and Salmān-i Savājī) is often contemptuous, especially when compared with the contemplation of beauty as a source of a superior form of intoxication. This attitude is particularly frequent in the *Ṭayyibāt*:
Warm up your voice O minstrel, and sing Saʿdi's poems!
Bring over the liquor of affection, as wine is not what I enjoy.
[3.47] Saʿdi YE, 119.
In other cases, Saʿdi juxtaposes the intoxication deriving from wine with the higher degree of ecstatic obnubilation of the senses generated by the contemplation of the beloved:
Wine intoxicates people, but no elation they derive from contemplation.
So much he inebriates me, that no wine I want to imbibe.
[3.48] Saʿdi YE, 173. Other lines highlight the coexistence of diverging ethical stands (probably also reflecting Abū Bakr's and Saʿd I's different moral attitudes):
O cup-bearer, I am already intoxicated by this passion:
Pour me another drop, and you'll take me away from myself!
Narrow is their mind, short their sight, yet forgive them and toast!
My companions are drunk from libations, and I from contemplation!
[3.49] Saʿdi YE, 126.
For a survey of the culture of wine-drinking in medieval Iran and its representation in Persian Literature, see Floor 2014; Karimi-Hakkak 2014; Kazemi 2020, 565–71. Cf. Franklin Lewis's observations on the symbolism of wine in Rumi's poetry (Lewis 2000, 324–26), which may also apply to some of Saʿdi's representations of bacchanalia. For a compelling note on the physiological association between wine-induced intoxication and the effects of *samāʿ*, see Bākharzi 1345/1966, 229. See also Purjavādi 2008; 2012.

103 Saʿdi might have decided to underline the "spiritual" dimension of *samāʿ* (*samāʿ-i rūḥānī*) in order to emphasize the metaphysical ends of the theo-erotic quest staged in the ghazal. However, Bākharzī, in his chapter on *samāʿ*, defines the expression *samāʿ-i rūḥānī* as "a *samāʿ* session in which no food is served or consumed, and the only sweets, fragrances, and rosewater that are provided proceed from the unseen [*ghayb*]." Bākharzi 1345/1966, 228. Cf. Saʿdi's line on the sweetness descending from the unseen:
As sweet beauties appear from the invisible world [*ʿālam-i ghayb*]
The salt of passion opens wounds in the hearts of the intimate masters. (See chapter 8, p. 414).

In the following line from the *Khavātīm*, the poet juxtaposes the social space in which *samāʿ* is performed as a shared spiritual undertaking with the mental milieu in which the lyric subject revisits in solitude the visual "taste" of the invisible world:

> After congregating, they all left the circle [*dāyira*] and followed their path.
> We stayed, lingering and contemplating your mental image [*khayāl-i tu*].
> *Khavātīm* 673[104]

In the line from the *Ṭayyibāt* below too, Saʿdi stages the transition from the physical presence of an object of desire to a parallel between a *samāʿ* session taking place in a physical space and its imaginal analogue:

> The candle will soon fade away, stay with us O accommodating boy.
> Contemplating your face at dawn brings about the midday sunshine.
>
> The minstrel of the companions just left, the cup bearer of drunkards is asleep
> The sacred body of our beautiful witness [*shāhid*] is still here, our gathering goes on!
> *Ṭayyibāt* 224[105]

The difference between contemplating the beloved early in the morning and appreciating his or her beauty more thoroughly under the midday light appears in al-Ghazālī's example illustrating the parallels between, on the one hand, mental and optical vision, and, on the other, spiritual cognition (*maʿrifa*) and supernal contemplation (*mushāhada*).[106] We may refer to al-Ghazālī's example as the main framework through which Saʿdi juxtaposes the mental vision of archetypal beauty with the *entelechia* of the optical perception of a mundane beloved. The chronology of the micro-narrative contained in the two distichs sets out the transition from the enjoyment of an ideal setting—in which beautiful objects of contemplation are praised in the context of a lyrical ritual—to the solitude of the visionary experiences. In this imaginal setting, the mundane *shāhid* is converted into the incommensurable beauty of *our shāhid* as a form translating the celestial archetypes of beauty, and the

104 [3.50] Saʿdi YE, 301.
105 [3.51] Ibid., 105.
106 See Chapter 3 (pp. 168–70).

gathering turns into *our* mental gathering, where the conjunction between the heart and the Preserved Tablet takes shape.[107]

Through Sa'di's staged reciprocity between bodies and words, the ghazal fully acquires the performative function to which we alluded at the beginning of this chapter: the text incorporates within itself not only the body of the object of desire, but also the social ritual. In the next chapter we will explore the different levels of this transition, from the ghazal as a transcription of visual and performance experience to the composition of lyric poetry expected to stimulate the sacred eroticism that characterizes the ecstatic goal of *samāʿ* as a ritual. As we shall see, the final level of this process of textualization of the body generates the idea and the practice of ghazal composition as an analogue of the ritual, as if it were to substitute *samāʿ* altogether and act upon the senses of the reader through literary performativity even without performance.

107 Compare the implied metaphysics of these lines from Sa'di's early divan, the *Ṭayyibāt*, with the line analyzed immediately before: while the former de facto deny the relevance of the phenomenal experience, the latter—taken from the *Khavātīm*—produces a conflation between the physical and the metaphysical dimensions of the visionary experience.

CHAPTER 10

The Ghazal as Description of Performance, Ritualized Script, and "Performative" Analogue of *Samā'*

As novices, the people of the world follow the path of my poetry [*murīd-i sukhanam*],
For I trained [*riyāżat-kash*] my soul by praying by the *miḥrāb* of your eyebrows.
Badāyi' 497[1]

•••

My eyes see no one whom I could ever compare to him
No simulacrum of the beloved can ever appear in the lovers' eyes....

Sa'di, you wish to describe the visage of the beloved, over and over
Yet the beauty of the rose escapes the profuse comparisons of the eloquent nightingale.
Ṭayyibāt 172[2]

Even though Sa'di's name is not usually associated with the practice of *samā'*, we have seen how direct or indirect references to the lyrical ritual are ubiquitous in his works. The aim of this final chapter is to reconsider Sa'di's multilayered observations on *samā'* in light of the nexus between performance and performativity as aspects of the text that show the porosity between the surface of language and the world. Having reassessed the centrality of the visionary experience of *mushāhada* in Sa'di's ghazals in contexts that blend philosophical, Sufi, and lyrical discourses, we can now discern more clearly

1 [3.52] Sa'di YE, 228.
2 [3.53] Sa'di YE, 82.

 | DOI:10.1163/9789004435902_015

the potential connections that most of his poems might have had with the socio-cultural institution of *samāʿ* even in cases in which the spiritual aspect of the practice is not directly mentioned. The following ghazal, for instance, does not immediately read as a text that could revolve around the psychology of *mushāhada*. However, once we track down a few key signposts, the considerations exposed in the previous chapter will help us recognize how these lines can involve performance and performativity as a lyrical embodiment of the experience of *samāʿ*:

> I never said that fasting does not last for long:
> Spiritual purification [*riyāżat*] will end, along with hardship.
>
> Privation will be necessarily followed by serenity,
> But patience is all that man needs!
>
> For how long will the end of Ramadan hide its countenance?
> Will we see the new moon, similar to an eyebrow?
>
> Why do you close the garden in this season?
> Open its gates, so that the heart may open up!
>
> Tell the boys to burn aloe and incense,
> And let the girls sprinkle musk around,
>
> For I believe that the beloved, as tall as a cypress,
> As beautiful as a painting, is about to come greet us! …
>
> When the beloved is spoken of in the gathering,
> Ask the singer to refrain from reciting any songs,
>
> For poetry in such a gathering is not befitting,
> Unless it is Saʿdi who composed the lines!
>
> *Badāyiʿ* 463[3]

As soon as the description of the end of Ramadan comes to a close, Saʿdi's sudden shift to the laud of the beloved urges us to reconsider the metaphorical level of the ghazal: the celebration of breaking the fast turns out to be an allegorical representation of the spiritual training (*riyāżat*) that the Sufi manuals

3 [3.54] Saʿdi YE, 213.

describe as a preparation for the visionary experience.[4] The metaphorical association between the new moon appearing to the fasting beholder and the beauty of the beloved signals the preparation for the peak of the experience of *mushāhada* ("for the beloved [...] is about to come greet us!"). From this angle, we can also make better sense of the recommendation not to read poetry during *such* a gathering, which may constitute an ironic innuendo to the antithetical relationship between poetry and remembrance of God (*ẕikr*) prescribed by some Sufi authors. With these premises, Saʿdi's declaration stands out: it is his poetry that should be recited during *such* gatherings. In a way, through this approach, not only does Saʿdi tell us about *samāʿ*, but he also presents his poetry as a script for *samāʿ* and, simultaneously, even a performative analogue of *samāʿ* itself. The text enacts the performance until turning into the very body of performance.

This final part of the book opened with a passage from Roland Barthes's *Fragments d'un discours amoureux* in which the French critic compares language to one's skin. We may regard this metaphor, especially in light of its sensual innuendo ("I rub my language against the other"; "My language trembles with desire"), as an illustration of Saʿdi's representation of *his* ghazals as a form of embodiment of *samāʿ* in the context of the beholder's experience of the connection between the physical world and the realm of the unseen.

If we follow Austin's speech acts theory, we can look at Saʿdi's representation of *samāʿ* through the lens of three different functions, which can help us define the poet's complex approach to this ritual from the perspective of what words can *do* in their historical contexts of composition and circulation. Some of Saʿdi's ghazals may simply talk about *samāʿ* as "meta-ritualistic" or, in Austin's terms, "locutionary" texts. Other poems, as we shall see, present themselves or act as textual scripts to be recited on the occasion of a *samāʿ* session. In Austin's terms, these would be "illocutionary" texts, i.e., poems that directly or indirectly call for a performative occasion: ghazals that "ought to" be recited for the sake of being incorporated into the physical mechanism of a performance. In this case, the text *acts* in synergy with the ritual, it blends with the voices, the sounds, and the bodies that make the ritual possible. Other texts, finally, can function as analogues of the *samāʿ* experience itself, as "epideictic" or performative compositions, in the "perlocutionary" sense of the concept.[5]

---

4 See Chapter 9, pp. 472–75.

5 My reappropriation of Austin's (1975) distinction between illocutionary and perlocutionary texts is based on Barbara Cassin's and Jonathan Culler's assessment of the possibility of conceiving lyric performativity in terms of speech acts. See Cassin 2009; 2011; and Culler 2015, 125–31.

A ghazal with a meta-ritualistic or locutionary function is a text that may talk about or mention the practice of *samāʿ* as an extra-textual performance. Such ghazals read as documents attesting to the practice of *samāʿ* as it was performed in a variety of *milieux* and used as a psycho-physiological technique placed at the service of the imaginal exploration of the unseen. We may regard these poems as historical attestations to the practice of *samāʿ* and compare Saʿdi's scattered observations on this ritual with Sufi manuals circulating immediately before, during, and slightly after his lifetime.

The "illocutionary" function highlights the ghazal as a text acting as a script to be performed during a *samāʿ* session. In these cases, the text acts almost as an operatic libretto that exists in dynamic tension with the actual *samāʿ* ritual. Finally, the epideictic or "perlocutionary" function emerges from the possibility of bringing all traces of external contexts of performativity into the core of the lyric: the ghazal turns into the performative experience itself, as a linguistic substitute for the practice of *samāʿ*. Through their inherent epideictic dimension, certain ghazals reach an intimate level of independence from the external world that allows their circulation amidst a plurality of historical contexts.

The study of the illocutionary aspect of some of Saʿdi's ghazals is a necessary step to understanding the mechanisms that contribute to the constitution of his lyrics as epideictic texts capable of embodying the *samāʿ* ritual. The illocutionary function of Saʿdi's ghazals, i.e., the either direct or indirect possibility for the text to offer itself as the script for a performance ritual, can appear in poems that were actually performed in specific historical settings, poems that meta-ritually mention the practice of *samāʿ*, and poems whose intrinsic formal and thematic structure calls for a performative reading.[6]

The first class of instances reveals Saʿdi's creative engagement with the composition of ghazals crafted to meet the demands of specific strands of the literary market in the arena of *samāʿ* rituals. We may classify Saʿdi's praise of his own poetic talent from the perspective of the different audiences that circulated his ghazals in response to their specific socio-political, aesthetic, and spiritual expectations. We have discussed Saʿdi's reluctance to present himself as a court poet during the early phase of Abū Bakr's rule. With prince Saʿd II, his son Muḥammad, and the last male atabegs of the Salghurid dynasty,

6 This aspect refers to specific formal characteristics of a ghazal (meter, internal rhymes, alliteration, consonances, etc.) that facilitate the act of performing its lines. Even though critics often praise the smoothness of Saʿdi's poetry, the link between his lyrical style and its musical subtext still lacks an in-depth study. A good point of departure for filling this gap in the scholarship might be a comparison between Saʿdi's ghazals and Rumi's *Dīvān-i Shams*, whose intrinsic musicality has been the object of several studies. See Shafiʿi-Kadkani 1377/1998, xxiii–xxviii.

Muḥammad-Shāh and Saljūq-Shāh, Saʿdi's rhetorical posture shifted to meet the aesthetic needs of a plurality of audiences, which explains the spectrum of his registers, ranging between the purely courtly, the spiritual, the pedagogical, and even the obscene. After the mid-1260s, the geopolitical horizon of the formative phase of the Ilkhanid empire was shaped by the Juvaynī brothers, ʿAṭā' Malik and Shams al-Dīn, who relied on a plurality of Sufi networks to exert their power pervasively.[7] Saʿdi must have seen the practice of *samāʿ* as the perfect venue to broadcast his literary renown in a trans-regional setting.

Saʿdi's intimations as to the necessity of reading his poetry as illocutionary texts to be performed in order to enliven the *samāʿ* rituals show the courtly derivation of his literary pride. In such instances, the mention of the *majlis* acts as a reminiscence of his activity at court and a reflection on the role that a professional lyric poet can take up when offering his rhetorical skills in the cause of spiritual aesthetics in a ritualized setting:

> Soon enough people will imagine that the morning
> Shines in the middle of the night, if you display the sun of your face....
>
> Clear the pages of thinking, recite the poems Saʿdi composed:
> Bring forth a load of pearls and scatter them around the gathering!
>
> *Ṭayyibāt* 54[8]

Other ghazals are closer to the one with which we opened this chapter, as the imagery that they feature speaks directly to the Sufi context of the performance that Saʿdi wished to orchestrate through the recitation of his own verse:

> The morals inspector chases the libertines, but
> Does he know about the Sufis chasing the boys for sacred ends [*ṣūfiyān-i shāhid-bāz*]? ...
>
> No nightingale knows about this story,
> No singer can perform with this voice.
>
> All goods arise from a precious source:
> Sugar from Egypt, Saʿdi from Shiraz!
>
> *Ṭayyibāt* 199[9]

7 See General Introduction, pp. 22–23.
8 [3.55] Saʿdi YE, 28.
9 [3.56] Saʿdi YE, 93–94.

Sa'di's comparison between luxury commodities and poetry reminds us of how different sources attest to the success of Sa'di's "marketing" strategy. In Anatolia, poets such as Rumi and Sayf-i Farghānī, for whom *samā'* constituted one of the key elements of their Sufi orthopraxis, would often make use of Sa'di's lines, through recitation and literary imitation, to enrich the spiritual and aesthetic discourses of their own communities.[10] Various hagiographic accounts, including *Siyar al-awliyā'* (composed by Amīr Khʷard in the 1350s), provide extensive descriptions of how Sa'di's ghazals were featured prominently in the *samā'* sessions taking place at the *khānaqāh* of the Chishti Sufi master Niẓām al-Dīn Awliyā' (d. 1325) in Delhi.[11] The case of the intertextual relations between Sa'di and Humām-i Tabrizī is particularly telling, as we may regard the latter as a key link between the spiritual policies of the Juvaynī family and the Persian-speaking literary arena during the second half of the 13th century.[12] The exceedingly positive outcome of Sa'di's "illocutionary" ambition is also attested to by Humām's declaration that, in the context of *samā'* sessions, sublime sensation (*ẕawq*) can only be achieved through the recitations of ghazals crafted in Shiraz.[13]

Among the ghazals in which Sa'di does not directly allude to the performance of *samā'*, some texts have received such a high degree of attention by his contemporaries that one may consider them as scripts intended to be

---

10 See Yazdānparast 1393/2014, 1: 696–725, 729–34. Sayf-i Farghānī, for instance, incorporated the last line of the ghazal quoted above to frame his own renown through Sa'di's fame:
It is now your turn, Sayf of Fergana:
Cast commotion into the world with your poetry,
For "sugar from Egypt and Sa'di from Shiraz"
Praise the beauty of your speech.
[3.57] Sayf Farghāni 1341–44/1962–65, 2: 95.

11 Ibid., 1: 738–46. On the role of *samā'* in the Chishti order during the epoch of the Delhi Sultanate, see Ernst and Lawrence 2002, 34–46.

12 Some manuscripts copied in the 14th and 15th centuries reveal that Humām was perceived as an active imitator of Sa'di's poetry. See for instance the reference that a miscellaneous collection of poems, Lālā Ismā'īl 487 (copied between 1340 and 1343), makes to their "poetic interactions" (*mu'ārażāt*, see Ingenito 2014, 77–78), and the several instances in which the copyist of an early Timurid manuscript transmitting Humām's *dīvān* quotes the first lines of the ghazals by Sa'di that were the object of Humām's responses. See Ms. Or., Suppl. persan 1531, ff. 15a, 27b, 44a, 73a, 73b, 74a. A similar list has been found in the oldest manuscript collecting Humām al-Dīn's works, copied in 1338–39. See Ms. Mar'ashi 16509, ff. 105b–107b. On Humām's role in the circulation of Sa'di's ghazals among the political elite of his time after the death of the older poet, see General Introduction, p. 25.

13 In their lyrical ritual [*samā'*] the seekers of "sublime sensations" [*ẕawq*]
ought to listen [*istimā'*] to the poetry created in Shiraz!
[3.1] Homām-e Tabrizi, 1351/1972, 106.

circulated on the occasion of lyrical rituals. In one of these ghazals, Saʿdi stages the psychological effects of the epiphany of beauty:

> What a wondrous sedition your beauty cast into the world:
> Not for a single breath could one cast his glances away from you.
> *Badāyiʿ* 468[14]

In his creative response, Humām alludes to the context of *samāʿ* by mentioning the performative event that prompted his composition as a re-appropriation of Saʿdi's rhythm of images:

> Once again, O minstrel, you cast a song [*ḥadīs̱ī*] among us:
> You cast such a sedition amidst the gathering of the lords of the heart!
>
> You disclosed our mystery among the elites and the commoners
> And cast this story onto the lips of all these people.
>
> You brought the beholders and the beautiful boys to the *samāʿ*
> And cast the intoxicated nightingales in the middle of the rose garden.[15]

The reference to a song or an "account" (*ḥadīs̱ī*) in verse could be read as an allusion to Saʿdi's ghazal, which was presumably performed during a *samāʿ* session that prompted Humām's *javāb*. The intrinsic illocutionary function of this specific ghazal by Saʿdi is also attested to by the responses of Sayf-i Farghānī (who directly quotes one of Saʿdi's hemistichs)[16] and a twofold response by Fakhr al-Dīn ʿIrāqī, one part of which alludes to the specific habit of entrusting one's cloak to the performer (*qavvāl*) as a result of ecstatic rapture (*vajd*):

> Moved by a sublime sensation [*ẕawq*], anyone who had a heart
> Cast it away upon listening to the song [*ḥadīs̱*] of your beauty....
>
> When ʿIrāqī heard the song lauding the beloved [*ḥadīs-i dust*] during the lyrical ritual,
> He cast not his cloak to the singer [*qavvāl*], but his own soul.[17]

---

14 [3.58] Saʿdi YE, 215.
15 [3.59] Homām-e Tabrizi, 1351/1972, 144.
16 Sayf- Farghāni 1341–44/1962–65, 2: 215–17.
17 [3.60] ʿErāqi 1375/1996, 146.

In Bīsutūn's second draft of his introduction to the *Kulliyāt*, we have a compelling source of evidence for the propensity to make use of Saʿdi's ghazals as scripts to be enacted in the context of ritualized gatherings. His account, quoted in full in the introduction the third part of this book, demonstrates that Saʿdi's ghazals were performed during *samāʿ* sessions as a primary source for the achievement of "sublime sensations" well into the 14th century. Even though Bīsutūn mentions that only the first four lines of the text were recited, a close look at the remainder of the ghazal can provide some insight into the rhetorical strategies through which Saʿdi crafted his poem as a "pre-scriptive" catalyst of the entrancing experience that his audiences wished to gain from *samāʿ*:

> The gaze of God's beholders seeks no lust;
> There are no erroneous steps in the journey of the passionate wayfarers.
>
> Over and over the beholders contemplate human beauty with their gazes,
> Only one glance is accorded to the commoners: forbidden is the second.
>
> A florid plant you ought to be when the morning breeze blows,
> Not a lifeless mineral that stands inert when grazed by the zephyr.
>
> What bliss if you die with your heart fully alive:
> A new life you'd enjoy which no end can dissolve.
>
> Set your eyes upon whomever cleanses your being from darkness:
> May God prevent you from staring at those bereft of any purity.
>
> You don't ask about your friends? What city are you from?
> Maybe in the country where you are no loyalty survives?
>
> Should the beholders' bones burn as reeds catching fire,
> They'd feel no pain, like the tambour when it is struck.
>
> Others shall recount [*ḥikāyat*] all that I may say about love
> But as no experience [*muʿāmalat*] they have, their words lack insight!
>
> *Ṭayyibāt* 301[18]

18 [3.61] Saʿdi YE, 138. I have edited the text on the basis of Ms. Kabul 1325, 384. In the manuscripts of the Bīsutūn recension (see, for instance, Ms. Tehran 1352, 5; Ms. Qom 1371, f. 2a) the first line features *zi sar-i havā* ("out of lust") instead of *ṭalab-i havā* ("seeking

In this ghazal we witness how Saʿdi suggests the existence of a form of reciprocity between the horizon of poetic diction and the physical experience of the world. Overall, the poem reads as a key to access the transition from the contained eroticism of the textual experience of *samāʿ* to the psychological awareness with which the "cognizers/beholders" may set their eyes on the physical bodies that inhabit the world and let their gaze dwell well beyond what is allowed to inexperienced commoners. In the last line, Saʿdi explicitly confronts the lyric tradition by claiming that his own lyricism (and not that of the "others") attains and provides spiritual insight by means of the peculiar experience of transcendent desire that characterizes his pragmatic understanding of the invisible meanings inhabiting human beauty.[19] At the risk of overinterpreting Saʿdi's wording, one may be tempted to recognize in this contextual use of the word *ḥikāyat* (lit., the "narration" or the "depiction") the Avicennian psychological paradigm of the compositive imagination, which translates into images the intimations that the practical intellect receives from the soul of the fixed stars.[20] What Saʿdi offers is therefore the visualization of the spiritual understanding of beauty as an experience that words can reproduce by converting spiritual bewilderment into aesthetic ecstasy.

In a certain way, Saʿdi presents his own literary identity as the inspired individual whom al-Ghazālī describes in the passage analyzed in the eighth chapter (the fourth phase of the visionary experience): the subject who, once he has "tasted" the contact between his intellect and the Preserved Tablet, knows how to "recognize" the invisible though the contemplation of the forms of the world. The blinding experience of *ẕawq* corresponds to the confusion of the individual when contemplating beauty without possessing the cognitive and spiritual resources that would allow him to make sense of it beyond

---

lust"). This slight semantic variation implies different approaches to the contemplation of human beauty for spiritual ends, for *ṭalab-i havā* signals the possibility of an active erotic quest, similar to the third phase of the model of the visionary experience illustrated by al-Ghazālī.

19 Compare Saʿdi's statement on his privilege as an inspiration that derives directly from "real" experience with the following lines:
Anyone who falls in love in the alley of the anemone-cheeked beauties
By no means will ever come back to his reason....
What kind of *miḥrāb*s are your seductive eyes?
Should the heathens see them, they would embrace our prayer....
With this pain, I scream my shouts from the heat of my lungs,
Unlike the others, whose words stem from futile affectations [*majāz*].
[3.62] Saʿdi YE, 208–209.

20 See chapters 6 and 7.

the phenomenal forms.[21] In the fourth phase, the spiritually inspired beholder acquires the capability of simultaneously perusing both the visible and the supernal dimensions of reality. This leap bridges the gap between the theory of spiritual cognition and the poetic authorship that turns the ghazal into an aesthetic map poised to guide the reader through the experience of *samāʿ* as a form of psychological training.

1 From Descriptive Locution to Scripted Performance

Musician! Retune your melody, for I'm on the brink
Of letting the tune that you sing reveal my secret.

No one in this epoch has wept for the beloved as much as I have:
The breath of my words will leave Shiraz to reach the farthest lands.

They would often tell me: "Saʿdi, come back to your senses for one breath!"
"For the sake of the beloved, one should not be but beside oneself."

Ṭayyibāt 259[22]

The following ghazal constitutes one of the cases in which a text explicitly mentioning the technical vocabulary that pertains to *samāʿ* was presumably composed to be performed during a lyrical ritual. The textual discrepancies that appear in the manuscripts suggest that the ghazal was the object of multiple authorial renditions, probably in the context of different instances of recitation on the occasion of *samāʿ* performances. While the main body of the text enacts the relationship between moral judgment and visionary experience in the context of the role of the senses in their approach to erotic contemplation and poetry recitation, the final line introduces Saʿdi as the guiding voice through which the listener may vicariously experience the "meaning" of the ghazal:

21 Al-Ghazālī clarifies on multiple occasions that some spiritual practitioners turn senseless and have no recollection of their trance-like state. Others (whose "faculty of imagination," in Avicennian terms, "may happen to have been created strong and dominant." Gutas 2006b, 345) do recall their visionary experience and are capable of describing it as translated by their internal senses. *Kimiyā*, 1: 91–92, 490.

22 [3.63] Saʿdi YE, 120.

Ecstatically [*ba ẕawq*] the wind reveals the fragrance of the garden.
The morning arises, the night is gone: extinguish the candle!

If it's true that—as you did to me—you can intoxicate and ravish all men,
Reveal your face to the pious man, offer the ascetic a taste of your liqueur.

Those who vilify the spiritual beholders [*ʿārifān*] cannot hear the secret of *samāʿ*.
Play for us mellifluous melodies, so that those joyless folks may leave us alone.

Forsake the cloak, serve some wine, bring that liquor, forget about hardship!
Unaware is the rationalizer of the pleasurable life of those who have lost their senses....

The forearms and curls of the sorcerers secretly plunge their blade.
Why silently cry: who shall listen to our desperate shouts?

A lawful dance you desire [*raqṣ-i ḥalāl*]: follow the path of the spiritual beholders [*ahl-i maʿrifat*]!
Stomp while dancing on this world, and move your hands to the rhythm of the hereafter!

Will you keep urging me not to run after the beautiful ones?
I have no choice: my passion [*shawq*] pushes me forth, against my will....

The springtime breeze and the fragrance of the roses beg for your voice, Saʿdi:
You are an eloquent nightingale, shame on all this silence!

Ṭayyibāt 151[23]

---

23 [3.64] I have edited the ghazal on the basis of Ms. Kabul 1325, 333. Cf. Saʿdi YE, 72–73 and, for the substantial variants found in the manuscript tradition, ibid., 414. The meter of this ghazal is a "doubled" (*mukarrar*) *rajaz* meter (*rajaz-i muṣamman-i maṭvī va makhbūn*), as it features a caesura in the middle of each hemistich that replicates the metrical pattern of the first half of each *bayt*. The peculiar structure of this meter creates an internal system of repetitions that makes it particularly apt for musical performances. The Kabul manuscript features some non-standard (albeit permissible) metrical characteristics that are not found in other manuscripts. For instance, the first halves of the second and fourth hemistichs close with words ending in "overlong" (rather than long) syllables:

The drama that in Saʿdi's "early ghazals" derives from the confrontation of the lyric subject against its ethical underpinnings is also the source of the dynamic continuity between poetry and experience that surfaces throughout Saʿdi's lyric output. Some of these early ghazals, like the one quoted above, showcase the performative quest of the lyric self in a fashion that breaks free from the scholastic context of *samāʿ* and places this practice in conversation with the act of composing poetry as an experience that is simultaneously biographical and fictive.

In the following text, the poet's meditations on his own life and experience are elevated to a higher degree of awareness of the lyric function vis-à-vis the psychology supporting the delicate mechanics of accessing beauty through one's physical eyes. The contrast between the unspoken ethical imperative of not nourishing carnal desire and the necessity of contemplating physical beauty to access the unseen is reminiscent of the frustration of the beholder when (in the third phase of the visionary experience exemplified by al-Ghazālī) he witnesses the discrepancy between the world of sense and the supernal realm:

1 Hold your beloved, even when the horizons are filled with enemies:
As he is the soothing balm, when the others sting you deeply.

2 O comely form! Before your countenance all the beauties of our time
Are but laconic talismans, timidly withering in their solitude.

3 Walk one morning toward the orchard, and you shall see
how the cypress will be uprooted from the banks of the stream.

4 How bitterly some commoners face the vexations of beautiful youths.
But listen to a sincere believer: sugar is what they scatter around!

---

shab guẕasht (instead of *rūz shud*, as attested by other manuscripts), and *namāy* (instead of *namā*). On this specific meter and the irregular caesurae of the doubled meters, see Thiesen 1982, 118–19, 162–63; Elwell-Sutton 1976, 88, 122–25). These non-standard endings suggest that (in a way not dissimilar from modern singing performances of classical Persian poetry) the first halves of the hemistichs of the opening lines were sung with an emphatic pause before the singer moved on to the rest of the *miṣrāʿ*. From this we may infer that the text transmitted by the Kabul manuscript reveals a trace of a preliminary unpolished rendition, which Saʿdi subsequently redrafted and circulated through other channels of transmission.

5 O austere devotee on the path of the heart: shut your eyes!
These beauties are renowned for snatching the people's hearts.

6 You may have to cast a veil upon your contemplative [*ta'ammul*] eyes,
Or entrust your heart, and all veils shall be lifted from your beholding.

7 I have no care for my life, but my frail heart is the jewel box
That preserves your secret: may it never break apart!

8 So rare in our epoch are my poetry and your beauty:
My eyes upon you, while everyone's ears enjoy my verses.

9 How could one contemplate the beloved's beauty as he truly *is*?
You ought to behold him through the path that Sa'di's glances have set.

Ṭayyibāt 206[24]

The main hermeneutical key to this ghazal lies in the meaning of the sixth line of the text, whose second hemistich is interpreted by most commentators as follows: "they will lift the veil from your actions"—with the implication that the subject of the sentence is the "beautiful ones" of the previous two lines. This reading generates a misunderstanding that resurfaces every time modern commentators interpret the imagery connected with the topic of the veil (*parda*) along the lines of ethical readings—the "veil" covering one's faults or hypocritical intentions—rather than as an epistemological (either cognitive or metaphysical) barrier that screens the subject from the truthful contemplation of the beloved.[25] The latter interpretation is supported by the syntax of the clause, in which the verb *bar afkanand* (lit. "they lift") acts as in an impersonal voice, which in English can be translated as a passive form: the veil shall be lifted, or "so that your veil may be lifted." This reading befits the ghazal's overarching theme of the contemplation of the beloved (here explicitly referred to as *ta'ammul*) as a practice that enables the beholder to conjoin his heart with the unseen and find a correspondence between the physical traces of beauty (the outstandingly beautiful "form" of the second line, *ṣūrat*) and the invisible, archetypal ideas (*ma'ānī*) that the internal senses of the lyric subject translate into mental images. The ethical modality of this ghazal exudes from the idea that Sa'di expresses in his last line, and according to which the spiritual value of the object of contemplation is contingent upon the modality of the gaze on

24 [3.65] Sa'di YE, 97.

25 Barzegar-Khāleqi 1386/2008, 1: 546; Niyāzkār 1390/2012, 668.

his body. The reiterated emphasis that lines five, six, and seven place on the heart brings us to the spiritual cardiology that we have explored in the second part of this study.

The heart, which al-Ghazālī represented as a conflation of the psychological and epistemological functions of Avicenna's rational soul, reappears in these lines as an organ that meditates on the physical beauty of the objects of desire (line five), opens up toward the metaphysics of the contemplation of beauty (line six), and finally preserves the cypher of the correspondence between the mental image of the beloved and its supernal ideal (the beloved's "secret," *sirr*—line seven). Moreover, al-Ghazālī's dual approach to spiritual knowledge as a potentially conflictual epistemological posture that can either dismiss the value of sensorial perception (what he calls the "path of the Sufis") or rely on the senses to achieve *maʿrifa* through syllogistic observation of the world (*iʿtibār*, *tafakkur*, *taʾammul*) is reflected in the dramatic conundrum of the fifth and sixth lines: on the one hand, the pious subject's desire to gaze upon the beloved's body and, on the other, the ethical necessity of withdrawing one's glances from potential sources of temptation.

The twist in the lyric narrative that turns this ghazal into an excellent source of theorization for Saʿdi's poetics of spiritual and cognitive performativity appears in the penultimate line, in which the poetic persona traces a correlation between the unique beauty of the beloved and the inimitability of Saʿdi's poetic style. By means of this parallel, Saʿdi anchors the value of the poetic description of the beloved to the meaning of the contemplative experience of beholding his beauty. He offers an abstracted physical experience transfigured into literary representation as a psychological tool that urges its audience to cognize the beloved as *he is* (*chunān ki ūst*).

The ontological problem of cognizing the true nature of the beloved implies the opposition between levels of reality that are hierarchically more or less "true" than others. Our previous discussion of the Avicennian foundations of the aspects of Saʿdi's poetry that fit al-Ghazālī's spiritual aesthetics of cognition showed us that we cannot conclude that the true nature of the beloved—the beloved as he quintessentially *is*—corresponds to a vaguely mystical manifestation of God. As maintained in the second part of the book, the depiction of the beloved as a divine infusion (referred to as incarnationism, *ḥulūl*) is a heterodox inference from both a theological and a psychological perspective—the latter being a flaw to which the estimative faculty (*vahm*) may succumb.

Considering the eccentricity of incarnationism in the theological and psychological tradition to which Saʿdi's aesthetics are anchored, the possibility of the lyric subject seeing God in the face of the beloved is an intellectual conflation that the logic of the ghazal can only support as a deviation from the lyric subject's cognitive system. On the contrary, what the lyric subject may "see" is the ideal essence of the beloved as it is reflected onto his own heart through the process of conjunction with what al-Ghazālī calls the "Preserved Tablet," and Avicenna, the soul of the fixed stars. In the seventh line, the vagueness with which Saʿdi alludes to an unspecified "secret" ("[…] my frail heart is the jewel box / That preserves your secret […]") certainly relates to the common theme of the secretive and forbidden affection between the lover and the beloved—a topic that exudes from the entire history of medieval lyric poetry. However, considering the aesthetics of the visionary context in which this ghazal takes shape, we could read the "secret" ingrained in the heart of the lyric persona in light of al-Ghazālī's theorization of the secret that inhabits the human heart and participates in the contemplation of the visible forms of the world as traces of a supernal equilibrium. The juxtaposition of the spiritual aesthetics of the heart's secret with the sudden praise of the unrivaled preeminence of the poet's own style along with the beloved's beauty involves a transition from the performativity of the quest for the invisible to the incorporation of any possible experience into the poetic diction. It is the same poetic diction that Saʿdi regulates and offers to his audience as the linguistic translation of the visual truth that his eyes can experience as it *is* or, as it *were* to *be*.

2 Transfiguring the Text into a Performative Experience

> You said that you would never contemplate beautiful bodies:
> You shall, if you experience gazing in the fashion of Saʿdi.
> *Ṭayyibāt*/*Badāyiʿ* 181[26]

The psychological link between the mundane aspect of the lyric subject's perusal of phenomenal reality and the spiritual understanding of the invisible constitutes the spine of Saʿdi's constant emphasis on the presentation of his literary persona as a fictitious author engaged in the active exploration of the world. As often remarked in the second chapter, in the context of the *Gulistān*, the kaleidoscopic multiplicity of experiences through which Saʿdi stages his own persona as an inspired anthropologist *ante litteram* offers an extraordinary vantage point for the exploration of the poet's lyric enactment of experience. The more Saʿdi offers his audience semi-fabricated (and yet credible) accounts of his worldly peregrinations, the more his abstracted lyricism conveys the sensation of real presences, tangible possibilities of the transmutation

26 [3.66] Saʿdi YE, 85–86.

of reality into delicate rhythms and compelling images. Saʿdi's lyrical effort eventually emerges as a rarefied form of experience that allows the reader to reenact the psychological journey of the poetic persona from physical contact with the world to inspired perception of the supernal realities. Far from being the description of an experience, the ghazal presents itself as the experience that can survive and find meaningful continuity well beyond the controlled environment of not only reclusive meditation on the divine, but even the mundane circles of the *samāʿ* sessions.

Poetry composition transitions from the status of mere literary exercise to the incorporation of bodily and spiritual experiences that guide the reader through the meanderings of the visible world, at its intersection with the supernal meanings that the signs of tangible reality constantly signify beyond themselves:

> I explored the world, contemplated it, and then returned:
> No one's form may ever compete with the beauty of the *imaginings* [*taṣāvīr*] of him.
>
> O Saʿdi, sweet is your tongue, why all this commotion?
> Our *shāhid* is a sacred sign [*āyat*], and *all this* is the exegesis [*tafsīr*] of his presence.
>
> *Badāyiʿ* 604[27]

"All this" (*īn hama*) attests to the function of lyric poetry to act as a transcription of both the lyric subject's participative perusal of the world and the recognition of ideal forms. Although these may be applied to specific objects of desire that belong to the poet's real objects of contemplation, they ultimately pertain to language itself, and attest to the psychological inspection of the invisible as an act that reads as the linguistic translation of vision. The *shāhid*, the young man bearing witness to the supernal sources of beauty, ceases to be an object of tangible contemplation placed alongside all the other forms of the world, and enters the language of the poet as an ideal of beauty that temporarily nullifies the aesthetic value of the visible world. The commotion that the presence of the mental *shāhid* generates attests to the limits of language vis-à-vis the representation of ideal beauty in a space that constantly oscillates between the sexual possibilities of imagination and the tension pulling the heart toward the heavenly archetypes. Notwithstanding the incapability of the lyric subject to fathom ideal beauty through language, it is the logical power of

27 [3.67] Saʿdi YE, 604.

poetry that overcomes the confusing commotion that the ecstatic moment of inward contemplation generates. The final hemistich addresses this very commotion and offers the parallel between the imaginal body of the ideal beloved and the Quranic correlation between the divine nature of its verses (*āyāt*) and the mundane aspect of its traditional exegetical act (*tafsīr*): the imaginal body turns into a sacred scripture capable of translating the truth into lyric links between the text and the world.

Verbalization of the imaginal content that aspires to mental representation of ideal beauty as a form of control of the interaction between the body of the subject, the world, and the supernal realm involves a renewed approach to the meaning of sensual attraction. In the following lines, Saʿdi explores the body of the beloved as if it were a book capable of embodying the perception of a real presence inhabiting the world and the realm of imagination, in which mental representations oscillate between wakefulness and dreams:

> The beauty of your downy beard is but a chapter from the book of your nature;
> The sweetness of your portrayals are but a letter from an entire book....
>
> You took sleep away from the eyes of the Masters of Gazes:
> Do you fear they may dream about your image while asleep?
>
> From my fiery poetic nature my words flow like water:
> As the blazes of your face, dripping sensual sweat.
>
> All my companions are with the beloved, while I long in pain:
> Everyone drinks from a source of water, but Saʿdi draws upon a mirage.
> *Ṭayyibāt/Badāyiʿ* 131[28]

The lines above eloquently portray both the sensual carnality of Saʿdi's lyricism and the spiritual dimension of his sacred eroticism. The establishment of an analogy between the author's poetic creativity and the seductive sweat of the beloved entrusts literary imagination with the key to the realm of the invisible without need for recurring to specific spiritual practices, such as contemplative seclusion or inspired lyrical rituals. The poet's praise of his own poetic skills eventually constitutes a strategy for him to reinvigorate the apparently static set of images that constitute the conventions of the lyric canon with a

---

28 [3.68] Saʿdi YE 63–64. Most manuscripts feature this ghazal in the *Badāyiʿ*. See ibid., 406. My edition is based on Ms. Kabul 1325, 324.

creative operation that stages life and literature in a simultaneous interplay within the text itself.

Sa'di showcases this process in a ghazal that represents one of the peaks of his lyric creativity. The poem with which I wish to conclude this book attests to Sa'di's lifetime quest for turning his own poetry into an everlasting monument capable of embracing all the diverse facets of his anthropological élan:

> I have never seen a man as splendid as you are!
> Look at your forms, your features ... you must be an angel! ...
>
> We have written our book, it enacts our love for you:
> And you, so ruthless in your heart, are effacing our story....
>
> Bewilderment overtakes me when I try to describe you:
> Beauty has its limits, but you transgress them all!
>
> The spiritual beholders of Fars lower their heads before the lines of your beard:
> Perhaps it is a line by Sa'di that they read, which you inscribed on your countenance?
>
> *Badāyi'* 398[29]

These lines stand out as the most accomplished manifesto of Sa'di's lyric project, as they combine the psychological theo-eroticism of beholding the unseen with the poet's inscription of his own fictitious subjectivity upon the face of the object of contemplation. The mention of Fars anchors the text to a level of external reality (al-Ghazālī's fourth phase) that speaks to the performative context that Sa'di incorporates within the representation of an object of desire which is simultaneously erotically mundane, semiotically spiritual, and fictitiously literary. The closing line represents the downy beard of the beloved, *khaṭ(ṭ)*, in a fashion similar to the ghazals in which Sa'di describes the fuzzy lines on his cheeks as the scripture attesting to the unfathomable power of the divine creation:

> On the page-like cheek of the beautiful ones they see the downy-beard [*khaṭ*],
> Short is their sight! But the beholder [*'ārif*] contemplates the pen of God's creation.

29 [3.69] Sa'di YE, 185; Ms. Tehran 1296, 427.

> Everyone's eyes peruse your face with so much passion, but
> The self-worshippers discern no difference between Truth and lust.[30]

As analyzed in the fourth chapter, the modality of the spiritual beholder's gaze is a rational-inferential posture capable of overcoming the base urges of the flesh. The final goal of this rationalized access to beauty is the establishment of what we have called the "imaginal-cosmological" psychology of the visionary experience. During the transition between these two modalities, the bodily presence of both the onlooker and the object of gazing constitute the main filter capable of potentially leading to a twofold error: incarnationism (*ḥulūl*) or lustful desires that do not seek "meanings" other than the physical surface of the flesh.

The line on the spiritual beholders of Fars directly implies this very tension. However, in the second hemistich, Sa'di brings about a twist that radically transforms the framework of the contemplative theo-eroticism from the point of view of its performative agency: whilst the fine beard of the beloved is a sign attesting to the divine power for the beholders' perusal, it also *reads* as a line from Sa'di's own poetry, which the beloved figuratively inscribes on his own face through his newly-sprouted downy marks of beauty: "Perhaps it is a line by Sa'di that they read, which you inscribed on your countenance?"

If we compare the line on the page-like face of the beloved with that on the beholders of Fars, the extraordinary implication of Sa'di's manipulation of the imagery related to the spiritual eroticism of the beloved's downy beard lies in the poet's implicit presentation of himself as the analogue of the divine presence, while his poetry figuratively replaces the creation of God. In the second hemistich of the line on the beholders of Fars, the adverb *magar* ("perhaps") establishes an ingenious correspondence between the physical presence of the beloved and the lyrical transmutation of his body into poetic representation. By doing so, Sa'di stages within the same line both the body of sensual experience and the lyrical repetition of the same body as a source of dual inspirational possibility for the audience. Through this process, the reader is converted into both the listener and the beholder of an experience that comes to the surface of poetry as a result of the lyrical domestication of spiritual audition and inspired contemplation with no need for either audition proper or material perusal of a bodily presence.

Sa'di's project involves both the domestication of the erotic experience and the lyrical reification of the lyrical ritual: the only body that is left to the audience is the incorporation, within his poetic output, of the sensorial effects of

30 [2.3] See Chapter 5 (p. 275).

visual desire and the spiritual "taste" of *samāʿ* regardless of the actual modality of exposure to these texts. This means that whatever tension the potentially metaphysical and potentially obscene possibilities of desire may involve, they are conflated within the aesthetic autonomy of the ghazal as a lyric discourse that binds together eroticism and spirituality through the representation of the sublime (the ecstatic *vajd* of the onlookers) as a linguistic act. *As if* the world of experience were to be enacted by the texture of the lyric. And *as if* the poet were to defy the divine act of creation, and introduce his language into the world as a constant creative act of lyrical manipulation, between the visible and the invisible facets of the secret of beauty.

Epilogue: Poetry as a Mirror for Experience

Almost like the titles of Saʿdi's works inscribed in the globes that appear in the frontispieces of the oldest manuscripts of the *Kulliyāt* (see plates III, IV), sensual desire, visionary spirituality, ethical insight, and political wisdom rotate around the core of the literary genius of the Shirazi poet. The inimitable balance that smoothly, almost invisibly, holds these different souls of Saʿdi's poetic language together constitutes the real wonder that inhabits the *Ṭayyibāt*, the *Badāyiʿ*, and the *Khavātīm* as nuanced condensations of the entirety of the poet's literary corpus.

If there is a humanistic value in Saʿdi's poetry (as has been occasionally claimed), it ought to be sought in the point of contact between the different dimensions of Saʿdi's multifaceted lyrical genius: their contribution to the poet's attempt to explore reality and the literary tradition to which he belongs, with a view to generating in his varied audiences the sort of impact that would provoke them to peruse the world and constantly meditate on human experiences. The value of experience (performed in all its different contextual possibilities: political, erotic, courtly, metaphysical, ludic, etc.) constitutes Saʿdi's ultimate ethical teaching. And it is toward the quest for experience that the poet oriented the entire spectrum of his rhetorical skills, in a fashion that, as we have seen in the last part of this book, tends to convert poetry into experience itself.

In Saʿdi's ghazals, political reality, carnal desire, the visible world and the realm of the unseen are not depicted as mimetic representations of some form of truth. Rather, they are alluded to through the inspiring power of poetic language, which provides readers and listeners with metaphorical thrusts that generate a constant interplay between images and words. Saʿdi's language, therefore, explores the subtle gap between what exists and what might come into existence, between the visualized and the envisioned, between recollection of past events and reveries of future forms of serene fulfillment.

With these final remarks on the intended psychological impact of Saʿdi's poetry, I wish to establish a dynamic point of contact between this book and a publication by Justine Landau that appeared a few years ago, and which investigates the poetics and the logical essence of medieval Persian poetry from the perspective of two 13th-century scholars, Shams-i Qays-i Rāzī (d. ca. 1230s) and Naṣīr al-Dīn Ṭūsī (d. 1274), who contributed in different ways to the shaping of the intellectual life of the Salghurid and Ilkhanid courts. *De rythme & de raison*, which is the title of Landau's seminal monograph, offers a peculiar approach to the logic of poetry that speaks directly to the balance between

 DOI:10.1163/9789004435902_016

rhythmical creativity and the controlled exercise of reason that characterizes Saʿdi's lyricism. By expanding on the Aristotelian and Avicennian foundations of Naṣīr al-Dīn's observations on the physiology of the moving effects of poetry, Justine Landau emphasizes the "efficacy of the poetic discourse in the eyes of the philosophers" as an action that, unlike illusions, "insinuates into the soul images capable of generating an emotional response without hindering the faculty of judgment."[1]

What Saʿdi's obscene fragments, political praise poems, and *samāʿ*-oriented performative lyrics have in common is the effort to generate a portrayal of sensual, ethical, and supernal realities that, on the one hand, corresponds to what the senses can witness, and on the other appeals to the tremendous capabilities of the intellect and the imaginative faculties. Landau elaborates on the pleasure and awe that Avicenna associates with the contemplation and the recognition of the work of art when it is partially disconnected from its original form. Similarly, the poetic imitation of the external forms, as we have seen with Saʿdi's perusal of the intimate body parts of the object of desire as well as the pure "meanings" descending from the unseen, does not produce resemblance, but a form of verisimilitude that translates into a "possibility of existence."[2]

Just as al-Ghazālī represents the Preserved Tablet as a mirror reflecting the spectrum of past events or future possibilities, Naṣīr al-Dīn frames poetry as a logic that, far from persuading through a rational discourse, is capable of depicting the lingering effects of past actions or previewing potential future states.[3] According to al-Ghazālī and the Sufi and poetic traditions that followed his intuitions, the goal of the spiritual cleansing of the heart that leads to the contemplation of the supernal realities is the acquisition of eternal bliss in the hereafter. On the other hand, the interplay that poetry generates between the imperfect imitation of reality and the depiction of credible fictive forms aims to move the souls of listeners and readers and induce them toward action—*as if* the events poetry describes were real.

Naṣīr al-Dīn's description of the physiological responses to the solicitation caused by poetry (symptoms such as "contraction," *qabż*, and "dilatation," *basṭ*) reflects the role that Saʿdi ascribes to his own lyric as an embodiment of the experience of *samāʿ*: a tool to access the invisible through the enjoyment of the forms of the world and their repetition within the boundaries of poetic language. A similar representation of the physiological function of poetry is found in the anonymous introduction to the early 14th-century anthology that

1 Landau 2013, 254.
2 Ibid., 232.
3 Ibid., 243–46.

contains one of the oldest selections of Saʿdi's poetry, including ghazals, *qasidas* and obscene pieces. The collector of the original anthology, probably writing only a few years after Saʿdi's death, points out that obscene and serious poetry (*hazl va jidd*) equalize nature's uneven alternation of contractions and dilatations: whenever readers are under the pressure of contractions, they may find relief in the levity of the obscene, whereas serious poetry may offer relief from excessive dilatation.[4]

From this point of view, while Saʿdi crafted his *qasidas* to attract the favor of his patrons and simultaneously promote the values of justice and good governance as mirrors intended to perfect the moral qualities of the rulers, he entrusted to his ghazals the function of stimulating the imagination of the reader as a form of aesthetic training for the external and internal senses in their experience of the physical and the metaphysical world:

> No form [*ṣūratī*] could ever contain all this meaning [*maʿnī*]
> No *sūra* [*sūratī*] could ever contain the signs of all these sacred verses [*āyat*].
>
> Descriptions cannot convey the perfection of your body's beauty,
> Unless a mirror reflects it and mimics it [*ḥikāyat*] as it is.
>
> My words and cogitations reached their apogee and ultimate boundaries,
> But the description of your beauty is yet to reach its pinnacle.
> *Ṭayyibāt* 149[5]

The object of desire surfaces to the senses as a conglomeration of signs that are both sensual (as the emergence of meanings seeking formal expression) and, through the reference to the Quranic verses (*āyāt*), scriptural—as divine impressions on the Preserved Tablet, also referred to as *umm al-kitāb*, or the celestial archetype of the Qurʾān. Ultimately, the manifestation of beauty, regardless of its origin, belongs to the sensory perception that the poet strives to induce through the imaginal power of language.

However, just as the mirror of the heart/intellect cannot mimic the supernal meanings "as they are" without transmuting them into images though the intervention of the internal senses, the mirroring effort of language to repeat and mimic (*ḥikāyat*) beauty ought to recognize its own limits. Poetry cannot repeat the indescribable splendor of beauty, because descriptions cannot seize

4 Ms. Tehran 1296, 2.

5 [3.70] Saʿdi YE, 72. For the order of the lines, I have followed Ms. Tehran 1296, 432.

the essence of things as they are.[6] What poetry can do—and here I return to Justine Landau's intuition—is to produce physiological impressions in the souls of listeners and offer them as analogues of the experience of contemplation. This is exactly what Saʿdi expresses at the end of the ghazal quoted above:

No one's ears ever heard Saʿdi's scripture of farewell
Without being pervaded by the pain that his verses convey.

Saʿdi's seems to have learned from Alexander's final judgment the lesson that Niẓāmī provided in his anecdote on the competition between Chinese and Greek painters: artistic mastery requires both mimetic polishing and the creation of fictitious yet credible forms, just like the accomplished *ʿārif*—Saʿdi's *ʿārif*, a beholder active in the world—ought to peruse reality through the external senses and imagine the invisible by means of the internal faculties. Unfortunately, this piece of wisdom did not assist Alexander in his journey through the realm of darkness, as he failed to reach the magical spring of the "water of life."

Probably inspired by Shams-i Qays, the rhetorician who flourished at the Salghurid court of Abū Bakr and who envisaged a new stylistic sensibility for the rhythmical and metaphorical aesthetics of the Persian verse,[7] Saʿdi found (like the prophet Khiżr, but in another form) the water of eternal life in the possibility of repeating, through poetry, the visual harmony of the world. In spite of the hundreds of years that separate us from 13th-century Shiraz, we may still read Saʿdi's poetry as the ultimate invitation to contemplate the manifestations of beauty surrounding us, both through our eyes open into the visible world, and through the filter of the linguistic reflection of its unfathomable source:

Here I am, O painting: while the birds and the fish were asleep
My poor eyes stayed awake all night long, longing for your countenance.

This interminable night might kill me while desiring you,
yet the morning breeze will bring me back to life.

6 "Si l'on suit Avicenne dans son raisonnement, Dieu seul connaît la « chose ». Il la connaît de toute éternité, comme il connait l'essence de toute chose avant même qu'elle accède à l'existence. Car c'est Dieu qui accord aux essences de passer de l'état de simple « possibilité » à l'existence véritable. Mais alors, que reste-t-il à l'homme pour comprendre la « chose »? Le versant esthétique de l'avicennisme offre peut-être la réponse : s'il ne peut saisir la « chose » par la pensée, l'homme est toujours capable de se la représenter en imagination." Landau 2013, 245.

7 Landau 2013, 151–52 ; 197–212.

I strive to hide the pain of love from my friends,
But my poetry is on fire: it will testify to my passion.

For the entire day Saʿdi's pen travels like Khiżr:
No wonder if the water of life will spring from this darkness.

Ṭayyibāt 89[8]

---

8 [3.71] Saʿdi YE, 44.

APPENDIX

Original Texts

1.1

یکی لطیفه ز من بشنو ای که در آفاق
سفر کنی و لطایف ز بحر وکان آری
گرت بدایع سعدی نباشد اندر بار
به پیش اهل قبایل چه ارمغان آری

1.2

مرا روی تو محراب است در شهر مسلمانان
وگر جنگ مغول باشد نگردانی ز محرابم

1.3

عافیت خواهی نظر در منظر خوبان مکن
ورکنی بدرود کن خواب و قرار خویش را
گبر و ترسا و مسلمان هر کسی در دین خویش
قبله‌ای دارند و ما زیبا نگار خویش را

1.4

سعدی اینک به قدم رفت و به سر باز آمد
مفتی ملت اصحاب نظر باز آمد
فتنهٔ شاهد و سودا زدهٔ باد بهار
عاشق نغمهٔ مرغان سحر باز آمد

 | DOI:10.1163/9789004435902_017

تا نپنداری کآشفتگی از سر بنهاد
تا نگویی که ز مستی به خبر بازآمد
دل بی‌خویشتن و خاطر شورانگیزش
همچنان یاوگی و تن به حضر بازآمد
سالها رفت مگر عقل و سکون آموزد
تا چه آموخت کز آن شیفته‌تر بازآمد
عقل بین کز بر سیلاب غم عشق گریخت
عالمی گشت و به گرداب خطر بازآمد
تا بدانی که به دل نقطهٔ پابرجا بود
که چو پرگار بگردید و به سر بازآمد
وه که چون تشنهٔ دیدار عزیزان می‌بود
گوییا آب حیاتش به جگر بازآمد
خاک شیراز همیشه گل خوشبوی دهد
لاجرم بلبل خوشگوی دگر بازآمد
پای دیوانگیش برد و سر شوق آورد
منزلت بین که به پا رفت و به سر بازآمد
میلش از شام به شیراز به خسرو مانست
که به اندیشهٔ شیرین ز شکر بازآمد
جرمناکست ملامت مکنیدش که کریم
بر گنهکار نگیرد چو ز در بازآمد
چه ستم کو نکشید از شب دیجور فراق
تا بدین روز که شبهای قمر بازآمد
بلعجب بود که روزی به مرادی برسید
فلک خیره کش از جور مگر بازآمد
دختر بکر ضمیرش به یتیمی پس از این
جور بیگانه نبیند که پدر بازآمد
نی چه ارزد دو سه خرمهره که در پیلهٔ اوست

خاصه اکنون که به دریای گهر بازآمد
چون مسلم نشدش ملک هنر چاره ندید
به گدایی به در اهل هنر بازآمد

1.5

هر دم از عمر می رود نفسی
چون نگه می کنم نمانده بسی
ای که پنجاه رفت و در خوابی
مگر این پنج روز دریابی

1.6

بیا ای که عمرت به هفتاد رفت
مگر خفته بودی که بر باد رفت
[...]
چو پنجاه سالت برون شد ز دست
غنیمت شمر پنج روزی که هست

1.7

پدرم بندهٔ قدیم تو بود
عمر در بندگی به سر بردست
بندهزاده که در وجود آمد
هم به روی تو دیده برکردست
خدمت دیگری نخواهم کرد
که مرا نعمت تو پروردست

1.8

همه قبیله من عالمان دین بودند
مرا معلم عشق تو شاعری آموخت

1.9

کف عطای تو گر نیست ابر رحمت حق
چه نعمت است که بر بر و بحر می‌باری

1.10

به تیغ و طعنه گرفتند جنگجویان ملک
تو بر و بحر گرفتی به عدل و همت و رای

1.11

مدیح شیوهٔ درویش نیست تا گویم
مثال بحر محیطی و ابر آذاری
نگویمت که به فضل از کرام ممتازی
نگویمت که به عدل از ملوک مختاری
وگرچه این همه هستی نصیحت اولیتر
که پند راه خلاص است و دوستی باری
[...]
هزار سال نگویم بقای عمر تو باد
که این مبالغه دانم ز عقل نشماری

1.12

دیار مشرق و مغرب مگیر و جنگ مجوی
دلی به دست کن و زنگ خاطری بزدای

1.13

سماع مجلست آواز ذکر و قرآنست
نه بانگ مطرب و آواز چنگ و نالهٔ نای

1.14

جهان بر آب نهادست و زندگی بر باد
غلام خاطر آنم که دل بدو ننهاد

1.15

شمایلی که نیاید به وصف در اوهام
خصایصی که نگنجد به ذکر در افواه
[...]
شهنشهی که زمین از فروغ طلعت او
منورست چنان کاسمان به طلعت ماه

1.16

به دولتت همه افتادگان بلند شدند
چو آفتاب که بر آسمان برد شبنم
مگر کمینهٔ آحاد بندگان سعدی
که سعیش از همه بیشست و حظش از همه کم

1.17

دلم از صحبت شیراز به کلی بگرفت
وقت آن است که پرسی خبر از بغدادم
هیچ شک نیست که فریاد من آنجا برسد
عجب ار صاحب دیوان نرسد فریادم
سعدیا حب وطن گر چه حدیثیست صحیح
نتوان مرد به سختی که من این جا زادم

1.18

اینان مگر ز رحمت محض آفریده‌اند
کآرام جان و انس دل و نور دیده‌اند

1.19

ای چشم تو دلفریب و جادو
در چشم تو خیره چشم آهو
در چشم منی و غایب از چشم
زآن چشم همی‌کنم به هر سو
این چشم و دهان و گردن و گوش
چشمت مرساد و دست و بازو
مه گر چه به چشم خلق زیباست
تو خوبتری به چشم و ابرو
با این همه چشم زنگی شب
چشم سیه تو راست هندو
صد چشمه ز چشم من گشاید
چون چشم برافکنم بر آن رو

چشمم بستی به زلف دلبند
هوشم بردی به چشم جادو
هر شب چو چراغ چشم دارم
تا چشم من و چراغ من کو
سعدی به دو چشم تو که دارد
چشمی و هزار دانه لولو

1.20

ماهرویا روی خوب از من متاب
بی خطا کشتن چه می بینی صواب
دوش در خوابم در آغوش آمدی
وین نپندارم که بینم جز به خواب
از درون سوزناک و چشم تر
نیمه‌ای در آتشم نیمی در آب
هر که بازآید ز در پندارم اوست
تشنه مسکین آب پندارد سراب
ناوکش را جان درویشان هدف
ناخنش را خون مسکینان خضاب
او سخن می گوید و دل می‌برد
و او نمک می ریزد و مردم کباب
حیف باشد بر چنان تن پیرهن
ظلم باشد بر چنان صورت نقاب
خوی به دامان از بناگوشش بگیر
تا بگیرد جامه‌ات بوی گلاب
فتنه باشد شاهدی شمعی به دست
سرگران از خواب و سرمست از شراب

بامدادی تا به شب رویت مپوش
تا بپوشانی جمال آفتاب
سعدیا گر در برش خواهی چو چنگ
گوشمالت خورد باید چون رباب

1.21

دختران طبع را یعنی سخن با این جمال
آبرویی نیست پیش آن زیبا پسر

1.22

مراد اهل طریقت لباس ظاهر نیست
کمر به خدمت سلطان ببند و صوفی باش

1.23

کجا همی رود این شاهد شکرگفتار
چرا همی نکند بر دو چشم من رفتار
به آفتاب نماند مگر به یک معنی
که در تأمل او خیره می‌شود ابصار
نظر در آینهٔ روی عالم افروزش
مثال صیقل از آیینه می‌برد زنگار
برات خوبی و منشور لطف و زیبایی
نبشته بر گل رویش به خط سبز عذار
به مشک سودهٔ محلول در عرق ماند
که برحریر نویسد کسی به خط غبار
لبش ندانم و خدش چگونه وصف کنم

که این چو دانهٔ نارست و آن چو شعلهٔ نار
چو در محاورت آید دهان شیرینش
کجا شدند تماشاکنان شیرین کار
نسیم صبح بر اندام نازکش بگذشت
چو بازگشت به بستان بریخت برگ بهار
متابع توام ای دوست گر نداری ننگ
مطاوع توام ای یار اگر نداری عار
تو در کمند من آیی کدام دولت و بخت
من از تو روی بپیچم کدام صبر و قرار
حدیث عشق تو با کس همی نیارم گفت
که غیرتم نگذارد که بشنود اغیار
همیشه در دل من هرکس آمدی و شدی
تو برگذشتی و نگذشت بعد از آن دیار
تو از سر من و از جان من عزیزتری
بخیلم ار نکنم سر فدا و جان ایثار
حلال نیست محبت مگر کسانی را
که دوستی به قیامت برند سعدی‌وار

1.24

همه دانند که من سبزه خط دارم دوست
نه چو دیگر حیوان سبزه صحرایی را

1.25

آدمی نیست مگر کالبدی بی‌جان است
آنکه گوید که مرا میل به دیدار تو نیست

1.26

سعدی خط سبز دوست دارد پیرامن خد ارغوانی
این پیر نگر که همچنانش از یاد نمی‌رود جوانی

1.27

گویند اگر آن خوش پسر آید چه آری در نظر
در چشم من چندین گهر بهر نثار کیست این
[…]
گلگون انار انگیخته گیسو کمند آویخته
دل خسته و خون ریخته چابک سوار کیست این

1.28

تو آن شهره یاری و آن شهریاری
که خسرو نشانی و خسرو نشانی
[…]
ندانم کدامی که دامی دلم را
ز نسل کیانی که اصل کیانی
[…]
ترا نار پستان به از نار بستان
که سیب از ترنجت کند بوستانی

1.29

کلید از دست بستانبان فتاده
ز بستان نار پستان در گشاده

دلی کان نار شیرین کار دیده
ز حسرت گشته چون نار کفیده

1.30

شمع چه می کنیم ما نور رخ تو شمع بس
برفکن از رخ چو مه خیز نقاب ای پسر

1.31

نقاب از رخ خوب آن خوش پسر
برانداز و در صورت جان نگر

1.32

دختران نعش را کاسد شود بازار حسن
گر چو یوسف پرده بردارد به دعوی روی تو

1.33

مگر تو روی بپوشی و فتنه بازنشانی
که من قرار ندارم که دیده از تو بپوشم

1.34

تویی لیلی تویی لیلی تویی دردِ مرا درمان
منم مجنون منم مجنون منم مجنونِ سرگردان
تویی شیرین به عهد خسرو پرویز بنشسته

منم فرهاد کوه افکن به بادم رفته شیرین جان
تویی شیرین تویی شیرین تویی شیرین چو جان در تن
منم خسرو منم خسرو گرفتار شب هجران
تویی عذرا تویی عذرا گرفتارم به درد تو
منم وامق منم وامق بکن درد مرا درمان
تویی گلشه تویی گلشه تویی گلبوی همچون مه
منم ورقه منم غرقه به بحر هجر بی پایان
تویی ویس گل اندام ز جانت بسته در دام
منم رامین که می سوزد دلم در غم ترا دامان
ز جان گویم ثنای آن جهانداری که او باقیست
که دادستم به لطف خود هم جان و هم ایمان

1.35

در آن آیینه دید از خود نشانی
چو خود را یافت بی‌خود شد زمانی

1.36

رفتی و نمی‌شوی فراموش
می‌آیی و می‌روم من از هوش

1.37

از ما به یک نظر بستاند هزار دل
این آبروی و رونق بازار بنگرید

1.38

سلطان صفت همی‌رود و صد هزار دل
با او چنان که در پی سلطان رود سپاه

1.39

گوشم به راه تا که خبر می‌دهد ز دوست
صاحب خبر بیامد و من بی‌خبر شدم

1.40

مطرب مجلس بساز زمزمهٔ عود
خادم ایوان بسوز مجمرهٔ عود
قرعهٔ همت برآمد آیت رحمت
یار درآمد ز در به طالع مسعود
دوست به دنیا و آخرت نتوان داد
صحبت یوسف به از دراهم معدود
وه که ازو جور و تندیم چه خوش آید
چون حرکات ایاز بر دل محمود
روز گل افشان نوبهار چه خسبی
خیز مگر پر کنیم دامن مقصود
باغ مزین چو بارگاه سلیمان
مرغ سحر برکشیده نغمهٔ داود
راوی روشندل از عبارت سعدی
ریخته در بزم شاه لولوی منضود
وارث ملک عجم اتابک اعظم
سعد ابوبکر سعد زنگی مودود

1.41

خلق گویند برو دل به هوای دگر ده
نکنم خاصه در ایام اتابگ دوهوایی

1.42

چو ترک دلبر من شاهدی به شنگی نیست
چو زلف پرشکنش حلقه فرنگی نیست
دهانش ار چه نبینی مگر به وقت سخن
چو نیک درنگری چون دلم به تنگی نیست
قوی به چنگ من افتاده بود دامن وصل
ولی دریغ که دولت به تیزچنگی نیست
به تیغ غمزه خون خوار لشکری بزنی
بزن که با تو در او هیچ مرد جنگی نیست
دوم به لطف ندارد عجب که چون سعدی
غلام سعد ابوبکر سعد زنگی نیست

1.43

کسان سفینه به دریا برند و سود کنند
نه چون سفینه سعدی به چون تو دریایی

1.44

تبارک الله از آن نقشبند ماء مهین
که نقش روی تو بستست و چشم و زلف و جبین
چنانکه در نظری در صفت نمی آیی

منت چه وصف بگویم تو خود در آینه بین
مه از فروغ تو بر آسمان نمی تابد
چه جای ماه که خورشید لایکاد یبین
خدای تا گل آدم سرشت و خلق نگاشت
سلالهای چو تو هرگز نیافرید از طین
نه در قبیلهٔ آدم که در بهشت خدای
بدین کمال نباشد جمال حورالعین
چنین درخت نروید به بوستان ارم
چنین صنم نبود در نگارخانهٔ چین
مگر درخت بهشتی بود که بار آرد
بنفشه و گل و بادام و لاله و نسرین
ز بس که دیدهٔ مشتاق در تو حیرانست
ترنج و دست به یک بار می‌برد سکین
طریق اهل نظر خامشی و حیرانیست
که در نهایت وصفت نمی‌رسد تحسین
حکایت لبت اندر دهان نمی گنجد
لب و دهان نتوان گفت در درج ثمین
گر ابن مقله دگربار با جهان آید
چنانکه دعوی معجز کند به سحر مبین
به آب زر نتواند کشید چون تو الف
به سیم حل ننویسد مثال ثغر تو سین
بیا بیا که به جان آمدم ز تلخی هجر
بگوی از آن لب شیرین حکایتی شیرین
ترنجبین وصالم بده که شربت صبر
نمی کند خفقان فاد را تسکین
دریغ اگر قدری میل از آن طرف بودی

کزین طرف همه شوقست و اضطراب و حنین
تو را سریست که با ما فرو نمی‌آید
مرا سری که حرامست بی‌تو بر بالین
میان حظ من و دشمنانت فرقی نیست
منت به مهرهمی میرم و حسود به کین
اگر تو بر دل مسکین من نبخشایی
چه لازمست که جور و جفا برم چندین
به صدر صاحب دیوان ایلخان نالم
که در ایاسهٔ او جور نیست بر مسکین
خدایگان صدور زمان و کهف امان
پناه ملت اسلام شمس دولت و دین
جمال مشرق و مغرب، صلاح خلق خدای
مشیر مملکت پادشاه روی زمین
که اهل مشرق و مغرب به شکر نعمت او
چو اهل مصر به احسان یوسفند رهین
بسی نماند که در عهد رأی و رأفت او
به یک مقام نشینند صعوه و شاهین
ز گوسپند بدوزد، رعایت نظرش
دهان گرگ و بدرد دهان شیر عرین
معین خیر و مطیع خدای و ناصح خلق
به رای روشن و فکر بلیغ و رای رزین
زهی به سایهٔ لطف تو خلق را آرام
خهی به قوت رای تو ملک را آیین
گر اقتضای زمان دور باز سرگیرد
بنات دهر نزایند بهتر از تو بنین
تو آن یگانهٔ دهری که در وسادهٔ حکم
به از تو تکیه نکردست هیچ صدرنشین

چو فیض چشمهٔ خورشید بامداد پگاه
که در تموج او منطمس شود پروین
فروغ رای تو مصباح راههای مخوف
عنان عزم تو مفتاح ملکهای حصین
خدای، مشرق و مغرب به ایلخان دادست
تو بر خزاین روی زمین حفیظ و امین
قضا موافق رایت بود که نتوان بود
خلاف رای تو رفتن مگر ضلال مبین
مخالفان تو را دست و پای اسب مراد
بریده باد که بی دست و پای به تنین
تمام ذکر تو ناگفته ختم خواهم کرد
که خوض کردم و دستم نمی‌دهد تبیین
لن مدحتک سبعین حجة دأبا
لما اقدرت علی واحد من السبعین
کمال فضل تو را من به گرد می‌نرسم
مگر کسی کند اسب سخن به زین به ازین
ورای قدر منست التفات صدر جهان
که ذکر بندهٔ مخلص کند علی‌التعیین
برای مجلس انست گلی فرستادم
که رنگ و بوی نگرداندش مرور سنین
تو روی دختر دلبند طبع من بگشای
که پیر بود و بدادم به شوهر عنین
بریده می کنم از نسل وصلتش درگور
که بخت درخور حسنش نمی دهد کابین
ستایش سخن خویشتن مکن سعدی
که زشت خوب نگردد به جامهٔ رنگین
اگر نه بنده‌نوازی از آن طرف بودی

که زهره داشت که دیبا برد به قسطنطین
که می برد به عراق این بضاعت مزجاة
چنانکه زیره به کرمان برند و کاسه به چین
تو را شمامهٔ ریحان من که یاد آورد
که خلق از آن طرف آرند نافهٔ مشکین
چه لایق مگسانست بامداد بهار
که در مقابلهٔ بلبلان کند طنین؟
که نشر کرده بود طی من در آن مجلس
که برده باشد نام ثری به علیین
به شکر بخت بلند ایستاده‌ام که مرا
به عمر خویش نکردست هرگز این تمکین
میان عرصهٔ شیراز تا به چند آخر
پیاده باشم و دیگر پیادگان فرزین؟
چو بیدبن که تناور شود به پنجه سال
به پنج روز به بالاش بردود یقطین
ز روزگار به رنجم چنانکه نتوان گفت
به خاک پای خداوند روزگار، یمین
بلی به یک حرکت از زمانه خرسندم
که روزگار به سر می رود به شدت وکین
دوای خسته و جبر شکسته کس نکند
مگر کسی که یقینش بود به روز یقین
یقین قلبی انی انال منک غنی
ولایزال یقینی من‌الهوان یقین
سخن بلند کنم تا بر آسمان گویند
دعای دولت او را فرشتگان آمین
همیشه خاتم اقبال در یمین تو باد
به عون ایزد و در چشم دشمنانت نگین

به رغم دشمن و اعجاب دوستان بادا
همیشه چشمهٔ رزقت معین و بخت معین
حزین نشسته حسودان دولتت همه سال
تو گوش کرده بر آواز مطربان حزین
مباد دشمنت اندر جهان وگر باشد
به زندگانی در سجن و مرده در سجین
دوان عیش تو بادا پس از هلاک عدو
چنانکه پیش تو دف می‌زنند و خصم دفین
ز دوستان تو آواز رود و بانگ سرود
بر آسمان شده وز دشمنان زفیر و انین
هزار سال جلالی بقای عمر تو باد
شهور آن همه اردی بهشت و فروردین

1.45

تو روی دختر دلبند طبع من بگشای
که خانگیش برآوردهام نه بازاری
چو همسریش نبینم به ناقصی ندهم
خلیفه‌زاده تحمل چرا کند خواری

1.46

گرفت پایهٔ تخت خدایگان زمین
قرارگاه همایون براوج علییّن
جهانگشای جوانبخت اتابک عادل
پناه سلغریان،شهریار روی زمین
مظفّرالدّین بوبکرسعد بن زنگی
که روی ملک کیانست وپشت ملّت ودین

1.47

صدای نوبت عدلت باصفهان برسید
چوطاس چرخ زآوای اوگرفت طنین

1.48

عروس طبع مرا ازثنای فایح شاه
همه زعنبر ومشک است بستر و بالین

1.49

دوبنده رابدرشاه رهنمون شده ام
یکی زماء مهین ویکی زماء معین
یکی بمعنی پاک ازعطای روح قدس
یکی بصورت خوب ازنژادحورالعین
یکی بزلف وخط آشوب وفتنۀ دلها
یکی بچهرۀ زیبا،نگارخانۀ چین
یکی زبهرتمنّای گوش معنی جوی
یکی زبهرتماشای چشم صورت بین
یکی گشاده میانست لیک بس دلبند
یکی ببسته میان لیک بس گشاده جبین
یکی سپیدولیکن چوچشم ودل روشن
یکی سیاه ولیکن چوعقل وجان شیرین

1.50

من آن مرغ سخندانم که در خاکم رود صورت
هنوز آواز می آید به معنی از گلستانم

1.51

گیرم که حال غرقه ندانند دوستان
باری در این سفینه ببینند ترسخن
در می‌چکد ز منطق سعدی به جای شعر
گرسیم داشتی بنوشتی به زرسخن

1.52

هم بود شوری در این سر بی‌خلاف
کاین همه شیرین زبانی می کند

1.53

سعدی شیرین زبان این همه شور از کجا
شاهد ما آیتیست وین همه تفسیر او

1.54

سعدی شیرین زبان این همه شور از کجا
تو شیرین زبانی ز سعدی بگیر

1.55

امشب آن نیست که در خواب رود چشم ندیم
خواب در روضه رضوان نکند اهل نعیم
خاک را زنده کند تربیت باد بهار
سنگ باشد که دلش زنده نگردد به نسیم
بوی پیراهن گم کرده خود می‌شنوم

گر بگویم همه گویند ضلالیست قدیم
عاشق آن گوش ندارد که نصیحت شنود
درد ما نیک نباشد به مداوای حکیم
توبه گویندم از اندیشه معشوق بکن
هرگز این توبه نباشد که گناهیست عظیم
ای رفیقان سفر دست بدارید از من
که بخواهیم نشستن به در دوست مقیم
ای برادر غم عشق آتش نمرود انگار
بر من این شعله چنان است که بر ابراهیم
مرده از خاک لحد رقص کنان برخیزد
گر تو بالای عظامش گذری وهی رمیم
طمع وصل تو می‌دارم و اندیشه هجر
دیگر از هر چه جهانم نه امید است و نه بیم
عجب از کشته نباشد به در خیمه دوست
عجب از زنده که چون جان به درآورد سلیم
سعدیا عشق نیامیزد و شهوت با هم
پیش تسبیح ملایک نرود دیو رجیم

1.56

شاهدان ز اهل نظر روی فراهم نکشند
بار درویش تحمل بکند مرد کریم

1.57

ما دگر کس نگرفتیم به جای تو ندیم
الله الله تو فراموش مکن عهد قدیم
هر کس از دایره جمع به راهی رفتند

ما بماندیم و خیال تو به یک جای مقیم
باغبان گر نگشاید در درویش به باغ
آخر از باغ بیاید بر درویش نسیم
گر نسیم سحر از زلف تو بویی آرد
جان فشانیم به سوغات نسیم تو نه سیم
بوی محبوب که بر خاک احبا گذرد
نه عجب باشد اگر زنده کند عظم رمیم
ای به حسن تو صنم چشم فلک نادیده
ای به مثل تو ولد مادر ایام عقیم
حال درویش چنان است که خال تو سیاه
جسم دلریش چنان است که چشم تو سقیم
چشم جادوی تو بی واسطه کحل کحیل
طاق ابروی تو بی شائبه وسمه وسیم
ای که دلداری اگر جان منت می باید
عشقبازی نه طریق حکما بود ولی
چشم بیمار تو دل می‌برد از دست حکیم
چاره‌ای نیست در این مسأله الا تسلیم
سعدیا عشق نیامیزد و عفت با هم
چند پنهان کنی آواز دهل زیر گلیم

1.58

دی بدان رستهٔ صرافان من بر در تیم
پسری دیدم تابنده‌تر از در یتیم
زین سیه چشمی جادو صنمی طرفه چو ماه
بی‌نظیری که نظیریش نه در هفت اقلیم
با دلم گفتم ای کاشکی این میر بتان

کندی بر من بیچاره دل خویش رحیم
رفتم و چشمگکی کردم و شد بر سر کار
کودکک جلد بد و زیرک و دانا و فهیم
گفتم او را ز کجایی و بگو نام تو چیست
گفت کز بلخم و نامست مرا قلب کریم
گفتم ای جان پدر آیی مهمان پدر
گفت چون نایم و رفتیم همی تا سوی تیم
هر دو در حجره شدیم آنگه و در کرده فراز
خوب شد آنهمه دشوار و شدم کار سلیم
دست شادی و طرب کردن و می خوردن برد
او چنان میری و منش راست بمانند ندیم
چون بشد مست و ز باده سر او گشت گران
کرد وسواس مرا در دل شیطان رجیم
گفتم او را که سه بوسه دهی ای جان پدر
گفت خواهی شش بگشای در کیسهٔ سیم
ده درم داشتم از گاه پدر مانده درست
کردم آن ده درم خویش بدان مه تسلیم
بند شلوارش بگشاده نگه کردم من
جفته‌ای دیدم آراسته با هر چه نعیم
سینه بر خاک نهاد آن بت باریک میان
تاب ماهی برسید از برسیمینش نسیم
شکم و نافه اش چون قله پر تو و پنیر
وآن سرین گاهش همچون شکم ماهی شیم
گنبدی از بر چون نقره برآورده سفید
کرده آن نقرهٔ سیمینش به الماس دو نیم
پاره‌ای بردم از این روغن ابلیس به کار
الف خویش نهان کردم در حلقهٔ میم

او به زیر من چون کبک که در چنگل باز
من بر آن گنبد او راست چو بر طور کلیم

1.59

امشب مگر به وقت نمی‌خواند این خروس
عشاق بس نکرده هنوز از کنار و بوس
پستان یار در خم گیسوی تابدار
چون گوی عاج در خم چوگان آبنوس
یک شب که دوست فتنه خفتست زینهار
بیدار باش تا نرود عمر بر فسوس
تا نشنوی ز مسجد آدینه بانگ صبح
یا از در سرای اتابک غریو کوس
لب بر لب چو چشم خروس ابلهی بود
برداشتن بگفته بیهوده خروس

1.60

آن را که نظر به سوی هر کس باشد
در دیدهٔ صاحبنظران خس باشد
قاضی به دو شاهد بدهد فتوی شرع
در مذهب عشق شاهدی بس باشد

1.61

شهربند هوای نفس مباش
سگ شهر استخوان شکار کند
هر شبی یار شاهدی بودن

روز هشیاریت خمار کند
قاضی شهر عاشقان باید
که به یک شاهد اختصار کند
سر سعدی سرای سلطانست
نادر آن جا کسی گذار کند

1.62

مکن عیب خردمندی که در بند هوا ماند
در آن صورت که عشق آید خردمندی کجا ماند
[...]
هوادار نکورویان نیندیشد ز بدگویان
بیا گر روی آن داری که طعنت در قفا ماند
[...]
اگر بر هر سر کویی نشیند چون تو بت رویی
بجز قاضی نپندارم که نفسی پارسا ماند
جمال محفل و مجلس امام شرع رکن‌الدین
که دین از قوت رایش به عهد مصطفی ماند

1.63

پیش از آب و گل من در دل من مهر تو بود
با خود آوردم از آنجا نه به خود بر بستم

1.64

معلمت همه شوخی و دلبری آموخت
جفا و ناز و عتاب و ستمگری آموخت

غلام آن لب ضحاک و چشم فتانم
که کید سحر به ضحاک و سامری آموخت
تو بت چرا به معلم روی که بتگر چین
به چین زلف تو آید به بتگری آموخت
هزار بلبل دستان سرای عاشق را
بباید از تو سخن گفتن دری آموخت
برفت رونق بازار آفتاب و قمر
از آن که ره به دکان تو مشتری آموخت
همه قبیله من عالمان دین بودند
مرا معلم عشق تو شاعری آموخت
مرا به شاعری آموخت روزگار آن گه
که چشم مست تو دیدم که ساحری آموخت
مگر دهان تو آموخت تنگی از دل من
وجود من ز میان تو لاغری آموخت
بلای عشق تو بنیاد زهد و بیخ ورع
چنان بکند که صوفی قلندری آموخت
دگر نه عزم سیاحت کند نه یاد وطن
کسی که بر سر کویت مجاوری آموخت
من آدمی به چنین شکل و قد و خوی و روش
ندیده‌ام مگر این شیوه از پری آموخت
به خون خلق فروبرده پنجه کاین حناست
ندانمش که به قتل که شاطری آموخت
چنین بگریم از این پس که مرد بتواند
در آب دیده سعدی شناوری آموخت

1.65

تا خبر دارم از او بی‌خبر از خویشتنم
با وجودش ز من آواز نیاید که منم
پیرهن می‌بدرم دم به دم از غایت شوق
که وجودم همه او گشت و من این پیرهنم
ای رقیب این همه سودا مکن و جنگ مجوی
برکنم دیده که من دیده از او برنکنم
خود گرفتم که نگویم که مرا واقعه‌ایست
دشمن و دوست بدانند قیاس از سخنم
در همه شهر فراهم ننشست انجمنی
که نه من در غمش افسانه آن انجمنم
برشکست از من و از رنج دلم باک نداشت
من نه آنم که توانم که از او برشکنم
گر همین سوز رود با من مسکین در گور
خاک اگر بازکنی سوخته یابی کفنم
گر به خون تشنه‌ای اینک من و سر باکی نیست
که به فتراک تو به زان که بود بر بدنم
مرد و زن گر به جفا کردن من برخیزند
گر بگردم ز وفای تو نه مردم که زنم
شرط عقلست که مردم بگریزند از تیر
من گر از دست تو باشد مژه بر هم نزنم
تا به گفتار درآمد دهن شیرینت
بیم آنست که شوری به جهان درفکنم
لب سعدی و دهانت ز کجا تا به کجا
این قدر بس که رود نام لبت بر دهنم

1.66

ماه منظور آن بت زیبای من
سرو روزافزون جان افزای من
کاندرین شهر از کمند موی اوست
بند بر پای جهان پیمای من
هر کسی با حریفی سرخوشست
وآن من کنگیست همبالای من
[...]
دوست میدارم که در کونش برم
نازنینتر عضوی از اعضای من
راضیم با خوی او کز خوی او
کم نخواهد بودن استقسای من
این قناعت بین که عارف میکند
تا کجا باشد قیامت جای من

1.67

این عشق را زوال نباشد به حکم آنک
ما پاک دیدهایم و تو پاکیزه دامنی

1.68

هر کجا سرو قامتی بینی
چشم در روی کن و خیو در مشت
چون نه کونش دری و نه شلوار
بی گاهت کسی نخواهد کشت

1.69

ز چشم مست تو امید خواب میبینم
تو خوش بخفت که ما را قرار خفتن نیست
بدیدن از تو قناعت نمی توانم کرد
حکایتی دگرم هست و جای گفتن نیست

1.70

چشمی که تو را یبند و در قدرت بی چون
مدهوش نماند نتوان گفت که ییناست

1.71

تشریف داد و رفت ندانم ز بیخودی
کاین دوست بود در نظرم یا خیال دوست
هوشم نماند و عقل برفت و سخن نبست
مقبل کسی که محو شود در کمال دوست

1.72

در دام تو محبوسم در دست تو مغلوبم
وز ذوق تو مدهوشم در وصف تو حیرانم

1.73

لب از ترشح می پاک کن برای خدا
که خاطرم به هزاران گنه موسوس شد

1.74

دوش بی روی تو آتش به سرم بر می‌شد
و آبم از دیده می‌آمد که زمین تر می‌شد
تا به افسوس به پایان نرود عمر عزیز
همه شب ذکر تو می‌رفت و مکرر می‌شد
[…]
از خیال تو به هر سو که نظر می‌کردم
پیش چشمم در و دیوار مصور می‌شد

1.75

کیر میگفت به کس کای بت برگزیده من
دوش بی روی تو آتش به سرم بر میشد
کس بدو گفت به جان تو که با کون امشب
همه شب ذکر تو میرفت و مکرر میشد
با خیال تو به هر سو که نظر میکردم
پیش چشمم در و دیوار مصور میشد
ز آرزوی قد و بالای تو تا روز سپید
آبم از دیده همی رفت و زمین تر میشد

1.76

قلم به یاد تو در مشت من نمی گنجد
که دیر شد کی نگشته است در دوات امید
تو را دوات سیه کرد روزگار و هنوز
مرا ز چشم قلم می چکد مداد سپید

1.77

بر حدیث من و حسن تو نیفزاید کس
حد همین است سخندانی و زیبایی را
سعدیا نوبتی امشب دهل صبح نکوفت
یا مگر روز نباشد شب تنهایی را

1.78

با یاد توام سعدی در شعر نمی گنجد
چون دوست یگانه شد با غیر نیامیزم

1.79

یک روز به شیدایی در زلف تو آویزم
زان دو لب شیرینت صد شور برانگیزم
[...]
بس توبه و پرهیزم کز عشق تو باطل شد
من بعد بدان شرطم کز توبه بپرهیزم

1.80

دوش گفتم ز عشق توبه کنم
که گه رفتن از جهان آمد
توبه کردم از این سخن که مرا
یاد آن یار دلستان آمد
بر زبان نام کون او بردم
کیر را آب بر دهان آمد

1.81

ای دیده به هرزه لولو ناب مریز
بر روی چو زر اشک چو سیماب مریز
شرطست کی از پس خوشی ریزند آب
تو هیچ خوشی ندیده ای آب مریز

1.82

ای لعبت خندان لب لعلت که مزیدست
وی باغ لطافت به رویت که گزیدست
شاهدتر از این میوه همه عمر کی خوردست
شیرین‌تر از این خربزه هرگز کی بریدست
ای خضر حلالت نکنم چشمه حیوان
دانی که سکندر به چه محنت طلبیدست
آن خون کسی ریخته‌ای یا می سرخ است
یا توت سیاهست که بر جامه چکیدست
با جمله برآمیزی و از ما بگریزی
جرم از تو نباشد گنه از بخت رمیدست
نیکست که دیوار به یک بار بیفتاد
تا هیچ کس این باغ نگویی که ندیدست
بسیار توقف نکند میوه بر بار
چون عام بدانست که شیرین و رسیدست
گل نیز در آن هفته دهن باز نمی کرد
و امروز نسیم سحرش پرده دریدست
در دجله که مرغابی از اندیشه نرفتی
کشتی رود اکنون که تتر جسر بریدست
رفت آن که فقاع از تو گشاییم دگربار

ما را بس از این کوزه که بیگانه مکیدست
سعدی در بستان هوای دگری زن
وین کشته رها کن که در او گله چریدست

1.83

این ریش تو سخت دیر بر می آید
موی زنخت بزیر بر می آید
با این همه چون کون تو می آرم یاد
آبم به دهان کیر بر می آید

1.84

بدنت در میان پیرهنت
همچو روحیست رفته در بدنی
وآن که بیند برهنه اندامت
گوید این پرگل است پیرهنی

1.85

خوش بود عیش با شکردهنی
ارغوان روی و یاسمن بدنی
روز و شب همسرا و هم دکان
در دکان مرد و در سرای زنی
گاه برهم نهاده دست ادب
همچو سرو ایستاده در چمنی
گه چنان تنگ رفته در آغوش

کی دو تن را بس است پیرهنی
میل در سرمه دان چنان شده سخت
که بن شمع در سرلگنی
نیم گز خورده سر و بن تا ناف
وز منی در میان پای منی
تخت زرین پادشه را نیست
آن لطافت کی پشت سیمتنی
من به بوسی رضا دهم هیات
نادرست این سخن ز مثل منی
زخمه ای در میان هر دو سرون
به کی هفتاد بوسه بر دهنی
سخن این است دشمنان را گوی
تا نگویند هر یکی سخنی

1.86

ور جماع آرزوت می باشد
تا به خاتم فرو کنی انگشت
حاصل آن بیش نیست آخر کار
که شود با تو نرم کنگ درشت

1.87

ندیدم امرد سی ساله چون تو در اسلام
عجوبهای چنین آخرالزمان باشد
اگر دو دست تو یک هفته در قفا بندند
به هفته دگرت ریش تا میان باشد

1.88

عروسان مقنع بی شمارند
عروسی در نکاح آور معمم
که گر بیرون کنی شلوارش از پای
تو پنداری که خرواریست شلغم

1.89

آنکه سروش به قد و بالا نیست
با همه راستست و با ما نیست

1.90

خوش بود دلبستگی با دلبری
ماه رویی مهربانی مهتری
جمجمی در پای مردانه لطیف
بر سرش خربندگانه میزری
امردی را کو پلاسی در برست
خوشترست از دختری در چادری
دختران را زر و زیور حاجت است
تا برانگیزند مهر شوهری
خط زنگاری و خال مشکبوی
در نمی باید به حسنش زیوری
مقنعی گر حوری بر سر کند
من گلیمی دوست دارم در بری
وآن گلیم از پیش بستن بر قفا
شرح آن چون من نداند دیگری

تا چو در روی اوفتد سیمین زنخ
زیوری گسترده باشد بستری
شاهد مطبوع شهری را بس است
آفتابی بس بود در کشوری
پادشاهان خواب بر منظر کنند
عارفان بر پشت زیبا منظری
این عصا کندر میان ران من است
بشکند گر آهنین باشد دری
بیش از این در نامه نتوانم نبشت
این حکایت را بباید دفتری

2.1

صورت کند زیبا بر پرنیان و دیبا
لیکن بر ابروانش سحر مبین نباشد

2.2

راه عشق از روی عقل از بهر آن بس مشکلست
کان نه راه صورت و پایست کان راه دلست
[…]
فرق کن در راه معنی کار دل با کار گل
کاین که تو مشغول آنی ای پسر کار گلست

2.3

دیده از دیدار خوبان برگرفتن مشکلست
هر که ما را این نصیحت می کند بی‌حاصلست

[...]

پیش از این من دعوی پرهیزگاری کردمی
باز می گویم که هر دعوی که کردم باطلست

[...]

من قدم بیرون نمی‌یارم نهاد از کوی دوست
دوستان معذور داریدم که پایم در گلست

[...]

آن که می گوید نظر در صورت خوبان خطاست
او همین صورت همی‌بیند ز معنی غافلست

[...]

ساربان آهسته ران کآرام جان در محملست
چارپایان بار بر پشتند و ما را بر دلست

2.4

گر رخسار چو ماهت صنما می‌نگرم
به حقیقت اثر لطف خدا می‌نگرم
تا مگر دیده ز روی تو بیابد اثری
هر زمان صد رهت اندر سر و پا می‌نگرم
تو به حال من مسکین به جفا می‌نگری
من به خاک کف پایت به وفا می‌نگرم
آفتابی تو و من ذره مسکین ضعیف
تو کجا و من سرگشته کجا می‌نگرم
سر زلفت ظلمات است و لبت آب حیات
در سواد سر زلفت به خطا می‌نگرم
هندوی چشم میناد رخ ترک تو باز
گر به چین سر زلفت به خطا می‌نگرم

راه عشق تو دراز است ولی سعدی وار
می‌روم وز سر حسرت به قفا می‌نگرم

2.5

گر کسی را حسد آید که تو را می‌نگرم
من نه در روی تو، در صنع خدا می‌نگرم
من از آن توام و هر چه مرا هست توراست
روشن است این که به چشم تو تو را می‌نگرم
خصم گوید که روا نیست نظر در رویش
من اگر هست و اگر نیست روا می‌نگرم
تشنه‌ام نیست شگفت ار طلبم آب حیوة
دردمندم نه عجب گر به دوا می‌نگرم
نور حسنی ست در آن روی بدان ملتفتم
من در آن آینه از بهر صفا می‌نگرم
روی زیبای تو آرام و قرار از من برد
من دگر باره در آن روی چرا می‌نگرم
هر طرف می‌نگرم تا که ببینم رویت
چون تو در جان منی من به کجا می‌نگرم
به حیات خودم امید نمی‌ماند هیچ
چون به حال خود و انصاف شما می‌نگرم
مدتی شد که به من روی همی ننمایی
عیب بخت است نه آن تو چو وامی‌نگرم
سیف فرغانی در غیر نظر چند کنی
گل چو دستم ندهد ز آن به گیا می‌نگرم
ور میسر نشود دیدن رویت چه کنم
می‌روم وز سر حسرت به قفا می‌نگرم

2.6

خوشا سپیده‌دمی باشد آنکه بینم باز
رسیده بر سر الله اکبر شیراز
بدیده بار دگر آن بهشت روی زمین
که بار ایمنی آرد نه جور قحط و نیاز
نه لایق ظلماتست بالله این اقلیم
که تختگاه سلیمان بدست و راه حجاز
هزار پیر و ولی بیش باشد اندر وی
که کعبه بر سر ایشان همی کند پرواز
به ذکر و فکر و عبادتهای شیخ کبیر
به حق روزبهان و به حق پنج نماز
که گوش دار تو این شهر نیکمردان را
ز دست ظالم بد دین و کافر غماز
به حق کعبه و آن کس که کرد کعبه بنا
که باد مردم شیراز در تنعم و ناز
هر آن کسی که کند قصد قبةالاسلام
بریده باد سرش همچو زر و نقره به گاز
که سعدی از حق شیراز روز و شب می گفت
که شهرها همه گنجشک و ملک ما شهباز

2.7

عبادت به تقلید گمراهی است
خنک رهروی را که آگاهی است

2.8

در من این هست که صبرم ز نکورویان نیست
زرق نفروشم و زهدی ننمایم کان نیست
ای که منظور ببینی و تأمل نکنی
گر تو را قوت این هست مرا امکان نیست
ترک خوبان ختا عین صوابست ولیک
چه کند بنده که بر نفس خودش فرمان نیست
من دگر میل به صحرا و تماشا نکنم
که گلی همچو رخ تو به همه بستان نیست
ای پری روی ملک صورت زیباسیرت
هر که با مثل تو انسش نبود انسان نیست
چشم برکرده بسی خلق که نابینایند
مثل صورت دیوار که در وی جان نیست
درد دل با تو همان به که نگوید درویش
ای برادر که تو را درد دلی پنهان نیست
آن که من در قلم قدرت او حیرانم
هیچ مخلوق ندانم که در او حیران نیست
سعدیا عمر گران مایه به پایان آمد
همچنان قصه سودای تو را پایان نیست

2.9

پیش رخ تو باید بر خاک سر نهادن
شرط است سجده بردن آیینه خدا را
عکس روی تو چون نگار خود بین در آینه
تا بدانی قدرت صورت نگار خیش را

2.10

مردم از ترس خدا سجده رویت نکنند
بامدادت که بینند و من از حیرانی

2.11

آمد به نماز آن صنم کافر کیش
ببرید نماز مومنان و درویش
می گفت امام مستمند دلریش
ای کاش من از پس بدمی وی از پیش

2.12

ای برتر از خیال و قیاس و گمان و وهم
وز هر چه گفته اند و شنیدیم و خوانده ایم

2.13

هر کسی را نتوان گفت که صاحب نظر است
عشقبازی دگر و نفس پرستی دگر است
نه هر آن چشم که بینند سیاه است و سپید
یا سپیدی ز سیاهی بشناسد بصر است
هر که در آتش عشقش نبود طاقت سوز
گو به نزدیک مرو کآفت پروانه پر است
گر من از دوست بنالم نفسم صادق نیست
خبر از دوست ندارد که ز خود با خبر است
آدمی صورت اگر دفع کند شهوت نفس

آدمی خوی شود ور نه همان جانور است
شربت از دست دلارام چه شیرین و چه تلخ
بده ای دوست که مستسقی از آن تشنه‌تر است
من خود از عشق لبت فهم سخن می‌نکنم
هرچ از آن تلخترم گر تو بگویی شکر است
گر به تیغم بزنی با تو مرا خصمی نیست
خصم آنم که میان من و تیغت سپر است
من از این بند نخواهم به در آمد همه عمر
بند پایی که به دست تو بود تاج سر است
دست سعدی به جفا نگسلد از دامن دوست
ترک لؤلؤ نتوان گفت که دریا خطر است

2.14

خواب خوش من ای پسر دستخوش خیال شد
نقد امید عمر من در طلب وصال شد
[...]
بر من اگر حرام شد وصل تو نیست بوالعجب
بوالعجب آن که خون من بر تو چرا حلال شد
پرتو آفتاب اگر بدر کند هلال را
بدر وجود من چرا در نظرت هلال شد
زیبد اگر طلب کند عزت ملک مصر دل
آن که هزار یوسفش بنده خال وحال شد
طرفه مدار اگر ز دل نعره بیخودی زنم
کآتش دل چو شعله زد صبر در او محال شد
سعدی اگر نظر کند در تو مگیر بر خطا
کاو نه به رسم دیگران بنده زلف و خال شد

2.15

اندر غزل خویش نهان خواهم گشتن
تا بر لب تو بوسه دهم چونش بخوانی

2.16

فضل خدای را که تواند شمار کرد
یا کیست آنکه شکر یکی از هزار کرد
آن صانع لطیف که بر فرش کائنات
چندین هزار صورت الوان نگار کرد
ترکیب آسمان و طلوع ستارگان
از بهر عبرت نظر هوشیار کرد
بحر آفرید و بر و درختان و آدمی
خورشید و ماه و انجم و لیل و نهار کرد
مسمار کوهسار به نطع زمین بدوخت
تا فرش خاک بر سر آب استوار کرد
اجزای خاک مرده به تأثیر آفتاب
بستان میوه و چمن و لالهزار کرد
ابر آب داد بیخ درختان تشنه را
شاخ برهنه پیرهن نوبهار کرد
در چوب خشک میوه و در نی شکر نهاد
وز قطره دانهای دررّ شاهوار کرد
آثار رحمتی که جهان سر به سر گرفت
احمال منتی که فلک زیر بار کرد
چندین هزار منظر زیبا بیافرید
این آب داد بیخ درختان تشنه را
تا کیست کو نظر ز سر اعتبار کرد

2.17

ای حلقهٔ درگاه تو هفت آسمان سبحانه
وی از تو هم پر هم تهی هر دو جهان سبحانه

2.18

یار من آن که لطف خداوند یار اوست
بیداد و داد و رد و قبول اختیار اوست
[...]
صاحبدلی نماند در این فصل نوبهار
الا که عاشق گل و مجروح خار اوست
باور مکن که صورت او عقل من ببرد
عقل من آن ببرد که صورت نگار اوست
گر دیگران به منظر زیبا نظر کنند
ما را نظر به قدرت پروردگار اوست
[...]

2.19

اینجا حلول کفر بود اتحاد هم
کین وحدتی است لیک به تکرار آمده
یک صانع است و صنع هزاران هزار بیش
جمله ز نقد علم نمودار آمده

2.20

کردی ظلمات و آب حیوان
معروف هم از لب و هم از خال

در یوسف مصر کس ندیده است
آن لطف که در تو بینم امسال
سربسته از آن بگفتم این حرف
تا بو که حلولیی کند حال
اینجا که منم حلول نبود
استغراق است و کشف احوال

2.21

هر ساعت از نو قبله‌ای با بت پرستی می‌رود
توحید بر ما عرضه کن تا بشکنیم اصنام را
می با جوانان خوردنم باری تمنا می کند
تا کودکان در پی فتند این پیر دردآشام را
[...]
جایی که سرو بوستان با پای چوبین می چمد
ما نیز در رقص آوریم آن سرو سیم اندام را

2.22

زین سان که وجود توست ای صورت روحانی
شاید که وجود ما پیشت عدمی باشد
گر جمله صنم‌ها را صورت به تو مانستی
شاید که مسلمان را قبله صنمی باشد

2.23

سفر قبله درازست و مجاور با دوست
روی در قبله معنی به بیابان نرود

2.24

وه که گر من باز بینم روی یار خویش را
تا قیامت شکر گویم کردگار خویش را
[...]
گبر و ترسا و مسلمان هر کسی در دین خویش
قبله‌ای دارند و ما زیبا نگار خویش را

2.25

آن که نقشی دیگرش جایی مصور می‌شود
نقش او در چشم ما هر روز خوشتر می‌شود
[...]
آب شوق از چشم سعدی می‌رود بر دست و خط
لاجرم چون شعر می‌آید سخن تر می‌شود

2.26

نشاط زاهد از انواع طاعت است و ورع
صفای عارف از ابروی نیکوان دیدن

2.27

سعدیا زنده عارفی باشی
گر برآید در این طلب جانت

2.28

و گر بهشت مصور کند عارف را
به غیر دوست نشاید که دیده بردارد

2.29

ای پسر دلربا وی قمر دلپذیر
از همه باشد گریز وز تو نباشد گزیر
تا تو مصور شدی در دل یکتای من
جای تصور نماند دیگرم اندر ضمیر

2.30

حرف‌های خط موزون تو پیرامن روی
گویی از مشک سیه بر گل سوری رقمند

2.31

چشم کوته نظران بر ورق صورت خوبان
خط همی‌بیند و عارف قلم صنع خدا را
همه را دیده به رویت نگرانست ولیکن
خودپرستان ز حقیقت نشناسند هوا را

2.32

گر اهل معرفتی هر چه بنگری خوبست
که هر چه دوست کند همچو دوست محبوبست
کدام برگ درختست اگر نظر داری
که سر صنع الهی برو نه مکتوبست

2.33

هر آن ناظر که منظوری ندارد
چراغ دولتش نوری ندارد
چه کار اندر بهشت آن مدعی را
که میل امروز با حوری ندارد
چه ذوق از ذکر پیدا آید آن را
که پنهان شوق مذکوری ندارد
میان عارفان صاحب نظر نیست
که خاطر پیش منظوری ندارد
اگر سیمرغی اندر دام زلفی
بماند تاب عصفوری ندارد
طبیب ما یکی نامهربانست
که گویی هیچ رنجوری ندارد
ولیکن چون عسل بشناخت سعدی
فغان از دست زنبوری ندارد

2.34

چشم خدا بر تو ای بدیع شمایل
یار من و شمع جمع و شاه قبایل
جلوه کنان می‌روی و باز می آیی
سرو ندیدم بدین صفت متمایل
هر صفتی را دلیل معرفتی هست
روی تو بر قدرت خدای دلایل
قصه لیلی مخوان و غصه مجنون

عهد تو منسوخ کرد ذکر اوایل
نام تو می‌رفت و عارفان بشنیدند
هر دو به رقص آمدند سامع و قایل

2.35

به جهان خرم از آنم که جهان خرم ازوست
عاشقم بر همه عالم که همه عالم ازوست
به غنیمت شمر ای دوست دم عیسی صبح
تا دل مرده مگر زنده کنی کان دم ازوست
نه فلک راست مسلم نه ملک را حاصل
آنچه در سر سویدای بنی آدم ازوست
به حلاوت بخورم زهر که شاهد ساقیست
به ارادت ببرم درد که درمان هم ازوست
زخم خونینم اگر به نشود به باشد
خنک آن زخم که هر لحظه مرا مرهم ازوست
غم و شادی بر عارف چه تفاوت دارد
ساقیا باده بده شادی آن کاین غم ازوست
پادشاهی و گدایی بر ما یکسانست
که برین در همه را پشت عبادت خم ازوست
سعدیا گر بکند سیل فنا خانهٔ دل
دل قوی دار که بنیاد بقا محکم ازوست

2.36

بامدادی که تفاوت نکند لیل و نهار
خوش بود دامن صحرا و تماشای بهار

صوفی از صومعه گو خیمه بزن بر گلزار
که نه وقتست که در خانه بخفتی بیکار
بلبلان وقت گل آمد که بنالند از شوق
نه کم از بلبل مستی تو، بنال ای هشیار
آفرینش همه تنبیه خداوند دلست
دل ندارد که ندارد به خداوند اقرار
این همه نقش عجب بر در و دیوار وجود
هر که فکرت نکند نقش بود بر دیوار
کوه و دریا و درختان همه در تسبیح‌اند
نه همه مستمعی فهم کند این اسرار
خبرت هست که مرغان سحر می گویند
آخر ای خفته سر از خواب جهالت بردار
هر که امروز نبیند اثر قدرت او
غالب آنست که فرداش نبیند دیدار
[…]
وقت آنست که داماد گل از حجلهٔ غیب
به در آید که درختان همه کردند نثار

2.37

سعدیا راست روان گوی سعادت بردند
راستی کن که به منزل نرود کجرفتار

2.38

قدیمی نکوکار نیکی پسند
به کلک قضا در رحم نقش بند

ز مشرق به مغرب مه و آفتاب
روان کرد و گسترد گیتی بر آب
زمین از تب لرزه آمد ستوه
فرو کوفت بر دامنش میخ کوه
دهد نطفه را صورتی چون پری
که کردست بر آب صورتگری
نهد لعل و پیروزه در صلب سنگ
گل و لعل در شاخ پیروزه رنگ
ز ابر افکند قطره‌ای سوی یم
ز صلب افکند نطفه‌ای در شکم
از آن قطره لولوی لالا کند
وز این صورتی سرو بالا کند

2.39

اگر مطالعه خواهد کسی بهشت برین را
بیا مطالعه کن گو به نوبهار زمین را
شگفت نیست گر از طین به درکند گل و نسرین
همانکه صورت آدم کند سلالهٔ طین را
حکیم بارخدایی که صورت گل خندان
درون غنچه ببندد چو در مشیمه جنین را
سزد که روی عبادت نهند بر در حکمش
مصوری که تواند نگاشت نقش چنین را
نعیم خطهٔ شیراز و لعبتان بهشتی
ز هر دریچه نگه کن که حور بینی و عین را

2.40

ای فتنه نوخاسته از عالم قدرت
غایب مشو از دیده که در دل بنشستی
[...]
در روی تو گفتم سخنی چند بگویم
رو باز گشادی و در نطق ببستی
[...]
سعدی غرض از حقه تن آیت حق است
صد تعبیه در توست و یکی باز نجستی
نقاش وجود این همه صورت که بپرداخت
تا نقش ببینی و مصور بپرستی

2.41

ای نظر آفتاب هیچ زیان داردت
گر در و دیوار ما از تو منور شود
گر نگهی دوستوار با طرف ما کنی
حقه همان کیمیاست وین مس ما زر شود
[...]
چون متصور شود در دل ما نقش دوست
همچو بتش بشکنیم هر چه مصور شود
پرتو خورشید عشق بر همه افتد ولیکن
سنگ به یک نوع نیست تا همه گوهر شود

2.42

ایها الناس جهان جای تن آسانی نیست
مرد دانا به جهان داشتن ارزانی نیست
خفتگان را چه خبر زمزمهٔ مرغ سحر
حیوان را خبر از عالم انسانی نیست
داروی تربیت از پیر طریقت بستان
کادمی را بتر از علت نادانی نیست
روی اگر چند پری چهره و زیبا باشد
نتوان دید در آیینه که نورانی نیست
شب مردان خدا روز جهان افروزست
روشنان را به حقیقت شب ظلمانی نیست
پنجهٔ دیو به بازوی ریاضت بشکن
کاین به سرپنجگی ظاهر جسمانی نیست
طاعت آن نیست که بر خاک نهی پیشانی
صدق پیش آر که اخلاص به پیشانی نیست
حذر از پیروی نفس که در راه خدای
مردم افکن تر ازین غول بیابانی نیست
عالم و عابد و صوفی همه طفلان رهند
مرد اگر هست به جز عارف ربانی نیست
با تو ترسم نکند شاهد روحانی روی
کالتماس تو به جز لذت نفسانی نیست

2.43

گفتم اگر نبینمت مهر فرامشم شود
می روی و مقابلی غایب و در تصوری

2.44

از بس که در نظرم خوب آمدی صنما
هر جا که می‌نگرم گویی که در نظری

2.45

بصر روشنم از سرمه خاک در توست
قیمت خاک تو من دانم کاهل بصرم
سرو بالای تو در باغ تصور بر پای
شرم دارم که به بالا صنوبر نگرم

2.46

ای جدل پیشه شفای خود ازین قانون ساز
کین اشارات نباشد پسر سینا را

2.47

درد و رنجوری ما را داروی غیر تو نیست
ای تو جالینوس جان و بوعلی سینای من

2.48

دل از دریچه فکرت به نفس ناطقه داد
نشان حالت زارم که زارتر می گشت

2.49

که یارب مر سنایی را سنایی ده تو در حکمت
چنان کز وی به رشک افتد روان بوعلی سینا

2.50

تا نقش خیال دوست با ماست
ما را همه عمر خود تماشاست

2.51

گر چه نفس هوا ز مشکست
ورچه سلب زمین ز دیباست
هر چند شکوفه بر درختان
چون دو لب دوست پر ثریاست
هر چند میان کوه لاله
چون دیده میان روی حوراست
چون دولت عاشقی در آمد
اینها همه از میانه برخاست

2.52

تا نقش خیال دوست با ماست
ما را همه عمر خود تماشاست
آن جا که وصال دوستانست
والله که میان خانه صحراست
وان جا که مراد دل برآید

یک خار به از هزار خرماست
چون بر سر کوی یار خسبیم
بالین و لحاف ما ثریاست
چون در سر زلف یار پیچیم
اندر شب قدر قدر ما راست
چون عکس جمال او بتابد
کهسار و زمین حریر و دیباست
از باد چو بوی او بپرسیم
در باد صدای چنگ و سرناست
بر خاک چو نام او نویسیم
هر پاره خاک حور و حوراست
بر آتش از او فسون بخوانیم
زو آتش تیزاب سیماست
قصه چه کنم که بر عدم نیز
نامش چو بریم هستی افزاست
آن نکته که عشق او در آن جاست
پرمغزتر از هزار جوزاست
وان لحظه که عشق روی بنمود
این ها همه از میانه برخاست
خامش که تمام ختم گشته ست
کلی مراد حق تعالا ست

2.53

شوری ز شراب خانه برخاست
برخاست غریوی از چپ و راست
تا چشم بتم چه فتنه انگیخت

کز هر طرفی هزار غوغاست
تا جام لبش کدام می داد
کز جرعهاش هر که هست شیداست
ساقی قدحی که مست عشقم
و آن باده هنوز در سر ماست
آن نعرهٔ شور همچنان هست
وآن شیفتگی هنوز برجاست
کارم، که چو زلف توست در هم
بی قامت تو نمیشود راست
مقصود تویی مرا ز هستی
کز جام، غرض می مصفاست
آیینهٔ روی توست جانم
عکس رخ تو درو هویداست
گل رنگ رخ تو دارد ارنه
رنگ رخش از پی چه زیباست
ور سرو نه قامت تو دیده است
او را کشش از چه سوی بالاست
باغی است جهان، ز عکس رویت
خرم دل آن که در تماشاست
در باغ همه رخ تو بیند
از هر ورق گل آن که بیناست
از عکس رخت دل عراقی
گلزار و بهار و باغ و صحراست

2.54

بوی گل و بانگ مرغ برخاست
هنگام نشاط و روز صحراست
فراش خزان ورق بیفشاند
نقاش صبا چمن بیاراست
ما را سر باغ و بوستان نیست
هر جا که تویی تفرج آن جاست
گویند نظر به روی خوبان
نهیست نه این نظر که ما راست
در روی تو سر صنع بی چون
چون آب در آبگینه پیداست
چشم چپ خویشتن برآرم
تا چشم نبیندت به جز راست
هر آدمیی که مهر مهرت
در وی نگرفت سنگ خاراست
روزی تر و خشک من بسوزد
آتش که به زیر دیگ سوداست
نالیدن بی حساب سعدی
گویند خلاف رای داناست
از ورطه ما خبر ندارد
آسوده که بر کنار دریاست

2.55

گر متصور شدی با تو برآویختن
حیف نبودی وجود در قدمت ریختن

فکرت من در تو نیست در قلم قدرتیست
کو بتواند چنین صورتی انگیختن

2.56

صبحی مبارکست نظر بر جمال دوست
بر خوردن از درخت امید وصال دوست
بختم نخفته بود که از خواب بامداد
برخاستم به طالع فرخنده فال دوست
از دل برون شو ای غم دنیا و آخرت
یا خانه جای رخت بود یا مجال دوست
خواهم که بیخ صحبت اغیار برکنم
در باغ دل رها نکنم جز نهال دوست
تشریف داد و رفت ندانم ز بیخودی
کاین دوست بود در نظرم یا خیال دوست
هوشم نماند و عقل برفت و سخن نبست
مقبل کسی که محو شود در کمال دوست
سعدی حجاب نیست تو آیینه پاک دار
زنگارخورده چون بنماید جمال دوست

2.57

رفتی و همچنان به خیال من اندری
گویی که در برابر چشمم مصوری
فکرم به منتهای جمالت نمی‌رسد
کز هر چه در خیال من آمد نکوتری

مه بر زمین نرفت و پری دیده برنداشت
تا ظن برم که روی تو ماه است یا پری
تو خود فرشته‌ای نه از این گل سرشته‌ای
گر خلق از آب و خاک تو از مشک و عنبری
[...]
گر چشم در سرت کنم از گریه باک نیست
زیرا که تو عزیزتر از چشم در سری
[...]
سعدی به وصل دوست چو دستت نمی‌رسد
باری به یاد دوست زمانی به سر بری

2.58

در تو حیرانم و اوصاف معانی که تو راست
و اندر آن کس که بصر دارد و حیران تو نیست
آن چه عیبست که در صورت زیبای تو هست
وان چه سحرست که در غمزه فتان تو نیست
[...]
از خدا آمده‌ای آیت رحمت بر خلق
وان کدام آیت لطفست که در شأن تو نیست

2.59

بازآی که در دیده بماندست خیالت
بنشین که به خاطر بگرفتست نشانت

2.60

چنان تصور معشوق در خیال من است
که دیگرم متصور نمی‌شود معقول

2.61

برکناری شو ز هر نقشی که آن آید پدید
تا تو را نقاش مطلق زان میان آید پدید
بگذر از نقش دو عالم خواه نیک و خواه بد
تا ز بی نقشیت نقشی جاودان آید پدید
تو ز چشم خویش پنهانی اگر پیدا شوی
در میان جان تو گنجی نهان آید پدید
[…]
جز خیالی چشم تو هرگز نبیند از جهان
از خیال جمله بگذر تا جهان آید پدید

2.62

در اندیشه ببستم قلم وهم شکستم
که تو زیباتر از آنی که کنم وصف و بیانت

2.63

آن چنان وهم در تو حیران است
که نمی‌داندت نشان گفتن

2.64

هر شب اندیشه دیگر کنم و رای دگر
که من از دست تو فردا بروم جای دگر
بامدادان که برون می‌نهم از منزل پای
حسن عهدم نگذارد که نهم پای دگر
هر کسی را سر چیزی و تمنای کسیست
ما نداریم به غیر از تو تمنای دگر
زان که هرگز به جمال تو در آیینه وهم
متصور نشود صورت و بالای دگر
وامقی بود که دیوانه عذرا بودی
منم امروز و تویی وامق و عذرای دگر
وقت آنست که صحرا گل و سنبل گیرد
خلق بیرون شده هر قوم به صحرای دگر
[…]
بازگویم نه که ایام بقا این همه نیست
سعدی امروز تحمل کن و فردای دگر

2.65

فکرم به منتهای جمالت نمی‌رسد
کز هر چه در خیال من آید نکوتری

2.66

راستی گویم به سروی ماند این بالای تو
در عبارت می‌نیاید چهره مهرافزای تو
چون تو حاضر می‌شوی من غایب از خود می‌شوم

زانکه حیران می‌بماند وهم در سیمای تو
کاشکی صد چشم از این بی خوابتر بودی مرا
تا نظر می کردمی در منظر زیبای تو
ای که در دل جای داری بر سر چشمم نشین
کاندر آن بیغوله ترسم تنگ باشد جای تو

2.67

سر قلم قدرت بی چون الهی
در روی تو چون روی در آیینه پدید است

2.68

ندانمت به حقیقت که در جهان به که مانی
جهان و هر چه در او هست صورتند و تو جانی
به پای خویشتن آیند عاشقان به کمندت
که هر که را تو بگیری ز خویشتن برهانی
مرا مپرس که چونی به هر صفت که تو خواهی
مرا مگوی که چه نامی به هر لقب که تو خوانی
چنان به نظرت اول ز خلق می ببری دل
که باز می‌نتواند گرفت نظرت ثانی
تو پرده پیش گرفتی و ز اشتیاق جمالت
ز پرده‌ها به درافتاد رازهای نهانی
بر آتش تو نشستیم و دود شوق برآمد
تو ساعتی ننشستی که آتشی بنشانی
چو پیش خاطرم آید خیال صورت خوبت
ندانمت که چه گویم ز اختلاف معانی
مرا نگاه نباشد نظر به روی جوانان

که پیر داند مقدار روزگار جوانی
تو را که دیده ز خواب و خمار باز نباشد
ریاضت من شب تا سحر نشسته چه دانی
من ای صبا ره رفتن به کوی دوست ندانم
تو می‌روی به سلامت سلام من برسانی
سر از کمند تو سعدی به هیچ روی نتابد
اسیر خویش گرفتی بکش چنان که تو دانی

2.69

بامدادی که تفاوت نکند لیل و نهار
خوش بود دامن صحرا و تماشای بهار
صوفی از صومعه گو خیمه بزن بر گلزار
که نه وقتست که در خانه بخفتی بیکار
بلبلان وقت گل آمد که بنالند از شوق
نه کم از بلبل مستی تو بنال ای هشیار
آفرینش همه تنبیه خداوند دلست
دل ندارد که ندارد به خداوند اقرار
این همه نقش عجب بر در و دیوار وجود
هر که فکرت نکند نقش بود بر دیوار
کوه و دریا و درختان همه در تسبیح‌اند
نه همه مستمعی فهم کنند این اسرار
خبرت هست که مرغان سحر می گویند
آخر ای خفته سر از خواب جهالت بردار
هر که امروز نبیند اثر قدرت او
غالب آنست که فرداش نبیند دیدار
[...]

وقت آنست که داماد گل از حجلهٔ غیب
به در آید که درختان همه کردند نثار

2.70

ای طراوت برده از فردوس اعلا روی تو
نادرست اندر نگارستان دنیا روی تو
گر چه از انگشت مانی برنیاید چون تو نقش
هر دم انگشتی نهد بر نقش مانی روی تو
از گل و ماه و پری در چشم من زیباتری
گل ز من دل برد یا مه یا پری نی روی تو
دختران نعش را کاسد شود بازار حسن
گر چو یوسف پرده بردارد به دعوی روی تو
ماه و پروین از خجالت رخ فروپوشد اگر
آفتاب آسا کند در شب تجلی روی تو
چشمم از زاری چو فرهاد است و شیرین لعل تو
عقلم از شورش چو مجنون است و لیلی روی تو
مردم چشمش بدرد پرده عمیان ز شوق
گر درآید در خیال چشم اعمی روی تو
روی هر صاحب جمالی را به مه خواندن خطاست
گر رخی را ماه باید خواند باری روی تو
چون به هر وجهی بخواهد رفت جان از دست ما
خوبتر وجهی بباید ساخت اولی روی تو
رسم تقوا می‌نهد در عشقبازی رای من
کوس غارت می‌زند در ملک تقوا روی تو
ملک زیبایی مسلم گشت فرمان تو را

تا چنین خطی مزور کرد افشا روی تو
خرده بر سعدی مگیر ای جان که جای خرده نیست
سوختن در عشق وان گه ساختن بی روی تو

2.71

پای سرو بوستانی در گل است
سرو ما را پای معنی در دل است

2.72

ما پراکندگان مجموعیم
یار ما غایب است و در نظر است
برگ تر خشک می‌شود به زمان
برگ چشمان ما همیشه تر است

2.73

خیال روی کسی در سرست هر کس را
مرا خیال کسی کز خیال بیرونست

2.74

سوی حق شاهراه نفس و نَفَس
آینهٔ دل زدودن آمد و بس

2.75

گوید آنکس درین مقام فضول
که تجلی نداند او ز حلول
گرت باید که بر دهد دیدار
آینه کژ مدار و روشن‌دار

2.76

در گمان تو نیامد ای عجب هرگز غلط
لوح محفوظست پنداری ترا اندر گمان

2.77

ور قضا تومار دیوان سازد اندر مدح تو
لوح محفوظ اندر آن دیوان و تومار آورد

2.78

نسختی از لوح محفوظ است گویی خاطرت
کاندرو بینی و دانی بودنیها بر یقین

2.79

از کن اول برآرد شعبده استاد فکر
وز پی آخر درآرد تیر مه باد صبا
دیده گوید تا چه می‌جوید برون از لوح روح
نفس گوید تا چه می‌خواند برون دل ذکا

2.80

تو را دل لوح محفوظ است و علم از فلسفی گیری
تو را خورشید همسایه چراغ از کوچه گیرانی

2.81

دل آینه‌ای است پشت او تیره
گر بزدایی بروی وا گردد
گل دل گردد چو پشت گردد رو
ظلمت چو رود همه ضیا گردد

2.82

دل آینه صورت غیب است ولیکن
شرط است که بر آینه زنگار نباشد

2.83

ای دوست برآور دری از خلق به رویم
تا هیچ کسم واقف اسرار نباشد

2.84

روز و شب می‌باشد آن ساعت که همچون آفتاب
می نمایی روی و دیگر باز روزن می بری

2.85

روی تو خوش می‌نماید آینه ما
کآینه پاکیزه است و روی تو زیبا
چون می روشن در آبگینه صافی
خوی جمیل از جمال روی تو پیدا
هر که دمی با تو بود یا قدمی رفت
از تو نباشد به هیچ حال شکیبا
صید بیابان سر از کمند بپیچد
ما همه پیچیده در کمند تو عمدا
طایر مسکین که مهر بست به جایی
گر بکشندش نمی‌رود به دگر جا
غیرتم آید شکایت از تو به هر کس
درد احبا نمی‌برم به اطبا
برخی جانت شوم که شمع افق را
پیش بمیرد چراغدان ثریا
گر تو شکرخنده آستین نفشانی
هر مگسی طوطیی شوند شکرخا
لعبت شیرین اگر ترش ننشیند
مدعیانش طمع کنند به حلوا
مرد تماشای باغ حسن تو سعدیست
دست فرومایگان برند به یغما

2.86

سعدی بشوی لوح دل از نقش غیر او
علمی که ره به حق ننماید جهالت است

2.87

دیگر از آن جانبم نماز نباشد
گر تو اشارت کنی که قبله چنینست
آینه‌ای پیش آفتاب نهادست
بر در آن خیمه یا شعاع جبینست
گر همه عالم ز لوح فکر بشویند
عشق نخواهد شدن که نقش نگینست

2.88

در که خواهم بستن آن دل کز وصالت برکنم
چون تو در عالم نباشد ور نه عالم تنگ نیست
شاهد ما را نه هر چشمی چنان بیند که هست
صنع را آیینه‌ای باید که بر وی زنگ نیست

2.89

عمرها در سینه پنهان داشتیم اسرار دل
نقطهٔ سر عاقبت بیرون شد از پرگار دل
گر مسلمانی رفیقا دیر و زنارت کجاست
شهوت آتشگاه جانست و هوا زنار دل
[...]
آخر ای آیینه جوهر دیده‌ای بر خود گمار
صورت حق چند پوشی در پس زنگار دل
این قدر دریاب کاندر خانهٔ خاطر ملک
نگذرد تا صورت دیوست بر دیوار دل

ملک آزادی نخواهی یافت و استغنای مال
هر دو عالم بندهٔ خود کن به استظهار دل
در نگارستان صورت ترک حظ نفس گیر
تا شوی در عالم تحقیق برخوردار دل
نی تو را از کار گل امکان همت بیش نیست
با تو ترسم درنگیرد ماجرای کار دل
سعدیا با کر سخن در علم موسیقی خطاست
گوش جان باید که معلومش کند اسرار دل

2.90

در زلف تو دادند نگارا خبر دل
معذورم اگر آمده‌ام بر اثر دل
یا دل بر من باز فرست ای بت مه رو
یا راه مرا باز نما تو به بر دل
نی نی که اگر نیست ترا هیچ سر ما
ما بی تو نداریم دل خویش و سر دل
چندین سر اندیشه و تیمار که دارد
تا گه جگر یار خورد گه جگر دل
بی عشق تو دل را خطری نیست بر ما
هر چند که صعب ست نگارا خطر دل
تا دل غم عشق تو در بست به شادی
بستیم به جان بر غم عشقت کمر دل

2.91

صورت نبندد ای صنم بی زلف تو آرام دل
دل فتنه شد بر زلف تو ای فتنهٔ ایام دل

ای جان به مولای تو دل غرقهٔ دریای تو
دیری است تا سودای تو بگرفت هفت اندام دل
تا جان به عشقت بنده شد زین بندگی تابنده شد
تا دل ز نامت زنده شد پر شد دو عالم نام دل
جانا دلم از چشم بد نه هوش دارد نه خرد
تا از شراب عشق خود پر باده کردی جام دل
پیغامت آمد از دلم کای ماه حل کن مشکلم
کی خواهد آمد حاصلم ای فارغ از پیغام دل
از رخ مه گردون تویی وز لب می گلگون تویی
کام دل من چون تویی هرگز نیابم کام دل
ای همگان را همدمی شادی من از تو غمی
عطار را در هر دمی جانا تویی آرام دل

2.92

کرا در شهر برگویم غم دل
که آید در دو عالم محرم دل
دلی دارم همیشه همدم غم
غمی دارم همیشه همدم دل
دل عالم نمی‌دانم یقین دان
از آن افتاده‌ام در عالم دل
دلی و صد هزاران آه خونین
ز حد بگذشت الحق ماتم دل
کنار مرحمت ار باز گیری
به خرواران فرو ریزم غم دل

2.93

حلقه دل زدم شبی در هوس سلام دل
بانگ رسید کیست آن گفتم من غلام دل
موج ز نور روی دل پر شده بود کوی دل
کوزه آفتاب و مه گشته کمینه جام دل
عقل کل ار سری کند با دل چاکری کند
گردن عقل و صد چو او بسته به بند دام دل

2.94

خوشتر از خلد برین آراستند ایوان دل
تا به شادی مجلس آراید درو سلطان دل
هم ز حسن خود پدید آرد بهشت آباد جان
هم به روی خود برآراید نگارستان دل
در سرای دل چو سلطان حقیقت بار داد
صف زدند ارواح عالم گرد شادروان دل
جسم چبود پرده‌ای پرنقش بر درگاه جان
جان چه باشد پرده‌داری بر در جانان دل
عقل هر دم نامه‌ای دیگر نویسد نزد جان
تا بود فرمان نویسی در بر دیوان دل
مرغ همت برتر از فردوس اعلی زان پرد
تا مگر یابد نسیم روضهٔ رضوان دل
حسن بی‌پایان دل گرد جهان ظاهر شود
هر که را چشمی بود باشد چو جان حیران دل
خضر جان گرد سرابستان دل گردد مدام
تا خورد آب حیات از چشمهٔ حیوان دل

[...]

ظاهر و باطن نگه کن اول و آخر ببین
تا تو را روشن شود کز چیست چار ارکان دل
طاق ایوانش خم ابروی جانان من است
قبلهٔ جان من آمد زین قبل ایوان دل
تا به رنگ خود برآرد هر که یابد در جهان
شعله‌ای هر دم برافروزد رخ تابان دل
چون نگار من به هر رنگی بر آید هر زمان
لاجرم هر دم دگرگون می‌شود الوان دل
خود دو عالم در محیط دل کم از یک شبنم است
کی پدید آید نمی در بحر بی‌پایان دل
از بهشت و زینت او در جهان رنگی بود
کان بهشت آراستند اعنی سرابستان دل
بر بساط دل سماط عیش گستردند لیک
در جهان صاحبدلی کو تا شود مهمان دل
حیف نبود در جهان خوانی چنین آراسته
وانگهی ما بیخبر از حسن و از احسان دل
از ثنای دل عراقی عاجز آمد بهر آنک
هر کمالی کان بیندیشد بود نقصان دل

2.95

شاید این طلعت میمون که به فالش دارند
در دل اندیشه و در دیده خیالش دارند
که در آفاق چنین روی دگر نتوان دید
یا مگر آینه در پیش جمالش دارند

2.96

دوش در صحرای خلوت گوی تنهایی زدم
خیمه بر بالای منظوران بالایی زدم
خرقه‌پوشان صوامع را دو تایی چاک شد
چون من اندر کوی وحدت گوی تنهایی زدم
عقل کل را آبگینه ریزه در پای اوفتاد
بس که سنگ تجربت بر طاق مینایی زدم
پایمردم عقل بود آنگه که عشقم دست داد
پشت دستی بر دهان عقل سودایی زدم
دیو ناری را سر از سودای مایی شد به باد
پس من خاکی به حکمت گردن مایی زدم
تاب خوردم رشته وار اندر کف خیاط صنع
پس گره بر خبط خود بینی و خود رایی زدم
تا نباید گشتم گرد در کس چون کلید
بر در دل ز آرزو قفل شکیبایی زدم
گر کسی را رغبت دانش بود گو دم مزن
زانکه من دم درکشیدم تا به دانایی زدم
چون صدف پروردم اندر سینه در معرفت
تا به جوهر طعنه بر درهای دریایی زدم
بعد ازین چون مهر مستقبل نگردم جز به امر
پیش ازین گر چون فلک چرخی به رعنایی زدم
کنیت سعدی فرو شستم ز دیوان وجود
پس قدم در حضرت بیچون مولایی زدم

2.97

بارکشیده جفا پرده دریده هوا
راه ز پیش و دل ز پس واقعه‌ایست مشکلم
معرفت قدیم را بعد حجاب کی شود
گر چه به شخص غایبی در نظری مقابلم
آخر قصد من تویی غایت جهد و آرزو
تا نرسم ز دامنت دست امید نگسلم
ذکر تو از زبان من فکر تو از خیال من
چون برود که رفته‌ای در رگ و در مفاصلم
مشتغل توام چنان کز همه چیز غایبم
مفتکر توام چنان کز همه خلق غافلم
گر نظری کنی کند کشته صبر من ورق
ور نکنی چه بر دهد بیخ امید باطلم

2.98

که نور عالم علوی فرا هر روزنی تابد
تو اندر صومعش دیدی و ما در کنج میخانه

2.99

شستم به آب غیرت نقش و نگار ظاهر
کاندر سراچه دل نقش و نگار دارم

2.100

دریچه‌ای ز بهشتش به روی بگشایی
که بامداد پگاهش تو روی بنمایی
جهان شب است و تو خورشید عالم آرایی
صباح مقبل آن کز درش تو بازآیی

2.101

گر کسی وصف او ز من پرسد
بی دل از بی نشان چه گوید باز
عاشقان کشتگان معشوقند
بر نیاید ز کشتگان آواز

2.102

ای فتنه نوخاسته از عالم قدرت
غایب مشو از دیده که در دل بنشستی

2.103

دیدار یار غایب دانی چه ذوق دارد
ابری که در بیابان بر تشنه‌ای ببارد
ای بوی آشنایی دانستم از کجایی
پیغام وصل جانان پیوند روح دارد
[...]
دانی چرا نشیند سعدی به کنج خلوت
کز دست خوبرویان بیرون شدن نیارد

2.104

کشته بینند و مقاتل نشناسند که کیست
کین خدنگ از نظر خلق نهان می آید

2.105

بزرگ دولت آن کز درش تو آیی باز
بیا بیا که به خیر آمدی کجایی باز
رخی کز او متصور نمی شود آرام
چرا نمودی و دیگر نمی‌نمایی باز
در دو لختی چشمان شوخ دلبندت
چه کرده‌ام که به رویم نمی گشایی باز
[…]
شراب وصل تو در کام جان من ازلیست
هنوز مستم از آن جام آشنایی باز
دلی که بر سر کوی تو گم کنم هیهات
که جز به روی تو بینم به روشنایی باز
[…]
عوام خلق ملامت کنند صوفی را
کز این هوا و طبیعت چرا نیایی باز
اگر حلاوت مستی بدانی ای هشیار
به عمر خود نبری نام پارسایی باز
گرت چو سعدی از این در نواله‌ای بخشند
برو که خو نکنی هرگز از گدایی باز

2.106

تو در میان خلایق به چشم اهل نظر
چنان که در شب تاریک پاره نوری

2.107

بلای عشق تو نگذاشت پارسا در پارس
یکی منم که ندانم نماز چون بستم
نماز کردم و از بیخودی ندانستم
که در خیال تو عقد نماز چون بستم
نماز مست شریعت روا نمی‌دارد
نماز من که پذیرد که روز و شب مستم
چنین که دست خیالت گرفت دامن من
چه بودی ار برسیدی به دامنت دستم

2.108

دل عارفان ببردند و قرار پارسایان
همه شاهدان به صورت تو به صورت و معانی
[...]
مده ای رفیق پندم که نظر بر او فکندم
تو میان ما ندانی که چه می‌رود نهانی

2.109

آنک از جنت فردوس یکی می آید
اختری می گذرد یا ملکی می آید
هر شکرپاره که در می‌رسد از عالم غیب

بر دل ریش عزیزان نمکی می آید
تا مگر یافته گردد نفسی صحبت دوست
نفسی می‌رود از عمر و یکی می آید
سعدیا لشکر سلطان غمش ملک وجود
هم بگیرد که دمادم یزکی می آید

2.110

کیست این ماه منور که چنین می گذرد
تشنه جان می دهد و ماء معین می گذرد
سرو اگر نیز تحول کند از جای به جای
نتوان گفت که زیباتر از این می گذرد
حور عین می گذرد در نظر سوختگان
یا مه چارده یا لعبت چین می گذرد
کام از او کس نگرفتست مگر باد بهار
که بر آن زلف و بناگوش و جبین می گذرد
مردم زیر زمین رفتن او پندارند
کآفتابست که بر اوج برین می گذرد
پای گو بر سر عاشق نه و بر دیده دوست
حیف باشد که چنین کس به زمین می گذرد
هر که در شهر دلی دارد و دینی دارد
گو حذر کن که هلاک دل و دین می گذرد
از خیال آمدن و رفتنش اندر دل و چشم
با گمان افتم و گر خود به یقین می گذرد
گر کند روی به ما یا نکند حکم او راست
پادشاهیست که بر ملک یمین می گذرد

سعدیا گوشه نشینی کن و شاهدبازی
شاهد آنست که بر گوشه نشین می گذرد

2.111

روزی بت من مست به بازار برآمد
گرد از دل عشاق به یک بار بر آمد
صد دلشده را از غم او روز فرو شد
صد شیفته را از غم او کار برآمد
رخسار و خطش بود چو دیبا و چو عنبر
باز آن دو بهم کرد و خریدار برآمد
در حسرت آن عنبر و دیبای نو آیین
فریاد ز بزاز و ز عطار برآمد
رشک ست بتان را ز بناگوش و خط او
گویند که بر برگ گلش خار برآمد
آن مایه بدانید که ایزد نظری کرد
تا سوسن و شمشاد ز گلزار برآمد
و آن شب که مرا بود به خلوت بر او بار
پیش از شب من صبح ز کهسار برآمد

2.112

سرمست ز کاشانه به گلزار برآمد
غلغل ز گل و لاله به یک بار برآمد
مرغان چمن نعره زنان دیدم و گریان
کین غنچه که از طرف چمنزار برآمد

آب از گل رخساره او عکس پذیرفت
و آتش به سر غنچه گلنار برآمد
سجاده نشینی که مرید غم او شد
آوازه اش از خانه خمار برآمد
زاهد چو کرامات بت عارض او دید
از چله میان بسته به زنار برآمد
بر خاک چو من بی‌دل و دیوانه نشاندش
اندر نظر هر که پری وار برآمد
من مفلس از آن روز شدم کز حرم غیب
دیبای جمال تو به بازار برآمد
کام دلم آن بود که جان بر تو فشانم
آن کام میسر شد و این کار برآمد
سعدی چمن آن روز به تاراج خزان داد
کز باغ دلش بوی گل یار برآمد

2.113

ای ماهروی حاضر غایب که پیش دل
یک روز نگذرد که تو صد بار نگذری
[…]
بازآی کز صبوری و دوری بسوختیم
ای غایب از نظر که به معنی برابری
[…]
تا خود برون پرده حکایت کجا رسد
چون از درون پرده چنین پرده می‌دری

2.114

وه که جدا نمی‌شود نقش تو از خیال من
تا چه شود به عاقبت در طلب تو حال من
ناله زیر و زار من زارتر است هر زمان
بس که به هجر می دهد عشق تو گوشمال من
نور ستارگان ستد روی چو آفتاب تو
دست نمای خلق شد قامت چون هلال من
پرتو نور روی تو هر نفسی به هر کسی
می رسد و نمی‌رسد نوبت اتصال من
خاطر تو به خون من رغبت اگر چنین کند
هم به مراد دل رسد خاطر بدسگال من
برگذری و ننگری بازنگر که بگذرد
فقر من و غنای تو جور تو و احتمال من
چرخ شنید ناله‌ام گفت منال سعدیا
کآه تو تیره می‌کند آینه جمال من

2.115

ای دل و جان کاملان گم شده در کمال تو
عقل همه مقربان بی خبر از وصال تو
جمله تویی به خود نگر جمله ببین که دایما
هجده هزار عالم است آینهٔ جمال تو
تا دل طالبانت را از تو دلالتی بود
هرچه که هست در جهان هست همه مثال تو
جملهٔ اهل دیده را از تو زبان ز کار شد
نیست مجال نکته‌ای در صفت کمال تو

چرخ رونده قرن‌ها بی سر و پای در رهت
پشت خمیده می‌رود در غم گوشمال تو
[…]
مانده‌اند دور دور اهل دو کون از درت
زانکه وجود گم کند خلق در اتصال تو
خشک شدیم بر زمین پرده ز روی برفکن
تا لب خشک عاشقان تر شود از زلال تو
گر چه فرید در جهان هست فصیحتر کسی
رد مکنش که در سخن هست زبانش لال تو

2.116

شمع شب‌ها به جز خیال تو نیست
باغ جان‌ها به جز جمال تو نیست
رو که خورشید عشق را همه روز
طالعی به ز اتصال تو نیست
[…]
نیم روز آرزوی تو دورست
نیم شب خالی از خیال تو نیست

2.117

طمع مدار که دوری گزینم از رخ خوب
که نیست شرط محبت جدائی از محبوب
[…]
چو اتصال حقیقی بود میان دو دوست
کجا ز یوسف مصری جدا بود یعقوب

[…]
ز صورت تو کند نور معنوی حاصل
دل شکسته که هم سالکست و هم مجذوب

2.118

نظر بعین طبیعت مکن که از خوبان
مراد اهل نظر اتصال روحانیست
پری رخا چکنم گر نخوانمت شب و روز
چرا که چارهٔ دیوانگان پری خوانیست
[…]
مپوش چهره که از طلعت تو خواجو را
غرض مطالعهٔ سر صنع یزدانیست

2.119

من چون تو به دلبری ندیدم
گلبرگ چنین طری ندیدم
مانند تو آدمی در آفاق
ممکن نبود پری ندیدم
وین بوالعجبی و چشم بندی
در صنعت سامری ندیدم
با روی تو ماه آسمان را
امکان برابری ندیدم
لعلی چو لب شکرفشانت
در کلبه جوهری ندیدم
چون در دو رسته دهانت

نظم سخن دری ندیدم
مه را که خرد که من به کرات
مه دیدم و مشتری ندیدم
وین پرده راز پارسایان
چندان که تو می‌دری ندیدم
دیدم همه دلبران آفاق
چون تو به دلاوری ندیدم
جوری که تو می کنی در اسلام
در ملت کافری ندیدم
سعدی غم عشق خوبرویان
چندان که تو می‌خوری ندیدم
دیدم همه صوفیان آفاق
مثل تو قلندری ندیدم

2.120

ساعتی کز درم آن سرو روان بازآمد
راست گویی به تن مرده روان بازآمد
پیر بودم ز جفای فلک و جور زمان
باز پیرانه سرم عشق جوان بازآمد
بخت پیروز که با ما به خصومت می‌بود
بامداد از در من صلح کنان بازآمد
دوست بازآمد و دشمن به مصیبت بنشست
باد نوروز علی رغم خزان بازآمد
مژدگانی بده ای نفس که سختی بگذشت
دل گرانی مکن ای جسم که جان بازآمد
باور از بخت ندارم که به لطف از در من

آن بت سنگ دل سخت کمان بازآمد
تا تو بازآمدی ای مونس جان از در غیب
هر که در سر هوسی داشت از آن بازآمد
عشق روی تو حرامست مگر سعدی را
که به سودای تو از هر که جهان بازآمد
دوستان عیب مگیرید و ملامت مکنید
کاین حدیثیست که از وی نتوان بازآمد

2.121

تو از هر در که بازآیی بدین خوبی و زیبایی
دری باشد که از رحمت به روی خلق بگشایی
ملامتگوی بی‌حاصل ترنج از دست نشناسد
در آن معرض که چون یوسف جمال از پرده بنمایی
به زیورها بیارایند وقتی خوبرویان را
تو سیمین تن چنان خوبی که زیورها بیارایی

2.122

دیدار تو حل مشکلات است
صبر از تو خلاف ممکنات است
دیباچهٔ صورت بدیعت
عنوان کمال حسن ذات است
چون روی تو صورتی ندیدم
در شهر که مبطل صلات است

2.123

همه کس عیب هوس باختن ما بکند
مگر آن کس که به دام هوسی افتادست

2.124

در همه عمرم شبی بی‌خبر از در درآی
تا شب درویش را صبح برآید به شام
[...]
ای که ملامت کنی عارف دیوانه را
شاهد ما حاضر است گر تو ندانی کدام

2.125

مگر تو روی بپوشی و گر نه ممکن نیست
که اهل معرفت از تو نظر بپرهیزند

2.126

بارها گفته‌ام این روی به هر کس منمای
تا تأمل نکند دیده هر بی بصرت
بازگویم نه که این صورت و معنی که تو راست
نتواند که ببیند مگر اهل نظرت

2.127

کبر یک سو نه اگر شاهد درویشانی
دیو خوش طبع به از حور گره پیشانی

آرزو می کندم با تو دمی در بستان
یا به هر گوشه که باشد که تو خود بستانی
با من کشته هجران نفسی خوش بنشین
تا مگر زنده شوم زآن نفس روحانی
گر در آفاق بگردی به جز آیینه تو را
صورتی کس ننماید که بدو می‌مانی
هیچ دورانی بی فتنه نگویند که بود
تو بدین حسن مگر فتنه این دورانی
مردم از ترس خدا سجده رویت نکنند
بامدادت که ببینند و من از حیرانی
[...]
این توانی که نیایی ز در سعدی باز
لیک بیرون روی از خاطر او نتوانی

2.128

ز حسن روی تو بر دین خلق می ترسم
که بدعتی که نبوده است در جهان آری

2.129

گرم بازآمدی محبوب سیم اندام سنگین دل
گل از خارم برآوردی و خار از پا و پا از گل
ایا باد سحرگاهی گر این شب روز می‌خواهی
از آن خورشید خرگاهی برافکن دامن محمل
گر او سرپنجه بگشاید که عاشق می کشم شاید
هزارش صید پیش آید به خون خویش مستعجل
گروهی همنشین من خلاف عقل و دین من

بگیرند آستین من که دست از دامنش بگسل
ملامتگوی عاشق را چه گوید مردم دانا
که حال غرقه در دریا نداند خفته بر ساحل
به خونم گر بیالاید دو دست نازنین شاید
نه قتلم خوش همی آید که دست و پنجه قاتل
اگر عاقل بود داند که مجنون صبر نتواند
شتر جایی بخواباند که لیلی را بود منزل
ز عقل اندیشه‌ها زاید که مردم را بفرساید
گرت آسودگی باید برو عاشق شو ای عاقل
مرا تا پای می پوید طریق وصل می‌جوید
بهل تا عقل می گوید زهی سودای بی‌حاصل
عجایب نقش‌ها بینی خلاف رومی و چینی
اگر با دوست بنشینی ز دنیا و آخرت غافل
در این معنی سخن باید که جز سعدی نیاراید
که هرچ از جان برون آید نشیند لاجرم بر دل

2.130

کاشکی پرده برافتادی از آن منظر حسن
تا همه خلق ببینند نگارستان را
همه را دیده در اوصاف تو حیران ماند
تا دگر عیب نگویند من حیران را
لیکن آن نقش که در روی تو من می‌بینم
همه را دیده نباشد که ببینند آن را
چشم گریان مرا حال بگفتم به طبیب
گفت یک بار ببوس آن دهن خندان را

3.1

طالبان ذوق را گو در سماع
استماع شعر شیرازی کنید

3.2

این مطرب از کجاست که برگفت نام دوست
تا جان و جامه بذل کنم بر پیام دوست
دل زنده می‌شود به امید وفای یار
جان رقص می کند به سماع کلام دوست

3.3

یار من آن که لطف خداوند یار اوست
بیداد و داد و رد و قبول اختیار اوست
[...]
باور مکن که صورت او عقل من ببرد
عقل من آن ببرد که صورت نگار اوست
گر دیگران به منظر زیبا نظر کنند
ما را نظر به قدرت پروردگار اوست

3.4

روی تو خوش می نماید آینه ما
کاینه پاکیزه است و روی تو زیبا

3.5

لیکن آن نقش که در روی تو من میبینم
همه را دیده نباشد که بینند آن را

3.6

هر کسی را نتوان گفت که صاحب نظر است
عشقبازی دگر و نفس پرستی دگر است

3.7

چندین هزار منظر زیبا بیافرید
تا کیست کو نظر ز سر اعتبار کرد

3.8

همه را دیده به رویت نگرانست ولیکن
خودپرستان ز حقیقت نشناسند هوا را

3.9

شب عاشقان بی‌دل چه شبی دراز باشد
تو بیا کز اول شب در صبح باز باشد
عجبست اگر توانم که سفر کنم ز دستت
به کجا رود کبوتر که اسیر باز باشد
ز محبتت نخواهم که نظر کنم به رویت
که محب صادق آنست که پاکباز باشد

به کرشمه عنایت نگهی به سوی ما کن
که دعای دردمندان ز سر نیاز باشد
سخنی که نیست طاقت که ز خویشتن بپوشم
به کدام دوست گویم که محل راز باشد
چه نماز باشد آن را که تو در خیال باشی
تو صنم نمی گذاری که مرا نماز باشد
نه چنین حساب کردم چو تو دوست می گرفتم
که ثنا و حمد گویم و جفا و ناز باشد
دگرش چو بازبینی غم دل مگوی سعدی
که شب وصال کوتاه و سخن دراز باشد
قدمی که برگرفتی به وفا و عهد یاران
اگر از بلا بترسی قدم مجاز باشد

3.10

نه از چینم حکایت کن نه از روم
که من دل با یکی دارم در این بوم
هر آن ساعت که با یاد من آید
فراموشم شود موجود و معدوم
ز دنیا قسم ما غم خوردن آمد
نشاید خوردن الا رزق مقسوم
رطب شیرین و دست از نخل کوتاه
زلال اندر میان و تشنه محروم
از آن شاهد که در اندیشه ماست
ندانم زاهدی در شهر معصوم
به روی او نماند هیچ منظور

به بوی او نماند هیچ مشموم
نه بی او عیش می‌خواهم نه با او
که او در سلک من حیف است منظوم
رفیقان چشم ظاهربین بدوزید
که ما را در میان سریست مکتوم
همه عالم گر این صورت ببینند
کس این معنی نخواهد کرد مفهوم
چنان سوزم که خامانم نبینند
نداند تندرست احوال محموم
مرا گر دل دهی ور جان ستانی
عبادت لازم است و بنده ملزوم
نشاید برد سعدی جان از این کار
مسافر تشنه و جلاب مسموم
چو آهن تاب آتش می‌نیارد
چرا باید که پیشانی کند موم

3.11

ز حسن روی تو بر دین خلق می ترسم
که بدعتی که نبوده است در جهان آری

3.12

عوام خلق ملامت کنند صوفی را
کز این هوا و طبیعت چرا نیایی باز

3.13

چنین که دست خیالت گرفت دامن من
چه بودی ار برسیدی به دامنت دستم

3.14

مردم از ترس خدا سجده رویت نکنند
بامدادت که ببینند و من از حیرانی

3.15

گر کسی سرو شنیدست که رفتست این است
یا صنوبر که بناگوش و برش سیمین است
نه بلندیست به صورت که تو معلوم کنی
که بلند از نظر مردم کوته‌بین است
خواب در عهد تو در چشم من آید هیهات
عاشقی کار سری نیست که بر بالین است
همه آرام گرفتند و شب از نیمه گذشت
وآنچه در خواب نشد چشم من و پروین است
خود گرفتم که نظر بر رخ خوبان کفر است
من از این بازنگردم که مرا این دین است
وقت آن است که مردم ره صحرا گیرند
خاصه اکنون که بهار آمد و فروردین است
چمن امروز بهشت است و تو در می‌بایی
تا خلایق همه گویند که حورالعین است
هر چه گفتیم در اوصاف کمالیت او
همچنان هیچ نگفتیم که صد چندین است

آنچه سرپنجهٔ سیمین تو با سعدی کرد
با کبوتر نکند پنجه که با شاهین است
من دگر شعر نخواهم که نویسم که مگس
زحمتم می‌دهد از بس که سخن شیرین است

3.16

مونس من ماه و پروینست هر شب تا به روز
زان رخ چون ماه و زان دندان چون پروین تو

3.17

نشان بخت بلند است و طالع میمون
علی الصباح نظر بر جمال روزافزون
علی الخصوص کسی را که طبع موزون است
چگونه دوست ندارد شمایل موزون

3.18

آن نه روی است که من وصف جمالش دانم
این حدیث از دگری پرس که من حیرانم
همه بینند نه این صنع که من می‌بینم
همه خوانند نه این نقش که من می‌خوانم
عجب آن نیست که سرگشته بود طالب دوست
عجب این است که من واصل و سرگردانم
سرو در باغ نشانند و تو را بر سر و چشم
گر اجازت دهی ای سرو روان بنشانم
به سرت کز سر پیمان محبت نروم

گر بفرمایی رفتن به سر پیکانم
باش تا جان برود در طلب جانانم
که به کاری به از این بازنیاید جانم
هر نصیحت که کنی بشنوم ای یار عزیز
صبرم از دوست مفرمای که من نتوانم
عجب از طبع هوسناک منت می آید
من خود از مردم بی طبع عجب می‌مانم
عشق من بر گل رخسار تو امروزی نیست
دیر سال است که من بلبل این بستانم
گفته بودی که بود در همه عالم سعدی
من به خود هیچ نیم هر چه تو گویی آنم
گر به تشریف قبولم بنوازی ملکم
ور به تازانه قهرم بزنی شیطانم

3.19

ذوقی چنان ندارد بی دوست زندگانی
دودم به سر برآمد زین آتش نهانی
شیراز در نبسته‌ست از کاروان ولیکن
ما را نمی گشایند از قید مهربانی
شرح غمت نگویم در صورتم نگه کن
دفتر دراز باشد دیباچه اش بخوانی
اشتر که اختیارش در دست خود نباشد
می بایدش کشیدن باری به ناتوانی
خون هزار وامق خوردی به دلفریبی
دست از هزار عذرا بردی به دلستانی
صورت نگار چینی بی خویشتن بماند

گر صورتت ببیند سر تا به سر معانی
ای بر در سرایت غوغای عشقبازان
همچون بر آب شیرین آشوب کاروانی
تو فارغی و عشقت بازیچه می‌نماید
تا خرمنت نسوزد تشویش ما ندانی
می گفتمت که جانی دیگر دریغم آید
گر جوهری به از جان ممکن بود تو آنی
سروی چو در سماعی بدری چو در حدیثی
صبحی چو در کناری شمعی چو در میانی
اول چنین نبودی باری حقیقتی شد
دی حظ نفس بودی امروز قوت جانی
شهر آن توست و شاهی فرمای هر چه خواهی
گر بی عمل بخشی ور بی گنه برانی
روی امید سعدی بر خاک آستان است
بعد از تو کس ندارد یا غایة الامانی

3.20

هر که به شب شمعوار در نظر شاهدی است
باک ندارد به روز کشتن و آویختن

3.21

دیدار یار غایب دانی چه ذوق دارد
ابری که در بیابان بر تشنه‌ای ببارد

3.22

هر که ز ذوقش درون سینه صفاییست
شمع دلش را ز شاهدی نگزیرد

3.23

عاشق آن است که بی خویشتن از ذوق سماع
پیش شمشیر بلا رقص کنان می آید

3.24

تا به کرم خرده نگیری که من
غایبم از ذوق حضور ای صنم

3.25

کیست آن کش سر پیوند تو در خاطر نیست
یا نظر با تو ندارد مگرش ناظر نیست
نه حلالست که دیدار تو بیند هر کس
که حرامست بر آن کش نظری طاهر نیست
همه کس را مگر این ذوق نباشد که مرا
کان چه من می‌نگرم بر دگری ظاهر نیست

3.26

[…]
جان در تن مشتاقان از ذوق به رقص آید
چون باد بجنباند شاخی ز گلستانت

دیوار سرایت را نقاش نمی باید
تو زینت ایوانی نه صورت ایوانت
[…]
شاید که در این دنیا موتش نبود هرگز
سعدی که تو جان دارد بل دوستتر از جانت
بسیار چو ذوالقرنین آفاق بگردید ست
این تشنه که می میرد بر چشمه حیوانت

3.27

گرش ببینی و دست از ترنج بشناسی
روا بود که ملامت کنی زلیخا را

3.28

جز خداوندان معنی را نغلطاند سماع
اولت مغزی بباید تا برون آیی ز پوست

3.29

نه مطرب که آواز پای ستور
سماع است اگر عشق داری و شور
[…]
نه بم داند آشفته سامان نه زیر
به آواز مرغی بنالد فقیر
سراینده خود می نگردد خموش
ولیکن نه هر وقت باز است گوش
چو شوریدگان می پرستی کنند

به آواز دولاب مستی کنند
به چرخ اندر آیند دولاب وار
چو دولاب بر خود بگریند زار
به تسلیم سر در گریبان برند
چو طاقت نماند گریبان درند
مکن عیب درویش مدهوش مست
که غرق است از آن می‌زند پا و دست
نگویم سماع ای برادر که چیست
مگر مستمع را بدانم که کیست
گر از برج معنی پرد طیر او
فرشته فرو ماند از سیر او
وگر مرد لهو است و بازی و لاغ
قوی تر شود دیوش اندر دماغ
چه مرد سماع است شهوت پرست
به آواز خوش خفته خیزد نه مست
پریشان شود گل به باد سحر
نه هیزم که نشکافدش جز تبر
جهان پر سماع است و مستی و شور
ولیکن چه بیند در آیینه کور؟
نبینی شتر بر نوای عرب
که چونش به رقص اندر آرد طرب
شتر را چو شور طرب در سر است
اگر آدمی را نباشد خر است

3.30

اینان که به دیدار تو در رقص می آیند
چون می روی اندر طلبت جامه درانند

3.31

شبی بر ادای پسر گوش کرد
سماعش پریشان و مدهوش کرد
همی گفت و بر چهره افکنده خوی
که آتش به من در زد این بار نی
ندانی که شوریده حالان مست
چرا بر فشانند در رقص دست
گشاید دری بر دل از واردات
فشاند سر دست بر کاینات
حلالش بود رقص بر یاد دوست
که هر آستینیش جانی در اوست

3.32

از در درآمدی و من از خود به در شدم
گفتی کز این جهان به جهان دگر شدم

3.33

و گر ز مغز حقیقت به پوست خرسندی
تو نیز جامه ازرق بپوش و سر بترش

3.34

شاهدبازم هر آنک انکار کند
چون در نگری روز و شب این کار کند
آنها که ببینی همه شاهدبازند
آن زهره ندارند که انکار کند

3.35

نام سعدی همه جا رفت به شاهدبازی
وین نه عیبست که در ملت ما تحسینیست

3.36

بر یاد دوست هر شب با شاهد خیال
پا در فراش ودست در آغوش می کنیم
ما در سماع خرقه خود چون قمیص گل
پاره ز عشق سرو قبا پوش می کنیم

3.37

پاکیزه روی را که بود پاکدامنی
تاریکی از وجود بشوید به روشنی
گر شهوت از خیال دماغت به در رود
شاهد بود هر آنچه نظر بر وی افکنی
ذوق سماع مجلس انست به گوش دل
وقتی رسد که گوش طبیعت بیا کنی

3.38

مطرب از دست من به جان آمد
که مرا طاقت شنیدن نیست
دست بیچاره چون به جان نرسد
چاره جز پیرهن دریدن نیست
[…]
گفتم ای بوستان روحانی
دیدن میوه چون گزیدن نیست
گفت سعدی خیال خیره مبند
سیب سیمین برای چیدن نیست

3.39

یار از برای نفس گرفتن طریق نیست
ما نفس خویشتن بکشیم از برای یار
[…]
یاران شنیده‌ام که بیابان گرفته‌اند
بی طاقت از ملامت خلق و جفای یار
من ره نمی‌برم مگر آن جا که کوی دوست
من سر نمی‌نهم مگر آن جا که پای یار
[…]
بستان بی مشاهده دیدن مجاهدست
ور صد درخت گل بنشانی به جای یار
ای باد اگر به گلشن روحانیان روی
یار قدیم را برسانی دعای یار
[…]

هر کس میان جمعی و سعدی و گوشه‌ای
بیگانه باشد از همه خلق آشنای یار

3.40

مطرب همین طریق غزل گو نگاه دار
کاین ره که برگرفت به جایی دلالت است

3.41

هر آن کس کو شناسد این سه حالت
بداند وضع الفاظ و دلالت

3.42

جمله تویی به خود نگر جمله ببین که دایما
هجده هزار عالم است آینهٔ جمال تو
تا دل طالبانت را از تو دلالتی بود
هرچه که هست در جهان هست همه مثال تو

3.43

گرچه شد معنی درین صورت پدید
صورت از معنی قریبست و بعید
در دلالت همچو آبند و درخت
چون بماهیت روی دورند سخت

3.44

یک قافیه درین سخن از دال خالی است
و آن نیز بر ملالت طبع دلالت است

3.45

سعدی بشوی لوح دل از نقش غیر او
علمی که ره به حق ننماید جهالت است

3.46

انیس خاطر سعدی سماع روحانی است
چه جای زمزمه عندلیب و سجع حمام
در این سماع همه شاهدان نیکوروی
برین شراب همه صوفیان درد آشام

3.47

بنال مطرب مجلس بگوی گفته سعدی
شراب انس بیاور که من نه مرد نبیدم

3.48

قوم از شراب مست و ز منظور بی‌نصیب
من مست از او چنان که نخواهم شراب را

3.49

من خود ای ساقی از این شوق که دارم مستم
تو به یک جرعه دیگر ببری از دستم
هر چه کوته نظرانند بر ایشان پیمای
که حریفان ز مل و من ز تامل مستم

3.50

هر یک از دایره جمع به راهی رفتند
ما بماندیم و خیال تو به یک جای مقیم

3.51

شمع بخواهد نشست بازنشین ای غلام
روی تو دیدن به صبح روز نماید تمام
مطرب یاران برفت ساقی مستان بخفت
شاهد ما برقرار مجلس ما بردوام

3.52

لا جرم خلق جهانند مرید سخنم
که ریاضت کش محراب دو ابروی توام

3.53

کس به چشمم در نمی آید که گویم مثل اوست
خود به چشم عاشقان صورت نبندد مثل دوست
[...]

سعدیا چندان که خواهی گفت وصف روی یار
حسن گل بیش از قیاس بلبل بسیارگوست

3.54

نگفتم روزه بسیاری نپاید
ریاضت بگذرد سختی سر آید
پس از دشواری آسانیست ناچار
ولیکن آدمی را صبر باید
رخ از ما تا به کی پنهان کند عید
هلال آنک به ابرو می‌نماید
سرابستان در این موسم چه بندی
درش بگشای تا دل برگشاید
غلامان را بگو تا عود سوزند
کنیزک را بگو تا مشک ساید
که پندارم نگار سروبالا
در این دم تهنیت گویان درآید
سواران حلقه بربودند و آن شوخ
هنوز از حلقه‌ها دل می‌رباید
چو یار اندر حدیث آید به مجلس
مغنی را بگو تا کم سراید
که شعر اندر چنین مجلس نگنجد
بلی گر گفته سعدیست شاید

3.55

دور نباشد که خلق روز تصور کنند
گر بنمایی به شب طلعت خورشیدوار

[…]
دفتر فکرت بشوی گفته سعدی بگوی
دامن گوهر بیار بر سر مجلس ببار

3.56

محتسب در قفای رندانست
غافل از صوفیان شاهدباز
[…]
هیچ بلبل نداند این دستان
هیچ مطرب ندارد این آواز
هر متاعی ز معدنی خیزد
شکر از مصر و سعدی از شیراز

3.57

نوبت تست سیف فرغانی
به سخن شور در جهان انداز
کآفرین می کند بر سخنت
شکر از مصر و سعدی از شیراز

3.58

چه فتنه بود که حسن تو در جهان انداخت
که یک دم از تو نظر بر نمی‌توان انداخت

3.59

باز ای مطرب حدیثی در میان انداختی
فتنه ای در مجلس صاحب دلان انداختی
راز ما را فاش کردی در میان خاص و عام
وین حکایت در زبان این و آن انداختی
عارفان را با پری رویان کشیدی در سماع
بلبلان مست را در گلستان انداختی

3.60

حدیث حسن تو هر جا که در میان آمد
ز ذوق هر که دلی داشت در میان انداخت
[…]
چو در سماع عراقی حدیث دوست شنید
بجای خرقه به قوال جان توان انداخت

3.61

نظر خدای بینان طلب هوا نباشد
سفر نیازمندان قدم خطا نباشد
همه وقت عارفان را نظرست و عامیان را
نظری معاف دارند و دگر روا نباشد
به نسیم صبح باید که نبات زنده باشی
که جماد مردگان را خبر از صبا نباشد
اگرت سعادتی هست که زنده دل بمیری
به حیاتی اوفتادی که دگر فنا نباشد
به کسی نگر که ظلمت بزداید از وجودت

نه کسی نعوذبالله که در او صفا نباشد
تو خود از کدام شهری که ز دوستان نپرسی
مگر اندر آن ولایت که تویی وفا نباشد
اگر اهل معرفت را چو نی استخوان بسوزد
چو دفش به هیچ سختی خبر از قفا نباشد
اگرم تو خون بریزی به قیامتت نگیرم
که میان دوستان این همه ماجرا نباشد
نه حریف مهربانست حریف سست پیمان
که به روز تیرباران سپر بلا نباشد
تو در آینه نگه کن که چه دلبری ولیکن
تو کی خویشتن ببینی نگهت به ما نباشد
تو گمان مبر که سعدی ز جفا ملول گردد
که گرش تو بی جنایت بکشی جفا نباشد
دگری همین حکایت بکند که من ولیکن
چو معاملت ندارد سخن آشنا نباشد

3.62

به کوی لاله رخان هر که عشقباز آید
امید نیست که دیگر به عقل بازآید
[…]
ندانم ابروی شوخت چگونه محرابیست
که گر ببیند زندیق در نماز آید
[…]
خروشم از تف سینه‌ست و ناله از سر درد
نه چون دگر سخنان کز سر مجاز آید

3.63

مطرب آهنگ بگردان که دگر هیچ نماند
که از این پرده که گفتی به درافتد رازم
کس ننالید در این عهد چو من در غم دوست
که به آفاق نفس می‌رود از شیرازم
چند گفتند که سعدی نفسی باز خود آی
گفتم از دوست نشاید که به خود پردازم

3.64

سخت به ذوق میدهد باد ز بوستان نشان
صبح دمید و شب گذشت خیز و چراغ وا نشان
گر همه خلق را چو من بی دل و مست می کنی
روی به صالحان نمای خمر به زاهدان چشان
منکر حال عارفان سر سماع نشنود
زمزمه‌ای بیار خوش تا بروند ناخوشان
خرقه بگیر و می بده باده بیار و غم ببر
بی‌خبر است عاقل از لذت عیش بیهشان
سوختگان عشق را دود به سقف می‌رود
وقع ندارد این سخن پیش فسرده آتشان
ساعد و زلف جادوان تیغ نهفته می زند
گوش کجا که بشنود ناله زار خامشان
رقص حلال بایدت سنت اهل معرفت
دنیی زیر پای نه دست به آخرت فشان
چند نصیحتم کنی کز پی نکوان مرو
چون نروم که بی خودم شوق می برد کشان

بوی بهشت می دمد ما به عذاب در گرو
آب حیات میرود ما تن خویشتن کشان
باد بهار و بوی گل متفقند سعدیا
چون تو فصیح بلبلی حیف بود ز خامشان

3.65

با دوست باش گر همه آفاق دشمنند
کو مرهم است اگر دگران نیش می‌زنند
ای صورتی که پیش تو خوبان روزگار
همچون طلسم پای خجالت به دامنند
یک بامداد اگر بخرامی به بوستان
بینی که سرو را ز لب جوی برکنند
تلخ است پیش طایفه‌ای جور خوبروی
از معتقد شنو که شکر می پراکنند
ای متقی گر اهل دلی دیده‌ها بدوز
کاینان به دل ربودن مردم معینند
یا پرده‌ای به چشم تأمل فروگذار
یا دل بنه که پرده ز کارت برافکنند
جانم دریغ نیست ولیکن دل ضعیف
صندوق سر توست نخواهم که بشکنند
حسن تو نادر است در این عهد و شعر من
من چشم بر تو و همگان گوش بر منند
گویی جمال دوست که بیند چنان که اوست
الا به راه دیده سعدی نظر کنند

3.66

تو که گفته‌ای تأمل نکنم جمال خوبان
بکنی اگر چو سعدی نظری بیازمایی

3.67

در همه گیتی نگاه کردم و باز آمدم
صورت کس خوب نیست پیش تصاویر او
سعدی شیرین سخن این همه شور از کجا
شاهد ما آیتیست این همه تفسیر او

3.68

ای حسن خط از دفتر اخلاق تو بابی
شیرینی از اوصاف تو حرفی ز کتابی
[...]
بر دیده صاحب نظران خواب ببستی
ترسی که ببینند خیال تو به خوابی
[...]
آب سخنم می‌رود از طبع چو آتش
چون آتش رویت که از او می‌چکد آبی
یاران همه با یار و من خسته طلبکار
هر کس به سر آبی شد و سعدی به سرابی

3.69

من آدمی به حسن تو دیگر ندیده‌ام
این صورت و صفت که تو داری فرشته‌ای
[...]
ما دفتر از حکایت عشقت نبسته‌ایم
تو سنگدل حکایت ما درنوشته‌ای
[...]
من در بیان وصف تو حیران بمانده‌ام
حدیست حسن را و تو از حد گذشته‌ای
سر می‌نهند پیش خطت عارفان پارس
بیتی مگر ز گفته سعدی نبشته‌ای

3.70

به هیچ صورتی اندر نباشد این همه معنی
به هیچ سورتی اندر نباشد این همه آیت
کمال حسن وجودت به وصف راست نیاید
مگر هم آینه گوید چنان که هست حکایت
مرا سخن به نهایت رسید و فکر به پایان
هنوز وصف جمالت نمی‌رسد به نهایت
فراقنامه سعدی به هیچ گوش نیامد
که دردی از سخنانش در او نکرد سرایت

3.71

منم ای نگار و چشمی که در انتظار رویت
همه شب نخفت مسکین و بخفت مرغ و ماهی

و گر این شب درازم بکشد در آرزویت
نه عجب که زنده گردم به نسیم صبحگاهی
غم عشق اگر بکوشم که ز دوستان بپوشم
سخنان سوزناکم بدهد بر او گواهی
خضری چو کلک سعدی همه روز در سیاحت
نه عجب گر آب حیوان به درآید از سیاهی

Bibliography

As highlighted in the introductory notes on transliteration, I have chosen to adopt a simplified system (previously referred to as "modern Persian"). For the bibliographical entries of publications in Arabic, I have made no distinction between long and short vowels except for the long and short /a/ (*a* / *ā*).

In most cases, I have referred to the modern translations of primary sources through the names of the translators and not the names of the original authors. I have made an exception for the cases in which the translations do not showcase literary revisittions or scholarly analyses of the original texts. In rare cases, and mainly to follow the customary practice of some scholarly traditions in specific subfields (see, for instance, Rahman's edition of the section on psychology of Avicenna's *Shifā'*), I have referred to the names of the authors of specific critical editions rather than the composers of the texts.

For the sake of practicality, I reproduce below all the abbreviations that I have signaled in the general introduction of the book. For the retrieval of the titles, see the specific "name-year" entries in the lists of manuscript, primary, and secondary sources.

Abbreviations

Bustān	Sa'di 1363/1984.
*EI*²	*Encyclopaedia of Islam*. New Edition. Edited by P. Bearman, Th. Bianquis, C. E. Bosworth, E. van Donzel and W. P. Heinrichs, 11 vols. Leiden: Brill, 1960–2009.
*EI*³	*Encyclopaedia of Islam*, Three. Edited by Gudrun Krämer, Denis Matringe, John Nawas, and Everett K. Rowson. Leiden: Brill, 2007–.
EIr	*Encyclopaedia Iranica*. General ed. Ehsan Yarshater. London: Routledge & Kegan Paul, 1982–. Also online at http://www.iranicaonline.org.
Golestān	Sa'di 1368/1989.
Kimiyā	al-Ghazāli 1380/2001.
Ms. Tehran 1296	Ms. Majles 900
Ms. Berlin 1306	Or Oct. 3451
Ms. Tehran 1321	Ms. Majles 2569
Ms. Dublin 1320s	Per 109
Ms. Kabul 1325	Ms. 3144
Ms. Paris 1320s	Supplément Persan 1796

Ms. London 1328	Ethé 1117 (Islamic 876)
Ms. Dushanbe 1310s	Ms. 502
Ms. Dublin 1340s	Per 113
Ms. Tehran 1340s	Ms. Majles 2570
Ms. Tehran 1352	Ms. Majles 7773
Ms. Qom 1340s	Ms. 1453
Ms. Mashhad 1364	Ms. 10412
Ms. Paris 1366	Supplément Persan 1778
Ms. Qom 1371	Ms. 11920
Ms. Paris 1384	Supplément Persan 816
Ms. Paris 1390s	Supplément Persan 817
Ms. London 1416	Ethé 1118 (Islamic 287)
Ms. Yale 1432	Ms. Persian 7
Ms. Paris 1461	Supplément Persan 1357
Sa'di YE	Sa'di 1385/2006a.
Sa'di KhE	Sa'di 1386/2007.

Primary sources

Manuscripts

Academy of Sciences of the Republic of Tajikistan, Dushanbe
Ms. 502: *Kulliyāt* of Sa'di, not dated, but late 13th to early 14th centuries (see Plate 2)
Berlin Staatsbibliothek
Or Oct. 3451: *Dīvān* of Sa'di, 706/1306
Bibliotheca Bodmeriana, Cologny, Geneva
Ms. 529: *Kulliyāt* of Sa'di, 720/1320
Bibliothèque nationale de France
Supplément Persan 816: *Kulliyāt* of Sa'di; *varia*, 786/1384
Supplément Persan 817: *Kulliyāt* of Sa'di, not dated, but late 14th century
Supplément Persan 1357: *Kulliyāt* of Sa'di, 865/1461
Supplément Persan 1531: *Dīvān* of Humām al-Dīn Tabrīzī, 816/1413
Supplément Persan 1778: *Kulliyāt* of Sa'di, 767/1366
Supplément Persan 1796: *Kulliyāt* of Sa'di, not dated, but early 14th century (see Plate 1)
British Library, India Office Library Collections, London
Ethé 1117 (Islamic 876): *Kulliyāt* of Sa'di, 728/1328
Ethé 1118 (Islamic 287): *Kulliyāt* of Sa'di, 819/1416
Chester Beatty Library, Dublin
Per 109: *Kulliyāt* of Sa'di, not dated, but late 13th to 14th centuries
Per 113: *Kulliyāt* of Sa'di, not dated, but mid-14th century (see Plate 3)

Majles Library, Tehran
Ms. Majles 900: *Taẕkira-yi shuʿarā*, not dated, but early 14th century
Ms. Majles 2569: *Kulliyāt* of Saʿdi, 721/1321
Ms. Majles 2570: *Kulliyāt* of Saʿdi, not dated, but mid- 14th century
Ms. Majles 7773: *Kulliyāt* of Saʿdi, 753/1352
Marʿashi Library, Qom
Ms. 11920: *Kulliyāt* of Saʿdi, 773/1371
Ms. 1453: *Kulliyāt* of Saʿdi, undated (erroneously catalogued as late 13th century), but mid-14th century
Ms. 16509: *Dīvān* of Humām al-Dīn Tabrīzī, 739/1338–39
Mashhad Shrine Library (Āstān-e Qods-e Razavi)
Ms. 10412: *Kulliyāt* of Saʿdi, 766/1364
National Archives of Afghanistan, (King Muhammad Zahir Shah's Personal Library Collection)
Ms. 3144 (de Beaurecueil 99): *Kulliyāt* of Saʿdi, 726/1325 (see book cover, and Plate 4)
Yale (Beinecke Rare Book and Manuscript Library)
Ms. Persian 7: *Kulliyāt* of Saʿdi, 845/1432

Printed Editions

ʿAbd al-Moʾmen Esfahāni, Abu Mansur (1364/1985). [*Tarjome-ye*] *Avāref al-maʿāref, taʾlif-e Shahāb al-Din Sohravardi, tarjome-ye abu Mansur ʿAbd al-Moʾmen Esfahāni*, edited by Qāsem Ansāri. Tehran: Sherkat-e Enteshārāt-e ʿElmi va Farhangi.

Abu al-Najib Suhrawardi, ʿAbd al-Qāhir (1977). *A Sufi Rule for Novices.* Kitāb Ādāb al-Murīdīn *of Abū al-Najīb al-Suhrawardī: An Abridged Translation and Introduction*, translated by Menahem Milson. Cambridge: Harvard University Press.

Abu al-Najib Suhrawardi, ʿAbd al-Qāhir (1977). *Kitāb ādāb al-muridin*, edited by Menahem Milson. Jerusalem: Hebrew University of Jerusalem.

Ahmad Ghazāli (1359/1980). *Savāneh*, edited by Nasrollāh Purjavādi. Tehran: Boniyād-e Farhang-e Irān.

Ahmad Ghazāli (1368/1989). *Savāneh*, edited by Helmut Ritter. Tehran: Markaz-e Nashr-e Dāneshgāhi.

Amini Haravi, Sadr al-Din Ebrāhim (1383/2004). *Fotuhāt-e shāhi*, edited by Mohammad-Rezā Nasiri. Tehran: Anjoman-e Āsār-o Mafākher-e Farhangi.

Amir Khword, Mohammad b. Mobārak Kermāni (1978). *Seyar al-awliyāʾ: Dar ahvāl-o malfuzāt-e mashāyekh-e chesht*, edited by Mohammad Ershād Qorayshi. Lahore: Moʾassase-ye Enteshārāt-e Eslāmi.

Amir Khosrow Dehlavi (1975). *Dibāche-ye divān-e ghorrat al-kamāl*, edited by Vazir al-Hasan ʿĀbedi. Lahore: Nāshnal Kumiti Barāy-e Sāt-e Su Sāle Taqribāt-e Amir Khosrow.

Amir Khosrow Dehlavi (1387/2008). *Divān-e Amir Khosrov-e Dehlavi: Motābeq-e noskhe-ye Yamin al-Din abu al-Hasan Khosrow*, edited by Eqbāl Salāh al-Din. Tehran: Negāh.

Amir Moʿezzi, Mohammad b. ʿAbd al-Malek (1385/2006). *Kolliyāt-e divān-e Amir Moʿezzi-ye Nishāburi*, edited by Mohammad-Rezā Qonbari. Tehran: Zavvār.

Astarābādi, Mohammad Qāsem Hendushāh (1387/2008). *Tārikh-e fereshte*, 2 vols, edited by Mohammad Rezā Nasiri. Tehran: Anjoman-e Mafākher-e Farhangi.

ʿAtāʾi, ʿIzz al-Din (1391/2012). *ʿEshq-nāme*, edited by Sārā Sāvar Soflā. Tehran: Ketāb-khāne, Muze va Markaz-e Asnād-e Majles-e Shurā-ye Eslāmi.

ʿAttār, Farid al-Din (1319/1940). *Divān-e qasāyed va ghazaliyāt-e shaykh Farid al-Din abu Hāmed Mohammad ebn-e abu Bakr Ebrāhim ebn-e Eshāq Attār-e Nishāburi*, edited by Saʿid Nafisi. Tehran: Eqbāl.

ʿAttār, Farid al-Din (1321/1942). *Ketāb-e tazkerat al-awliyā*ʾ, edited by Mirzā Mohammad Khān Qazvini. Tehran: Markaz.

ʿAttār, Farid al-Din (1391/2012). *Tazkerat al-awliyā*ʾ, edited by Mohammad Esteʿlāmi. Tehran: Zavvār.

ʿAttār, Farid al-Din (1392/2013). *Divān-e ʿAttār-e nishāburi. Matn-e enteqādi bar asās-e noskhehā-ye khatti-ye kohan*, edited by Mahdi Madāyeni and Mehrān Afshāri. Tehran: Cheshme.

Anvari, Awhad al-Din Mohammad (1337/1958). *Divān-e Anvari*, edited by Mohammad-Taqi Modarres-e Razavi, 2 vols. Tehran: Bongāh-e Tarjome va Nashr-e Ketāb.

ʿAyn al-Qozāt Hamadāni (1348–50/1969–71). *Nāmehā-ye ʿAyn al-Qozāt Hamadāni*, edited by ʿAli Naqi Monzavi and ʿAfif ʿOssayrān, 2 vols. Tehran: Boniyād-e Farhang-e Irān.

ʿAyn al-Qozāt Hamadāni (1373/1994). *Tamhidāt*, edited by ʿAfif ʿOssayrān. Tehran: Manuchehri.

ʿAziz al-Din Nasafi (1341/1962). *Majmuʿe-ye rasāʾel mashhur be ketāb al-ensān al-kāmel*, edited by Marijan Molé. Tehran: Qesmat-e Irānshenāsi-ye Anstitu-ye Irān va Farānse.

ʿAziz al-Din Nasafi (1391/2012). *Kashf al-haqāyeq*, edited by Seyyed ʿAli Ashghar Mirbāqeri-fard. Tehran: Sokhan.

Azraqi Haravi (1336/1957). *Divān-e Azraqi-ye Haravi*, edited by Saʿid Nafisi. Tehran: Zavvār.

Bākharzi, Abu al-Mafākher Yahyā (1345/1966). *Awrād al-ahbāb va fosus al-ādāb*, edited by Iraj Afshār. Tehran: Dāneshgāh-e Tehrān.

Banākati, Dāvud ibn Mohammad (1348/1969). *Tārikh-e Banākati*, edited by Jaʿfar Sheʿār. Tehran: Selsele-ye Enteshārāt-e Anjoman-e Āsār-e Melli.

Bayhaqi, Abu al-Fazl Moḥammad b. Hosayn (1388/2009). *Tārikh-e Bayhaqi*, edited by Mohammad Jaʿfar Yāhaqqi and Mahdi Sayyadi, 2 vols. Tehran: Sokhan.

Bayzāvi, ʿAbdallāh b. ʿOmar (1382/2002). *Nezām al-tavārikh*, edited by Mir Hāshem Mohaddes. Tehran: Boniyād-e Mowqūfāt-e Doktor Mahmud-e Afshār.

Boshāq, At'ame-ye Shirāzi (1382/2003). *Kolliyāt-e Boshāq At'ame-ye Shirāzi*, edited by Mansur Rastgār-Fasā'i. Tehran: Mirās-e Maktub.

al-Daylami, Abu al-Hasan (1955). *Sirat al-shaykh al-kabir abu 'abdallāh ebn al-khafif al-shirāzi*, edited by Annemarie Schimmel. Ankara: Türk Tarih Kurumu Basimevi.

Dawlatshāh Samarqandi (1385/2007). *Tazkerat al-sho'arā*, edited by Fāteme 'Alāqe. Tehran: Pazhūheshgāh-e 'Olum-e Ensāni va Motāla'āt-e Farhangi.

Ebn Bazzāz Ardabili (1373/1994). *Safvat al-safā': dar tarjome-ye ahvāl va aqvāl va karāmāt-e shaykh Safi al-Din Eshāq Ardabili*, edited by Gholām Rezā Tabātabā'i-Majd. Tabriz.

Ebn Zarkub Shirāzi, Ahmad b. Abi al-Khayr (1389/2010). *Shirāz-nāma*, edited by Mohammad-Javād Jeddi, and Ahsanollāh Shokrallāhi. Tehran: Farhangestān-e Honar.

'Erāqi, Fakhr al-Din (1371/1992). *Lama'āt*, edited by Mohammad Khwājavi. Tehran: Mavā.

'Erāqi, Fakhr al-Din (1375/1996). *Kolliyāt-e shaykh Fakhr al-Din Ebrāhim motekhallas be 'Erāqi*, edited by Sa'id Nafisi. Tehran: Ketāb-khāne-ye Sanā'i.

Farid Esfahāni [Esfarāyeni], Farid al-Din (1381/2002). *Divān-e Farid-e Esfahāni* (*Esfarāyeni*), edited by Mohsen Kayāni. Tehran: Anjoman-e Āsār va Mafākher-e Farhangi.

Farrokhi Sistāni, Abu al-Hasan 'Ali (1380/2001). *Divān-e hakim Farrokhi-ye* Sistāni, edited by Mohammad Dabir-Siyāqi. Tehran: Zavvār.

al-Ghazāli, Abu Hāmid Muhammad (1957). *Ihyā' 'ulum al-din*, edited by Badawi Tabana, 4 vols. Cairo: Dār Ihyā' al-Kutub al-'Arabiyya.

al-Ghazāli, Abu Hāmid Muhammad (1964). *Mīzān al-'amal*, edited by Sulaymān Dunyā. Cairo: Dār al-Ma'ārif.

al-Ghazāli, Abu Hāmid Muhammad (1971). *Al-Maqsad al-asnā fi sharh ma'āni asmā' Allāh al-husnā*, edited by Fadlou A. Shehadi. Beyrouth [Beirut]: Dar el-Machreq.

al-Ghazāli, Abu Hāmid Muhammad (2000). *The Incoherence of the Philosophers* [*Tahāfut al-falāsifa*], edited and translated by Michael E. Marmura. Provo, Utah: Brigham Young University Press.

al-Ghazāli, Abu Hāmed Mohammad (1380/2001). *Kimiyā-ye sa'ādat*, edited by Hoseyn Khadivjam, 2 vols. Tehran: Sherkat-e 'Elmi va Farhangi.

Hāfez, Shams al-Din Mohammad (1362/1983). *Divan-e Hāfez*, edited by Parviz Nātel Khānlari, 2 vols. Tehran: Khwārazmi.

Hāfez, Shams al-Din Mohammad (1384/2005). *Divān-e Hāfez: bar asās-e noskhe-ye now-yāfte-ye besiyār kohan*, edited by Sādeq Sajjādi and 'Ali Bahrāmiyān. Tehran: Fekr-e Ruz.

Hāfez, Shams al-Din Mohammad (1386/2007). *Daftar-e degarsānihā dar ghazalhā-ye Hāfez*, edited by Salim Naysāri, 2 vols. Tehran: Farhangestān-e Zabān-o Adab-e Fārsi.

Hojviri, Abu al-Hasan ʿAli (1387/2008). *Kashf al-mahjub*, edited by Mahmud ʿĀbedi. Tehran: Sorush.

Homām-e Tabrizi (1351/1972). *Divān-e Homām-e Tabrizi*, edited by Rashid ʿAyvazi. Tabriz: Dāneshgāh-e Tabriz.

Ibn Sinā (1353/1974) *Tabiʿiyyāt. Dāneshnāme-ye ʿalāʾi*, edited by Seyyed Mohammad Meshkāt. Tehran: Ketābforushi-ye Dehkhodā.

Ibn Sīnā (1381/2002). *Al-ishārāt wa al-tanbīhāt*, edited by Mojtabā Zāreʿi. Qom: Būstān-e Ketāb-e Qom.

Jahān Malek Khātun (1374/1995). *Divān-e kāmel-e Jahān Malek Khātun*. Edited by Purāndokht Kāshānirād and Kāmel Ahmad-nezhād. Tehran: Zavvār.

Ibn al-Fuwatī (1416/1995). *Majmaʿ al-ādāb fī muʿjam al-alqāb*, edited by Mohammad al-Kāzem, 6 vols. Tehran: Vezārat-e Farhang va Ershād-e Eslāmi.

Ibn al-Jawzi (1975). *Talbis iblis*. Beirut: Dār al-Kutub al-ʿIlmiyya.

Ibn al-Jawzi (1983). *Talbis iblis*. Beirut: Dār al-Qalam.

Ibn Miskawayh, Ahmad b. Mohammad (1966). *Tahzib al-akhlāq*, edited by Qustantin Zurayq. Beirut: American University of Beirut.

Ibn Miskawayh, Ahmad b. Mohammad (2002 [1968]). *The Refinement of Character: A Translation from the Arabic of Aḥmad ibn-Muḥammad Miskawayh's Tahdhīb al-akhlāq*, translated by Costantine K. Zurayk. Chicago: Kazi Publications.

Junayd Shirāzi (1328/1949). *Shadd al-izār fi hatt al-awzār ʿan zawwār al-mazār*, edited by Mohammad Qazvini and ʿAbbās Eqbāl. Tehran: Markazi.

Kamāl al-Dīn Esfahāni (1348/1970). *Divān-e khāleq al-maʿāni, Abu al-Fazl Kamāl al-Din Esmāʿil-e Esfahāni*, edited by Hosein Bahr al-ʿOlumi. Tehran: Ketāb-forushi-ye Dehkhodā.

Kāshāni, ʿEzz al-Din Mahmud (1367/1998). *Ketāb mesbāh al-hedāye va meftāh al-kefāye*, edited by Jalāl al-Din Homāʾi. Tehran: Chāpkhāne-ye Majles.

Kermāni, Awhad al-Din (1366/1987). *Divān-e robāʿiyāt-e Awhad al-Din Kermāni*, edited by Ahmad Abu Mahbub. Tehran: Sorush.

Khāqāni Shervāni, Afzal al-Din (1382/2003). *Divān-e Afzal al-Din Badil ben ʿAli Najjār Khāqāni Shervāni*, edited by Ziyāʾ al-Din Sajjādi. Tehran: Zavvār.

Khwāju Kermāni (1369/1990). *Divān-e ashʿār-e khwāju-ye Kermāni*, edited by Ahmad Soheyli-Khwānsari, Tehran: Pazhang.

Lonbāni, Rafiʿ al-Din (1369/1990). *Divān-e Rafiʿ al-Din Lonbāni*, edited by Taqi Binesh. Tehran: Pazhang.

Majd al-Din b. Ahmad Hamgar. (1375/1996). *Divān-e Majd-e Hamgar*, edited by Ahmad Karami. Tehran: Mā.

Maybodi, Rashid al-Din (1382/2003). *Kashf al-asrār va ʿoddat al-abrār*, edited by ʿAli-Asghar Hekmat, 11 vols. Tehran: Amir Kabir.

Mohammad b. Monavvar (1366/1987). *Asrār al-towhid fi maqāmāt al-shaykh abi Saʿid*, edited by Mohammad-Rezā Shafiʿi-Kadkani, 2 vols. Tehran: Āgāh.

Mohammad Tabrizi (1380/2001). *Safine-ye Tabriz*, edited by ʿAbd al-Hoseyn Hāʾeri and Nasrollāh Purjavādi. Tehran: Markaz-e Nashr-e Dāneshgāhi.

Mostawfi, Hamdallāh (1364/1985). *Tārikh-e gozide*, edited by ʿAbd al-Hoseyn Navāʾi. Tehran: Amir Kabir.

Nasir al-Din Tusi, Mohammad b. Mohammad (2536/1977). *Akhlāq-e nāseri*, edited by Mojtabā Minovi and ʿAli-Rezā Haydari.

Nezāmi ʿAruzi (1336/1957). *Chahār maqāle*, edited by Mohammad Qazvini and Mohammad Moʿin. Tehrān: Dāneshgāh-e Tehrān.

Nezāmi Ganjavi (1313/1934). *Khosrow-o Shirin*, edited by Vahid Dastgerdi. Tehran: Armaghān.

Nezāmi Ganjavi (1316/1937), *Sharaf-Nāme*, edited by Vahid Dastgerdi. Tehran: Armaghān.

Nezāmi Ganjavi (1392/2013). *Khosrov-o Shirin*, edited by Behruz Sarvatiyān. Tehran: Amir Kabir.

ʿObayd Zākāni, Nezām al-Din (1374/1995). *Akhlāq al-ashrāf*, edited by ʿAli Ashghar Halabi. Tehran: Asātir.

ʿObayd Zākāni, Nezām al-Din (1999). *Kolliyāt-e ʿObayd-e Zākāni*, edited by Mohammad-Jaʿfar Mahjub. New York: Bibliotheca Persica.

ʿObayd Zākāni, Nezām al-Din (1384/2005). *Kolliyāt-e ʿObayd-e Zākāni*, edited by Parviz Atābaki. Tehran: Zavvār.

Olfati Tabrizi (1362/1983). *Rashf al-alhāz fi kashf al-alfāz*, edited by Najib Māyel Herāvi. Tehrān: Mowlā.

ʿOnsori Balkhi (1363/1984). *Divān-e Onsori-ye Balkhi*, edited by Seyyed Mohammad Dabir-Siyāqi. Tehran: Ketāb-khāne-ye Sanāʾi.

Qoshayri, ʿAbd al-Karim (1391/2012). *Tarjome-ye resale-ye qoshayriyye*, translated by Abu ʿAli Hasan b. Ahmad ʿOsmāni [11th century], edited by Mahdi Mahabbati. Tehran: Hermes.

Qushayri, ʿAbd al-Karim (1988). *Al-Risāla al-qushayriyya fi ʿilm al-tasawwuf*, edited by Maʿruf Zurayq and ʿAli ʿAbd al-Hamid Baltaji. Damascus, Beirut: Dār al-Khayr.

Qushayri, ʿAbd al-Karim (2007). *Al-Qushayri's Epistle on Sufism*: al-Risala al-Qushayriyya fi ʿilm al-tasawwuf, translated by Alexander D. Knysh. Reading: Garnet Publishing.

Rāduyāni, Mohammad (1380/2001). *Tarjomān al-balāghe*, edited by Ahmed Ātash. Tehran: Anjoman-e Āsār va Mafākher-e Farhangi.

Rāmi, Sharaf al-Din (1325/1946). *Anis al-ʿoshshāq*, edited by ʿAbbās Eqbāl Ashtiyāni. Tehran: Anjoman-e Nashr-e Āsār-e Irān.

Rashid al-Din, Fazlallāh Hamadāni (1389/2011). *Jāmeʿ al-tavārikh. Tārikh-e Salghoriyān*, edited by Mohammad Rowshan. Tehran: Mirās-e Maktub.

Rāzi, Fakhr al-Din Mohammad b. ʿOmar (1382/2003). *Jāmeʿ al-ʿolum-e ʿsettini*, edited by Seyyed ʿAli Āl-e Dāvud. Tehran: Boniyād-e Mowqufāt-e Doktor Mahmud-e Afshār.

Rumi, Jalāl al-Din (1925–40). *Masnavī: The Mathnawí of Jaláluʾddín Rúmí*, edited and translated by Reynold A. Nicholson, 8 vols. London/Leiden: Luzac/Brill.

Rumi, Jalāl al-Dīn (1393/2014). *Masnavi-ye maʿnavi*: ākharin- tashih-e Reynuld A. Nikolsun va moqābale-ye mojaddad bā noskhe-ye Qoniye, edited by Renynold A. Nicholson and Hasan Lāhuti, 4 vols. Tehran: Mirās-e Maktub.

Rumi, Mawlānā Jalāl al-Dīn Mohammad Mawlavi (1376/1997). *Divān-e Shams-e Tabrizi*, edited by Badiʿ al-Zamān Foruzānfar. Tehran: Amir Kabir.

Ruzbehān Baqli (1958). *Le Jasmin des Fidèles d'amour. Kitâb-e* [sic] *ʿabhar al-ʿâshiqîn. Traité de soufisme en persan publié avec une double introduction et la traduction du chapitre premier, par Henry Corbin et Mohammad Moʾin*. Tehran: Institut Français d'Iranologie de Téhéran.

Ruzbehān Baqli (1351/1972). *Resālat al-qods va resāle-ye ghalatāt al-sālekin*, edited by Javād Nurbakhsh. Tehran: Ferdowsi.

Ruzbehān Baqli (1981). *Commentaire sur les paradoxes des soufis* (*Sharh-e Shathîyāt*). *Texte persan publié avec une introduction en français et un index par Henry Corbin*, edited by Henry Corbin. Tehran: Institut Français d'Iranologie de Téhéran. Paris: Librairie d'Amérique et d'Orient A. Maisonneuve.

Ruzbehān-e Sāni, Sharaf al-Din Ebrāhim (1349/1970). *Tohfat ahl al-ʿerfān*, edited by Javād Nurbakhsh. Tehran: Enteshārāt-e Khāneqāh-e Neʿmatollāhi.

Saʿdi Shirāzi, Mosharref al-Din Mosleh (1363/1984). *Bustān-e Saʿdi* (*Saʿdi-nāme*), edited by Gholām-Hoseyn Yusofi. Tehran: Khwārazmi.

Saʿdi Shirāzi, Mosharref al-Din Mosleh (1368/1989). *Golestān-e Saʿdi*, edited by Gholām-Hoseyn Yusofi. Tehran: Khwārazmi.

Saʿdi Shirāzi, Mosharref al-Din Mosleh (1385/2006a). *Ghazalhā-ye Saʿdi*, edited by Gholām-Hoseyn Yusofi. Tehran: Sokhan.

Saʿdi Shirāzi, Mosharref al-Din Mosleh (1385/2006b). *Kolliyāt-e Saʿdi; golestān bustān, ghazaliyāt, qasaʾed, qeteʿāt, rasāʾel va hazliyyāt az ru-ye qadimtarin noskhehā-ye mowjud*, edited by Mohammad ʿAli Foroughi. Tehran: Zavvār.

Saʿdi Shirāzi, Mosharref al-Din Mosleh (1386/2007). *Kolliyāt-e Saʿdi*, edited by Mohammad-ʿAli Foroughi and Bahā al-Din Khorramshāhi. Tehran: Nāhid.

Salmān Sāvaji (1383/2004). *Kolliyāt-e Salmān-e Sāvaji*, edited by ʿAbbās-ʿAli Vafāʾi. Tehran: Anjoman-e Āsār-o Mafākher-e Farhangi.

Sanāʾi, Majdud b. Ādam (1362/1983). *Divān-e hakim abu al-Majdud ben Ādam Sanāʾi-ye Ghaznavi*, edited by Mohammad-Taqi Modarres-e Razavi. Tehran: Sanāʾi.

Sanāʾi, Majdud ben Ādam (1382/2003). *Hadiqat al-haqiqa va shariʿat al-tariqa* (*Fakhri-nāme*), edited by Maryam Hoseyni. Tehran: Markaz-e Nashr-e Dāneshgāhi.

Sanāʾi, Majdud ben Ādam (1389/2010). *Divān-e hakim Sanāʾi*, edited by Mozāher Mosaffā, edition revised by Shāhrokh Hekmat. Tehran: Zavvār.

Sanā'i, Majdud ben Ādam (1397/2018). *Hadiqat al-haqiqa*, edited by Mohammad Ja'far Yāhaqqi and Seyyed Mehdi Zarqāni, 2 vols. Tehran: Nashr-e Sokhan.

Sayf Farghāni, Sayf al-Din Mohammad (1341–44/1962–65). *Divān-e Sayf al-Din Mohammad Farghāni*, edited by Zabih Allāh Safā, 3 vols. Tehran: Dāneshgāh-e Tehran.

Shabānkāre'i, Mohammad (1363/1984). *Majma' al-ansāb*, edited by Mir Hāshem Mohaddes. Tehran: Amir Kabir.

Shabestari, Mahmud (2535/1976). *Golshan-e rāz*, edited by Javād Nurbakhsh. Tehran: Enteshārāt-e Khānaqāh-e Ne'matollāhi.

Shams-e Qays, Shams al-Din Mohammad b. Qays al-Rāzi (1388/2009). *Al-mo'jam fi ma'āyir ash'ār al-'ajam*, edited by Mohammad Qazvini, Modarres-e Razavi, and Sirus Shamisā. Tehran: 'Elm.

Shojā' (2536/1977). *Anis al-nās*, edited by Iraj Afshār. Tehran: Bongāh-e Tarjome va Nashr-e Ketāb.

Sudi Bosnavi (1349/1970). *Sharh-e Sudi bar golestān-e Sa'di*, edited and translated by Haydar Khosh-Tinat, Zeyn al-'Ābedin Chāvoshi, and 'Ali Akbar Kāzemi. Tehran, Tabriz: Ketāb-forushi-ye Tehrān.

[al-] Suhrawardi, Shihāb al-Din Abu Hafs 'Umar b. Muhammad (1971). *Awārif al-ma'ārif*, vol. 1, edited by 'Abd al-Halim Mahmud and Mahmbud b. al-Sharaf. Cairo: Matba'at al-Sa'āda, Dār al-Kutub al-Haditha.

[al-] Suhrawardi, Shihāb al-Din Abu Hafs 'Umar b. Muhammad (2000). *Awārif al-ma'ārif*, vol. 2, edited by 'Abd al-Halim Mahmud and Mahmbud b. al-Sharaf. Cairo: Dār al-Ma'ārif.

Suzani Samarqandi (1338/1959). *Divān-e hakim Suzani Samarqandi*, edited by Nāser al-Din Shāh-Hoseyni. Tehran: Amir Kabir.

Tāj al-Din Oshnovi (1368/1989). *Majmu'e-ye āsār-e fārsi-ye sheykh abu Mohammad Mahmud ben Khodādād ben Yusof, mashhur be Tāj al-Din Oshnovi* (*qarn-e sheshom-o haftom-e hejri*), edited by Najib Māyel Heravi. Tehran: Tahuri.

al-Tusi, Ahmad b. Muhammad (1938). *Bawāriq al-ilmā'*, edited and translated by James Robson. London: Royal Asiatic Society.

Vassāf (1259/1852). *Tajziyat al-amsar va tazjiyat al-a'sār*, edited by Mohammad Mehdi Esfahani. Bombay.

Vā'ez Kāshefi, Hosayn (1369/1990) [1977]. *Badāye' al-afkār fi sanāye' al-ash'ār*, edited by Rahim Mosalmān-Qalif; reprinted by Mir Jalāl al-Din Kazzāzi. Tehran: Nashr-e Markaz.

Vatvāt, Rashid al-Din (1339/1960). *Divān-e Rashid al-Din Vatvāt*, edited by Sa'id Nafisi. Tehran.

Zangi Bokhāri (1372/1993). *Zangi-nāme*, edited by Iraj Afshār. Tehran: Tus.

Secondary Sources

ʿAbbāsi, Habib Allāh (1396/2017). "Az tarjome tā ta'lif: Moqāyese-ye sākhtāri-mohtavā'i-ye do tarjome-ye ketāb-e *avāref al-maʿāref.*" *Nashriye-ye Tārikh-e Adabiyāt* 9.2 (1396/2017): 99–112.

Abdul-Raof, Hussein (2010). *Schools of Qur'anic Exegesis: Genesis and Development.* London, New York: Routledge.

Abrahamov, Binyamin (1991), "Ibn Sīnā's Influence on al-Ghazālī's Non-Philosophical Works." *Abr Nahrain* 29 (1991): 1–17.

Abrahamov, Binyamin (1993). "Al-Ghazālī's Supreme Way to Know God." *Studia Islamica* 77 (1993): 141–168.

Abrahamov, Binyamin (1995). "The *Bi-lā Kayfa* Doctrine and Its Foundations in Islamic Theology." *Arabica* 42.3 (1995): 365–379.

Abrahamov, Binyamin (2003). *Divine Love in Islamic Mysticism: The Teachings of al-Ghazâlî and al-Dabbâgh.* New York: Routledge.

Abrahamov, Binyamin (2015). "Al-Ghazālī and the Rationalization of Sufism." In *Islam and Rationality: The Impact of al-Ghazālī, Papers Collected on His 900th Anniversary, Volume 1*, edited by Georges Tamer, 35–48. Leiden: Brill.

Afary, Janet (2009). *Sexual Politics in Modern Iran.* Cambridge: Cambridge University Press.

Afshār, Iraj (1385/2006). "Irān-shenāsi: tāzehā va pārehā-ye irān-shenāsi." *Bokhārā* 50 (1385/2006): 76–91.

Ahmad, Nazir (1381/2002). "Saʿdi-ye Shirāzi va amir-e moghul amir ankiyānu." *Nāme-ye Anjoman* 2.2 (1381/2002): 24–31.

Aigle, Denise (1997). "Le soufisme sunnite en Fars: Šayḫ Amin-al-din Balyāni." in *L'Iran face à la domination mongole*, edited by Denise Aigle, 233–61. Tehran: Institut Français de Recherche en Iran.

Aigle, Denise (2005). *Le Fârs sous la domination mongole: Politique et fiscalité (XIIIe–XIVe s.).* Paris: Association pour l'avancement des études iraniennes.

Ali, Samer M. (2010). *Arabic Literary Salons in the Islamic Middle Ages: Poetry, Public Performance, and the Presentation of the Past.* Notre Dame: University of Notre Dame Press.

Al-Kassim, Dina (2008). "Epilogue: Sexual Epistemologies, East in West." In *Islamicate Sexualities: Translations across Temporal Geographies of Desire*, edited by Kathryn Babayan and Afsaneh Najmabadi, 297–339. Cambridge: Harvard University Press.

Altmann, Alexander (1969) "The Delphic Maxim in Medieval Islam and Judaism." In *Studies in Religious Philosophy and Mysticism*, 1–40. Ithaca: Cornell University Press.

Aminrazavi, Mehdi, ed. (2014). *Sufism and American Literary Masters.* Albany: State University of New York Press.

Andrews, Walter G. (1985). *Poetry's Voice, Society's Song: Ottoman Lyric Poetry*. Seattle: University of Washington Press.

Andrews, Walter G., and Mehmet Kalpaklı (2005). *The Age of Beloveds: Love and the Beloved in Early-modern Ottoman and European Culture and Society*. Durham: Duke University Press.

Anwar, Etin (2003). "Ibn Sīnā's Philosophical Theology of Love: A Study of the *Risālah fī al-ʿIshq*." *Islamic Studies* 42.2 (2003): 331–345.

Arberry, A. J. trans. (1945). *Kings ad Beggars: The First Two Chapters of Saʿdī's* Gulistān, translated by A. J. Arberry. London: Luzac.

Aryanpur, ʿAli-Rezā (1986). *Pazhuheshi dar shenākht-i bāghhā-ye Irān va bāghhā-ye tārikhi-ye Shirāz*. Tehran: Farhangsārā.

Aubin, Jean (1953). "Les princes d'Ormuz du XIIIe au XVe siècle." *Journal asiatique* 24.1 (1953): 77–138.

Austin, John Langshaw (1975). *How to Do Things with Words*, edited by J. O. Urmson and Marina Sbisà. Cambridge: Harvard University Press.

Avery, Kenneth S. (2004). *A Psychology of Early Sufi* Samāʿ*: Listening and Altered States*. New York, London: Routledge.

Avery, Peter (2007). *The Collected Lyrics of Háfiz of Shíráz*. Cambridge: Archetype.

Baffioni, Carmela (1998) "From Sense Perception to the Vision of God: A Path towards Knowledge According to the Iḫwān al-Ṣafāʾ." *Arabic Sciences and Philosophy* 8.2 (1998): 213–231.

Bahār, Mohammad Taqi (1349/1970). *Sabk-shenāsi*, 3 vols. Tehran: Amir Kabir.

Bakhtin, Mikhail (1984). *Rabelais and His World*, translated by Hélène Iswolsky. Bloomington: Indiana University Press.

Balafrej, Lamia (2019) "Compilations of the Bustān of Saʿdī in Iran, Central Asia, and Turkey, ca. 1470–1550." *Iranian Studies* 52.5–6 (2019): 691–715.

Balda-Tillier, Monica (2014). "*ʿUdhrī* Love and *Mujūn*: Opposites and Parallels." In *The Rude, the Bad and the Bawdy: Essays in Honour of Professor Geert Jan van Gelder*, edited by Adam Talib, Marlé Hammond, and Arie Schippers, 123–140. Cambridge: Gibb Memorial Trust.

Baldick, R. Julian (1973). "The Authenticity of ʿIrāqī's *ʿUshshāq-nāma*." *Studia Iranica* 2.1 (1973): 67–78.

Baneth, David Z. (1938). "The Common Teleological Source of Baḥya ibn Paqūda and al-Ghazālī." In *Sefer Magnes* (*Magnes Anniversary Book*), edited by Yitzhak F. Baer, 23–30. Jerusalem: Hebrew University.

Bargigli, Rita (1995). *I poeti della Pleiade ghaznavide*. Milano: Ariele.

Bargneysi, Kāzem (1380/2001). *Ghazaliyyāt-e Saʿdi bar asās-e chāphā-ye shādravānān Mohammad-ʿAli Forughi va Habib-e Yaghmāyi*. Tehran: Fekr-e Ruz.

Barthes, Roland (1989). "*The Reality Effect*." In *The Rustle of Language*, translated by Richard Howard, edited by François Wahl, 141–48. Berkeley: University of California Press.

Barthes, Roland (2010a). *A Lover's Discourse: Fragments*, translated by Richard Howard. New York: Hill and Wang.

Barthes, Roland (2010b). *Camera Lucida: Reflections on Photography*, translated by Richard Howard. New York: Hill and Wang.

Barzegar-Khāleqi, Mohammad-Rezā, and Turaj ʿAqdā'i (1386/2008). *Sharh-e ghazalhā-ye Saʿdi*, 2 vols. Tehran: Zavvār.

Bashari, Javād (1388/2009). "Ashʿāri now-yāfte az Jahān Malek Khātun." *Payām-e Bahārestān* 3 (1388/2009): 740–766.

Bashari, Javād (1398/2020). *Ahvāl-e sheykh-e ajall Saʿdi*. Tehran: Tak Barg.

Bashear, Suliman (2004). *Studies in Early Islamic Tradition*. The Hebrew University of Jerusalem: The Max Schloessinger Memorial Foundation.

Bashir, Shahzad (2011). *Sufi Bodies: Religion and Society in Medieval Islam*. New York: Columbia University Press.

Baudrillard, Jean (1990). *De la séduction*, translated by Brian Singer as *Seduction*. Montreal: New World Perspectives.

Bausani, Alessandro, and Antonio Pagliaro (1968). *Storia dell letteratura persiana*. Milan: Nuova Accademia Editrice.

Bec, Pierre (1984). *Burlesque et obscénité chez les troubadours: Pour une approche du contre-texte médieval*. Paris: Stock.

Bell, Gertrude (1995) [1897]. *Poems from the Divan of Hafiz*. London, W. Heinemann, 1897; reissued as *The Hafez Poems of Gertrude Bell*. Bethseda: IranBooks, 1995.

Bell, J. Norment (1986). "Avicenna's Treatise on Love and the Nonphilosophical Muslim Tradition." *Der Islam* 63.1 (1986): 73–89.

Belo, Caterina (2007). *Chance and Determinism in Avicenna and Averroes*. Leiden: Brill.

Bentley, Joseph (1970). "Satire and the Rhetoric of Sadism." in *The Perverse Imagination: Sexuality and Literary Culture*, edited by Irving Buchen, 55–73. New York: New York University Press.

Berlekamp, Persis (2011). *Wonder, Image, and Cosmos in Medieval Islam*. New Haven: Yale University Press.

Biran, Michal (2005). *The Empire of the Qara Khitai in Eurasian History: Between China and the Islamic World*. Cambridge: Cambridge University Press.

Biran, Michal (2016). "Music in the Conquest of Baghdad: Ṣafī al-Dīn Urmawī and the Ilkhanid Circle of Musicians." In *The Mongols' Middle East: Continuity and Transformation in Ilkhanid Iran*, edited by Bruno De Nicola and Charles Melville, 131–154. Leiden, Boston: Brill.

Biran, Michal (2018). "Violence and Non-Violence in the Mongol Conquest of Baghdad." In *Violence in Islamic Thought from the Mongols to European Imperialism*, edited by Robert Gleave and István Kristó-Nagy, 15–31. Edinburgh: Edinburgh University Press.

Black, Deborah L. (1993). "Estimation (*Wahm*) in Avicenna: The Logical and Psychological Dimensions." *Dialogue: Canadian Philosophical Review*, 32.2 (1993): 219–258.

Black, Deborah L. (1998). "Beauty." In "Aesthetics in Islamic Philosophy." In Routledge Encyclopedia of Philosophy Online, edited by Edward Craig. Taylor and Francis. Available online at https://www.rep.routledge.com/articles/thematic/aesthetics-in-islamic-philosophy/v-1/sections/beauty. Accessed on 3 February 2018.

Black, Deborah L., trans. (2009) "Avicenna: *Shifāʾ* (*Healing*), *Al-Nafs* (*Psychology*), Book 4.", by Avicenna. Unpublished translation by Deborah L. Black. Available online at http://individual.utoronto.ca/dlblack/WebTranslations/shifanafs41-3.pdf.

Blair, Sheila S. (1993). "The Ilkhanid Palace." *Ars Orientalis* 23 (1993): 239–248.

Blair, Sheila S. (2014). *Text and Image in Medieval Persian Art*. Edinburgh: Edinburgh University Press.

Bloch, Howard E. (1986). *The Scandal of the Fabliaux*. Chicago, London: The University of Chicago Press.

Bloch, Howard E. (1991). *Medieval Misogyny and the Invention of Western Romantic Love*. Chicago, London: The University of Chicago Press.

Blochet, Edgard (1927). *Catalogue des manuscrits persans de la Bibliothèque Nationale*, 3rd volume. Paris: Réunion des Bibliothèques Nationales.

Boone, Joseph A. (2014). *The Homoerotics of Orientalism*. New York: Columbia University Press.

Bosworth, Clifford Edmund (1963). *The Ghaznavids: Their Empire in Afghanistan and Eastern Iran, 994–1040*. Edinburgh: Edinburgh University Press.

Bosworth, Clifford Edmund (1966). "Mahmud of Ghazna in Contemporary Eyes and in Later Persian Literature." *Iran* 4.1 (1966): 85–92.

Bosworth, Clifford Edmund (1968). "The Development of Persian Culture under the Early Ghaznavids." *Iran* 6.1 (1968): 33–44.

Bosworth, Clifford Edmund (1978). "The Heritage of Rulership in Early Islamic Iran and the Search for Dynastic Connections with the Past." *Iranian Studies* 11 (1978): 7–34.

Bosworth, Clifford Edmund (1991). "Farrukhī's Elegy on Maḥmūd of Ghazna." *Iran* 29.1 (1991): 43–49.

Bosworth, Clifford Edmund (1996). *New Islamic Dynasties: A Chronological and Genealogical Manual*. New York: Columbia University Press.

Bosworth, Clifford Edmund, and Mohsen Ashtiany, trans. (2011). *The History of Beyhaqi (The History of Sultan Masʿud of Ghazna, 1030–1041), by Abu'l-Faẓl Beyhaqi*, 3 vols. Boston: Ilex Foundation; Washington, D.C.: Center for Hellenic Studies.

Böwering, Gerhard (1980). *The Mystical Vision of Existence in Classical Islam: The Qur'ānic Hermeneutics of the Ṣūfī Sahl al-Tustarī (d. 283/896)*. Berlin: Walter de Gruyter.

Boyle, John Andrew (1961). "The Death of the Last 'Abbasid Caliph: A Contemporary Muslim Account." *Journal of Semitic Studies* 6 (1961): 145–161.

Boyle, John Andrew (1968). "Dynastic and Political History of the Īl-Khāns." In *The Cambridge Hitory of Iran*, vol. 5, edited by John Andrew Boyle, 303–421. Cambridge: Cambridge University Press.

Brookshaw, Dominic Parviz (2003). "Palaces, Pavilions and Pleasure-Gardens: The Context and Setting of the Medieval Majlis." *Middle Eastern Literatures* 6 (2003): 199–223.

Brookshaw, Dominic Parviz (2005). "Odes of a Poet-Princess: The Ghazals of Jahan-Malik Khatun." *Iran* 43 (2005): 173–195.

Brookshaw, Dominic Parviz (2009). "To be Feared and Desired: Turks in the Collected Works of 'Ubayd-i Zākānī." *Iranian Studies* 42.5 (2009): 725–744.

Brookshaw, Dominic Parviz (2012). "'Have You Heard the One about the Man from Qazvin?' Regionalist Humor in the Works of 'Ubayd-i Zākāni." In *Ruse and Wit: The Humorous in Arabic, Persian, and Turkish Narrative*, edited by Dominic Parviz Brookshaw, 44–69. Boston: Ilex Foundation.

Brookshaw, Dominic Parviz (2014). "Lascivious Vines, Corrupted Virgins, and Crimes of Honour: Variations on the Wine Production Myth as Narrated in Early Persian Poetry." *Iranian Studies* 47.1 (2014): 87–129.

Brookshaw, Dominic Parviz (2019). *Hafiz and His Contemporaries. A Study of Fourteenth-century Persian Lyric Poetry*. London: I. B. Tauris.

Buchman, David, trans. (1998). *The Niche of Lights* [*Mishkāt al-anwār*]. *Parallel English-Arabic text translated, introduced, and annotated by David Buchman*, by Abu Hāmid Muhammad al-Ghazāli. Provo: Brigham Young University Press.

Bürgel, Johan Christoph (2005). "The Mighty Beloved: Images and Structures of Power in the Ghazal from Arabic to Urdu." *In Ghazal as World Literature I: Transformations of a Literary Genre*, edited by Thomas Bauer and Angelika Neuwirth, 283–309. Beirut, Würzburg: Ergon.

Burrell, David, and Nazih Daher, trans. (1992). *The Ninety-Nine Beautiful Names of God. Al-Maqsad al-asnā fi sharah ma'āni asmā' Allāh al-husnā*, by Abu Hāmed Mohammad al-Ghazāli. Cambridge: Islamic Text Society.

Camille, Michael (2014). "Dr Witkowski's Anus: French Doctors, German Homosexuals and the Obscene in Medieval Church Art." In *Medieval Obscenities*, edited by Nicola McDonald, 17–38. Woodbridge: York Medieval Press.

Cassin, Barbara (2009). "Sophistics, Rhetorics, and Performance; or How to Really Do Things with Words." *Philosophy & Rhetoric* 42.4 (2009): 349–372.

Cassin, Barbara (2011). "La performance avant le performative, ou la troisième dimension du langage." In *Genèse de l'acte de parole*, edite by Barbara Cassin and Carlos Levy, 122–128. Turnhout: Brepols.

Chalisova, Natalia (2009). "Persian Rhetoric: 'Elm-e Badi' and Elm-e Bayān." In *A History of Persian literature, vol. 1: General Introduction to Persian Literature*, edited by Johannes T. P. de Bruijn, 139–171. London: I. B. Tauris.

Chittick, William C. (2013). *Divine Love: Islamic Literature and the Path to God.* New Haven: Yale University Press.

Collot, Michel (2014). *Pour une géographie littéraire.* Paris: Corti.

Compagnon, Antoine (2004). *Literature, Theory, and Common Sense*, translated by Carol Cosman. Princeton: Princeton University Press.

Cooperson, Michael, trans. (2020). *Impostures*, by al-Ḥarīrī. New York: New York University Press.

Coppens, Pieter (2018). *Seeing God in Sufi Qur'an Commentaries: Crossing between This World and the Otherworld.* Edinburgh: Edinburgh University Press.

Cross, Cameron (2015). *The Poetics of Romantic Love in* Vis & Rāmin. Phd dissertation, University of Chicago.

Culler, Jonathan (2015). *Theory of the Lyric.* Cambridge: Harvard University Press.

Culler, Jonathan (2017). "Lyric Words, not Worlds." *Journal of Literary Theory* 11.1 (2017): 32–39.

Darling, Linda. "'The Vicegerent of God, from Him We Expect Rain': The Incorporation of the Pre-Islamic State in Early Islamic Political Culture." *Journal of the American Oriental Society* 134.3 (2014): 407–29.

Davidson, Herbert A. (1992). *Alfarabi, Avicenna and Averroes on Intellect: Their Cosmologies, Theories of the Active Intellect, and Theories of Human Intellect.* New York, Oxford: Oxford University Press.

Davidson, James (2007). *The Greeks and Greek Love: A Bold New Exploration of the Ancient World.* New York: Random House.

Davidson, Olga (1998). "The Text of Ferdowsi's *Shâhnâma* and the Burden of the Past." *Journal of the American Oriental Society*, 118.1 (1998): 63–69.

Davis, Dick (1999). "Sufism and Poetry: A Marriage of Convenience?" *Edebiyat* 10.2 (1999): 279–292.

Davis, Dick (2013). *Faces of Love: Hafez and the Poets of Shiraz.* London: Penguin Books.

Davis, Glenn (2014). "The Exeter Book Riddles and the Place of Sexual Idiom in Old English Literature." In *Medieval Obscenities*, edited by Nicola McDonald, 39–54. Woodbridge: York Medieval Press.

de Beaurecueil, Serge (1964). *Manuscrits d'Afghanistan.* Cairo: Institut Français d'Archéologie Orientale.

de Blois, François (2004). *Persian Literature: A Bio-Bibliographical Survey. Volume V: Poetry of the Pre-Mongol period*. London, New York: Routledge.

de Blois, François, and Nicholas Sims-Williams, ed. (2006). Dictionary of Manichaean Texts. Volume II: Texts from Iraq and Iran (Texts in Syriac, Arabic, Persian and Zoroastrian Middle Persian). Turnhout: Brepols.

de Bruijn, Johannes T. P. (1983). *Of Piety and Poetry: The Interaction of Religion and Literature in the Life and Works of Ḥakīm Sanāʾī of Ghazna*. Leiden: Brill.

de Bruijn, Johannes T. P. (1997). *Persian Sufi Poetry: An Introduction to the Mystical Use of Classical Persian Poems*. Richmond: Curzon.

de Callataÿ, Godefroid (2014). "Philosophy and Bāṭinism in al-Andalus: Ibn Masarra's *Risālat al-Iʿtibār* and the *Rasāʾil Ikhwān al-ṣafāʾ*." *Jerusalem Studies in Arabic and Islam* 41 (2014): 261–312.

de Fouchécour, Charles-Henri (1969). *La description de la nature dans la poésie lyrique persane du XI*e *siècle: inventaire et analyse des thèmes*. Paris: C. Klincksieck.

de Fouchécour, Charles-Henri (1986). *Moralia: Les notions morales dans la littérature persane du 3*e*/9*e *au 7*e*/13*e *siècle*. Paris: Éditions Recherche sur les Civilisations.

de Fouchécour, Charles-Henri, trans. (2006). *Le Divân: Oeuvre lyrique d'un spirituel en Perse au XIV*e *siècle*, by Shams al-Din Mohammad Hāfez. Lagrasse: Verdier.

Dehqāni, Mohammad (1394/2014). "Safarhā-ye donkishutvār-e Saʿdi." *Negāh-e Now* 23.101 (1394/2014): 101–108.

Dehqāni, Mohammad (2016). "Moruri bar *Saʿdi, shāʿer-e ʿeshq-o zendegi*." *Irān Nāme* 30.3 (2016): 298–307.

De Nicola, Bruno (2014). "Patrons or *Murīds*? Mongol Women and Shaykhs in Ilkhanid Iran and Anatolia." *Iran* 52.1 (2014): 142–156.

De Nicola, Bruno, and Charles Melville, eds. (2016). *The Mongols' Middle East: Continuity and Transformation in Ilkhanid Iran*. Leiden, Boston: Brill.

De Nicola, Bruno (2017). *Women in Mongol Iran: The Khātūns, 1206–1355*. Edinburgh: Edinburgh University Press.

Derāyati, Mostafā, ed. (1390–/2011–). *Fehrestegān: Noskhehā-ye khatti-ye irān (fankhā)*, 45 vols. Tehran: Sāzemān-e Asnād-o Ketābkhāne-ye Melli-ye Jomhuri-ye Eslāmi-ye Irān.

D'Erme, Giovanni M., trans. (2005). *Dissertazione letifica: Racconti e satire dalla Shiraz del Trecento*, by ʿObayd Zākāni. Roma: Carocci.

Dillon, Emma (2014). "Representing Obscene Sound." In *Medieval Obscenities*, edited by Nicola McDonald, 55–84. Woodbridge: York Medieval Press.

Donaldson, E. Talbot (1954). "Chaucer the Pilgrim." *PMLA* 69.4 (1954): 928–936.

Dragonetti, Roger (1960). *La Technique poétique des trouvères dans la chanson courtoise*. Bruges: De Tempel.

Dunton-Downer, Leslie (1998). "Poetic Language and the Obscene." In *Obscenity: Social Control and Artistic Creation in the European Middle Ages*, edited by Jan M. Ziolkowski, 19–37. Leiden, New York: Brill.

During, Jean (1988). *Musique et extase: l'audition mystique dans la tradition soufie*. Paris: Albin Michel.

Ebstein, Michael (2014). "Ḏū l-Nūn al-Miṣrī and Early Islamic Mysticism." *Arabica* 61 (2014): 559–612.

Eco, Umberto (1989). *The Open Work*. Translated by Anna Cancogni. Cambridge: Harvard University Press.

Elamrani-Jamal, Abdelali (1984). "De la multiplicité des modes de la prophétie chez Ibn Sīnā." In *Études sur Avicenne*, edited by Jean Jolivet and Roshdi Rashed, 125–142. Paris: Les Belles Lettres.

Elias, Jamal J. (2012). *Aisha's Cushion: Religious Art, Perception, and Practice in Islam*. Cambridge, London: Harvard University Press.

El-Rouayheb, Khaled (2005). *Before Homosexuality in the Arab-Islamic World, 1500–1800*. Chicago: University of Chicago Press.

El Shamsy, Ahmed (2016). "Reading *The Wisdom in God's Creations* (*al-Ḥikma fī makhlūqāt Allah*)." In *Islam and Rationality: The Impact of al-Ghazālī. Papers collected on his 900th Anniversary*, vol. 2, edited by Frank Griffel, 90–112. Leiden and Boston, MA: Brill.

Elwell-Sutton, Laurence Paul (1976). *The Persian Metres*. Cambridge: Cambridge University Press.

Emerson, Ralph Waldo (1911). *The Complete Poetical Works of Ralph Waldo Emerson*. Boston: Houghton Mifflin.

Endress, Gerhard (2006). "Reading Avicenna in the *Madrasa*: Intellectual Genealogies and Chains of Transmission of Philosophy and the Sciences in the Islamic East." in *Arabic Theology, Arabic Philosophy: From the Many to the One. Essays in Celebration of Richard M. Frank*, edited by James E. Montgomery, 371–422. Leuven: Peeters.

Eqbāl Āshtiyāni, ʿAbbās (1328/1949). "Ketāb al-hekmat fi al-adʿiyat al-mowʿezat l'el-ommat." *Yādgār* 5.7/8 (1328/1949): 124–31.

Eqbāl Āshtiyāni, ʿAbbās (1377/1998). "Zamān-e tavallod va avā'el-e zendegāni-ye Saʿdi." *Saʿdi-shenāsi* 1 (1377/1998): 9–23.

Ernst, Carl W. (1985). *Words of Ecstasy in Sufism*. Albany: State University of New York Press.

Ernst, Carl, W. (1994). "Rūzbihān Baqlī on Love as 'Essential Desire.'" In *Gott ist schön und Er liebt die Schönheit/God is Beautiful and He Loves Beauty: Festschrift für Annemarie Schimmel*, edited by Alma Giese and J. Christoph Bürgel, 181–189. Bern: Peter Lang.

Ernst, Carl W. (1996). *Rūzbihān Baqlī: Mysticism and the Rhetoric of Sainthood in Persian Sufism*. Richmond: Curzon.

Ernst, Carl W., and Bruce B. Lawrence (2002). *Sufi Martyrs of Love: Chishti Sufism in South Asia and Beyond*. New York: Palgrave Macmillan.

Esin, Emel (1979). "Turk-i Māh Chihrah (the Turkish Norm of Beauty in Iran)." In *Akten des VII. internationalen Kongresses für iranische Kunst und Archäologie, München, 7–10 September 1976*, 449–460. Berlin: D. Reimer.

Esin, Emel (1983). "Descriptions of Turks and 'Tatars' (Mongols) of the Thirteenth Century, in Some Anatolian Sources." In *Documenta Barbarorum: Festschrift für Walther Heissig zum 70. Geburtstag*, edited by Klaus Sagaster and Michael Weiers, 81–87. Wiesbaden: Harrassowitz.

Est'elāmi, Mohammad (1382/2003). *Dars-e Hāfez: Naqd-o sharh-e ghazalhā-ye khwāje Shams al-Din Mohammad Hāfez*, 2 vols. Tehran: Sokhan.

Ethé, Hermann (1903). *Catalogue of Persian Manuscripts in the Library of the India Office*, 2 vols. Oxford.

Ettinghausen, Richard (1947). "Al-Ghazzālī on Beauty." In *Art and Thought: Issued in Honor of Dr. Ananda K. Coomaraswamy on the Occasion of His 70th Birthday*, edited by K. Bharatna Iyer, 160–165. London: Luzac.

Fackenheim, Emil L., trans. (1945). "A Treatise on Love by Ibn Sina (Translated by Emil L. Fackenheim)." *Mediaeval Studies* 7.1 (1945): 208–228.

Fati, Hushang (1379/2000). "Sa'di va shaykh-e dānā-ye morshed—Shahāb." *Sa'di-shenāsi* 2 (1379/2000): 196–210.

Fausto-Sterling, Anne (2007). "Frameworks of Desire." *Daedalus* 136.2 (2007): 47–57.

Fausto-Sterling, Anne (2012). *Sex/Gender: Biology in a Social World*. New York, London: Routledge.

Feuillebois-Pierunek, Ève (2002). *A la croisée des voies célestes. Faxr al-Din 'Erâqi: poésie mystique et expression poétique en Perse médiévale*. Tehran: Institut Français de Recherche en Iran, 2002.

Floor, Willelm (2014). "The Culture of Wine Drinking in Pre-Mongol Iran." In *Wine Culture in Iran and Beyond*, edited by Bert G. Fragner, Ralph Kauz, and Florian Schwarz, 165–210. Vienna: Verlag der Österreichischen Akademie der Wissenschaften.

Foucault, Michel (1978). *The History of Sexuality, Volume 1: An Introduction*, translated by Robert Hurley. New York: Pantheon.

Foruzānfar, Badi' al-Zamān (1316/1938). "Sa'di va Sohravardi." *Sa'di-nāme*, edited by Habib Yaghmā'i, *Majlale-ye Ta'lim va Tarbiyat* 11–12 (1316/1938): 71–90.

Foruzānfar, Badi' al-Zamān (1347/1968). *Sharh-e masnavi-ye sharif*. Tehran: Chāpkhāne-ye Dāneshgāh-e Tehrān.

Foruzānfar, Badi' al-Zamān, ed. (1347/1969). *Manāqeb-e Awḥad al-Dīn Ḥāmed ben abī al-Fakhr Kermāni*, edited by Badi' al-Zamān Foruzānfar. Tehran: Bongāh-e Tarjome va Nashr-e Ketāb.

Fotuhi, Mahmud, and Mohammad Afshin Vafā'i (1388/2009). "Mokhāteb-shenāsi-ye Hāfez dar sade-ye hashtom-o nohom-e hejri bar asās-e ruykard-e tārikh-e adabi-ye hermenutik." *Naqd-e adabi* 2.6 (1388/2009): 71–128.

Fradenburg, Louise, and Carla Freccero, eds. (1996). *Premodern Sexualities*. London, New York: Routledge.

Frank, Richard M. (1991–1992). "Al-Ghazālī on *Taqlīd*: Scholars, Theologians, and Philosophers." *Zeitschrift für Geschichte der arabisch-islamischen Wissenschaften* 7 (1991–1992): 207–252.

Frank, Richard M. (1992). *Creation and the Cosmic System: Al-Ghazālī & Avicenna*. Heidelberg: C. Winter.

Frank, Richard M. (1994). *Al-Ghazālī and the Ashʿarite School*. Durham/London: Duke University Press.

Gadamer, Hans-Georg (1989). *Truth and Method*. Translated and edited by Joel Weinsheimer and Donald G. Marshall. London: Sheed & Ward.

Garden, Kenneth (2014). *The First Islamic Reviver: Abū Ḥāmid al-Ghazālī and his* Revival of the Religious Sciences. Oxford: Oxford University Press.

Gaunt, Simon (1999). "Orality and Writing: The Text of the Troubadour Poem." In *The Troubadours: An Introduction*, edited by Simon Gaunt and Sarah Kay, 228–246. Cambridge: Cambridge University Press.

Gaunt, Simon (2014). "Obscene Hermeneutics in Troubadour Lyric." In *Medieval Obscenities*, edited by Nicola McDonald, 85–104. Woodbridge: York Medieval Press.

Geertz, Clifford (1973). *The Interpretation of Cultures: Selected Essays*. New York: Basic Books.

Ghafuriyān, Maryam (1398/2019). *Sheykh-e ajall dar maktab-e emām-e morshed: barresi-ye tatbiqi va ta'sir-paziri-ye Sa'di dar* Bustān *va* Golestān *az* ehyiā' 'olum al-din-*e Ghazāli*. Tehran: Sāyeh-Gostar.

Ghani, Qāsem (1356/1977). *Bahs dar āsār-o afkār-o ahvāl-e Hāfez*, 2 vols. Tehran: Zavvār.

Ghofrāni, Jahrami (1366/1987) In *Zekr-e jamil-e Saʿdi: Majmuʿe-ye maqālāt va ashʿār be monāsabat-e bozorgdāsht-e hasht-sadomin sālgard-e sheykh-e ajall Saʿdi*, edited by Kumisiyun-e melli-ye yunesko, vol. 3, 93–112. Tehran: Edāre-ye Koll-e Enteshārāt va Tablighāt-e Vezārat-e Ershād-e Eslāmi.

Gianotti, Timothy J. (2001). *Al-Ghazālī's Unspeakable Doctrine of the Soul: Unveiling the Esoteric Psychology and Eschatology of the Iḥyā'*. Leiden: Brill.

Gibb, H. A. R., trans. (1958). *The Travels of Ibn Baṭṭūṭa, A.D. 1325–1354*, by Ibn Battuta, 4 vols. Cambridge: Cambridge University Press, [Vol. 1] 1958; London: Hakluyt Society, [vols. 2–3].

Gibb, H. A. R., trans. (2011). *Travels in Asia and Africa, 1325–1354*, by Ibn Battuta. London: Routledge.

Gilli-Elewy, Hend (2000). *Bagdad nach dem Sturz des Kalifats: Die Geschichte einer Provinz unter ilhanischer Herrschaft (656–735/1258–1335)*. Berlin: Schwarz.

Gilli-Elewy, Hend (2011). "The Mongol Court in Baghdad: The Juwaynī Brothers Between Local Court and Central Court." In *Court Cultures in the Muslim World: Seventh to Nineteenth Centuries*, edited by Albrecht Fuess and Jan-Peter Hartung, 168–81. London/New York: Routledge.

Glünz, Michael (1993). *Die panegyrische Qaṣīda bei Kamāl ud-Dīn Ismāʿīl aus Isfahan: Eine Studie zur persischen Lobdichtung um den Beginn des 7./13. Jahrhunderts*. Beirut, Stuttgart: Franz Steiner.

Glünz, Michael. (1995). "The Sword, the Pen and the Phallus: Metaphors and Metonymies of Male Power and Creativity in Medieval Persian Poetry." *Edebiyât* 6 (1995): 223–243.

Glünz, Michael (1996). "Poetic Tradition and Social Change: The Persian Qasida in Post-Mongol Iran." In *Qasida Poetry in Islamic Asia and Africa, vol. 1. Classical Traditions and Modern Meanings*, edited by Stefan Sperl and Christopher Shackle, 183–205. Leiden, New York, Köln: Brill.

Goldziher, Ignaz (1897). "Du sens propre des expressions Ombre de Dieu, Khalife de Dieu, pour désigner les chefs d'Islam." *Revue de l'histoire des religions* 35 (1897): 331–338.

González Ginocchio, David (2013). "Avicenna's Philosophy of the Animal Soul in Context." In *Animals and Otherness in the Middle Ages: Perspectives Across Disciplines*, edited by Francisco García García, Monica Ann Walker Vadillo, María Victoria Chico Picaza, 63–74. Oxford: Archaeopress.

Goodman, Lenn E. (2005). *Avicenna*. London: Routledge.

Goodman, Lenn E., and Richard McGregor (trans.), by Ikhwān al-Ṣafāʾ (2009). *The Case of the Animals versus Man Before the King of the Jinn: A Translation from the* Epistles of the Brethren of Purity. Oxford: Oxford University Press.

Grabar, Oleg (1977). "Islam and Iconoclasm." In *Iconoclasm: Papers Given at the Ninth Spring Symposium of Byzantine Studies, University of Birmingham*, edited by Anthony Bryer and Judith Herrin, 45–52. Birmingham, UK: Centre for Byzantine Studies.

Gramlich, Richard, trans. (1976). *Gedanken über die Liebe*, by Ahmad Ghazālī. Wiesbaden: F. Steiner.

Greenblatt, Stephen (1997). "The Touch of the Real." *Representations* 59 (1997): 14–29.

Gribetz, Arthur (1991). "The *Samāʿ* Controversy: Sufi vs. Legalist." *Studia Islamica* 74 (1991): 43–62.

Griffel, Frank (2004). "al-Ġazālī's Concept of Prophecy: The Introduction of Avicennian Psychology into Ašʿarite Theology." *Arabic Sciences and Philosophy* 14 (2004): 101–144.

Griffel, Frank (2009a). *Al-Ghazālī's Philosophical Theology*. Oxford, New York: Oxford University Press.

Griffel, Frank (2009b). "Al-Ghazālī's Cosmology in the Veil Section of His *Mishkāt al-Anwār*." In *Avicenna and his Legacy: A Golden Age of Science and Philosophy*, edited by Tzvi Langermann, 27–49. Turnhout: Brepols.

Griffel, Frank (2011). "Al-Ghazālī's Use of 'Original Human Disposition' (*fiṭra*) and Its Background in the Teachings of al-Fārābī and Avicenna." *The Muslim World* 102.1 (2011): 1–32.

Gust, Geoffrey W. (2018). *Chaucerotics: Uncloaking the Language of Sex in* The Canterbury Tales *and* Troilus and Criseyde. New York: Palgrave.

Gutas, Dimitri (2006a). "Intellect Without Limits: The Absence of Mysticism in Avicenna." In *Intellect et imagination dans la philosophie médiévale. Actes du XIe congrès international de philosophie médiévale de la société internationale pour l'étude de la philosophie médiévale, (S.I.E.P.M), Porto, du 26 au 31 août 2002*, edited by Maria Cândida Pacheco and José F. Meirinhos, vol. 1, 351–372. Turnhout: Brepols.

Gutas, Dimitri (2006b). "Imagination and Transcendental Knowledge in Avicenna." In *Arabic Philosophy, Arabic Theology; From the Many to the One: Essays in Celebration of Richard M. Frank*, edited by James E. Montgomery, 337–354. Leuven: Peeters.

Gutas, Dimitri (2011). "Philosophy in the Twelfth Century: one View from Baghdad, or the Repudiation of al-Ghazālī." In *In the Age of Averroes: Arabic Philosophy in the Sixth/Twelfth Century*, edited by Peter Adamson, 9–26. London, Turin: The Warburg Institute, Nino Aragno Editore.

Gutas, Dimitri (2013). "Avicenna's philosophical project." In *Intepreting Avicenna: Critical Essays*, edited by Peter Adamson, 28–47. Cambridge: Cambridge University Press.

Gutas, Dimitri (2014a). *Avicenna and the Aristotelian Tradition: Introduction to Reading Avicenna's Philosophical Works. Second, Revised and Enlarged Edition, Including an Inventory of Avicenna's Authentic Works*. Leiden: Brill.

Gutas, Dimitri (2014b). *Orientations of Avicenna's Philosophy: Essays on His Life, Method, Heritage*. Farnham: Ashgate Variorum.

Haidari, A. A. (1986). "A Medieval Persian Satirist." *Bulletin of the School of Oriental and African Studies, University of London* 49.1 (1986): 117–127.

Haider, Najam (2013). "Contesting Intoxication: Early Juristic Debates over the Lawfulness of Alcoholic Beverages." *Islamic Law and Society* 20.1–2 (2013): 48–89.

Halabi, 'Ali Asghar (1364/1985). *Moqaddameyi bar tanz va shukh-tab'i dar Irān*. Tehran: Payk.

Halabi, 'Ali Asghar (1998). *'Obayd-e Zākāni*. Tehran: Tarh-e now.

Hall, Robert E. (2004). "Intellect, Soul and Body in Ibn Sīnā: Systematic Synthesis and Development of the Aristotelian, Neoplatonic and Galenic Theories." In *Intepreting Avicenna: Science and Philosophy in Medieval Islam. Proceedings of the Second Conference of the Avicenna Study Group*, edited by Jon McGinnis and David C. Reisman, 62–86. Leiden: Brill.

Hall, Robert E. (2006). "The '*Wahm*' in Ibn Sina's Psychology." In *Intellect et imagination dans la philosophie médiévale. Actes du XIe congrès international de philosophie médiévale de la société internationale pour l'étude de la philosophie médiévale, (S.I.E.P.M), Porto, du 26 au 31 août 2002*, edited by Maria Cândida Pacheco and José F. Meirinhos, vol. 1, 533–549. Turnhout: Brepols.

Halperin, David (2003). "The Social Body and the Sexual Body." In *Sex and Difference in Ancient Greece and Rome*, edited by Mark Golden and Peter Toohey, 131–150. Edinburgh: Edinburgh University Press.

Hamidiyān, Sa'id (1383/2004). *Sa'di dar ghazal*. Tehran: Nashr-e Qatre.

Hanaway, William L. (1976). "Paradise on Earth: The Terrestrial Garden in Persian Literature." In *The Islamic Garden*, edited by Elisabeth B. Macdougall, and Richard Ettinghausen, 41–68. Washington: Dumbarton Oaks.

Hanaway, William L. (1993). "Iranian Identity." *Iranian Studies* 26.1–2 (1993): 147–150.

Hasanli, Kāvus (1388/2009). "'Kāri nime-tamām az mardi tamām': 'Ghazalhā-ye Sa'di, tashih-e [bedun-e] tozih-e Doktor Gholām-Hoseyn Yusofi." *Pazhuhesh-nāme-ye Zabān-o Adabiyāt-e Fārsi* 1.1 (1388/2009): 95–106.

Hassan, Mona (2016). *Longing for the Lost Caliphate: A Transregional History*. Princeton, Oxford: Princeton University Press.

Hasse, D. Nikolaus (2000). *Avicenna's* De Anima *in the Latin West: The Formation of a Peripatetic Philosophy of the Soul 1160–1300*. London: Warburg Institute.

Haydari, 'Ali (1392/2013). "Degarguni-ye Sa'di dar ghazal." *Pazhuhesh-nāme-ye Adab-e Ghenā'i-ye Dāneshgāh-e Sistān-o Baluchestān* 21 (1392/2013): 83–102.

Haydari-Yasāvoli, 'Ali (1396/2017). "Dast-nevisi kohan az divān-e Homām al-Din Tabrizi (abiyāt va nekāt-e now-yāfte)." *Mirās-e Shahāb* 90 (1396/2017): 135–184.

Heath, Peter (1992). *Allegory and Philosophy in Avicenna (Ibn Sînâ) With a Translation of the Book of the Prophet Muhammad's Ascent to Heaven*. Philadelphia: University of Pennsylvania Press.

Heinrichs, Wolfhart P. (1984). "On the Genesis of the *Ḥaqîqa-Majâz* Dichotomy." *Studia Islamica*, 59 (1984): 111–140.

Heinrichs, Wolfhart P. (2016). "On the figurative (*majāz*) in Muslim interpretation and legal hermeneutics." In *Interpreting Scriptures in Judaism, Christianity and Islam: Overlapping Inquiries*, edited by Mordechai Z. Cohen and Adele Berlin, 249–265. Cambridge: Cambridge University Press.

Henderson, Jeffrey (1991). *The Maculate Muse: Obscene Language in Attic Comedy*. New York, Oxford: Oxford University Press.

Herdt, Gilbert (2014). *The Sambia: Ritual, Sexuality, and Change in Papua New Guinea*. Belmont, CA: Wadsworth.

Hillenbrand, Carole (1988). "Islamic Ortodoxy or Realpolitik: Al-Ghazālī's Views on Government." *Journal of the British Institute of Persian Studies* 26 (1988): 81–94.

Hillenbrand, Carole (1994). "Some Aspects of Al- Ghazālī's Views on Beauty." In *Gott ist schön und Er liebt die Schönheit/God is Beautiful and He Loves Beauty: Festschrift für Annemarie Schimmel*, edited by Alma Giese and J. Christoph Bürgel, 249–265. Bern: Peter Lang.

Hillenbrand, Carole (2013). "The *Kimiya-yi sa'adat* (*The Alchemy of Happiness*) of al-Ghazali: a misunderstood work?" In *Ferdowsi, the Mongols and the History of Iran. Art, literature and culture from early Islam to Qajar Persia. Studies in Honour of Charles Melville*, edited by Robert Hillenbrand, A. C. S. Peacock and Firuza Abdullaeva, 59–69. London: I. B. Tauris.

Hillenbrand, Robert (2014). "Wine in Islamic Art and Society." In *Court and Craft: A Masterpiece from Northern Iraq*, edited by Rachel Ward, 38–45, London: Paul Holberton Publishing.

Hindley, John Hoddon (1800). *Persian Lyrics, or Scattered Poems from the Diwan-i Hafiz: with Paraphrases in Verse and Prose, a Catalogue of the Gazels as Arranged in a Manuscript of the Works of Hafiz in the Chetham Library at Manchester, and Other Illustrations*. London: Harding.

Homā'i, Jalāl al-Din (1347/1995). *Fonun-e balāghat-o sanā'āt-e adabi*. Tehran: Tus.

Hoseyni, Maryam. (1391/2012) "Moqāyese-ye tatbiqi-ye qasāyed-e Sanā'i va Sa'di." *Sa'di-shenasi* 15 (1391/2012): 132–151.

Hunt, Lynn, ed. (1993). *The Invention of Pornography: Obscenity and the Origins of Modernity, 1500–1800*. New York: Zone Books.

Inaba, Minoru (2103). "Sedentary Rulers on the Move: The Travels of the Early Ghaznavid Sultans." In *Turko-Mongol Rulers, Cities and City Life*, edited by David Durand-Guédy, 75–98. Leiden; Boston: Brill.

Inati, Shams C. (1996). *Ibn Sīnā and Mysticism. Remarks and Admonitions: Part Four*. London, New York: Kegan Paul International.

Ingenito, Domenico (2009). "Quattro divān attuali: Hāfez tra ricezione e traduzione." *Oriente Moderno*, Nuova Serie, 89.1 (2009): 151–172.

Ingenito, Domenico (2010). "« Sedavo il dolore ardente dei giorni con l'acqua del canto poetico »: I versi della Dama del Mondo (Jahān Malek Khātun)." *Semicerchio: rivista di poesia comparata* 43 (2010): 40–60.

Ingenito, Domenico (2011). "Questi versi una fica li ha cantati—La Dama del Mondo (Jahān Malek Khātun): la maggiore poetessa dell'islam medievale." *Testo a Fronte: teoria e pratica della traduzione letteraria* 44 (2011): 37–76.

Ingenito, Domenico. (1391/2012). "Hāfez dar itāliyā." In *Hāfez, zendegi va andishe*, edited by Kāzem Musavi Bojnurdi and Asghar Dādbeh, 337–351. Tehran: Dāyerat al-Ma'āref-e Bozorg-e Eslāmi.

Ingenito, Domenico (2014). "'Tabrizis in Shiraz Are Worth Less than a Dog': Sa'dī and Humām, a Lyrical Encounter." in *Politics, Patronage and the Transmission of Knowledge in 13th–15th Century Tabriz*, edited by Judith Pfeiffer, 77–127. Leiden/ Boston: Brill.

Ingenito, Domenico (2018a). "Jahān Malik Khātūn: Gender, Canon, and Persona in the Poems of a Premodern Persian Princess." In *The Beloved in Middle Eastern Literatures: The Culture of Love and Languishing*, edited by Alireza Korangy, Hanadi Al-Samman, and Michael Beard, 177–212. London, New York: I.B. Tauris.

Ingenito, Domenico (2018b). "Hafez's 'Shirāzi Turk': A Geopoetical Approach." *Iranian Studies* 51.6 (2018): 851–887.

Ingenito, Domenico (2019). "'A Marvelous Painting': The Erotic Dimension of Sa'di's Praise Poetry." *Journal of Persianate Studies* 12.1 (2019): 103–166.

Ingenito, Domenico (2020). "Mahmud's New Garden in Balkh: A Literary Approach to Ephemeral Architecture." In *The City of Balkh: The History and Culture of a Great Islamic Capital*, edited by Edmund Herzig, Arezou Azad, Philippe Marquis, and Paul Wordsworth, [forthcoming] London: I. B. Tauris.

Ingenito, Domenico, and Camilla Miglio (2013). "Die Reise des Hāfez von Shiraz über Istanbul und Wien nach Weimar: Oder: 'Europa hatte nie eine reine Seele'." *Rivista dell'Istituto Italiano di Studi Germanici* 2 (2013): 247–265.

Iser, Wolfgang (1974). *The Implied Reader: Patterns of Communication in Prose Fiction from Bunyan to Beckett*. Baltimore: Johns Hopkins University Press.

Jabre, Farid [Farid Jabr] (1958). *La notion de la* ma'rifa *chez Ghazali*. Beyrouth [Beirut]: Editions Les Lettres Orientales.

Jabre, Farid [Farid Jabr] (1970). *Essai sur le lexique de Ghazālī*. Beirut: Université Libanaise.

Jackson, Peter (1999). *The Delhi Sultanate. A Political and Military History*. Cambridge: Cambridge University Press.

Jackson, Peter (2017). *The Mongols and the Islamic World: From Conquest to Conversion*. New Haven: Yale University Press.

Jackson, Virginia, and Yopie Prins, eds. (2014). *The Lyric Theory Reader: A Critical Anthology*. Baltimore: John Hopkins University Press.

Jacobi, Renate (1990). "The *Khayāl* Motif in Early Arabic Poetry." *Oriens* 32 (1990): 50–64.

Jacobi, Renate (1992). "Theme and Variations in Umayyad Ghazal Poetry." *Journal of Arabic Literature* 23.2 (1992): 109–119.

Jacobi, Renate (1999). "'Udhrī." *Encylopedia of Arabic Literature*, edited by Julie Scott Meisami, and Paul Starkey, vol. 2, 789–791. London, New York: Routledge.

Jahanpour, Farhang (2014). "Emerson on Hafiz and Sa'di: The Narrative of Love and Wine." In *Sufism and American Literary Masters*, edited by Mehdi Aminrazavi, 117–152. Albany: State University of New York Press.

Jakobson, Roman (1987). "On Realism in Art." In *Language in Literature*, edited by Krystyna Pomorska and Stephen Rudy, 19–27. Cambridge: Harvard University Press.

Janos, Damian (2016). "Intuition, Intellection, and Mystical Knowledge: Delineatig Fakhr al-Dīn al-Rāzī's Cognitive Theories." In *Islam and Rationality: The Impact of al-Ghazālī*, vol. 2., edited by Frank Griffel, 189–228. Leiden: Brill.

Janssens, Jules (1986). "Le Dānesh-Nāmeh d'Ibn Sīnā: un texte à revoir?" *Bulletin de philosophie médiévale* 28 (1986): 163–177.

Janssens, Jules (1993). "Le *Ma'ârij al-quds fī madârij ma'rifat al-nafs*: Un élément-clé pour le dossier Ghazzâlî-Ibn Sînâ?" *Archives d'histoire doctrinale et littéraire du Moyen Âge* 60 (1993): 27–55.

Janssens, Jules (1996). "The Problem of Human Freedom in Ibn Sînâ." *Actes del Simposi Internacional de l'Edat Mitjana*, edited by Paloma Llorente, Agustí Boadas, Francesc J. Fortuny, Andreu Grau, and Ignasi Roviró, 112–118. Vic: Patronat d'Estudis Osonencs.

Janssens, Jules (2001). "Al-Ghazzālī's *Tahāfut*: Is it Really a Rejection of Ibn Sīnā's Philosophy?" *Journal of Islamic Studies* 12.1 (2001): 1–17.

Janssens, Jules (2003). "Al-Ghazzâlî and his Use of Avicennian Texts." In *Problems in Arabic Philosophy*, edited by Miklós Maróth, 37–49. Piliscaba: Avicenna Institute of Middle East Studies.

Janssens, Jules, and Daniel De Smet (2002). *Avicenna and His Heritage*. Leuven: Leuven University Press, 2002.

Jauss, Hans Robert, and Elizabeth Benzinger (1979). "Literary History as a Challenge to Literary Theory." *New Literary History* 2.1 (1970): 7–37.

Jauss, Hans Robert, and Timothy Bahti (1979). "The Alterity and Modernity of Medieval Literature." *New Literary History* 10.2 (1979): 181–229.

Jones, Sir William (1771). *A Grammar of the Persian Language*. London: W. and J. Richardson.

Karamustafa, Ahmet T. (2007). *Sufism: The Formative Period*. Edinburgh: Edinburgh University Press.

Karimi-Hakkak, Ahmad (2014). "*Āb-e Ātash-Zāy* (Fire Breeding Liquid): The Nature and Functions of Wine in Classical Persian Poetry." In *Wine Culture in Iran and Beyond*, edited by Bert G. Fragner, Ralph Kauz, and Florian Schwarz, 311–330. Vienna: Verlag der Österreichischen Akademie der Wissenschaften.

Katouzian, Homa (1999). "Sufism and Sa'di, and Sa'di on Sufism." In *The Heritage of Sufism (Volume 2): The Legacy of Medieval Persian Sufism (1150–1500)*, edited by Leonard Lewisohn, 191–201. Oxford: Oneworld.

Katouzian [Katuziyān], Homa [Homā] (2006a). *Sa'di: shā'er-e 'eshq-o zendegi*. Tehran: Nashr-e Markaz.

Katouzian, Homa (2006b). *Sa'di: The Poet of Life, Love, and Compassion*. Oxford: Oneworld.

Katouzian, Homa (2016). *Saʿdi in Love: The Lyrical Verses of Persia's Master Poet*. London: I. B. Tauris.

Kaukua, Jari (2007). *Avicenna on Subjectivity: A Philosophical Study*. Jyväskylä: Jyväskylä University.

Kazemi, Ranin (2020). "Doctoring the Body and Exciting the Soul: Drugs and consumer culture in medieval and early modern Iran." *Modern Asian Studies* 54.2 (2020): 554–617.

Kennedy, Hugh (2008). "Al-Jāḥiẓ and the Construction of Homosexuality at the Abbasid Court." In *Medieval Sexuality: A Casebook*, edited by April Harper and Caroline Proctor, 175–188. New York, London: Routledge.

Keshavarz, Fatemeh (2015). *Lyrics of Life: Saʿdi on Love, Cosmopolitanism and Care of the Self*. Edinburgh: Edinburgh University Press.

Key, Alexander (2018). *Language between God and the Poets: Maʿnā in the Eleventh Century*. Oakland: University of California Press.

Khatib-Rahbar, Khalil (1367/1988). *Divān-e ghazaliyāt-e ostād-e sokhan Saʿdi-ye Shirāzi: Bā maʿni-ye vāzhehā va sharh-e abiyāt va zekr-e vazn va bahr-e ghazalhā va barkhi noktehā-ye dasturi va adabi va amsāl va hekam*, 2 vols. Tehran: Mahtāb.

Khorramshāhi, Bahāʾ al-Din (1366/1987). *Hāfeznāme: sharh-e alfāz, aʿlām, mafāhim-e kelidi va abiyāt-e doshvār-e Hāfez*, 2 vols. Tehran: Sorush.

Kiening, Christian (2003). *Zwischen Körper und Schrift: Texte vor dem Zeitalter der Literatur*. Frankfurt: Fischer.

King, Anya H. (2017). *Scent from the Garden of Paradise: Musk and the Medieval Islamic World*. Leiden: Brill.

Klein, Yaron (2014). "Music, Rapture and Pragmatics: Ghazālī on Samāʿ and Wajd." In *No Tapping around Philology: A Festschrift in Honor of Wheeler McIntosh Thackston Jr.'s 70th Birthday*, edited by Alireza Korangy and Daniel J. Sheffield, 215–242. Wiesbaden: Harrassowitz Verlag.

Kozah, Mario (2015). *The Birth of Indology as an Islamic Science: Al-Bīrūnī's Treatise on Yoga Psychology*. Leiden: Brill.

Kraemer, Joel L. (1986). *Humanism in the Renaissance of Islam: The Cultural Revival During the Buyd Age*. Leiden: Brill.

Kukkonen, Taneli (2012). "Receptive to Reality: Al-Ghazālī on the Structure of the Soul." *The Muslim World* 102 (2012): 541–561.

Lambton, Ann K. S. (1988). *Continuity and Change in Medieval Persia: Aspects of Administrative, Economic, and Social History, 11th–14th Century*. Albany: The Persian Heritage Foundation.

Landau, Justine (2012). "Naṣīr al-Dīn Ṭūsī and Poetic Imagination in the Arabic and Persian Philosophical Tradition." In *Metaphor and Imagery in Persian Poetry*, edited by Ali Asghar Seyed-Gohrab, 15–65. Leiden: Brill.

Landau, Justine (2013). *De rythme & de raison. Lecture croisée de deux traités de poétique persans du XIIIe siècle*. Paris: Presses de la Sorbonne Nouvelle / IFRI.

Lane, George (2003). *Early Mongol Rule in Thirteen-Century Iran: A Persian Renaissance*. London, New York: Routledge.

Lange, Christian (2016). *Paradise and Hell in Islamic Traditions*. New York: Cambridge University Press.

Laoust, Henri (1970). *La politique de Ġazālī*. Paris: Librairie Orientaliste de Paul Geuthner.

Layiān, Sa'id (1394/2015). "Barresi va naqd-e ghazalhā-ye Sa'di-ye tashih-e Gholām-Hoseyn Yusofi va Parviz Atābaki." *Āyene-ye Mirās* 36 (1394/2015): 131–162.

Lazarus-Yafeh, Hava (1975). *Studies in al-Ghazzālī*. Jerusalem: Magnes.

Lee, Joo-Yup. "The Historical Meaning of the Term *Turk* and the Nature of the Turkic Identity of the Chinggisid and Timurid Elites in Post-Mongol Central Asia." *Central Asiatic Journal* 59.1–2 (2016): 101–132.

Lescot, Roger (1944). "Essai d'une chronologie de l'oeuvre de Hafiz." *Bulletin d'Études Orientales* 10 (1944): 57–100.

Levron, Pierre (2010). "Mélancolie et scatologie: de l'humeur noire aux vents et aux excréments." *Questes* 21 (2010): 72–88.

Levy, Reuben (1969). *An Introduction to Persian Literature*. New York: Columbia University Press.

Lewis, Franklin D. (1995). *Reading, Writing and Recitation: Sanā'ī and the Origins of the Persian Ghazal*, 2 vols. PhD dissertation, University of Chicago.

Lewis, Franklin D. (2000) *Rumi: Past and Present, East and West. The Life, Teachings and Poetry of Jalâl al-Din Rumi*. Oxford: Oneworld.

Lewis, Franklin D. (2001a). "Golestān-e Sa'di." *Encyclopaedia Iranica*, see online edition for print edition reference, http://www.iranicaonline.org/articles/golestan-e-sadi. Accessed on 30 July 2019.

Lewis, Franklin (2001b). "The Modes of Literary Production: Remarks on the Composition, Revision and Publication' of Persian Texts in the Medieval Period." *Persica* 17: 69–83.

Lewis, Franklin D. (2006). "The Transformation of the Persian Ghazal: From Amatory Mood to Fixed Form." In *Ghazal in World Literature, vol. 2, From a Literary Genre to a Great Tradition*, edited by Angelika Neuwirth, Michael Hess, Judith Pfeiffer, and Boerte Sagaste, 121–39. Beirut: Ergon Verlag.

Lewis, Franklin (2009), "Sexual Occidentation: The Politics of Boy-love and Christian-love in 'Attar." *Iranian Studies* 42: 693–723.

Lewis, Franklin (2010a). "The Semiotics of Dawn in the Poetry of Ḥāfiẓ." In *Hafiz and the Religion of Love in Classical Persian Poetry*, edited by Leonard Lewisohn, 251–278. London: I.B. Tauris.

Lewis, Franklin D. (2010b). "Sincerely Flattering Panegyrics: The Shrinking Ghaznavid Qasida." in *The Necklace of the Pleiades: 24 Essays on Persian Literature, Culture and Religion*, edited by Franklin D. Lewis and Sunil Sharma. Leiden, Amsterdam, 209–250. Leiden: Leiden University Press.

Lewis, Franklin D. (2014a). "Towards a Chronology of the Poems in the *Dīwān-i Shams*: A Prolegomenon for a Periodization of Rumi's Literary Oeuvre." In *The Philosophy of Ecstasy: Rumi and the Sufi Tradition*, edited by Leonard Lewisohn, 145–176. Bloomington: World Wisdom.

Lewis, Franklin D. (2014b). "Ut Pictura Poesis: Verbal and Visual Depictions of the Practice of Poetry in the Medieval Period." In *No Tapping around Philology: A Festschrift in Honor of Wheeler McIntosh Thackston Jr.'s 70th Birthday*, edited by Alireza Korangy and Daniel J. Sheffield, 53–70. Wiesbaden: Harrassowitz Verlag.

Lewis, Franklin D. (2018a). "To Round and Rondeau the Canon: Jāmī and Fānī's Reception of the Persian Lyrical Tradition." In *Jāmī in Regional Contexts: The Reception of ʿAbd al-Raḥmān Jāmī's Works in the Islamicate World, ca. 9th/15th–14th/20th Century*, edited by Thibaut d'Hubert and Alexandre Papas, 463–571. Leiden: Brill.

Lewis, Franklin D. (2018b). "Authorship, Auctoritas and the Management of Literary Estates in Pre-Modern Persian Literature." *Jerusalem Studies in Arabic and Islam* 54 (2018): 73–125.

Lewisohn, Leonard (1989). "Shabestari's *Garden of Mysteries*: The Aesthetics and Hermeneutics of Sufi Poetry." *Temenos* 10 (1989): 177–207.

Lewisohn, Leonard (1995). *Beyond Faith and Infidelity: The Sufi Poetry and Teachings of Mahmud Shabistari*. Richmond: Curzon.

Lewisohn, Leonard (1997). "The Sacred Music of Islam: *Samāʿ* in the Persian Sufi Tradition." *British Journal of Ethnomusicology* 6 (1997): 1–33.

Lewisohn, Leonard, ed. (2010). *Hafiz and the Religion of Love in Classical Persian Poetry*. London: I.B. Tauris.

Lewisohn, Leonard (2014a). "Sufism's Religion of Love, from Rābiʿa to Ibn ʿArabī." In *The Cambridge Companion to Sufism*, edited by Lloyd Ridgeon, 150–180. Cambridge: Cambridge University Press.

Lewisohn, Leonard (2014b). "Principles of the Philosophy of Ecstasy in Rūmī's Poetry." In *The Philosophy of Ecstasy: Rumi and the Sufi Tradition*, edited by Leonard Lewisohn, 35–80. Bloomington: World Wisdom.

Lizzini, Olga L. (2009). "Vie active, vie contemplative et philosophie chez Avicenne." In *Vie active et vie contemplative au Moyen Âge et au seuil de la Renaissance*, edited by Christian Trottmann, 207–239. Rome: École Française de Rome.

Lobel, Diana (2007). *A Sufi-Jewish Dialogue: Philosophy and Mysticism in Baḥya ibn Paqūda's* Duties of the Heart. Philadelphia: University of Pennsylvania Press.

Loloi, Parvin. (2004). *Hāfiz, Master of Persian Poetry: A Critical Bibliography. English Translations since the Eighteenth Century*. London: I. B. Tauris.

Loloi, Parvin (2014). "Emerson and aspects of Sa'di's Reception in Nineteenth Century America." In *Sufism and American Literary Masters*, edited by Mehdi Aminrazavi, 91–116. Albany: State University of New York Press.

Losensky, Paul E. (1994). "'The Allusive Field of Drunkenness': The Safavid-Moghul Responses to a Lyric by Bābā Fighānī." in *Reorientations/Arabic and Persian Poetry*, edited by Suzanne Pinckney Stetkevych, 227–262. Bloomington: Indiana University Press.

Losensly, Paul E. (1997). "Demand, Ask, Seek": The Semantics and Rhetoric of the Radīf *Ṭalab* in the Persian Ghazal." *Turkish Studies Association Bulletin* 21.2 (1997): 19–40.

Losensky, Paul E. (1998a). *Welcoming Fighani: Imitation and Poetic Individuality in the Safavid-Mughal Ghazal*. Costa Mesa: Mazda Publishers.

Losensky, Paul E. (1998b). "Linguist and Rhetorical Aspects of the Signature Verse (*Takhalluṣ*) in the Persian *Ghazal*." *Edebiyāt* 8 (1998): 239–271.

Losensky, Paul E. (2003). "The Palace of Praise and the Melons of Time: Descriptive Patterns in 'Abdī Bayk Šīrāzī's *Garden of Eden*." *Eurasian Studies* 2.1 (2003): 1–29.

Losensky, Paul E. (2004). "'The Equal of Heaven's Vault': The Design, Ceremony, and Poetry of the Hasanabad Bridge." in *Writers and Rulers: Perspectives on Their Relationship from Abbasid to Safavid Times*, edited by Beatrice Gruendler and Louise Marlow, 95–216. Wiesbaden: Reichert.

Losensky, Paul E. (2009a). "Poetics and Eros in Early Modern Persia: *The Lovers' Confection* and *The Glorious Epistle* by Mohtasham Kāshāni." *Iranian Studies* 42.5 (2009): 745–764.

Losensky, Paul E., trans (2009b). *Farid ad-Din 'Attār's Memorial of God's Friends. Lives and Sayings of Sufis*. Translated and introduced by Paul Losensky. New York, Mahwah: Paulist Press.

Losensky, Paul E. (2012). "Sa'di." *Encyclopedia Iranica*, online edition, available at http://www.iranicaonline.org/articles/sadi-sirazi. Accessed on 30 July 2019.

Lonsensky, Paul E. (2013). "To Revere, Revise, and Renew: Ṣā'ib of Tabriz Reads the Ghazals of Rūmī." *Mawlana Rumi Review* 4 (2013): 10–49.

Losensky, Paul E. (2015). "'Square Like a Bubble': Architecture, Power, and Poetics in Two Inscriptions by Kalim Kāshāni." *Journal of Persianate Studies* 8 (2015): 42–70.

Losensky, Paul E. and Sunil Sharma (2013). *In the Bazaar of Love: The Selected Poetry of Amīr Khusraw*. New York: Penguin Global.

Lumbard, Joseph E. B. (2007). "From Ḥubb to 'Ishq: The Development of Love in Early Sufism." *Journal of Islamic Studies* 18.3 (2007): 345–385.

Lumbard, Joseph E. B. (2016). *Aḥmad Al-Ghazālī, Remembrance, and the Metaphysics of Love*. Albany: SUNY Press.

MacDonald, Duncan B. (1901a). "*Emotional Religion in Islām as Affected by Music and Singing*. Being a Translation of a Book of the *Iḥyā* [sic.] *'Ulūm ad-dīn* of al-Ghazzālī with Analysis, Annotation, and Appendices (Part I.)" *Journal of the Royal Asiatic Society* (Apr., 1901): 195–252.

MacDonald, Duncan B. (1901b). "*Emotional Religion in Islām as Affected by Music and Singing*. Being a Translation of a Book of the *Iḥyā* [sic.] *'Ulūm ad-dīn* of al-Ghazzālī with Analysis, Annotation, and Appendices (Part II.)" *Journal of the Royal Asiatic Society* (Oct., 1901): 705–748.

MacDonald, Duncan B. (1902). "*Emotional Religion in Islām as Affected by Music and Singing*. Being a Translation of a Book of the *Iḥyā* [sic.] *'Ulūm ad-dīn* of al-Ghazzālī with Analysis, Annotation, and Appendices (Part III.)" *Journal of the Royal Asiatic Society* (Jan., 1902): 1–28.

Macdougall, Elisabeth B., and Richard Ettinghausen, eds. (1976). *The Islamic Garden*. Washington: Dumbarton Oaks.

Maes, Hans (2012). "Who Says Pornography Can't Be Art?" In *Art and Pornography: Philosophical Essays*, edited by Hans Maes and Jerrold Levinson. Oxford: Oxford University Press.

Mahmudpur, Loqmān (1395/2016). "Barresi-ye hoviyyat-e ʿabu al-faraj ben jowzi bannā bar eshārāt-e saʿdi dar golestān." *Fonun-e Adabi* 8.3 (1395/2016): 169–184.

Māyel Heravi, Najib. (1379/2000). *Tārikh-e noskhe-pardāzi va tashih-e enteqādi-ye noskhehā-ye khatti*. Tehran: Ketābkhāne, Muze va Markaz-e Esnād-e Majles-e Shurā-ye Eslāmi.

Manoukian, Setrag (1991). *L'argento di un povero cuore: centouno ghazal di Saʿdi Shirāzi*. Rome: Istituto culturale della Repubblica islamica d'Iran in Italia.

Marcotte, Roxanne (2007). "Suhrawardi." *The Stanford Encyclopedia of Philosophy* (*Summer 2019 Edition*) edited by Edward N. Zalta, available online at https://plato.stanford.edu/archives/sum2019/entries/suhrawardi/.

Marmura, Michael E., trans. (1963). "On the Proof of Prophecies and the Interpretation of the Prophet's Symbols and Metaphors." By Avicenna, in *Medieval Political Philosophy*, edited by Ralph Lerner and Muhsin Mahdi, 112–121. New York: Glencoe.

Marmura, Michael E. (1985). "Divine Omniscience and Future Contingents in Alfarabi and Avicenna." In *Divine Omniscience and Omnipotence in Medieval Philosophy: Islamic, Jewish and Christian Perspectives*, edited by Tamar Rudavsky, 81–94. Dordrecht: Reidel.

Massé, Henri (1919). *Essai sure le poète Saadi: suivi d'une bibliographie*. Paris: P. Geuthner.

Massé, Henri (1972). "Le divan de la princesse Djehane." In *Mélange d'iranologie en mémoire de feu Said Naficy*, edited by Parimarz Naficy, 1–42.

Māyel Heravi, Najib (1364/1985). "Tarjome-ye ʿAvāref al-Maʿāref-e Sohravardi." *Nashr-e Dānesh* 32 (1364/1985): 34–40.

Māyel Heravi, Najib (1390/2011). "Safine-ye Nuh." *Gozāresh-e Mirās* 5.47–48 (1390/2011): 11–15.

McDonald, Nicola, ed. (2014). *Medieval Obscenities*. Woodbridge: York Medieval Press.

McGinnis, Jon, ed. (2004). *Interpreting Avicenna: Science and Philosophy in Medieval Islam. Proceedings of the Second Conference of the Avicenna Study Group*. Leiden: Brill.

McGinnis, Jon (2007). "Making Abstraction Less Abstract: The Logical, Psychological, and Metaphysical Dimensions of Avicenna's Theory of Abstraction." *Proceedings of the American Catholic Philosophical Association* 80 (2007): 169–183.

McGinnis, Jon (2010). *Avicenna*. Oxford: Oxford University Press.

McGinnis, (2013a) "New Light on Avicenna." In *Philosophical Psychology in Arabic Thought and the Latin Aristotelianism of the 13th Century*, edited by Luis Xavier López-Farjeat and Jörg Alejandro Tellkamp, 41–57. Paris: J. Vrin.

McGinnis, Jon (2013b). "Pointers, Guides, Founts and Gifts: The Reception of Avicennan Physics in the East." *Oriens* 41 (2013): 433–456.

McGinnis, Jon (2016). "Naṣīr al-Dīn al-Ṭūsī (d. 1274), *Sharḥ al- Ishārāt*." In *The Oxford Handbook of Islamic Philosophy*, edited by Khaled El-Rouayheb and Sabine Schmidtke, 326–347. New York: Oxford University Press.

Mehren, August Ferdinand (1894). *Traités mystiques d'Abou Alî al'Hosain b. Abdallâh b. Sînâ ou d'Avicenne. IIIème Fascicule*. Leyde (Leiden): Brill.

Meier, Fritz (1999). "The Dervish Dance." In *Essays on Islamic Piety and Mysticism*, translated by John O'Kane, 23–48. Leiden: Brill.

Meisami, Julie Scott (1985). "Allegorical Gardens in the Persian Poetic Tradition: Nezami, Rumi, Hafez." *International Journal of Middle East Studies* 17 (1985): 229–260.

Meisami, Julie Scott (1987). *Medieval Persian Court Poetry*. Princeton: Princeton University Press.

Meisami, Julie Scott (1990a) "Ghaznavid Panegyrics: Some Political Implications." *Iran* 28.1 (1990a): 31–44.

Meisami, Julie Scott (1990b). "Medieval Persian Panegyric: Ethical Values and Rhetorical Strategies." In *Courtly Literature: Culture and Context. Proceedings of the 5th Triennial Congress of the International Courtly Literature Society, Dalfsen, The Netherlands, 09–16 August 1986*, edited by Keith Busby and Erik Kooper, 439–458. Amsterdam, Philadelphia: John Benjamins.

Meisami, Julie Scott (1990c). "Persona and Generic Conventions in Medieval Persian Lyric." *Comparative Criticism* 12 (1990c): 125–151.

Meisami, Julie Scott (1991). "The Ghazal as Fiction: Implied Speakers and Implied Audience in Hafiz's Ghazals." In *Intoxication, Earthly and Heavenly: Seven Studies on the Poet Hafiz of Shiraz*, edited by Michael Glünz and Johann Christoph Bürgel, 89–103. Bern: Peter Lang.

Meisami, Julie Scott (1993). "Arabic *Mujūn* Poetry: The Literary Dimension." In *Verse and the Fair Sex: Studies in Arabic Poetry and in the Representation of Women in Arabic Literature*, edited by Fredrick de Jong, 8–30. Utrecht: M. Th. Houtsma Stichtung.

Meisami, Julie Scott (1995). "The Body as Garden: Nature and Sexuality in Persian Poetry." *Edebiyat* 6 (1995): 245–274.

Meisami, Julie Scott (1996). "Poetic Microcosms: The Persian Qasida to the End of the Twelfth Century." in *Qasida Poetry in Islamic Asia and Africa, vol. 1. Classical Traditions and Modern Meanings*, edited by Stefan Sperl and Christopher Shackle, 137–182. Leiden, New York, Köln: Brill.

Meisami, Julie Scott (1997). "Mixed Prose and Verse in Medieval Persian Literature." In *Prosimetrum: Cross-Cultural Perspectives on Narrative in Prose and Verse*, edited by Joseph Harris and Karl Reichl, 295–319. Cambridge: D. S. Brewer.

Meisami, Julie Scott (2001). "The Poet and His Patrons: Two Ghaznavid Panegyrists." *Persica* 17 (2001): 91–105.

Meisami, Julie Scott (2003). *Structure and Meaning in Medieval Arabic and Persian Poetry*. London, New York: Routledge.

Meisami, Julie Scott (2005). "The Persian Ghazal between Love Song and Panegyric." In *Ghazal as World Literature I: Transformations of a Literary Genre*, edited by Thomas Bauer and Angelika Neuwirth, 327–342. Beirut, Würzburg: Ergon.

Meisami, Julie Scott (2010). "A Life in Poetry: Hafiz's First Ghazal." In *The Necklace of the Pleiades: 24 Essays on Persian Literature, Culture and Religion*, edited by Franklin D. Lewis and Sunil Sharma, 163–181. Leiden: Brill.

Melchert, Christopher (2015). "The Early Controversy Over Whether the Prophet Saw God." *Arabica* 62 (2015): 459–476.

Melikian-Chirvani, Assadullah Souren (1971). "Le royaume de Salomon: Les inscriptions persanes des sites achéménides." In *Le monde iranien et l'Islam*, edited by Jean Aubin, vol. 1, 1–41. Geneva: Droz, Paris: Minard.

Melikian-Chirvani, Assadullah Souren (1974). "L'évocation litteraire du Bouddhisme dans l'Iran musulman." *Le monde iranien et l'Islam* 2 (1974): 1–72.

Melikian-Chirvani, Assadullah Souren (1985). "The Aesthetics of Islam." In *Treasures of Islam*, edited by Toby Falk, 20–24. London: Sotheby's/Philip Wilson Publishers.

Meneghini, Daniela (2003). Review of *'Obayd Zākāni, Collected Works*, ed. M. J. Mahjoub, New York, 1999, *Middle Eastern Literatures* 6.2 (2003): 241–245.

Merçil, Erdoğan (1975). *Fars atabegleri Salgurlar*. Ankara: Türk Tarih Kurumu.

Merguerian, Gayane Karen and Afsaneh Najmabadi (1997). "Zulaykha and Yusuf: Whose 'Best Story'?" *International Journal of Middle East Studies* 29.4 (1997), 485–508.

Michot, Yahya [Jean] (1984). "*L'épître sur la connaissance de l'âme rationnelle et de ses états* attribuée à Avicenne." *Revue philosophique de Louvain* 82.56 (1984): 479–499.

Michot, Yahya [Jean] (1985). "Prophétie et divination selon Avicenne: Présentation, essai de traduction critique et index de l'« Épître de l'âme de la sphère. »" *Revue Philosophique de Louvain* 83.60 (1985): 507–535.

Michot, Yahya [Jean] (1986). *La destinée de l'homme selon Avicenne: Le retour à Dieu (ma'ād) et l'imagination*. Leuven: Peeters.

Michot, Jean (1993). "La pandémie Avicennienne au VIe/XIIe siècle. Présentation, *editio princeps* et traduction de l'introduction *du Livre de l'advenue du monde* (*Kitāb ḥūduth al-'ālam*) d'Ibn Ghaylān al-Balkhī." *Arabica* 40.3 (1993): 287–344.

Mikkelson, Jane (2019). "Flights of Imagination: Avicenna's Phoenix ('Anqā) and Bedil's Figuration for the Lyric Self." *Journal of South Asian Intellectual History* 2 (2019): 28–72.

Miller, James E. (1998). "Walt Whitman's Omnisexual Vision." In *The Chief Glory of Every People: Essays on Classic American Writers*, edited by Matthew J. Bruccoli, 235–239. Carbondale and Edwardsville: Southern Illinois University Press.

Miller, Matthew T. (2018). "Embodying the Beloved: Embodiment, (Homo)eroticism, and the Straightening of Desire in the Hagiographic Tradition of Fakhr al-Dīn 'Irāqī." *Middle Eastern Literatures* 21.1 (2018): 1–27.

Minovi, Mojtabā (1338/1959). "Taḥqīqātī dar bāre-ye kolliyāt-e Sa'di." *Yaghmā* 11.9 (1338/1959): 385–391.

Minovi, Mojtabā (1353/1974). "*Resāle-ye sāhebiyye* az shaykh-e ajall Sa'di-ye Shirāzi dar nasihat-e arbāb-e mamlekat." *Majalle-ye Dāneshkade-ye Adabiyāt-o 'Olum-e Ensāni-ye Dāneshgāh-e Ferdowsi* 10.1 (1353/1974): 25–65.

Morrison, Robert (2009). "*Falsafa* and Astronomy after Avicenna: An Evolving Relationship." In *Avicenna and his Legacy: A Golden Age of Science and Philosophy*, edited by Tzvi Langermann, 307–326. Turnhout: Brepols.

Mortazavi, Manuchehr (1365/1986). *Maktab-e Hāfez*. Tehran: Tus.

Motallebi-Kāshāni, Nāder (1389/2011). "Nāme-ye 'Allāme Mohammad Qazvini be Zokā' al-Molk Mohammad-'Ali Foroughi." *Nāme-ye Bahārestān* 17, 207–2014.

Movahhed, Ziyā' (1391/2012). "Hazliyāt-e Sa'di." *Sa'di-shenāsi* 15 (1391/2012): 47–52.

Moynihan, Elizabeth B. (1979). *Paradise as a Garden in Persia and Mughal India*. New York: G. Braziller.

Mozaffari, 'Alirezā, and 'Ali Dalā'i-Milān (1392/2013). "Barresi-ye mabāni-ye falsāfi-ye 'erfāni-ye hasti-shenāsi-ye sanā'i dar hadiqe." *Zabān-o adab-e fārsi* (*dāneshgāh-e tabriz*) 228 (1392/2013): 165–184.

Murata, Kazuyo (2017). *Beauty in Sufism: The Teachings of Rūzbihān Baqlī*. Albany: SUNY Press.

Murray, Stephen O., and Will Roscoe, eds. (1997). *Islamic Homosexualities: Culture, History, and Literature*. New York, London: New York University Press.

Naaman, Erez (2013). "Women Who Cough and Men Who Hunt: Taboo and Euphemism (*kināya*) in the Medieval Islamic World." *Journal of the American Oriental Society* 133.3 (2013): 467–493.

Nafisi, Sa'id (1341/1962). *Mohit-e zendegi va ahvāl-o ash'ār-e Rudaki*. Tehran: Ebn-e Sinā.

Nagy, Gregory (1996). *Poetry and Performance: Homer and Beyond*. Cambridge: Cambridge University Press.

Najmabadi, Afsaneh (1988). “Reading for Gender Through Qajar Art.” In *Royal Persian Paintings: The Qajar Epoch 1785–1925*, edited by Layla S. Diba, and Maryam Ekhtiar, 76–89. Brooklyn: Museum of Arts, in association with I. B. Tauris (London).

Najmabadi, Afsaneh (2005). *Women with Mustaches and Men without Beards: Gender and Sexual Anxieties of Iranian Modernity*. Berkeley and Los Angeles: University of California Press.

Nasr, Seyyed Hossein (1993). *An Introduction to Islamic Cosmological Doctrines: Conceptions of Nature and Methods Used for its Study by the Ikhwān al-Ṣafā’, al-Bīrūnī, and Ibn Sīnā. Revised Edition*. Albany: SUNY Press.

Necipoğlu, Gülrü (1995). *The Topkapı Scroll: Geometry and Ornament in Islamic Architecture*. Santa Monica: Getty Center for the History of Art and the Humanities.

Necipoğlu, Gülrü (2015). “The Scrutinizing Gaze in the Aesthetics of Islamic Visual Cultures: Sight, Insight, and Desire.” *Muqarnas* 32 (2015): 26–31.

Nicholson, Reynold A., trans. (1976 [1911]). *The Kashf al-Mahjùb: The Oldest Persian Treatise on Sufism by Alí B. Uthmán al-Jullábi al-Hujwírí. Translated from the text of the Lahore edition, compared with mss. in the India office and British Museum*, by Abu al-Hasan ʿAli Hojviri. London: Luzac.

Niyāzkār, Farah (1390/2012). *Sharh-e ghazaliyāt-e Saʿdi*. Tehran: Hermes.

Niyāzkār, Farah (1392/2013). “Samāʿ-e ahl-e tasavvof va ruykarde Saʿdi bedān.” *Adabiyāt-e ʿErfāni va Osture-shenākhti* 33 (1392/2013): 269–296.

Nowruzi, Jahānbakhsh (1388/2009). “Che kasi ghazaliyāt-e saʿdi rā be chahār daste taqsim nemude? Va be che ʿellat?” *Majalle-ye bustān-e adab-e dāneshgāh-e shirāz* 2 (1388/2009): 157–178.

Nurbakhsh, Javād (1984). *Sufi Symbolism I: The Nurbakhsh Encyclopedia of Sufi Terminology* (*Esoteric Symbolism of the Parts of the Beloved’s Body*), translated by Leonard Lewisohn. London: KNP.

Oberhelman, Steven M. (1997). “Hierarchies of Gender, Ideology, and Power in Ancient and Medieval Greek and Arabic Dream Literature.” In *Homoeroticism in Classical Arabic Literature*, edited by J. W. Wright Jr. and Everett K. Rowson, 55–93. New York: Columbia University Press.

Obermayer, Hans Peter (1998). *Martial und der Diskurs über männliche “Homosexualität” in der Literatur der frühen Kaiserzeit*. Tübingen: Narr.

Ohlander, Erik (2008). *Sufism in an Age of Transition: ʿUmar al-Suhrawardī and the Rise of the Islamic Mystical Brotherhoods*. Leiden: Brill.

Omar, Sara (2012). “From Semantics to Normative Law: Perceptions of *Liwāṭ* (Sodomy) and *Siḥāq* (Tribadism) in Islamic Jurisprudence (8th–15th Century CE).” *Islamic Law and Society* 19 (2012): 222–256.

Omidsalar, Mahmoud (2002). "Orality, Mouvance, and Editorial Theory in *Shāhnāma* Studies." *Jerusalem Studies in Arabic and Islam* 27 (2002): 245–283.

Oppenheimer, Paul (1989). *The Birth of the Modern Mind: Self, Consciousness, and the Invention of the Sonnet*. Oxford: Oxford University Press.

Opwis, Felicitas (2011). "Shifting Legal Authority from the Ruler to the *'Ulama*: Rationalizing the Punishment for Drinking Wine during the Saljuq Period." *Der Islam* 86 (2011): 65–92.

Ormsby, Eric Linn (1991). "The Taste of Truth: The Structure of Experience in al-Ghazālī's al-*Munqidh min al-Ḍalāl*," in), *Islamic Studies Presented to Charles J. Adams*, edited by Wael B. Hallaq and Donald P. Little, 133–152. Leiden: Brill, 1991.

Orsatti, Paola (2019). "Persian Language in Arabic Script: The Formation of the Ortographic Standard and the Different Graphic Traditions of Iran in the First Centuries of the Islamic Era." In *Creating Standards: Interactions with Arabic Script in 12 Manuscript Cultures*, edited by Dmitry Bondarev, Alessandro Gori, and Lameen Souag, 39–72. Berlin, Boston: De Gruyter.

Pellò, Stefano (2013). "A Paper Temple: Mani's *Arzhang* in and around Persian lexicography" In *Sogdians, their Precursors, Contemporaries and Heirs. Based on proceedings of* [sic] *conference "Sogdians at Home and Abroad" held in memory of Boris Il'ich Marshak (1993–2006)*, edited by P. B. Lurje and A. I. Torgoev, 252–265. St. Petersburg: The State Hermitage Publishers.

Peraino, Judith (2011). *Giving Voice to Love: Song and Self-Expression from the Troubadours to Guillaume de Machaut*. Oxford: Oxford University Press.

Petchesky, Rosalind (2007). "Sexual Rights Policies Across Countries and Cultures: Conceptual Frameworks and Minefields." In *Sex politics: Reports from the Front-lines*, edited by Richard Parker, Rosalind Petchesky, and Robert Sember, 9–25. Rio de Janeiro: Sexuality Policy Watch.

Pfeiffer, Judith (2006). "Reflections on a 'Double Rapprochement': Conversion to Islam Among the Mongol Elite During the Early Ilkhanate." In *Beyond the Legacy of Genghis Khan*, edited by Linda Komaroff, 369–389. Brill: Leiden.

Picone, Michelangelo (2000). "Traditional Genres and Poetic Innovation in Thirteenth—Century Italian Lyric Poetry." In *Medieval Lyric: Genres in Historical Content*, edited by William Paden, 146–157. Urbana, Chicago: Universiy of Illinois Press.

Piemontese, Angelo Michele (1995). "La leggenda persiana del contrasto fra pittori greci e cinesi." In *L'arco di fango che rubò la luce alle stelle: Studi in onore di Eugenio Galdieri per il suo settantesimo compleanno*, edited by Michele Bernardini et alii, 293–302. Lugano: Edizioni Arte e Moneta.

Pinder-Wilson, Ralph (1976). "The Persian Garden: Bagh and Chahar Bagh." In *The Islamic Garden*, edited by Elisabeth B. Macdougall and Richard Ettinghausen, 69–86. Washington: Dumbarton Oaks.

Pines, Shlomo (1987). "Quelques notes sur les rapports de l'*Iḥyâ' 'ulûm al-dîn* d'al-Ghazâlî avec la pensée d'Ibn Sînâ." In *Ghazâlî: La raison et le miracle. Table ronde UNESCO, 9–10 decembre 1982*, 11–16. Paris: Maisonneuve et Larose.

Pormann, Peter E. (2013). "Avicenna on Medical Practice, Epistemology, and the Physiology of the Inner Senses." In *Interpreting Avicenna: Critical Essays*, edited by Peter Adamson, 91–108. Cambridge: Cambridge University Press.

Purjavādi, Nasrollāh (1370/1991). "Mas'ale-ye ta'rif-e alfāz-e ramzi dar she'r-e 'āsheqāne-ye fārsi." *Ma'āref* 24 (1370/1991): 240–277.

Purjavādi, Nasrollāh (1378/1999). "Sa'di va Ahmad Ghazāli." *Nashr-e dānesh* 16.1 (1378/1999): 3–16.

Purjavādi, Nasrollāh (1389/2000). "Dar havāpeymā, hamrāh bā 'Obayd." *Nashr-e Dānesh* 17.2 (2000): 66–68.

Purjavādi, Nasrollāh (1381/2002). *Do mojadded: pazhuheshhā'i dar bāre-ye Mohammad-e Ghazzāli va Fakhr-e Rāzi / Two Renewers of Faith. Studies on Muhammad-i Ghazzālī and Fakhruddīn-i Rāzī*. Tehran: Markaz-e Nashr-e Dāneshgāhi.

Pourjavady [Purjavādi], Nasrollah (2005). "Stories of Aḥmad al-Ghazālī 'Playing the Witness' in Tabrīz (Shams-i Tabrīzī's Interest in *shāhid-bāzī*)." Translated by Scott Kugle, in *Reason and Inspiration in Islam: Theology, Philosophy, and Mysticism in muslim Thought*, edited by Todd Lawson, 200–220, London: I.B. Tauris.

Proust, Marcel (1957). *Swann's Way*, translated by C. K. S. Moncrieff. New York: Penguin Books.

Purjavādi, Nasrollāh (1387/2008). *Bāde-ye 'eshq: pazhuheshi dar ma'nā-ye bāde dar she'r-e 'erfāni-ye fārsi*. Tehran: Kārnāme.

Pourjavady [Purjavādi], Nasrollah (2012). "Love and the Metaphors of Wine and Drunkenness in Persian Sufi poetry." In *Metaphor and Imagery in Persian Poetry*, edited by Ali Asghar Seyed-Gohrab, 125–136. Leiden: Brill.

Purnāmdāriyān, Taqi (1382/2003). *Gomshode-ye lab-e daryā: Ta'amoli dar ma'ni va surat-e she'r-e Hāfez*. Tehran: Sokhan.

Qayyumi, Samira (1386/2007). "Negāhi digar be bayti az masnavi." *Motāla'āt-e 'Erfāni* 5 (1386/2007): 119–130.

Qazvini, Mohammad (1377/1998). "Mamduhin-e sheykh Sa'di." *Sa'di-shenāsi* 1 (1377/1998): 25–90.

Rahman, Fazlur (1952). *Avicenna's Psychology. An English Translation of* Kitāb al-Najāt, *Book II, Chapter VI*, London, New York: Oxford University Press.

Rahman, Fazlur (1959). *Avicenna's De anima: Being the Psychological part of* Kitāb al-Shifā'. London, New York: Oxford University Press.

Rapoport, Michael A. (2018). *The Life and Afterlife of the Rational Soul: Chapters VIII–X of Ibn Sīnā's* Pointers and Reminders *and Their Commentaries*. PhD dissertation, Yale University.

Ravalde, Esther (2016). “Shams al-Dīn Juwaynī, Vizier and Patron: Mediation between Ruler and Ruled in the Ilkhanate.” In *The Mongols' Middle East: Continuity and Transformation in Ilkhanid Iran*, edited by Bruno De Nicola and Charles Melville. Leiden/Boston: Brill.

Richard, Francis (1997). *Splendeurs persanes: Manuscrits du XIIe au XVIIe siècle*. Paris: Bibliothèque Nationale de France.

Richard, Francis (2013). *Catalogue des manuscrits persans. Bibliothèque nationale de France, Département des manuscrits. Tome II: Le supplément persan. Première partie, 1–524; Deuxième partie, 525–1000*, 2 vols. Rome: Insituto per l'Oriente C.A. Nallino.

Richlin, Amy (1992). *The Garden of Priapus: Sexuality and Aggression in Roman Humor*. New York, Oxford: Oxford University Press.

Ridgeon, Lloyd (1998). *ʿAzīz Nasafī*. Richmond: Curzon.

Ridgeon, Lloyd (2002). *Persian Metaphysics and Mysticism: Selected Treatises of ʿAzīz Nasafī*. Richmond: Curzon.

Ridgeon, Lloyd (2012). “The Controversy of Shaykh Awḥad al-Dīn Kirmānī and Handsome, Moon-Faced Youths: A Case Study of *Shāhid-Bāzī* in Medieval Sufism.” *Journal of Sufi Studies* 1.1 (2012): 3–30.

Ridgeon, Lloyd (2014). *Morals and Mysticism in Persian Sufism: A History of Sufi-*futuwwat *in Iran*. London: Routledge.

Ridgeon, Lloyd (2015). “Mysticism in Medieval Sufism.” In *The Cambridge Companion to Sufism*, edited by Lloyd Ridgeon, 125–149. Cambridge: Cambridge University Press.

Ridgeon, Lloyd (2017). *Awḥad al-Dīn Kirmānī and the Controversy of the Sufi Gaze*. London: Routledge.

Rind, Bruce (1998). “Biased Use of Cross-Cultural and Historical Perspectives on Male Homosexuality in Human Sexuality Textbooks.” *The Journal of Sex Research* 35.4 (4): 397–407.

Ritter, Hellmut (2003). *The Ocean of the Soul: Man, the World and God in the Stories of Farid al-Din ʿAttar*, translated by John O'Kane. Leiden: Brill.

Rowson, Everett K. (1991). “The Categorization of Gender and Sexual Irregularity in Medieval Arabic Vice Lists.” In *Body Guards: The Cultural Politics of Gender Ambiguity*, edited by Julia Epstein and Kristina Straub, 50–79. New York: Routledge.

Rowson, Everett K. (1998). “Mujūn.” *Encylopedia of Arabic Literature*, edited by Julie Scott Meisami and Paul Starkey, vol. 2, 546–548. London, New York: Routledge.

Rubanovich, Julia (2006). “Aspects of Medieval Intertextuality: Verse Insertions in Persian Prose *dāstāns*.” *Jerusalem Studies in Arabic and Islam* 32 (2006): 247–268.

Rubanovich, Julia (2009). “Metaphors of Authorship in Medieval Persian Prose: A Preliminary Study.” *Middle Eastern Literatures* 12.2 (2009): 127–153.

Rudgar, Qanbar ʿAli (1384/2005). “Khāndān-e Zangi-ye Faryumadi.” *Motālaʿāt-e Eslāmi* 68 (1384/2005): 163–79.

Rundgren, Frithiof (1978–1979). "Avicenna on Love: Studies in the *'Risāla fī māhıyat al-'ishq'*." *Orientalia Suecana* 27–28 (1978–1979): 42–62.

Rustomji, Nerina (2009). *The Garden and the Fire: Heaven and Hell in Islamic Culture*. New York: Columbia University Press.

Rypka, Jan (1968). *History of Iranian Literature*. Dordrecth: D. Reidel.

Sabur, Dariyush (1384/2005). *Āfāq-e ghazal-e fārsi*. Tehran: Zavvār.

Saccone, Carlo, trans (2007). *Aḥmad Ghazâlî: Delle occasioni amorose*, by Ahmad Ghazāli. Roma: Carocci.

Safā, Zabih-Allāh (1368/1989). *Tārikh-e adabiyyāt dar Irān*, 5 vols, Tehran.

Safi, Omid. "Bargaining with *Baraka*: Persian Sufism, 'Mysticism,' and Pre Modern Politics." *The Muslim World* 90 (2000): 259–288.

Schimmel, Annemarie (1975a). *Mystical Dimensions of Islam*. Chapel Hill: The University of North Carolina Press.

Schimmel, Annemarie (1975b). "Turk and Hindu: A Poetical Image and its Application to Historical Fact." In *Islam and Cultural Change in the Middle Ages*, edited by Speros Vryonis 107–128. Wiesbaden: Harassowitz.

Schimmel, Annemarie (1976). "The Celestial Garden in Islam." in *The Islamic Garden*, edited by Elisabeth B. Macdougall and Richard Ettinghausen, 11–40. Washington: Dumbarton Oaks.

Schimmel, Annemarie (1988). "The Genius of Shiraz: Sa'di and Hafez." in *Persian Literature*, edited by Ehsan Yarshater, 214–225. Albany: Bibliotheca Persica.

Schimmel, Annemarie (1992). *A Two-Colored Brocade: The Imagery of Persian Poetry*. Chapel Hill: University of North Carolina Press.

Schmidtke, Sabine (1999). "Homoeroticism and homosexuality in Islam: a review article." *Bulletin of the School of Oriental and African Studies, University of London* 62.2 (1999): 260–266.

Schoeler, Gregor (2014). "Abū Nuwās' Poem to the Zoroastrian Boy Bihrūz: An Arabic *sawgand-nāma* with a Persian *kharja*." In *The Rude, the Bad and the Bawdy: Essays in Honour of Professor Geert Jan van Gelder*, edited by Adam Talib, Marlé Hammond, and Arie Schippers, 66–79. Cambridge: Gibb Memorial Trust.

Schultz, James A. (1997). "Bodies That Don't Matter: Heterosexuality Before Heterosexuality in Gottfried's *Tristan*." In *Constructing Medieval Sexuality*, edited by Karma Lochrie, Peggy McCracken, and James A. Schultz, 91–110. Minneapolis, London: University of Minnesota Press.

Schultz, James A. (2006). *Courtly Love, the Love of Courtliness, and the History of Sexuality*. Chicago and London: The University of Chicago Press.

Sebti, Meryem (2003). "La distinction entre intellect pratique et intellect théorique dans la doctrine de l'âme humaine d'Avicenne." *Philosophie* 77 (2003): 23–44.

Sebti, Meryem (2005). "Le statut ontologique de l'image dans la doctrine avicennienne de la perception." *Arabic Sciences and Philosophy* 15.1 (2005): 109–140.

Sells, Michael A. (1996). *Early Islamic Mysticism: Sufi, Qur'ān, Mi'raj, Poetic and Theological Writings*. New York: Paulist.

Seybold, John (1994). "The Earliest Demon Lover: The *Ṭayf al-khayāl* in *al-Mufaḍḍalīyāt*." In *Reorientations/Arabic and Persian Poetry*, edited by Suzanne P. Stetkevych, 180–189.

Seyed-Gohrab, Ali Asghar (2003). *Love, Madness and Mystic Longing in Nizami's Epic Romance*. Leiden: Brill.

Seyed-Gohrab, Ali Asghar (2012). "Waxing Eloquent: The Masterful Variations on Candle Metaphors in the Poetry of Ḥāfiẓ and his Predecessors." In *Metaphor and Imagery in Persian Poetry*, edited by Ali Asghar Seyed-Gohrab, 81–124. Leiden: Brill.

Shafi'i-Kadkani, Mohammad-Rezā, ed. (1377/1998). *Gozide-ye ghazaliyāt-e Shams*. Tehran: Sherkat-e Enteshārāt-e 'Elmi va Farhangi.

Shafi'i-Kadkani, Mohammad-Rezā (1382/2003). "Khāqāni va mohit-e adabi-ye Tabriz." *Nāme-ye Bahārestān* 7–8 (1382/2003): 159–164.

Shafi'i-Kadkani, Mohammad (1386/2007). "In Kimiyā-ye hasti: 'āmel-e musiqā'i dar takāmol-e jamālshenāsi-ye she'r-e Hāfez." In *Zamine-ye ejtemā'i-ye she'r-e Fārsi*, 317–353. Tehran: Akhtarān.

Shah-Kazemi, Reza (2002). "The Notion and Significance of *Ma'rifa* in Sufism." *Journal of Islamic Studies* 13.2 (2002): 155–181.

Shamisā, Sirus (1370/1991). *Seyr-e ghazal dar she'r-e fārsi*. Ferdows: Tehran.

Shamisā, Sirus (1381/2002). *Shāhed-bāzi dar adabiyāt-e fārsi*. Tehran: Ferdows.

Shams, Mohammad-Javād (1383/2004). "Bozghosh-e Shirāzi." *Dāyerat al-ma'aref-e bozorg-e eslāmi*, vol. 12, edited by Mohammad-Kāzem Musavi Bojnurdi, 79–81. Tehran: Markaz-e Dāyerat al-Ma'āref-e Bozorg-e Eslāmi.

Shari'at, Mohammad-Javād (1366/1987). "Kohantarin noskhe-ye divān-e Sa'di va rāh-e estefāde az ān." In *Zekr-e jamil-e Sa'di: Majmu'e-ye maqālāt va ash'ār be monāsabat-e bozorgdāsht-e hasht-sadomin sālgard-e shaykh-e ajall Sa'di*, edited by Kumisiyun-e Melli-ye Yunesko, vol. 2, 309–319. Tehran: Edāre-ye Koll-e Enteshārāt va Tablighāt-e Vezārat-e Ershād-e Eslāmi.

Sharifi-Sahi, Mohsen (1392/2013). "Ash'āri now-yāfte dar jong-e khatti-ye 900-e majles." 17 (1392/2013): 45–60.

Sharlet, Jocelyn (2010). "A Garden of Possibilities in Manuchehri's Spring Panegyrics." *Journal of Persianate Studies* 3.1 (2010): 1–25.

Sharma, Sunil (2000). *Persian Poetry at the Indian Frontier: Mas'ûd Sa'd Salmân of Lahore*. Delhi: Permanent Black.

Sharma, Sunil (2004). "The City of Beauties in Indo-Persian Poetic Landscapes." *Comparative Studies of South Asia, Africa and the Middle East* 24.2 (2004): 73–81.

Sharma, Sunil (2005). *Amir Khusraw: The Poet of Sultans and Sufis*. Oxford: Oneworld.

Sharma, Sunil (2011). "'If There is a Paradise on Earth, It Is Here': Urban Ethnography in Indo-Persian Poetic and Historical Texts." In *Forms of Knowledge in Early Modern Asia: Explorations in the Intellectual History of India and Tibet, 1500–1800*, edited by Sheldon Pollock, 240–256. Durham: Duke University Press.

Sharma, Sunil (2012). "Representation of Social Groups in Mughal Art and Literature: Ethnography or Trope?" In *Indo-Muslim Cultures in Transition*, edited by Alka Patel and Karen Leonard, 17–36. Leiden: Brill.

Sharma, Sunil (2017). *Mughal Arcadia: Persian Literature in an Indian Court*. Cambridge: Harvard University Press.

Shehadi, Fadlou (1995). *Philosophies of Music in Medieval Islam*. Leiden: Brill.

Shihadeh, Ayman (2016a). *Doubts on Avicenna: A Study and Edition of Sharaf al-Dīn al-Masʿūdī's Commentary on the Ishārāt*. Leiden, Boston: Brill.

Shihadeh, Ayman (2016b). "Al-Rāzī's (d. 1210) Commentary on Avicenna's *Pointers*: The Confluence of Exegesis and Aporetics." In *The Oxford Handbook of Islamic Philosophy*, edited by Khaled El-Rouayheb and Sabine Schmidtke, 296–325. New York: Oxford University Press.

Shiloah, Amnon (1995). *Music in the world of Islam: A Socio-Cultural Study*. Detroit: Wayne State University Press.

Shiloah, Ammon. (1997). "Music and Religion in Islam." *Acta Musicologica* 69.2 (1997): 143–155.

Singer, Irving (1984). *The Nature of Love, Volume 1: Plato to Luther*. Chicago: Chicago University Press.

Skellie, Walter James 2010 [1938]. [al-Ghazāli's] Kitāb sharḥ 'ajā'ib al-qalb, *The Marvels of the Heart. Book 21 on the* Iḥyā' ʿulūm al-dīn, *The Revival of the Religious Sciences. Translated from the Arabic with an* Introduction *and* Notes *by Walter James Skellie, with a* Foreword *by T. J. Winter*. Louisville: Fons Vitae. Was *The Religious Psychology of al-Ghazzali: A Translation of His Book of the Iḥiyā' on the Explanation of the Wonders of the Heart*. PhD Dissertation, Hartford Seminary.

Soucek, Priscilla (1972). "Niẓāmī on Painters and Painting." in *Islamic Art in the Metropolitan Museum of Art*, edited by Richard Ettinghausen. 9–21. New York: Metropolitan Museum.

Soucek, Priscilla P. (2000). "The Theory and Practice of Portraiture in the Persian Tradition." In *Muqarnas: An Annual on the Visual Culture of the Islamic World*, edited by David J. Roxburgh. Leiden: Brill, 97–108.

Soreth, Marion (1964). "Text- und quellenkritische Bemerkungen zu Ibn Sīnā's Risāla fī l-ʿIšq." *Oriens*, 17 (1964): 118–131.

Southgate, Minoo S. (1984). "Men, Women, and Boys: Love and Sex in the Works of Saʿdī." *Iranian Studies* 17.4 (1984): 413–452.

Sperl, Stefan, and Christopher Shackle, eds. (1996). *Qasida Poetry in Islamic Asia and Africa*. Leiden: Brill.

Spitzer, Leo (1946). "Note on the Poetic and the Empirical 'I' in Medieval Authors." *Traditio* 4 (1946): 414–422.

Sprachman, Paul (1981). *The Comic Works of 'Ubayd-i Zâkâni: A Study of Medieval Persian Bawdy, Verbal Aggression, and Satire*. PhD dissertation, University of Chicago.

Sprachman, Paul (1988). "Persian Satire, Parody and Burlesque: A General Notion of Genre." In *Persian Literature*, edited by Ehsan Yarshater, 226–248. Albany: Bibliotheca Persica.

Sprachman, Paul (1995). *Suppressed Persian: An Anthology of Forbidden Literature*. Costa Mesa: Mazda.

Sprachman, Paul (2012). *Licensed Fool: The Damnable, Foul-Mouthed 'Obeyd-e Zākāni*. Costa Mesa: Mazda.

Squires, Geoffrey (2014) *Hafez: Translations and Interpretations of the Ghazals*. Oxford: Miami University Press.

Stetkevych, Jaroslav (1993). *The Zephyrs of Najd: The Poetics of Nostalgia in the Classical Arabic Nasīb*. Chicago, London: University of Chicago Press.

Stetkevych, Suzanne Pinckney (1993). *The Mute Immortals Speak: Pre-Islamic Poetry and the Poetics of Ritual*. Ithaca, London: Cornell University Press.

Strohmaier, Gotthard (1988). "Avicennas Lehre von den 'inneren Sinnen' und ihre Voraussetzungen bei Galen." In *Le opere psichologice di galeno: Atti del terzo colloquio galenico internazionale (Pavia: 10–12 settembre 1986)*, edited by Paola Manuli and Mario Vegetti, 231–242. Naples: Bibliopolis.

Stroumsa, Sarah, and Sara Sviri (2009). "The Beginnings of Mystical Philosophy in al-Andalus: Ibn Masarra and His *Epistle on Contemplation*." *Jerusalem Studies in Arabic and Islam* 36 (2009): 201–253.

Suerbaum, Almut (2010). "Paradoxes of performance: Autobiography in the songs of Hugo von Montfort and Oswald von Wolkenstein." In *Aspects of the Performative in Medieval Culture*, edited by Manuele Gragnolati and Almut Suerbaum, 143–164. Berlin, New York: De Gruyter.

Sviri, Sara (2012). "Sufism: Reconsidering Terms, Definitions and Processes in the Formative Period of Islamic Mysticism." In *Les maîtres soufis et leurs disciples. IIIe–Ve siècles de l'hégire (IXe–XIe s.). Enseignement, formation et transmission*, edited by Geneviève Gobillot and Jean-Jacques Thibon, 17–34. Beirut: Institut Français du Proche-Orient.

Szombathy, Zoltan (2013). Mujūn*: Libertinism in Medieval Muslim Society and Literature*, Cambridge: Gibb Memorial Trust.

Takeshita, Masataka (1987). "Continuity and Change in the Tradition of Shirazi Love Mysticism: A Comparison between Daylamī's *'Atf al-Alif* and Rūzbihan Baqlī's *'Abhar al-'Āshiqīn*." *Orient* 23 (1987): 113–131.

Tally, T. Robert, Jr. (2013). *Spatiality*. London: Routledge.

Tally, T. Robert, Jr., ed. (2017). *The Routledge Handbook of Literature and Space*. New York: Routledge.

Testori, Giovanni. (1973). *Nel tuo sangue*. Milano: Rizzoli.

Tetley, Gillies (2009). *The Ghaznavid and Seljuq Turks: Poetry as a Source for Iranian History*. London, New York: Routledge.

Thackston, Wheeler M., tr. (2008). *The Gulistan (Rose Garden) of Saʿdi: Bilingual English and Persian Edition with Vocabulary*. Bethesda: Ibex.

Thiesen, Finn (1982). *A Manual of Classical Persian Prosody: with Chapters on Urdu, Karakhanidic and Ottoman Prosody*. Wiesbadem: Harrassowitz.

Thiesen, Finn (2003). "Pseudo-Håfez: A Reading of Wilberforce Clarke's Rendering of *Divån-e Håfez*." *Orientalia Suecana* 51–52 (2003): 437–460.

Thomas, Alfred (1998). "Alien Bodies: Exclusion, Obscenity and Social Control in *The Ointment Seller*." In *Obscenity: Social Control and Artistic Creation in the European Middle Ages*, edited by Jan M. Ziolkowski, 214–230. Leiden, New York: Brill.

Toulalan, Sarah (2017). "Pornography, Procreation and Pleasure in Early Modern England." In *The Cambridge Companion to Erotic Literature*, edited by Bradford K. Mudge, 105–112. Cambridge: Cambridge University Press.

Treiger, Alexander (2011). "Al-Ghazālī's 'Mirror Christology' and Its Possible East-Syriac Sources." *The Islamic World* 101.4 (2011): 698–713.

Treiger, Alexander (2012). *Inspired Knowledge in Islamic Thought: Al-Ghazālī's Theory of Mystical Cognition and Its Avicennian Foundation*. London, New York: Routledge.

Treiger, Alexander (2020). "Al-Ghazālī's Philosophical Soteriology." In *Light upon Light: Essays in Islamic Thought and History in Honor of Gerhard Bowering*, edited by Jamal J. Elias and Bilal Orfali, 383–400. Leiden: Brill.

Tuft, Anthony K. (1983). "The *Ruʾyā* Controversy and the Interpretation of Qur'ān Verse VII (*al-Aʿrāf*): 143." *Hamdard Islamicus* 6.3 (1983): 3–41.

Tuft, Anthony K. (1979). *The Origins and Development of the Controversy over 'Ruʾyā' in Medieval Islam and its Relation to Contemporary Visual Theory*. PhD dissertation, University of California, Los Angeles.

Utas, Bo (2007). "Sufi texts as literature or literature as Sufi texts." In *Religious Texts in Iranian Languages. Symposium held in Copenhagen May 2002*, edited by Fereydun Vahman and Claus V. Pedersen, 293–300. København: Det Kongelige Danske Videnskabernes Selskab.

Vadet, Jean-Claude (1968). *L'Esprit courtois en Orient dans les cinq premiers siècles de l'Hégire*. Paris: Maisonneuve et Larose.

Vajda, Georges (1972). "Le *maʿāriǧ al-quds fī madāriǧ maʿrifat al-nafs* attribué à al-Ġazālī et les écrits d'Ibn Sīnā." *Israel Oriental Studies* 2 (1972): 470–473.

van den Berg, Gabrielle (1988). "The Nasībs in the Dīvān of Farrukhī Sīstānī: Poetical Speech versus the Reflection of Reality." *Edebiyāt* 9.1 (1998): 17–34.

van Ess, Joseph. "The Logical Structure of Islamic Theology." In *Logic in Classical Islamic Culture*, edited by Gustave E. von Grunebaum, 21–50. Wiesbaden: O. Harrassowitz.

van Gelder, G. Jan (1988). *The Bad and the Ugly: Attitudes towards Invective Poetry* (Hijāʾ) *in Classical Arabic Literature*. Leiden: Brill.

van Gelder, G. Jan (2003). "Inspiration and 'Writer's Block' in Classical Arabic Poetry." In *Poetica medievale tra oriente e occidente*, edited by Paolo Bagni and Maurizio Pistoso, 61–71. Rome: Carocci.

van Ruymbeke, Christine (2007). *Science and Poetry in Medieval Persia: The Botany of Nizami's* Khamsa. Cambridge: Cambridge University Press.

van Ruymbeke, Christine (2008). "L'histoire du Concours des peintres Rumis et Chinis chez Nizami et Rumi. Deux aspects du miroir." In *Miroir et Savoir. La transmission d'un thème platonicien, des Alexandrins à la philosophie arabo-musulmane. Actes du colloque international tenu à Leuven et Louvain-la-Neuve, les 17 et 18 novembre 2005*, edited by Daniel De Smet, Meryem Sebti, and Godefroid de Callataÿ, 273–291.

van Ruymbeke, Christine (2009). "The Hellenistic Influences in Classical Persian Literature." In *A History of Persian Literature. Volume I: General Introduction to Persian Literature*, edited by J.T.P. de Bruijn, 345–368. London, New York: I. B. Tauris.

Vasvári, Louise O. (1998). "Fowl Play in My Lady's Chamber: Textual Harassment of a Middle English Pornithological Riddle and Visual Pun." In *Obscenity: Social Control and Artistic Creation in the European Middle Ages*, edited by Jan M. Ziolkowski, 108–133. Leiden, New York: Brill.

Vílchez, José Miguel Puerta (2017). *Aesthetics in Arabic Thought: From Pre-Islamic Arabia through al-Andalus*, translated by Consuelo López-Morillas. Leiden: Brill.

Vinyoli, Joan (1979). *Obra poètica, 1975–1979*. Barcelona: Editorical Crítica.

Virani, Shafique N. (2019). "Persian Poetry, Sufism and Ismailism: The Testimony of Khwājah Qāsim Tushtarī's *Recognizing God*." *Journal of the Royal Asiatic Society* 29.1 (2019): 17–49.

von Grunebaum, Gustave E. (1944). "Observations on City Panegyrics in Arabic Prose." *Journal of the American Oriental Society* 64 (1944): 61–65.

von Grunebaum, Gustave E. (1952). "Avicenna's *Risâla fî ʾl-ʿišq* and Courtly Love." *Journal of Near Eastern Studies* 11.4 (1952): 233–238.

Wagner, Peter (1988). *Eros Revived: Erotica of the Enlightenment in England and America*. London: Secker & Warburg.

Walbridge, John (1992). *The Science of Mystic Lights: Quṭb al-Dīn Shīrāzī and the Illuminationist Tradition in Islamic Philosophy*. Cambridge: Harvard University Press.

Walzer, Richard (1957). "Al-Fārābī's Theory of Prophecy and Divination." *The Journal of Hellenic Studies* 77.1 (1957): 142–148.

Walzer, Richard, trans. (1998). *On the Perfect State (Mabādiʾ ārāʾ ahl al-madīnat* [sic] *al-fāḍilah): Revised Text with Introduction, Translation, and Commentary by Richard Walzer*, by Abu Nasr al-Farābi. Chicago: Kazi.

Watt, William Montgomery (1961). "Created in his Image: A Study in Islamic Theology." *Transactions of the Glasgow University Oriental Society* 18 (1961), 38–49.

Wendt, Gisela (1978). *Aḥmad Ghazzālī: Gedanken über die Liebe*. Amsterdam: Castrum Peregrini.

Whittingham, Martin (2007). *Al-Ghazālī and the Qur'ān: One Book, Many Meanings*. London: Routledge.

Wickens, George Michael (1974). *Morals Pointed and Tales Adorned: The Būstān of Sa'dī*. Leiden: Brill.

Wilber, Donald Newton (1979). *Persian Gardens and Garden Pavilions*. Washington: Dumbarton Oaks.

Wilcox, Andrew (2011). "The Dual Mystical Concepts of *Fanā'* and *Baqā'* in Early Sūfism." *British Journal of Middle Eastern Studies* 38.1 (2011): 95–118.

Wilkinson, J. V. S., ed. (1959). *The Chester Beatty Library. A Catalogue of the Persian Manuscripts and Miniatures. Volume I MSS. 101–105*. By A. J. Arberry, M. Minovi, and the late E. Blochet. Dublin: Hodges Figgis.

Williams, Gerhild Scholz (2016). "Body Language: Keeping Secrets in Early Modern Narratives." In *Mapping Gendered Routes and Spaces in the Early Modern World*, edited by Merry E. Wiesner-Hanks, 101–116. London, New York: Routledge.

Williams, Craig (2010). *Roman Homosexuality*. Oxford, New York: Oxford University Press.

Wisnovsky, Robert (2013) "Avicenna's Islamic Reception." In *Intepreting Avicenna: Critical Essays*, edited by Peter Adamson, 190–213. Cambridge: Cambridge University Press.

Wolfson, Elliot R. (1997). *Through a Speculum that Shines: Vision and Imagination in Medieval Jewish Mysticism*. Princeton: Princeton University Press.

Wolfson, Harry A. (1935) "The Internal Senses in Latin, Arabic and Hebrew Philosophic Texts." *Harvard Theological Review* 28 (1935): 70–133; reprinted in *Studies in the History of Philosophy and Religion*, vol. 1, 250–314. Cambridge: Harvard University Press. Paris: A. and W. Galignani.

Wordsworth, William (1835?). *The Poetical Works of William Wordsworth*. Complete in One Volume.

Wright Jr, J. W., and Everett K. Rowson, eds. (1997). *Homoeroticism in Classical Arabic Literature*. New York: Columbia University Press.

Wright, Elaine (2012). *The Look of the Book: Manuscript Production in Shiraz, 1303–1452*. Washinghton, DC: Freer Gallery of Art.

Yaghmā'i, Habib, ed. (1316/1938). *Sa'di-nāme. Majalle-ye Ta'lim va Tarbiyat* 11–12 (1316/1938).

Yaghoobi, Claudia (2016). "Yusuf's 'Queer' Beauty in Persian Cultural Production." *The Comparatist* 40 (2016): 245–266.

Yāhaqi, Mohammad Ja'far (1379/2000). "Khorāsān dar khayāl-e Sa'di." *Sa'di-shenāsi* 3 (1379/2000): 124–140.

Yarshater, Ehsan (1986). "Persian Poetry in the Timurid and Safavid Periods." In *The Cambridge History of Iran. Volume 6: The Timurid and Safavid Periods*, edited by Peter Jackson and Lawrence Lockhart, 965–994. Cambridge: Cambridge University Press.

Yarshater, Ehsan (2000). "Love-related Conventions in Sa'di's Ghazals." In *Studies in Honor of Clifford Edmund Bosworth. Volume II. The Sultan's Turret: Studies in Persian and Turkish Culture*, edited by Carole Hillenbrand, 420–439. Leiden: Brill.

Yarshater, Ehsan (2006). "ḠAZAL ii. CHARACTERISTICS AND CONVENTIONS." *Encyclopædia Iranica*, online edition, available at http://www.iranicaonline.org/articles/gazal-2 (accessed on 13 May 2019).

Yāsemi, Rashid (1316/1938) "Sa'di va "eshq." *Sa'di-nāme*, edited by Habib Yaghmā'i, *Majalle-ye Ta'lim va Tarbiyat* 11–12 (1316/1938): 208–215.

Yazdānparast, Hamid (1393/2014). *Ātash-e Pārsi. Derangi dar ruzegār, zendegi va andishe-ye Sa'di*, 2 vols. Tehran: Ettelā'āt.

Yazdānparast, Hamid (1394/2015). "Sa'di va tabi'at-dusti." *Ettelā'āt-e Hekmat-o Ma'refat* 10.2 (1394/2015): 44–51.

Yohannan, John D. (1977). *Persian Poetry in England and America: a 200-Year History*. Delamr: Caravan Books.

Yohannan, John D. (1987). *The Poet Sa'di: A Persian Humanist*. Lanham: University Press of America.

Zaehner, Robert Charles (1969). *Hindu and Muslim Mysticism*. New York: Schocken.

Zargar, Cyrus A. (2011). *Sufi Aesthetics: Beauty, Love, and the Human Form in the Writings of Ibn 'Arabi and 'Iraqi*. Columbia: University of South Carolina Press.

Zarqāni, Seyyed Mahdi (1390/2011). "Tatavvor-e mafhum-e mohākāt dar neveshtārhā-ye falsafi-eslāmi." *Jostārhā-ye Novin-e Adabi* 44.127 (1390/2011): 1–28.

Zarrinkub, 'Abd al-Hossein (1386/2007). *Hadis-e khwosh-e Sa'di: dar bāre-ye zendegi va andishe-ye Sa'di*, edited by K. Ejtemā'i-Jandaqi. Tehran: Sokhan.

Ze'evi, Dror (2006). *Producing Desire: Changing Sexual Discourse in the Ottoman Middle East, 1500–1900*. Berkeley, Los Angeles: University of California Press.

Ziai, Hossein (1995). "Hâfez, Lisân al-Ghayb of Persian Poetic Wisdom." In *Gott ist schön und Er liebt die Schönheit/God is Beautiful and He Loves Beauty: Festschrift für Annemarie Schimmel*, edited by Alma Giese and J. Christoph Bürgel, 449–469. Bern: Peter Lang.

Zibā'i-Nezhād, Maryam (1385/2006). "Hamsuyi-ye andishe dar āsār-e shaykh-e eshrāq-o Sa'di-ye Shirāzi." *Sa'di-shenāsi* 9 (1385/2006): 135–164.

Ziolkowski, Jan M. (1998). "Obscenity in the Latin Grammatical and Rhetorical Tradition." In *Obscenity: Social Control and Artistic Creation in the European Middle Ages*, edited by Jan M. Ziolkowski, 41–59. Leiden, New York: Brill.

Zipoli, Riccardo (1364/1995). "Āyyine dar ash'ār-e Farrokhi, Sa'di, Hāfez, hamrāh bā pishnehādi dar zamine-ye barresi-ye āmāri-tatbiqi." In *Zekr-e jamil-e Sa'di:*

Majmuʿe-ye maqālāt va ashʿār be monāsabat-e bozorgdāsht-e hasht-sadomin sālgard-e shaykh-e ajall Saʿdi, edited by Kumisiyun-e Melli-ye Yunesko, vol. 2, 231–256. Tehran: Edāre-ye Koll-e Enteshārāt va Tablighāt-e Vezārat-e Ershād-e Eslāmi.

Zipoli, Riccardo (1993). *The Technique of the* Ǧawāb*: Replies by Nawāʾī to Ḥāfiẓ and Ǧāmī.* Venice: Cafoscarina.

Zipoli, Riccardo (1994). "Oscenità poetiche neopersiane: due tarjîʿ-band sulla masturbazione." *Annali di Ca' Foscari* 33.3 (1994): 249–291.

Zipoli, Riccardo (1995). "I Carmina Priapea di Sûzanî." *Annali di Ca' Foscari* 34.3 (1995): 205–256.

Zipoli, Riccardo (1996). "Elementi osceni nella lessicografia neopersiana." *Annali di Ca' Foscari* 35.3 (1996): 249–289.

Zipoli, Riccardo (1997). "Le *khabīthāt* oscene di Saʿdī." *Annali di Ca' Foscari* 36.3 (1997): 179–214.

Zipoli, Riccardo (2001). "The Obscene Sanâ'i." *Persica* 17 (2001): 173–194.

Zipoli, Riccardo (2009). "Poetic Imagery." In *A History of Persian literature, vol. 1: General Introduction to Persian Literature*, edited by Johannes T. P. de Bruijn, 172–232. London: I. B. Tauris.

Zipoli, Riccardo (2011). "Obscene vocabulary in Steingass's dictionary." In *The Persian language in history*, edited by Mario Maggi and Paola Orsatti, 297–305. Wiesbaden: Reichert.

Zipoli, Riccardo (2015). *Irreverent Persia: Invective, Satirical and Burlesque Poetry from the Origins to the Timurid Period (10th to 15th Centuries)*. Leiden: Leiden University Press.

Ziyā', Mohammad-Rezā (1390/2011). "Dar bāre-ye maqāle-ye 'Safine-ye Nur.'" *Gozāresh-e Mirās* 49 (1390/2011): 49.

Zumthor, Paul (1987). *La lettre et la voix: De la 'littérature' médiévale*. Paris: Seuil.

Zumthor, Paul (2000). *Essai de poétique médiévale*. Paris: Seuil.

Zumthor, Paul (2002). *Toward a Medieval Poetics*, translated by Philip Bennet. Minneapolis: University of Minnesota Press.

Index

Abaqa (Ilkhanid ruler) 21–24, 29, 304
Abbasid caliphate 17, 57, 85, 110, 178, 190, 240, 334
ʿAbd Allāh Tabbākh, Shahāb al-Dīn 41
Abhar al-ʿāshiqīn 219
Abish Khātūn (Salghurid princess) 20, 23–24, 31
Abū Bakr b. Saʿd I (Salghurid ruler) 10–19, 21, 90–92, 97, 101, 109, 110–112, 114–115, 123–133, 150, 157, 218–20, 291, 304–305, 458, 460n24, 488, 496n102, 502, 522 *see also* Salghurid dynasty
Abū Ḥulmān 261
Abū Nuwās 196n113
Abū Saʿīd (Ilkhanid ruler) 22, 446
Abū Saʿīd b. Abī al-Khayr 249–50, 495n100
Ādāb al-murīdīn (Abū al-Najīb Suhravardī) 475n50
Adam 94, 138, 155, 263, 272, 274
aesthetics 1, 7–8, 16, 28, 46, 53, 58, 66–69, 84–85, 93, 141,150, 170, 210–11, 225, 242–43, 395, 397, 462
  spiritual 22, 73, 135, 216, 219, 230, 255–59, 280, 289, 291–92, 313–16, 346–47, 363, 415, 404, 437–38, 444–45, 465–66, 472–73
Aḥmad Tegüder 23–24
Akhlāq-i nāṣirī *see* Naṣīr al-Dīn Ṭūsī
ʿAlāʾ al-Dīn Muḥammad Fariyūmadī (Ilkhanid minister) 22, 30, 446 *see also* Saʿdi: Sufi lodge
ʿālam-i qudrat (world of divine power) 292–93, 295 see also *ghayb*
Alexander the Great (*Iskandar*) 362, 392–95, 397, 439, 470, 522 *see also* Greek and Chinese painters
Altājū (Ilkhanid commander) 19
Amīn al-Dīn Baliyānī 491
Amīn al-Dīn Ḥājī Bulah 471–73, 483
Amīr Inkiyānū (Ilkhanid governor) 21–22, 304
Amīr Khusraw of Delhi 24, 75n45, 234, 472n42
Amīr Muʿizzī 92, 194–95, 197, 370–71
Amīr Muqarrab al-Dīn Masʿūd (Salghurid vizier) 19
ʿAmmāra, Abū Manṣūr (Samanid poet) 249–50
amrad (beardless boy) 403, 406, 413 *see also* homoeroticism; *shāhid*
Anatolia 7, 9, 23n78, 212, 217, 504
Anvarī 156, 175n61, 178, 380, 402, 469n38
Arabic poetry 90n80, 178, 240, 482
  Udhri poetry 178, 240
Arghun (Ilkhanid ruler) 24
ʿārif (Gnostic, mystic, spiritual beholder) 8, 151, 201, 271–72, 275–77, 280–81, 297–98, 360, 411–12, 432, 467, 509 see also *maʿrifa*
  Avicenna's definition 298–99, 345–48
asceticism (*zuhd*) 59, 114, 232, 271, 297–99, 345, 366, 417–19, 456–57, 474–75, 487–91, 493, 509
Ashʿarism 228n52, 229, 236, 239, 265n71, 288, 318n50
Asīr al-Dīn Akhsīkatī 471
Asrār al-tawḥīd 249–50
ʿAṭāʾī 220n21
ʿAṭṭār 76n47, 225, 260n54, 362–63, 372, 494n98
  comparison with Saʿdi 257n49, 260n54, 334–35, 362, 363n26, 380, 424–25, 469n38
Austin, John Langshaw 159, 179–80, 445, 472n42, 501–502 *see also* speech acts
Avicenna (Ibn Sīnā) 8, 21, 211, 227, 231, 263n62, 282–83, 297–98
  Active Intellect (*al-ʿaql al-faʿʿāl*) 299n65, 319–21, 323, 326n73 331–32, 346, 355, 356, 370n42, 375n75, 387, 413, 423
  Aristotelian influences 164, 229, 263, 266, 299, 314–15, 318, 320, 325n72, 336n96, 356, 520
  al-Ishārāt wa al-tanbīhāt (*Pointers and Reminders*) 280n22, 302–305, 324, 345, 374, 412–13
  brain anatomy 323, 325–26, 329–30, 353–54, 375–76, 396, 478–79, 481, 483, 492
  common sense (*al-ḥiss al-mushtarak*) 325–30, 333–32, 346, 357, 361, 364, 376, 387, 393, 396, 409, 412, 417

compositive imagination (*takhayyul*) 328–31, 336, 353–54, 356, 365, 369, 376, 396, 417, 420, 507
Correct Guessing (*ḥads*) 343–45, 410–11
cosmology 8–9, 231, 293–94, 321–22, 340, 348–51, 354, 355–57, 360–61, 366n33, 374, 375n57, 381, 388, 405n35, 414–15, 423–24, 461, 473
Dānish-nāma (*Book of Knowledge*) 323–24, 365, 369, 374, 376
Epistle on Love 263n62, 266, 306n22, 312–20, 402
estimative faculty (*wahm*) 330–33, 335–38, 358, 376–77, 433–34, 479–80
intellection and cognition 298–99, 304, 354–57, 359–60
intellect or rational soul 231, 294, 298, 305, 313, 319–20, 366, 413, 464 *see also* heart
intelligibles 320–21, 326, 331, 334, 344–45, 354–56, 369, 387
internal senses 8, 164, 168n45, 203, 211, 230, 265, 282–86, 300, 303n7, 306, 324–33, 393–94, 396, 401, 406–407, 413–17, 420–22, 425n59, 427, 431, 478–79, 484–85, 511, 521
Kitāb al-Shifāʾ (*The Book of Healing*) 303, 305n20, 328n76, 329n78, 357n13
Persian poetry 304–306
practical intellect (*al-ʿaql al-ʿamalī*) 320–21, 329, 340, 354–57, 360, 66, 365–396, 412, 429, 431, 484, 507
psychology 138, 269–70, 306–307, 313–16, 318–23, 354, 412 *see also* Avicenna: intellect; internal senses
reception and influence 302–309, 312–13, 324
retentive imagination (*khayāl*) 329, 333–34, 342, 353–54, 356, 363–64, 371, 409, 412–13, 417, 420
Risāla fī aḥwāl al-nafs 355
soul of the fixed stars (as analogue of *malakūt*, *lawḥ-i maḥfūẓ*) 231, 329n77, 348–49, 356–57, 360, 363, 369–70, 375, 385, 387, 396, 412, 414–15, 420, 461, 484, 507, 513
syllogistic thinking 230, 237, 286–87, 318n50, 321–23, 338, 340, 343–45, 358–59, 361n20, 385–87
theoretical intellect (*al-ʿaql al-naẓarī*) 320–21, 354–56, 387, 394n10
ʿAwārif al-maʿārif 222, 475n50, 486n71
see also Suhravardī; Suhravardiyya
Persian translations 223n36
Awḥad al-Dīn Kirmānī 224–26, 242n24, 458, 466n34, 485n67, 489–92
Awrād al-aḥbāb va fuṣūs al-ādāb 225, n40, 247n34, 275n50, 486n72 *see also* Bākharzī
Ayāz 79, 82n57, 89
ʿAyn al-Qużāt Hamadānī 132, 225, 233, 247n33, 272–74, 313, 396, 398–99, 401, 404n34, 433–34, 489
Azraqī 370n45, 371n45

Baghdad 6, 16, 17, 21–22, 56n4, 85, 110, 129n75, 178n70, 211, 222–24, 227, 229, 291, 303–304, 446, 458, 487, 489
Mongol conquest 9, 12n25, 17, 48n18, 56–57, 111, 157n18, 190–91, 218
Niẓāmiyya school 11, 13, 229, 304, 451
al-Baghdādī, ʿAbd al-Laṭīf 304
Bahrain 12
Bahrāmshāh (Ghaznavid ruler) 219n17, 308n30
Bākharzī, Yaḥyā b. Aḥmad 225n40, 247n34, 445, 466n34, 473n45, 474n48, 475n50, 476n53, 483n62, 486n72, 490n90, 496n102
Balkh 121
Banakātī, Abū Sulaymān 25n88, 34
Barthes, Roland 53, 146–147, 501
Baudrillard, Jean 15–152, 159–60
Bec, Pierre 178–79
Beloved
as a divine sign 175, 202, 207, 225–26, 233–36, 243–44, 247, 257–58, 274–77, 282 311–12, 332, 340–44, 350–51, 398–99, 411, 435, 514–15
as a mirror of the unseen 340–44
departure as veiling of the "supernal meanings" 408–409, 422–25, 429–31, 511–12
downy-beard (*khaṭṭ*) 192, 197, 271, 274–77, 351
gender and identity 74, 80–82, 151, 194–97, 243–44
physical traits 75–79, 258
veiled 76–79

Benjamin, Walter 52
Bernart de Ventadorn 181
Bidel (Bedīl) 227
al-Bisṭāmī 264–65
Bīsutūn, ʿAlī 29–30, 447, 471–72, 506 *see also* Saʿdi: Bīsutūn recension
Bloch, Howard 183
Bloom, Harold 227
Boccaccio, Giovanni 159
Brethren of Purity (Ikhwān al-Ṣafāʾ) 229n52, 254n45, 282–83, 313, 314n43, 325n72
Brookshaw, Dominic 48n6, 88n76
Buddhism 21, 144
Bukhara 9, 180, 247n34, 374
Būstān 10, 25, 135, 223, 228
  Composition 87–88
  Dedicatees 10–11, 87n73, 470
  Samāʿ 480–82
  teleological aesthetics 290–91
Byzantium (*Rūm*) 95, 393n7, 437

Central Asia 9, 39n154, 58, 79, 84, 90n80, 91, 141–42, 144, 149, 180, 212, 269, 392, 393n7
Chaucer, Geoffrey 136, 159
China 144n105, 214, 392, 393n7, 455–57
Chorasmia (Khwārazm) 11n19, 14n32, 141–44, 150
Christians 2, 21, 23, 247n37, 269, 276, 379, 395n14
Cooperson, Michael 107
Culler, Jonathan 51n9, 106–18, 152, 167, 180, 443–44, 445n8, 472n42, 501

Damascus 22, 261
dance see *samāʿ*
Dante Alighieri 2, 135
Dawlatshāh Samarqandī 180
Delhi 24, 504
desire *see* eroticism
Diḥya Kalbī (companion of the Prophet) 403–406, 412
dreams and visions 50–52, 54, 163, 169, 177n74, 302, 317, 324n69, 327, 329, 340, 356–57, 368–70, 376–77, 402, 406, 412–14, 461, 515

Eco, Umberto 113
Egypt 76–78, 260n54, 503
El-Rouayheb, Khaled 49n7, 66–69, 131
eroticism 47–55, 118–123, 153–55, 163–72, 179–80, 185–91, 430 *see also* homoeroticism; lust
  erotic epistemology 242–255, 257–58, 272, 279–81, 350
  sacred (theo-eroticism) 73, 132, 192, 208–12, 207–214, 219–21, 223–26, 236–45, 240, 242, 246–50, 261–65, 271–73, 275–78, 294–96, 311–12, 314–16, 332, 335–51, 396–98, 403–405, 407–409, 417–19, 444, 455–58, 465–67, 468, 489–98 see also *shāhid* and *shāhid-bāzī*
  sexual desire 3, 7–8, 9, 47, 49, 54, 59–60, 63–64, 66–67, 92, 103, 123, 131–33, 137–41, 148–50, 153–58, 162–68, 171–75, 179, 185–87, 193–95, 230, 235, 240–43, 245–46, 249–52, 259–61, 274–75, 294–97, 316, 334, 347–50, 372, 402, 410, 418–20, 431–32, 444–45, 448–49, 492–95, 519–20

Fabliaux 159–60, 183
Fakhr al-Dīn Abū Bakr (Salghurid vizier) 18, 18n48, 101n8
Farhād 80
Farīd Iṣfahānī (Salghurid poet) 16n42, 87n73, 110n37, 469n38
Farrukhī Sīstānī 33, 92, 144n105, 219n17
Fars 4, 10n14, 12, 14n31, 16–24, 29–31, 87n73, 91, 101, 111–12, 211, 217, 219, 222, 228, 261, 304, 306, 410, 446, 458, 516–17
fayż (divine effluence) 294, 299, 320, 343, 423n57
Fighānī Babā 208
fitna (temptation) *see* lust
de Fouchécour, Charles-Henry 3, 101n8, 102–104, 106–107
Forughi, Mohammad-ʿAli 3n8, 26, 29n107, 35, 37n143, 41

gardens 57, 89, 100–101, 104, 105, 112, 232, 289, 292, 347, 353, 360, 407, 418–22, 463, 505
  in Shiraz 7, 23, 62n14, 100n6, 451
Gaunt, Simon 182–84
gaze (*naẓar, nigāh*)

contemplation (*ta'ammul*) 255–59, 265–66, 271–77, 283–86, 308–309, 409–10, 506, 511
naẓar-bāzī 223, 414
permissibility 242–55, 259–61, 413, 430, 448, 454, 470
geopoetics 180, 213, 217–19, 457
ghayb (realm of the unseen) 9, 165, 255, 265, 281, 324, 338–42, 347–49, 359, 366, 404, 412–15, 419–22, 442, 444
al-Ghazālī, Abū Ḥāmid Muḥammad 165, 167, 183, 272, 274–75 see also *Iḥyā' 'ulūm al-dīn*; *Kīmiyā-yi sa'ādat*
Avicenna's influence on 230–31, 263n62, 264n65, 282–83, 286n34, 287, 293–94, 307–309, 312–14, 319, 320n56, 323–24, 329n77, 331, 343, 354, 361, 363, 366–69, 404, 412–13, 486–7, 512
influence on Sa'di 6, 211, 225, 227, 239, 289–94, 362–64, 366–67, 372–74, 395–96, 424, 428–29, 492–94, 512
parallels with Sa'di 227
science of unveiling (*mukāshafa*) 358, 362–66, 479, 487
spiritual cardiology 8, 229–30, 305–306, 354, 366–71, 422–23
tale of the Greek and Chinese painters 393–94
Tahāfut al-falāsifa (*Precipitance of the Philosophers*) 168n45, 320n56, 324, 370n42
teleology 229–30, 254n46, 258n51, 282–84, 287–89
witnessing (*mushāhada*) 363–66, 392
Ghazālī, Aḥmad 225, 247n33, 266–67, 269, 272, 313, 319, 378, 398
Savāniḥ 266–67, 378
Ghazan (Ilkhanid ruler) 25, 234
Ghaznavids 33, 85–89, 91–92, 112n43, 116, 144, 177n66, 190, 219n17, 334
Ghiyās al-Dīn Balban 24
God
affinity with mankind (*munāsaba, mushākala, tashabbuh*) 52, 263–65, 267–68, 272–74, 411
as a painter, fashioner 94, 234, 255–59, 258n51, 271–75, 292–93, 334, 453
attributes 226, 238, 256n48, 281–83, 294–95
beauty of 8, 50, 52, 109, 322, 398, 411
vision of (*ru'yat Allāh*) 226, 233, 236–45, 261, 273n6, 287, 290, 346–47, 358–59, 361, 424–25, 512
Greek and Chinese painters (tale) 392–95, 435–40
Guilhèm de Peitieus 179
Gujarat 14
Gulistān 7, 10, 25, 152, 183–84
Anecdote of Ibn al-Jawzī's intimations on music 487–88
composition 17, 88, 101, 110–114, 451
contents 101–104, 136–137
dedicatees 10–11, 17–18, 88, 101, 109–123
implied reader 109–114, 117–123
lyricism 116–123, 124–133, 141–150, 445n8, 463
manuscripts 101n8, 112n45
patronage 103–104, 124–133, 470
pseudo-biographism 104–109, 133–137, 139–150
style 101–102
story of the judge who fell in love with a young man 124–133
story of the prince and the dervish 116–123
story of Sa'di's encounter with a boy in Kashgar 140–150, 152, 406–407, 417
visionary experience 217, 358–61, 365–66, 402–403, 407, 415, 417–18, 421–22, 451–52

Ḥadīqat al-ḥaqīqa 161–62, 358n15, 366n33
Hāfez Shirazi 28, 46–48, 88n76, 105, 144–145, 171, 180, 197, 214n12, 218n15, 219n17, 233n3, 234, 247n35, 299n67, 425, 452n7, 454n12, 460n25, 461n28, 496n102
debate on homoeroticism 72n37
hajv 173
al-Ḥallāj, Manṣūr 220, 263–64
Hamburger, Käte 106–108, 118–120, 135, 152, 167, 443–44
Hamidian, Sa'id 3, 32, 226
hazl 156–58, 161–62, 172–77
heart (*dil, qalb*)
as a mirror reflecting the unseen 8, 57, 236–37, 265, 274, 283, 297, 306, 327, 368–69, 372–77, 379–80, 396, 398, 410–11, 422–23, 479, 494, 512, 521 see also *ghayb*

heart (*dil, qalb*) (*cont.*)
as analogue of the Rational Soul 231, 294, 368
hermeneutics
spiritual 221n26, 239, 245–50, 254–55, 342, 438, 458, 491, 514–15
radical mystical symbolism 8, 59n9, 211, 225, 226n42, 231–233, 233n3, 234n4, 247, 248n36, 277, 292, 301–302, 312, 317, 322, 339, 342, 344n117, 357, 423, 444, 446, 451n3, 512
homoeroticism 7, 8, 54, 70n32, 151, 196, 274–77, 413–14, 417–19, 485 *see also* Saʿdi: homoeroticism
androgyny 68, 75–82, 188–90
binary approaches 68, 79, 83
constructivism 83–85, 92
denial 54, 59–60, 71–74, 87, 125n67
essentialism 66–67
intergenerational 73, 121–133, 192–93, 199, 259–61, 403, 406–407
Islamicate societies and literatures 66–69, 199
legal aspects 126–133
Persian poetry 70n32, 72n37, 80–92
political symbolism 88–98, 114–123, 190–91, 201–203, 465–67
Hujvīrī, Abū al-Ḥasan 250–55, 259–61, 278n17
Hülegü 17–21, 23, 29, 87n73
ḥulūl (incarnationism) 259–60, 273–74, 399, 478
as an estimative error 331–33, 433–34, 479–80, 512
Humām-i Tabrīzī 23, 25, 234–36, 443, 446n10, 504–506

Ibn Baṭṭūṭa 62
Ibn al-Fuwaṭī 11
Ibn al-Haytham 169–70, 299–300
Ibn al-Jawzī 259n52, 486–88
Ibn Khafīf 218–20, 376
Ibn Khaldūn 394
Ibn Zarkūb 210, 220n21, 491
Ibrāhīm Sulṭān 41
ʿibrat (inference) 251–52, 254–59, 277–78, 342–45, 453
Iḥyāʾ ʿulūm al-dīn 165, 229, 262, 287, 288n41, 364n40, 367n34, 375, 386, 393, 437, 476n52, 485n70, 487

Ilkhanids 7, 17, 29, 57, 87, 212, 291–92, 458, 504
iltibās 238 *see also* Rūzbihān-i Baqlī
imaginal-cosmological modality 9, 293–96, 299–300, 354, 356–57, 360–61, 384–89, 404–22, 448, 467–68, 493–94, 501
imagination (*khayāl*) 51, 120, 163–69, 181–82, 231, 271–72, 308–309, 326–28, 353–54, 412, 444
India 24, 45, 213
Injuids 30–32, 36, 38–39
Intertextuality 27, 178–74, 194–97, 208–209, 212–14, 234–35, 311–12, 418–22 *see also* Saʿdi: intertextuality
Iraq 7, 15n34, 56, 111
ʿIrāqī, Fakhr al-Dīn 71n36, 211n7, 220n21, 247n34, 305, 309–12, 371–72, 381–83, 399–400, 433, 446, 505–506
Iser, Wolfgang 113
Iskandar Sultān 41
Islam 1, 23, 56–57, 101, 112n43, 133, 138, 302, 427
Islamic law 59, 67, 115, 124, 128–30, 132, 165, 170, 228, 251, 324, 410, 411n42, 461
istiqbāl 208–13 *see also* intertextuality; Saʿdi: intertextuality
ittiḥād (unification, infusion) 264, 399, 478 *see also* incarnationism

Jahān Malik Khātūn 79–81, 454n13
Jāmī, ʿAbd al-Raḥmān 2n, 234
Jāmiʿ al-ʿulūm *see* Rāzī, Fakhr al-Dīn
javāb 208–13, 505 *see also* intertextuality; *istiqbāl*
jinās-i tāmm (paranomasia) 63, 130n78, 268–69, 353–54, 395 *see also* Saʿdi: style
Joseph *see* Yūsuf
Junayd Shīrāzī 11n19, 22n76
al-Jurjānī, Aḥmad b. Muḥammad 172
Juvaynī, ʿAtāʾ Malik 6, 19–21, 291–92, 465n33, 503
Juvaynī, Shams al-Dīn 4, 6, 19–25, 29, 37, 56–60, 68, 90n81, 93–98, 219n17, 220, 234, 291, 446, 503

Kaʿba 218 see also *qibla*
Kamāl al-Dīn Iṣfahānī 97, 197, 469n38
Kashf al-maḥjūb 238n18, 250–55, 262 *see also* Hujvīrī

Kashgar 104, 140–150, 152, 406, 417
Keshavarz, Fatemeh 3, 70–71, 102n11, 141n101
Khān Malik Ṣulṭān Muḥammad (governor of Multan) 24
Khāqānī 425n59, 469n38, 471
Khiżr 188, 377, 383, 522–23
Khorasan 91, 228, 229, 259, 306–308, 319n53, 339, 366
Khusraw va Shīrīn (Niẓāmī) 5, 81
Khwājū Kirmānī 75n45, 234, 425–26
Kiening, Christian 153, 164, 179
Kīmiyā-yi sa'ādat (*Alchemy of Bliss*) 165–72, 229, 305–306, 329n77, 489
  love for God 261–66, 473
  on poetry and music 166–67, 246–50
  on *samā'* 473–80, 485n70
  paradigm of the visionary experience (five stages) 402–12
  spiritual aesthetics 282–89, 363–65, 485
  spiritual cardiology 165, 367–71, 422–23
Kitāb al-Manāẓir 169

Landau, Justine 12n25, 180n75, 519–22
Levron, Pierre 181
Lewis, Franklin D. 28n105, 59n8, 70n32, 102n10, 109n33, 129n75, 248n36, 308n30, 452, 459, 496n102
Lewisohn, Leonard 72n37, 248n36
Loqmān-Adham, Mohammad-Hoseyn 29, 35
Losensky, Paul 12, 70n33, 208–209, 213n10, 452
lust (*havā, shahvat*) 255, 259–61, 275–78, 294–96, 314–15, 404–405, 407, 410–12, 418, 429–30, 432, 447–48, 455, 491–92 *see also* desire: sexual desire
lyric poetry
  as ritual 445n8, 466, 468, 501–503
  external reality and experience 74–75, 105–109, 126–127, 141–50, 168–70, 181–82, 275–77, 326–28, 334–36, 406, 457, 507, 510, 517–23
  embodiment 137–140, 179, 187, 207–208, 239–40, 400–401, 443, 448–49, 457, 467, 501
  fiction 81–2, 100, 104–109, 133–37, 152, 201, 443–44, 458, 462
  poetic "I" (persona) 108, 118–20, 135–37, 152–53, 201, 231, 250, 455, 459, 462–64, 512
  psychology of lyric subject 357, 405–406, 412, 429–30

Maḥmūd of Ghazna 79, 82n57, 86n67, 89, 219n17, 370
majāz and *ḥaqīqat* dichotomy 397–401, 411–12, 417–18
Majd al-Dīn Rūmī 18
Majd-i Hamgar (Salghurid poet) 21, 111–12, 469n38
Majnūn 80, 436
malakūt (supernal realm, *ākhira*) 284, 293, 306n23, 340, 348–51, 354, 358, 360, 368–72, 376, 462–63 see also *ghayb*; Preserved Tablet
Mānī 349–50, 392
ma'nī (pl. *ma'ānī*)
  mental content 169n48, 230, 269–70, 273–75, 330, 332–33, 337–38, 341–43, 493
  spirit 208, 251, 269, 273–74
  supernal meanings 170, 208–209, 230, 251, 252n42, 253, 268, 279n17, 306n23, 339–45, 366–67, 403–404, 406–12, 414–15, 426, 430–34, 456, 464, 466, 472, 477, 480–81, 484, 493–94, 511
ma'rifa (spiritual cognition) 276–86, 290, 308–309, 339, 392 see also *'ārif*; Sa'di: *ma'rifa*
  definitions 278–79, 477–78
  aesthetic aspects 280–85, 322–23, 342–43, 474, 512
Maybudī, Rashīd al-Dīn 77–78
Mecca 22, 217, 269
Mengü Temür (Ilkhanid prince) 23
Mikkelson, Jane 4n, 227
mimesis (*muḥākāt, ḥikāyat*, imaginal translation) 163–64, 274, 336–65, 374, 376, 396–97, 412, 421–22, 479, 507, 511
Minovi, Mojtabā 35, 36, 111n39
mirror 58, 81, 94
  imagination as a 324, 336–37
  beloved as mirror of divine beauty 215–16, 234–35, 341,423, 478 *see also* heart: as a mirror
  poetry as a 247n33
Mishkāt al-anwār (*The Niche of Lights*) 264–65, 274–75, 321n58, 331n85

Mongols 1, 4, 7, 9, 19, 21, 23, 25, 56, 86, 93, 95, 98, 188–90, 212, 218–20 *see also* Ilkhanids
mouvances (or "variances") 25, 27–28, 33
muʿāmala (spiritual transaction) 278, 360, 421, 506
Muḥammad Khwārazmshāh 141, 144, 150
Muḥammad b. Saʿd II (Salghurid prince) 11, 17–18, 24, 29, 31, 87–88, 115, 116n54, 454, 502–503
Muḥammad (Prophet) 273n6, 365, 404
Muḥammad-Shāh (Salghurid prince) 17–18, 111n42, 157n18, 503
Muḥammad b. Vāsiʿ 260–61
mukāshafa (unveiling) 9, 169, 351, 354, 358–60, 362–66, 479, 487 *see also* visionary experience
mulk (world of sense) 293, 348–49, 354–55, 376 *see also malakūt*
murāʿāt-i naẓīr (observance of the similar) 214
mushāhada (manifestation) 9, 231, 237, 260–61, 290, 325–26, 345–47, 351, 354, 363, 383–84, 386, 392, 397, 403–405, 408–11, 435, 493, 497, 499–501 *see also* visionary experience
al-Mustaʿṣim (caliph) 9, 57n4, 111
Mustawfī, Ḥamd-Allāh 11n19, 19n57, 489n83
Muzaffarids 31, 40–41, 88n76

Nafisi, Saʿid 10
nafs (carnal soul) 137–38, 252, 259n52, 277, 284, 364–65, 429, 431–33 *see also* Avicenna: animal soul; lust
Najīb al-Dīn Buzghush 21, 222, 304, 459
Najmabadi, Afsaneh 60n11, 68n28, 69, 76
Nasafī, ʿAzīz al-Dīn 319n53, 325n71, 335
  Kashf al-ḥaqāyiq 374–76
  Kitāb al-insān al-kāmil 306, 374, 376–77
al-Nāṣir (Abbasid caliph) 222
Naṣr II (Samanid ruler) 180
Naṭanzī, Saʿd al-Dīn 304
Nawrūz 194
New Criticism 207
New Historicism 207–208
Neysāri, Salim 28
Niẓām al-Dīn Awliyāʾ 504
Niẓāmī ʿArūżī
  Chahār maqāla 324
Nizāmī Ganjavī 39, 76n45, 81, 392–93

obscene poetry 3, 151, 153–63, 171–72, 235–36, 444, 521 see also *hazl*; Saʿdi: *Khabīsāt*
  as counter-text 153–55, 161–62, 165–66, 178–84, 192–93, 200–201
  ʿawrat 172–77, 183–84, 190
  critical dismissal 155, 157–58
  euphemisms 184–91
  Marxist readings 159
  mujūn 178
  reification of the body 176, 239, 246, 316, 480
  scatological reductionism 174
  spiritual fetishization of the body 176, 239, 246–47, 316
  studies 158–60

panegyric poetry (*qasida*) 80, 86–98, 176–77, 180 *see also* Saʿdi: patrons; *qasidas*
paradise 17n42, 94, 118, 181, 200, 217, 238n18, 272, 280, 284, 291, 349, 363, 364n28, 365, 381, 382, 384, 397–94, 398, 414–16, 419–20, 460, 467
performance and performativity 3, 9, 16, 23, 28, 50, 86, 94–95, 108–109, 120, 159, 165–71, 179–80, 444–49, 467–68, 499–523
Persian Gulf and Kish 12, 12n25
pornography 7, 49, 151–52, 158–62, 171–72, 177–78, 189n101, 316, 480
Preserved Tablet (*lawḥ maḥfūẓ*) 231, 329n77, 340, 348–51, 360–61, 368–77, 393–94, 412, 414, 432, 474, 494, 507
  in Persian poetry 370–74
Proust, Marcel 450

Qazvini, Mohammad 37n143, 41
qibla 2, 261, 378, 382
  of love 266–70
Qurʾān 16, 76–79, 89, 114, 119n58, 126, 138, 207, 231, 236, 254n46, 257–58, 273, 286, 289, 290n47, 291, 295, 338–40, 348, 364n30, 370, 469n36, 515, 521
Qushayrī, ʿAbd al-Karīm 259, 278n16, 282, 287n37, 339, 361n22, 326n23, 485n67, 485n67
Quṭb al-Dīn Shīrāzī 64–65

Rafīʿ al-Dīn Lunbānī (Salghurid poet) 15n34
Ramadan 168, 500
rational-inferential modality (*tafakkur, fikrat*) 8, 230–31, 255–59, 275–77, 286–90, 292–93, 298, 302, 322, 338, 342–45, 385–86, 392, 397–98, 404, 448–89, 474, 512 see also *ʿibrat*
Rāzī, Fakhr al-Dīn 303n8, 305n20, 306–307, 324, 335, 344n118, 364n29
Richard, Francis 3740
riyāżat (spiritual training) 297–98, 375–76, 417, 474, 475n51, 499–500
Rūdakī Samarqandī 180
Rukn al-Dīn abū Yaḥyā (Salghurid judge) 132–133
Rumi, Jalāl al-Dīn 46, 59n8, 211n7, 233n3, 305n20, 309–12, 381, 394–95, 445n7, 446, 452n7, 494n98, 496n102, 502n6, 504
Rūzbihān-i Baqlī 218–20, 225, 238–39, 294–96, 304, 313, 319n53, 396, 458, 475n51, 485n67, 490n90
Rūzbihān-i Sānī 220

Saʿd I (Salghurid ruler) 13n31, 15, 87n73, 112n45, 114, 220n21
Saʿd II b. Abī Bakr 10–11, 14–17, 18n48, 20, 24, 87–92, 105, 109–123, 134, 149, 157n18, 219n17, 220, 291, 308n30, 454, 460n24, 464–65, 470, 488, 490n88, 502–503 *see also* Salghurid dynasty
Saʿdi, *see also Būstān*; *Gulistān*; eroticism, sacred
  anthropology of vision 216–17, 225, 229–30, 242–43, 279–82, 306, 326–28, 332–33, 346–47, 372–74, 416–17
  as a *ʿārif* (spiritual beholder) 271–73, 345–47 see also *ʿārif*
  Badāyiʿ 4, 6n10, 93, 120n60, 145, 190, 221, 458–64, 490, 499–500, 519
  Bīsutūn recension 29–30, 36, 38–41, 88, 90, 112n45, 119, 125, 447, 451n4, 494n97, 495n101, 506
  celebration of God 214–17, 285–86, 255–58, 289–91, 346–47
  celebration of Ilkhanid power 19–20, 92–97
  chronology of works 4, 16, 29, 31, 36, 145–147, 190, 221–22, 451–52, 503
  contemplation of beauty 255–59, 267–70, 289–93, 309–12, 316, 346, 505–507
  death 10
  father 12
  ghazal collections 20, 24n83, 26–27, 31, 181–82, 207–208, 221–22
  homoeroticism 56–66, 70–71, 77–78, 86–98, 114–133, 139–150, 183, 186, 198–203, 224, 243–46, 274–77, 416–18, 458–59, 490–92, 503
  internal senses 326–28, 333–38, 341–43, 353–54, 358–61, 416–20
  intertextuality 97, 121–123, 182, 208–214, 234–35, 311–12, 402, 418–22, 425–27, 491, 502–505
  Khavātīm 6n10, 31, 209, 221–22, 458, 462–68, 497, 498n107
  life 10–25, 87–88, 141, 149–150, 190, 224–25, 239–40, 272, 451–52, 457, 459, 487, 510
  lyric innovations 210–12, 224, 229–30, 234–35, 240, 244–45, 275–78, 309, 316, 334–38, 253–54, 373–74, 395, 400, 438–40, 459, 507, 513–15
  malik al-shuʿarā (king of the poets) 1, 1n4, 34
  maʿrifa 274–77, 279–82, 322, 359
  maʿānī as non-sensible attributes of the beloved 332–33, 337–38
  manuscripts 13, 13–14n31, 26, 29–42, 87n73, 96–97, 119, 154–55n9, 256n48, 350n127, 509n23
  mystical interpretations 54, 211, 225–26, 233–34, 240, 244n26, 248n36, 301–302, 357, 423–24, 444, 484
  mufti of the Masters of Gazes 5–6, 8, 241, 409
  name 10, 14, 34, 447
  obscene poetry (*Khabīsāt*) 7, 34, 61–63, 151, 153–58, 163–64, 171–72, 178, 185–94, 197–203, 235–36, 480
  patrons 11, 14–17, 29, 86–98, 103–104, 110–114, 156–57, 217–20, 239–40, 292–93, 304, 444, 449, 459–60, 464–66, 470, 488–89, 502–504
  pen name 11, 14, 16, 88–89
  philosophical influences 209, 304–306, 316, 318, 322, 326–45, 349–51, 358–61, 373–74, 395–96, 412–15, 424, 462

Sa'di (*cont.*)
pre-Bīsutūn recensions 29–31, 35–38, 88, 119n59, 125, 154n9, 452–53, 457–58
qasidas 13–14, 18, 21, 38–39, 57n4, 57–58, 86–98, 191, 255–57, 289–90, 292–93, 346–47, 464–67, 489n82
renown 15–16, 23–24, 30, 40, 62, 142, 149–150, 183, 212, 272, 425, 446, 459, 472n42, 490–91, 502–505
Risāla-yi 'aql va 'ishq 304, 359–60, 402–403
romantic interpretations 49, 54, 59, 70, 107–108, 226, 312
Sa'dī-yi ākhar al-zamān 15–16
Ṣāḥibiyya collection 12, 25, 36
sahl-i mumtana' ("inimitable smoothness") 32–33
samā' (lyric ritual) 446n10, 446–49, 467–68, 480–88, 499–523 *see also* speech acts
self-praise 6, 15–16, 95–96, 109–110, 118n56, 127, 142, 461, 500–501, 503–504
spiritual sobriety 220, 229–30, 238–39, 309, 322
Sufi influences 115–124, 211, 217–27, 234–36, 240, 267–70, 272–73, 275–78, 359–61, 374–77, 402, 419, 427–28, 430–34, 459, 464, 468–72, 481–88, 503–505
Sufi lodge 6, 22–23, 30, 37, 93, 220, 234, 391, 446, 488–89, 491
style 2, 32, 47, 49–53, 58, 88–89, 133, 140, 178, 189, 208, 214, 268–70, 432, 505
Ṭayyibāt 24n83, 31, 50, 88n75, 90n81, 110n38, 120, 125, 221, 223, 255, 415, 452–58, 469, 490, 496n102, 497, 498n107
themes 3–9, 100–101
travels 11, 14n31, 21–22, 24, 135, 141, 217–19, 222–23, 451–52
visionary experience of the lyric subject (five phases) 405, 408–12, 414–35, 462–64, 493–94, 499–501
works 25–30, 34–42, 47, 145, 448
Safavids 2n7, 62, 208, 210, 212
Ṣafī al-Dīn Ardabīlī 62, 183, 459, 491
Safīna-yi Tabrīz 471–72
ṣāḥib-dil (Master of the Heart) see *'ārif*; *Gulistān*; visionary experience
ṣāḥib dīvān see Juvaynī, Shams al-Dīn
Salghurid dynasty 6–7, 9–25, 29, 31, 87–92, 157, 218–20, 376, 459, 490 *see also* Abū Bakr b. Sa'd I; Sa'd II
Salghūr-Shāh (Abū Bakr b. Sa'd I's brother) 18, 157
Saljūq-Shāh (Salghurid prince) 18–19, 93, 157
Salmān Sāvajī 494n98
samā' (lyrical ritual) 9, 16, 28, 30, 120, 223, 304, 403, 445–49, 466–67, 470–98 *see also* performance and performativity
and sexual desire 488–98
as a catalyst for the visionary experience 472, 479
Bīsutūn's account 447–49
in the *Safīna-yi Tabrīz* 477
lawfulness 165–72, 250–55, 486–88
spiritual physiology of 473–90, 505–508
Samarkand 9, 40, 156, 194
Sanā'ī Ghaznavī 121–123, 144n105, 156, 161–62, 177, 179, 208–212, 219n17, 307–309, 334, 366n33, 371, 380, 418–22, 459, 461n27, 469n38
Sayf Farghānī 76n47, 212–17, 305, 425, 491, 504
Sebti, Meryem 326n73, 328n76, 396
Shabistarī, Maḥmūd 247n34, 248n36, 255, 494n98
shāhid and *shāhid-bāzī* 4, 8, 50, 52, 57, 72n37, 73, 119–120, 128–133, 192, 201, 223, 259–61, 273–74, 297–98, 317–18, 378, 398–99, 406, 411–12, 416–17, 432, 434–35, 456, 489–98, 503
Shakespeare 2
Shams-i Qays-i Rāzī 12n25, 15n34, 115n51, 150, 490n88, 519, 522
Shams-i Tabrīzī 59n8, 224
Sharma, Sunil 452, 669
Shiraz 5–6, 9, 19, 57, 96, 114–115, 150, 217–19, 451–52, 457, 503–504, 508
shirk (associationism, polytheism) 259, 265 *see also ḥulūl*
speech acts 159, 179–80, 472n42 *see also* Austin, John Langshaw
locutionary texts 501–502
illocutionary texts 501, 504–13
perlocutionary texts 501
spiritual beholder see *'ārif*

Spitzer, Leo 135
Sufism 21, 30, 50–51, 115–124, 134, 165, 218–29, 234–37, 240, 242, 245–55, 259–61, 282–90, 294–96, 305–309, 312–14, 339–40, 359–62, 374–85, 394–96, 403–409, 433–34, 445–49, 464, 468–72, 475–80, 486–92, 500–502
Suhravardī, Shahāb al-Dīn Abū Ḥafs 222–24, 303–304, 458, 475n50, 486n71
Suhravardī, Shahāb al-Dīn (Shaykh-i ishrāq) 299n67, 325n70
Suhravardiyya order 21, 24n84, 222, 304, 495
Sūzanī Samarqandī 156–57, 161, 178–79, 194–97
Syar al-awliyā' (Amīr Khward) 504
syllogistic thinking 287, 512 see also *tafakkur*

Tabriz 4, 19, 20, 22, 24, 87, 95, 444, 471, 477, 495
tafakkur (*fikrat*) 230, 286–290, 308, 322, 338, 343–45, 383–86, 392, 397, 405, 418, 474, 512 *see also* rational-inferential modality
Tāj al-Ḥalāvī 3n
tajallī (spiritual epiphany) 238, 294–95, 350, 399
Talbīs Iblīs (*The Deceit of Satan*) see Ibn al-Jawzī
Terken Khātūn (Salghurid princess) 18–19, 465n33
Timurids 2n7, 31, 40–41, 208, 210–12, 222, 504n12
Tuḥfat ahl al-ʿirfān 220n21 *see also* Rūzbihān-i Sānī
Turkān Pass (Fars) 14n31
Ṭūsī, Naṣīr al-Dīn 303n8, 324, 325n70, 335, 519–20

ʿUbayd Zākānī 61–62, 156, 178, 180–83
Ulfatī Tabrīzī 247n34
ʿUnṣurī Balkhī 173, 370
ʿUshshāq-nāma 220n21 *see also* ʿAṭā'ī
Ushnuhī, Ṣad al-Dīn Muḥammad 304

Vāʿiẓ-i Kāshifī 32–33, 214
varidāt (spiritual inspirations) 252n42, 484–85, 485n67
Vaṣṣāf (historian) 12n25, 17n46, 18n54, 21, 115–16, 116n53
Vaṭvāṭ, Rashīd al-Dīn 32–33
Vinyoli, Joan 45
visionary experience (*mukāshafa*, *mushāhada*) 3, 9, 169, 231, 236–37, 260, 345–47, 354, 359–60, 368–72, 378–83, 392, 397, 501 *see also* imaginal-cosmological modality; five phases (al-Ghazālī's paradigm)
  dangers on the path (phase five) 411–12
  imaginal translation (phase two) 406–407, 412–21
  preliminary contact (phase one) 405, 412
  renewal of the imaginal contact (phase four) 409–10, 426–30, 507–508
  return to the external senses (phase three) 407–409, 422–26, 510–11

wahm *see* Avicenna: estimative faculty
wajd (ecstatic rapture) 359, 445n7, 476, 482, 485, 495, 505, 518
Wright, Elaine 38, 40–41
Wine 496

Yarshater, Ehsan 70, 84n65, 233n3
Yohannan, John 3, 219n17
Yusofi, Gholām-Hoseyn 26–31, 40, 101n9
Yūsuf (Joseph) 76–79, 94, 118–119, 243, 350, 425, 429

Ẓahīr Fāryābī 471
zandaqa (heresy) 250–51
Zangī Bukhārī, Muḥammad b. Maḥmūd 400
Zangī b. Mawdūd 219n17
Zargar, Cyrus 73
ẕawq (sublime sensation) 238, 443, 449, 464, 468–72, 495, 504, 505, 507
ẕikr 16, 120, 280, 363–64, 384, 467–68, 478, 501
Zipoli, Riccardo 155–56, 161
Zulaykhā 78–79
Zumthor, Paul 27, 153

www.ingramcontent.com/pod-product-compliance
Lightning Source LLC
Chambersburg PA
CBHW050300010526
44108CB00040B/1898